Project of History of Indian Science,
Philosophy and Culture

Publications in PHISPC—CONSSAVY Series

HISTORY OF SCIENCE, PHILOSOPHY AND CULTURE IN INDIAN CIVILIZATION

General Editor & Project Director D.P. Chattopadhyaya

Conceptual Volumes

*	Part 1	Science, Philosophy and Culture: Multi-disciplinary Exploration	D.P. Chattopadhyaya & Ravinder Kumar (eds.)
*	Part 2	Science, Philosophy and Culture: Multi-disciplinary Exploration	D.P. Chattopadhyaya & Ravinder Kumar (eds.)

VOLUME I The Dawn and Development of Indian Civilization

*	Part 1	The Dawn of Indian Civilization (up to c. 600 bc)	G.C. Pande (ed.)
*	Part 2	Life, Thought and Culture in India (from c. 600 bc to c. ad 300)	G.C. Pande (ed.)
➢	Part 3	India's Interaction with South East Asia	G.C. Pande (ed.)
➢	Part 4	A Golden Chain of Civilization: Indian, Iranian, Semitic and Hellenic	G.C. Pande (ed.)
➢	Part 5	Purāṇas, History and Itihāsa	Vidya Niwas Misra (ed.)

VOLUME II Life, Thought and Culture in India (AD 300-1100)

*	Part 1	Life, Thought and Culture in India (AD 300–1000)	K. Satchidananda Murty (ed.)
*	Part 2	Advaita Vedānta	R. Balasubramanian (ed.)
*	Part 3	Theistic Vedānta	R. Balasubramanian (ed.)
*	Part 4	Origin and Development of the Vaiśeṣika System	Anantalal Thakur
➢	Part 5	A Social History of India in the First Millennium AD	B.D. Chattopadhyaya (ed.)
➢	Part 6	Purva Mīmaṁsā from an Interdisciplinary Point of View	K.T. Pandurangi (ed.)

VOLUME III Development of Philosophy, Science and Technology in India and Neighbouring Civilizations

*	Part 1	History of Indian Science, Technology and Culture (ad 1000–1800)	A. Rahman (ed.)
*	Part 2	India's Interaction with China, Central and West Asia	A. Rahman (ed.)
*	Part 3	Development of Nyāya Philosophy and its Social Context	Sibajiban Bhattacharyya (ed.)
➢	Part 4 & 5	Philosophical Concepts relevant to Science in Indian Tradition	Pranab Kumar Sen (ed.)
➢	Part 6	Twenty Centuries of Mutual Vibrations between Indian and Chinese Civilizations	Tan Chung & Geng Yinzeng (eds.)
➢	Part 7	History of Indian Ocean: India and Littoral Countries	Om Prakash (ed.)

VOLUME IV Fundamental Indian Ideas of Physics, Chemistry, Life Sciences and Medicine

*	Part 1	Chemistry and Chemical Techniques in India	B.V. Subbarayappa (ed.)
*	Part 2	Life Sciences and Medicine in India	B.V. Subbarayappa (ed.)
➢	Part 3	Indian Perspective in the Physical World	B.V. Subbarayappa
➢	Part 4	History of Indian Astronomy and Mathematics	B.V. Subbarayappa

VOLUME V Agriculture in India

➢	Part 1 & 2	A History of Agriculture in India	Lallanji Gopal & V.C. Srivastava (eds.)

VOLUME VI Culture, Language, Literature and Arts

➢	Part 1	Aesthetic Theories and Forms in Indian Tradition	S.S. Barlingay, D.P. Chattopadhyaya and Kapila Vatsyayan (eds.)
*	Part 2	Indian Art: Forms, Concerns and Development in Historical Perspective	B.N. Goswamy (ed.)
➢	Part 3	Architecture in India	M.A. Dhaky (ed.)
➢	Part 4	Language, Grammar and Linguistics in Indian Tradition	V.N. Jha (ed.)
•	Part 5-10	PHISPC in Regional Languages and Literatures	

VOLUME VII The Rise of New Polity and Life in Villages and Towns

➢	Part 1 & 2	Social History of Medieval India	J.S. Grewal (ed.)
➢	Part 3, 4 & 5	Religious Systems of India	S.R. Saha, N.S.S. Raman, M. Rafique and others (eds.)

VOLUME VIII Economic History of India

➢	Part 1	Economic History of India from Thirteenth to Seventeenth Century	Irfan Habib (ed.)
➢	Part 2 & 3	Economic History of India from Eighteenth to Twentieth Century	B.B. Chaudhuri (ed.)

VOLUME IX Colonial Period

*	Part 1	Medicine in India: Modern Period	O.P. Jaggi
➢	Part 2	Women in India: Ancient and Medieval Period	Bhuvan Chandel (ed.)
➢	Part 3	Women in India: Colonial and Post-colonial Period	Bharati Ray (ed.)

VOLUME X Towards Independence

*	Part 1	Development of Indian Philosophy from Eighteenth Century Onwards	Daya Krishna
➢	Part 2	Colonial Development, Education and Social Awareness up to 2000	S. Gopal, Ravinder Kumar & S. Bhattacharya (eds.)
*	Part 3	Historical Perspectives of Warfare in India: Some *Morale* and *Material Determinants*	S.N. Prasad (ed.)
➢	Part 4	Cultural Foundations of Mathematics: The Nature of Mathematical Proof and the Transmission of the Infinitesimal Calculus from India to Europe in the 16th c. CE	C.K. Raju (ed.)

. . . contd. at the back of this volume

History of Science, Philosophy and Culture in Indian Civilization

General Editor D.P. Chattopadhyaya

Volume IV Part 3

Indian Perspectives on the Physical World

B.V. SUBBARAYAPPA

Project of History of Indian Science, Philosophy and Culture

CENTRE FOR STUDIES IN CIVILIZATIONS

Publication of this Volume and much of the research it represents have been made possible by continuing grants with full financial assistance from the Department of Higher Education, Ministry of Human Resources Development, Government of India, which has supported multidisciplinary exploration of the Project of History of Indian Science, Philosophy and Culture.

First published in 2004
by Professor Bhuvan Chandel, Member Secretary
CSC, 36 Tughlakabad Institutional Area, New Delhi 110 062

Distributed by
Munshiram Manoharlal Publishers Pvt. Ltd.
54, Rani Jhansi Road
New Delhi 110 055.

ISBN: 81-87586-17-6

Typeset in HACC Indic, 12/14 pts.

*Typeset by Digigrafics and
Printed at Pauls Press, New Delhi*

Dedicated to

Acharya P. C. Ray	*B. N. Seal*
M. Hiriyanna	*S. N. Sen*

Centre for Studies in Civilizations

Governing Board

Professor D.P. Chattopadhyaya	Member, *Chairman*
Professor G.C. Pande	Member
Professor Daya Krishna	Member
Professor Arjun Sengupta	Member
Professor Yash Pal	Member
Professor J.V. Narlikar	Member
Professor Kireet Joshi	Member
Shri T.N. Chaturvedi	Member
Professor V.R. Mehta	Member
Professor Bhuvan Chandel	Member, *Member-Secretary*

Contents

Preface

Over the ages, an incessant human endeavour has been to understand, among others, the observed world of matter, energy, qualities, motion, space and time. Alongside, the pristine origin of the Universe as well as the knowledge of the terrestrial-celestial relationship or the microcosmic macroscopic consonance also engaged the attention of thinkers of ancient cultures in one form or the other. Such knowledge, however, was an integral part of a holistic vision of Man *in* Nature and seldom in terms of a dichotomy of Man *and* Nature or Man *against* Nature.

Of all the ancient cultures, the Indian culture-area has been noted for fostering a holistic view of the Universe on the matrix of which several concepts were developed encompassing matter or the substance, its diverse qualities, atomism, motion, space and time. Some epistemological attempts too were made for their rational interpretation, albeit their limitations. The sources dealing with these ideas are in Sanskrit and not unoften mixed with ontological or metaphysical issues. The viewpoints of both the orthodox and heterodox systems (the Bauddha, Jaina, Cārvāka and the like) have been examined in the context of their approach to the physical world.

An attempt is thus made in this Volume to present a perspective on these and related Indian thoughts. Wherever necessary and possible, a brief review of the concerned ideas of the other cultures has been given to facilitate a comparative understanding. Relevant Sanskrit passages have also been given under references with a view to enabling an interested reader to have access to the original sources for further critical evaluation. An extensive bibliography along with a glossary of Sanskrit terms has been appended in the hope that they would enhance the value of this publication.

I am grateful to Professor D.P. Chattopadhyaya Ji, Chairman, CSC and Project Director, PHISPC for his constant encouragement. My special thanks are due to Professor Bhuvan Chandel, Project-Coordinator, PHISPC and Shri S. Sreekumaran, Administration-cum-Accounts Officer of PHISPC for their help in various ways.

I am indeed beholden to Professor D. Prahladachar, Vice-Chancellor, Rashtriya Sanskrit Vidyapeetha, Tirupati, for going through the manuscript in detail and giving several suggestions, specially with regard to the portion relating to the Nyāya-Vaiśeṣika. He has also kindly agreed to include his two articles (Appendices 3 and 4) in this volume. I am grateful to Swamy Prabhananda, Secretary, The Ramakrishna Mission Institute of Culture, Kolkata for according permission to reproduce the article: "Geographical Knowledge in Ancient and Medieval India" (Appendix 2) written by Sashibhushan Chaudhuri and published in *The Cultural Heritage of India*, Vol VI. 2001, pp. 5-17.

The permission granted by the Permissions Administrator of M/s. Taylor and Francis Group, London, for the reproduction of the article: 'Time and Eternity in Indian Thought' (Appendix 1) published in *Man and Time*, Routledge and Kegan Paul, London, 1958, pp. 173-200, is gratefully acknowledged.

I am deeply appreciative of the assistance of Professor C. Ramanathan who worked as Research Associate throughout the preparation of this Volume. I offer my special thanks to Dr. Sudha Gopinath (Bangalore University) for reading the manuscript as well as giving suggestions, and to Dr. B.S. Ramakrishna Rao who has spared no efforts in going through the proofs meticulously. It gives me great pleasure to thank specially Ms. Bindu Menon for going through the proofs thoroughly and meticulously. Her devoted efforts are indeed exemplary. Thanks are also due to S.G. Srinivasa Murthy for efficient typing, and to Digigrafics as well as Pauls Press for their concerted efforts which have led to this elegant publication.

B.V. Subbarayappa

General Introduction

I

It is understandable that man, shaped by Nature, would like to know Nature. The human ways of knowing Nature are evidently diverse, theoretical and practical, scientific and technological, artistic and spiritual. This diversity has, on scrutiny, been found to be neither exhaustive nor exclusive. The complexity of physical nature, life-world and, particularly, human mind is so enormous that it is futile to follow a single method for comprehending all the aspects of the world in which we are situated.

One need not feel bewildered by the variety and complexity of the worldly phenomena. After all, both from traditional wisdom and our daily experience, we know that our own nature is not quite alien to the structure of the world. Positively speaking, the elements and forces that are out there in the world are also present in our body-mind complex, enabling us to adjust ourselves to our environment. Not only the natural conditions but also the social conditions of life have instructive similarities between them. This is not to underrate in any way the difference between the human ways of life all over the world. It is partly due to the variation in climatic conditions and partly due to the distinctness of production-related tradition, history and culture.

Three broad approaches are discernible in the works on historiography of civilization, comprising science and technology, art and architecture, social sciences and institutions. Firstly, some writers are primarily interested in discovering the general laws which govern all civilizations spread over different continents. They tend to underplay what they call the noisy local events of the external world and peculiarities of different languages, literatures and histories. Their accent is on the unity of Nature, the unity of science and the unity of mankind. The second group of writers, unlike the generalists or transcendentalists, attach primary importance to the distinctiveness of every culture. To these writers human freedom and creativity are extremely important and basic in character. Social institutions and the cultural articulations of human consciousness, they argue, are bound to be expressive of the concerned people's consciousness. By implication they tend to reject concepts like archetypal consciousness, universal mind and providential history. There is a third group of writers who offer a composite picture of civilizations, drawing elements both from their local as well as common characteristics. Every culture has its local roots and peculiarities. At the same time, it is pointed out that due to demographic migration and immigration over the centuries an element of compositeness emerges almost in every culture. When due to a natural calamity or political exigencies people move from one part of the world to another, they carry with them, among other things, their language, cultural inheritance and their ways of living.

In the light of the above facts, it is not at all surprising that comparative anthropologists and philologists are intrigued by the striking similarity between different language families and the rites, rituals and myths of different peoples. Speculative philosophers of history, heavily relying on the findings of epigraphy, ethnography, archaeology and theology, try to show in very general terms that the particulars and universals of culture are 'essentially' or 'secretly' interrelated. The spiritual aspects of culture like dance and music, beliefs pertaining to life, death and duties, on analysis, are found to be mediated by the material forms of life like weather forecasting, food production, urbanization and invention of script. The transition from the oral culture to the written one was made possible because of the mastery of symbols and rules of measurement. Speech precedes grammar, poetry prosody. All these show how the 'matters' and 'forms' of life are so subtly interwoven.

II

The PHISPC publications on History of Science, Philosophy and Culture in Indian Civilization, in spite of its unitary look, do recognize the differences between the areas of material civilization and those of ideational culture. It is not a work of a single author. Nor is it being executed by a group of thinkers and writers who are methodologically uniform or ideologically identical in their commitments. In conceiving the Project we have interacted with, and been influenced by, the writings and views of many Indian and non-Indian thinkers.

The attempted unity of this Project lies in its aim and inspiration. We have in India many scholarly works written by Indians on different aspects of our civilization and culture. Right from the pre-Christian era to our own time, India has drawn the attention of various countries of Asia, Europe and Africa. Some of these writings are objective and informative and many others are based on insufficient information and hearsay, and therefore not quite reliable, but they have their own value. Quality and view-points keep on changing not only because of the adequacy and inadequacy of evidence but also, and perhaps more so, because of the bias and prejudice, religious and political conviction, of the writers.

Besides, it is to be remembered that history, like Nature, is not an open book to be read alike by all. The past is mainly enclosed and only partially disclosed. History is, therefore, partly objective or 'real' and largely a matter of construction. This is one of the reasons why some historians themselves think that it is a form of literature or art. However, it does not mean that historical construction is 'anarchic' and arbitrary. Certainly, imagination plays an important role in it.

But its character is basically dependent upon the *questions* which the historian raises and wants to understand or answer in terms of the ideas and actions of human beings in the past ages. In a way, history, somewhat like the natural sciences, is engaged in answering questions and in exploring relationships of cause and effect between events and developments across time. While in the natural sciences, the scientist poses questions about nature in the form of hypotheses, expecting to elicit authoritative answers to such questions, the historian studies the past, partly for the sake of understanding it for its own sake and partly also for the light which the past throws upon the present, and the possibilities which it opens up for moulding the future. But the difference between the two approaches must not be lost sight of. The scientist is primarily interested in discovering laws and framing theories, in terms of which different events and processes can be connected and anticipated. His interest in the conditions or circumstances attending the concerned events is secondary. Therefore, scientific laws turn out to be basically abstract and easily expressible in terms of mathematical language. In contrast, the historian's main interest centres round the *specific* events, human ideas and actions, not *general* laws. So, the historian, unlike the scientist, is obliged to pay primary attention to the circumstances of the events he wants to study. Consequently, history, like most other humanistic disciplines, is concrete and particularist. This is not to deny the obvious truth that historical events and processes consisting of human ideas and actions show some trend or other and weave some pattern or other. If these trends and patterns were not there at all in history, the study of history as a branch of knowledge would not have been profitable or instructive. But one must recognize that historical trends and patterns, unlike scientific laws and theories, are not general or purported to be universal in their scope.

III

The aim of this Project is to discover the main aspects of Indian culture and present them in an interrelated way. Since our culture has influenced, and has been influenced by, the neighbouring cultures of West Asia, Central Asia, East Asia and South-East Asia, attempts have been made here to trace and study these influences in their mutuality. It is well known that during the last three centuries, European presence, both political and cultural, in India has been very widespread. In many volumes of the Project considerable attention has been paid to Europe and, through Europe, to other parts of the world. For the purpose of a comprehensive cultural study of India, the existing political boundaries of the South Asia of today are more of a hindrance than help. Cultures, like languages, often transcend the bounds of changing political territories.

If the inconstant political geography is not a reliable help to the understanding of the layered structure and spread of culture, a somewhat comparable problem is encountered in the area of historical periodization. Periodization or segmenting time is a very tricky affair. When exactly one period ends and another begins is not precisely ascertainable. The periods of history designated as ancient, medieval and modern are purely conventional and merely heuristic in character. The varying scopes of history, local, national and continental or universal, somewhat like the periods of history, are unavoidably fuzzy and shifting. Amidst all these difficulties, the volume-wise details have been planned and worked out by the editors in consultation with the Project Director and the General Editor. I believe that the editors of different volumes have also profited from the reactions and suggestions of the contributors of individual chapters in planning the volumes.

Another aspect of Indian history which the volume editors and contributors of the Project have carefully dealt with is the distinction and relation between civilization and culture. The material conditions which substantially shaped Indian civilization have been discussed in detail. From agriculture and industry to metallurgy and technology, from physics and chemical practices to the life sciences and different systems of medicines—all the branches of knowledge and skill which directly affect human life—form the heart of this Project. Since the periods covered by the PHISPC are extensive—prehistory, proto-history, early history, medieval history and modern history of India—we do not claim to have gone into all the relevant material conditions of human life. We had to be selective. Therefore, one should not be surprised if one finds that only some material aspects of Indian civilization have received our pointed attention, while the rest have been dealt with in principle or only alluded to.

One of the main aims of the Project has been to spell out the first principles of the philosophy of different schools, both pro-Vedic and anti-Vedic. The basic ideas of Buddhism, Jainism and Islam have been given their due importance. The special position accorded to philosophy is to be understood partly in terms of its proclaimed unifying character and partly it is to be explained in terms of the fact that different philosophical systems represent alternative world-views, cultural perspectives, their conflict and mutual assimilation.

Most of the volume editors and at their instance the concerned contributors have followed a middle path between the extremes of narrativism and theoreticism. The underlying idea has been this: If in the process of working out a comprehensive Project like this every contributor attempts to narrate all those interesting things that he has in the back of his mind, the enterprise is likely to prove unmanageable. If, on the other hand, particular details are consciously forced into a fixed mould or pre-supposed theoretical structure, the details lose their particularity and interesting character. Therefore, depending on the nature of the problem of discourse, most of the writers have tried to reconcile in their presentation, the specificity of narrativism and the generality of theoretical orientation. This is a conscious editorial decision. Because, in the absence of a theory, however inarticulate it may be, the factual details tend to fall apart. Spiritual network or theoretical orientation makes historical details not only meaningful but also interesting and enjoyable.

Another editorial decision which deserves spelling out is the necessity or avoidability of duplication of the same theme in different volumes or even in the same volume. Certainly, this Project is not an assortment of several volumes. Nor is any volume intended to be a miscellany. This Project has been designed with a definite end in view and has a structure of its own. The character of the structure has admittedly been influenced by the variety of the themes accommodated within it. Again it must be understood that the complexity of structure is rooted in the aimed integrality of the Project itself.

IV

Long and in-depth editorial discussion has led us to several unanimous conclusions. Firstly, our Project is going to be *unique,* unrivalled and discursive in its attempt to integrate different forms of science, technology, philosophy and culture. Its comprehensive scope, continuous character and accent on culture distinguish it from the works of such Indian authors as P.C. Ray, B.N. Seal, Binoy Kumar Sarkar and S.N. Sen and also from such Euro-American writers as Lynn Thorndike, George Sarton and Joseph Needham. Indeed, it would be no exaggeration to suggest that it is for the first time that an endeavour of so comprehensive a character, in its exploration of the social, philosophical and cultural characteristics of a distinctive world civilization—that of India—has been attempted in the domain of scholarship.

Secondly, we try to show the linkages between different branches of learning as different modes of experience in an *organic* manner and without resorting to a kind of reductionism, materialistic or spiritualistic. The internal dialectics of organicism without reductionism allows fuzziness, discontinuity and discreteness within limits.

Thirdly, positively speaking, different modes of human experience—scientific, artistic, etc. have their own individuality, not necessarily autonomy. Since all these modes are modification and articulation of *human* experience, these are bound to have between them some finely graded commonness. At the same time, it has been recognized that reflection on different areas of experience and investigation brings to light new insights and findings. Growth of knowledge requires humans, in general, and scholars, in particular, to identify the distinctness of different branches of learning.

Fourthly, to follow simultaneously the twin principles of: (a) individuality of human experience as a whole, and (b) individuality of diverse disciplines, are not at all an easy task. Overlap of themes and duplication of the terms of discourse become unavoidable at times. For example, in the context of *Dharmaśāstra*, the writer is bound to discuss the concept of value. The same concept also figures in economic discourse and also occurs in a discussion on fine arts. The conscious editorial decision has been that, while duplication should be kept to its minimum, for the sake of intended clarity of the themes under discussion, their reiteration must not be avoided at high intellectual cost.

Fifthly, the scholars working on the Project are drawn from widely different disciplines. They have brought to our notice an important fact that has clear relevance to our work. Many of our contemporary disciplines like economics and sociology did not exist, at least not in their present form, just two centuries ago or so. For example, before the middle of nineteenth century, sociology as a distinct branch of knowledge was unknown. The term is said to have been coined first by the French philosopher Auguste Comte in 1838. Obviously, this does not mean that the issues discussed in sociology were not there. Similarly, Adam Smith's (1723–90) famous work *The Wealth of Nations* is often referred to as the first authoritative statement of the principles of (what we now call) economics. Interestingly enough, the author was equally interested in ethics and jurisprudence. It is clear from history that the nature and scope of different disciplines undergo change, at times very radically, over time. For example, in India *arthaśāstra* does not mean the science of economics as understood today. Besides the principles of economics, it discusses at length those of governance, diplomacy and military science.

Sixthly, this brings us to the next editorial policy followed in the Project. We have tried to remain very conscious of what may be called indeterminacy or inexactness of translation. When a word or expression of one language is translated into another, some loss of meaning or exactitude seems to be unavoidable. This is true not only in the bilingual relations like Sanskrit-English and Sanskrit-Arabic, but also in those of Hindi-Tamil and Hindi-Bengali. In recognition of the importance of language-bound and context-relative character of meaning we have solicited from many learned scholars, contributions, written in vernacular languages. In order to minimize the miseffect of semantic inexactitude we have solicited translational help of that type of bilingual scholars who know both English and the concerned vernacular language, Hindi, Tamil, Telugu, Bengali or Marathi.

Seventhly and finally, perhaps the place of technology as a branch of knowledge in the composite universe of science and art merits some elucidation. Technology has been conceived in very many ways, e.g. as autonomous, as 'standing reserve', as liberating or enlargemental, and alienative or estrangemental force. The studies undertaken by the Project show that, in spite of its much emphasized mechanical and alienative characteristics, technology embodies a very useful mode of knowledge that is peculiar to man. The Greek root words of technology are *techne* (art) and *logos* (science). This is the basic justification of recognizing technology as closely related to both epistemology, the discipline of valid knowledge, and axiology, the discipline of freedom and values. It is in this context that we are reminded of the definition of man as *homo technikos*. In Sanskrit, the word closest to *techne* is *kalā* which means any practical art, any mechanical or fine art. In the Indian tradition, in *Śaivatantra*, for example, among the arts (*kalā*) are counted dance, drama, music, architecture, metallurgy, knowledge of dictionary, encyclopaedia and prosody. The closeness of the relation between arts and sciences, technology and other forms of knowledge are evident from these examples and was known to the ancient people. The human quest for knowledge involves the use of both head and hand. Without mind, the body is a corpse and the disembodied mind is a bare abstraction. Even for our appreciation of what is beautiful and the creation of what is valuable, we are required to exercise both our intellectual competence and physical capacity. In a manner of speaking, one might rightly affirm that our psychosomatic structure is a functional connector between what we are and what we could be, between the physical and the beyond. To suppose that there is a clear-cut distinction between the physical world and the psychosomatic one amounts to denial of the possible emergence of higher logico-mathematical, musical and other capacities. The very availability of aesthetic experience and creation proves that the supposed distinction is somehow overcome by what may be called the bodily self or embodied mind.

V

The ways of classification of arts and sciences are neither universal nor permanent. In the Indian tradition, in the *Ṛgveda*, for example, *Vidyās* (or sciences) are said to be four in number: (i) *Trayī*, the triple Veda; (ii) *Ānvīkṣikī*, logic and metaphysics; (iii) *Daṇḍa-nīti*, science of governance; (iv) *Vārttā*, practical arts such as agriculture, commerce, medicine, etc. Manu speaks of a fifth *vidyā*, viz. *Ātma-vidyā*, knowledge of self or of spiritual truth. According to many others, *vidyā* has fourteen divisions, viz. the four *Veda-s*, the six *Vedāṅga-s*, the *Purāṇa-s*, the *Mīmāṁsā*, *Nyāya*, and *Dharma* or law. At times, the four *Upa-veda-s* are also recognized by some as *vidyā*. *Kalās* are said to be 33 or even 64.

In the classical tradition of India, the word *Śāstra* has at times been used as the synonym of *vidyā*. *Vidyā* denotes instrument of teaching, manual or compendium of rules, religious or scientific treatise. The word *Śāstra* is usually found after the word referring to the subject of the book, e.g., *Dharma-śāstra*, *Artha-śāstra*, *Alaṅkāra-śāstra* and *Mokṣa-śāstra*. Two other words which have been frequently used to denote different branches of knowledge are *jñāna* and *vijñāna*. While *jñāna* means knowing, knowledge, especially the higher form of it; *vijñāna* stands for the act of distinguishing or discerning, understanding, comprehending and recognizing. It means worldly or profane knowledge as distinguished from *jñāna*, knowledge of the divine.

It must be said here that the division of knowledge is partly conventional and partly administrative or practical. It keeps on changing from culture to culture, from age to age. It is difficult to claim that the distinction between *jñāna* and *vijñāna* or that between science and art is universal. It is true that even before the advent of modern age, both in the East and the West, two basic aspects of sciences started gaining recognition. One is the *specialized character* of what we call scientific knowledge. The other is the concept of *trained skill* which was brought close to scientific knowledge. In the medieval Europe, the expression 'the seven liberal sciences' has so often been used simultaneously with 'the seven liberal arts', meaning thereby, the group of studies by the *Trivium* (Grammar, Logic and Rhetoric) and *Quadrivium* (Arithmetic, Music, Geometry and Astronomy).

It may be observed here, as has already been alluded to earlier, that the division between different branches of knowledge, between theory and practice, was not pushed to an extreme extent in the early ages. *Praxis*, for example, was recognized as the prime *techne*. The Greek word, *technologia* stood for systematic treatment, for example, of Grammar. *Praxis* is not the mere application of *theoria*, unified vision or integral outlook, but it also stands for the active impetus and base of knowledge. In India, one often uses the terms *Prayukti-vidyā* and *Prayodyogika-vidyā* to emphasize the practical or applicative character of knowledge. *Prayoga* or application is both the test and base of knowledge. Doing is the best way of knowing and learning.

That one and the same word may mean different 'things' or concepts in different cultures and thus create confusion has already been stated before. Two such words which in the context of this Project under discussion deserve special mention are *dharma* and *itihāsa*. Ordinarily, *dharma* in Sanskrit-rooted languages is taken to be conceptual equivalent of the English word *religion*. But, while the meaning of religion is primarily theological, that of *dharma* seems to be manifold. Literally, *dharma* stands for that which is established or that which holds people steadfastly together. Its other meanings are law, rule, usage, practice, custom, ordinance and statute. Spiritual or moral merit, virtue, righteousness and good works are also denoted by it. Further, *dharma* stands for natural qualities like burning (of fire), liquidity (of water) and fragility (of glass). Thus one finds that meanings of *dharma* are of many types—legal, social, moral, religious or spiritual, and even ontological or physical. All these meanings of *dharma* have received due attention of the writers in the relevant contexts of different volumes.

This Project, being primarily historical as it is, has naturally paid serious attention to the different concepts of history—epic-mythic, artistic-narrative, scientific-causal, theoretical and ideological. Perhaps the point that must be mentioned first about history is that it is not a correct translation of the Sanskrit word *itihāsa*. Etymologically, it means what really happened (*iti-ha-āsa*). But, as we know, in the Indian tradition *purāṇa* (legend, myth, tale, etc.), *gāthā* (ballad), *itivṛtta* (description of past occurrence, event, etc.), *ākhyāyikā* (short narrative) and *vaṃśa-carita* (genealogy) have been consciously accorded a very important place. Things started changing with the passage of time and particularly after the effective presence of Islamic culture in India. Islamic historians, because of their own cultural moorings and the influence of the Semitic and Graeco-Roman cultures on them, were more particular about their facts, figures and dates than their Indian predecessors. Their aim to bring history close to statecraft, social conditions and the lives and teachings of the religious leaders imparted a mundane character to this branch of learning. The Europeans whose political appearance on the Indian scene became quite perceptible only towards the end of the eighteenth century brought in with them their own view of historiography in their cultural baggage. The impact of the Newtonian Revolution in the field of history was very faithfully worked out, among others, by David Hume (1711–76) in *History of Great*

Britain from the Invasion of Julius Caesar to the Revolution of 1688 (6 vols., 1754–62) and Edward Gibbon (1737–94) in *The History of the Decline and Fall of the Roman Empire* (6 vols., 1776–88). Their emphasis on the principles of causality, datability and continuity/linearity of historical events introduced the spirit of scientific revolution in European historiography. The introduction of English education in India and the exposure of the elites of the country to it largely account for the decline of the traditional concept of *itihāsa* and the rise of the post-Newtonian scientific historiography. Gradually, Indian writers of our own history and cultural heritage started using more and more European concepts and categories. This is not to suggest that the impact of the European historiography on Indian historians was entirely negative. On the contrary, it imparted an analytical and critical temper which motivated many Indian historians of the nineteenth century to try to discover and represent our heritage in a new way.

VI

The principles which have been followed for organizing the subjects of different volumes under this Project may be stated in this way. We have kept in view the main structures which are discernible in the decomposible composition of the world. The first structure may be described as physical and chemical. The second structure consists, broadly speaking, of biology, psychology and epistemology. The highest and the most abstract structure nests many substructures within it, for example, logic, mathematics and musical notes. It is well known that the substructures within each structure are interactive, i.e. not isolable. The more important point to be noted in this connection is that the basic three structures of the world, viz., (a) physico-chemical, (b) bio-psychological, and (c) logico-mathematical are all simultaneously open to upward and downward causation. In other words, while the physico-chemical structure can causally influence the bio-psychological one and the latter can causally influence the most abstract logico-mathematical, the reverse process of causation is also operative in the world. In spite of its relative abstractness and durability, the logico-mathematical world has its downward causal impact on our bio-psychological and epistemological processes and products. And the latter can also bring about change in the structures of the physical world and its chemical composition. Applied physics and bio-technology make the last point abundantly clear.

Many philosophers, life-scientists, and social scientists highlight the point that nature loves hierarchies. Herbert Simon, the economist and the management scientist, speaks of four steps of partial ordering of our world, namely; (i) chemical substances, (ii) living organisms, tissues and organs, (iii) genes, chromosomes and DNA, and (iv) human beings, the social organizations, programmes and information process. All these views are in accord with the anti-reductionist character of our Project. Many biologists defend this approach by pointing out that certain characteristics of biological phenomena and process like unpredictability, randomness, uniqueness, magnitude of stochastic perturbations, complexity and emergence cannot be reduced without recourse to physical laws.

The main subjects dealt with in different volumes of the Project are connected not only conceptually and synchronically but also historically or diachronically. For pressing practical reasons, however, we did not aim at presenting the prehistorical, proto-historical and historical past of India in a continuous or chronological manner. Besides, it has been shown in the presentation of the PHISPC that the process of history is non-linear. And this process is to be understood in terms of human praxis and an absence of general laws in history. Another point which deserves special mention is that the editorial advisors have taken a conscious decision not to make this historical Project primarily political. We felt that this area of history has always been receiving extensive attention. Therefore, the customary discussion of dynastic rule and succession will not be found in a prominent way in this series. Instead, as said before, most of the available space has been given to social, scientific, philosophical and other cultural aspects of Indian civilization.

Having stated this, it must be admitted that our departure from conventional style of writing Indian history is not total. We have followed an inarticulate framework of time in organizing and presenting the results of our studies. The first volume, together with its parts, deals with the prehistorical period to AD 300. The next two volumes, together with their parts, deal with, among other things, development of social and political institutions and philosophical and scientific ideas from AD 300 to the beginning of the eleventh century AD. The next period with which this Project is concerned spans from the twelfth century to the early part of the eighteenth century. The last three centuries constitute the fourth period covered by this Project. But, as said before, the definition of all these periods by their very nature are inexact and merely indicative.

Two other points must be mentioned before I conclude this General Introduction to the series. The history of some of the subjects like religion, language and literature, philosophy, science and technology cannot for obvious reason be squeezed within the cramped space of the periodic moulds. Attempts to do so result in thematic distortion. Therefore, the reader will often see the overflow of some ideas from one period to another. I have already drawn attention to this tricky and fuzzy and also the misleading aspects of the periodization of history, if pressed beyond a point.

Secondly, strictly speaking, history knows no end. Every age rewrites its history. Every generation, beset with new issues, problems and questions, looks back to its history and reinterprets and renews its past. This shows why history is not only contemporaneous but also futural. Human life actually knows no separative wall between its past, present and future. Its cognitive enterprises, moral endeavours and practical activities are informed of the past, oriented by the present and addressed to the future. This process persists, consciously or unconsciously, wittingly or unwittingly. In the narrative of this Project, we have tried to represent this complex and fascinating story of Indian civilization.

D.P. Chattopadhyaya
General Editor

Centre for Studies in Civilizations
New Delhi

CHAPTER 1

An Overview

THE PHYSICAL WORLD is the knowable world through the human senses and mind engendered by the associated intellection. It is the world of matter and energy, their diverse nature and manifold manifestations inclusive of the varied properties of matter as well as motion, space and time. The physical world exists independently of our understanding it, and is regarded as being different from the organic one, though the latter derives its substratum and sustenance from the former, with a symbiotic relationship.

The origins of the physical world and the emergence of life in or on it have been fascinating and baffling alike. Their precise beginnings are still enigmatic despite the spectacular scientific advances in both the physical and the biological realms. Nevertheless, the search for the primordial world–stuff and the first appearance of life has been continuing incessantly. The saga of human knowledge or a holistic vision, however, goes back to the early civilizations—the Mesopotamian, the Egyptian, the Indian and the Chinese. The main characteristic of that knowledge was what may be called the triple-stranded, *man–spirit–cosmos view,* a vision that was the fountain-source of all forms of knowledge and experience of which a knowledge of the physical world was an integral component. It was not long before several religious and mythological ideas were woven into this triple-stranded view.

In the early civilizations (over 5000 years ago) there were parallel developments as regards their concerns about the celestial sphere as well as the terrestrial world. Those concerns were in the nature of forging a correspondence or a consonance between the two, which was not only a way of thinking but also the very process of living in harmony with nature, with all that is non-self. It is true that, in the first millennium B.C., a few pre-Socratic thinkers attempted to blaze new trails towards an understanding of the essence or the first principle of the physical world. But Pythagoras and his followers, Plato, Aristotle and others developed ideas, in their own way, not altogether devoid of, and in fact in furtherance of the man–spirit–cosmos view. Chinese too were no exception and the concept of Tao had an irresistible appeal to them as a way of life. Much later, some Islamic savants and Sufis also became its exponents. Of all the ancient cultures, probably the Indian culture-area was, and continues to be, the most committed one, for fostering the man–spirit–cosmos inter-relationship for a meaningful living in the matrix of the fourfold *puruṣārthas*. With this mind-set sciences like astronomy, mathematics, medicine as well as plant science were conceived and their progress determined. Alongside were also some speculations on matter, qualities, motion, space and time as well as the epistemological issues generated by them.

The innate strength of science lies in its methodology and the triumph of science is the triumph of its method. But the scientific method encompasses only the sensorial data and is thus limited to the knowledge gained through the senses and mind. It needs to be recognized that science is one form of human knowledge, notwithstanding its vast and variegated spectrum of exciting achievements.

Some explanation is desirable, indeed necessary, when the word 'science' is used in the ancient and medieval context. The word 'science' is derived from the Latin word 'cientia' which generally means 'to know or "the knowledge' in the same way as 'Veda' connotes. The latter, however, in the way it has come down to us is more comprehensive than 'cientia'. Yet, 'cientia' also encompassed all that was knowable or interpretable including natural philosophy. In fact, early modern science in the post-Renaissance period was identified with natural philosophy. It is significant to note that Isaac Newton in the Seventeenth century A.D., titled his seminal books on the laws of motion as *The Mathematical Principles of Natural Philosophy* (abbreviated as *Principia*). It was around the middle of the nineteenth century, the usage of word, *science,* became more pronounced and it discarded any type of its affiliation with philosophy or religion, not on ideological but on methodological grounds. The innate strength of science lies in its powerful method and the applicability of its methods governed generally by experiment, observation and inference. Such a rigorous method was not the forte of scientific pursuits in all of the ancient and early medieval cultures. Nevertheless, there were attempts at observation and inference as well as speculations concerning the origin of the universe, matter and motion, space and time as well as the epistemological issues.

Endeavours such as these were also noticeable among the Greeks, Greco-Romans, Eastern and Western Islam and early medieval Europe where theology became the 'queen of sciences'. So far as the exact sciences were concerned, it was what is generally termed a 'Dark Age' for Europe (*c.* 400-1200 A.D.), despite the commentaries and translations into Latin, of the works of Plato and Aristotle by thoughtful theologians like Bioethius, Macrobius and Martianus Capella (about the fifth cent. A.D.), studies of the 'trivium' (grammar, dialectic and rhetoric) as well as the 'quadrivium' (geometry, arithmetic, astronomy and music), Pliny's *Natural History* (first century A.D.) and the earlier Lucretius' (first cent. B.C.) *On the Nature of Things,* among others, exerted some influence on the medieval Christian thinkers. There was, however, the other side, namely, the influences of Neoplatonism which, through the works of Hypatia and St. Augustine, entered into

Christianity with the core concept of the relationship of microcosm and macrocosm. And Augustine had a dislike for the phenomenal knowledge except the medical practices. His call was 'Return to thyself. In inner man dwells truth' (Singer p. 125). In India, on the other hand, around this time, the exponents of Nyāya-Vaiśeṣika, Sāṃkhya, Jaina and the Sarvāstivādins (Buddhist) put forth their own ideas and interpretations of the phenomenal world. Their approaches and disputations were in marked contrast with those of the medieval European scholars. More importantly, the inseparable relation between microcosm and macrocosm was recognized in India even in the Vedic times long before it assumed some importance in Europe.

The foregoing sketch, though brief, is important for understanding the history of science, because it was Europe that emerged as the home of modern science from the time of the scientific Renaissance there till the middle of the nineteenth century. The question as to why and how a new way of looking at and a new method of studying the natural phenomena occurred only in Europe and not in the Orient including India, China and the Islamic culture-area, is a difficult one indeed. Although precise answers to it may not be found easily, it should be borne in mind that in Europe, at the time of Renaissance in Letters and the Arts, Indian scientific ideas in astronomy, mathematics and medicine as also some works of Aristotle and other Greek thinkers were available to the European intellects. It was an age of translation of the works written in Arabic into Latin which eventually became the language of science. Indian astronomical texts of Brahmagupta were translated into Arabic at the Abbasid Caliphate; likewise, the medical classics the *Caraka* and *Suśruta saṃhitās* and *Mādhava nidāna*. It may be noted that Adelard of Bath (*c.* 12th cent. A.D.) translated into Latin the Arabic work of Al-Khwārizmī which contained Indian arithmetic and number system. At the same time he rendered into Latin the Arabic work on Euclid. Al-Rāzi's medical compendium, *Kitāb-al-hawi*, which contained Indian medical practices was also rendered into Latin.

There were other translators like Robert of Chester, Domenigo Ganzalez, John of Seville, Gerard of Cremona, Michael the Scot and Moses Farachi (12th–13th cent. A.D.) who made available in Latin the Arabic version of the scientific thoughts of the Greek, Indian and Islam. There emerged thus a variegated and intellectually stimulating corpus of knowledge. Albertus Magnus, St. Thomas Aquinas, Witelo, Roger Bacon and others, reflected upon this knowledge-spectrum and began to tread new paths of thinking in the thirteenth century. A new scholasticism surfaced; knowledge from different sources and regions assimilated and discussed. Several universities sprang up in England, France, Italy and other places. The medieval universities energized a meeting of the minds and encouraged discourses; old ideas of Aristotle and others began to be questioned; new vistas of thinking opened up in astronomy, mathematics, matter and motion, related to space and time. It is not insignificant that great scientific personages like Copernicus, Galileo, Kepler and Newton were also products of one medieval university or the other. If St. Augustine had exhorted: 'Go not out of doors and return to thyself' which held sway over the mind of Europe for nearly a thousand years, the post-Renaissance period in Europe witnessed the thinkers going out of doors and studying the phenomena outside. There came about a confluence of several streams of knowledge some of which began to swell into a scientific one.

In India

The Indian situation was altogether different, may be because of the hierarchical or caste-ridden, social organization, or the political upheavals that came up from time to time, or the absence of medieval universities of the type that sprang up in Europe or the emphasis on preceptor–disciple relationship, or the importance given to spiritual pursuits and adherence to values of life. Perhaps it was all of them and many others put together that led to a circumscription of the traditionally fostered knowledge more than a stimulation for treading new paths of inquiry into the natural phenomena.

Even then, Indian thought-structure with its intertwined strands of intricacies has been vibrant and complex alike. Vibrant, because of its excursus of diverse character into the inseparable relationship between man and the universe, between the self and all that is non-self; complex, because of its several types of religio-philosphical speculations even beyond the sensorial experience, but not discarding altogether the sensorially knowable physical world. While one may understand by studying the extant texts, the origin and growth of Indian astronomy, mathematics, medicine, plant science and ecological concerns, one has perforce to examine carefully the extensive religio-philosophical and related literature to arrive at the Indian perspectives on the physical world. The task is by no means easy; for, it would appear that ontological and allied issues are not unoften mixed up with those of the physical world, with the result that the ideas of matter and motion specially, appeared to have taken a back seat in their much needed interpretation on a rationally perceivable foundation. It would, however, appear that there was free-thinking as well as logical discourses, albeit the preceptor–disciple relationship, on both material and non-material issues excepting perhaps the Cārvākas to whom the material objects or the sensorial data were alone real. The spectrum of Indian thought including that of the Jaina and the Bauddha is indeed a broad one including that of the physical world. A close examination even of the early literature, both primary and secondary, reveals that, when compared with the thoughts of Egyptians and Sumerians or Babylonians, Indian approach to the physical world has been a multifaceted one in a holistic matrix.

Even accepting the existence and the importance of the physical world, Indian ethos is characterised by the four *puruṣārtha* or human goals, namely, *dharma* (right duty and conduct); *artha* (wealth), *kāma* (desire) and *mokṣa* (salvation). It needs to be recognized that the Indian way of meaningful living over the ages has never stood for the total denial of the enjoyment of life. The *Ṛgveda* exhorts: 'Let us see a hundred autumns, Let us enjoy a hundred autumns'. The materially enriched life, however, has to be tempered with the life-sustaining values by following the path of *dharma,* while *artha* as well as *kāma* is to be subordinated towards *mokṣa* or the liberation from bondage. Further, the Indian view of life is that one must *act* or *work*, but with a sense of detachment or without craving for the fruits of action, as the *Bhagavadgītā* succinctly advocates. It is enjoined that the foundation for such action is to be a moral one with virtues like self-restraint, honesty, non-violence, fortitude and a conscious feeling of oneself with all that is non-self, both animate and inanimate, based on *dharma*. The Prabhākara school of Mīmāṃsā rightly asserts that *dharma* is the ultimate value, an end in itself and not a means to an end. It may be observed that, while the spiritual realization is the most exalted or of supreme value, it is by and large individualistic; but *dharma* has social dimensions vis-à-vis the shared material world.

It would be naïve to categorise the systems of Indian religio-philosophy into those that are mainly concerned with the manner of understanding the knowable world, like the Vaiśeṣika, Nyāya, Sāṃkhya as well as the Vedānta, and those that are deeply involved in the refinement of human nature and conduct, like the Yoga, the Bauddha and the Jaina. There is no denying that all the systems have emphasized the importance, in ways more than one, of right living and action, meditation and disciplined thought and practice from birth to the day of deliverance, apart from the imperative need for following the path of *dharma* which is the kernel of Indian thought and the way of life.

It would be an oversimplification, therefore, if one were to identify Indian thought only with spirituality and salvation (*mokṣa*) or the liberation from the presumed cycle of births and deaths and from the sufferings in life. It would be as superficial and erroneous as the statement of some westerners that India is a land of rope-walkers and snake-charmers. Equally erroneous would it be if one were to ascribe a totally materialistic view to the Indian way of thinking and action. Human mind is capable of circumscription and transcendence—circumscription by the play of senses tuned to the occurrences in the physical world; transcendental, beyond the senses, beyond the observable material world into an experience of an undifferentiated oneness or that which is real or Absolute, incommunicable and inexpressible. In several ways Indian thought-structure is an admixture of both. In essence it represents not only the yearnings of human mind to understand the physical world but also the great heights which human mind could reach beyond the ambience of the physical world.

Early Ideas

How far can one go back to find the early ideas on the physical world? The Indus Valley civilization or the Harappa culture as the archaeologists prefer to call it, flourished between *c.* 2750 and 1900 B.C. and had a decadent phase till *c.* 1600. This vast civilization covered an extensive area of about 1.3 million sq. km. and was noted for functional town-planning, inter-linked drainage system, public bath, standardized burnt-brick constructions, tiled-flooring, spinning and weaving, terracotta craft and, more significantly the copper-bronze technology of casting by cire-purdue or lost-wax process, a tradition that continues even to this day for casting icons. We are, however, in the dark about the Harappan thoughts on the physical world, as also their astronomy, mathematics and medicine, since the script forms on the seals, sealings and other inscribed objects numbering about 3000, have not been deciphered yet satisfactorily. The available archaeological evidence, nevertheless, appears to point out some relationship between what are known as Vedic people who are supposed to have made their appearance *c.* 1500 B.C. and the Harappans. It seems likely that the Vedic thoughts could well have been those of the Harappan priestly class, controversies apart.

The story is, however, agreeably different from the Vedic period (*c.* 1500–1000 B.C.) onwards. The four Vedas, specially the *Ṛgveda*, provide an insight into certain lofty thoughts, even amidst the rather elaborate Ṛgvedic mythology. It is significant that a comparison of the Ṛgvedic and the Mesopotamian mythologies reveals some noticeable parallels.

The word 'Mesopotamian' is used here in a large sense inclusive of the Sumerian, Akkadian, Assyrian, the general nomenclature of the Babylonian, and the admixtures which took place during the fourth-third millennium B.C. Some minor differences apart, they had common perceptions of their gods, including their attributes and deeds.

In the Mesopotamian mythology,[1] the Universe was divided into two parts and three regions. Each of the latter had a god-head: (i) *Anu*—ruler of sky or heaven; *Enlil*—ruler of the earth, and *Ea*—the governor of waters. *Anu* was the supreme god and the other gods regarded him as their 'father' or chief. He was all-powerful but meted out justice whenever the need arose. He created stars to destroy the wicked and the stars were known as 'the soldiers of Anu'. He never descended to the earth, but walked in an exclusively reserved portion of the sky, which was designated as *Anu's* way; (ii) Enlil whose domain was the earth, was the Lord of the Air too. He was the god of the hurricane and his weapon was *amaruk* (the deluge). In his anger sometimes he caused the deluge to annihilate the recalcitrant human race; (iii) *Ea* or *Enki* ruled over waters and the name meant 'House of Water'. But he was not the sovereign of marine waters, but of *Apsu* (the stretch of fresh water that encircled the earth and on which the earth floated). Ea was invoked in incantations and was the patron of artisans. In course of time, this triad of gods was replaced by *Marduk* (also spelt as *Merdoch*) who absorbed all the other gods with supreme authority. He was supposed to be the son of Ea, having arisen from *Apsu*. There was thus the conception of an all-powerful god-head among gods. Such a conception of god-head or the omnipotent god is also noticeable in the *Ṛgveda,* but in a refined form, and this is called by the Vedic scholars the monotheism or henotheism or kathenotheism.[2]

Among the Mesopotamian gods, there was also the triad of what may be called the sidereal divinities, namely, (i) *Sin* (not to be confused with the English word in modern sense) or the Moon-god, who was venerated specially at Ur, was regarded as the destroyer of nocturnal evil-doers by his illumination in the night. He was also a measure of time and full of wisdom; (ii) *Shamash*, the Sun-god who was known for his vigour and courage and who was regarded as the god of Justice, 'bore the title of Judge of the Heavens and the Earth' and no evil action escaped from his purview; and (iii) *Ishtar*, the daughter of *Anu*, was the goddess of morning and evening. She was the personification of the planet Venus. She was voluptuous and even a war-goddess (*Larousse Encyclopedia of Mythology*, pp. 49-72).

Apart from these divinities, there was *Adad*, the god of lightning and tempest, standing on a bull and grasping thunderbolt in each hand. He was the god of rains, inundation and fertilization. Like Shamash, he was also the Lord of revealing future. *Gibil* was the fire-god and was regarded as the son of *Anu*. But *Nusuku*, another fire-god represented the sacred fire and was invoked during sacrifices as the sublime messenger carrying sacrificial fragrance to the gods. It is significant to note the role of Vedic fire-god, *Agni,* as the messenger of sacrificial offerings to gods.

In the Vedic ensemble, the division of the Universe into two parts *Dyauḥ* and *Pṛthivī* and the three regions, each with a god-head, the concepts of nature in terms of Aditi, Aryaman's way, Soma identified with the Moon, Sūrya (the Sun) and Agni or Fire (whom the Vedic sages extolled in diverse ways), are somewhat similar to, if not exactly identical with, those of the Mesopotamian gods, viz., Anu, and Anu's way, Sin, Shamash and Gibil (as well as Nusuku) respectively (see the footnotes).*3

* **Mesopotamian**	**Ṛgvedic**
1. Universe conceived in terms of celestial and terrestrial parts (male-female symbolism)	Dyāvā-Pṛthivī or celestial terrestrial male-female symbolism
2. Two regions of the Universe and the triad of gods:	Dyusthāna (celestial); Antarikṣasthāna (atmospheric); and Pṛthivīsthāna (terrestrial):
(i) Anu: God of Sky and heaven	(i) Sūrya (celestial)
(ii) Enlil: God of Air and Hurricane	(ii) Vāyu (atmospheric)
(iii) Ea or Enki: Lord of the Earth and Water surrounding the Earth	(iii) Agni (Earth)
	Other Gods:
	Celestial: Ādityas, Dyaus, Varuṇa, Aryaman; Savitṛ, Uṣas, Pūṣan, Viṣṇu
	Atmospheric: Indra, Apāmnapāt, Rudra, Parjanya
	Terrestrial: Pṛthvī, Soma, Bṛhaspati, and rivers.
3. Anu's way	Aryaman's path
4. The Sidereal deities:	Candramā (Moon); Sinīvālī,
(i) Sin (Moon)	fourteenth day of the New Moon-half of a month.
(ii) Shamash (Sun)	Sūrya
(iii) Ishtar (Goddess of morning and evening)	Uṣas (Goddess of Dawn)
5. Giebil and Nusuku (fire-gods): Nusuku was the sublime messenger for carrying sacrifical fragrance and offerings to gods	Agni: messenger carrying sacrifical fragrance and offerings to heaven
6. Adad: The god of lightning and tempest; carrying thunderbolt in each hand	Indra's weapon was thunderbolt
7. Neargal, the warrior-god and his variant Dibarra were associated with the destruction of cities to establish their supremacy over humans	Indra associated with the destruction of cities of demons like Vṛtra.
8. Performance of sacrifices to propitiate gods	Similar ritual practices
9. Gods were fond of intoxicating drinks	Soma was the most favoured intoxicating drink offered to gods
10. Gods with animal connections	Similar ideas
(i) Shamash (Sun): Eagle and Later driven by horses;	(i) Sun: Eagle flying through space; also in a chariot driven by horses
(ii) Ea: Antelope and serpent	(ii) Indra: White horse
(iii) Adad: Pig	(iii) Maruts or Vāyu: Antelope or deer
(iv) Merodoch: Bull	(iv) Agni: Red horse
(v) Ishtar: Lion (Female goddess)	(v) Savitṛ: Tawny horse
	(vi) Aśvins: Ass
	(vii) Uṣas: Red cow

Ṛta

The *Ṛgveda*, in its ten *maṇḍalas* and 10552 *mantras* under 1028 *sūktas* or hymns, has several ideas concerning the universe, but within a divine framework—'God solidified the molten earth, established the moving mountains, created the heavenly regions and firmly fixed the skies'[4] (II.12.2), the first and foremost being *ṛta*, the natural order or law, that governs the entire universe, including the movements and occurrences therein. It would appear such a conception was seminal to the Vedic thought processes and one does not find a parallel to it in as detailed a manner as in the *Ṛgveda,* in other cultures at that point of time. *Ṛta* was not only described as the immanent power or force causing the flow of rivers, seasonal changes, alternation of day and night, and the movement of the Sun but it was also regarded as the very face of the Sun itself. Even the gods were enjoined to follow *ṛta*. The idea of *ṛta* was physical and moral alike. In the Vedic thinking, sin meant the transgression of the natural law. Later, this approach gradually gave rise to the notion of Dharma that has been an inseparable component of Hinduism and other religions. *Yajña* (sacrifice) was conceived as the 'navel of the Univese' (*bhuvanasya nābhiḥ*) and the abode of *ṛta* (*ṛtasya dhāma*). The very act of performing *yajña* meant the protection of *ṛta*, the cosmic order. In this manner, the triple-stranded man–spirit–cosmos view runs through, in one form or the other, throughout the Vedic literature. It was, nevertheless, a cyclic-dynamic view as the *Ṛgveda*[5] says that the Creator created the Sun, the Moon and the firmament over and over again.

Cosmography, Cosmogony and Related Ideas

The cosmos which is named as *Bhūmikośa* in the *Chāndogya Upaniṣad*[6] has been described as of round shape, having the form of human body in three parts. 'Its middle in the form of human belly is the atmosphere, its lower portion is earth, and its mouth is the heaven, while its quarters are intermittent joints'. The tripartite structure of cosmos was believed to encompass the three *lokas* or worlds: of the *Dyaus* or *Svar* (celestial region); (ii) *Antarikṣa* (sky or firmament or atmosphere); and (iii) the *Pṛthivī* (earth). Such a tripartite speculation was not peculiar to the Vedic Indians. It was also prevalent among the Greeks, specially among the Pythagoreans and others as the locales respectively of the gods, demons or spiritual creatures, and mortals.[7] The Vedic imagery, however, does not regard them as water-tight compartments, but presents them as an integrated whole. While the holistic view of the cosmos or universe persists, there are some variations. The *Aitareya Brāhmaṇa*[8] states: 'The sky rests on the air; the air on the earth; the earth on the waters; the waters on the reality (*satya*); the reality on Brahman; and Brahman, on *tapas* or creative fervour. The *Aitareya Āraṇyaka*[9], on the other hand, refers to four worlds, of *Ambhas, Marīci, Mara* and *Ap;* that *Ambhas* (water) is above the heaven; Marīci (lights) are the sky; Mara (mortal) is the earth, and waters under the earth are the Ap world; Here two types of Waters have been thought: of one above the heaven (or the heaven itself), and the other below the earth. It may be noted that water has been projected to be the primordial element in some of the Upaniṣads, although the *Ṛgveda* in its *Nāsadīya Sūkta*[10] refers to it with a question as to whether it was so.

A somewhat different picture of the universe is presented in the *Bṛhadāraṇyakopaniṣad,*[11] when it refers to as many as ten worlds including air, Sun, Moon, stars and gods, ending with Prajāpati and Brahman. On the other hand, another *upaniṣad*[12] speaks of seven nether worlds: Atala, Pātāla, Vitala, Sutala, Rasatala, Mahatala and Talatala. These and allied passages in the Vedic literature reveal only certain speculative endeavours that do not throw much light on the structure of the physical world. There is an interesting presentation in the *Maitreya Upaniṣad* that Brahman is the soul of the Sun and from the Sun emanate the Moon, planets and stars as well as the year (time) itself.

In the Purāṇa-s

However, speculations persisted in the *Purāṇa-s* which present rather a detailed description of the three *Lokas,* (*Bhūḥ, Bhuvaḥ, Svaḥ* and *Janaḥ, tapaḥ* and *Satya*) each of Brahmā, Viṣṇu and Śiva, the mythological trinity, or the Creator, the Sustainer and the Destroyer of the universe, respectively. The *Viṣṇu Purāṇa*[13] (II. 7, 16-20) has an interesting account of these *Lokas* as well as their subsidiary ones, in terms of *yojana-s* thus giving a spatial matrix. According to this Purāṇa, the solar disc (*Sauramaṇḍalam*) is hundred thousand *yojana-s* from the Earth; from the Solar disc, the Moon is a hundred thousand *yojana-s;* from the Moon, The *nakṣatra maṇḍala* (asterisms) is again a hundred thousand *yojana-s*. The Purāṇa also states that ten million *yojana-s* above *Dhruva* lies what is called the *Maharloka,* twice this distance above is *Janaloka,* four times this distance lies *Tapoloka* and six times this distance above situates the *Satyaloka.* An interesting aspect of this four-tiered world is that it relates to the inhabitants therein respectively as those (i) who live for one *kalpa* (see p. 221) or a day of Brahmā, (ii) who cannot be devoured by fire, and (iii) those who are immortal. Such a classification is a graded one culminating in the *Satya Loka,* also called *Brahmaloka,* the abode of the Creator.

The *Vāyu purāṇa*[14] presents the three worlds as *Bhūḥ, Bhuvaḥ* and *Svaḥ,* stating that the terrestrial world is a part of *Bhūloka,* also indirectly pointing out the teresstrial–celestial correspondence. The sphere that extends from *Bhūḥ* to the Sun is stated to be the residence of the *siddhas* and *munis* (those who are enlightened and have acquired divine status) and is called *Bhuvarloka*. This *Purāṇa* also states, in quantitative terms, that the region extending from the Sun and Dhruva encompassing a vast span of fourteen thousand *yojanas*, is *Svarloka*.[15] This idea goes back to the period of the Brāhmaṇas. The *Śatapatha Brāhmaṇa* (XI. 1.6.1.ff) speaks of how Prajāpati rose from the golden egg which swam about for a year in the waters which desired to propagate themselves and, for that purpose mortified themselves giving rise to the golden egg. Prajāpati was born after a year by breaking open the egg. It has been stated that one year after, he tried to speak and he said 'bhūh' and this word became the Earth; he uttered *bhuvah* and this word became the atmosphere; the word *svar* spoken by him became the sky. Alongside, from the five syllables which form these three words, he made the five seasons of the year (spring, summer, rainy, autumn and winter). This hierarchical approach appears to be symbolic of the thought—processes of human beings from the mundane to the finest state. The word *loka,* significantly also means to *shine* or to *perceive*. The *Purāṇa-s* recognize in all 14 *lokas*—seven rising from the earth one above the other (*Bhūloka, Bhuvarloka, Svarloka, Maharloka, Janaloka, Tapoloka* and *Satyaloka*), and seven lower regions (Atala, Pātāla etc.)[16] descending from the earth one below the other. In course of time, this presentation emphasised the geocentric view, although from a standpoint different from the astronomical one. One can also perceive in this presentation the man–spirit–cosmos integration attempted in a different way.

The *Nāsadīya sūkta,* a cosmogonic hymn of the *Ṛgveda* (X. 129; see next chapter for details) posited the idea of the unknowable nature of the world-ground. But the *Ṛgveda* also thought of a godhead, Prajāpati, the Lord of all creatures. The *Puruṣasūkta*[17] presented an array of creation from a Cosmic Person. There was also a concept of Hiraṇyagarbha (golden egg) as well as of Viśvakarman in the context of creation. The source or the origin of creation of the universe as a whole is expounded as being everlasting.

As for the shape of the universe, there are early references in the *Ṛgveda*[18] to indicate that the universe was regarded as a sphere, or a disc. The Greeks like Xenophobes and Parmanedes, on the other hand, thought of the universe as being circular. Empedocles emphasized the globular idea of the Universe but at its primordial stage a view which was accepted by both Plato and Aristotle.

In Indian belief there was the idea of Mount Meru, which was supposed to be located on the highest mountain, in the center of the world. This idea recurs in Indian astronomy as the pivotal point around which the planets would revolve. Another belief was that on this point, Brahmā, the creator, resided and this was thus another way of expressing the man–spirit–cosmos relationship.

In the Upaniṣad-s

But the man–spirit–cosmos view attained new height with the elucidation of the concept of Brahman, specially in the Upaniṣads. Brahman was conceived in terms of the creator, preserver and the destroyer of the World, the last one being thought of as the world going back to Brahman itself or himself. The Upaniṣads proclaim that Brahman is not dual nor plural; but an all-inclusive one, the inanimate and the animate; also identified with self or ātman. The *Aitareya upaniṣad*[19] says: 'This one (the self) is Brahman; this is Indra, this is Prajāpati; this is all these gods; and this is these five elements, namely, earth, air, ākāśa, water and fire; and this is all these (big creatures), together with the tiny ones, that are the procreators of others, those that are born of eggs, of wombs, of moisture and of the earth, viz., horses, cattle, men, elephants, and all the creatures that are there, which move or fly and those which do not move.'

The Upaniṣad goes a step further and declares: 'All these are impelled by consciousness; all these have consciousness as the giver of their reality; the universe has consciousness as its eye and consciousness is its end. Consciousness is Brahman'. The upaniṣadic approach, then, is to have an undifferentiated view of the physical and biological worlds as well as the concept of Supreme Consciousness equated with Brahman or Self which is essentially consciousness itself.

The *Muṇḍaka upaniṣad*[20] has an imagery: 'As a spider spreads out and withdraws (its threads), as on the earth grow herbs and trees, and as from a living man issues out hair (on the head and body), so out of the Imperishable does the Universe emerge here (in this phenomenal creation)'.

The Upaniṣadic position, if stated in general terms, is that, though the world is characterised by attributes, relations, actions and events as well as by the elements of space, time and even a type of causality, Brahman has none of these. Śaṅkara's Advaita, however, points out that Brahman is both *mūrta* (corporeal) and *amūrta* (subtle or incorporeal), *parā* (supreme) and *aparā* (lower). Endowed with qualities (*saguṇa*), this aspect of Brahman is designated by Śaṅkara as Īśvara who is regarded as being both the material and the efficient or the instrumental cause of the world, and Māyā is the power of Īśvara. Thus qualified Brahman manifests himself as the world by his Māyā. There is the well known upaniṣadic saying: 'all this is Brahman (*sarvam khalvidam Brahma*); 'all this' according to Śaṅkara, stands for the phenomenal world; but this is real for the ignorant and, when the ignorance (*avidyā*) is removed and enlightenment attained through the pathways of meditation and the like, the physical world would appear to be unreal to an enlightened person. It would seem that advaita does not disregard the existence of the physical world, although it does not throw much light on it either. Though the upaniṣadic or the Vedāntic approach to Brahman and Māyā[21] scaled new heights with the discourses of Śaṅkara, the upaniṣadic postulate of five elements, despite their metaphysical and also physical characteristics, did not appear to have appealed very much to Śaṅkara.

The Five Elements

The *pañcamahābhūta-s*—*pṛthivī, ap, tejas, vāyu* and *ākāśa*—had, from their roots in the Upaniṣads, become already integrated into the philosophical systems of the Sāṃkhya and the Vaiśeṣika. This doctrine of five elements, an important thought-structure from the point of view of the physical world, had its adherents to whom not only an error free knowledge of the physical world was necessary but also, through it, the attainment of the life's highest value (*nihśreyas* or *apavarga*). The orthodox systems that provide an integrated insight of the five elements—the Sāṃkhya, the Vaiśeṣika and the syncretic Nyāya-Vaiśeṣika—merit special attention.

Sāṃkhya: Perhaps the oldest of the six orthodox systems, the Sāṃkhya regards Prakṛti as the unmanifested potential or the first principle of the universe, which is also referred to as *Pradhāna* or *Avyakta*. It has been explained that the world of experience is finite or limited with its apparent diversities and, therefore, there should be an all-inclusive and eternal source which, according to Sāṃkhya, is Prakṛti which itself is the unity of three *guṇa-s* – *sattva, rajas* and *tamas*. In other words, Prakṛti is constituted of these three *guṇa-s*, intertwined like the three strands (*guṇas*) of a rope. *Sattva* is all that is bright and good; *rajas*, the principle of motion and restless activity; while *tamas*, meaning literally darkness, is the principle of inertia and ignorance. They are symbolically presented in terms of colours: *sattva* (white): *rajas* (red); and *tamas* (black). They are not separate from Prakṛti; for, together they themselves form Prakṛti in a state of equilibrium.

The Sāṃkhya, a dualistic system, has projected, besides Prakṛti, another reality or entity by the name of Puruṣa, the spirit or the subject, uncaused and as eternal as Prakṛti. But unlike the latter, as noted before, Puruṣa is not composed of the three *guṇas*. But, according to Īśvarakṛṣṇa, the author of the *Sāṃkhya-kārikā*, Puruṣa is a witness (*sākṣi*) of these *guṇas*, but even beyond them. Puruṣa is regarded as an intelligent principle for experiencing the empirical world, and also as pure consciousness and an *adhiṣṭhāna* or the foundation of all knowledge. Through the interaction between Puruṣa and Prakṛti, an unfolding takes place leading to *Buddhi* or *Mahān, ahaṅkāra* or ego, encompassing the five subtle states called the *tanmātra-s*, the mind and the five elements (*mahābhūtāni*). Like the Mīmāṃsā and the Jaina, the Sāṃkhya thinks of the plurality of the Puruṣa-s or selves, although it is stated that the selves are alike and their essence is nothing but consciousness.

The Sāṃkhya system, like the other Indian systems, is not one of mere explanation of the objective physical world and the subjective self, but of eventual emancipation back to the original Puruṣa in relation to the Prakṛti, to the proximity (*sānnidhya*) of the three *guṇas* away from the worldly bondage. The Puruṣa, as stated already, is himself beyond the three *guṇa-s*, but the bound selves have these *guṇas* in different degrees leading to their plurality. Each self, then, has his own Prakṛti, but with a commonality of the gross physical world constituted of the five elements.

According to Sāṃkhya, Prakṛti and Puruṣa are in the relation of each needing the other, and for the creation or the unfolding, they have to interact with each other, Prakṛti being dynamic and Puruṣa, being the inactive one. But this interaction is not in the nature of a direct contact, but is stated to be due to the proximity of the Puruṣa, which would be causative of the disturbance of the equilibrium of the three *guṇas* (Prakṛti) leading to the evolution or *pariṇāma* of Prakṛti. Nevertheless, some Sāṃkhya followers argue that there would also be a semblance of, though not a real, contact between Prakṛti and Puruṣa.

In the Sāṃkhya duality, despite its own incongruities, the uncaused Prakṛti, but the first cause of the universe, through its evolution or sequential change, ends up with the five elements of physical nature. Prakṛti, therefore, is the material cause and all aspects of the physical world including space and time are supposed to be contained in it. Its dynamic character is suggestive of its being even in motion. It may be noted that the Sāṃkhya (*nirīśvara*) system with its 24 principles (excluding Puruṣa) did dispense with the notion of God as a Creator, although later a god-head was superimposed (*seśvara Sāṃkhya*). The evolution, as contemplated in the Sāṃkhya, is teleological as it is intended for the purpose of Puruṣa whose ultimate aim is liberation from the worldly confines.

To return to the five elements: These are the evolutes of the corresponding five subtle states called *tanmātra-s*, an idea that goes back to the *Praśnopaniṣad*. As for the seed ideas of the Sāṃkhya, it may be noted that certain upaniṣadic thoughts influenced the origin of the Sāṃkhya system. In its evolutionary scheme, interestingly the *tammātra-s* are related to *ahaṅkāra* or ego which is said to be of three types in consonance with the three *guṇas* of Prakṛti—the *vaikārika* or *sāttvika*, the *taijasa* or *rājasika*, and *bhūtādi* or *tāmasika*. It is from the last that the five *tanmātra-s* or 'things-in-themselves' or subtle essences that are related respectively to the five sensorial attributes, namely, smell, taste, visual (or colour), touch and sound, from which, according to the Sāṃkhya, the five gross elements are derived. The Sāṃkhya view in this respect is in contradistinction to that of the Nyāya – Vaiśeṣika which thinks of the five specific qualities of the elements: *pṛthvī* (smell); *ap* (taste); *tejas* (colour); *vāyu* (touch) and *ākāśa* (sound), without any mention specifically of their essence in the form of tanmātra-s. The Nyāya-Vaiśeṣika, however, has thought of the atomic states of the first four elements and the atoms also are regarded as possessing the respective specific attributes.

The Sāṃkhya exposition of Prakṛti appears to be an abstract one. It is not in reality what may be generally referred to as the composite Nature or the observable material world. Its theory of causation is known as *satkāryavāda* or the *pariṇāmavāda* or the modification of Prakṛti. This theory does not admit any new production except the view that the production is a part of evolutionary process. In other words, the effect is the very essence of its material cause, and the production is only a concretization of that which already exists potentially[22] (*Sāṃkhya-Kārikā*, 9). "There are certain special features of evolution (Sāṃkhya), which deserve notice. First, it is based on a belief in the indestructibility of matter and the persistence of force. Something cannot come out of nothing; and whatever is, has always been. Production is only the manifestation (*abhivyakti*) of what is already in a latent form, and is not a new creation (*ārambha*). ...Evolution is conceived as cyclic or periodical. That is, there are periods of evolution and dissolution alternating so that it is not a process of continuous progress in one direction only".[23]

In the Sāṃkhya scheme the gross elements owe their evolution to the *tanmātra-s* with an increasing degree of differentiation: *Ākāśa* emerges from *śabda tanmātra* with only sound as its manifest quality; *vāyu* emerges from both *śabda* and *sparśa tanmātra-s* with two qualities, namely, sound and touch; *tejas* arises from these two and the *rūpatanmātra*, thus possessing three qualities—sound; touch and colour; *ap* comes about from the aforesaid three and the *rasa tanmātra*, having thus four qualities, namely, sound, touch, colour and taste; and lastly, *pṛthivī* emerges from the preceding four as well as the *gandha tanmātra* and has all the five qualities—sound, touch, colour, taste, and smell. According to the *Yoga-sūtra-bhāṣya*,[24] each element consists of finite discrete particles called *paramāṇu-s*. But, this does not represent in any manner a Sāṃkhya atomism. For Indian atomism, one has to turn to the Nyāya-Vaiśeṣika, Jaina and certain schools of Buddhism.

Nyāya-Vaiśeṣika

Though the Nyāya and the Vaiśeṣika had independent origins, the Vaiśeṣika perhaps being earlier, they became syncretic by about the tenth century A.D., and hence they are clubbed together. The Vaiśeṣika system expounds a pluralism, believing in the diversity of the observed world of matter, attributes and motion.

The nomenclature or the title, the *Vaiśeṣika,* is indeed interesting. There is a general agreement among scholars that this nomenclature owes its origin to the fifth of its six categories (*padārtha-s*), namely, *viśeṣa,* a category that does not find a place in the other orthodox or heterodox systems. Udayana, however, thinks that, though the title is derived from *Viśeṣa,* it means the ascertainment of the true characteristics of the entities. According to H. Ui,[25] the Vaiśeṣika also means 'superior' or 'distinguished' perhaps from the Sāṁkhya that had its own strong exponents. The author or the propounder of the Vaiśeṣika model is generally believed to be the sage, Kaṇāda variously called Kaṇabhuk, Kaṇabhakṣa, Kaṇacara and Kaṇavṛta, the word, *kaṇa,* meaning particle or atom, and thus the author's name signifying the one who is an eater of particles. The commentator Śrīdhara has, however a different version, i.e., that Kaṇāda used to live on grains scattered in fields or on roads.

The Vaiśeṣika is also called *Aulūkya darśana* and the story goes that a divinity appeared before Kaṇāda in the form of an owl (*ulūka*) and inspired him to write the Vaiśeṣika aphorisms. The *Sarvadarśana saṅgraha* of Mādhavācārya, speaks of *Aulūkya darśana.* There are differing views as to whether Kaṇāda was a believer in god or not. But, according to Praśastapāda, Kaṇāda could well have been a devotee of Śiva and was an exponent of *dharma, niḥśreyas* and *mokṣa.* Kaṇāda begins his *sūtras* by saying that he would now explain *dharma*[26] and in the next *sūtra,* he speaks of *niḥśreyas.*[27] There are equally differing opinions about the date of Kaṇāda. One of the arguments to the effect that he was pre-Buddhist is that there is no reference whatsoever either to the Buddha or the Buddhist tenets in the *Vaiśeṣika sūtra-s.* According to Winternitz[28] one Rohagupta, a learned Jain, adopted the Vaiśeṣika categories in his expositions. In any case, the Vaiśeṣika system has a distinct position in the history of Indian philosophical thought.

There is a long interregnum between the time of the *Vaiśeṣika sūtra-s* of Kaṇāda and the appearance of their authentic and lucid exposition by Praśastapāda (*c.* 4th cent. A.D.). Possibly there might have been a couple of commentaries in between, since references to some of their contents are found in later works. Like the Vaiśeṣika, Nyāya also thinks of '*apavarga* and *niḥśreyas*' in its introductory verses.

Generally Nyāya means 'argumentation', (though it literally means 'going back') and an analytical method. It is also called *hetu-vidyā* or the science of causes. The Nyāya-Vaiśeṣika, therefore, is concerned with a methodology of understanding or a logical interpretation of pluralistic realism. It tacitly accepts the reality of the world, like the Vaiśeṣika, the basic postulate of which is that knowledge is always in relation to objects and the objects are not only independent of knowledge but also of one another.

Of all the Indian systems of thought, the Vaiśeṣika provides its own original approach to the understanding of the physical world. In an analytical manner it has projected six categories or *padārtha-s* (called the *bhāvapadārtha-s* or being) and a seventh one (*abhāva*), apparently non-existent which the later Vaiśeṣikas elaborated upon. A *padārtha* generally means an object of knowledge, characterised by its existence (*astitva*), knowability (*jñeyatva*) and nameability (*abhidheyatva*). The main six categories of the Vaiśeṣika are: (i) substance (*dravya*); (ii) quality or attribute (*guṇa*); (iii) action (*karma*); (iv) generality (*sāmānya*); (v) particularity (*viśeṣa*); and (vi) inherence (*samavāya*).

The *Vaiśeṣika sūtra-s* along with the *Upaskāra* of Śankaramiśra and other texts deal in succinct manner with the six categories, definitions of nine substances including space and time, soul and mind, the qualities and their inherence, atoms, action or motion, determinate and indeterminate perception, the nature of sense organs and their objects, three types of causes and allied aspects. Over the centuries, engendered by the rigour of logic provided by the Nyāya, there ensued subtle distinctions and discourses among the commentators of this system, ably defending their position vis-à-vis that of their opponents. What is of relevance to us, however, is the meticulousness with which this system is delineated in considerable detail. More relevant are the perspicacious mind-set behind it and its refreshingly original approach to the knowledge of the physical world, despite its limitations.

Substance

The Vaiśeṣika concept of substance is indeed interesting. Substance is defined as the substratum in which both the qualities and actions inhere. In other words, the latter have no independent existence apart from the substance which is regarded as self-subsistent and independent. Nor can a substance in its name and form or even otherwise remain divorced from attribute or action. The generic substance is pluralistic inasmuch as it is of nine types: the five elements, time, space, self or spirit or the knower, and mind or the internal organ. Each of the five elements has a specific quality, namely, earth: smell; water: taste; fire: colour; air: touch; and *ākāśa*: sound, corresponding to the five senses. This type of relationship is obviously of considerable significance because it brings about a complementarity of the pathways (senses) of seeking knowledge of objects and the objects themselves. Such a correspondence is not noticeable in respect of the five elemental theory either of the Greeks or of the Chinese. Moreover the creation and the dissolution of the Universe have been explained in terms of the four of the Indian five elements as follows. Neither the Greeks nor the Chinese made such an attempt.

The *Sṛṣṭisaṃhārakāraṇam* of the *Praśastapādabhāṣya*,[29] has provided a clear exposition of how the process of creation and destruction takes place involving the four elements and their atomic states.

'When a hundred years, according to the measure adopted in the case of Brahmā, have elapsed, there comes the moment for the liberation of the Brahmā ruling at that time; and then for the sake of the resting at night [i.e. for a short while] of all living beings wearied by their wandering [through series of births], there arises in the mind of the Supreme Lord (Maheśvara) who is the ruler of all the world, a desire to destroy [all created things]. Simultaneously with such a desire, there comes about a cessation of the operations of the various *adṛṣṭa-s* inhering in all the selves, *adṛṣṭa-s* which are causes of their [=the selves] bodies and sense organs as well as the gross material elements. Next, due to the desire of the Supreme Lord as well as the moments produced by the conjunction of the self with the atoms, there comes about disjunction in the atoms constituting bodies and sense organs as a result of which the conjunctions cease. And this brings about the destruction of all [created] things up to the state of the [indivisible] atoms'.

'In the same manner, there comes about a successive destruction of the gross material elements, namely, earth, water, fire and air one after the other. After this, the atoms remain by themselves in their isolated condition and the selves too, as characterized by the particular *dharma* (virtue); and *adharma* (vice), and tendencies (*saṃskāra*), remain for the same amount of time'.

'Then, again, to make possible the experiences [of pleasure and pain] to be gained by the living beings, there arises in the mind of the Supreme Lord, a desire for creating things. Such a desire is followed by the production of movements in the atoms of air, the movements being due to the conjunction of the self with the atoms under the influence of the *adṛṣṭa-s* located in all the selves, which then become operative. These moments bring about the mutual conjunctions of the air atoms, and next, there appears, in the order of the dyad etc., finally the gross air which remains vibrating in the sky. After this, in that very gross air, there appears, in the same order, out of the water-atoms, the great reservoir of water [gross water] which remains surging there'. In this thoughtful approach, Praśastapāda has accorded a distinct place to the role of atoms.

These ideas of Praśastapāda have been elaborated upon by Vyomaśivācārya and Udayana in their works, *Vyomavatī* and *Kiraṇāvalī* respectively. It has been pointed out that first the atoms of air combine, eventually into *māhān vāyu* (Great Air) and subsequently a big reservoir of water (due to the combination of watery atoms) is produced which remains flowing owing to the velocity of air. At this stage, the huge earth in a solid form comes into being, as a result of the combination of earth-atoms; and subsequently, a big heap of fire.

After the formation of the five elements (*mahābhūta-s*) one after another, according to these texts, through the Divine Will (*saṅkalpa*), a huge cosmic egg is produced, which is but from the atoms of fire, assisted by those of earth. The texts further point out that Brahmā, with four lotus-like faces, becomes himself produced and engaged by the Divine Will in the production of living beings. It is Brahmā who is the source of further creation including gods, sages and human beings, the four *varṇa-s* and the like, incorporating in them, according to their past deeds, different degrees of *dharma, jñana, aiśvarya,* etc.[30] Even though the Vaiśeṣika adopted a bold approach towards an explanation of the origin of creation in terms of atoms, it chose to join the mainstream of mythological lore, perhaps to gain some credibility to its own ideas among the common people to whom mythology had a special appeal.

Atomism

The word 'atom' is called *aṇu* or *paramāṇu* in the Nyāya-Vaiśeṣika texts, although the word *aṇu* has been used in some upaniṣads in the sense of 'very minute' or 'extremely small'.[31]

In the *Vaiśeṣika sūtra-s,* the word' *aṇu*[32] is consciously used for denoting an atom. The *sūtra-s,* deal with the proof of atoms, though indirectly, as well as their qualities. More importantly, that the atoms are all globular (*pārimāṇḍalya*)[33] has been emphasised in the *sūtra.*

It is only Praśastapāda, who for the first time elaborated upon the nature and structure of the Vaiśeṣika atomism that was further developed by the later Vaiśeṣikas with the epistemic support from the Naiyāyikas. The *Nyāya-bhāṣya* (of Vātsyāyana), *Nyāya-kusumāñjalī* of (Uddyotakara), *Vyomavatī* (of *Vyomaśivācārya*), *Nyāya-Kandalī* (of Śrīdhara) and Kiraṇāvalī (of Udayana) are of special importance from the point of view of what may be generally called the Nyāya-Vaiśeṣika atomism to which Uddyotakara specially made significant contributions in his exposition of the concerned *Nyāyasūtra-s* (4.2, 17-25).

As produced things or sensorially perceived objects, the four elements, earth, water, fire and air, are regarded as non-eternal, but are held to be eternal in their atomic states. The firm belief in the eternality led to the Vaiśeṣika or the Nyāya-Vaiśeṣika atomism with the conviction that, the concept of atom would be a logical necessity. An atom has been described as eternal, spherical, in motion at the primordial stage, indestructible and supra-sensible in the same way as the pre-Socratic Greek savants, Democritus and Leucippus, expounded their atomic postulate. Unlike them, however, the Nyāya-Vaiśeṣika thought of four classes of atoms, each for earth, water, fire and air. More importantly, the Nyāya-Vaiśeṣika atoms share the characteristics or special attributes of the respective gross states as noted earlier. While Democritus viewed that even 'soul' would be composed of atoms in a strictly materialistic manner the Vaiśeṣika abhorred such a view; likewise, the Greek exposition that atoms and void were real was not acceptable to the Nyāya-Vaiśeṣika. The Greek atomism did not explain in any detail as to how the gross bodies were formed from the atoms. The Vaiśeṣika, on the other hand, delineated a structure in terms of dyads (*dvyaṇuka*: two atoms), triads (*tryaṇuka* or *trasareṇu*: three dyads) and so on. As for the different properties observed in a gross substance, the Vaiśeṣika exposition was that it was due to the structural arrangement (*vyūha*) of atoms or dyads or triads. It is interesting to note that, while the Greek atomism lay dormant from about the first century A.D. to the seventeenth century, Indian atomism, including the Jaina atomism, was a vibrant thought specially between the fourth and the fourteenth centuries A.D.

The Greek atomism, after its revival by such thinkers as Gassendi, Boyle and Newton, was prone to provide a new stimulus to the development of modern physics and chemistry in the nineteenth century. The Vaiśeṣika atomism, with its four types of atoms and just logically determined dyads, triads etc. did not appear to have the potential to move along fresh vistas of thinking in respect of the nature and composition of matter and its diversities. The concept of mass as a measurable entity was noted for its absence in the Nyāya-Vaiśeṣika model. It may be observed that Newton in the seventeenth century propounded the idea of mass in his now familiar laws of motion. The Nyāya-Vaiśeṣika deliberated upon motion in rather a restricted way under its category of action (*karma*). In a rudimentary manner, it sought to explain five types of motion: upwards, downwards, general (horizontal or in any direction), expansion and contraction. Motion along with the determinants of space and time was never thought of, and a measurable approach involving mass, space and time was a desideratum. Significantly, it was this approach and the experiments associated with it that marked the beginnings of physics in the 15th–16th century in the West, characterized by the science of measurement, reproducibility and verifiability.

The World-stuff

In one respect, nevertheless, the Nyāya-Vaiśeṣika was far ahead conceptually, namely, its exposition of the category of *dravya* or substance. This included, as noted before, the four material elements, the ubiquitous *ākāśa* (not to be equated with the Aristotelian ether), time and space, self and mind. The inclusion of *self*, the knower, and *mind*, the knowing faculty, proved to be of great significance even from the modern scientific point of view. With all its powerful methodology, sophisticated experimentation and mathematical models, modern science is still unable to arrive at what is called the world-stuff or substance. Even the current unified field theory of four types of force has remained still with all the nuances of its plurality, although there seems to be certain reconciliation among some of them. Whether the essentially sense-based modern science would be able to explain in its own terms or the limitation of human mind itself is reached in the field of modern science is a moot point, the main reason being that modern science excludes the observer or the self with his mind, in all of its experimental methods based on sensorial encounters. The Vaiśeṣika, on the other hand, had realized the necessity of the inclusion of the self and mind in its concept of substance even over two thousand years ago. Such an approach was not, however, based on any experimental or mathematical model like modern science. It was essentially in the nature of a thought-model, but became effective for the Nyāya-Vaiśeṣika portrayal of reality in tune with its approach to the knowledge of the phenomenal world.

Qualities

As regards the qualities or attributes, Kaṇāda, the author of the Vaiśeṣika sūtra-s, has mentioned 17 of them and his scholiast of the fifth century A.D., Praśastapāda in his *bhāṣya* has added seven more including gravity (*gurutva*) as an attribute but only of earth and water, perhaps keeping in mind that the other two, fire and air, would have no heaviness in them. In any case, the idea of gravitational pull or attraction has not been dealt with in measurable terms. However, Annam Bhaṭṭa (17th cent. A.D.) in his *Tarkasaṅgraha* defines *gurutva* or gravity as 'the non-inherent cause of the first fall,' thus in a way making a suggestion of gravitational pull or attraction (personal communication from D. Prahlādācār). Even in the West such an idea did not take the form of a law of universal gravitation till the seventeenth century when it was Newton who first enunciated it. But the recognition of the fact that the two elements—earth and water—in their gross form possess the quality of heaviness was a novel idea, since even around the fifth century A.D., neither the Greco-Roman nor the Chinese appeared to have thought of gravity in any meaningful manner.

Generality, Particularity and Inherence

The three categories, substance, qualities and action or motion, are related among themselves. This mutual relationship coupled with the three other categories—generality, particularity and inherence—appear to be disparate; but it should be noted that there is an inter—relatedness among all of them. The generality (*sāmānya*), that encompasses the common characteristics of objects is regarded as one, eternal and universal. In any case it is not a subjective concept, but objectively considered as the universal. It is regarded as being of two types: the higher one or the being (*sattā*) which includes the largest number of objects or the entities; and the lower one, which covers a limited number of things. For, example, *pṛthvītva* (objects having *pṛthvī* element); *ghaṭatva* (the abstract of the objects of pottery) and the like. The Vaiśeṣika generality is not an equivalent of Platonic 'Idea' as it has a far greater significance than the latter towards an understanding of the relata of the observable world.

The observed objects, however, are different from one another in several ways and each has its own character. If generality is an inclusive one, there needs to be another entity that accounts for differentiation. The Vaiśeṣika has, therefore, projected another category called *viśeṣa* or particularity in the case of those which otherwise resemble one another, but not those which have perceivable differentiation. In fact, the Vaiśeṣika system, as noted already, derives its nomenclature mainly because of this approach, in addition to the category of generality or *sāmānya*. However, the category, *viśeṣa*, has its ambiguity; for, according to Vaiśeṣika, the viśeṣa relates to both the qualitative and quantitative differences, meaning thereby that only in such cases it is applicable.

The sixth category of the Vaiśeṣika is *samavāya* or inherence, or an inseparable, eternal relation. According to the *Praśastapāda bhāṣya*, inherence is the relationship subsisting among the things that are inseparable and standing to one another in the relation of the container and the contained. They are five types of objects which alone are permissive of *samavāya* : (i) substance and qualities; (ii) substance and action; (iii) generality and its possessor; (iv) particularity and eternal substance; and (v) the whole and parts or the material cause and the effect. It is tempting to argue that, after all, inherence could be in the nature of conjunction (*saṃyoga*). But the Nyāya-Vaiśeṣika position is that inherence is not conjunction which is thought of as an attribute or quality in relation to a substance and not as an independent category. Moreover, conjunction is stated to be a quality possessed by all the nine types of substance, along with the disjunction (*vibhāga*); in other words, conjunction occurs between two separable objects, while inherence is in the related objects which are inseparable. Conjunction, therefore, is in the nature of an external relation or adventitious, while inherence is eternal as an internal relation. The concept of whole and its parts is an important one. It is pointed out that the whole is different from the parts of which it is constituted.

Valid Knowledge

Both the Nyāya and the Vaiśeṣika approach to the knowledge of reality lies in their belief that without right knowledge, ignorance reigns supreme resulting in bondage and suffering. And liberation from them is the ultimate goal. As indicated already, the Vaiśeṣika developed a model of categories as an exposition of the world of reality. Nyāya supplemented it by delineating the means and the manner of the acquisition of right knowledge towards the attainment of the highest good (*niḥśreyas; apavarga*). As noted earlier, the Vaiśeṣika presented six categories (and later seven by including *abhāva*) and classified all the knowable and nameable objects under them in an integrated manner. The Nyāya provided sixteen categories. The Vaiśeṣika's six categories can come under one of them called *prameya* or the objects of knowledge. *Prameya* is the second in the series of sixteen categories, the first one being *pramāṇa* or instrument of the acquisition of knowledge. With this approach, significantly, Nyāya-Vaiśeṣika believes that not only the acquired knowledge is about the perceived objects but even the nature of knowledge itself could be definitive. Towards this end, the Nyāya-Vaiśeṣika epistemology was meticulously structured.

Accepting that the external world is real, the Nyāya-Vaiśeṣika emphasises that knowledge has to be logically obtained. The Vaiśeṣika, like Buddhism, regards the direct perception (*pratyakṣa*) and inference (*anumāna*) as the logical means of arriving at the right or valid knowledge of the observed world. Nyāya, in addition, includes verbal testimony (*śabda*) and comparison (*upamāna*) as the other two pathways towards the confirmation or strengthening of one's argument leading eventually to valid or error-free knowledge. Nyāya emphasises that since the self through its senses is in direct contact with the object, the data acquired can never be false. But error may arise when complex objects are not property perceived and the resulting complex cognition could be false. 'If the complex content of our knowledge has a complex corresponding to it in the objective world, we have truth; otherwise error'.[34] Nyāya has examined in detail the possibilities of error in direct perception and how to find out whether the knowledge obtained is true or not by subjecting the so gained knowledge to practical tests in a logical manner.

Gautama or Gotama who is supposed to be the author of *Nyāya sūtra-s*, thinks of a triple classification of inference: *pūrvavat* (reasoning based on resemblance or similarity that which has been observed in the past); *śeṣavat* (reasoning by the process of elimination); and *sāmānytodṛṣṭa* (reasoning, based upon sensorial object, about that which is even beyond it). The reasoning in respect of the existence of mind or even God belongs to this category. Generally a five-membered syllogism is adopted to arrive at valid inference. Nyāya holds the view that deduction and induction are inseparably related. It may be noted that the Aristotelian syllogism which is three-membered, is mainly deductive and verbal. But according to Nyāya, the inference is meant also for convincing others. The point worthy of note is that Nyāya accords as distinct a position to inference as it does to direct perception. In this connection, it may be desirable to point out that the progress of modern science over the centuries is by and large due to inference based on the observed data, besides to some extent the process of induction and mathematical modelling. But, as has been rightly said by Eddington, 'Observation is the Court of Appeal in Science'. Even the mathematically inferred ones, at some stage or the other, are to be tested on the anvil of direct observation. Modern scientific methodology recognizes no authority save the experiments, observation and inference. Even the concept of a great scientist is not accepted just because he is a recognized authority, unless and until it is tested by the related scientific method. Personal authority is a *persona non grata* in science and it is only the proven and verifiable scientific method that is the accepted authority.

The Nyāya, on the other hand, has introduced verbal testimony (*śabda*) under *pramāṇa-s* along with direct perception and inference. The verbal testimony is the statement of an *āpta*, a trustworthy person whose views are regarded as true knowledge. The teachings of the Veda are accepted as valid, since the Veda is held to be a revealed knowledge or authored by God and thus free from blemishes. The position of Nyāya in this respect appears to be woefully retrograde from the point of view of meaningful epistemology; for, in the course of acquiring valid knowledge, if there emerges an idea that is not in conformity with what is stated in the Veda or by an authoritative person, the supremacy of the latter becomes acceptable. The fourth instrument of knowledge is by way of comparison (*upamāna*) which is the knowledge of similarity or resemblance. The *Nyāya* holds that *upamāna* will be instrumental in realising the relation of denotation between a word and its meaning.

Causation

The theory of causation as conceived and developed by Nyāya-Vaiśeṣika has some merits, albeit its limitation. It is called *asatkāryavāda* or *ārambhavāda* in contradistinction to the *satkāryavāda* or the *pariṇāmavāda* of the Sāṃkhya. According to the Nyāya-Vaiśeṣika theory of causation, the effect or the product is a new thing and the cause produces the effect. In the *satkāryavāda*, as noted earlier, the new production is not recognised, clinging to the view that the effect pre-exists in the cause, and the effect is just a manifestation of that which is already contained in the material cause. The *pariṇāmavada*, however, seems to believe that the effect is real, but as a transformation of the material cause.

According to Nyāya-Vaiśeṣika, there are three types of causes: (i) the inherent cause (*samavāyī*) or the material cause; (ii) the non-inherent cause (*asamavāyī*), but supposed to be contained in the material cause; and (ii) the efficient cause (*nimitta*) that helps the material cause to produce its effect. The material cause is considered to be always a substance (*dravya*) while the non-inherent cause can be quality or action. The efficient cause may be a substance, quality (*guṇa*) or action (*karma*).

A tangential aspect of the Nyāya theory of causation is the distinction made between what it calls *sādhāraṇa* (ordinary or general) and *asādhāraṇa* (extraordinary) cause. The latter encompasses the instrumental or efficient cause. But the former includes space, time, God's knowledge, the will of God, merit, demerit, prior non-existence and the absence of the counteracting factors (in all eight in number). In the Nyāya-Vaiśeṣika atomism, the primordial motion of atoms is explained as being due to *adṛṣṭa*, the unseen power, that is to say, a power or force external to atoms which, however, are the material cause. The concept of an unseen power represents the limitation of the Nyāya-Vaiśeṣika theory of causation which otherwise has its rational dimensions even from the modern scientific point of view. Causation and the conception of God or divine dispensation both have their role, each in its own way, in the Nyāya-Vaiśeṣika.

Svabhāvavāda

It is interesting to note that the *Śvetāśvatara upaniṣad*[35] refers to both *Yadṛchhāvāda* or *ākasmikavāda* or *animittavāda* (accidentalism) and *Svabhāvavāda* (naturalism). The former believes that the observed order of the physical and biological world is due to a chance; and chaos is self-determined and it is the necessity that governs all phenomena. More importantly, it is stated that necessity is neither due to any external agency, nor due to any definite cause. In other words, this approach discarded the notions of cause either as such or in relation to its effect even for an understanding or explanation of the physical or knowable world. The *animittavāda* too espoused the view that was at total variance with the circumscribed Vedic or the Brāhmanical (priestly) ideas, and also with the upaniṣadic metaphysical idealism. According to Hiriyanna (pp. 103-105), the conceptual approach of the followers of the *svabhāvavāda* and the *animittavāda* was in the nature of heterodoxy, denying the transmigration of soul as well as the *karma* doctrine. Udayana, however, in his *Nyāyakusumāñjali* (I. 5) has argued in favour of causality and the need for it for a rational understanding of the knowable world.

Jaina Views

The Jaina perspective on the physical world is an inseparable part of the realistic as well as relativistic approach of Jainism itself to the universe. The Jainas believe that change or mode is the essential character of all reals and hence all that is real is dynamic. The entire universe is viewed as being constituted of *Jīva* (life or soul) and *Ajīva* (non-living). 'As surely as there is a subject that knows, Jainism says, so surely is there an object that is known. Of them, the *ajīva* has its own specific nature; but that nature cannot be properly understood until it is contrasted with the *jīva*. That is why it is designated as *'not jīva'* or the contradictory of *jīva*. The latter is the higher and the more important category, which accounts for its independent designation, although that can also be well understood only when contrasted with the *ajīva* or non-spirit. ...The *jīva's* relation to matter explains also the somewhat peculiar Jaina view of knowledge. Knowledge is not something that characterises the *jīva*. It constitutes its very essence. The *jīva* can, therefore, know everything unaided directly and exactly as it is; only there should be no impediment in its way'.[36]

The Jaina view of the physical world was also a part of Jaina astronomy which, though strange and ununderstandable in its conceptions, adopted *mutatis mutandis* the Brāhmaṇic astronomical parameters specially of the *Vedāṅga jyotiṣa*. One of the peculiar conceptions relates to the Jaina view of two Suns, two Moons and two sets of 27 *nakṣatra-s* or asterisms. This was in tandem with their two sets of ideas, one, that the earth is a series of flat concentric rings of land formation; and the second, that they are separated by concentric ocean rings. Of them, the central circle called Jambūdvīpa, in the middle of which lay a mountain by name Sudarśa Meru encircled by the salt ocean. Beyond it was supposed to be another Dvīpa (*Dhātuki*) encircled by black ocean, and beyond it lay yet another Dvīpa (*Puṣkara*) with impassable mountain range. The Jambūdvīpa was believed to comprise four quarters, the southernmost being Bhāratavarṣa a nomenclature also found in the Hindu cosmography but in a different way. The Sun, the Moon and the stars were believed to move around the earth's surface in circles, but around Mount Meru. It has been explained in the *Sūrya prajñapti*, a Jaina work in *ardhamāgadhī* script with an extensive commentary by *Malayagiri,* that the two Suns called Bhārata and Airāvata would move through half a diurnal circle in the course of 30 *muhūrta-s* and complete a full diurnal circle in 60 *muhūrta-s* or 2 days. Another peculiar view was that Bhārata (the Sun) which would move in the southern hemisphere would illumine the Bhārata Khaṇḍa, while the Airāvata which would traverse the same circle in the southern hemisphere would illuminate the Airāvata areas.[37] It is very difficult to understand the rationale behind such views, although there are attempts by some Jaina scholars in support of these views of Jaina cosmography.

Ajīva

Be that as it may, the Jaina view of the world of matter has its own originality, despite its rather circumscribed approach. The relationship between *jīva* (life or soul) and *ajīva,* or the living and the non-living has been noted already, the latter not having life and the associated consciousness. *Ajīva* is further divided into *kāla* (time), *ākāśa*, *dharma*, *adharma* and *pudgala*. *Ākāśa* is space, *dharma* and *adharma* are respectively the principles of motion (or dynamics) and stability or static. The Jaina postulate of *ākāśa* is entirely different from that of either the Sāṃkhya or the Nyāya-Vaiśeṣika.

As for time, it is regarded as infinite, but with a cyclic idea built into it. Each cycle is supposed to have two eras of equal duration (*avasarpiṇī* and *utsarpiṇī*). But, these eras are related to virtues of life. In *avasarpiṇī*, a descending era, virtue is stated to be gradually on the decline, while in *utsarpiṇī*, the virtue would be on the ascendency. Time is conceived as being partless, while the other four *ākāśa*, *dharma*, *adharma* and *pudgala* are regarded as possessing parts (*astikāya*). *Ākāśa* or space is also regarded as infinite; nevertheless, in two parts: *lokākāśa* in which movements occur; and *alokākāśa*, characterised by the absence of any type of motion, and hence it is an empty space. It is only in *lokākāśa* that *pudgala* or matter is believed to be atomic, capable of being divided into infinite number of *ākāśāṇus* called *pradeśas* and each such unit being occupied by each atomic unit of matter (*pudgala paramāṇu*). In the Jaina view *dharma* (motion) and *adharma* (state of rest) have also parts and appear to be physical in their connotation (in Jainism), in contradistinction to their respective meanings of virtue and vice in some other systems of thought. In any case, the Jaina view of space atoms or points as well as of time in terms of *kālāṇu-s* (time atoms) is in sharp contrast with that of the Nyāya-Vaiśeṣika approach to space and time.

However, the atoms of time are viewed as the ultimate ones, discrete and infinitesimal while time itself, called the *niścaya kāla,* is considered to be eternal and motionless. It is also regarded as the basis or support for what is thought of as the *vyavahāra kāla*—the present, the past and the future—and referred to as *samaya*. Thus the Jainas (the Digambaras) do not appear to be definitive about time as one and all-pervasive. Further, it has been pointed out that there are distinctive time-units corresponding to distinctive human experiences. Nevertheless, like the Nyāya-Vaiśeṣika, Jainas regard time and space as real.

Jainism asserts that the world is not merely a changing phenomena but is also beginningless and endless. There is in Jainism no conception of God as the creator, preserver and destroyer of the world, while the idea of God is a tacit premise of the orthodox Hindu systems. More importantly, Jainas regard the atoms as the material cause of the world. As noted before, *pudgala* is one of the five categories of the non-living and its two recognised states are atomic (*aṇu*) and aggregate (*skandha*). According to Kundakundācārya, *pudgala* is that which can be experienced by the five senses and has forms or states. In general, its six types of grossness (*bādara*) are: gross–gross; gross; gross–fine; fine–gross; fine; and fine–fine. The first one stands for huge objects like mountains (perceptible) and the last one, for those surpassing or beyond perception. This categorization in permutation and combination encompasses, in the Jaina view, all that is knowable. However, the finest one, the holistic perception or *kevalajñāna* or *sakala pratyakṣa* is possible only for the enlightened and liberated souls.

Jaina Atomism

The Jaina thinkers have put forward an atomism that, to some extent, resembles the Greek atomism. It is, however, conceptually and structurally different from that of the Nyāya-Vaiśeṣika. The material atoms of Jainas are of one class (not of four types as conceived by the Nyāya-Vaiśeṣika) similar to the Greek atoms. But an atom, the subtlest, partless and indivisible ultimate particle, is believed to change in relation to colour, taste, smell and touch, i.e., the qualities of the four elements: *tejas (fire), ap (water), pṛthivī (earth)* and *vāyu (air)*. An atom is also regarded as a point with reference to *kṣetra* or field, and momentary with reference to *kāla* or time. According to Jaina atomism, two or more atoms combine to form an aggregate, called *skandha*, and the physical world is regarded as a *mahāskandha*. A *skandha* may be formed either by atoms or by the dissociation of a larger *skandha* into smaller ones. In other words, like the Nyāya-Vaiśeṣika postulate of dyad, triad, etc. leading to gross matter, the Jaina view takes cognizance of the reverse direction also, although it thinks of *dvipradeśa skandha* (from two atoms), *tripradeśa skandha* (three atoms) and so on. Besides, the *skandha-s* of countable units and infinite units with several combinations are also thought of. Further, in relation to vibration and non-vibration, there could be varieties of *skandhas* according as the component atoms vibrate, non-vibrate and partly-vibrate, possibly to explain the differing behaviours of various substances. It may be noted that the elements—earth, water, fire and air—the four-fold divisions through which the physical world is sought to be understood are, according to Jaina thinkers, not the primary but secondary ones. They are formed out of atoms which, in reality, are not distinguishable from one another. Nevertheless, because of the characteristics of attributes like odour, taste, colour and the like, the atoms give rise to the world of diverse character.

An interesting aspect of Jaina atomism is that the combination of atoms is stated to be due to their inherent attributes, unlike the referral concept of the Nyāya-Vaiśeṣika. The attributes are in terms of an attractive force (*snigdha*), repulsive force (*rūkṣa*) and even a combination of the two, viz., attractive alternative *cum* repulsive force. The significant point to note is that the Jaina savants have viewed these as natural to or inherent not only in the atoms but even in respect of the aggregates. Jaina atoms recognize no outside or unseen force or *adṛṣṭa* of the Nyāya-Vaiśeṣika. According to Umāsvāti, the author of the *Tattvārthādhigamasūtra* (*c.* 2nd century. A.D.), the combination of similar or dissimilar atoms takes place when there is a difference of at least two units of attraction or repulsion between them, although what that unit quantitatively has not been specified. In other words, atoms cannot enter into combination if they have equal degree of *snigdha* and *rūkṣa*; likewise, two atoms, each having only either *snigdha* and *rūkṣa* cannot combine, according to the Jaina atomists. As for the aggregate formed out of atoms, their view is that it is not a new substance, like the dyad or the triad of the Nyāya-Vaiśeṣika, but a special form of aggregated atoms. The Jaina atomists believe that an atom may not be active always, but sometimes it vibrates or revolves by itself in a regular (*samita*) or in an irregular way (*nimita*). Some of the Jaina texts like the *Bhagavatī sūtra* and the *Sthānāṅga sūtra* provide considerable details about the vibration of atoms form the point of view of time, movement form one point of space to another, its direction and speed, resistance encountered and the like—all in a speculative manner. It would appear that the concept of *pudgala* and atomism is a well knit part of Jainism which also believes that even *karma* which is described as the keynote of the Jaina system is supposed to be composed of subtle particles.

Though Jainism accepts the reality of the world or universe, it emphasizes that the universe needs to be looked at from several points of view, each of which may lead to a conclusion that it might be different from the other. It is likened to each of the blind person's arriving at his own conclusion while examining an elephant. That the reality is not determinate but complex and there are seven ways or steps (*sapta bhaṅgī*) for comprehending it, led the Jaina thinkers to postulate what is known as *Syādvāda* or the doctrine of 'may be'. According to this standpoint, each understanding or comprehension is in the nature of our judgements that will have but a partial view of reality. In Jaina thought, the permanent as well as the changes or modifications, are both equally real with the result that it might lead to an erroneous judgement if only one aspect of it is examined and considered as fully valid. It is true that the Vedāntins like Śaṅkarācārya and Rāmānuja, and the Buddhists like Dharmakīrti and Śāntarakṣita have vehemently criticized the Syādvāda from their own philosophical positions. The Syādvada, however, advocates the necessity of examining all possible ways of knowing the empirical world without any fixed notion about its origin and manifestations or modifications. Nevertheless, it is not in the nature of uncertainty but of practical necessity or compulsion towards a total examination of the sensorial world. The Jaina exposition of *kevala jñāna* indicates that at the highest level of knowledge, the objects or their transformations are capable of comprehension with little or no possibility of erroneous judgements. In any case, Jainism does not accept any form of Absolutism. In any case, that the Jaina thought-structure of the physical or knowable world, through tangential and materialistic here and there, poses more questions than solving them on the canvas of the cause and effect relationships.

Buddhist Approach

The twelve-spoked wheel of what is called *pratītyasamutpāda* or dependent origination, the foundational idea of the Buddha, encompasses six sense organs including mind, sense–object contact and sense experience (*vedanā*), variously, called *bhavacakra, dharmacakra, pratītyasamutpāda cakra* and the like. But the Buddhist approach to the sensorial world is entirely different from that of the orthodox systems and Jainsim. The self as well as the material world is regarded as a flux (*santāna*), and the objects are regarded as having no stability and in incessant motion, a series of similar states or a fleeting ordered succession. And such an order does not owe its origin to any supernatural agency, but is governed by necessity and is dependent upon certain conditions in the absence of which the series could terminate. Buddhism admits that all phenomena can be known by their causes, but every phenomenon changes from moment to moment. The Buddhist (Sarvāstivādin) doctrine of momentariness (*kṣaṇabhaṅgavāda*), also called the theory of flux or ceaseless flow (*santānavāda*), emphasizes that everything is momentary, and change or the very process associated with objects is alone real, and not the objects by themselves.

Buddhists professing Śūnyavāda (Mahāyāna) or the nihilist school aver that there is no persisting substance either as an object or a subject of knowledge. The former, they argue, is generally material, but that matter is not the ultimate reality. If there is no real object of knowledge, there cannot be any real subject to know it. Thus the knower and the known are not all substantial and, hence the world of our experience cannot but be an unreal void, according to them.

The *Vijñānavāda* (Idealist) school of Buddhism is in general agreement with the nihilists, but do not subscribe to the nihilists' concept of absolute void. In their view, absolute void has no meaning since it is contradicted by the conscious perception or an idea which comes up every moment and this alone is undeniable real.

The *Sthaviravāda* (or Theravāda in Pali) of the Hīnayāna Buddhism denies that matter *per se* is eternal and regards the four elements: earth, water, fire and air that constitute matter, as a series of their atomic states, i.e., matter is but an aggregate or a collocation of momentary atoms. It is hard to understand the implications of this approach to the world of matter, although the followers of this line of thinking called the Sarvāstivādins, are stated to believe in the existence as such.

The Sarvāstivādins who admit the atomic state of matter, but within their general thoughts on momentariness, have tried to explain atomism as part of their concept of *rūpa* or that which has the capacity to affect sense organs, considering that an atom is the minutest unit of *rūpa*. The term, *rūpa*, is explained etymologically as meaning not in terms of matter or quality, but as of evanescence. The Bauddha atoms share the characteristics of momentariness in the sense that they are presumed to undergo phase changes continually. Gross matter is regarded as a conglomeration or aggregation of independent atoms, a sort of a cluster having one atom at the centre and the others around it. The aggregation is supposed to consist of eight atoms—four fundamental and four secondary ones. The former are those of earth, water, fire and air. The secondary ones are those of colour, odour, taste and touch, thus in a way following the specific attributes of the Nyāya-Vaiśeṣika postulate of the four classes of atoms. As regards their aggregation leading to the formation of gross objects, there are differing views of the Bauddha as to whether it is a case of straight combination or they are in close proximity with one another with some intervening space among them. These speculative ideas also include that of eight atoms constituting an aggregate, besides the view that each secondary atom requires four fundamental or primary atoms for its support, i.e., an aggregate is supposed to consist of 20 atoms ($4 \times 4 + 4$), if the aggregate does not sound and, if it does, it would require 25 atoms.

The Bauddha atomism is totally at variance with that of Nyāya-Vaiśeṣika. It does not think of atoms as indivisible, or the ultimate material particles of matter; instead it regards them as force or energy. The reality is dynamic, according to the Buddhist view, and all the elements of the external world are mere forces. It has been explained that the hard atom is not an atom of stuff characterized by hardness, and the fiery atom is nothing but the energy of heat; the atom of motion, nothing but kinetic energy. The hard atom means repulsion and the liquid one means attraction or cohesion. A further characteristic of these atoms is that all bodies consist of the same aggregates. If a physical body appears as a flame, another body appears as water or some metal, it has been explained that this is due not to the quantitative predominance of the corresponding element, but to its intensity. The Buddhist theory of matter is a dynamic one.[38]

Cārvākas and Materialistic Approach

The foundational idea of Cārvāka or the Lokāyata is one of material life and its enjoyment. Strangely the origin of this thinking is attributed to one Bṛhaspati who is supposed to be the preceptor of divinities and hence a sage of exalted thinking, and also a treasure house of all forms of knowledge including that concerned with the worldly life. The Cārvāka accepted the reality of four elements, earth water, fire and air but not as part of the holistic *pañcabhūta-s* adopted by the Sāṃkhya, Nyāya-Vaiśeṣika; nor in the way the Jainas expounded. The Cārvākas did not develop any type of meaningful epistemology, accepting only the direct perception as the means of acquiring valid knowledge.

While considering the Indian materialist speculation, a reference needs to be made to Uddālaka-Āruṇi. In his exposition on the possible primal state of matter and the production of gross material, Āruṇi thought of a type of chaotic mass in the beginning which gradually, through the combination of particles as well as their separation, gave rise to various types. There is a view[39] that the materialistic ideas of Āruṇi might have contained the germs of atomism. In this context, the dialogue between him and his son Śvetaketu is interesting. When asked by his son as to how did this enormously gross world of matter come into being or take shape out of the most minute entity of reality (*sat*), Āruṇi tried to explain it with a fig fruit, asking his son to go on crushing it. Upon doing so continuously, Śvetaketu eventually said that he could not find or observe anything further. Āruṇi, however, explained that there are invisible particles or grains that go to make the fig fruit and that from a small fig seed the great fig tree grows with all its branches and innumerable leaves. In the same way, he sought to convince his son that from the minutest *sat*, the visible physical world would spring up. Whether Āruṇi's *sat* means the primordial matter is a moot point. The fact that Āruṇi's exposition is in the upaniṣadic matrix seems to suggest that the word *sat* stands for Brahman who, in the general upaniṣadic thought structure is the creator, preserver and destroyer of the created world in the sense that it would get back into Brahman.

Āruṇi's material elements are not as distinct from each other as they are in the Vaiśeṣika five elements. Besides, he seems to favour the view that an effect is a transformation of the cause[40] in much the same way as the Sāṃkhya does. In the history of Indian atomism, Āruṇi's material and other expositions deserve close examination.

Western Ideas: Some Aspects

In the Greek and the Greco-Roman culture—areas from about 700 B.C. to 3rd or 4th century A.D., the human mind was astir in several ways. The pre-Socratic thinkers—Thales of Miletus, Anaximander, Anaximenes, Heraclitus and others had made bold attempts towards an understanding of the 'essence' of the physical world in terms of the first element, either water, air or fire respectively. Another Greek savant, Empedocles added the element, earth; and the four elements with their primary but opposite qualities of hot and cold, dry and moist, led to an explanation of the material world and its changes or modifications. What is worthy of note is that in this conceptual approach no supernatural force or ontological Being was accepted, though Heraclitus had thought of being–becoming in his own way.

The pro-Socratic intellectual giant, Plato put forward his doctrine of *Ideas* and thought that form was the essence. He even regarded that 'soul' was the place of all forms that could be defined. Mathematical principles lay at bottom of his intellectual endeavours and his source of inspiration in this respect was Pythagoras to whom mathematics, specially numbers, was the basis of all things. An interesting aspect was that the Pythagoreans, through the manipulation of equilateral triangles and squares in three dimensions, discerned four 'regular solids' or figures (forms) with all their sides and angles being equal like the basic equilateral. These were the four-sided tetrahedron, the six-sided cube, the eight-sided octahedron and the twenty-sided icosahedrons. More importantly, their identification was sought to be done with the four elements of the physical world earth, air, fire and water. Later, the twelve-sided dodecahedron was arrived at not by the combination of equilateral triangles, but by the construction of five-sided (pentagon) plane figures. These five regular forms became known as 'Platonic bodies' for reasons not definitely known. The dodecahedron was related to the Universe.

If the pre-Socratic thinkers expounded a material concept of the world and Empedocles considered the four elements as the 'roots of the world', Plato and his followers including the Pythagoreans emphasised that it was the form, the **Idea** and mathematics put together that encompasses everything, and therefore the real one. Plato's pupil, Aristotle, took a different but reconciliatory view that mathematics would deal only with abstraction and it would be erroneous if the very nature of matter was excluded, and the observed changes or modifications ignored. Aristotle emphasized that matter was the actuality of form. His world-view was dualistic in the sense of his differentiation between the terrestrial one (with an inter-play of the four elements as well as their four qualities) and the celestial one composed of the quintessence or the fifth element, Ether. He believed that the Universe was limited in space contained as it would be within an outer sphere, but unlimited in time, and thought that it was subjected neither to creation nor destruction as a whole.

While Plato thought of the Creator, Aristotle projected the idea of an Unmoved Mover in his exposition of the Universe and movement of planetary and other astral bodies. IIis was a geo-centric Universe which comprised several spheres centering round the earth: the firmament; water, air and fire; planetary spheres, the sphere of fixed stars and Primum Mobile. Aristotle made a subtle distinction between the celestial and the terrestrial motion, by presenting the view that stars and planets would move with uniform circular velocity in crystalline spheres. The circular movement was regarded by him as the perfect one, while on the earth, motion would be rectilinear, earth being an imperfect one. The celestial–terrestrial distinction was noticeable not only in the Aristotelian concept but also among the Pythagoreans and others even before him.

Aristotle was opposed to the atomic view of matter propounded by Leucippus and Democritus who lived about 150 years before him. He held that matter was continuous and not composed of discrete units—a view which he shared with his preceptor, Plato. As for the motion, while Aristotle maintained the uniform circular velocity of the planetary bodies, he had an erroneous idea that bodies would fall with velocities proportional to their weights and inversely proportional to the densities of the media through which they fall. This idea persisted till Galileo (16th century) attempted to show experimentally that bodies fall with the same velocity irrespective of their weights in a given medium. It is important to note that right from the Greeks, matter and motion engaged the attention of several thinkers in one way or the other and it was the problem of motion in space and time, and the experimental approach to understand it that marked the turning point in ushering in what is known as early modern science from about the 14th century.

Scientific Renaissance

It is well known that the Greek and the Indian elements had found their way into Europe through the translation of Arabic works in the 12th–14th century A.D. Their contributions to the scientific renaissance, a new way of understanding of nature and the phenomena were no less significant. The emerging tradition of scholasticism began to be associated with experimentation, observation and inference. There came about new interpretations of the motion of heavenly bodies leading to a conception of the helio-centric system by Copernicus. There was also a new world-view put forward by Tycho Brahe who expounded a planetary system with the Earth being at the center of the orbits of the Moon and the Sun, and also central to the fixed stars. In his scheme, however, the Sun would revolve round the Earth in 24 hours carrying the other planets with it. Mathematically, the Tycho system was more or less akin to that of Copernicus. Tycho's pupil, Kepler, put forth the idea that the planets move round the Sun not in circles, but in ellipses, the Sun being one of the foci, and that a planet moves out uniformly in such a way that a line drawn from it to the Sun sweeps out equal areas of the ellipse in equal times.

While the celestial motion assumed a new dimension with Kepler, the motion of bodies on the earth too began to be examined on fresh lines in a measurable manner, thus heralding the dawn of the science of mechanics applicable to all tangible objects. Early in the seventeenth century Galileo became a pioneer in this direction and led the way towards developing a picture of a mechanical universe.

He put forward in a rational and verifiable way his ideas on matter, motion and acceleration. In the late seventeenth century, Newton reinforced the mechanical conception through his laws of motion and the law of universal gravitation which emphasized that the laws of motion are the same for both the celestial and terrestrial bodies. His concept of mass provided a quantitative methodology for the understanding and interpretation of matter and motion, velocity and acceleration.

Before Galileo, whether air was material and whether it had weight or not was one of speculation without any experimental approach. Though Galileo believed that air had weight, he was unable to explain the failure of suction pump to lift water higher than 35 feet. His pupil, Toricelli, constructed barometer filled with mercury, the word 'barometer' meaning weight-measurer. On his own, Galileo invented a thermometer. Earlier, he had also constructed a telescope, (though he was not its inventor) and observed the sun spots, surface of the Jupiter and Mars. The heavens as well as the nature and structure of the planets observed through a telescope on the one hand and on the other, the flora and micro-organisms observed through a microscope opened up new vistas of scientific investigations. Alongside, physical principles began to be applied to physiology and William Harvey's measurement of blood circulation provided new stimuli for the emergence of modern medicine. Though the emerging science had the appellation of natural philosophy, it was prone to carve out a niche for itself based on its methodology, verifiability, reproducibility and even falsifiability in the 18th and 19th centuries. In the 20th century, it scaled new heights with spectacular achievements. The origins of what is generally called western science, and its subsequent growth lay in the European culture-area and later mostly in the other western countries.

But the European culture-area was in an intellectually stagnant state till about the 12th cent. A.D. so far as a new or a rational way of investigating the natural phenomena was concerned. By that time it had begun to receive a corpus of knowledge through the Latin translations of the treatises of several Arabic savants who themselves had inherited a wide spectrum of knowledge specially from the Greek, Greco-Roman and Indian sources. They had also generated some fresh ideas; but within the Islamic framework. The Chinese culture-area too had its own speculations about the Universe, although they did not influence in any manner the Latin medieval European approaches. A brief reference to the foregoing may not be out of place here; in fact they may enable us to appreciate the Indian perspectives on the physical world in a better manner.

Islamic Culture-area

Between the 9th and the 14th centuries, there were certain developments in the Islamic culture-area, both in Eastern and Western Islam as is generally designated.

In the former of which Baghdad was an important center of academies, Indian elements specially in astronomy, mathematics and medicine had been absorbed, along with Hindu numerals and the decimal place-value system through the translations into Arabic of the works of *Brahmagupta* and *Āryabhaṭa*, the medical treatises of Caraka, Suśruta, Vāgbhaṭa and Mādhava as well as the Indian materia medica. Some Islamic savants too blazed new trails. These were two contemporary luminaries in the eleventh century A.D.—Ibn al-Haytham (known in the West as Alhazen) and Al-Bīrūnī. Ibn al-Haytham had a definite preference for the Platonic tradition and in many ways remained an Aristotelian. However he discarded the theory of both Euclid and Ptolemy concerning the manner of direct perception that the eyes send out visual rays to the object of vision. He put forward the view that the form of the perceived object passes into eyes and is transmuted by their lens which he called the 'transparent body'. He also dealt with the propagation of light, the colours and optical reflection, for which he performed experiments for the determination of the angles of incidence of light and reflection. Besides, Alhazen examined the refraction of light rays through transparent media like air and water. These and other investigations of Alhazen became landmarks of science in the Islamic culture-area. Al-Bīruni, the eleventh century encyclopediast, astronomer, mathematician, physician and geographer, was also known for his exact determination of the specific weights of eighteen precious stones and metals. He also determined the circumference and diameter of the Earth by using spherical trigonometry, as well as the Sun's declination and zenithal movement. While al-Haytham was a pioneer in the mathematics-based approaches to the understanding to the physical world, Al-Bīrūni did not appear to have thought of along those lines. However, he sojourned in the north-western parts of India, learnt Sanskrit and became an effective transmitter of specially Indian astronomy, but not much of Indian ideas on the physical world. Around this time, there was what was known as the Brethern of Purity, the members of which dealt with natural phenomena on scientific lines and exerted some influence on the thinkers in Western Islam, specially in Spain. Al-Khwārizmī, and Al-Kindi, were the noted transmitters of Indian mathematics, while Al-Bīrūnī, Al-Maimonides and Averroes examined the Hellenistic astronomy as well as the then prevalent world-view afresh, and exerted some influence over the subsequent developments in Latin Medieval Europe.

Chinese Ideas

In the Chinese thought-structure, which cannot claim as much antiquity as the three ancient civilizations as well as the Vedic and the Upaniṣadic ideas, there were, according to Needham, 'two fundamental tendencies which paradoxically helped the germs of science on the one hand and injured them on the other'. One was Confucianism that was basically rationalistic and opposed to any superstitious or even supernatural forms of religion. But on the other side its intense concentration of interest upon human social life to the exclusion of non-human phenomena negatived all investigations of *Things*, as opposed to *Affairs*. Hence, not for the last time in history, not only in China, rationalism proved itself less favourable than mysticism, to the progress of science'. The Confucian attitude to knowledge was that the affairs of human society in general and of man in particular needed to be investigated, and in this frame work, traditional rites and ceremonies were emphasised. The nature of man, his goodness and evil tendencies, and the necessity of cultivating the good were of fundamental importance for the Confucians.

The opponents of Confucianism were the Taoists or those who believed and meditated upon the *Tao of Nature*. Their approach to knowledge was that it should be related to the observation of nature. They were experimentalists too in such areas as alchemy and pharmaceutics. At the same time they were also mystics and grew in the ambience of ancient shamans and magical practices. However, their conception of Tao or the Way as the one which determined the activities of the Universe, as the order of Nature, which, according to Needham, 'was not metaphysical. '. . . . We believe that the Chinese mind throughout the ages did not, on the whole, feel the need of metaphysics; physical nature with all that implied at the highest levels sufficed. The Chinese were extremely loath to separate the One from the Many or the 'spiritual' from the 'material'. Organic naturalism was their *philosphia perennis*. In all of the happenings or actions, it is the necessity that operates and governs, was the refrain of Taoists'.[41]

Taoists believed in the unity of Nature and in its uncreated eternity. At the individual level a Taoist aspired to attain material immortality (without death) through several practices like respiratory techniques, heliotherapeutic technique, sexual and dietary techniques, and alchemical aspects through which a Taoist was to become a 'Perfect Immortal' or *hsien*, corresponding to the Indian *siddha*, the physical body being as important as the physical world.

Two fundamental ideas of the Taoists, namely, the theory of the five elements and the Yin-Yang postulate need special mention. The Chinese theory of five elements (*c.* 4th or 3rd cent. B.C.) is not as old as either the Indian or the Greek, but is entirely different in conception from either of them. In their evolution or systematisation, the Chinese thinker, Tsou Yen, played an important role. The Chinese five elements were more in the nature of a relationship or processes than representing five kinds of matter. The five elements were: Water, Fire, Wood, Metal, and Earth. Their natural properties were given due recognition: thus, water stood for liquidity, fluidity and solution; Fire, heat and combustion; wood, solidity involving workability; Metal, solidity involving mouldability; and Earth, nutrivity. Certain tastes were also associated with them Water (saltiness); Fire (bitterness); Wood (sourness); Metal (acridity); and Earth (sweetness). It is significant to note that 'air' that has an important position both in the Indian and the Greek scheme of five elements is conspicuous by its absence in the Chinese five elemental theory.

The association of tastes with the elements has been explained by Needham in a sympathetic, (but rather unconvincing, if not far fetched) manner as follows: 'The association of saltiness with water, while natural indeed to coastal people, suggests primitive experiments and observations on solutions and crystallization. The association of bitterness with fire, while perhaps the least oblivious of the Fire, may imply the use of heat in preparing decoctions of medicinal plants, which would be the bitterest of substances likely to be known. There would be a connection of 'hot' and 'bitter' in spices. The association of sourness with wood can readily be explained, since wood, as vegetal, would be connected with all kinds of plant substances which become sour on decomposition. The association of acridity with metal points directly to smelting operations, many of which give off highly acrid fumes, e.g., sulphur dioxide. Lastly, the association of sweetness with earth would be due to the finding of honey in bee's nests in the earth, and to the general sweet taste of bees'.[42] It is true that in Āyurveda, the combination of elements has been envisaged to explain the six tastes: sweet (earth and water); sour (fire and earth); salty (water and fire); bitter (*ākāśa* and air); pungent (fire and air); and astringent (earth and air). Āyurveda emphasises that the corresponding two elements alone do not constitute a particular taste (*rasa*); only these two are predominant in it while the other three would also enter into its composition. Thus Āyurveda has maintained the holistic nature of the doctrine of five elements in a way different from that of the Chinese.

A curious aspect of the Chinese five elements is that each in a successive manner was taken as a symbol of the concerned emperor, extending it to the dynasties as well as the rise and fall of the rulers, attributing to them the qualities and the dominance as well as the reign of the related element. Heaven was regarded as having the five elements, first wood followed by Fire, Earth, Metal and Water. A type of 'Father-and-son relationship' among the elements was also thought of as follows: Wood produces Fire; Fire produces Earth; Earth produces metal; and metal produces Water. This was supposed to be the Tao of Heaven. The five elements were also explained in the context of the five seasons and twelve months of a year as well as the cardinal points and also numbers. It would appear that the Chinese five elements represented a spectrum of Chinese thinking that was really disjointed, though it appeared to be an all-encompassing one.

Somewhat clearer in its conceptual approach and contextual interpretation was the Chinese Yin-Yang theory or the two fundamental forces. A succinct statement has been made in one of the texts (fifth chapter of the fifth appendix of the I–Ching of the third century B.C.), namely, 'One Yin and one Yang; that is the Tao'. Yin was associated with darkness, and Yang with light; Yin being feminine and Yang, masculine. There was also the view, specially of Wang Chung (first century A.D.), that heaven was synonymous or equated with Yang, but earth with Yin. Though he was a naturalist, he believed in 'Chance and strife in Nature as well as necessity'. This male–female imagery (Yin and Yang) provided some sort of a foundation for both Chinese alchemy and medicine.

As for the Chinese world-view, there was a two-in-one concept *Li* and *Chhi,* which were supposed to be present both in heaven and earth. But *Li* was regarded as *one* and its functions manifold. It was believed that the Tao organised all forms from above, while *Chhi* was the instrument composing all forms below. In general *Li* was the cosmic principle of organization, and *Chhi*, a composite of matter energy. Both *Li* and *Chhi* were regarded as being inseparable, the former inhering in the latter.

The conception of God, as the omnipotent and omnipresent Creator, or the Being–Becoming or of the Universal spirit, was not the forte of the Chinese thinking. Not that superstitious ideas and practices or irrational attitudes were absent in the spectrum of Chinese thought. Some of them were the generic bases for the emergence of alchemy and associated practices. It is rather difficult to identify a particular thread of thought that would be characteristic of the Chinese view of the physical world. The Chinese world-view depended upon a totally different line of thinking from what one notices in India and Greece of ancient lines. 'The harmonious cooperation of all beings arose, not from the orders of a superior authority external to themselves, but from the fact that they were all parts in a hierarchy of wholes forming a cosmic pattern, and what they obeyed were the internal dictates of their own natures. And lastly there was always the environment of Chinese social and economic life, out of which arose the transition from feudalism to bureaucratism which could not but condition at every step the science and philosophy of the Chinese people. All we can say is that science of Nature which then would have developed is that it would have been profoundly organic and non-mechanical'.[43]

SOURCES: AN OUTLINE

The sources that provide an insight into the Indian perspectives on the physical world are indeed wide and varied. In this section an attempt is being made to present a bird's eye view of the literary sources, original as well as commentaries, that have been bequeathed to us over the millennia. Such sources are mainly in

Sanskrit language, relating to the Indian perspectives on the physical world that have been a fountain source of the extensive and diverse Indian thought-structures. The manuscript-wealth of India in Sanskrit and other languages is very large. The most important, if not all, of them have been studied, commented upon and their contents are fairly well known. However, from the point of view of historiography, the data-base needs to encompass also the hitherto unstudied manuscripts some of which might contain certain seminal ideas and interpretations. But the task is a hard one and the coverage would be enormous. In any case, the spectrum of the generated and assiduously fostered knowledge is a very broad one, and the perspectives on the physical world have been an integrated component of the preserved knowledge. An outline of these sources presented below includes those of the Hindu, Jaina and the Bauddha.

Of necessity, one has to begin with the Vedic literature since the so-called Indus Script, as noted before, has not been deciphered satisfactorily. The origin of the Vedas is still controversial. In any case the Vedic seers or sages (*ṛṣis*)and their exponents have left behind substantial literary works that go by the name of the Vedas, Brāhmaṇas, Āraṇyakas and Upaniṣads. The Vedas have been presumed to be revealed knowledge. As noted before, the term, *Veda*, means 'to know' or knowledge itself. It is interesting to note that the Latin word, '*cientia*' from which the modern word, science, is derived also means knowledge. But *Veda* encompasses in several ways the totality of human knowledge of the outer world and the inner man far more than the western *cientia*, besides being much more ancient than the latter. In fact the Vedas are the earliest literary compositions in human history transmitted for a long time through an oral tradition that was noted for different schools engendered by preceptor–disciple relationship. But the Vedic preceptors were not the authors of the Vedas, but only exponents of the revealed knowledge which was, then as now, held as being sacred and of unquestionable authority. The Vedas are called *śrutis* (the heard ones) and it is amazing that they have been preserved by oral transmission over a very long period with little or no variation or interpolation either in their contents or in their articulation.

The four Vedas are: the *Ṛgveda,* the *Yajurveda,* the *Sāmaveda* and the *Atharvaveda.* Their associated *Brāhmaṇas* and the major *Upaniṣads* are as follows:

The *Ṛgveda: Aitareya Brāhmaṇa; Aitareya upaniṣad* and *Kauśītakī upaniṣad.*

The *Yajurveda;* in two *śākhā-s (schools): Black (Kṛṣṇa) Yajurveda– Taittirīya, Maitrāyaṇī, Kāṭhaka, and Kaṭha-kāpiṣṭhala; Upaniṣads: Taittirīya, Kāṭhaka, Śvetāśvatara; Maitrāyaṇīya* and *Mahānārayaṇa. White (Śukla) Yajurveda— Vājasaneyī; Śatapathabrāhmaṇa;* and *Upaniṣads: Bṛhadāraṇyaka* and *Īśa.*

The *Sāmaveda: Pañcaviṃśabrāhmaṇa* or *Tāṇḍyamahābrāhmaṇa, Ṣaḍviṃśa Jaiminīya Brāhmaṇa;* Upaniṣads: *Chāndogya Upaniṣad and Kena (Talavakāra) Upaniṣad.*

The Atharvaveda: *Gopatha brāhmaṇa,* Upaniṣads: *Māṇḍūkya, Praśna, Muṇḍaka upaniṣad-s* and several others.

It may be noted that the relationship between the *Brāhmaṇa-s* with their specialization in various liturgical aspects, and the *Upaniṣad-s* with their metaphysical or philosophical speculations, is not direct, but in several cases it is through the *Āraṇyakas* (*lit.* forest treatises). These also deal with certain types of ritual and allegorical explanations that paved the way for the Upaniṣadic thoughts. In respect of the *Sāmaveda,* however, the position of *Āraṇyaka* is not very clear. The broad distinctions between a *Brāhmaṇa, Āraṇyaka* and an *Upaniṣad,* according to Deussen, 'are by no means always correctly observed; e.g., among the Aitareyans the matter of the Brāhmaṇa extends into the Āraṇyaka, while with the Taittirīyakas, the close of the *Brāhmaṇa* extends into the Āraṇyaka agree throughout, and the dividing line is arbitrary. This state of things is to be explained probably only on the supposition that the entire teaching material of each *śākhā* (school) formed originally a consecutive whole, and that this whole was in the later times distinguished into Brāhmaṇa, Āraṇyaka and Upaniṣad on a principle which did not depend upon the character of the subject matter alone, but, which through general correspondence with it, was in fact imposed upon it'.[44] In any case, the Upaniṣads constitute the end of the Vedas (Vedānta) and formed the bedrock of the later metaphysical or philosophical speculations inclusive of those relating to the physical or knowable world. There emerged between the sixth century B.C. and early centuries of the Christian era, what are known as the *darśanas* (philosophical insights) of which six of them—Vaiśeṣika, Sāṃkhya, Nyāya, Yoga, Pūrva and Uttara-Mīmāṃsā—designated as the *ṣaḍ-darśanas.* These are generally called the orthodox systems in contradistinction to the heterodox ones, many the Bauddha and the Jaina, besides the Cārvāka and others. Before we go into the sources available to us, some reflection on the Vedic sources may be necessary.

The Ṛgveda

The *Ṛgveda,* regarded as the earliest among the four Vedas and datable to *c.* 1500 B.C., is an important source for an understanding of the world-ground or *one* in *many* and related issues. It comprises 1028 hymns (*sūkta-s*) under ten *maṇḍala-s* or segments as follows:

Maṇḍala	Sūktas	Mantras	Ṛsis
I	191	2006	Various ṛsis
II	43	429	Gṛtsamada
III	62	617	Viśvāmitra
IV	58	589	Vāmadeva and Gautama
V	87	727	Atri
VI	75	765	Bharadvāja
VII	104	841	Vasiṣṭha
VIII	103	1716	Kaṇva
IX	114	1108	Various ṛsis
X	191	1754	Various ṛsis

It will be observed that the *Ṛgveda*, though considered revealed knowledge, is not a composite one and has different levels obviously formulated in different periods. The codification of these is supposed to have been done by one Vedavyāsa of whom we know very little. Vedic scholars generally concede that the *maṇḍala* II to VIII are perhaps older than I and X, the last being the latest one. Maṇḍala IX which is devoted to Soma, the elixir plant which has been extolled for its elevating effects, seems to be much older perhaps belonging to the Indo-Iranian period. The *Ṛgveda* is an important primary source for its presentation of the three-fold division of the visible universe into the celestial, the atmospheric and the terrestrial regions. It has also certain astronomical ideas. Its cosmogonic hymn (X. 129) on the one hand and, on the other, its concept of ONE or unitary world-ground are of seminal importance, the latter perhaps culminating in the later Upaniṣadic concept of Brahman, the only one without a second as this Absolute is generally described.

The classification of the universe into celestial, atmospheric and terrestrial, as noted already, and the association of each of them with deities are in the nature of unity in diversity. The universe was supposed to be composed of two halves (*dyāvā-pṛthivī*) and the Vedic gods like Indra, Varuṇa, Maruts, Agni (fire god) and the Sun perhaps represented the natural forces or occurrences. Likewise, *Yajña* (sacrifice) was thought of in terms of its being the navel of the universe. The Creator (Prajāpati), and the stages of creation in a holistic manner had their own influences on the later Hindu thought.

The *Yajurveda*, a compendium of several sacrificial formulae in its two divisions (white and black) owes allegiance to the *Ṛgveda* and abounds in mantras, borrowed from the *Ṛgveda* with of course some variations. But it does not appear to contain any new idea about the physical world excepting its Brāhmaṇa, viz., the *Śatapatha* that provides valuable information on the Indian *nakṣatra* system. The *Atharvaveda* too does not offer any fresh ideas regarding the nature and structure of the physical world. However, there are over 60 hymns in praise of the Earth as goddess, which also throw some light on the physical geographical peculiarities as well as those that are in the nature of supporters and preservers of life. The *Atharvaveda* strangely recognizes time (*Kāla*) as the first cause of all existence. The *Brāhmaṇa-s* which Winternitz had described as the 'Science of Sacrifice', though contain details concerning astronomy, anatomy as well pathological and physiological ideas, they too do not contain any original ideas concerning the physical world that could well have been prevalent at that time.

It is the Upaniṣads, the final segment of Vedic literature, that are full of significance form the point of view of the Indian perspectives on the nature of the physical world or the universe as a whole. For, it may be noted that the Sāṃkhya model of thinking can be traced to them. Even Buddhism, though it had its independent origin, was influenced to some extent by some of the basic Upaniṣadic ideas. As Deussen says: To every Indian Brāhman today, the Upaniṣads are what the New Testament is to the Christian' (p. VIII). The metaphysical speculations of the Upaniṣads are not devoid of their approach to the knowable world. One of the Upaniṣads considers the four Vedas as 'inferior knowledge' (*aparā vidyā*) while the Upaniṣadic knowledge is regarded as 'superior knowledge' (*parāvidyā*).

The number of Upaniṣads is stated to be large. But the following Upaniṣads are of great importance: *Bṛhadāraṇyaka, Chāndogya, Taittirīya, Aitareya, Kauṣītakī, Kena, Kaṭha, Īśa, Śvetāśvatara, Muṇḍaka, Praśna, Maitrāyaṇīya and Māṇḍūkya*. Essentially, the Upaniṣadic intellectual discourses are on the Absolute; but they have one significant idea from the view point of an approach to the physical world, which may be designated as the doctrine of five elements (*Pañcamahābhūta-s*). This versatile doctrine also became an integral component specially of three of the *ṣaḍdarśana-s*, namely, the Vaiśeṣika, the Sāṃkhya and the Nyāya. It was also an expository ground for the heterodox Bauddha and Jaina schools as well as the Cārvākas.

The Vaiśeṣika and the Nyāya Sources

The foundational texts of the Vaiśeṣika and the Nyāya-schools are the origina *Vaiśeṣika sūtra* (*c*. 6th cent. B.C.) of Kaṇāda and the *Nyāya-sūtras* of Gautama (*c*. 5th-4th cent. B.C.). The *Padārthadharmasaṃgraha*, also known as *Praśastapādabhāṣya* (*c*. 4th or 5th cent. A.D.) by *Praśastapādācārya* (which though intended to be a commentary on the first, has its own originality) and the

Nyāya-bhāṣya of Vātsyāyana (*c.* 5th cent. A.D.) are also valuable primary sources. The other important texts are: *Nyāyavārtika of Uddyotakara* (9th cent. A.D.); and Vācaspati Miśra's *Nyāyavārtikatātparyaṭīkā* (*c.* 850); The 10th cent. witnessed the emergence of several important works. Among them are: *Vyomavatī* of Vyomaśivācārya which is a commentary on *Praśastapādabhāṣya; Nyāyamañjarī of Jayantabhaṭṭa* and *Nyāyasāra of Bhāsarvajña;* Udayana's *Nyāyakusumāñjali; Ātmaviveka or Bauddhadhikkāra; Lakṣaṇāvalī and Nyāyapariśiṣṭa.* as well as their commentaries— *Nyāya-Vārttikatātparyapariśuddhi* and *Kiraṇāvalī;* Śrīdharabhaṭṭa's *Nyāya Kandalī*— a commentary on *Praśastapādabhāṣya* and Śivāditya's *Saptapadārthī* (10th cent.).

Of the later texts special mention needs to be made of the *Tattvacintāmaṇi* of Gangeśopādhyāya (late 12th cent.); *Tārkikarakṣā* of Vallabhācārya; *Nyāya Līlāvatī*— a commentary on PPB by Vallabhācārya; *Nyāyalīlāvatīprakāśa; Kiraṇāvalīprakāśa; Nyāyapariśiṣṭaprakāśa; Nyāyanibandhaprakāśa; Kusumāñjaliprakāśa*—all by Vardhamāna Upādhyāya (13th cent.); *Tarkabhāṣā* of Keśavamiśra (13th cent.); *Upaskāra*—a commentary on Vai. Sū. as well as *Nyāyalīlāvatī–kaṇṭhābharaṇam,* and *Kalpalatā* by Śaṅkara Miśra (15th cent.); *Dīdhiti*—a commentary on *Tattvacintāmaṇi* and others as well as *Padārthatattvanirūpaṇa* by Raghunāthaśiromaṇi of Nadia (16th cent.); Rucidatta's commentary, *Nyāyakusumāñjaliprakāśamakaranda* (16th cent.); *Bhāṣāpariccheda* and *Siddhāntamuktāvalī* of Viśvanātha Pañcānana (17th cent.); *Tarkakaumudī* of Laugākṣi Bhāskara and Annaṁbhaṭṭa's *Tarkasaṁgraha* and *Tarkasaṁgrahadīpikā.*

It is indeed scholastically heartening that most of the important Nyāya-Vaiśeṣika texts have been critically examined and published over the last century and a half. The late Ganganatha Jha, Vindhyeshvari Prasad and other Indian savants as also some foreign scholars have spared no efforts in bringing to the fore the epistemic and the incisive intellectual approach to reality, as preserved in these texts for over 2500 years.

Sāṃkhya

Though the number of works on the Sāṃkhya system are not as many as those on the Nyāya-Vaiśeṣika, it has been alluded to and commented upon by the followers of the other systems and such expositions are equally important for a critical evaluation of the Sāṃkhya. There are two aspects—the pre-Classical and the Classical Sāṃkhya as also another two, the *nirīśvara* (without a god-head) and *seśvara* (with a god-head) Sāṃkhya that are discussed in the purāṇas, the *Sūryasiddhānta* and others.

The *Sāṃkhya-sūtra* ascribed to Kapila, though it contains the material that can go back to the fifth or fourth century before the Christian era, appears to be a much later work in the form in which it has come down to us. This text has six chapters, four of which deal with the Sāṃkhya concepts, one with the rival systems in a critical manner and the other gives the parables. The *Sāṃkhya-sūtra* has been commented upon by Vijñāna Bhikṣu, under the title: *Sāṃkhya-Pravacana-bhāṣya,* but with significant modifications vis-à-vis the Vedāntic doctrines.

The most important text of the Classical Sāṃkhya is undoubtedly the *Sāṃkhya-Kārikā* (*c.* 5th cent. A.D.) and its author is Īśvara Kṛṣṇa. It is also called the *Sāṃkhya saptati,* since it contains 70 stanzas which enumerate in a lucid manner, the Sāṃkhya principles of evolution in the context of Prakṛti (the unmanifested and inert) and Puruṣa (the sentient being) Vācaspati Miśra (9th century. A.D.) has commented upon the *Sāṃkhya-kārikā* and the commentary is known as the *Sāṃkhya tattva Kaumudī.* Īśvara Kṛṣṇa's work was rendered into Chinese (6th cent. A.D.) by one Paramārtha. *Tattva-Samāsa* is another work on Sāṃkhya in a concise form. The works on Yoga like Patañjali's *Yoga sūtra* are also the other sources since the Sāṃkhya and the Yoga are allied systems like the Nyāya-Vaiśeṣika.

Buddhist Sources

Buddhist sources comprise what is known as Pāli Buddhism or canonical Buddhism and those of later Buddhism of the Hīnayāna and Mahāyāna schools. It is the latter that are of significance from the point of view of the Indian perspectives on the physical world. The *Laṅkāvatāra sūtra; Lalitavistara;* Nāgārjuna's, *Mūlamādhyamīka-kārikā; Vigrahavyāvṛttanī,* and *Bhavaśāntisūtra* (restored into Sanskrit from the Tibetan and Chinese Versions); Āryadeva's *Cittaviśuddhi prakaraṇa,* Candrakīrti's *Prasannapadā* and *Mādhyamikāvatāra; Śāntideva's Śikṣāsamuccaya,* Asaṅga's *Mahāyānasūtrālaṅkāra;* Vasubandhu's *Vijñaptimātratāsiddhi* and *Abhidharmakośa;* Diṅnāga's *Pramāṇasamuccaya;* Dharmakīrti's *Nyāya-bindu, Pramāṇavārtika* and *Vādanyāya;* Dharmottara's *Nyāyabindutīkā;* Śāntarakṣita's *Tattvasaṅgraha;* and *Kumāraśīla's Tattvasaṅgrahapañjikā.* Besides, several texts of the orthodox systems, specially those of Nyāya-Vaiśeṣika, will have to be examined for their refutation of the Buddhist view on the material world.

Jaina Sources

Of the Jaina sources, special mention needs to be made of *Samayasāra, Pañcāstikāya* and *Ṣaṭprābhṛta* by Kundakundācārya, *Tattva* and *Pradīpikā* by

Amṛtacandra Sūri; *Tattvādhigamasutra* by Umāsvāti; and its commentaries; *Nyāyāvatāra* of Siddhasena Divākara; *Pramāṇamīmāṃsā* by Hemacandra; *Syādvādmañjari* of Malliṣeṇa; *Ṣaḍdarśanasamuccaya* by Haribhadra; and *Dravyasaṅgraha* by Nemicandra.

Besides, there are other texts like *Sarvārthasiddhi* of Pūjyapāda; *Tattvārtha Rājavārtika* of Akalaṅkadeva; *Tattvārtha Ślokavārtika* of Vidyānanda; *Prajñapti* and *Aṇuyogadvārasūtra ṣaṭtrimśikā* of Ratnasiṃha Sūri; and *Sthānāṅgasūtra* with *Ṭīkā* by Abhayasūri. The critical comments on the Jaina views as found in the texts of the orthodox systems also need to be examined.

Others

There is no authentic text concerning the Cārvāka materialistic approach. But, the *Cārvāka darśana*, which is briefly dealt with in the *Ṣaḍdarśana saṃgraha* of Mādhavācārya, and the counteraction of the views of Cārvāka by other schools are important. In addition, several sources, though called the secondary ones, by various eminent scholars, both Indian and foreign, in the eighteenth and nineteenth centuries as well as early in the twentieth century are equally valuable and they have been listed in the bibliography given on pp. 337-351.

REFERENCES

1. Spence, Lewis: *The Myths of Babylonia and Assyria*, London, 1941; Centenau, Georges: *Everyday life in Babylonia and Assyria*, London, 1954; Guirand, P.: *Assyrio-Babylonian Mythology*, Larausse Encyclopedia of Mythology, London, 1973

2. Dasgupta, S. N.: *History of Indian Philosophy*, Vol. I, Cambridge University Press, Cambridge, p. 16.

3. Subbarayappa, B. V., 'The Ṛgvedic people: Their Identity', *Sri Nagabhinandanam*, (Ed) L. K. Srinivasan and S. Nagaraju, M. S. Nagaraja Rao Felicitation Committee, Bangalore, 1995, pp. 83-89

4. यः पृथिवीं व्यथमानामदृंहद्
   यः पर्वतान् प्रकुपिताँ अरम्णात् ।
   यो अन्तरिक्षं विममे वरीयो
   यो द्यामस्तभ्रात्स जनास इन्द्रः ॥ RV II.12.2

5. सूर्याचन्द्रमसौ धाता यथापूर्वमकल्पयत् ।
   दिवं च पृथिवीं चान्तरिक्षमथो स्वः । RV X.190.3

6. सूर्याचन्द्रमसौ धाता यथापूर्वमकल्पयत् ।
   दिवं च पृथिवीं चान्तरिक्षमथो स्वः । RV. X.190.3
   अन्तरिक्षोदरः कोशो भूमिबुध्नो न जीर्यति

दिशो ह्यस्य स्रक्तयो द्यौरस्योत्तरं बिलं स एष

कोशो वसुधानस्तस्मिन् विश्वमिदं ततम् । - Ch. up. 3-15-1.

7. Colebrooke, H. T.; *Miscellaneous Essays* I, Trübner, London, 1879, p. 24.

8. द्यौरन्तरिक्षे प्रतिष्ठितान्तरिक्षं पृथिव्यां पृथिव्यप्स्वाप: सत्ये सत्यं ब्रह्मणि ब्रह्म तपसि ।
   Ait. Br. 11.6.3.

9. स ऐक्षत लोकान्नु सृजा इति स इमाँल्लोकानसृजत । अम्भो मरीचिर्मरं आप: अदो अम्भ: परेण दिवं द्यौ: प्रतिष्ठान्तरिक्षं
   मरीचय: पृथिवी मरो या अधस्तात्ता आप: । Ait.Br. 2.4.3,4

10. को अद्धा वेद क इह प्रवोचत्कुत आ जाता कुत इयं विसृष्टि: ।
    अर्वाग्देवा अस्य विसर्जनेनाथा को वेद यत आबभूव ॥ RV. X.129.6

11. गार्गीति कस्मिन्नु खलु वायुरोतश्च प्रोतश्चेत्यन्तरिक्षलोकेषु गार्गीति । ....कस्मिन्नु खलु आदित्यलोका
    ओताश्चप्रोताश्चेति .... कस्मिन्नु खलु चन्द्रलोका ओताश्च प्रोताश्चेति ..... कस्मिन्नु खलु नक्षत्रलोका ओताश्च
    प्रोताश्चेति ..... कस्मिन्नु खलु देवलोका ओताश्च प्रोताश्चेति ...... कस्मिन्नु खलु प्रजापतिलोका ओताश्च प्रोताश्चेति
    ..... कस्मिन्नु खलु ब्रह्मलोका ओताश्च प्रोताश्चेति । Br. up. 3.6.1.

12. चातलपाताल ..... वितल ..... सुतलरसातल ..... तलातलमहातल-ब्रह्माण्डं च विसजयेत् । *Āruṇeya. up.*
    I (*Atala, Vitala. . . .*)

13. पादगम्यं तु यत्किञ्चिद्वस्त्वस्ति पृथिवीमयम् ।
    स भूर्लोक: समाख्यातो विस्तरोऽस्ति मयोदित: ॥
    भूमिसूर्यान्तरं यच्च सिद्धादिमुनिसेवितम् ।
    भुवर्लोकस्तु सोऽप्युक्तो द्वितीयो मुनिसत्तम ॥
    ध्रुवसूर्यान्तरं यच्च नियुतानि चतुर्दश ।
    स्वर्लोक: सोऽपि गदितो लोकसंस्थानचिन्तकै: ॥
    त्रैलोक्यमेतत्कृतकं मैत्रेय परिपठ्यते ।
    जनस्तपस्तथा सत्यमिति चाकृतकत्रयम् ॥
    कृताकृतकयोर्मध्ये महर्लोक इति स्मृत: ।
    शून्यो भवति कल्पान्ते योऽत्यन्तं न विनश्यति । - *Viṣṇu. pur.*: 2.7. 16-20
    भूमेर्योजनलक्षे तु सौरं मैत्रेय मण्डलम् ।
    लक्षाद्दिवाकरस्यापि मण्डलं शशिन: स्थितम् ॥
    पूर्णं शतसहस्रे तु योजनानां निशाकरात् ।
    नक्षत्रमण्डलं कृत्स्नं उपरिष्टात् प्रकाशते ॥ Ibid, 2.7. 5,6

14. तारकासन्निवेशस्य दिवं यावद्धि मण्डलम् ।
    पर्यास: सन्निवेशस्य भूमेस्तावत्तु मण्डलम् ॥
    पर्यासापरिगाणेन भूगोरतुल्यं दिवं रगृतग् ।
    सप्तानामपि लोकानामेतन्मानं प्रकीर्तितम् ॥
    अण्डस्यान्तस्त्विमे लोका: सप्तद्वीपा च मेदिनी ।
    भूर्लोकश्च भुवश्चैव तृतीयस्स्वरिति स्मृत: ।
    महर्लोको जनश्चैव तप: सत्यश्च सप्तय: ॥
    एते सप्तकृता लोकाश्छत्राकारा व्यवस्थिता: ।

स्वकैरावरणैः सूक्ष्मैर्धार्यमाणाः पृथक् पृथक् ॥ *Vāyu purāṇa*: 50,75-78.

ग्रहान्निस्सृत्य सूर्यात्तु कृत्स्ने नक्षत्रमण्डले ।

वारस्यान्ते विशात्यर्कं धुवेण परिवेष्टितम् ॥ *Vāyu purāṇa*: 51-52.

15. ताऽअकामयन्त कथं नु प्रजायेमहीति

ताऽइश्राम्यँस्तास्तपोऽतप्यन्त तासु

तपस्तप्यमानासु हिरण्मयमाण्डं संबभूव

जातो ह तर्हि संवत्सरऽआस तदिदं

हिरण्मयमाण्डं यावत्संवत्सरस्य वेला

तावत्पर्यप्लवत । *Śat.Br.*, XI.1.6.1 ff.

16. उपवर्णितं भूमेर्यथासंनिवेशावस्थानं अवनेः अपि अधस्तात् सप्तभूमिवरा एकैकशो योजनायुतान्तरेणायाम-

विस्तरेणोपक्लृप्ता अतलं वितलं सुतलं तलातलं महातलं रसातलं पातालमिति । *Bhāg. pur*: 5.24.7.

17. तस्माद्विराडजायत विराजोऽधिपूरुषः ।

स जातो अत्यरिच्यत पश्चाद्भूमिमथो पुरः ।

RV. X.90.2.

18. मही समैरच्चम्वा समीची उभे ते अस्य वसुना न्यृष्टे ।

शृण्वे वीरो विन्दमानो वसूनि महदेवानामसुरत्वमेकम् ॥

इन्द्राय गिरो अनिशितसर्गा अपः प्रेरयं सगरस्य बुध्नात् ।

यो अक्षेणेव चक्रिया शचीभिर्विष्वक् तस्तम्भ पृथिवीमुत द्याम् ॥

RV. III.55.20; X.89.4.

19. एष ब्रह्मैव इन्द्र एष प्रजापतिरेते सर्वे देवा इमानि च पञ्चमहाभूतानि पृथिवीवायुराकाश अपो ज्योतींषीत्येतानीमानि

च क्षुद्रमिश्राणीव बीजानीतराणि चेतराणि चाण्डजानि च जरायुजानि च स्वेदजानि चोद्भिज्जानि चाश्वा गावः पुरुषा

हस्तिनो यत्किञ्चेदं प्राणि जङ्गमं च पतत्रि च यच्च स्थावरं सर्वम् । *Ait. up.* III.1.3.

20. यथोर्णनाभिः सृजते गृह्णते च यथा पृथिव्यामोषधयः सम्भवन्ति ।

यथा सतः पुरुषात्केशलोमानि तथाऽक्षरात्सम्भवतीह विश्वम् । *Muṇḍ.up.* I. 1.6.

21. माया इति अविद्यमानस्य आख्या इत्यभिप्रायः । *Māṇḍ. Kārikā*, IV.58,

न तु परमार्थतः धर्माणां जन्म नाशो वा युज्यते इत्यर्थः । *Ibid*, IV.59

22. असदकारणादुपादानग्रहणात्सर्वसंभवाभावात् ।

शक्तस्य शक्यकरणात् कारणभावाच्च सत्कार्यम् ॥ *Sām.Kārikā*, 9

23. M. Hiriyanna, *Outlines of Indian Philosophy*, p. 273.

24. पार्थिवस्याणोर्गन्धतन्मात्रं सूक्ष्मो विषयः ।

आप्यस्य रसतन्मात्रम् । तैजसस्य रूपतन्मात्रम् ।

वायवीयस्य स्पर्शतन्मात्रम् । आकाशस्य शब्दतन्मात्रम्

इति । तेषामहङ्कारः । अस्यापि लिङ्गमात्रं सूक्ष्मो

विषयः । लिङ्गमात्रास्याप्यलिङ्गं सूक्ष्मो विषयः ।

न चालिङ्गात्परं सूक्ष्ममस्ति । नन्वस्ति पुरुषः

सूक्ष्म इति? सत्यम् । यथा लिङ्गात्परं

अलिङ्गस्य सौक्ष्म्यं न चैवं पुरुषस्य । किंतु

लिङ्गस्यान्वयि कारणं पुरुषो न भवति, हेतुस्तु
भवतीति । अत: प्रधाने सौक्ष्म्यं निरतिशयं
व्याख्यातम् । *Yogasūtra Bhāṣya,* i.45

25. Ui. H: *The Vaiśeṣika Philosophy,* p. 4

कणादमिति तस्य कापोतीं वृत्तिमनुतिष्ठत: रथ्यानिपतितांस्तण्डुलकणान् आदाय प्रत्यहं कृताहारनिमित्ता संज्ञा । NK.
p.4

26. अथातो धर्मं व्याख्यास्याम: । VS. 1.1.

27. यतोऽभ्युदयनि:श्रेयससिद्धि: स धर्म: । VS. 1.1.2.

28. Winternitz, M: *Jainas,* in the *History of Indian Literature,* p. 26

29. चतुर्णां महाभूतानां सृष्टिसंहारविधिरुच्यते । ब्राह्मेण मानेन वर्षशतान्ते वर्तमानस्य ब्रह्मणोऽपवर्गकाले संसारे खिन्नानां
प्राणिनां निशि विश्रामार्थं सकलभुवनपतेमहेश्वरस्य सञ्जिहीर्षासमकालं शरीरेन्द्रियमहाभूतोपनिबन्धकानां
सर्वात्मगतानामदृष्टानां वृत्तिनिरोधे सति महेश्वरेच्छात्माणुसंयोगजकर्मभ्य: शरीरेन्द्रियकारणाणु-
विभागेभ्यस्तत्संयोगवृत्तौ तेषामापरमाण्वन्तो विनाश: । तथा पृथिव्युदकज्वलनपवनानामपि महाभूतानामनेनैव
क्रमेणोत्तरस्मिन्नुत्तरस्मिन् सति पूर्वस्य पूर्वस्य विनाश: । तत: प्रविभक्ता: परमाणवोऽवतिष्ठन्ते
धर्माधर्मसंस्कारानुविधाश्चात्मानस्तावन्तमेव कालम् । PPB.57.

30. Umesh Mishra, p. 271.

31. अणु: पन्था वितत: पुराणो मां स्पृष्टोऽनुवित्तो मयैव । *Br.up.* IV.4.8.
यदर्चिमद्यदणुभ्योऽणु च यस्मिंल्लोका निहिता लोकिनश्च । *Muṇḍ. up.* II.2.2
एषोऽणुरात्मा चेतसा वेदितव्यो यस्मिन् प्राण: पञ्चधा संविवेश । *Muṇḍ. up.* III.1.9.

32. अणोर्महत्तश्चोपलब्ध्यनुपलब्धी नित्ये व्याख्याते । VS. 7.1.8.

33. नित्यं पारिमाण्डल्यम् । VS. 7-1.20.

34. M. Hiriyanna, p. 252

35. काल: स्वभावो नियतिर्यट्टच्छा
भूतानि योनि: पुरुष इति चिन्त्या ।
संयोग एषां नत्वात्मभावादात्माप्यनीश:
सुखदु:खहेतो: ॥ *Śvet. up.* I.2.

36. Hiriyanna, M: *Outlines of Indian Philosophy,* pp. 157-158.

37. Sen, S. N: 'Astronomy', in A *Concise History of Science in India,* (Eds) Bose, D. M., Sen S.
N. and Subbarayappa, B.V., pp. 80-81.

38. Stcherbatsky, Th: *Buddhist Logic,* Vol. I, p. 191.

39. Ruben, W: '*Studies in Ancient Indian Thought, Uddālaka and Yājñavalkya',* pp. 77-90.

40. कुतस्तु खलु सोम्यैवं स्यादिति होवाच कथमसत: सज्जायेतेति सदेव सोम्येदमग्र आसीदेकमेवाद्वितीयम् । Ch. up.
VI. 2.2.

41. Needham, J.: *Chinese Science and Civilisation,* Vol. II, p. 12.

42. op. cit: pp. 244.

43. op. cit.: Vol III. pp. 582-83.

44. Deussen, P.: *The Philosophy of the Upaniṣads;* p. 4.

CHAPTER 2

Unitary Conceptions

IT is innate to human mind, despite its mundane desires and instinctive impulses leading to disharmonious tendencies and discordant actions, to ponder over the essence or the comprehensible unity in multiplicity. This is also the goal ever in sight (although not yet reached) of modern science which has been incessantly endeavouring towards this goal with its sophisticated methodology. Human mind, a complex one both in its internal structure and external manifestations, has proceeded principally along two lines: one of interacting and understanding the physical world through the associated senses; and the other of holistic or spiritual experience of undifferentiated oneness. These attitudes have characterized human intellectual endeavours in all culture-areas in one form or the other, more so in the Indian culture right from the Vedic times. The concept of THAT ONE or ONE becoming MANY has been a seminal one throughout the Indian (Hindu) religious as well as philosophical inquiries and religious as well as cultural history. It would be erroneous to think that this is an other-worldly approach. For, in Indian ethos, human life has been accorded an exalted status, and the zest for life has not taken a back seat. The *Ṛgveda* implores: 'Let us see a hundred autumns: let us live a hundred autumns; let us enjoy a hundred autumns. . . '.[1] To an Indian of both orthodox and heterodox positions, the worldly life and the spiritual experience are not incompatible; nor are they mutually exclusive. In fact they are considered to be complementary to each other in a holistic manner. The *Ṛgveda* implores that sight be given to the eyes and bodies so that they could survey and see the world in detail.[2] But such a detailed survey was intended to see the world in its totality, in its oneness. It was in pursuance of this attitude and because of the mind-set behind it that certain unitary conceptions could not but emerge and they did so in the Vedic period itself. The Vedic sages with their attuned mind and intense meditation envisioned the ONENESS of all, for they were seers through their inner eyes.

Ṛtam

That the Universe is an ordered whole and not capricious was recognized by the Vedic seers. Probably in no other culture at that time, was there such a recognition in a detailed manner as in the *Ṛgveda*. It is significant to note that modern science even in its earlier phase between the 14th and 18th centuries A.D., proceeded on the tacit 'belief' that there was an order in the universe and the scientific rationality should not only take cognizance of it but also discover it by its own methodology. In the middle of the last century, the well known mathematician and philosopher of science, A. N. Whitehead in his thoughtful book: *Science and the Modern World*[3] (p.4) stated: 'In the first place there can be no living science unless there is a widespread intuitive conviction in the existence of an order of things and in particular of an order of nature'. Scientific laws in a sense are a reiteration of the laws of nature. It is important to note that the Ṛgvedic seers had not only an instinctive conviction in the natural order but also delineated it in unequivocal terms. The word used for the natural law or order in the *Ṛgveda* is *ṛtam*.

There are nearly 160 references to *ṛta* in several *maṇḍalas* of the *Ṛgveda*. It needs to be mentioned at this stage, however, that, apart from its connotation involving the regularity of action or movements in the physical world, *ṛta* also refers to moral law and even the supreme will of God. In fact the Vedic idea of sin was in the context of the transgression of *ṛta*.[4] The Vedic gods too were enjoined to follow *ṛta* and also uphold it, and the Gods were expected to chant the songs of *ṛta*.[5] They were believed to be the lovers and cherishers of *ṛta*. They were also supposed to rejoice in the fulfilment of *ṛta*.[6] The Sun (Savitṛ) was eulogized as being a dweller in eternal law), and it was recognized that its movements take place along the right path because of *ṛta*. The Sun was supposed to withdraw its rays (in the evening) due to *ṛta*.[7] Uṣas, the morning goddess, was to follow the path of *ṛta*, without violating it.[8] She was even imagined to wake up from the stratum of *ṛta* and illumine with the reddish effulgence.[9]

Agni, the ruler of sacrifice, was invoked as the guardian of the eternal law, and within the lap of *ṛta*, Agni lay.[10] As the knower of *ṛta*, Agni was even implored to pay attention to the fire-rituals and the offering of prayers.[11] He was considered to have been born, before humans, as the follower of the eternal law.[12] Vedic seers, after the performance of a sacrifice to which they offered Soma juice, thought that the immortal Soma juice exuded from *ṛta*[13] and that it emanated from the hall of sacrifice (*yajña*) which itself was considered to be the abode of *ṛta*.[14] In the Vedic symbolism, *ṛta* was visualized as even the thread of sacrifice,[15] which was in the nature of a terrestrial and celestial correspondence or consonance.

Another Vedic divinity, Bṛhaspati, was extolled as the destroyer of guilt and evil, in order to uphold the all-powerful law.[16] The two other celestial entities, Mitra–Varuṇa occupied a special place as the custodians of *ṛta*.[17] The *Ṛgveda* states that Indra, the powerful god, lights up and energizes the whole world. All phenomena, the cyclic events, the flow of rivers, changes of seasons, day and night, and the like occur in accordance with *ṛta* according to Vedic seers who thus perceived a unitary principle, ever-active and omnipresent as the governing agent in an immanent form. It would appear that the idea of *ṛta* in course of time shaped itself into not only the *Mīmāṁsā* conception of *apūrva* that confirms the future enjoyment resulting from the rituals performed now, but also the Nyāya-Vaiśeṣika concept of *adṛṣṭa* and into the general conception of *Karma* itself.[18]

It would appear that the idea of natural order and moral law goes back to a period earlier than the *Ṛgveda*, to the possible integrated group of what are generally known as Indo-Aryans and Iranians. The latter called it *aśa* and this finds some elucidation in the Avestan literature. In the *Ṛgveda*, *Varuṇa*, of all the Vedic gods, was intimately associated with *ṛta* and was regarded as the upholder of moral law and the laws of nature. He was regarded as the regulator of the seasons and months, rains and the movements of the Sun and the Moon. Varuṇa perhaps corresponded to the Avestan Ahura Mazda in the sense that Ahura Mazda was also hailed by the Iranians as the divine person known for his wisdom and morality. It is significant to note that the disciplined routine followed by pious men in the path of *ṛta* is generally called *vrta*. It needs to be pointed out that neither the much later Greek *moira* nor the Chinese *Tao* which admits that the universe is an ordered whole is comparable to the much older and wider notion of *ṛta*.

Yajña

Ṛta was intimately associated with the religious kernel of the Vedic people, namely *Yajña* or the performance of sacrifices of diverse intent. *Yajña*, as noted already, was regarded as the abode of *ṛta,* and the act of sacrifice itself was considered to protect *ṛta* by which the happenings both in the physical world and the celestial sphere would continue to be orderly and harmonious. In fact, *yajña* was conceived as the navel (*nābhi*)[19] of the world. It was considered to be in the nature of a pathway leading to the divine dispensation, and eventually to the Creator. The *Śulba sūtra-s* of the *Kalpa*, one of the six auxiliaries of the Vedas, deal with the construction of several forms of sacrificial altars. Apart from the geometrical and arithmetical spin-offs from such constructions, the fundamental concept behind them appeared to be the recognition that the performer of sacrifices would transcend into an enlightened state away from the mundane shackles, through the mediation of Agni placed in the forms of altars; for, Agni is indeed formless and energetic, the terrestrial Agni being one of the aspects of the celestial light or energy, and associated with *ṛta*. The concept of *yajña* is synonymous with the assimilation of the individual self into the expanse of cosmic energy, a terrestrial–celestial consonance and human–divine communion. Yajña along with Agni, is extolled in the very first *mantra* of the first *sūkta* of the first *maṇḍala* of the *Ṛgveda*[20] that has come down to us in the present form.

Yajña and the act of creation or even the Creator himself were inter-related. For example, according to the *Śatapatha Brāhmaṇa*, Prajāpati, made offerings to *Viśvayajña*, before creation. There were different kinds of sacrifices depending upon the performer's desire(s), one of them was also *Jñana yajña,* a spiritual quest for achieving liberation. The Puruṣa in the *Puruṣa sūkta*[21] is generally described as the Cosmic Man and is stated to have been sacrificed in parts leading to five kinds of creation as follows: (i) creatures of air and land, wild and tame were born first; (ii) then the revelations (the Vedas) and the meters; (iii) next, from different parts of the body of Cosmic Man four different classes of men were born; (iv) then the two celestial lights and the gods Indra, Agni and Vāyu; and next (v) air, the sky and the earth came forth. The idea of Cosmic Man, as developed in the *Rgveda* was a unitary one, attempting to relate the different manifestations to a primordial source as follows: the organic and the inorganic, or the animate and the inanimate were integrated with a divine human form. A fourth of him was supposed to encompass all beings while three-fourths of him, that which was immortal in heaven. From the earthly quarter, he was believed to have given rise to animate and also inanimate objects in all directions.

Cosmic Energy

The Vedic seers regarded the unmanifested energetic ensemble as the cosmic energy, and the celestial light as its manifestation. The *Rgveda* speaks of cosmic light in diverse forms. Even the Vedic gods by their generic nomenclature, *deva,* have been extolled as natural forms of cosmic light. Uṣas, the goddess, was hailed as heaven's daughter in the eastern region (sunrise) attired in garments all of light.[22] The dawn was praised as the one that would give the light even to the Sun.[23] Savitṛ was known as the light immortal for all human beings.[24] The attainment of the light and the discovery of the gods have been alluded to in the *Rgveda* in the context of the Soma drink.[25]

More importantly, the cosmic light was conceived as the very principle of life and longevity, the 'soul of all gods' and the 'womb' of all created things.[26] *Aditi* which literally means the boundless or the unbounded and, according to Aurobindo, is the pure consciousness of infinite existence and the Light-infinite.[27] In the Vedic view, Aditi encompassed the celestial as well as the atmospheric regions. It was also visualized as the mother of all gods and creation, and gods were supposed to have been born of Aditi and hence they were an inseparable part of the Infinite-Light.[28] The idea of infinite light as an energetic unitary principle attained great height in the Upaniṣads in some of which Brahman is referred to as Self-Luminous Light. The whole world is illumined with his light[29] and thousands of Sun pale into nothingness before this Divine light, as explained in the *Bhagavadgītā*.

It is significant to note that several Vedic prayers are concerned with the invocation to Aditi. The offsprings of Aditi are the Ādityas. The Sun (Āditya) has a special role to play in the physical world. He is regarded as a form of Prajāpati (the Lord of Creatures). He has established himself, according to the *Bṛhaddevatā*,[30] in the three parts of the Universe (celestial, atmospheric and terrestrial): the atmospheric region is *antarikṣāgni* (lightning) and in the terrestrial region, *agni* (fire). That the unitary cosmic light is the primal source of all forms of energy was recognized by the Vedic seers who, in recognition of it, have in no unmistakable terms, saw in it the unfathomable divinity and hence worshipped it. To them Nature was one energetic entity, absolute and immanent, in all transformations or manifestations that are apparently diverse. The statements—the Universe is one (*Viśvamekam*) and it is one (*tadekam*)—as stated in the *Rgveda*[31] refer symbolically as well as by implication to the cosmic energetic principle. In pursuance of this thought, in the *Rgveda*, the Sun is regarded as the source of all generation and manifestation. Further the statement, 'Him who is the One Real, sages name variously,[32] represents the Vedic unitary conception par excellence.

Gods and God-head

The unitary approach can also be observed in the Vedic ensemble of gods. The number of Vedic gods may be 300, 3000 or 3, but 33 of them[33] could be classified under three heads: celestial (*dyulokastha*); atmospheric (*antarikṣastha*); and terrestrial (*pṛthivīstha*), each comprising eleven gods.[34] Several of them are personified forms of natural phenomena or forces. Agni is regarded as the Lord of the terrestrial gods, Vāyu (Air) of the atmospheric ones, and Āditya (the Sun), of the celestial gods. A striking feature of the *Rgveda* is its exposition of ONE amidst the multiplicity of gods. Hiriyanna rightly strikes the chord: 'The belief in a plurality of gods, which was a characteristic feature of early Vedic religion, loses its attraction; and the Vedic Indian, dissatisfied with the old mythology and impelled by that longing for simplicity of explanation so natural to man, starts upon seeking after not the causes of natural phenomena, but their first or ultimate cause. He is no longer content to refer observed phenomena to a multiplicity of gods, but strives to discover the one God that controls and rules over them all. The conception of a unitary god-head which becomes explicit now may be said to lie implicit already in the thought of the earlier period'.[35] One notices in the *Rgveda* not only a prayerful worship of several gods but also a reverential acceptance of the importance of a particular god, praising that god as the supreme one. There is a view as that of Max Muller that this attitude towards one god should be differentiated from monotheism (only one god) and Max Muller called it 'henotheism'. Apart from the controversy as to whether it is 'opportunistic monotheism' or it did pave the way for monotheism, it is important to recognise that the Vedic mind-set was to discover ONE amidst all. 'The key-note of the Vedic hymns is the same spiritual monism, the same immanent conception of the identity-in-difference which ultimately transcends even itself, the same indescribable absolutism, which holds both monism and pluralism within its bosom and which ultimately transcends both, which we find so beautifully and poetically developed in the Upaniṣads. To read anthropomorphic polytheism, and then henotheism and monotheism in the Vedas is, 'to borrow a phrase from Gauḍapāda, 'to see the footprints of birds in the air'.[36]

In this connection it may be noted that in the *Bṛhadāraṇyakopaniṣad*,[37] there is an enchanting dialogue between Vidagdha Śākalya and Yājñavalkya that runs as follows:

(Q) Śākalya: Yājñavalkya, Gods are how many?
(A) Yājñavalkya: three hundred and three thousand three.
(Q) How many gods?
(A) Thirty-three
(Q) How many gods?
(A) Three
(Q) How many gods?
(A) Two
(Q) How many gods?
(A) One and a half
(Q) How many gods?
(A) One
(Q) Who is the only one god?
(A) He is *Prāṇa*, He is *Brahma*, He is *That*.

One would not fail to notice that in the multiplicity of gods, the concept of ONE fundamental principle was pronounced.[38] Apart from the monistic idea, the *Ṛgveda* itself succinctly states: 'the real essence of the gods is ONE'[39] (III.55); and 'only the wide awake, the mindful, know the ultimate Abode of the Lord'.

The personification of the creative power of nature, Prajāpati (*lit.* the Lord of living beings), according to the *Śatapatha Brāhmaṇa,* is the thirty-fourth god who includes the other thirty-three gods in him. The *Ṛgveda* thinks of Prajāpati as the one and the one only who encompasses the entire universe or all created things and even beyond it.[40] In contradistinction to the *Ṛgvedic* personification of the godhead, the *Atharvaveda* thinks of *Prāṇa* or spiritual force[41] and even Cosmic Time[42] as the creator and destroyer. The Vedic idea of god is both transcendental and immanent, and the concept of ONE is a dominant gene of all Vedic thought processes. This has found expression in several ways in the *Ṛgveda*. For example, it unequivocally exhorts that the Primordial ONE is the source of the MANY (*Ekaṃ vā idaṃ vi babhūva sarvam*).[43]

Cosmogonic Ideas

The quintessence of the Vedic conviction in ONE can be found in what is called the *Nāsadīya Sūkta* (RV. X. 129)[44] which has cosmogonic undertones as follows:

(1)
Non-being, then existed not, nor being,
There was no air, nor sky that is beyond it,
What was concealed? Wherein? In whose protection?
And was there deep unfathomable water?

(2)
Death then existed not, nor life immortal,
Of neither night nor day was any token,
By its inherent force, the one breathed windless
No other thing than that beyond existed.

(3)
Darkness there was at first by darkness hidden,
Without distinctive marks, this all was water,
That which becoming, by the void, was covered,
That One by force of heat came into being.

(4)
Desire entered the One in the beginning,
It was the earliest seed of thought, the product,
The sages searching in their hearts with wisdom,
Found out the bond of being in non-being.

(5)
Their ray extended light across the darkness,
But was the One above or was it under?
Creative force was there and fertile power,
Below was energy, above was impulse.

(6)
Who knows for certain? Who shall here declare it?
Whence was it born, and whence came this creation?
The gods were born after the world's creation,
Then who can know from whence it has arisen.

(7)
None knoweth whence creation has arisen,
And whether he has or has not produced it,
He who surveys it in the highest heaven,
He only knows or haply, he may know not.

—— (Macdonell's translation)

A close examination of the *Nāsadīya sūkta* reveals that it expounds the First Cause without any mythological or supernatural elements. It speaks of an inward *fervour* or warmth and thereafter the *desire*, the *primal seed* or germ. The thought-structure of this hymn speaks volumes about the type of high thinking in the Vedic times about creation with an open-mindedness, but still with a question about the origin of the world itself. The ultimate principle is called *Tad Ekam* or *That One*, formless and indistinguishable.

The statement that there was no existent, nor non-existent needs some explanation. The existent in its manifestation was not there in the beginning, but, on this basis, it cannot be deemed to have been non-existent. For, it is the very first from which all existence issued forth. The assertion that the ONE breathed windless is similar to if not identical with the Aristotelian concept of the Unmoved Mover in his scheme of the Universe. Likewise, in China, Lao-Tzu thought of the one, nameless, formless yet complete and dependent on nothing except itself.[45] But the Aristotelian or Lao-Tzian concept was at least a thousand years later than the Ṛgvedic lofty concept.

The *Ṛgveda*,[46] in a figurative way goes on to exclaim: 'What indeed was the wood? What was that tree from which they fashioned heaven and earth? In the *Puruṣa sūkta*, as noted before, Cosmic Man is presented as the one Being from whom the different parts of the universe emanated. 'The Moon was gendered from his mind; and from his eye, the Sun had its birth; Indra and Agni from his mouth were born; and Vāyu from his breath. Forth from his navel came mid-air; the sky was fashioned from his head; Earth from his feet, and from his ear, the regional; Besides, came forth horses, cattle, goats, sheep and other animals, the four castes of people—all when sacrifice was performed with Puruṣa as an oblation. If the *Puruṣa sūkta* at a personified level deals with the origins that can be traced to Cosmic Man whose sacrifice gave rise to the varieties of the knowable universe, the *Nāsadīya sūkta* at an impersonal level expresses the unknowability of the origin of the Universe in an inquisitive mixture of opposites.

The idea of a primordial or cosmic man with mythical undertones was existent in several ancient cultures. In the Scandinavian Edda mythology, the creation process was associated with the dismemberment of a gigantic person called Ymir, the progenitor of a lineage of gigantic beings. His blood was supposed to have created the sea and waters; his flesh, the soiled firmament; his bones, the mountains; his skull, the dome of the sky; his brain, the clouds; and his eye brows, the dwellings of the human race. And finally human beings were born.[47] In China too there was a legend that projected the idea of the emergence of the Universe from the organs of the body of primordial person referred to as 'The Ancient ONE'. When this man died, his head became the mountains; his eyes became the Sun and the Moon; his fat became seas and bays; his hair became plants and trees.[48] But such conceptions as these can in no manner be construed as unitary ones similar to the *Puruṣa* and the *Nāsadīya sūkta*.

Both the *Puruṣa sūkta* and the *Nāsadīya sūkta*, however, are in the tenth *maṇḍala* of the *Ṛgveda*, which, according to several scholars, is the latest in the *Ṛgvedic* compendium. In the first *maṇḍala* which is supposed to be not the earliest, there is the concept of ONE, but in the context of different names, perhaps relating to gods. From an attitude of praising gods through an identification of one particular god or god-head among gods, Viśvakarman as the creator and governor of the universe, and the cosmic egg (*hiraṇyagarbha*),[49] and eventually a Cosmic Person or *Puruṣa*, the Vedic sages envisioned a unitary world-ground which they perceived to be the only reality, although its origin was recognized to be beyond the human comprehension. The Vedic imageries gradually led to an exposition of the understandable or the recognizable world-stuff.

The *Śatapatha Brāhmaṇa*[50] has an interesting speculation on the origin as well as certain components of the Universe. It starts with the primeval water as the only one that existed in the beginning and the Waters (plural) desired to propagate their kind. Through their own churning (mortification), a golden egg originated in them, and swam in the waters for about a year. After another year, the cosmic person, Prajāpati, arose out of it breaking open the golden egg which, however, continued to float for another year. Prajāpati, uttered *bhūḥ*, it became the earth; his word *bhuvaḥ* became the atmosphere; and his utterance 'svar', became the sky beyond. The text goes on to say that out of these three words which have five syllables, Prajāpati made the five seasons of the year (spring, summer, raining, autumn and winter). The conception of the primeval water in the *Śatapatha Brāhmaṇa*, apparently is similar to that of Thales (Greek); but in reality it differs substantively, because the latter thought of water as the ultimate physical world-ground.

Brahman and Māyā: The Phenomenal World

The word 'brahman' used in the *Ṛgveda* had the connotation of the spiritual power of prayer in a magical or supernatural context or magical esoterism. At the same time, it acquired the meaning of sacred knowledge being synonymous with the Vedic knowledge itself as well as an exalted divinity during the performance of sacrifices.

In the Upaniṣads, Brahman began to signify the fundamental cause or the primordial or the highest principle, a cosmic principle which pervades the Universe—the Absolute Reality. The *Chāndogya*[51] describes Brahman as that from which the world is born, into which it returns and by which it is supported, i.e.,

Brahman is the creator, destroyer and preserver of the universe. The *Katha* projects the Brahman as the self-luminous, immortal and the supporter of all the worlds,[52] while the *Bṛhadāraṇyaka* describes Brahman as the one in which all beings, all gods, all worlds, all organs are contained.[53] The five elements, *pṛthvī, ap, tejas, vāyu,* and *ākāśa,* the building entities of the physical world as conceived by Indian thinkers, are supposed to have been created by Brahman (see next chapter). In fact all aspects of the inorganic and organic nature are stated to be Brahman, assuming different names and forms. The organic beings are divided into three categories: (i) born from the egg; (ii) born alive; (iii) born from the germ, besides a later one, namely, those born from sweat.[54] In each and all of these, Brahman is believed to live. Brahman treated as being synonymous or identical with ātman, the innate soul in contradistinction to the physical body frame. It is regarded as all-pervading. The *Bṛhadāraṇyaka* says:[55] '. . .When it breathes, it is called breath; when it speaks, voice; when it hears, ears; when it thinks, mind. These are merely the names of its activities. . . . Ātman does not appear as a whole and it is immanent in all of its manifestations'. The true self is not equated with mind but is regarded as the intelligent and knowable spirit in man, as a philosophical concept, along with Brahman. Brahman, according to the Upaniṣads, is omnipotent and imperishable.[56] The highest monism of Indian thought in terms of Brhaman-ātman, the indescribable and incommunicable non-dual experience of the blissful state, is indeed fascinating; but its discourse is beyond the scope and purpose of the present volume. The concept of Māyā, nevertheless, needs some consideration as it is supposed to be the first cause of the physical or the knowable world.

Māyā: The seed ideas of Māyā (illusion) or *avidyā* (ignorance) can be found in the upaniṣads[57] (*Praśna,* I. 16; *Bṛh.* II 4.14; *Śve,* IV. 9; *Īśa.* 15). Śaṅkara, the most powerful exponent of Advaita (non-dual) viewed the phenomenal world caused by Māyā as not real; but since it is known to us, this world is not unreal in that sense only. The advaitic exposition is that the objects of the perceived world are *jaḍa* and depend upon the universal spirit for their being or existence. It is difficult, according to the position of a strict advaitin, to classify the world in an analytical manner since it is not the ultimate one. The reality is relative and thus an appearance. Māyā is akin to *avidyā*[58] that is responsible for creating illusion. It has been explained that Māyā is the potency or *śakti* that is inherent in *Īśvara* which through the instrumentality of the former, manifests the objective world in all its diverse forms and associated names. In other words, the source of the universe is not Māyā that is only in the nature of an accessory to *Īśvara* in the creation of the world of objects out of itself. Further, it is pointed out that the world is an appearance to *Īśvara* but not to those who have experienced the unity or non-duality. For those with their *avidyā,* the world looks to be real. Brahman is the original, the world is its translation in space–time; and the translating agency being Māyā. Brahman has two aspects: The *nirguṇa* Brhaman and the *saguṇa* Brahman; it is the latter aspect of which the phenomenal world is the effect, *nirguṇa* Brahman being not the cause of the world of objects. The concept of *Īśvara* is in the context of *saguṇa* Brahman. Devotion to *Īśvara*, it is stated, would prepare the seeker to meditate upon the real Brahman.

According to Śaṅkara,[59] 'Māyā is indescribable and indefinable, for it is neither real nor unreal nor both (*sadasadanirvacanīya*). It has a phenomenal and relative character (*vyāvahārikasattā*); but it is only appearance. It is of the nature of super imposition (*adhyāsa*) and therefore wrong cognition but removable by right knowledge. When *vidyā* dawns *avidyā* vanishes. The locus (*āśraya*) as well as object (*viṣaya*) is Brahman, but Brahman is untouched by it. Māyā is not only the absence of knowledge but it is also wrong knowledge (*mithyācāra rūpa*). But Māya is something positive (*bhāvarūpa*) but ultimately unreal. The relation of Māyā and Brahman is unique and is called *tādātmya*. It is not identity, nor difference nor both' (C. Sharma, p. 274). A proper understanding of Māyā is very essential for a critical appreciation of the Vedāntins' approach to the physical world.

It is not intended here to present various aspects of Advaita, nor its place in Indian philosophy *vis-a-vis* the other systems of thought. But it may be desirable to reflect, briefly though, on the effect of the advaitic approach to the understanding of the reality of the physical world. It would, however, appear that there are some parallels between the advaita and the modern scientific position relating to the possible unified dimension of the physical world.

According to Sreekantan:[53] "The Advaita philosophy has the closest parallelism to some of the insights of modern physics. The three fundamental aspects on which this parallelism of insights are strikingly apparent, are:

 (i) There is only one entity that is real and everything else is some kind of a modification of it.

 (ii) The phenomenal world arises as a result of the intrinsic nature of this reality itself.

(iii) Reality *per se* depends on the observer and his viewpoint.

The Advaita philosophy is expounded by Śaṅkara in the form of *ślokas* (stanzas) in several texts in Sanskrit. I will quote a few of them from *Vivekacūḍāmaṇi* which means: "the Crest Jewel of Discrimination" with English translation as given by Swami Mādhavānanda.

The cardinal tenet of Advaita is: 'There is only one entity Brahman and nothing else'.

Now what is Brahman? The identity of Brahman is spelt out in the famous *mahāvākyas*—the great sayings: *Prajñānam Brahma* (Consciousness is Brahman: *Ait.up—Ṛgveda*); *Ayam ātmā Brahma* (The self is Brahman: *Māṇḍ.up—Yajurveda*);

Tattvamasi (That thou art: *Chandogya.up—Sāmaveda*); *Aham Brahmāsmi* (I am Brahman: *Bṛhadāraṇyaka up.*—Yajurveda).

In propounding his philosophy, Śaṅkara uses extensively an analysis of our daily experience under various circumstances and drives home his viewpoint by beautiful similes. Let me illustrate this with one line of argument:

Śaṅkara starts with a consideration of the three normal states of daily experience: the Waking State (*jāgrat*), the Dreaming State (*svapna*) and the Deep Sleep State (*suṣupti*). The Waking State is the one in which we all have common experience of an external world in which all the activities of both animate and inanimate objects take place in space and time. The most important aspect of this State is that the experiences can be shared by all of us. This State of common activity is called *Vyāvahārika* State. In contrast, the Dreaming State is highly individualistic and the experiences cannot be shared, nor can they be recorded by any instrument. As long as we are dreaming, the Waking State has ceased to exist. But in the Dreaming State, we have the same kind of experiences regarding material, animal and human objects and activities in space and time, though these have no direct relation to the Waking State. The moment we wake up, however, the realities of the Dreaming State, the objects, space, time and everything disappear and we interpret the dream as a creation of our mind. In the third State of Deep Sleep, our experience is very different. There is no space, time or objects. We seem to have merged with something that we do not comprehend clearly after waking up.

What Śaṅkara emphasises is that there is a common witness (*Sākṣī*)—the "I"—that experiences all the three states. This witness according to him is self (*ātman*) and is consciousness (*prajñā*).

So far everything is common experience. What Śaṅkara and the Vedāntins tell us further is that there is yet another higher state of awakening, of enlightenment, which has been attained by some of the sages and which can be attained by any one who undergoes training in disciplining the mind by meditation, contemplation and yoga practices. When one attains this state, the phenomenal world just merges with the one reality (Brahman). From this esoteric point of view of those who have seen the truth and experienced the ultimate reality, there is no world, no creation, no destruction and no God. There is only Brahman and nothing else. We come to the identity:

Self = Consciousness = Brahman = Everything.

The verdict of all discussions on the Vedānta is that the *Jīva* and the whole universe are nothing but Brahman, and that liberation means abiding in Brahman, the indivisible Entity. The *Śrutis* themselves are an authority (for the statement) that Brahman is none to second' according to Śaṅkara.

If Brahman is universal consciousness and there is nothing else, then how does the phenomenal world of matter, space and time, whose reality we cannot question based on our Waking State experience, arise? (This question is not in principle different from the one that physics has to answer—how from the empty space of quantum mechanical definition, does the phenomenal world of three spatial dimensions and time arise?)

In the following two verses (their translation in English is given below) Śaṅkara expresses the way the universe is envisaged in terms of the underlying reality and the modality of creation: (i) 'As the wave, the foam, the whirlpool, the bubble, etc., are all in essence but water, similarly the *Cit* (Knowledge Absolute) is all this, from the body up to egoism. Everything verily is the *Cit*, homogeneous and pure. . . . and (ii) 'In me, the ocean of Infinite Bliss, the waves of the universe are created and destroyed by the playing of the wind Māyā'.

The phenomenal world arises from Brahman through the play of Māyā, which is the creative aspect of Brahman itself. Māyā is rather a difficult and somewhat abstract concept. Māyā is recognized only through its action. It is the causative factor and is uncaused. (it is somewhat like the concept-fluctuation' that is used to describe creation in physics). Brahman, seen with this power of Māyā, naturally became the all powerful God, the Creator. As we have already seen from the point of view of the one who has identified himself with Brahman through realization, Māyā is unreal and like a mirage in the desert.

The role of Māyā and its characteristics are described in the following two *ślokas* (their translation in English is given below):

(i) 'Avidyā (nescience) or Māyā, called also the undifferentiated, is the power of the Lord. She is without beginning, is made up of the three *guṇa-s* and is superior to the effects (as their cause). She is to be inferred by one of clear intellect only from the effects. She produces. It is She who brings forth this whole universe;

(ii) 'From Mahat down to the gross body everything is the effect of Māyā: These and Māyā itself know thou to be the non-Self, and therefore unreal like the mirage in a desert.'

What happens to the phenomenal world for one who has (been liberated) seen the truth (*Jīvanmukta*). This is described in the following two *ślokas* (Eng. tr.):

(i) 'Where is the Universe gone, by whom is it removed, and where is it merged? It was just now seen by me. And has it ceased to exist?. It is passing strange!'

(ii) 'As, when a jar is broken, the space enclosed by it becomes palpably the limitless space, so when the apparent limitations are destroyed, the knower of Brahman verily becomes Brahman itself.'

Thus the phenomenal world, according to the advaita philosophy, is both real and unreal. It is *real* from the point of view of the common man to which category we all belong, and *unreal* from the point of view of one who has realized the truth.

What do these Parallelisms of Insights Mean?

These insights of the Vedānta philosophy are very ancient and those of advaita philosophy, as propounded by Śaṅkarācārya, about 1200 years belong to an era much before the advent of Modern Science. These insights would have had no relevance in the heydays of classical physics when the reductionism method reigned supreme, and the external world was regarded as objective, and determinism and causality were unquestioned. However, as we have seen over the last hundred years, because of the discovery of a variety of new phenomena and the development of quantum mechanics and relativity, there has been a major transformation in the viewpoint of physics, especially since it has been realized that the role of the conscious observer cannot be extricated in the analysis of the objective world. It has now become a participatory universe with the subject-object relation being of a very special kind. One has to wait for further developments in the field of life sciences to understand clearly the role of consciousness in the physical interpretation. This can come about only when one has a clear picture of what consciousness itself is.

. . . The ancient philosophers of the advaita type do not have to depend on modern physics for their substantiation inasmuch as modern physics need not to depend on the ancient philosophies for its progress. However, from the point of view of philosophy of science, it would be wrong to ignore the parallelism of insights and thoughts from wherever they may be and to whatever period they may belong" (extracted from B. V. Sreekantan's paper: 'Modern Science and Ancient Indian Philosophies', *Science in the West and India: Some Historical Aspects*, pp. 445-449).

Some Ideas in the West

In the history of the human understanding of the universe, one notices some parallel developments in other cultures even in ancient times. Such developments in the Mesopotamian culture-area (Akkadians, Sumerians, Assyrians and Babylonians included) have been dealt with already. In the Mesopotamian Epic of Creation, which has come down to us in the form of seven cuneiform tablets, now preserved in the British Museum, London, Water is the primordial element—*apsu*, a kind of abyss filled with fresh water from which all beings including, gods were supposed to have been born, and *Tiamat* (salt water). The Sumerian incantation states that in the beginning nothing as yet existed, no heaven and earth, save the abyss of primeval water. The *Nāsadīya* of the *Ṛgveda*, as noted before, also states that there was neither existent nor non-existent, there was not firmament nor sky beyond, and speaks of water also the word, *āpaḥ*, in the Sanskrit texts is generally in plural sense a reminiscent of *apsu* and *Tiamat*.

It was at least a millennium or two before that there was a marked departure from the gods and the heavens in the speculation concerning the origin or the nature of the universe. This came about with the Greek thinkers around the sixth century B.C. and a few centuries later. The Ionian Thales of Miletus discarded the divine dispensation of Mesopotamian Merdoch as well as Egyptian gods, and expounded that the ultimate essence of all things was Water. He was followed by others like Anaximander, Anaximenes, Heracleitus and Pythagoras. While Anaximander thought of an undifferentiated entity, Anaximenes postulated that Air was the primordial stuff. Hereaclitus, on the other hand, believed in the state of flux and stressed that change was alone real. In pursuance of this idea, he regarded fire as the basic element. Empedocles, another Greek thinker, added Earth, and put forward his scheme of four elements. Later in Athens, between *c.* 400 and 300 B.C, the two great savants, Plato and Aristotle, endeavoured to provide a unified picture of the universe, each in his own way. Plato was greatly influenced by Pythagorean vision and in his *Timaeus* he described the universe as a living one with a 'soul':

"*Timaeus* tries to give a physical account of how the 'soul' moves in body. The 'soul' is in movement and the body moves because it is interwoven with it. The Creator compounded the Soul–substance out of the elements and divided it according to the harmonic numbers so that it might have an innate perception of harmony and that its motion might be with movements well attuned. He bent its straight line into a circle. This he divided into two circles united at two common points. One of these he divided into seven circles (the orbits of the seven planets) in such wise that the motions of the heavens are the motions of the soul" [*De Anima of Aristotle*].[60]

Plato's pupil, Aristotle, attempted to pursue the Platonic view, but in a slightly different manner through his exposition of the relationship between the general description of the Universe ('Physis') and the study of living beings. He thought that the objects were either 'with soul' (psyche) or 'without soul' (apsychic) and that 'matter is identical with potentiality, form with actuality, the 'soul' being that which gives the form or actuality in living things'. In contrast to his master's view, Aristotle did not think of 'soul' as having a separate existence. As for the living beings, he proposed a Ladder of Nature in a graded manner starting with lower plants. Aristotle was both a vitalist and a teleologist, believing that the soul had a purpose and would work towards it. Nevertheless, he differentiated between the earth and the celestial sphere—a duality that was akin to either the contemporaneous or earlier neo-Platonic view of macrocosm and microcosm, of the heavens and man on the earth. This view found the support of St. Augustine

(354-430 A.D.) and through him it found its way into Christianity in the fifth century A.D. As noted already, the intimate consonance between man and Universe, the terrestrial–celestial inseparable relationship were already expounded in a mature way in the *Ṛgveda* itself about 2000 years earlier.

Aristotle's duality was not only in relation to the composition of the heavens of which *ether* was an integral component but also in the context of celestial motion that all stars and planets would move with uniform circular velocity and in spheres, centred round the earth. The motion of celestial bodies would be perfect circular motion, while the motion on the imperfect earth would be linear. This duality continued to hold sway over the European thinking till Newton (17th cent), demolished it by his law of universal gravitation. Earlier Kepler had demonstrated that the planets would move round the Sun not in circles, but in elliptical paths.

An older contemporary of Newton, Thomas Hobbes, whose unorthodox opinions incurred the wrath of the Church, was basically a materialist who believed that all knowledge owed itself to sensorial experience. His was a mechanical conception of nature, just as he thought that human thoughts and emotions were a consequent of the motions of atoms in the body. His slightly junior contemporary, Rene Descartes, the noted French mathematician and philosopher, propounded the idea '*cogito ergo sum*' or 'I think, therefore I am', alluding to the complementarity of *being* and *thought*, of the relationship between consciousness and existence. He thought of a Perfect Being, arguing that if the idea of perfection (from our own imperfections) was to be a valid one, then there should be one of perfection. Descartes also expounded the duality of mind and matter, the former being involved in the process of thinking and the latter, occupying space. He was well known for his theory of vortices to explain the motion of the celestial bodies.

In contradistinction to the Cartesian duality, Spinoza thought of a universal unity called the 'substance', pointing out that reality was the substratum or substance of all phenomena. Though he discarded the idea of a cosmic purpose, he expounded the idea of nature, and defined the purposes at work in nature. He, however, did not accept the immortality of soul as also the free will.

Bishop Berkeley emphasised that mind was alone real and nothing existed apart from perception. The things or objects were in the nature of our ideas, according to Berkeley, who strongly opposed the materialistic views. His junior contemporary, David Hume, on the other hand, vehemently argued against Berkeley's views and his emphasis on mind. His was a materialistic present and he pointed out that there was no mind, no substance, no reality, no permanence, no immutability, beyond the world of our experience.

Immanuel Kant tried to reconcile these extreme positions through his well known exposition of the 'thing-in-itself', the phenomenon and the noumenon. He stressed the importance of *a priori* knowledge and his *Critique of Pure Reason* and the *Critique of Practical Reason* became important for understanding the relationship between the human mind and the world of matter.

The position at present is that modern science is still unable to arrive at scientifically that ONE principle or the origin of the universe. Though the postulate of Big Bang may either provide answers to or explain some of the astronomically or physically observed characteristics of the Universe, it has its own limitations concerning the origin or the *why* the supposed first cause, the Big Bang (explosion), occurred some 13 millions of years ago. As Paul Dyson puts it: 'It explains everything except the explosion'. In the 17th century, Newton in a revolutionary way enunciated the laws of motion and the law of universal gravitation that govern both the celestial and the terrestrial phenomena. But he too thought of the solar system and the universe in terms of a deistic design. The questions as to how the gravitational force is transmitted across the space and how does any action at a distant place occur, still, remained enigmatic to Newton and his contemporaries. Perhaps his view also, according to some, was that 'God only knows. A deity or god is an expression that signifies in a way the limitations of human mind 'who knows?' Or 'whether even the god knows'? These are an admission perhaps of the incapability of human mind to traverse beyond the confines of the very processes of the mind. The exposition of the *Nāsadīya sūkta* around three thousand and five hundred years ago, as noted before, has pointed out the limitation of the human mind in trying to unravel the origin of the mysterious universe, by projecting a question: 'Who knows?', Max Planck, the exponent of the Quantum Theory which is seminal to modern physics, thought, 'that we ourselves are part of the mystery we are trying to solve'.[61]

There is no denying that the Western approach towards an understanding of the physical world has not been holistic, but analytic and reductionistic by and large. The Western metaphysical ideas too have been of the same genre. The Indian approach, on the other hand, has been a holistic one right from the Vedic times—an attitude that does not make any difference between mind and matter. the self and the non-self, or man and nature. The concept of ONE has been the forte of Indian thought-structure, and it permeates in one form or the other the Indian approach to, and perspectives on, the physical world.

REFERENCES

(The English translations of all the Ṛgvedic references are taken from the *The Hymns of the Rgveda* by Ralph T. H. Griffith.)

1. शतं जीव शरदो वर्धमान: शतं हेमन्ताञ्छशतमु वसन्तान् । शतमिन्द्राग्री सविता बृहस्पति: शतायुषा हविषेमं पुनर्दु: ।
   RV.X.161.4
   (Recurrence : AV. 3.11.4, 20.96.9, *Nighaṇṭu* 14-36)

Live, Waxing in thy strength, a hundred autumns, live through a hundred springs, a hundred winters.
Through hundred oblation Indra, Agni, Bṛhaspati, Savitar, Yield him for a hundred.

2. चक्षुर्नो धेहि चक्षुषे चक्षुर्विश्व्यै तनूभ्यः । सं चेदं वि च पश्येम । RV.X-158.4

Give sight unto our eyes, Give thou our bodies sight that they may see : May we survey, discern this world.

3. Whitehead, A.N : *Science and The Modern World,* London, 1942, p. 4.

4. ऋतेन यावृतावृधावृतस्य ज्योतिषस्पती । ता मित्रावरुणा हुवे । RV.I-23-5

Those who by law uphold the Law, Lords of the shining light of Law, Mitra I call and Varuṇa.

5. ऋतस्य या अभिरक्षन्ति गोपाः । RV.I.163.5

Those who guard the holy law keep it safely.

अभीमृतस्य दोहना अनूषत योनौ देवस्य । RV.I.144.2

To him sang forth the flowing streams of holy law, encompassed in the home and birth-place of god.

6. कथा ते अग्ने शुचयन्त आयोर्ददाशुर्वाजेभिराशुषाणाः ।

उभे यत् तोके तनये दधाना ऋतस्य सामन् रणयन्त देवाः ॥ RV.I.147.1

How, Agni, have the radiant ones, aspiring endued thee with the vigour of the living, so that on both sides fostering seed and offspring, the gods may joy in Holy Law's fulfilment?

7. ऋतेन देवः सविता शमायत ऋतस्य शृङ्गमुर्विया वि पप्रथे ।

ऋतं सासाह महि चित् पृतन्यतो मा नो वि यौष्टं सख्या मुमोचतम् । RV.VIII.86.5

8. ऋतस्य योषा न मिनाति धामाहरहर्निष्कृतमाचरन्ती ।

कन्येव तन्वा शाशदानाँ एषि देवि देवमियक्षमाणम् ॥ RV.I.123.9-10

एष दिवो दुहिता प्रत्यदर्शि ज्योतिर्वसाना समना पुरस्तात् ।

ऋतस्य पन्थामन्वेति साधु प्रजानतीव न दिशो मिनाति । RV.I.124.3

She who hath knowledge of the first day's nature is born refulgent white out of darkness. The maiden break not the law of order, day by day coming to the place appointed. I.123.9
There in the eastern region she, Heaven's Daughter, arrayed in the garments, all of light, appeareth.
Truly she followeth the path of order, nor faileth knowing well the Heavenly quarters. I.124.3

9. ऋतस्य देवीः सदसो बुधाना गवां न सर्गा उषसो जरन्ते । RV.IV.51.8

Awaking, from the seat of holy order, the Goddess Dawns come nigh like troops of cattle.

चुतधामानं बृहतीमृतेन ऋतावरीमरुणप्सुं विभातीम् । RV.V.80.1

Sublime, by Law true to eternal order, bright on her path, red-tinted, far-refulgent (Goddess Dawn who bringeth Sun Light).

10. ऋतस्य योनावशयद् दमूना जामीनामग्निरपसि स्वसॄणाम् । RV.III.1.11

Friend of the house, within the lap of Order lay Agni, in the sister River's service.

11. प्राग्रये बृहते यज्ञियाय ऋतस्य वृष्णे असुराय मन्म । RV.V.12.1

To Agni, lofty Asura, meet for worship seer of eternal law, my prayer I offer.

12. गोपा ऋतस्य दीदिहि स्वे दमे । RV.III.10.2

(Agni!) shine forth in thine own home as guardian of the law.

13. असृग्रमिन्दव: पथा धर्मन्नृतस्य सुश्रिय: । RV.IX.7.1

Forth on their way the glorious (Soma) drops have flowed for the maintenance of law.

14. ऋतस्य धामन् रणयन्त देवा: । RV.IV.7.7

Gods may rejoice in the home of the Order.

15. ऋतस्य तन्तुर्वितत: पवित्र आ जिह्वाया अग्रे वरुणस्य माययया । RV.IX.73.9

The thread of sacrifice spun in the cleansing sieve, on Varuṇa's tongue-tip, by super-natural night.

16. स ऋणचिद्वणया ब्रह्मणस्पतिर्द्रुहो हन्ता मह ऋतस्य धर्तरि । RV. II.23.17

Him, too, who threatens us without offence of ours the evil-minded, arrogant, sapacious man, Him turn thou from our path away, Bṛhaspati give us fair access to this banquet of the Gods (sacrifice).

17. ऋतमृतेन सपन्तेषिरं दक्षमाशाते । अद्रुहा देवौ वर्धेते । RV.V.68.4

Carefully tending Law with Law they have attained their vigorous might the two Gods were devoid of guile.

18. S.C. Chatterjee and D. M. Dutta, *An Introduction to Indian Philosophy*, p. 17.
    RV. IX. 121.1; X. 37.5

19. यज्ञो भुवनस्य नाभि: । RV. I.164.35

Sacrifice indeed is the navel of the universe

20. अग्निमीळे पुरोहितं यज्ञस्य देवमृत्विजम् ।

होतारं रत्नधातमम् । RV. I.1.1.

21. तेन देवा अयजन्त साध्या ऋषयश्च ये ।

तस्माद्यज्ञात् सर्वहुत: संभृतं पृषदाज्यम् । पशूंस्ताँश्चक्रे वायव्यान् आरण्यान् ग्राम्याश्च ये । तस्माद्यज्ञात्सर्वहुत: ऋच: सामानि जज्ञिरे । छंदांसि जज्ञिरे तस्मात् यजुस्तस्मादजायत । तस्मादश्वा अजायन्त ये के चोभयादत: । गावो ह जज्ञिरे तस्मात् तस्माज्जाता अजावय: । यत्पुरुषं व्यदधु: कतिधा व्यकल्पयन् । मुखं किमस्य कौ बाहू का ऊरू पादा उच्येते । ब्राह्मणोऽस्य मुखमासीत् बाहू राजन्य: कृत: । ऊरू तदस्य यद्वैश्य: पद्भ्यां शूद्रो अजायत । चन्द्रमा मनसो जात: चक्षो: सूर्यो अजायत । मुखादिन्द्रश्चाग्निश्च प्राणाद्वायुरजायत । नाभ्या आसीदन्तरिक्षम् शीष्र्णो द्यौ: समवर्तत । पद्भ्यां भूमिर्दिश: श्रोत्रात् तथा लोकाँ अकल्पयन् । RV.X-90. 7-14

With him the Deities and all Sādhyas and Ṛsis sacrificed.
From the great general sacrifice the dripping fat was gathered up. He formed the creatures of the air and animals, both wild and tame.
From that great general sacrifice ṛcas and Sāma hymns were born.
There from were spells and charms produced; the yajus had its birth from it.
From it were horses born; from it all cattle with two rows of teeth;
From it were generated kine, from which the goats and sheep were born,
When they divided .... how many portions did they make?

What do they call his mouth, his arms?
What do they call his thighs and feet?
That *Brāhmaṇa* was his mouth,
of both his arms was *Rājanya* made.
His thighs became the *Vaiśya*; from his feet the *Śūdra* was produced.
The moon was gendered from his mind, and from his eye the sun had birth.
Indra and Agni from his mouth were born, and Vāyu from his breath.
From his navel came the mid-air; the sky was fashioned from his head;
Earth from his feet, and from his ears the regions.
Thus they formed the worlds.

22. एषा दिवो दुहिता प्रत्यदर्शि ज्योतिर्वसाना समना पुरस्तात् । ऋतस्य पन्थानमन्वेति साधु प्रजानतीव न दिशो मिनाति ।
(also ref.7) RV.I.124.3

इदमु त्यत् पुरुतमं पुरस्ताज्ज्योतिस्तमसो वयुनावदस्थात् ।

नूनं दिवो दुहितरो विभातीगार्तुं कृणवन्नुषसो जनाय ॥ RV.IV.51.1

Forth from the darkness in the region eastward this most abundant splendid light hath mounted. Now, verily, the far-refulgent mornings, daughters of heaven bring welfare to the people.

23. ... अयं सूर्ये अदधाज्ज्योतिरन्तः । RV.VI.44.23

The Dawns he wedded to a glorious consort and set within the Sun the light that lights him.

24. उदु ज्योतिरमृतं विश्वजन्यं विश्वानरः सविता देवो अश्रेत् ।

क्रत्वा देवानामजनिष्ट चक्षुराविरकभुर्वनं विश्वमुषाः ॥ RV.VII.76.1

Savitar God of all men hath sent upward his light, designed for all mankind, immortal, Through the God's power that Eye was first created. Dawn has made all the universe apparent.

25. अपाम सोमममृता अभूमागन्म ज्योतिरविदाम देवान् ।

किं नूनमस्मान् कृणवदरातिः किमु धूर्तिरमृतं मर्त्यस्य ॥ RV.VIII.48.3

We have drunk Soma and become immortal; we have attained the light, the Gods discovered. Now what may foeman's malice do harm to us? What, O immortal, mortal man's deception?

26. इदं श्रेष्ठं ज्योतिषां ज्योतिरागाच्चित्रः प्रकेतो अजनिष्ट विभ्वा ।

यथा प्रसूता सवितुः सवायँ एवा रात्र्युषसे योनिमारैक् । RV.I.113.1

27. Aurobindo, Sri: *On the Vedas*. Aurobindo Ashram, Pondicherry, 1964, pp. 464 ff.

28. अदितिर्द्यौरदितिरन्तरिक्षमदितिर्माता स पिता स पुत्रः ।

विश्वे देवा अदितिः पञ्च जना अदितिर्जातमदितिर्जनित्वम् ॥ RV.I.89.10

Aditi is the heaven, Aditi is mid-air, Aditi is the Mother and the sire and the son. Aditi is all Gods, Aditi five-classed men, Aditi all that has been born and shall be born.

29. न तत्र सूर्यो भाति न चन्द्रतारकं नेमा विद्युतो भान्ति कुतोऽयमग्निः ।

तमेव भान्तमनुभाति सर्वं तस्य भासा सर्वमिदं विभाति । Katha.up.5.15

The Sun shines not there, nor the moon and stars, these lightnings shine not, much less this (earthly) fire. After Him, as He shines, doth every thing shine. This whole world is illumined with His Light.

30. Bhagavadgītā, Ch. XI.

31. एजद् ध्रुवं पत्यते विश्वमेकं चरत् पतत्रि विषुणं वि जातम् । RV.III.54.8

One all is Lord of what is fixed and moving, that walks, that flies, this multiform creation.

32. एकं सद्विप्रा बहुधा वदन्ति । RV. I. 164.46

33. त्रीणि शता त्री सहस्राण्यग्निं त्रिंशच्च देवा नव चासपर्यन् ।

औक्षन् घृतैरस्तृणन् बर्हिरस्मा आदिद्धोतारं न्यसादयन्त ॥ RV.III.9.9

Three times a hundred Gods and thrice a thousand, and three times ten and nine have worshipped Agni.

For him spread sacred grass with oil bedewed him and stabilised him as priest and sacrificer.

34. आ नासत्या त्रिभिरेकादशैरिह देवेभिर्यातं मधुपेयमश्विना ।

प्रायुस्तारिष्टं नी रपांसि मृक्षतं सेधतं द्वेषो भवतं सचाभुवा ॥ RV.I.34.11

Come, O Nāsatyas, with the thrice eleven gods; Come, O Aśvins, to the drinking and make long our days of life, and wipe out all our sins; ward off our enemies, be with us even more.

ये देवासो दिव्येकादश स्थ पृथिव्यामध्येकादश स्थ ।

अप्सुक्षितो महिनैकादश स्थ ते देवासो यज्ञमिमं जुषध्वम् ॥ RV.I.139.11

O Ye eleven Gods, whose home is heaven, O ye eleven who make earth your dwelling, ye who with sight, eleven, live in waters, accept this sacrifice, O Gods, with pleasure.

35. Hiriyanna, M: op. cit, p. 38.

36. Sharma, C: *A Critical Survey of Indian philosophy*; p. 16

37. अथ हैनं विदग्धः शाकल्यः पप्रच्छ कति देवा याज्ञवल्क्येति स हैतयैव निविदा प्रतिपेदे यावन्तो वैश्वदेवस्य निविदुच्यन्ते

त्रयश्च त्री च शता त्रयश्च त्री च सहस्रेत्योमिति होवाच कत्येव देवा याज्ञवल्क्येति त्रयस्त्रिंशदित्योमिति होवाच कत्येव

देवा याज्ञवल्क्येति षडित्योमिति होवाच कत्येव देवा याज्ञवल्क्येति त्रय इत्योमिति होवाच कत्येव देवा याज्ञवल्क्येति

द्वावित्योमिति होवाच कत्येव देवा याज्ञवल्क्येत्यध्यर्ध इत्योमिति होवाच कत्येव देवा याज्ञवल्क्येत्योमिति होवाच

कतमे ते त्रयश्च त्री च शता त्रयश्च त्रीच सहस्रेति ॥ *Br.up.*3.9.1

38. इन्द्रं मित्रं वरुणमग्निमाहुरथो दिव्यः स सुपर्णो गरुत्मान् ।

एकं सद् विप्रा बहुधा वदन्त्यग्निं यमं मातरिश्वानमाहुः ॥ RV.I.164.46

They call him Indra, Mitra, Varuṇa, Agni and he is heavenly nobly-winged garutmĭn. To what is one, sages give many a title, they call it Agni, Yama, Mātariśvan.

39. RV. III.55.19

40. प्रजापते न त्वदेतान्यन्यो विश्वा जातानि परि ता बभूव ।

यत् कामास्ते जुहुमस्तन्नो अस्तु वयं स्याम पतयो रयीणाम् ॥ RV.I.121.10

Prajāpati! thou only comprehendest all these created things, and none beside thee Grant us our heart's desire when we invoke thee. May we have store of wealth in possession.

41. प्राणादेवान्नादेनान्नमत्ति य एवं वेद । AV.15.14.22

     He who hath the knowledge of the Omnipresent God, preserves his spiritual force as life-preserve. etc.

42. कालोऽमूं दिवमजनयत् काल इमाः पृथिवीरुत । कालो ह भूतं भव्यं चेषितं ह वि तिष्ठते ॥
     AV.19.53.5

     The Kāla created these heavenly spheres, Kāla has also made these terrestrial spheres. In the Kāla is verily stationed, in various forms, all that was created before, and all that shall be created in future, and all that is moving on.

43. एक एवाग्निर्बहुधा समिद्धः

     एकः सूर्यो विश्वमनु प्रभूतः ।

     एकैवोषाः सर्वमिदं वि भा-

     त्येकं वा इदं वि बभूव सर्वम् ॥ RV. VIII. 58.2.

44. नासदासीन्नो सदासीत् तदानीं नासीद्रजो नो व्योमा परो यत् । किमावरीवः कुह कस्य शर्मन्नम्भः किमासीद्गहनं गभीरम् । न मृत्युरासीदमृतं न तर्हि न रात्र्या अह आसीत् प्रकेतः । आनीदवातं स्वधया तदेकं तस्माद्धान्यन्न परः किंचनास । तम आसीत् तमसा गूळ्हमग्रेऽप्रकेतं सलिलं सर्वमा इदम् । तुच्छ्येनाभ्वपिहितं यदासीत् तपसस्तन्महिनाजायतैकम् । कामस्तदग्रे समवर्तताधि मनसो रेतः प्रथमं यदासीत् । सतो बन्धुमसति निरविन्दन् हृदि प्रतीष्या कवयो मनीषा । तिरश्चीनो विततो रश्मिरेषामधः स्विदासीदुपरि स्विदासीत् ।

     रेतोधा आसन् महिमान आसन्त्स्वधा अवस्तात् प्रयतिः परस्तात् । को अद्धा वेद क इह प्रवोचत् कुत आ जाता कुत इयं विसृष्टिः । अर्वाग्देवा अस्य विसर्जनेनाथा को वेद यत आबभूव । इयं विसृष्टिर्यत आबभूव यदि वा दधे यदि वा न । यो अस्याध्यक्षः परमे व्योमन्त्सो अङ्ग वेद यदि वा न वेद । RV.X.129

45. Nakamura, Hajime: *A Comparative History of Ideas*, p. 54.

46. किं स्विद् वनं क उ स वृक्ष आस यतो द्यावापृथिवी निष्टतक्षुः ।

     संतस्थाने अजरे इतऊती अहानि पूर्वीरुषसो जरन्त ॥ RV. X.31.7.

     What was the tree, what wood, in sooth, produced in, from which fashioned forth the earth and Heaven?

     These Twain stand fast and wax not old for ever, these have sung praise to many a day and morning. X-31-7

47. Spence, Lewis: *An Introduction to Mythology*, p. 170.

48. Nakamura, *op cit*. p.52.

49. RV. X.121

50. *Śat. Br.* 11.1.6.1

51. सर्वं खल्विदं ब्रह्म तज्जलानित्युपासीत । Ch.up.3.14.1

     (ब्रह्मणः जातं-ब्रह्मणि लीयते-अनिति प्राणिति Śaṅkara's comm.)

52. तमेव भान्तमनुभान्ति सर्वं तस्य भासा सर्वमिदं विभाति Kaṭha up. (5.15). ऊर्ध्वमूलमवाक्शाख एषोऽश्वत्थः सनातनः । तदेव शुक्रं तद्ब्रह्म तदेवामृतमुच्यते । तस्मिंल्लोकाः श्रिताः सर्वे तदु नात्येति कश्चन । एतद्वै तत् । *Kaṭha up*.6.1.

After Him, as He shines, doth everything shine This whole world is illumined with His light. Its root is above, its branches below, This eternal fig-tree! that root indeed in the pure, That indeed is called Immortal, On it all the worlds rest, And no one so ever goes beyond it, This, verily, is that!

53. अस्मिन्नात्मनि सर्वाणि भूतानि सर्वे देवाः सर्वे लोकाः सर्व एत आत्मानः समर्पिताः । *Br.up.*2.5.15

In this soul all things, all gods, all worlds, all breathing things, all these selves are held together.

54. तेषां खल्वेषां भूतानां त्रीण्येव बीजानि भवन्त्याण्डजं जीवजमुद्भिज्जमिति । *Ch.up.* 6.3.1

Now, of these beings here there are just three origins; (there are beings) born from an egg, born of living thing, born of a sprout.

55. एकैकेन भवत्यात्मेत्येवोपासीतात्र ह्येते सर्व

एकं भवन्ति तदेतत्पदनीयमस्य सर्वस्य

यदयमात्माऽनेन ह्येतत्सर्वं वेद यथा ह वै

पदेनानुविन्देदेवं कीर्तिं श्लोकं विन्दते य एवं वेद । *Br.up.* I. 4.7

56. तद्ध एतदक्षरं गार्ग्यदृष्टं द्रष्ट्रश्रुतं श्रोत्रममतं मन्त्रवज्ञातं विज्ञातृ नान्यदतोऽस्ति द्रष्टृ नान्यदतोऽस्ति श्रोतृ नान्यदतोऽस्ति

मन्तृ नान्यदतोऽस्ति विज्ञात्रेतस्मिन्नु खल्वक्षरे गार्ग्याकाश ओतश्च प्रोतश्चेति ॥ *Br.up.*3.8.11

Verily, O Gārgi, that imperishable is the unseen seer, the unheard Hearer, the unthought thinker, the ununderstood understander. Other than it there is naught that sees, other than it there is naught that hears. Other than it there is naught that thinks, other than it there is naught that understands.

Across this Imperishable O Gārgi, is space woven, warp and woof.

57. छन्दांसि यज्ञाः क्रतवो व्रतानि भूतं भव्यं यच्च वेदा भवन्ति ।

अस्मान् मायी सृजते विश्वमेतत् तस्मिंश्चान्यो मायया संनिरुद्धः । *Śvet. up.* 4-9

Sacred poetry, the sacrifices, the ceremonies, the ordinances,

The past, the future, and what the Vedas declare, this whole world the illusion maker projects out of this (Brahma).

And in it by illusion (Māyā) the other (soul) is confined.

58. अविद्यायामन्तरे वर्तमानाः स्वयं धीराः पण्डितं मन्यमानाः ।

जङ्घन्यमानाः परियन्ति मूढा अन्धेनैव नीयमाना यथान्धाः । *Muṇḍ.up.* 2.8

Those abiding in the midst of ignorance, self-wise, thinking themselves learned, hard smitten, go around deluded, like blind men led by one who is himself blind.

59. Sreekantan, B.V.: 'Modern Physics and Ancient Indian Philosophies', in *Science in the West and India*, (Eds) B. V. Subbarayappa and N. Mukunda, 1993, pp. 445-450

60. Singer, C : *A Short History of Science*, Clarendon Press, Oxford, 1948; p. 37.

61. Sreekantan, B.V, et al (Eds): *Scientific Studies on Consciousness*, National Institute of Advanced Studies, Bangalore, 1999, p. 7.

CHAPTER 3

Five Elements
(Pañcamahābhūta-s)

The doctrine of five elements—*pṛthivī, ap, tejas, vāyu* and *ākāśa*—is a seminal one in the Indian thought-structure. Its foundation, evolution and pervasiveness were such that it entered into several philosophical systems, both orthodox and heterodox. More importantly, it also provided several conceptual schemes for Āyurveda not only in respect of physiological processes, diagnosis of diseases and drug action but also for the maintenance of health as will be seen later. The concept of five elements was also an important one among the Greeks and the Chinese. But the nature and characteristics of the Greek and the Chinese elements, and the context in which they were conceived were totally different from the Indian, thus pointing to the fact that they originated independently of one another. Suffice it to say that, when compared with the Greek and the Chinese elements, the Indian five elements or the *Pañcabhūtas* were noted for their originality as well as viability.

Pañcabhūta-s or Pañcamahābhūta-s

Indian five elements called the *pañcabhūta-s* or *pañcamahābhūta-s* had their origins in an Upaniṣadic ontological framework, unlike the Greek or the Chinese ones. Central to this framework was the concept of Brahman as the Creator of the Universe. The Upaniṣadic postulate of *Brahman* and *Ātman,* both being synonyms and denoting the First Principle of the universe has been dealt with already in the preceding chapter.

Evolution of the concept of five elements: The *Taittirīya upaniṣad* says: By which creatures are born from life and after death, enter into it, you examine at, that is Brahma'.[1] The *Chāndogya* goes a step further when it asserts that 'Assuredly this universe is Brahman and it should be worshipped as *tajjalān*'.[2] According to the commentary on this by Śaṇkara, this includes the elements, fire, water, earth, etc.[3] In any case, the *Chāndogya* points out that : 'Alone existing...... was this (Brahman) in the beginning. It proposed, I will become many, will propagate myself; thereupon It created the heat. From heat water arises and from water, food (i.e., the earth). That divinity proposed: I will enter into these three (heat, water and earth) with this living self (the individual soul) and unfold thence name and form'. This Upaniṣad also speaks of three origins—born from egg; born from living being, and born of a sprout.[4] The *Bṛhadāraṇyaka* speaks of inorganic entities or the elements (*ākāśa, vāyu, agni* and *ap*) and points out that, if Brahman is worshipped as such, one would get certain types of benefits.[5]

It may be recalled that the concept of water as the first element is very old. It was speculated upon even in the *Ṛgveda*. Later, in the *Chāndogya*, came up the group of three wherein the water element was placed between the elements of fire and earth, each in succession from its predecessor.[6] The postulate of five elements is encountered perhaps first in the *Taittirīya*[7] which has an exposition as follows: 'From this *Ātman* (identical with Brahman) in reality, has arisen *ākāśa*; from *ākāśa, vāyu* (air), from *vāyu, agni* (fire), from *agni, ap* (water); and from *ap, pṛthivī,* (earth); from *pṛthivī, oṣadhi* (herbs); from *oṣadhi, anna* (food); *anna* transformed into seed and later *puruṣa* (human being). Śaṅkara, in his commentary on this passage, adds the attributes of the five elements in a progressive manner thus: '*ākāśa*—sound and providing space for all things that have forms; *Vāyu*—two attributes, namely, touch and sound (from its cause, *ākāśa*); Agni—three attributes, namely, its own quality, colour, and touch and sound; *Āpah*—four attributes: its own quality taste, colour, touch and sound; *Pṛthivī*—five attributes: its own quality of smell, and taste, colour, touch and sound.[8] The correlation of the five elements with the five sense organs had already been expounded by the *Sāṃkhya* and the *Vaiśeṣika* system as will be seen later.

The *Aitareya upaniṣad*,[9] in its exposition on the Self (identified with Brahman) states: 'He is Brahma; he is Indra, he is Prajāpati, (he is) all these gods; and these gross five elements (namely, earth, air, *ākāśa*, water and light.....'. It may be noted that this Upaniṣad has its own order of enumeration of the five elements and uses *jyotīṃṣi* for fire instead of *tejas* or *agni*.

As noted already, the first element in the Indian context is water, and the *Ṛgveda* speaks of water in its cosmogonic hymn (*Nāsadīya sūkta*). But this hymn exclaims: Who knows? (*Ko veda*).[10] It is very difficult to accept that the *Ṛgveda* propounded that Water was the only primordial principle. It also states that *Prajāpati* (Father-God or Supreme God) begets 'the great sparkling waters',[11] and of the primeval slime in which the beginnings of heaven and earth plunged.[12] It is interesting to note that in the Babylonian concept of creation, water as the primordial element has been clearly stated. The word used there is *apsu* (a combination of two types of water). Water was also thought of as having healing power in the *Ṛgveda*.[13]

The conception of primeval waters is also found in the Upaniṣads. In the *Bṛhadāraṇyaka* there is a statement that waters are the body of that *prāṇa* (*ādhidaivika prāṇa*).[14] The *Chāndogya* elucidates the extensiveness of water: 'This earth, the air, the heavens, the mountains, gods and men, domestic animals and birds, vegetables and trees, wild creatures down to worms, flies and ants are nothing but different forms of water'.[15] But, this approach is in the context of the *upāsanā* (adoration), identifying water with Brahman (*abbrahma*).[16] This strain of thinking continues in respect of *tejas* and *ākāśa*, projecting the idea that *tejobrahma* is superior to *abbrahma* and *ākāśabrahma* is superior to *tejobrahma*—a hierarchical approach under what is called *bhūmāvidyā*.[17] This also encompassed *Smarabrahma* (memory), *Āśābrahma* (hope) and *Prāṇabrahma* (vital breath) on the one hand and on the other, *Dhyānabrahma* (meditation), *Vijñānabrahma* (understanding), *Balabrahma* (strength) and *Annabrahma* (food).[18] It has been pointed out that *abbrahma* is superior to *annabrahma* which, in turn, superior to *balabrahma* and so on. It needs to be emphasized that the elements as conceived in the upaniṣads are more metaphysical than physical and are in the nature of certain steps towards a progressive understanding of Brahman as well as the latter's identification with each of them in consonance with the upaniṣadic fundamental conception that Brahman is the one and the only cosmic principle and that Brahman and Ātman are identical. Deussen writes (p. 39): 'Brahman, the power which presents itself to us materialized in all existing things, which creates, sustains, preserves, and receives back into itself again all worlds, this eternal divine power is identical with Ātman; with that which, after stripping off everything external, we discover our real most essential thing, our individual self, the soul. This is the fundamental thought of the Upaniṣads. It is briefly expressed by the great sayings: *tat tvam asi*[19] and *aham Brahma asmi* (I am Brahman).[20]

It will be observed from the foregoing that the concept and ramification of the Indian elemental theory emanated from a type of monism or the becoming of a Supreme Being, Brahman, the creator, preserver and even destroyer in the sense that all the created ones would eventually return to Brahman.

Sāṃkhya and the Five Elements

It is rather difficult to trace sequentially and rationally the transformation of the upaniṣadic metaphysical or ontological five elements into the physical entities as found in the Sāṃkhya and Vaiśeṣika systems. However, some reflection on Brahman and Ātman may be necessary to understand the basic premise of the Sāṃkhya of which the five elements are integral components. The *Chāndogya* refers to a question raised by some sages[21] as to who is ātmā or who is Brahma. Śaṅkara in his commentary elucidates that Brahman and Ātman are in the relation of *Viśeṣaṇa-viśeṣyabhāva*, (i.e., Brahman is the term to be defined and Ātman defines it). Further, 'by Brahman the co-notational limitation implied in ātman is removed and as Deussen puts it, and by Ātman, the conception of Brahman as a divinity to be worshipped is condemned'.[22]

There is an interesting series of passages in the Chāndogya. Five Brāhmaṇas seized with the questions: What is ātman? what is Brahman, go to the sage, Uddālaka Āruṇi who was contemplating the Ātman as the all-pervading universe. Since he was not sure of his own exposition, the Brāhmaṇas and Uddālaka proceeded to King Aśvapati Kaikeya who explained it as follows:[23]

'To judge from your observations, you all conceive of this Ātman Vaiśvānara as though it were something separate from yourselves, and thus you consume your food. He who worships this Ātman Vaiśvānara consumes food in all worlds, in all beings, in all selves. And of this very Ātman Vaiśvānara, the bright (heaven) is the head, the all-pervading Sun (*āditya*) is the eye, the Wind (*vāyu*) is the breath, the manifold (all-pervasive) *ākāśa* is its trunk, its bodily frame, water (*ap*) is its bladder, the earth, its feet.[24] Ātmā is not only the individual soul but also the Supreme Soul without sin, free from old age, from death and suffering and whose decree is true and that which should be sought after.[25] This Upaniṣad speaks of three ātman-s: the corporeal, the individual and the Supreme. The Taittirīya postulates five *ātman-s* in the context of living process, will power and knowledge as follows: *annamaya, prāṇamaya, manomaya, vijñānamaya* and *ānandamaya* (later known as sheaths or *koṣa-s*).[26] Casting off the sheaths one by one, the eventual stage i.e., bliss, the innermost essence of the being and nature.[27] It would appear that, to begin with, the concept that included the individual souls perhaps in a way led to a dualism of *puruṣa* (sentient being) and the eternal, unmanifest nature (*prakṛti*) as the two principles, without any postulate of God or the Creator or Brahman. Puruṣa, the knowing subject became distinct from *Prakṛti* comprising all that is objective, and both were thought of as being closely related from eternity. The *Śvetāśvatara* has the concept a duality in terms of female principle and male principle. Their interaction would unfold the *Prakṛti* in relation to each *Puruṣa* according to the Sāṃkhya system which encompasses 24 principles as follows:

The Classical Sāṃkhya enumerates the 24 principles as follows:

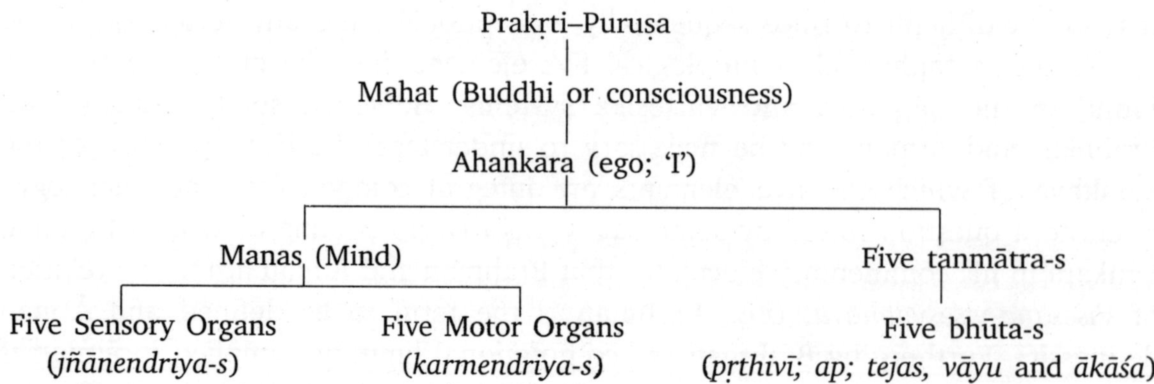

It may be observed that *Prakṛti* is the unmanifested one while *Puruṣa*, in plural (i.e., *Puruṣa-s*) is intimately related to it. Further, Prakṛti is the 'rootless root' of the universe and intertwined with the three *guṇas* (as in three stranded rope) namely *sattva* (bright, good) *rajas* (energetic); and *tamas* (dark and inert). Figuratively the *Śvetāśvatara upaniṣad* (4.5) states;[28]

That one she-goat, red and white and blackish

Casts many, young, which are fashioned like to her;

The one ram leaps on her in the ardour of love,

The other ram abandons her, his companion.[29] (tr. P. Deussen)

The relationship of many *Puruṣas* (many rams) to Prakṛti (she-goat) which is red, white and black, according to Śaṅkara, represent the three *guṇas* and foreshadow the Sāṃkhya doctrine of Puruṣa–Prakṛti.

Tanmātra-s: Of relevance to us are the *tanmātra-s* and the five elements of the Sāṃkhya. The former are considered to be subtle, invisible and associated with ego or *ahaṅkāra*, while the five *bhūta-s*, the produced ones, are regarded as non-eternal. It is rather difficult to define exactly the *tanmātra-s* in physical terms. They appear to represent the very essence of the concerned *bhūta* or element, possibly with their inherent power of influencing the respective senses, thus conferring on each element the corresponding specific sensorial quality.

The five *tanmātra-s*, according to the Sāṃkhya concept, are a part of what is called *liṅgam* or the 'mark' by which the individuals are distinguished. It is also deemed to be the 'fine body' (*sūkṣma śarīra*) that could pass on from one birth to the other. The *liṅgam* comprises, besides *tanmātra-s*, the *mahat* or *buddhi*, *ahaṅkāra* (ego), mind and the five sensory and motor organs. Thus each individual has his own *liṅgam* or characteristics, although all *liṅgam-s* are believed to originate from one *Prakṛti*. The different characteristics are stated to be due to the qualitative and quantitative variations in respect of the three *guṇas: sattva, rajas*, and *tamas*. Since the *tanmātra-s* are also a part of *liṅgam*, it follows that at each self-unfolding, the *bhūtas* or the gross five elements would also be in tune with the individual. In other words, each individual would have his own perceptions and experience of the gross world of matter. Significantly *ahaṅkāra* is central to *liṅgam* and the *tanmātra-s* on the one hand and mind on the other, emanate from or associated with it, while the five elements are an offshoot of the *tanmātra-s*.

The origin of the postulate of *tanmātra* (*lit.* subsisting from this alone) can be traced to some of the *upaniṣads*. For example, the *Praśna upaniṣad*[30] refers to *pṛthivī, ap, tejas, vāyu* and *ākāśa* also in terms of *pṛthivīmātrā, apomātrā, tejomātrā, vāyūmātra and ākāśamātra*. The *Maitrāṇayīya upaniṣad*[31] also speaks about *tanmātra* in a different vein. Sometimes subtle substances (*tanmātra-s*) are spoken of by the word 'element' (*bhūta*). Probably for the first time, the word *tanmātra*, occurs in the *Maitrāṇayīya upaniṣad*, with the appellation of *bhūta*, while the gross elements are called *mahābhūta-s*. Such ideas might have influenced the Sāṃkhya system at a later stage to include *tanmātra-s* in its evolutionary scheme. In the pre-classical Sāṃkhya as found, for instance, in the *Bhagavadgītā*, there is no mention of *tanmātra-s* at all. In any case, the *Sāṃkhya* followers found it appropriate to include the subtle states that *tanmātra-s* were supposed to be, as a step towards the production of gross bodies constituted of five elements either singly or in combination.

The generation or the production of five elements from the *tanmātrās* according to *Sāṃkhya–kārikā*[32] and Vācaspati Miśra's commentary on it, is as follows:

From Śabda (sound) *tanmātra* emerges *ākāśa* (an ubiquitous substance)

From Śabda and sparśa (touch) *tanmātra-s* emerge *vāyu* (air)

From Śabda, sparśa and rūpa (colour) *tanmātra-s* emerge *tejas* (light)

From Śabda, sparśa, rūpa and rasa (taste) *tanmātra-s* emerge *ap* (water)

From Śabda, sparśa, rūpa, rasa and gandha (odour) *tanmātrā-s* emerge *pṛthivī* (earth).

The above presentation means that *ākāśa* can only be heard; *vāyu*, heard and felt (touch); *tejas*, heard, felt and seen; *ap*, heard, felt, seen and tasted; and *pṛthvī* heard, felt, seen, tasted and smelt. Each element, however, is stated to have specific quality as follows: *ākāśa*—sound; *vāyu*—touch; *tejas*—colour, *ap*—taste; and *pṛthvī*—smell. They are also associated with the five sense organs, ears, skin, eyes, tongue and nose respectively. This idea also found the support of Kaṇāda and other exponents of the Nyāya-Vaiśeṣika.[33]

Apart from an evolutionary delineation in respect of the five elements, the Sāṃkhya system which owes its codification to certain aspects of the upaniṣadic or Vedāntic approach, does not appear to throw much light on the physical world. But, the later work, the *Vedāntasāra*[34] in a pluralistic, at the same time in a holistic manner, explains the five-fold character of the elements inasmuch as that half of each of the element is that element itself, while the other half would comprise the remaining four elements; for example, the element water consists of half of water with eighth each of earth, fire air, and *ākāśa*. It may be emphasized that the five elements—*pṛthivī, ap, tejas, vāyu,* and *ākāśa* are generally translated into English respectively as earth, water, fire, air and ether, The English equivalents do not convey fully the nature and significance of the Sanskrit words. Moreover, it would be erroneous to equate *ākāśa* with ether, a term used for the fifth element of the Greeks, since the Indian *ākāśa*, unlike the former, is also a part of the terrestrial bodies and its specific quality is sound, besides other qualities. It is considered as ubiquitous, non-material like time, space and self.[35]

Vaiśeṣika System

A more detailed account of the five elements has been provided by the Vaiśeṣika system in its approach towards an understanding of the physical world in terms of six categories of reals (*bhāva padārtha-s*) and a seventh one (*abhāva*). The *bhāva padārtha-s* are: *dravya* (substance); *guṇa* (attributes); *karma* (action); *sāmānya* (generality); *viśeṣa* (particularity); and *samavāya* (inherence).[36] In the generic category of substance, nine entities that are also called substances, have been included and they are: the five elements, time (*kāla*), ātma (self), mind (*manas*);[37] The first four elements: *pṛthivī, ap, tejas* and *vāyu* (earth, water, fire and air respectively) are considered to be atomic. While the importance of these nine entities will be discussed in the next chapter, it needs to be recognized that the five elements are an integral part of this model, and their qualities or attributes have been clearly presented as follows:

Pṛthivī (Earth): It is of two kinds; eternal in its atomic state and evanescent in the form of products.[38] The latter encompasses several types of objects that are commonly perceived. These include mud forms, rocks, minerals, various kinds of stones, gems, diamond and the like on the one hand and on the other, vegetables, grasses, herbs, trees, and their flowers and fruits. In general, earthly products are regarded as being threefold: (i) in the form of solid body; (ii) related objects of perception; (iii) the sense organ, olfactory (nose itself). The specific quality of earth in its gross form as well as in its atomic state is smell (*gandha*).[39] According to the Vaiśeṣika, earth possesses 14 other qualities: colour, taste, odour, touch, number, dimension, distinctness, conjunction, disjunction, distance, proximity, gravity, fluidity and faculty.[40]

Ap (Water): It is also of two kinds; eternal in its atomic state and non-eternal as products.[41] Like earth, it is three fold: (i) in the form of liquid bodies; (ii) several types of objects; (and) the sense organ, tongue itself. Its specific quality is taste. It is pointed out that its body is in the region of Varuṇa, the rain god.[42] The objects exist as rivers, oceans, hail, rain, and the like.[43] Even the Moon is regarded as of this element. The colour of water is stated to be white.[44] Similar to earth, it has fourteen qualities, colour, taste, touch, number, dimension, distinctness, conjunction, disjunction, distance, proximity, gravity, viscidity, fluidity, and faculty.[45]

The water element, has the intrinsic quality, namely, weight (*gurutva*)[46]. It shares this quality with the Earth element, and water falls down like rain when there is no conjunction of clouds with air. This is rather a curious explanation and not in tune with the common observation, but in consonance with the Vaiśeṣika position with regard to the categorized qualities of weight and conjunction. It may be noted that weight or *gurutva* is not regarded as a quality of the other three elements, namely, fire, air, and *akāśa*. For this reason, *gurutva* cannot be equated to the Newtonian notion of gravity which is a force that can manifest itself in all ponderable masses, celestial or terrestrial, big or small, and thus has its universality.

As for liquidity (*dravatva*), the Vaiśeṣika believed it to be the non-inherent cause for the flow of water. Strangely, the circulation of water in plants is said to be due to unseen (*adṛṣṭa*) factors. The concept of conjunction and disjunction is so appealing to the Vaiśeṣika that it explains thunder as being due to the conjunction of water with water, and disjunction of water from water[47] obviously referring to the mutual impact of water-bearing clouds. But the cause of such an impact has, remained unexplained. Associated with this sort of explanation, however, is the one that speaks of fire in the 'waters of *ākāśa*' and the thunder is its mark, perhaps indirectly alluding to the observed lightning and heard thunder.

The difference between the earth and the water element in respect of their qualities is that the former is associated with odour and proximity, while the latter has in their places taste and viscidity (odour and taste being the specific quality of earth and water respectively).

Tejas (Fire): Regarded as white and dazzling,[48] fire is also conceived as being in two forms: eternal in its atomic form and non-eternal in its ramifications or products.[49] The latter, as in the cases of earth and water, is also thought of in three aspects: (i) body stated to be in the region of Sun;[50] (ii) the sense organ (eyes);[51] and (iii) objects which are of four types earthly, heavenly, stomachic and mineral.[52] The earthly fire is that which is perceived ordinarily like wood-fire; the heavenly one obviously refers to the Sun, lightning and, perhaps, stars. The stomachic fire (*jaṭharāgni*) is the one that brings about digestion of the food taken in, a concept that influenced the Āyurvedic digestive metabolism as will be seen later. The mineral fire relates to the shining metals like gold and other metals.[53] The specific quality of fire is colour. It has eleven qualities: colour, touch, number, dimension, distinctness, conjunction, disjunction, distance, proximity, fluidity and faculty.[54] It does not possess the qualities of odour (specific to earth) taste (specific to water) and gravity (common to both earth water).

Vāyu (Air): It is also considered to be eternal in its atomic form and non-eternal in the form of its products.[55] Unlike the preceding three elements, the products of which are postulated as being threefold, those of air are believed to be of four types:[56] (i) its body that exists in the region of Maruts (atmosphere):[57] (ii) the sense organ, skin or tactile that pervades the surface of the body;[58] (iii) the object that is actually experienced as air (and is the substratum of tactile sensation);[59] and (iv) breath or air inside the body that moves various fluids, causing secretions on account of its movement inside the body.[60] The movement of air, its capacity to make the clouds move from one place to another in cris-cross direction as well as to cause the showering of rains have been included among the attributes of air.[61] It has also been pointed out that air lifts light substances upwards.[62] Such common observations apart, the specific quality of air is tactile sensation and the general ones, nine in number, are: touch, number, dimension, distinctness, conjunction, disjunction, proximity, distance and faculty.[63] Although in the Sāṃkhya sequence air is stated to emanate from the *śabda* (sound) and *sparśa* (touch) *tanmātrās*, the quality of sound has not been included among those of air.

Ākāśa (an ubiquitous substance): In contradistinction to earth, water, fire or light and air, *ākāśa* is not considered as material, nor generally atomic, but one and all-pervading.[64] Its special quality is sound and the auditory organ is of *ākāśa* itself. Its six qualities are:[65] sound, number, dimensions, distinctness, conjunction and disjunction.[66]

As far as the classification of the five elements is concerned, there is an intimate relationship among the elements and the senses in the Vaiśeṣika (later the Nyāya-Vaiśeṣika). The olfactory, gustatory, visual, tactile and auditory sense organs are supposed to comprise respectively the elements, earth, water, fire, air, and *ākāśa,* the gateways of perception leading to human knowledge. The principle governing this kind of relationship appears to be the like apprehending the like. The eyes apprehend colour, colour is therefore the attribute of fire element and so on. Kaṇāda, the propounder of the *Vaiśeṣika system*, in his *Vaiśeṣika sūtra-s* had indicated in all 17 attributes;[67] but Praśastapāda, an able exponent of the Vaiśeṣika system added 7 more in his *bhāṣya* and the 24 attributes form the corner stone of the second category of the system (*guṇa*).[68] It may be noted that these attributes have neither an independent existence, nor any motion of their own. They inhere in the concerned substance or material.[69]

Five Elements and their Role in Medicine

Āyurveda: Both the Sāṃkhya and the Vaiśeṣika along with its allied Nyāya system have provided a theoretical framework for the codified medical system, the Āyurveda. It needs to be emphasised that the philosophical approach, engendered by the aforesaid systems, is as much an integrated component of Āyurveda as are its concerns for total health, the cure of diseases, longevity and the like. An Āyurvedic physician was expected, then as now, to possess distinct knowledge of the various aspects of both the spiritual and material life. During the 6th–4th cent. B.C., the Upaniṣadic fervour and discourses provided a fillip to the systematization of a spectrum of ideas that were current then concerning the relation between man and nature, man and the observable world and the nature of man himself on the one hand and, on the other, the methodology needed for a thorough knowledge of the phenomenal world and the elevation of human mind with a control over the senses. These led to the emergence of the Sāṃkhya, Vaiśeṣika, Nyāya and Yoga. In the new mood and endeavour of systematization, the Upaniṣadic five elements loomed large. Their metaphysical nuances, however, receded to the background and their physical aspects came to the fore. The then floating medicinal ideas and practices too could not but be systematised in such a way that the Vedic religio-magical medicine was to be discarded and a standardised procedure of diagnosis and treatment developed with a sound theoretical basis.

Such a systematization became imperative in the emerging ambience of the second urbanization that India witnessed around that time to keep at bay the quackery as well as superstitions and superstitious practices that were presumed to ward off diseases. The new codified knowledge gave rise to a new class of physicians with new approaches to practices that derived their sustenance from the Sāṃkhya, Vaiśeṣika and Nyāya systems, but with *mutatis mutandis* modifications wherever it was felt necessary.

The thought-structure of Āyurveda, apart from its intricately worked out thereapeutics, is an example of intellectual coherence—a consistent way of looking at the phenomenal world in a holistic manner. Recognising the dynamic interaction between man (microcosm) and the Universe (macrocosm) the Āyurvedic theory of *loka-puruṣa-sāmya* envisages that an individual's health would be sound and vibrant if the inter-relationship is natural and wholesome, while the contrary would lead to a diseased state.

The *Caraka saṃhitā* and the *Suśruta saṃhitā,* the two Āyurvedic classics, have dealt with their fundamental postulates in the context of the Sāṃkhya, Vaiśeṣika and Nyāya systems. In the place of the term, *tattva* of the Sāṃkhya, the Āyurvedic term is *dhātu*[70] (a pre-classical Sāṃkhya term). However, the two texts have classified broadly the factors of evolution as *Prakṛti* and *Vikṛti*. The former includes intellect or consciousness, *ahaṅkāra* and the five subtle states (*tanmātrā-s*);[71] the latter comprises the five sense organs, mind and the five objects of senses (the gross elements).[72] There are other differences between the Sāṃkhya as is generally known and the one that is in the Āyurvedic classics which need not be discussed here. Suffice it to emphasise that the five elements and the concept of *dravya* or substance, the properties (of elements) and the logical postulates of Nyāya are of fundamental importance to Āyurveda.[73]

Āyurveda considers human body as a combination of the five elements and soul.[74] In the *Suśruta saṃhitā* there is a succinct delineation of the way in which the five elements enter into human body from its very conception. The foetus which has in it the energetic principles assumes its form by *vāyu*; the *tejas* element transforms it and maintains its temperature. The *ap* element preserves its moisture or fluidity, while the *pṛthivī* gives it size and shape, compactness and the requisite hardness.[75] *Ākāśa* offers expanse to the embryo and develops it. According to

SAMKHYA PHILOSOPHY AND ĀYURVEDA

I. Original (ādya) Samkhya as found in the *Agniveśa tantra* (*Caraka saṃhitā*)

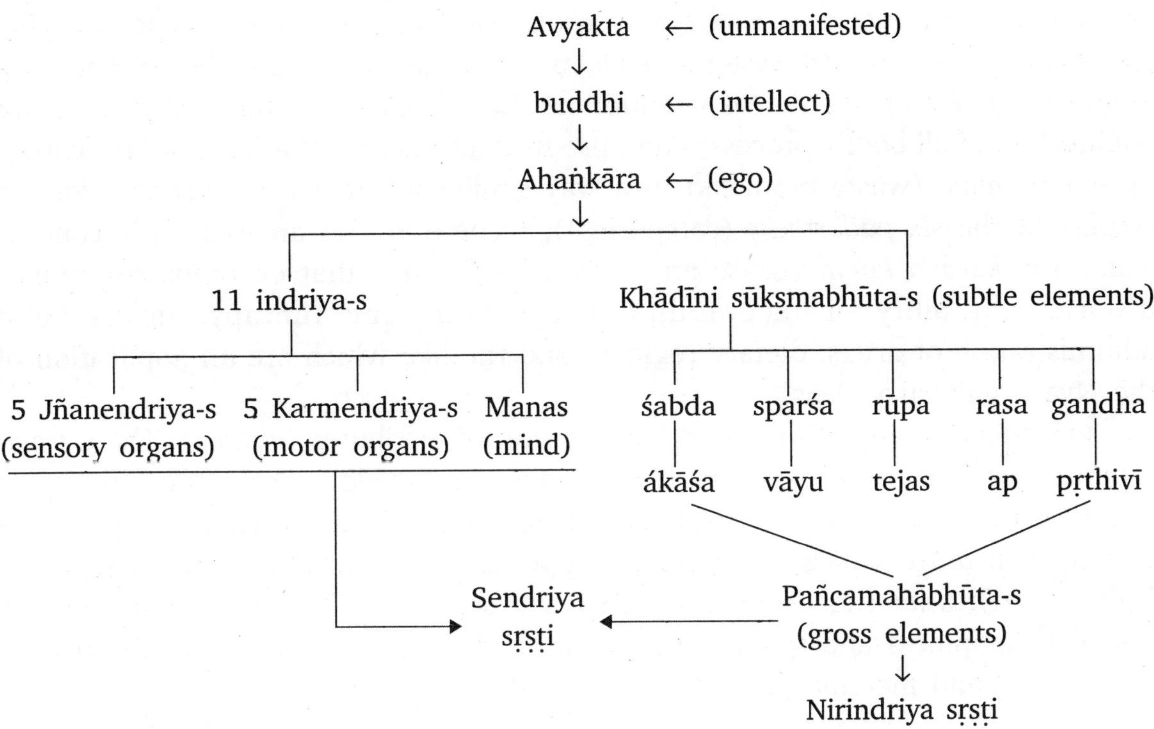

II. Sāṃkhya as found in the *Suśruta saṃhitā*

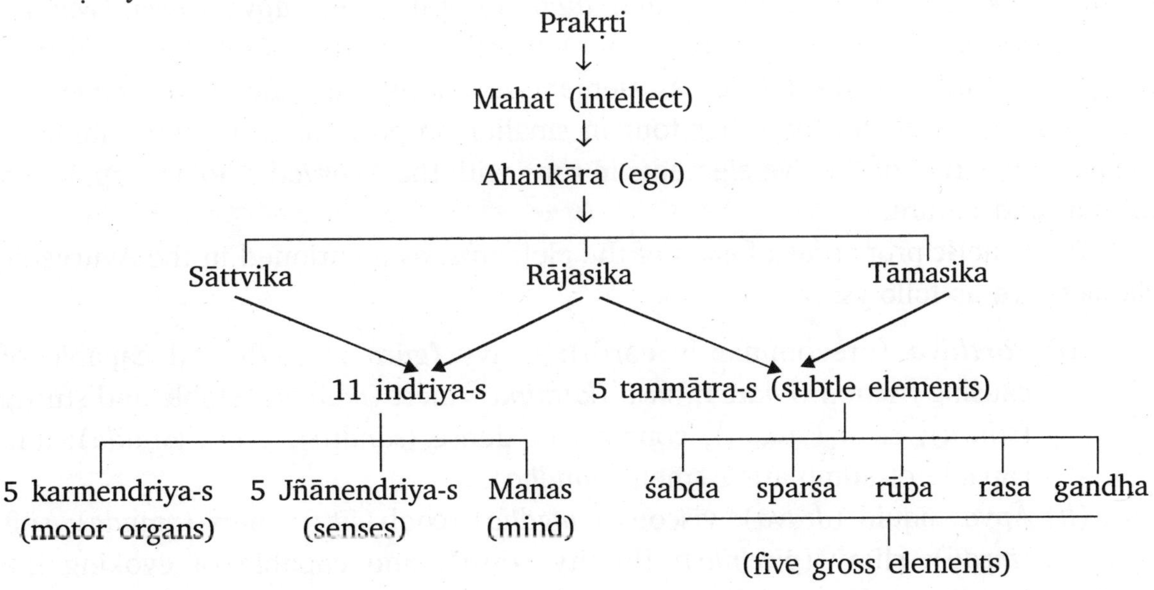

Source: B. G. Gopinath: 'Foundational Ideas of Āyurveda' in *MEDICINE AND LIFE SCIENCES*, (Ed) B. V. Subbarayappa, p. 95.

Āyurveda, the soul or the consciousness constitutes the sixth element.[76] The postulate of Agniveśa as explained in the *Caraka saṃhitā* is that the soul first of all unites with *ākāśa*, before uniting with the other elements for setting forth the creation or the formation of embryo.[77] *Caraka saṃhitā*, though it does not mention specifically the *Vaiśeṣika* system, deals with the six *kāraṇas*. The *kāraṇas* are employed generally for the explanation of the causation or the maintenance of equilibrium of all bodily processes and products like *doṣa* (vitiation), *dhātu* (causes of action) *mala* (waste products) in a way similar to what the Vaiśeṣika does in respect of the six *padārtha-s* (categories)).[78] There is also an Āyurvedic concept called the *kāraṇa kārya* (cause and effect) *siddhānta*[79] that encompasses health, disease, curability or incurability, drugs and drug therapy, dosage and administration of drugs, dietary regimen and the like which are an application of the Nyāya-Vaiśeṣika ideas.

Of special interest to us is the application of attributes (*guṇa-s*). The *Caraka saṃhitā* describes in all 41 attributes: 5 sensorial (*śabda, sparśa, rūpa, rasa* and *gandha* that are the characteristics of the five elements), 20 starting with *guru* and ending with *drava* which are mutually opposite in nature like guru (heavy) and *laghu* (light); *uṣṇa* (hot) and *śīta* (cold) and so on; 6 of internal character like intellect, happiness and misery; and 10 others like conjunction and disjunction, observation and metamorphosis.

Āyurveda recognizes five types of substances—*ākāśīya dravya* (relating to the elements *ākāśa*; *vāyavīyadravya* (air); *taijasadravya* (fire); *āpyadravya* (water); and *pārthivadravya* (earth).[80] Like the Vaiśeṣika and the Sāṃkhya, Āyurveda accepts that each of the five gross elements contains the concerned element in greater proportion and the other four in smaller proportions, thus subscribing to the holistic nature of the five elements in tune with the Āyurvedic holistic approach to man and nature.

The generic properties of each of the elements, as mentioned in the Āyurvedic classics, are as follows:

(i) **Pārthiva** (predominantly earth): heavy (*guru*); rough and capable of causing friction (*khara*); hard (*kaṭhina*); inert (*manda*); stable and sturdy (*sthira*); clear (*viśada*); compact or dense (*sāndra*); gross (*sthūla*); and capable of stimulating smell (*gandha*).

(ii) **Āpya**: liquid (*drava*); viscous (*snigdha*); cool (*śīta*); inert (*manda*); soft (*mṛdu*); slimy (*picchila*); fluidity (*rasa*); and capable of evoking the sensation of taste (*rasa*).

(iii) **Taijasa or Āgneya**: hot (*uṣṇa*); sharp or penetrating (*tīkṣṇa*); subtle (*sūkṣma*); light (*laghu*); rough (*rūkṣa*); clear, transparent (*viśada*); and capable of evoking visual sensations (*rūpa*).

> (*iv*) **Vāyavya:** light (*laghu*); cool (*śīta*); rough and also rarefied (*rūksa*); rough (*khara*); clear (*viśada*); subtle (*sūksma*) and capable of stimulating tactile sensations (*sparśa*).
>
> (*v*) **Ākāśīya or Nābhasa:** soft (*mrdu*); light (*laghu*); subtle (*sūksma*); cohesive (*ślaksna*); and inducing auditory sensations (*śabda*).

The elements fire (*agni*), air (*vāyu*) and *prthivī* (earth) play a special role in Āyurveda. Fire has been conceived under two heads: (i) *kāyāgni* that is mainly concerned with biochemical processes involved in gastro-intestinal digestion; (ii) *dhātvagni* that is involved in metabolism and nutrition. The former also is concerned with the excitation and secretion of the digestive juices—gastric, hepatic and pancreatic, so necessary for ensuring intestinal digestion. *Agni* constitutes *pitta* (generally bile) which is one of the *tridhātu-s–tridosa-s* or what are known as three humours, the other two being *vāta* (wind) and *kapha* (phlegm). Five types of *pitta* have been recognized, depending upon its position and the functions—*pācaka, sādhaka, rañjaka, ālocaka* and *bhrājaka*. The Āyurvedic classics have dealt in detail with these five aspects of fire. Likewise, they have dealt with the five aspects of *vāta* (wind; air) in terms of its voluntary actions and the discharge of waste products from the body through its five forms: *prāna* (air breathed into the lungs); *udāna* (that which enters head); *samāna* (essential for digestion); *vyāna* (diffused throughout the body); and *apāna* (that which goes out of the anus). The five aspects of *kapha* or phlegm that is constituted of the elements earth and water, are *kledaka, avalambaka, bodhaka, tarpaka* and *sleśmaka.*[81]

The *tridhātu-s* or *tridosa-s* are said to be formed out of the elements as follows: *vāta* from *vāyu* + *ākāśa; pitta* from *tejas;* and *kapha* from *prthvī* + *ap*. These, associated as they are with the five elements, determine, according, to Āyurveda, not only the physical and physiological processes in the human body but also the pathogenesis of diseases and symptoms. Their equilibrium or harmony is health, and their disequilibrium or disharmony is disease. The concept of restoring and maintaining equilibrium of the symbiotic relationship of body and mind in the overall ambience of soul is the forte of Āyurveda.

The five elements are also associated with the formation of six rasas or tastes as follows: *sweet* (madhura) from *prthivī* and *ap; sour* (āmla) from *tejas* and *prthivī; saltish* (lavana) from *ap* and *tejas; bitter* (tikta) from *ākāśa* and *vāyu;* pungent (katu) from *tejas* and *vāyu;* and *astringent* (kasāya) from *prthivī* and *vāyu*.

It would appear that neither the Greek medicine nor the Chinese one did develop itself upon the basis of five elements as much as Āyurveda. In fact, apart from the four humours of the Greek medicine which in a way is an offshoot of the Greek four elements, the Greek elements played no significant role in the evolution of Greek medicine. By and large, the Chinese medicine owed no notable allegiance to the five elements that were, of course, entirely different from the Greek elemental postulate.

Unāni:[82] The Unāni or Greco-Arabic medicine in India of which the *Canon of Medicine* of Ibn-Sīnā or Avicenna as known to the West, has accepted the Empedoclean four elements—earth, fire, air, and water, along with the four primary qualities hot and dry as well as cold and moist. The four elements have been formulated as primary constituents of the human body. Ibn-Sīna has used two words in Arabic to denote these elements: *arkan* (pillars) and *unsur* (element). Since the latter has the connotation of chemical elements, the word, *unsur*, is not generally used in the texts on unāni medicine; instead *arkan* has been employed for denoting the elements. The four qualities are referred to as the four states, two being active (hot and cold), and the other two, passive (moist and dry). It has been explained that the two members of each pair are antagonistic to each other and also not coexistent at any given point of time. A knowledge of the four combinations, hot and moist; cold and moist; cold and dry; hot and dry is also a part of Unāni medical ideas and practices.

Siddha system: The Siddha system of medicine, mostly prevalent in Tamil Nadu, owed its inspiration to the Chinese Patrology and the Yin-Yang theory. There is a proverb in Tamil, which states that a physician is the son of an alchemist. The alchemical supremo, mercury (male principle) and sulphur (female) as well as several minerals and metals with their elaborate processing constitute the medical armamentarium of the Siddha system. Hence, the five elements had no place to begin with in this system, the male–female categorization occupying an important position. However, from about the 15 or 16th cent. A.D. the Āyurvedic five elements were taken in by this system not only for diagnosis (*tridhātu–tridoṣa-*concept) but also in the prescription of drugs for the cure of diseases.[83] The drugs, though mineral often times, are extensively processed with a wide variety of plants. Nevertheless, one does not find in the Siddha texts any appreciable account of the five elements which, on the other hand, are a strong foundation of Āyurveda.

Cārvāka and the Elements

There was a school of materialism that went by the name of *Cārvāka*. There are several views on this nomenclature such as, that there was one *Cārvāka* who was the founder of this school and that *cārvāka* was not a proper name but the one given to a materialist who believed in 'eat, drink and be merry' (*carv* meaning to eat) or that a person who was sweet-tongued (*cāru-vāk*) and hence the ideas of Cārvāka have no profundity. In any case, a materialist would be a non-conformist or a heretic (*nāstika*) and the *Cārvāka* school was heretic with no faith in the concept of god or divine power. Unfortunately, there are no literary sources left behind by this school, excepting a much later work, the *Tattvopaplavasimha* of one Jayanta Bhaṭṭa, published in 1940 by the Oriental Research Institute of Baroda (modern Vadodara). However, references to the *Cārvāka* school and some its rather mundane ideas are found in some texts, like the *Sarvadarśana samgraha* of Mādhavācārya. (14th cent. A.D.).

In any case, Cārvāka, also called Lokāyata signifying common people, accepted only the total validity of direct perception and rejected even inference. It emphasized that the four elements—earth, fire, air and water—are the elements that are real, and that mind is only a product of matter. *Cārvākas* also held the view that even senses and perceived objects were the results of the different combinations of elements, and that even consciousness arose from the matter of these elements. As regards soul and liberation, they believed that the former was nothing but the conscious body while death alone would be liberation (Chandradhara Sharma, pp. 41-42). According to *Sarvadarśana samgraha,* the *Cārvākas* were vehemently, against Vedic rites and rituals and even called the authors or seers of the Vedas 'buffoons, knaves and demons'. Be that as it may, there is a little or no explanation, by the *Cārvākas* regarding the nature and structure of the four elements, nor of their physical characteristics. They had no epistemic approach of their own. The view of *Cārvākas* met with severe criticism by both the orthodox and heterodox systems in India.

Pūrva-Mīmāmsā

The Pūrva-Mīmāmsā, one of the six orthodox Indian systems of thought, believes, like the Nyāya-Vaiśeṣika, in the reality of the external world and also of the individual souls. It has also accorded a place to the five elements in its concept of substance (*dravya*). Its exposition of substances is, however, slightly different from that of the Nyāya-Vaiśeṣika although the approach is more or less similar to that of the Nyāya-Vaiśeṣika. While the Nyāya-Vaiśeṣika expounds nine types of substances, the *Pūrva-mīmāmsā* delineates eleven in this order, earth, water, fire, darkness, *ākāśa*, time, space, soul or self, mind and sound.[84]

However, Mīmāmsā accepts the specific qualities of earth, water, fire and air similar to the Nyāya-Vaiśeṣika, namely, smell, taste, colour, and touch respectively. But, unlike the Nyāya-Vaiśeṣika, it gives the status of a substance to sound, a quality, and thus does not accept that sound is the special quality of *ākāśa*. According to Mīmāmsā, sound is directly known through the sense organ, the ears, and thus this system does not subscribe to the mediation of *ākāśa* for sound; nor it accepts a sound as a specific quality of ears, as explained by the Nyāya-Vaiśeṣika. Even in respect of *tejas*, it thinks of the quality of hot and touch along with colour, the specific quality of fire element. Generally, the word, *vyoma* (a synonym for *ākāśa*) is used in the *Pūrva-mīmāṃsā* texts. Several arguments have been advanced to show that sound is an eternal substance like *ākāśa*. One of them is: 'Indeed, if sound were non-eternal, the eternality of the Vedas which are of the nature of sounds, would meet with ridicule (like hitting with a hare's horn *Mānameyodaya*. p. 233). As for the other qualities of the five elements, they are more or less the same as those enumerated by the Nyāya-Vaiśeṣika, although the Bhāṭṭa school of *Pūrva-mīmāṃsā* does not accept that a substance is the substratum of quality while the Nyāya-Vaiśeṣika emphasises that the qualities inhere in a substance and that they do not have a separate existence.

Jaina View

In Jainism, the elements constitute a part of what is called *pudgala* (matter), one of the five categories of *Ajīva* (unconscious non-spirit), the other four being *ākāśa* (space), *dharma* (motion), *adharma* (rest) and *kāla* (time). In fact, Jainism thinks of the whole universe under two heads: *Jīva* (conscious spirit) and *Ajīva*. Its postulate concerning the four gross elements: earth, water, fire and air, is interesting. Like the Nyāya-Vaiśeṣika, Jainism does not think of them in the produced states as eternal substances, but views them as being differentiated by developing the qualities of smell, taste, colour and touch. Umāsvāti, however, has dealt with the five elements including *ākāśa*. But the Jaina concept of *ākāśa* is at variance with that of the Nyāya-Vaiśeṣika inasmuch as *ākāśa*, according to Jaina, is inclusive of *dik* or space and it is one of the five constituents of *pudgala* or matter.

Bauddha

Siddhārtha who through his intense meditation became the Buddha, the Enlightened, was more an ethical teacher and a mystic than a metaphysician. However, Buddhism developed along two sects: Hīnayāna and Mahāyāna. According to the Sautrāntikas of the Hīnayāna, all elements exist only as sense data and not as actual substances. The elements, *ākāśa* and others are momentary since they are not capable of functioning effectively either successively or simultaneously. Buddhism does not in general accept realism of the type of Nyāya-Vaiśeṣika. The metaphysics of Hīnayāna is concerned largely with the doctrine called *Kṣaṇabhaṅgavāda*, i.e., the theory of momentariness or the theory of Flux or Ceaseless Flow (*Santānavāda*) which postulates that both mind and matter are momentary. Nevertheless, the Sautrāntikas admit the atomic view of matter, considering matter in the matrix of *rūpa*. They regard matter as a collocation consisting of the substratum of the four qualities—colour, taste, odour and touch, and for them, an atom is the minutest unit of *rūpa*. As for the four elements—earth, water, fire and air—it is pointed out that they are to be thought of in terms of their nature, activity and functions such as attraction, cohesion, capacity towards clustering and the like. It is also pointed out that the world of matter, sense organs and our bodies are all in the nature of aggregates from these elements and hence are called *bhautika* to indicate their secondary character . The Buddhists, in any case did not develop a concept of substance because of their philosophical compulsions of their doctrine of momentariness, although certain schools of Buddhism thought of the four elements in their atomic states. Even these schools have no definitive ideas about motion of bodies. This was in sharp contrast with the approach of Nyāya-Vaiśeṣika and other schools of thought. The concept of substance, qualities and motion are presented in the next chapter.

It would be desirable to understand, though briefly, the nuances of the Greek and the Chinese five elements, since this would enable us to appreciate the Indian five elements.

Greek Elements

The origin of the elementary postulate among the Greeks, as mentioned before can be traced to the Ionian Thales of Miletus (*c.* 624-565 B.C.), a versatile intellect and successful merchant. Well versed in astronomy as well as geometry and inclined to speculate on the essence of all that was observable in nature, Thales thought that *Water* was the substance or the primal matter or mobile essence. To him it was an embodiment of physical essence and a cycle of existence through the sky, the atmosphere and the earth as well as to the bodies of plants and animals, back to air and sky again, thus conserving itself amidst its observed changes. The Babylonians had also thought of water (*apsu*) as the primordial substance, but in a somewhat mythological setting. But Thales, a bold thinker as he was, set aside the mythological premise and attempted to explain the diversity of the world of matter in terms of a single substance water not in a metaphysical but in a physical matrix. Following the footsteps of Thales, his pupil, Anaximander (611-547 B.C.) who was meticulously interested in geography and astronomy, thought of the unity of matter, and expounded a limitless (infinite) substance as the first principle in terms of a qualitatively undifferentiated but eternal matter (*aperion*) that would always be in motion. Another Miletan, Anaximenes (570 B.C.), attempted to specify the concept of Anaximander and enunciated that the first or the primordial principle was *Air* (*pneuma*) that had perceivable, eternal motion and hence a dynamic one. He also speculated that the process of rarefaction or condensation would be causative of the varied transformations of the primary substance.

A remarkable Ionian philosopher was Heracleitus of Ephesus (*c.* 540-475 B.C.) who emphasised that everything was in a state of flux and that change alone was real. He argued that *Fire*, the most changing element, was the origin and image of all the observed things. It may be significant to note that the Heracleitan idea of flux is more or less similar to the Buddhist view.

Each of the foregoing monistic conceptions had its inherent limitations towards the explanation of the diverse observed phenomena. A Sicilian thinker, Empedocles (*c.* 500-430 B.C.) who was greatly influenced by the Pythagorean ideas, sought to provide a pluralistic but an integrated presentation of four elements by adding **Earth** as one more element with a view to explaining the multiplicity of phenomena. Calling them the 'roots' of the world, he postulated that love and strife or affinity and opposition would always be in operation everywhere and these would be responsible for all types of combinations and separations respectively. He held the view that the four elements were the causes of all occurrences even in macrocosm. In his scheme, the four primary qualities: heat and cold; moisture and dryness, exhibited affinity and opposition like the elements.

Plato (*c.* 427-347 B.C.), one of the great Greek thinkers, in his younger days and even later, was also inclined towards the Heracleitan view that 'things perceived by the senses were ever in a state of flux and there would no precise knowledge concerning them. He maintained, according to Aristotle, that 'there could be no real definition of things perceived by the sense because they were always changing. Those things which could alone be defined he called them *Ideas,* and things perceived by the senses, he said, were different from these Ideas and were all called after them'[85] (*Metaphysics,* quoted by Singer, p. 32).

Aristotle (384-322 B.C.), a pupil of Plato, expounded that the *Primary* or *Potential* matter as he called it, would undergo changes or transformations into different substances depending upon the nature and the extent of interaction among the four primary qualities. The four elements too were formed, according to him, by the primary qualities in pairs; thus Earth would be formed with the pair of Cold and Dry; Water with Cold and Wet; Fire with Hot and Dry; and Air with Hot and Wet. It needs to be emphasised that the elements Earth, Water, Fire and Air as conceived by Empedocles and explained by Aristotle, were the principles, but did not represent the observed or the phenomenal earth, water, fire and air. In a way, it was pluralistic monism, since it was conceived that Water would have a preponderance of that element, but it would also contain small amounts of the other three elements, and that their essences would be beyond the sensorial perceptions. Such an integration was also one of the characteristics of the Indian doctrine of five elements as will be observed later.

The Ionian, Pythagoras, an younger contemporary of Thales, but a native of Samos, attached great importance to mathematics, specially to numbers. The Phythagorean believed in 'harmony of the spheres' and extended this observation by stressing that the pitch of musical notes would depend on a simple numerical ratio of the length of the chords.

In any case, the Pythagoreans added a new dimension to the Greek theory of elements. They held that numbers had a real and distinct existence and, according to Aristotle (Singer, p. 18), the numbers were the elements of all things. They even conceived of the heaven or celestial sphere in terms of a musical and numerical scale, and the number *ten* was thought to be perfect, comprising in itself the whole nature of numbers. They believed that even justice, reason and opportunity or chance were capable of being expressed numerically. The Pythagorean exposition of what was called the 'harmony of the spheres', as noted above, emanated from their interest in the numerical scale of music. They were also noted for their interpretations of numbers in relation to geometrical forms. More importantly, the Pythagoreans, in a very succinct but curious manner, manipulated equilateral triangles and squares in three dimensions, and arrived at four regular solids, namely, four-sided pyramid (tetrahedron); the six-sided cube, the eight-sided or octahedron and the twenty-sided or icosahedron. These were regarded as representing the four elements. There was also a fifth one, the twelve-sided dodecahedron. Since the idea of a fifth element was later introduced by Aristotle known as the quintessence or *Ether* that was supposed to constitute the celestial bodies; the later Pythagoreans considered the dodecahedron as representing the Universe itself. The five regular solids became later known as 'Platonic bodies' which Plato described in his *Timaeus*, but were in reality the Pythagorean ones.

Aristotle projected a picture of the universe in the following order of spheres: the earth partly covered by ocean; the firmament; water; air and fire of elemental nature; planetary spheres; fixed stars; and Primum Mobile. In his scheme, the spheres of pure elements were regarded as inaccessible as the heavens; and beyond the elemental sphere, would be the region of the *Ether* (Greek word meaning 'shining') that would enter into the composition of celestial bodies. Aristotle regarded matter as continuous in contradistinction to the atomic theory expounded by his predecessors, Leucippus and Democritus. He emphasized that all terrestrial things were made up of four elements, while the celestial ones had Ether, the fifth element. Thus he sought to make a distinction between the terrestrial and celestial bodies on the basis of elements, although such a distinction was also speculated upon by earlier Greek savants in a different manner. In any case, The Greek doctrine of five elements became an important thought-structure among the exponents of the orthodox medieval theology, both Christian and Muslim alike. All the same, the five elements were understood in relation to their physical aspects, independently of either religious or metaphysical undertones to a considerable extent.

Chinese Five Elemental Theory

The Chinese theory of five elements had a different undertone and was developed by what were known as Naturalists. The Chinese five elements were: Water, Fire, Wood, Metal and Earth. It needs to be emphasised that Air (*pneuma*) which played an important role in the Greek postulates not only of the physical world but also in medicine, is noted for its absence as one of the elements in the Chinese model. Likewise, the latter differs from the Indian doctrine of five elements of which Air (*Vāyu*) is an important component. Moreover, Chinese five elements are not in the nature of any type of fundamental matter, but represent the five kinds of primary processes and relationship with certain qualities as follows:

WOOD:	accepting form by submitting itself to cutting and carving instruments	solidity involving sourness workability
FIRE :	heating, burning, ascending	heat, combustion, bitterness
EARTH:	producing edible vegetation sweetness	nutrition
METAL:	accepting form by moulding when in the liquid state, and the capacity of changing this form by re-melting and re-moulding.	solidity involving acridity congelation and re-congelation
WATER:	soaking, dripping, descending (dissolving?)	liquidity, saltiness fluidity, solution

(*Source*: Needham II, p. 243)

According to Needham: 'On this view the five elemental theory (of the Chinese) was an effort to reach a provisional classification of the basic properties, that is to say, which would only be manifested when they were undergoing change. It is often pointed out, therefore, that the term 'element' has never been satisfactory for *hsing*, the very etymology which had from the beginning the implication of movements. The five elements were five powerful forces in ever-flowing cyclic motion, and not passive motionless fundamental substances. One remarkably interesting aspect.... is the association of the five elements with the five tastes (and) it strongly suggests the chemical interests of the Naturalists.'[86]

There was a peculiar aspect of the Chinese elements, namely, their feudal association. The dynasty of Shun was supposed to have been ruled by the virtue of Earth; the Hsia dynasty by virtue of Wood; the Shang dynasty by Metal; and the Chow dynasty by Fire. Successive emperors had to choose their colour of official investiture so that the chosen colour would be in tune with the concerned element. There was also the concept of what was called Mutual Conquestion or Cyclical Conquest like 'Wood overcoming Earth, Metal overcoming Wood, Fire overcoming Metal, Water overcoming Fire, and (finally) Earth overcoming Water at which point the cycle commenced all over again. All changes in human history were thus considered manifestations of the same changes which could be observed at the lower inorganic levels and from which indeed the very conception of the elements had been derived'.[87]

The Chinese five elements were also involved in the prognostication of certain happenings vis-à-vis the emperors as well as during the cycle of the year when each element would be predominant and also reign during the concerned cyclical sign. When the element Wood reigned during spring, it was thought that the emperor would not grant favours, but if indulged in cutting and destroying, some one of his family would die. After 72 days when this period was over, the element Fire would begin to reign and the emperor would take hasty measures; there would be epidemics, drought and the destructions of plants and people. Seventy-two days later the element Earth would start its reign and in the ensuing 72 days if the emperor resorted to the construction of palaces and the like, his life would be in danger; and if the city walls were erected, his ministers would die. During the next 72 days it was the element Metal that would reign and during this period, if the emperor caused mining operations or pounding of rocks, his troops would be defeated in battle, his soldiers might die and he himself might lose his throne. The next 72 days would be the reign of Water when, if the emperor allowed the dykes to be cut, even his empress might die, and pregnant woman would have abortions.

In the Chinese scheme of elements, Wood was accorded the first place and Water the last, the Earth element being in the middle. In the chapter 'On the Five Elements', Tung Chung-Shu (middle of second century B.C.) justifies this order by asserting that 'Wood produces Fire, Fire produces Earth, Earth produces Metal and Metal produces Water; and Water produces Wood. He also points out that this relation is like that of father and son, saying: 'As transmitters they are fathers, as receivers they are sons. There is an unvarying dependence of the sons on fathers, and direction from the father to the sons. Such is the Tao of heaven.'[88] It was also thought that, of the five elements, it was the Earth that would bring forth the five elements and four seasons together, wood having its place in the east and lording over the essence (*chii*) in spring, Fire in the south having authority over summer, Metal in the West commanding autumn, and Water in the north having authority over winter.

Chinese theory of five elements was indeed a complex one. While it found favour among the Naturalists, the orthodox Confucians did not accept it. The latter even viewed with disdain the whole approach of Tsou Yen who had earlier elaborated upon the nature and relationship of the five elements. In any case, the correlation of five elements with the Yin-Yang concept of Taoists as well as the inclusion of the domesticated ones reveals the extent of the thought pervasiveness of the Chinese Naturalists. Wood was considered as of Yin in Yang or Lesser Yang; Fire: Yang or great Yang; Earth: equal balances; Metal: Yang in Yin or lesser Yin; Water: Yin or greater Yin. As for the planets, Jupiter, Mars, Saturn, Venus and Mercury were associated respectively with Wood, Fire, Earth, Metal and Water. Likewise, the weather forms of wind, heat, thunder, cold and rain. Green, red yellow, white and black were the respective colours; similarly, muscle, pulse (blood), flesh, skin and hair and bone marrow as parts of the body; eye, tongue, mouth, nose and ears (the sense organs), and sheep, fowl, dog and pig (domestic animals) were related to Wood, Fire, Earth, Metal and Water respectively. There were other symbolic correlations too with regard to these five elements. According to Needham, such wide correlations did, to some extent, act as a drag on the real observations of Nature and in a way had a negative effect on the real scientific movement in China.

The Chinese concept of five elements was to an appreciable extent at variance with both the Greek and the Indian five elemental theory, although there were some similarities in approach; for example, the correlation between the five elements and the sense organs. But such a correlation was somewhat tardy when compared with the Indian model that was conceived and developed in an entirely different context.

At this stage, some additional remarks on the Indian and the Greek approaches to the elemental postulate may be necessary. First, the Greek element, *Ether*; this was conceived by Aristotle to enter into the composition of the celestial bodies, while *ākāśa* was not thought of that way by Indian thinkers, but a substratum of sound, one and ubiquitous. The Indian concept of *ākāśa* was far more comprehensive than the Greek *ether* inasmuch as the former was even regarded as that from which everything arises, or out of which everything appears and into which everything is dissolved.[89] *Ākāśa* had an exalted position of the Absolute too. 'In *ākāśa* we rejoice (when we are together) and do not rejoice (when we are separated). In *ākāśa* everything is born, and towards it everything tends after it is born. Meditate on *ākāśa*. He who meditates on it as the Absolute (Brahman) obtains the worlds of *ākāśa* and of light, which are free from pleasure and pain, wide and spacious; he is, as it were, Lord and Master as far as *ākāśa* reaches'.[90] It is tempting to compare *ākāśa* with Anaximander's *apeiron*, the unlimited principle regarded as the origin of all manifestations and to which they were respected the return at their dissolution. It must, however, be noted that the concept as expounded in the *Chāndogya*, was much earlier and in the context of the Supreme Reality.

As regards, the Greek element, Air, the Indian counterpart being Vāyu, Anaximenes postulated the foundational material principle, Air, by drawing the analogy of microcosmos and macrocosmos, namely, just as air (aer) holds us together and sustains life, so does Air surround the whole Universe as a permanent substance.[91] Soon Air was raised to the level of divinity. Interestingly, the Latin word, *anima*, means both air and breath (life). The principle of air was an important approach to Greek and Greco-Roman medicine, from Hippocrates to Galen of Pergamum. One sees more or less a similar but independent development in India with regard to the concept of Air. The *Chāndogya* (IV.3) states that Vāyu is the *sūtra* (thread) that holds together this and other worlds, all beings and the organs of the body. The *Bṛhadāraṇyaka* has a similar imagery.[92] The breath of life, *prāṇa* has also been discussed in the Upaniṣads. In any case the exposition of *vāyu* and *prāṇa* antedate similar approach of the Greek thinkers.

Apart from the Heracletian postulate of Fire as the primordial element, the Greek god Zeus was referred to as the Supreme fire and immortal while the other gods including the Sun and the Moon, born out of it, would eventually die.[93] In the Ṛgveda as well as in the *Bṛhadāraṇyaka upaniṣad* there is a reference to Agni Vaiśvānara or the Universal Fire. The very first *mantra* of the first *maṇḍala* of the Ṛgveda is a laudatory one for Agni, the Fire-god.[94]

In one respect, namely, the numbers, the Indian approach was different. Though number-reckoning was on an ascending decimal scale and the exposition of huge numbers are evidenced in the Ṛgveda itself, and some magical association of numbers like seven, eighteen, twenty-four, a hundred and eight and its multiples are found in the post-Vedic and later literature, Indian speculation on numbers did not dwell upon them in terms of the principles of the Universe as the Pythagorieans did.

The concept of elements emerged as a seminal one in Indian thought and continued to have its influence in one way or the other on the different shades of thinking for a very long time.

REFERENCES

(The English translations of all the Upaniṣadic references are taken from *The Thirteen Principal Upaniṣads* by R. E. Hume.)

(All references to the *Praśastapādabhāṣya* (PPB) are taken from *Kiraṇāvalī* (ed) Jitendra S. Jetley; including the numbers of the Vaiśeṣika Sūtra-s mentioned).

1. यतो वा इमानि भूतानि जायन्ते । येन जातानि जीवन्ति । यत्प्रयन्त्यभिसंविशन्ति । तद्विजिज्ञासस्व । तद्ब्रह्मेति । *Tai.up*.3.1d

2. सर्वं खल्विदं ब्रह्म तज्जलानिति शान्त उपासीत । (*Ch.up*. 3.14.1)

   Verily this whole world is Brahman. Tranquil, let one worship It as that from which he came forth, as that into which he will be dissolved, as that in which he breathes.

3. इदं जगन्नामरूपविकृतं प्रत्यक्षादिविषयं ब्रह्मकारणं वृद्धतमत्त्वाद् ब्रह्म । Śaṅkara (on 3.14.1)

   This world which manifests itself as name and form and which has objects of perception, is caused by Brahma. As he is the oldest he is called Brahma.

4. तदैक्षत बहुस्यां प्रजायेयेति तत्तेजोऽसृजत तत्तेज ऐक्षत बहुस्यां प्रजायेयेति तदपोऽसृजत तस्माद्यत्र क्व च शोचति स्वेदते वा पुरुषस्तेजस एव तदध्यापो जायन्ते । ता आप ऐक्षन्त बह्व्यः स्याम प्रजायेमहीति ता अन्नमसृजन्त तस्माद्यत्र क्व च वर्षति तदेव भूयिष्ठमन्नं भवत्यद्भ्य एव तध्यन्नाद्यं जायते । (*Ch.up*. 6.2.3,4)

   (6.2.3) It bethought itself, 'would that I were many! Let me procreate myself! It emitted heat. That heat bethought itself. 'Would that I were many! Let me procreate myself!' It emitted water. Therefore whenever a person gives or perspires from the heat, then water is produced.

   The water bethought itself; 'would that I were many! Let me procreate myself'. It emitted food. Therefore whenever it rains, then there is abundant food. So food for eating is produced just from water. Ibid. p. 241.

   तेषां खल्वेषां भूतानां त्रीण्येव बीजानि भवन्त्याण्डजं जीवजमुद्भिज्जमिति । सेयं देवतैक्षत हन्ताहमिमास्तिस्रो देवता अनेन जीवेनात्मनाऽनुप्रविश्य नामरूपे व्याकरवाणीति । (*Ch.up*.6.3.1,2)

   Now of these beings here, there are just three origins, born from an egg, born from a living thing, born of a sprout.

   That divinity bethought itself; 'come! let me enter these three divinities with this living soul (Ātman) and separate out name and form!

5. स होवाच गार्ग्यो य एवायमाकाशे पुरुषः एतमेवाहं ब्रह्मोपास इति स होवाचाजातशत्रुर्मा मैतस्मिन्संवदिष्ठाः पूर्णमप्रवर्तीति वा अहमेतमुपास इति स य एतमेवमुपास्ते पूर्यते प्रजया पशुभिर्नास्यास्माल्लोकात्प्रजोद्वर्तते । (*Br.up*. 2.1.5)

   स होवाच गार्ग्यो य एवायं वायौ पुरुष एतमेवाहं ब्रह्मोपास इति स होवाचाजातशत्रुर्मा मैतस्मिन्संवदिष्ठा इन्द्रो वैकुण्ठोऽपराजिता सेनेति वा अहमेतमुपास इति स य एतमेवमुपास्ते जिष्णुर्हापराजिष्णुर्भवत्यन्यतस्त्यजायी। (*Br.up*. 2.2.6)

   स होवाच गार्ग्यो य एवायमग्नौ पुरुष एतमेवाहं ब्रह्मोपास इति स होवाचाजातशत्रुर्मा मैतस्मिन्संवदिष्ठा विषासहिरिति वा अहमेतमुपास इति स य एतमेवमुपास्ते विषासहिर्हि भवति विषासहिर्हास्य प्रजा भवति । (*Br.up*. 2.1.7)

   स होवाच गार्ग्यो य एवायमप्सु पुरुष एतमेवाहं ब्रह्मोपास इति स होवाचाजातशत्रुर्मा मैतस्मिन्संवदिष्ठाः प्रतिरूप इति वा अहमेतमुपास इति स य एतमेवमुपास्ते प्रतिरूपं हैवैनमुपगच्छति नाप्रतिरूपमथो प्रतिरूपोऽस्माज्जायते । (*Br.up*. 2.1.8)

Gārgya said: 'The person who is here in *ākāśa*. Him, indeed, I worship as Brahma'. Ajātaśatru said: 'Talk not to me about him! I worship him, verily, as the Full, the non-active. He who worships him as such is filled with off-spring and cattle. His offspring goes not forth from this earth'.

Gārgya said: 'The person who is here in wind, Him, indeed, I worship as Brahma.' (2.1.5) Ajātaśatru said: 'Talk not to me about him! Verily I worship as Indra, the terrible (*Vaikuntha*) and the unconquered army. He who worships him as such becomes indeed triumphant, unconquerable, and a conqueror of adversaries.'

Gārgya said : 'The person who is here in fire, Him, indeed, I worship as Brahma'. (2.1.6) Ajātaśatru said, 'talk not to me about him I worship him, verily, as the vanquisher. He who worships him as such becomes a vanquisher indeed, His offsprings become vanquishers'.

Gārgya said : 'The person who is here in water, Him, indeed, I worship as Brahma!' (2.1.8).

Ajātaśatru said, 'Talk not to me about him! I worship him verily as the counterpart (of phenomenal objects). His counterpart comes to him (in his children), not that which is not his counterpart.

His counterpart is born from Him.

6. *Ch. up.* 6.2.3

7. तस्माद्वा एतस्मादात्मन आकाशस्सम्भूतः । आकाशाद्वायुः । वायोरग्निः । अग्नेरापः । अद्भ्यः पृथिवी । पृथिव्या ओषधयः। ओषधीभ्योऽन्नम् । अन्नात्पुरुषः । स वा एष पुरुषोऽन्नरसमयः । (*Tai.up.* 2.1)

From this soul (Ātman), verily *ākāśa* arose; from *ākāśa*, wind (*vāyu*); from wind, fire; from water, the earth; from the earth, herbs; from herbs, food; from food, semen; from semen, the person.

This, verily, is the person that consists of the essence of food.

8. आकाशो नाम शब्दगुणोऽवकाशकरो मूर्तद्रव्याणाम् । तस्मादाकाशात्स्वेन स्पर्शगुणेन पूर्वेण च आकाशगुणेन शब्देन द्विगुणो वायुः । वायोश्च स्वेन रूपगुणेन पूर्वाभ्यां च त्रिगुणोऽग्निः संभूतः । अग्रेश्च स्वेन रसगुणेन पूर्वैश्च त्रिभिश्चतुर्गुणा आपः संभूताः। अद्भ्यः स्वेन गन्धगुणेन पूर्वैश्च चतुर्भिः पञ्चगुणापृथिवी संभूता ।

(Śaṅkara on *Tai. up.* 2.1)

Ākāśa indeed (is an element) which gives space for the corporeal objects to exist. Air has two qualities, viz. as a result of *ākāśa* it has sound, a quality of *ākāśa* and the quality of touch, a quality of its own. On account of air, (*vāyu*) two qualities and its own quality, colour; fire (*agni*) is the possessor of three qualities. On account of fire, with three qualities, and having its natural quality of taste, water becomes the possessor of four qualities. As a result of water (*ap*) with four qualities; and also having its natural quality of smell, the earth (*pṛthivī*) contains five qualities.

9. एष ब्रह्मैष इन्द्र एष प्रजापतिरेते सर्वे देवा इमानि च पञ्चमहाभूतानि पृथिवी वायुराकाश आपो ज्योतींषि । *Ait. up.*3.3

He is Brahma; he is Indra; he is Prajāpati, (he is) all these gods; and these five gross elements (*Mahābhūtāni*) namely earth (*Pṛthivī*), wind (*vāyu*), space (*ākāśa*), water (*āpas*), and light (*jyotīṃṣi*).

10. अर्वाग्देवा अस्य विसर्जनेनाथा को वेद यत आबभूव । RV.X.129.7

11. मा नो हिंसीज्जनिता य: पृथिव्या यो वा दिवं सत्यधर्मा जजान ।

यश्चापश्चन्द्रा बृहतीर्जजान कस्मै देवाय हविषा विधेम । RV. **X**.121.9

Never may he harm us who is earth's begetter, nor he whose laws are sure, the heaven's creator, He who brought forth the great and lucid waters, what god shall we adore with our oblation.

12. प्र केतुना बृहता यात्यग्निरा रोदसी वृषभो रोरवीति ।

दिवश्चिदन्ताँ उपमाँ उदानळपामुपस्थे महिषो ववर्ध ॥ RV.**X**.8.1

Agni advances with his lofty banner. The Bull is bellowing to the earth and heavens, He hath attained the sky's supremest limits, the steer has waxen in the lap of waters. 15.

13. आप: सर्वस्य भेषजीस्तास्ते कृण्वन्तु भेषजम् । RV. **X**.137.6

The waters have healing power, the waters drive diseases away.

14. अथैतस्य प्राणस्य आप: शरीरम् । *Br.up.* 1.5.13

The waters are the body of *Prāṇa*.

15. आप एवेमा मूर्ता येयं पृथिवी यदन्तरिक्षं यद्द्यौः यत्पर्वता: यद्देवमनुष्या: यत्पशवश्च वयांसि च तृणवनस्पतय:

श्वापदान्याकीटपतङ्गपिपीलिकं आप एवेमा मूर्ता: अप उपास्स्वेति । *Ch.up.*7.10.1

All these are forms of water, viz. This earth, the sky, the heavens, the mountains, these gods and men, the beasts and birds, the gross and the trees, the wild natures down to worms, flies and ants. All these are forms of water only; you propitiate water.

16. स योऽपो ब्रह्मेत्युपास्ते आप्नोति सर्वान्कामान् तृप्तिमान् भवति ।

He who propitiates water as Brahman attains all his desires and becomes satisfied. *Ch. up.* 7.10.2

17. यत्र नान्यत्पश्यति नान्यच्छृणोति नान्यद्विजानाति स भूमा । *Ch.up.* 7.24.1

When a man sees no other, hears no other, knows no other, that is infinite. (*Bhūmā*)

18. आपो वावान्नाद्भूयस्तस्माद्यदा सुवृष्टिर्न भवति व्याधीयन्ते प्राणा अन्नं कनीयो भविष्यति ....

तेजो वावाद्भ्यो भूयस्तद्धा एतद्वायुमागृह्याकाशमभितपति तदाहुर्निशोचति नितपति वर्षिष्यति वा इति तेज एव तत्पूर्वं दर्शयित्वाऽथाप: सृजते ।.....

आकाशो वाव तेजसो भूयान् आकाशे वै सूर्याचन्द्रमसौ उभौ विद्युन्नक्षत्राण्यग्निराकाशेन आह्वयति आकाशेन श्रृणोत्याकाशेन प्रतिश्रृणोति आकाशे रमते.....

स्मरो वावाकाशाद्भूयस्तस्माद्यप बहव आसीरन्न स्मरन्तो नैव ते किञ्चन श्रृणुयुर्न मन्वीरन्न विजानीरन् ...

आशा वाव स्मराद्भूयस्याशोद्धो वै स्मरो मन्त्रानधीते कर्माणि कुरुते पुत्रांश्च पशूंश्चेच्छत इमं च लोकममुं चेच्छत आशामुपास्स्वेति।

प्राणो वा आशाया भूयान्यथा वा अरा नाभौ समर्पिता एवमस्मिन् प्राणे सर्वं समर्पितम् ।.....

एष तु वा अतिवदति य: सत्येनातिवदति सोऽहं भगव: सत्येनातिवदानीति सत्यं त्वेव विजिज्ञासितव्यमिति सत्यं भगवो विजिज्ञास इति।

यदा वै विजानात्यथ सत्यं वदति नाविजानन् सत्यं वदति विजानन्नेव सत्यं वदति विज्ञानं त्वेव विजिज्ञासितव्यमिति विज्ञानं भगवो विजिज्ञास इति । *Ch.up.* 7.10 to 10–17;

19. स आत्मा तत्त्वमसि श्वेतकेतो इति । *Ch.up.* 6.8.7

That is Ātman, that art thou, śvetaketu.

20. य एवं वेदाहं ब्रह्मास्मीति स इदं सर्वं भवति । *Br.up.*1.4.10

Whoever thus knows 'I am Brahma' becomes this all.

21. प्राचीनशाल औपमन्यव: सत्ययज्ञ: पौलुषिरिन्द्रद्युम्नो भाल्लवेयो जन: शार्कराक्ष्यो बुडिल आश्वतराश्विस्ते हैते महाशाला

महाश्रोत्रिया: समेत्य मीमांसां चक्रु: को न आत्मा किं ब्रह्मेति । *Ch.up.* 5.11.1

Prācīnaśāla Aupamanyava, Satyayajña Pauluṣi, Indradyumna Bhāllaveya, Buḍila Āśvatarāśvi, Jana Śārkarākṣya—the great householders, greatly learned in sacred lore, having come together, pondered: 'who is our Ātman? What is Brahma?'

22. Deussen P: *The Philosophy of Upaniṣads*, pp. 86-87.

23. तान् होवाच अश्वपतिर्भगवन्तोऽयं कैकेय: संप्रति इममात्मानं वैश्वानरमध्येति तं हन्त अभ्यागच्छामेति तं हाभ्याजग्मु: ।
Ch.up. 5.11.4

(Uddālaka-Āruṇi) said to them, 'Revered ones! This Aśvapati Kaikeya knows Vaiśvānara well. We will go to him. They then went to him.

24. तान्होवाचैते वै खलु यूयं पृथगिवेममात्मानं वैश्वानरं विद्वांसोऽन्नमत्थ यस्त्वेतमेवं प्रादेशमात्रमभिविमानमात्मानं

वैश्वानरमुपास्ते स सर्वेषु लोकेषु सर्वेषु भूतेषु सर्वेष्वात्मस्वन्नमत्ति ।

तस्य ह वा एतस्यात्मनो वैश्वानरस्य मूर्धैव सुतेजाश्चक्षुर्विश्वरूप: प्राण: पृथग्वर्त्मात्मा सन्देहो बहुलो बस्तिरेव रयि: पृथिव्येव पादावुर एव वेदिर्लोमानि बर्हिर्हृदयं गार्हपत्यो मनोऽन्वाहार्यपचन आस्यमाहवनीय: । *Ch.up.* 5.18.1,2

Then he said to them; 'you eat food here, knowing this universal soul as if something separate. He, however, who reverences this universal Ātman that is of the measure of the span—this (yet) is to be measured by thinking of oneself—he eats food in all worlds, in all beings, in all selves.

The bright shining heaven is indeed the head of that universal Ātman. The manifold (Sun) is his eye.

That which possesses various paths (i.e. the wind) is his breath. This extended (*ākāśa*) is his body. Wealth (i.e., water) is indeed his bladder. The support (i.e., the earth) is indeed his feet. The sacrificial area is indeed his breast. The sacrificial grass is his hair. The *Gārhapatya* fire is his heart.

Anvāhārya pacana fire is his mind. The *Āhavanīya* fire is his mouth.

25. य आत्माऽपहतपाप्मा विजरो विमृत्युर्विशोको विजिघत्सोऽपिपास: सत्यकाम: सत्यसङ्कल्प: सोऽन्वेष्टव्य: स विजिज्ञासितव्य: स सर्वांश्च लोकानाप्नोति सर्वांश्च कामान्यस्तमात्मानमनुविद्य विजानातीति ह प्रजापतिरुवाच ।
Ch.up. 8.7.1

The self which is free from evil, ageless, deathless, sorrowless, hungerless, thirstless, whose desire is the Real, whose conception is the Real, He should be searched out, Him one should desire to understand. He obtains all worlds and all desires who has found out and who understands the self-thus spoke Prajāpati.

26. (i) अन्नं ब्रह्मेति व्यजानात् । *Tai.up.* 3.2

(ii) प्राणो ब्रह्मेति व्यजानात् । *Tai.up.* 3.3

(iii) मनो ब्रह्मेति व्यजानात् । *Tai.up.* 3.4

(iv) विज्ञानं ब्रह्मेति व्यजानात् । *Tai.up.* 3.5

(v) आनन्दो ब्रह्मेति व्यजानात् । *Tai.up.* 3.6

(i) (Vāruṇi) understood that Brahman is food.
(ii) He understood that Brahman is breath.
(iii) He understood that Brahman is mind.
(iv) He understood that Brahman is understanding.
(v) He understood that Brahman is bliss.

27. एतमन्नमयमात्मानमुपसङ्क्रामति । एतं प्राणमयमात्मानमुपसङ्क्रामति । एतं मनोमयमात्मानमुपसङ्क्रामति एतं विज्ञानमयमात्मानमुपसङ्क्रामति । एतमानन्दमयमात्मानमुपसङ्क्रामति । *Tai.up.* 2.8

(He who knows this, on departing from this world) proceeds on to the self which consists of food, then to the self which consists of breath, then to the self which consists of mind, then to the self which consists of conscious understanding and (ultimately) to the self which consists of bliss.

28. अजामेकां लोहितशुक्लकृष्णां

बह्वीः प्रजाः सृजमानां सरूपाः ।

अजो ह्येको जुषमाणोऽनुशेते

जहात्येकां भुक्तभोगामजोऽन्यः ॥ *Śvet.up.* 4.5

With the one unborn female, red, white and black. Who produces many creatures like herself, there lies the one unborn male taking this delight. Another unborn male leaves her with whom he has had his delight. R. E. Hume.

29. Tr. by Paul Deussen in *The Philosophy of Upaniṣads*, p. 251.

30. पृथ्वी च पृथ्वीमात्रा आपश्चापोमात्रा च तेजश्च तेजोमात्रा च वायुश्च वायुमात्रा चाकाशश्चाकाशमात्रा च चक्षुश्च द्रष्टव्यं च श्रोत्रं च श्रोतव्यं च घ्राणं च घ्रातव्यं च रसश्च रसयितव्यं च त्वक्च स्पर्शयितव्यं च वाक्च वक्तव्यं च आत्मनि संप्रतिष्ठते *Praśna* 4.8

Earth and the subtle element of the earth, water and the subtle element of water, heat and the subtle element of heat, wind and the subtle element of the wind, ākāśa and the subtle element of ākāśa, sight and what can be seen, hearing and what can be heard, smell and what can be smelt, taste and what can be tasted, the skin and what can be touched, speech and what can be spoken (exist in the Ātman).

31. पञ्चतन्मात्रा भूतशब्देनोच्यन्तेऽथ पञ्चभूतानि महाभूतशब्देनोच्यन्ते । *Mai.up.* 3.2

The five subtle elements are spoken of by the word 'element' (*bhūta*). Likewise, the five gross elements (*Mahābhūta*) are spoken of by the word 'great element.' *Mai.up.*3.2

32. (i) तत्र शब्दतन्मात्रादाकाशं शब्दगुणम् । *Ākāśa* possesses the quality of sound out of the subtle element of *śabda*, sound.

(ii) शब्दतन्मात्रसहितात् स्पर्शतन्मात्रात् वायुः शब्दस्पर्शगुणः ।

Air (*vāyu*) possesses the qualities: sound and touch due to the subtle element, touch, in association with the subtle element, sound.

(iii) शब्दस्पर्शतन्मात्रसहितात् रूपतन्मात्रात् तेजः शब्दस्पर्शरूपगुणम् ।

The element of heat possesses the qualities, sound, touch and colour due to the subtle element of colour in association with the subtle elements of sound and touch.

(iv) शब्दस्पर्शरूपतन्मात्रसहितात् रसतन्मात्रात् आप: शब्दस्पर्शरूपरसगुणा: ।

The element of water possesses the qualities of sound, touch, colour and taste due to the subtle element of taste in association with the subtle elements of sound, touch and colour.

(v) शब्दस्पर्शरूपरसतन्मात्रसहितात् गन्धतन्मात्रात् शब्दस्पर्शरूपरसगन्धगुणा पृथिवी ।

The element of earth possesses the qualities sound, touch, colour, taste and smell due to the subtle element of smell in association with the subtle elements of sound, touch, colour and taste (Vācaspatimiśra's com.. on SK. 22).

33. पृथिव्यादिरूपरसगन्धस्पर्शा द्रव्या नित्यत्वादनित्यत्वाच्च । VS. 7.1.2

Also the colour, taste, smell, touch of the earth inasmuch as substances are non-eternal, are non-eternal.

पृथिव्या रूपरसगन्धस्पर्शा:, जलस्य रूपरसस्पशां:, तेजसो रूपस्पर्शौ, वायो: स्पर्श: एतेषां नित्याश्रितानामनित्यत्वम् ।
Vivṛti on VS. 7.1.2

The colour, taste, smell and touch of the earth; the colour, taste, and touch of water; the colour and touch of fire; and touch of air, these inhering in the non-eternal are non-eternal.

34. आकाशादि पञ्चसु एकैकं द्विधा समं विभज्य तेषु दशसु भागेषु प्राथमिकान् पञ्चभागान् प्रत्येकं चतुर्धा समं विभज्य तेषु चतुर्णा भागानां स्वस्वद्वितीयार्धभागपरित्यागेन भागान्तरेषु योजनम् । *Vedāntasāra* (also see *Pañcadaśī*, 1.7)

35. आकाशकालदिगात्मनां सर्वगतत्त्वं, परममहत्त्वं, सर्वसंयोगिसमानदेशत्त्वं च । तत्राकाशस्य गुणा: शब्दसङ्ख्याचापरिमाणपृथक्त्व संयोगविभागा: । PPB. 19

Ākāśa, time (काल), space (दिग्) and self (Ātmā) are ubiquitous, all-pervading; and all corporeal objects exist in them.
Among them *ākāśa* has the following qualities (viz. sound, number, volume, separateness, conjunction and disjunction).

36. द्रव्यगुणकर्म-सामान्य-विशेष-समवायानां पदार्थानां साधर्म्य-वैधर्म्य-तत्त्वज्ञानं नि:श्रेयसहेतु: । PPB.2

A correct knowledge of the attributes of the objects viz. substance, attribute, action, generality, particularity, inherence leads to the removal of misery permanently.

37. तत्र द्रव्याणि पृथिव्यप्तेजोवाय्वाकाशकालदिगात्ममनांसीति सामान्यविशेषसंज्ञोक्तानि नवैव । PPB.4

There the substances are only nine (in numbers) as referred to in the *Vaiśeṣika sūtra*, viz. earth, water, fire, air, *ākāśa*, time, space, self and mind.

38. सा तु द्विविधा । नित्या चानित्या च । परमाणुलक्षणा नित्या । कार्यलक्षणा त्वनित्या । PPB.30

(Earth) is of two kinds viz. eternal and non-eternal. That which is characterised by an atom is eternal and that which is characterised as an effect is non-eternal.

त्रिविधं चास्या: कार्यम् । शरीरेन्द्रियविषयसंज्ञकम् । PPB.30

As a product (the earth) is of three kinds, viz. The organic element (*śarīra*), sense organ (*indriya*) and matter (*viṣaya*).

विषयस्तु द्रव्यणुकादिप्रक्रमेणारब्ध: मृत्पाषाणस्थावरलक्षण: । PPB. 33

The matter (of element earth) is a constituent of dyads and onwards appearing in the form of mud, rocks and immovable things (like trees).

39. क्षितावेव गन्ध: । PPB.29

Small is (the specific quality) only of earth.

40. रूप-रस-गन्ध-स्पर्श-सङ्ख्या-परिमाण-पृथक्त्व-संयोग-विभाग-परत्व-अपरत्व-गुरुत्व-द्रव्यत्व-संस्कारवत्यः ।
PPB.34

The earth element has the qualities; viz. colour, taste, smell, touch, number, dimension, separateness, conjunction, disjunction, distance, proximity, gravitation, viscidity, faculty of impression.

41. तास्तु पूर्ववद् द्विविधाः, नित्यानित्यभावात् । PPB. 37

The water, as stated earlier, is of two kinds. (viz. eternal and non-eternal).

42. तासां कार्यं च त्रिविधम् । शरीरेन्द्रियविषयसंज्ञकम् । तत्र शरीरं अयोनिजमेव वरुणलोके । इन्द्रियं रसव्यञ्जकं
विजात्यनभिभूतैर्जलावयवैः आरब्धं रसनम् । PPB.37-39

The constituent element water is of three kinds viz. body, sense-organ and matter. The body which is not organically born (*ayonija*) lies in Varuṇa's region. The sense organ is the tongue created by the constituents, untainted of water which is characterised by taste.

43. विषयस्तु सरित्समुद्रहिमकरकादिरिति । PPB.40

The matter (of water element) exists in rivers, sea, ice, etc.

44. शुक्लमधुरशीता एव रूपरसस्पर्शाः । PPB.36

The colour, taste and touch (of water element) are white, sweet and cold (respectively).

45. रूप-रस-स्पर्श-द्रवत्व-स्नेह-सङ्ख्या-परिमाण-पृथक्त्व-संयोग-विभाग-परत्व-अपरत्व-गुरुत्व-संस्कारवत्यः ।
PPB.34

The water element has the qualities viz. colour, taste, touch, fluidity, viscidity, number, magnitude, distance, proximity, conjunction, disjunction, gravity and faculty of impression.

46. अपां संयोगाभावे गुरुत्वात् पतनम् । VS. 5.2.3

The falling of water results from weight in the absence of conjunction.

47. अपां संयोगविभागाच्च स्तनयित्नोः । VS. 5.2.11

The rolling of thunder results from conjunction with water, disjunction from a cloud.

48. शुक्लं भास्वरं च रूपम् । उष्ण एव स्पर्शः । PPB.43

Its colour is white and bright. Its touch is hot (तद्रूपं तेजस एव । Therefore colour is the quality of fire only).

49. तदपि द्विविधमणुकार्यभावात् । कार्यं च शरीरादित्रयम् । PPB.44

That (element of fire) also is of two kinds viz. atomic and constituent.
As a product it is of three kinds such as body and others.

50. शरीरमयोनिजमादित्यलोके । PPB.45

The body, not organically born, lies in the Sun's region.

51. इन्द्रियं सर्वप्राणिनां रूपव्यञ्जकं अन्यावयवानभिभूतैः तेजोऽवयवैरारब्धं चक्षुः । PPB.46

The sense organ of all animals which manifests colour is the eye, unaffected by any defect, created by the constituents of fire.

52. विषयसंज्ञकं चतुर्विधम् – भौमं दिव्यमौदर्यमाकरजं च । PPB.47

The matters of fire element are, (i) earthly; (ii) heavenly; (iii) stomachic; and (iv) mineral.

53. तत्र भौमं काष्ठेन्धनप्रभवमूर्ध्वज्वलनस्वभावं पचन-दहन-स्वेदनादिसमर्थं च, दिव्यमबिन्धनं सौरविद्युदादि ।

भुक्तस्याहारस्य रसादिपरिणामार्थमुदर्यम् । आकरजं सुवर्णादि । PPB.47

The earthly (fire-element) has the nature of upward flame born of the wood; it is capable of digesting, burning and perspiring (in the animals).
The heavenly fire having water for fuel comprises the lightning and solar fire and such other (celestial lights).
The stomachic fire consists in changing (digesting) the food taken into digested food (*rasa*).
The element of fire in the mines is gold and others.

54. रूप-स्पर्श-सङ्ख्या-परिमाण-पृथक्त्व-संयोग-विभाग-परत्व-अपरत्व-द्रवत्व-संस्कारवत् (तेज:)   PPB.41

The element of fire has the following qualities; colour, touch, number, dimension, separateness, conjunction, disjunction, distance, proximity, fluidity, faculty of impression.

55. स चाऽयं द्विविधोऽणुकार्यभावात् । PPB.50

Air also is of two kinds viz. the atomic form and constituent form.

56. तत्र कार्यलक्षणश्चतुर्विध: शरीरमिन्द्रियं विषय: प्राण इति । PPB.51

The constituent air element is four-fold: The body, the sense organ, the matter and the vital breath.

57. तत्रायोनिजमेव शरीरं मरुतां लोके पार्थिवावयवोपष्टम्भाच्चोपभोगसमर्थम् । PPB.52

The body of the element of air lies in the region of maruts, being not born organically. Since it is the supporter of the constituents of the earth it is an object of use/experience.

58. इन्द्रियं सर्वप्राणिनां स्पर्शोपलम्भकं, पृथिव्याद्यनभिभूतैर्वाय्ववयवैरारब्धं शरीरव्यापि त्वगिन्द्रियम् । PPB.53

The sense organ of air (*vāyu*) of all the animals is the tactile organ, constituted by the constituents of air un-affected by the elements like earth, extending all over the body.

59. विषयस्तूपलभ्यमानस्पर्शाधिष्ठानभूत: स्पर्शशब्दधृतिकम्पलिङ्ग: । PPB.54

The matter of the element air is cognised being the substratum of touch experience and is marked (liṅga) by the touch, sound, sustenance and movement.

(Udayana : वायु: प्रत्यक्ष:, उपलभ्यमानस्पर्शाधिष्ठानत्वात् घटवदिति ।

(Udayana argues that air is perceptible.)
Vāyu is perceptible because it is the substratum for the experience of touch like a pitcher.

60. प्राणोऽन्त:शरीरे रसमलधातूनां प्रेरणादिहेतुरेक: सन् क्रियाभेदादपानादिसंज्ञां लभते । PPB.56

Air element which moves inside the body to promote the digestion of food and faces although one, acquires names such as *apāna* and others depending on its function.

61. तिर्यग्गमनस्वभावो मेघादिप्रेरणधारणासमर्थ: । PPB.54

(The earth element) has the nature of moving across and it is capable of moving and carrying the clouds.

62. सोऽपि सावयविनोर्वाय्वोरूर्ध्वगमनेनानुमीयते; तदपि तृणादिगमनेन । PPB.55

When two constituent airs collide they go upwards (a phenomena, although not perceived) is inferred. They lift (light things) like straw etc. upward (leading to such inference).

63. स्पर्शसङ्ख्याचापरिमाणपृथक्त्वसंयोगविभागपरत्वापरत्वसंस्कारवान् ।   PPB.48

(The element of air) has the qualities, viz. touch, number, dimension, separateness, conjunction, disjunction, distance, proximity and faculty of impression.

64. आकाशकालदिशामेकैकत्वादपरजात्यभावे पारिभाषिक्यस्तिस्रो संज्ञा भवन्ति । PPB.60

Ākāśa, Time and space are one each as there is no generality applicable to them. (In the absence of generality) the words, per se, define the objects

विभववचनात्परममहत्परिमाणम् । PPB.63

Because the word, *Vibhava* (all-pervading) is used in the sūtra (VS.7.1.22), it is all-pervading.

65. श्रोत्रं पुन: श्रवणविवरसंज्ञको नभोदेश: । PPB.66

The *ākāśa* region lies in the hollow region of the ear.

66. तत्राकाशस्य गुणा: शब्दसंख्यापरिमाणपृथक्त्वसंयोगविभागा: । PPB.61

The qualities of *ākāśa* are sound, number, magnitude, separateness, conjunction and disjunction.

67. रूपरसगन्धस्पर्शा: सङ्ख्या: परिमाणानि पृथक्त्वं संयोगविभागौ परत्वापरत्वे बुद्धि: सुखदु:खेच्छाद्वेषौ प्रयत्नाश्च गुणा: । VS. 1.1.6

Colour, taste, smell, touch, numbers, dimensions, separateness, conjunction and disjunction, distance and proximity, intellect, pleasure and pain, desire and hate, effort; these are attributes.

68. गुणा: रूपरसगन्धस्पर्शसङ्ख्याचापरिमाणपृथक्त्वसंयोगविभागपरत्वापरत्व-बुद्धिसुखदु:खेच्छाद्वेषप्रयत्नाश्चेति कणादोक्ता: सप्तदश । च शब्दसमुच्चिताश्च गुरुत्वद्रवत्वस्नेहसंस्काराद्दृष्टशब्दा: इत्येव चतुर्विंशतिर्गुणा: । PPB.5

The *Sūtrakāra* (Kaṇāda) has categorically stated that the qualities are seventeen, viz. colour, taste, smell, touch, number, magnitude, separateness, conjunction, disjunction, distance, proximity, intellect, pleasure, pain, desire, aversion and effort. But the word 'and' (*ca*), the total of attributes enumerated will be twenty-four viz. gravity, fluidity, viscidity, impression, fate (*dharma* and *adharma*), and sound.

69. रूपादीनां गुणानां सर्वेषां गुणत्वाभिसम्बन्धो द्रव्याश्रितत्वं निर्गुणत्वं निष्क्रियत्वम् । PPB.83

All the attributes such as colour are inherently connected with the genus of attribution. Substances are their substrates. They do not have quality of their own. The attributes have no motion.

70. पुनश्च धातुभेदेन चतुर्विंशतिक: स्मृत: । मनो दशेन्द्रियाण्यर्था: प्रकृतिश्चाष्टधातुकी ॥

Again from division of constituents (*dhātu*) Puruṣa is known as possessing twenty four entities as : mind, ten sense-organs, five sense objects, and Prakṛti consisting of eight entities (*avyakta, mahat, ahaṅkāra* and five elements). 1.1.51 *Caraka saṃhitā*

71. खादीनि बुद्धिरव्यक्तमहङ्कारस्तथाष्टम: । भूतप्रकृतिरुद्दिष्टा विकाराश्चैव षोडश ॥ *Caraka saṃhitā* 4.1.63-65

Ākāśa etc. (the five elements), *buddhi* (intellect-mahat), *avyakta* (the un-manifest primordial nature), and *ahaṅkāra* (ego), the eighth one, constitute the original source of creation (*bhūta-prakṛti*).

Note : *Ākāśa* etc. refer to the five subtle elements.

72. बुद्धीन्द्रियाणि पञ्चैव पञ्चकर्मेन्द्रियाणि च । समनस्काश्च पञ्चार्था विकारा इति संज्ञिता: ॥ op. cit.

The *vikāra-s* (modifications products) are sixteen, viz. five sense-organs, five motor-organs, the mind and five objects of senses (*bhūta-s*).

The word *artha* means, the objects of perception, entities of the physical world.

73. तत्राश्रिताः कर्मगुणाः कारणं समवायि यत् । तद्द्रव्यं समवायी तु निश्चेष्टं कारणं गुणः ॥ op. cit.

Substance is that where actions and properties are located and which is the material cause of its effect; *guṇa* is related with inherence to *dravya*; it is devoid of action; it is non-inherent cause of its effect.

74. जायते बुद्धिरव्यक्तादुबुद्धयाहमिति मन्यते । परं खादीन्यहङ्कारादुत्पद्यन्ते यथक्रमम् ॥ ततः संपूर्णसर्वाङ्गो जातोऽभ्युदित उच्यते। op. cit. 4.1.66-67

From the unmanifest, the intellect evolves, ego arises out of intellect and the five *bhūta-s* originate from ego in their respective order. Thus evolved and complete with all the organs, the person is born or is said as emerged.

75. शुक्रशोणितं गर्भाशयस्थं आत्मप्रकृतिः । तं चेतनावस्थितं वायुर्विभजति । तेज एनं पचति । आपः क्लेदयति । पृथिवी संहन्ति । आकाशं विवर्धयति । विकारसंमूर्छनं गर्भ इत्युच्यते । *Su.saṃ.* 3.5.3

The life principle is the semen and blood which exist in the embryo. Air gives shape to the foetus in the energetic principle. Heat maintains temperature. Water element provides fluidity. The Earth element hardens it. *Ākāśa* allows it to grow. This process of change is called the womb.

76. खादयश्चेतनाषष्ठा धातवः पुरुषः स्मृतः । चेतनाधातुरप्येकः स्मृतः पुरुषसंज्ञकः ॥

The aggregate of five *mahābhūta-s* and consciousness as the sixth one is known as Puruṣa. Consciousness alone is known also as Puruṣa. *Ca.saṃ.* 4.1.16

77. प्रलयात्यये सिसृक्षुर्भूतान्यक्षरभूत आत्मा सत्त्वोपादानः पूर्वतरं आकाशं सृजति, ततः क्रमेण व्यक्ततरगुणान् धातून् वाय्वादिकांश्चतुरः । तथा देहग्रहणेऽपि प्रवर्तमानः पूर्वमाकाशमेवोपादत्ते । 4.4.8

As the underlying self with a desire to create the being as the end of final destruction creates, with the psyche as the instrument, first of all, *ākāśa*; and, there after gradually the other four elements, viz. vāyu etc. which have more manifest qualities. At the time of putting on the body also. He takes up *ākaśa* as the first.

78. Gopinath B. G.: 'Foundational Ideas of Āyurveda' in *Medicine and Life Sciences*, (Ed) B. V. Subbarayappa, p. 73.

79. op.cit. p. 74 ff.

80. तस्य गुणाः शब्दादयः गुर्वादयश्च द्रवान्ताः, कर्म पञ्चविधमुक्तं वमनादि ।

Its properties are sound etc. and those from guru to *drava*, and its action has been said as five-fold *vamana* etc. (Ca.saṃ.1-26-10)

तत्र द्रव्याणि गुरु, खर, कठिन, मन्द, स्थिर, विशद, सान्द्र, स्थूल, गन्ध, गुण-बहुलानि पार्थिवानि, तानि उपचयसङ्घातगौरवस्थैर्यकराणि; द्रव-स्निग्ध, शीत, मन्द, मृदु, पिच्छल, रस, गुण-बहुलान्याप्यानि, तानि उपक्लेद, स्नेह, बन्ध, निष्यन्द, मार्दव, प्रह्लादकराणि; उष्ण, तीक्ष्ण, सूक्ष्म, लघु, रूक्ष, विशद, रूप, गुण-बहुलानि आग्नेयानि, तानि दाह, पाक, प्रभा, प्रकाश, वर्ण-कराणि; लघु, शीत, रूक्ष, खर, विशद, सूक्ष्म, स्पर्श-गुणबहुलानि वायव्यानि, तानि रौक्ष्य, ग्लानि, विचार, वैशद्य, लाघवकराणि; मृदु, लघु, सूक्ष्म, श्लक्ष्ण, शब्द, गुणबहुलानि आकाशात्मकानि, तानि मार्दव, सौषिर्य, लाघवकराणि ।

(Drugs) *Dravyas* which are predominant in properties of heavy, course, hard, dull, stable, non-slimy, solid, gross and smell are *Pārthiva* (constituted predominantly by *Pṛthivībhūta*). They exert actions like development, compactness, heaviness and firmness.

Those predominant in properties of liquid, unctuous, cold, dull, soft, slimy and taste are *āpya* (constituted predominantly by *apbhūta*). They exert actions like moistening, unition, binding, oozing, softening and exhilaration.

Dravya-s predominant in properties of hot, sharp, minute, light, rough, non-slimy and vision are *āgneya* (constituted predominantly by *agni-tejas bhūta*). They produce heat, digestion, lustre, light and complexion.

Those predominant in properties of light, cold, rough, coarse, non-slimy, minute and touch are *vāyavya* (constituted predominantly by *vāyubhūta*). They produce actions of roughness, depression, movement, non-sliminess, and lightness.

Dravya-s having predominance in the properties of soft, light, minute, smooth and sound are *ākāśya* (constituted predominantly by *ākāśa bhūta*). They exert action of softening, hollowing and lightness.

81. तेषां षण्णां रसानां सोमरसातिरेकान्मधुरो रसः, पृथिव्यग्निभूयिष्ठत्वादाम्लः, सलिलाग्निभूयिष्ठत्वाल्लवणः, वाय्वग्निभूयिष्ठत्वात् कटुकः, वाय्वाकाशातिरिक्तत्वात् तिक्तः, पवनपृथिवी व्यतिरेकात् कषाय इति ।   1.26.40

Of the six rasas, *madhura* (sweet) is produced from the dominance of Soma (water), *āmla* by that of *Pṛthivī* and *Agni*, *lavaṇa* by that of *Ap* and *Agni*; *kaṭu* by that of *Vāyu* and *Agni*; *tikta* by that of *Vāyu* and *Ākāśa;* and *kaṣāya* by that of *Vāyu* and *Pṛthivī.*

82. Rahman, Zillur: 'Unani Medicine in India', its *Origin and Fundamental Concepts'* in *Medicine and Life Sciences in India*, pp. 272-325.

83. Subbarayappa, B. V.: 'Siddha Medicine: An Overview', *Lancet*, **350**, 20-27, Dec, 1997, pp. 1841-44.

84. *Mānameyodaya*, p. 153.

85. Aristotle's *Metaphysics*, quoted by Singer, *A Short History of Science*, p. 32.

86. Needham, J.: *Science and Civilization in China*, Vol. II, p. 244.

87. Ibid, p. 239.

88. Ibid, p. 249.

89. *Ch. up.* VII.12.1; 1.9.1

90. *Ch. up.* VII.12.1-2

91. Guthrie, W. K. C.: *A History of Greek Philosophy*, 1962, pp. 128ff.

92. *Ch. up.* IV.3; *Br. up.* I. 5.12

93. Guthrie, op. cit. pp. 454-64.

94. RV. I.1.1

CHAPTER 4

Substance, Qualities and Motion

WHAT IS SUBSTANCE or the world-stuff or world-ground? This enigmatic question engaged the attention of thinkers over a long period in all ancient cultures. The elusive problem, the problem of ONE in MANY or ONE BECOMING MANY, was of fundamental importance to their wide and varied speculative endeavours. However, their world-view was not generally the one which was not exclusive of man, the knower himself. Thus there was an integration in one form or the other of the knower and the known, man and the world, and of the individual spirit and the cosmic spirit. In its earlier phase, this man–spirit–cosmos view, as noted before, that was prevalent in different culture-areas often in an esoteric mould, was inexorably mixed up with certain mythological elements. Gradually it attempted to free itself from such elements and began to acquire a philosophical foundation, the theological and ontological ideas notwithstanding.

Indian philosophical inquiry concerning the universal principle Brahman and Ātman has been dealt with already. This approach, it may be reiterated, transcended the conception of the basic substance of the knowable physical world through our senses, and was generally spiritual in character. There was, however, one philosophical system, the Vaiśeṣika and later the syncretic Nyāya-Vaiśeṣika that tried to look at the reality in a different perspective in a pluralistic but holistic manner. It has so happened that the spiritual approach specially of the Vedānta has established a continuity of its own over the centuries, while the Nyāya-Vaiśeṣika concept of reality has almost become a thing of the past except that it has some place as a discipline in academic institutions, as a system that merits some attention while studying the other systems of Indian thought.

The Vaiśeṣika model

The Vaiśeṣika has attempted to understand the world of matter, qualities and motion under six or seven categories or *padārtha-s* as follows:

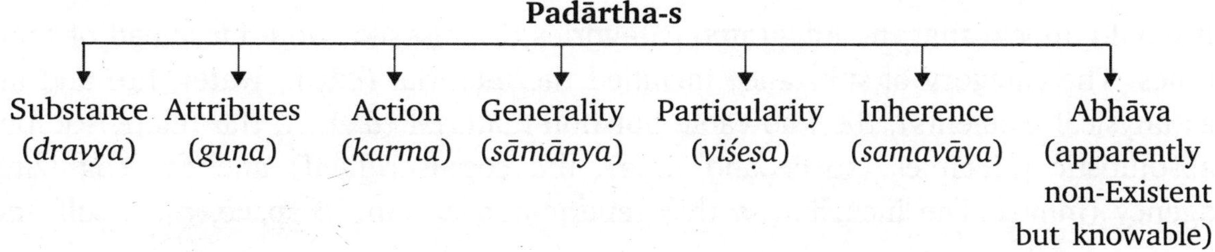

Their knowledge, it has been stated, leads one to the attainment of the highest good.[1]

The word '*padārtha*' means generally 'the meaning of word'; but in the Vaiśeṣika context it has the connotation of 'the object signified by a word',[2] and that all objects of knowledge (they are also reals) come under the umbrella of this term. The first six are known as the *bhāva padārtha-s* (being) and the seventh one is called *abhāva* (non-being) literally meaning apparently non-existing but knowable. The importance of this idea of *abhāva* lies in the recognition, as a logical necessity, of the possible counter-entity as it were for every knowable object. Hence it is regarded as real as the *bhāva padārtha-s*. According to Kumārila and his followers, the idea of negation is intuitive with reference to the object and it does not have ordinary cognition or *pramāṇa* to prove the existence of such a thing. From the point of view of syllogism, the concept of *abhāva* helped greatly the process of reasoning in the analytical interpretation of reality.[3]

The characteristics of a *padārtha* are: (i) its existence (*astitva*), nameabilitiy (*abhidheyatva*) and knowability (*jñeyatva*).[4] According to Kaṇāda, the propounder of the Vaiśeṣika, all types of knowledge indicate that there is an object independent of it and even beyond.[5] Significantly, the Vaiśeṣika categories relate to all the knowables that are regarded as real. Though they appear to be metaphysical, they deal with some physical entities of which the Vaiśeṣika concept of substance (*dravya*) is the most important one. The generic category of *dravya* comprises the five elements (*pṛthivī, ap, tejas, vāyu* and *ākāśa*), space (*diś*), time (*kāla*), the knower (self or *ātmā*) and mind (*manas*); each one of them is considered as substance also, it being inherent in the 'substanceness'.[6]

These nine under the first category of *dravya,* and the other five *padārtha-s,* have been conceived in such a manner that their knowledge would lead to an understanding of the reality or the world-stuff. It will be noted that the doctrine of five elements is an inseparable part of the generic substance itself.

The following schematic diagram (see next page) presents the analytical, but integrated, approach of the Vaiśeṣika towards matter in its twin aspects—the eternal and the non-eternal.

The Vaiśeṣika Substance

It would appear that the integrated categories of Vaiśeṣika were far ahead of their times. The category of substance included the material (earth, water, fire and air as physical elements), the knowable but non-material (*ākāśa*), the relativistic but absolutistic principles (space and time), the cogniser (self) and the cognizing agency (mind). The inclusion in this generic conception, of space, time, self and

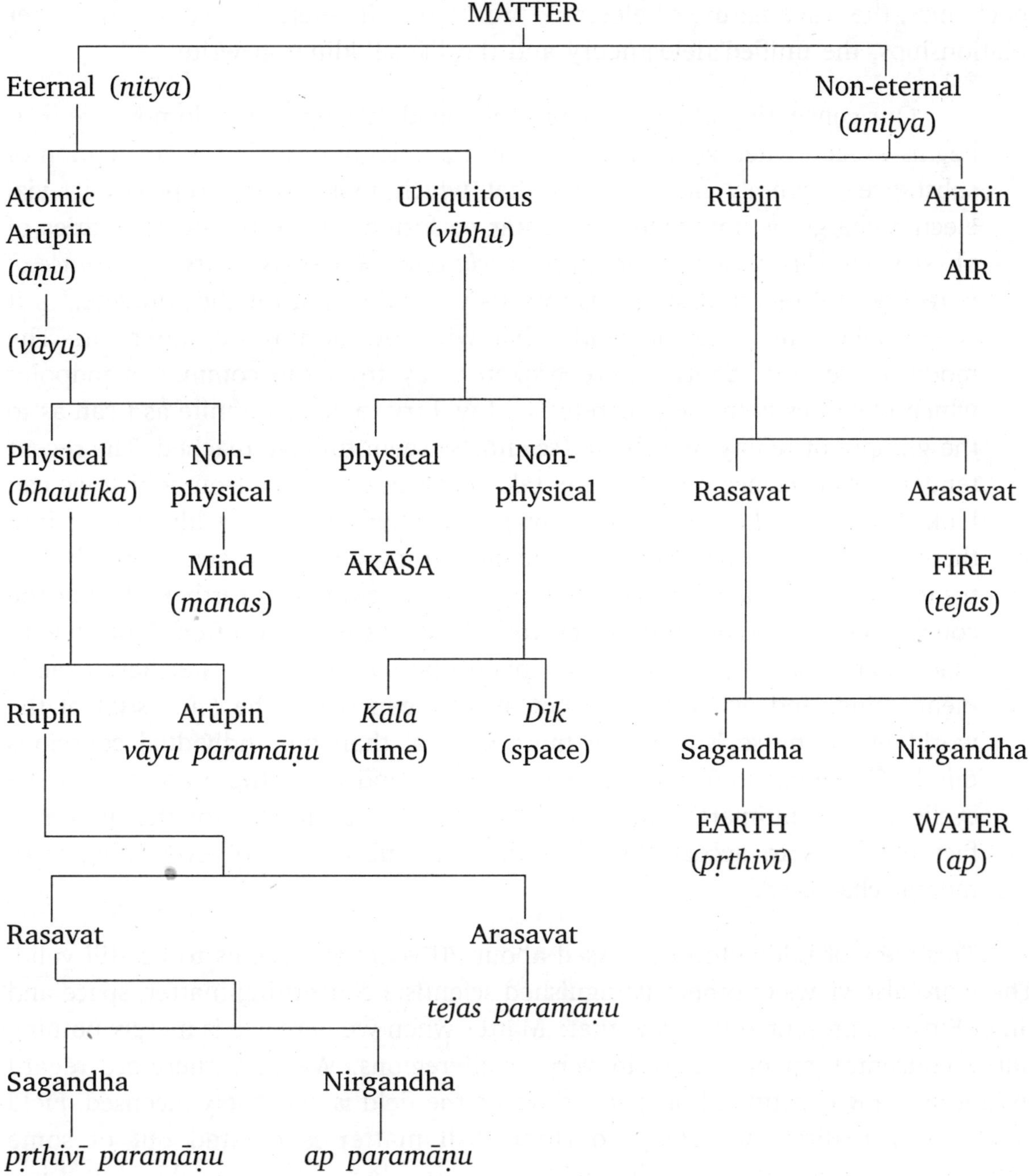

(**Source:** *Conception of Matter according to Nyāya-Vaiśeṣika*, U. Mishra, p. 56.).

mind is of seminal significance even from the standpoint of the advances made in modern theoretical physics. For, the question: What is substance? has remained still unresolved in modern science. This is evidenced by the vicissitudes and conceptual modifications through which the problems of matter and energy have passed from the last quarter of the nineteenth century to the present, namely, the law of conservation of mass, that of energy, the fundamental particles, quantum mechanics, the wave nature of electron, principle of indeterminacy, energy-matter relationships, the unified field theory and the like. Eddington writes:

> 'Our conception of substance is only vivid as long as we do not face it. It begins to fade when we analyse it..... In the scientific world the conception of substance is wholly lacking, and that which most nearly replaces it, viz. electric charge, is not exalted as a star performer above the other entities of physics. *For this reason the scientific world often shocks us by its appearance of unreality.* It offers nothing to us to satisfy our demand for the concrete...... It is not solely the scientific world that will now occupy our attention. The modern scientific theories have broken away from the common standpoint which identifies with the concrete....... I will try to be as definite as I can as to the glimpse of reality, which we (scientists) seem to have reached. The recent tendencies of science do, I believe, take us to an eminence from which we can look down into the deep waters of philosophy; and if I rashly plunge into them, it is not because I have confidence in my powers of swimming, but to try to show that the water is really deep'. Eddington adds further: 'To put the conclusion crudely the stuff of the world is *mind stuff*. As is often the way with crude statements, I shall have to explain that by 'mind' I do not here exactly mean mind, and by 'stuff' I do not at all mean stuff. The *mind stuff* of the world is, of course, something more general than our individual conscious minds. The *mind stuff* is not spread in space and time; these are part of the cyclic scheme ultimately derived out of it...... It is difficult for the matter of fact physicists to accept the view that the substratum of everything is of mental character'.[7]

This view of Eddington expressed about 70 years ago seems to be still valid. There are also views of other distinguished scientists concerning matter, space and time: Einstein presented the view that: 'Matter when we perceive is merely nothing but a concentration of energy in very small regions. We may therefore regard matter as being constituted of space in which the field is extremely incensed. Field is the only reality'. According to Dirac: 'All matter is created out of some imperceptible substratum. Nothingness; unimaginable and undetectable. But it is a peculiar form of nothing out of which all matter is created'. Steven Weinberg states: 'At the present level of understanding they seem to be all elementary fields. They are highly simple because they are governed by symmetries. These are not objects with which we are not familiar. In fact our ordinary *intuitive notions* (emphasis added) of space, time and causation, substance and so on really lose meaning on that scale'. Another postulate is that 'vacuum' is all of 'physics' and all things that existed or can exist is present potentially in the nothingness of space.[8]

Such assertions as these point out the enigmatic nature of reality or substance or the world-stuff. Modern science has been endeavouring to unravel this enigma more with mathematical models involving specially quantum mechanics with some observable experiments. The Big Bang concept does, however, explain most of the observed phenomenon of matter and energy, but modern cosmology is still unable to shed light on how the primordial or the "world-stuff" came into being.

In general, scientific methodology takes cognizance of the 'observables' or the sensorial data and the associated causal mechanism; the unobservables even at some stage or the other, in one form or the other, need to be understood, verified, reproduced or even falsified. In the scientific approach, the observational procedure, in the name of objectivity, excludes the observer, the participant in the whole process. The exclusion of the subjective element (i.e., the complex involving the motion of 'I', mind, senses, nerve impulses, brain functions and such other determinants involved in every inch of observation) seems to have come in the way of arriving at a definite conclusion regarding the substance or world-stuff. The Vaiśeṣika, it may be noted, has included in its conceptual presentation of substance, the self and mind, considering their role in observation and experience, and making some distinction between the two in respect of their attributes.

According to Vaiśeṣika, self has the following attributes: cognition, pleasure, pain, desire, aversion, effort, virtue and vice, faculty, number, dimension, distinctness, conjunction and disjunction. The Nyāya (Sūtra. I. 1.10) avers that these are the probans to prove the existence of *ātman,* since these attributes cannot exist without a substratum which can only be *ātman.* Śaṅkara Miśra, in his *Upaskāra*[9] thinks, and rightly so, that the motion or the cognition of the expression, 'I', refers to one's own *ātman* through the instrumentality of mind, but evidently not to one's physical body. Praśastapāda (*PPB.* 99, 69-70) adduces some commonsensical arguments like the functioning of vital airs in an organism, involuntary actions such as the opening and closing of eye-lids and the like, to prove the existence of *ātman,* the conscious agent. The Vaiśeṣika, nevertheless, also believes in the plurality of self—as many *jīvātman-s*—as there are living beings. But, at the same time, it accepts the existence of the Highest Self or God (*Maheśvara*) or *Paramātman.* On the other hand, the attributes of minds are: number, dimension, distinctness, conjunction, disjunction, priority, posteriority and faculty. It is important to note that the Vaiśeṣika considers mind as corporeal and even atomic. In fact in Indian thought generally there is no duality, like the Cartesian, between mind and matter. The Vaiśeṣika model of substance inclusive of self and mind, though speculative, has its own originality.

It is significant to note that the Vaiśeṣika has conceived of matter as something that does not possess consciousness and associated psychic potentials as well as their manifestations. Alongside, however, it has realized the seminal role of the conscious agent, *ātman*, in the totality of reality. In its scheme under *dravya*, therefore, apart from the conscious agent, it has explained eight aspects namely, the four *bhūtas* (*pṛthvī, ap, tejas* and *vāyu*); those involved in the process of creation, i.e., *ākaśa* and *kāla* (time) along with an entity of relative positions namely, *dik* (space) and more importantly, *manas* or mind which, of course, is intimately associated with self. The Vaiśeṣika also firmly believes in the consciousness of the Universe as a whole. It further believes that consciousness and the knowable matter are inseparable. It is not insignificant that modern science is also thinking of the nature of consciousness vis-à-vis the nature of the universe itself.

Views of Plato and Aristotle

It may be desirable, indeed necessary, to have at least a bird's eye view of some Greek concepts, specially of Plato and Aristotle, as that would throw some light by way of contrast, on the originality of the Vaiśeṣika categories. We have seen in the preceding chapter the origin and ramifications of the Indian doctrine of five elements and its philosophical context. A reference to the origin and nature of the Greek as well as the Chinese five elements has also been made in comparison. Around the time of appearance of the *Vaiśeṣika sūtra-s*, perhaps a century later, Athens was an intellectually active center (*c.* 400-300 B.C.), the towering thinkers there being Plato (pupil of Socrates) and Aristotle (pupil of Plato). Plato (427-347 B.C.) was well known for his *Doctrine of Ideas* and he regarded ideas of the mind as being more concrete than the percepts of the material word. On the Platonic 'idea' which by its nature would be divorced from matter, Aristotle in his *Metaphysics* writes:

> In his youth Plato became familiar with the doctrine of certain philosophers that all things perceived by the senses are even in a state of flux and there is no knowledge concerning them (Heraclitus). To these views he held even in later years. His reason was that there could be no real definition of things perceived by the senses because they were always changing. Those things that alone could be defined, he called *Ideas*, and things perceived by the senses, he said, were different from those *Ideas* and were all called after them.[10]

Plato repudiated the atomic views of Democritus and Leucippus who denied the existence of mind, the seat of *Ideas*, as a separate entity, and its attachment to phenomena or sensorial percepts. Plato was an accomplished mathematician with leanings towards Pythagoreans. To Plato, mathematical principles also had a special appeal. To him 'God was a Geometer' and mathematics, 'the portal to philosophy'.

It is even said that 'such works as Euclid's *Elements* is in essence a product of Plato's thought and of Plato's school. It is certainly no overstatement that, 'through Euclid, every schoolboy nowadays is a student of Plato'.[11] In his *Timaeus*, Plato projected the idea of the Universe as a living one with a 'soul' and this Platonic vision of the Universe led the neo-Platonics to conceive the intimate relation between macrocosm and microcosm.

The *Ideas*, according to Plato, would be the goal of any intellectual activity and, through intellectual analysis and synthesis could one arrive at a knowledge that the *Ideas* exist and are as real as universals. In the dialogue called *Phaedrus*, Plato states that a man must have intelligence of universals, and be able to proceed from the many particulars of the sense to one conception of reason.

Aristotle (384-322 B.C.) who established a school called the *Peripatetic* (Greek: walking around while lecturing) school in his garden known as Lyceum, during his sojourn in Athens for twelve years before his death, was in essence a naturalist. He also thought of the relation between living beings and 'Physics', which then for him was a general description of the universe. Although he was not strictly an evolutionist, he arranged different kinds of animate and inanimate ones in a series which came later to be known as Aristotle's 'Ladder of Nature'.[12] He was also a vitalist as well as teleologist and was opposed to the mechanical conceptions of Greek atomists and others. He believed in three forms of soul: (i) vegetative; (ii) animal (both (i) and (ii) being lower forms); and (iii) rational or conscious soul (higher) that characterizes human being.

To Aristotle, celestial bodies and the terrestrial ones were different. He subscribed to the Empedoclean theory of four elements, but added the fifth one, *Ether*, that would be peculiar to the celestial bodies. He emphasized that circular movements would be perfect and also that stars and planets move with uniform circular velocity in spheres, centered round the Earth. This geocentric picture of the universe and the associated circular movements held sway over astronomers, the Church leaders and others for nearly 2000 years till the time of Kepler who demolished the idea of circular movement of planets and instead scientifically established their elliptical orbits.

As for matter, Aristotle expounded that it was the *actuality* of form, and, as for motion, his view was that bodies would fall with velocities proportional to their weights and inversely proportional to the densities of the media through which they fall to the ground. He regarded that matter was not totally formless and that which was totally formless could not exist at all. He thought that matter was either unformed or partially formed. He called the Pure Form, God. In Aristotle's view, forms were immanent in nature more than transcendent, and his conception of God was entirely different, not as a Creator but as a cause of all movements in the world, He being unmoved, thus a Supreme Cause. The metaphysical God of

Aristotle was in the nature of a logical postulate to account for the existence and changes in the perceived world. Aristotle maintained that the contemplation of eternal truth or reality should be the highest goal of human intellect amidst the natural objects and occurrences. He tried to categorise these in his own logical way either in his scheme of the 'Ladder of Nature' or in his concentric picture of the universe. In any case, neither the pre-Socratic thinkers nor Plato and Aristotle appeared to have attempted to develop a model that would be viable enough for understanding the knowable world, apart from their unitary approach, however lofty it was. The Vaiśeṣika model, on the other hand, seems to be the first of its type in the history of scientific ideas, specially its all-inclusive concept of substance.

Qualities

The second category of the Vaiśeṣika model is *guṇa* or quality. Kaṇāda, as pointed out before, enunciated 17 qualities, while his scholiast but an original thinker, Praśastapāda, added seven more,[13] elaborated upon them perhaps in the context of the particle *ca* in the related *Vaiśeṣika sūtra*[14] The *Bhāṣāpariccheda*[15] a later work, echoes these twenty-four qualities as being 17+7.[16]

It may be reiterated that the 24 qualities of the Vaiśeṣika are: colour, taste, smell, touch, numbers, extension, individuality, conjunction and disjunction, priority and posteriority, intellection, pleasure and pain, desire, aversion, and volitions. Commenting on the word 'ca' of the *Sūtra, Praśastapāda* has added seven more, namely, (i) gravitation; (ii) fluidity; (iii) viscidity; (iv) tendency; (v) *dharma* (virtue); (vi) *adharma* (vice); and (vii) sound. He has also given succinct definitions of these qualities as follows: (see for original passages under References).

The 24 attributes together constitute the second category of the Vaiśeṣika and each of the nine substances has its attributes as shown in the following table (p. 115).

It is significant to observe that the five generic attributes *number, dimension, distinctness, conjunction* and *disjunction* are common to all the nine substances. These attributes are of fundamental importance to the Nyāya-Vaiśeṣika for a proper elucidation of its general approach to reality.

Colour: It is apprehended only by the sense organ eye. It exists or resides in three elements, viz. earth, water and light or fire and is of several kinds such as white and others. It is permanent in the atoms of substances like water atom, but is destroyed in the earth atoms in conjunction with heat or subjected to the action heat, and is destroyed when its substrates are destroyed.[17]

In this context, Śrīdhara adds that the substance is first destroyed and then the disjunction of the colour follows.[18]

Table
Different types of substances and their attributes

pṛithivī	*ap*	*tejas*	*vāyu*	*ākāśa*	*kāla*	*dik*	*ātman*	*manas*
eternal in atomic state corporeal principle of olfactory organ	eternal in atomic state corporeal principle of gustatory organ	eternal in atomic stage corporeal principle of visual organ	eternal in atomic state corporeal principle of tactile organ	eternal and one ubiquitous principle of auditory organ	eternal and one ubiquitous	eternal and one ubiquitous	eternal and one ubiquitous	eternal and one ubiquitous
specific quality **odour**	specific quality **taste**	specific quality- **colour**	specific quality- **touch**	specific quality- **sound**				
14 qualities; colour, taste, odour, touch, number, dimension, distinctness, conjunction, disjunction, distance, proximity, gravity, fluidity and faculty	14 qualities; colour, taste, touch, number, distinctness, dimension, conjunction, disjunction, distance, proximity, gravity, viscidity, fluidity and faculty	11 qualities; colour, touch, number, dimension, distinctness, conjunction, disjunction, distance, proximity, fluidity and faculty	9 qualities: touch, number, dimension, distinctness, conjunction, disjunction, proximity, distance and faculty	6 qualities: sound, number, dimension, distinctness, conjunction and disjunction	5 qualities: number, dimension, distinctness, conjunction and disjunction	5 qualities: number, dimension, distinctness, conjunction and disjunction	14 qualities: cognition, pleasure, pain, desire, aversion, effort, virtue, vice, faculty, number, dimension, distinctness, conjunction and disjunction	8 qualities: number, dimension, distinctness, conjunction, disjunction, priority, posteriority and faculty

Taste: The quality which is apprehended by the tongue is taste, that exists in two elements or substances—earth and water. It is stated to be the cause of life, nutrition, strength and health. The taste is of six kinds, viz., sweet, sour, salty, bitter, pungent and astringent (cf. six tastes of the Āyurveda); and it supports the organ of taste in their perception or experience. The eternality and non-eternality of taste are also similar to those of colour.[19]

Smell: It is the quality which is perceived by the sense organ of smell (nose) and exists only in the earth and plays a role in the assistance of nose for the experience of smell. It is of two kinds, fragrant and non-fragrant.[20]

Touch: The quality that is perceived by the sense organ of touch is tactile. It exists in earth, water, fire and air. It supports the perception of touch on the skin, and is of three kinds, viz., cold, hot and neither cold nor hot. Its eternality and non-eternality are similar to the aforesaid qualities.[21]

Number: The number exists in one or several substances where counting of one, two, etc., is involved. Of them the number that exists in one substance can be determined as eternal like the atom in water, and non-eternal as the constituent in water. The number that exists in many substances can range from two to *Parārdha* (10^{12}).[22]

Parimāṇa: The quality that can be employed for weighing or measuring, is called *Parimāna*, which is four-fold, atomic, large (*mahat*), long and short. Mahat is of two kinds; eternal and non-eternal. The eternal one lies in sky, time, space and self because they are supreme and all-pervading. The atomic one is also of two kinds: the eternal and the non-eternal. Between the two, the eternal atomic size, spherical as it is, relates to paramāṇu and mind. The non-eternal one is a constituent of dyad and through it of triad only.[23]

The eternality and non-eternity can be understood from the analogy of number, the difference being that in the case of number of *one-ness,* there is a comprehensive generality and non-comprehensive generality, but in the case of separateness (*pṛthaktva*) there is no non-comprehensive generality. Separateness can be cognized by means of number because the concepts of separateness emanates only from number.[24]

Conjunction: Conjunction, is that which brings in the conception of (two things) being conjuncted. This is also the cause of substance, quality and action. For example, conjunction of threads is the cause of the substance (say cloth), the conjunction of drum and sky is the cause of the quality of sound, While the conjunction of blowing air over a straw is the cause of movement (*karma*) in the straw.[25]

Conjunction is also the combination of two substances hitherto uncombined, and is of three kinds: (i) *anyatarakarmaja;* (ii) *ubhayakarmaja;* (iii) *saṃyogaja.*

The second one occurs when two moving objects moving in opposite directions collide, as in the case of two wrestlers or two rams (colliding with each other); the third and the last one is just produced or which was produced long time back is conjuncted with non constituent substances, like the yarn and shuttle.

Disjunction: Disjunction is that which gives rise to the conception, this is disjuncted from that. A disjunction is also that which is preceded by conjunction. It is the cause of sound. Like conjunction, disjunction is also of three kinds: (i) *anyatarakarmajaḥ*; (ii) *ubhayakarmajaḥ*; and (iii) *vibhāgakarmajaḥ*. Of them, the first two occur like in the case of conjunction only.[26]

Priority and Posteriority: 'This is temporally (in time) or spatially (in space) prior to that; 'This is (temporally or spatially)[27] posterior to that'; these conceptions arise from the qualities of Priority and Posteriority.

This notion is of two kinds: Proximity and remoteness of space as well as proximity and remoteness of time. That which gives rise to the conception of space in particular is either spatial proximity or remoteness. That which gives rise to the immediate (present) or remoteness of age is temporal proximity or remoteness. They are placed together because each is complementary to the other. Whatever is a product, it is sure to perish. When the inherent, the non-inherent and the efficient causes get destroyed, proximity is also destroyed. The destruction of remoteness also can be construed in the same way.

The words, *buddhi* (intellect), *upalabdhi* (apprehension), *jñānam* (knowledge) and *pratyaya* (conception) are all synonymous (in epistemology). *Buddhi* is of different kinds, because it has infinite objects (to apprehend) and it has independent relation in each (of them). Although, broadly speaking, it has relations with infinite objects, it is of two kinds: *vidyā* and *avidyā*.[28]

Avidyā is four-fold: doubt, erroneous knowledge, indeterminate cognition and dream. *Vidyā* also is four-fold: perception, inference, memory and supra-human cognition. Puruṣa experiences the forms assumed by the intellect.

Akṣa means sense organ. They are six in all, viz. nose, tongue, eye, skin, ear and mind.[29]

Pleasure: Pleasure is that which gives pleasant experience. When the desired objects like necklace etc. are acquired, the knowledge of the desired object, the proximity of the contact between the mind and the soul dharma is stated to be born, resulting in the feeling of joy, love and the brightening of eyes, which is pleasure.[30]

Pain: That which gives unfavourable experience is *duḥkha* (pain) the proximity of undesirable things like poison, the contact of the sense organs with them, and the union of soul and mind due to *adharma* all these together bring pain. This results in intolerance, agony and helplessness.[31]

Desire: Desire is that (which one feels) when one longs or forays for a desired object for oneself or the others. This arises from the contact of the soul with the mind assisted by joy (or memory).[32]

Aversion: Aversion is that which has in it hatred, i.e., while it exists, an animal (or man), gets the feelings of hate. Aversion arises when the soul and mind are in contact as a result of pain or (painful) memory; but it is also the cause of volition, memory, *dharma* and *adharma*.[33]

Effort: Effort, activity and energy are synonyms, and it is of two kinds: those emanating from the desire or hatred. The contact between the soul and mind related to *dharma* and *adharma* is called life (*jīvana*).[34]

***Gravity* (Weight):** Gravity is that quality from which the vertical downward movement originates in earth and water. It is not perceivable, by any sense organ, but can be inferred by the falling action of the objects. Gravity acts against conjunction, volition and tendentions (movement), like the qualities of water, etc. which remain eternal or non-eternal depending on their substrates in their eternal or non-eternal forms, i.e. their atomic or constituent forms.[35] A javelin or an arrow does not fall because of the momentum.[36]

Fluidity: Fluidity is the cause of the action of flowing. It exists in three substances, viz. earth, water and fire. It is two-fold, natural and artificial. Natural fluidity is the unique quality of the water element, while the artificial fluidity is the ordinary quality of the two elements, earth and fire. The eternality or the non-eternality of fluidity is similar to gravity. Artificial fluidity can be observed (as a quality) in earth, and heat as a result of fire.[37]

Viscidity: This is a special quality that exists only in water. It is the cause of making solidity in objects or of making them thick. The quality of fluidity also has eternality or non-eternality as in the case of gravity.[38]

Saṃskāra: This is a process or an in-built tendency which is of three kinds, viz., velocity, impress, and elasticity.[39]

Among them, velocity arises due to movement being assisted by particular but efficient causes of only five substances viz. earth, water, heat and air. It is the real cause of chain of action in a particular direction. It gets destroyed when it is impeded by tangible substances. Quite often it is caused by the velocity already inherent in the substrate.

Bhāvanā: It is in the nature of a reminiscent impression and is also the cause of recognition of objects, and can be known through inference. Elasticity is the tendency that exists in objects which have the quality of touch, and get back to the original condition which is altered differently in its substance as a result of intense conjunction among its constituents in a particular time. The quality of elasticity (of bringing back to the original position) is observed among the sentient as well as non-sentient things like a bow, a branch, tooth, bone, thread and cloth when they are constrained to be in a bending condition. The eternity and non-eternity of this quality also can be inferred as in the case of gravity.

Dharma: Dharma is a quality of the soul.[40] It is effective for well-being and is also the liberating cause of the soul. It transcends all senses, and is destroyed by the ultimate joy and self-realisation. *Dharma* originates from (i) the combination of man and his mind, and (ii) his will or resolve. It consists in the actions (detailed in scriptures) or performance of those who are in varṇas and āśramas.

Substances, qualities and actions also assist in attaining general or particular *dharmas*.

Adharma: *Adharma* is also a quality of the soul.[41] It is the cause or the means for pain. It transcends sense organs, and is destroyed by self-realisation.

Sound: The special quality of the *ākāśa* is sound. It can be perceived from the sense organ, the ears. It can be produced from conjunction or disjunction, and it exists in some part of its substrate.[42] Ordinary sound is that of the touch. As a wave rises immediately after the earlier wave recedes, sound also appears in the sky following immediately another sound.

Though a quality subsists in a substance, it has been pointed out that it does not have the potential of being endowed with another or additional quality; more importantly, it does not become an independent cause with regard to conjunction and disjunction, in respect of action or motion, which in turn does not depend upon anything to produce conjunction and disjunction. This distinction clarifies the Vaiśeṣika postulate that a substance is a substratum of both quality and motion, it being an inherent cause[43]. Motion is stated to be the common cause of conjunction and disjunction, i.e., it can cause disjunction from an object, and also create conjunction with another.[44]

But it has been emphasized that any type of action or movement cannot be the cause of an object or substance that experiences it. A substance is rightly regarded as the common cause of the first three categories, namely, substance itself, quality and motion, the cause being understandably an *inherent* one.[45] Alongside, quality also becomes the common cause of the three categories,[46] but quality as a cause would be a *non-inherent* one. Such distinctions have made the Vaiśeṣika explanation of the first three categories a rational one indeed. As for motion, it has no causative potential to give rise to a substance, nor of another type of motion,[47] either in its own substratum or in any other substratum. It has been argued that if two substances are in motion, they are two clear separate actions, while if two substances are in inherent relation, there could be only one action. As Śaṅkaramiśra states, when the consistent parts are moving, the whole is also moving; but when the whole is moving, we do not see the parts moving. Such examples are more metaphysical than physical explanations.

MOTION

According to *Vaiśeṣika sūtra*[48] motion is produced by *gurutva* (weight), *prayatna* (effort) and *saṃyoga* (conjunction). Praśastapāda adds one more, namely, *dravatva* (fluidity). Besides, *adṛṣṭa* (the unseen force), as noted already is considered to be a cause for motion,[49] in addition to the attribute *saṃskāra*.[50] Weight, that is stated to be an attribute of only earth and water elements, is regarded, of course qualitatively, as the cause of falling motion (*patana karma*). While such a cause it is generally held to be supra-sensible, Vallabhācārya in the *Nyāya-līlāvatī* (p. 69) thinks that it is perceived while in its downward operation. Nevertheless, that a motion of this type is accelerated due to gravity has not been indicated, but its neutralization by conjunction and other efforts has been thought of. An interesting explanation relates to the first initiative of falling (i.e. when a body is released to fall or there is disjunction between the hand and an object). It is pointed out that the first event of motion is due to weight alone, while the subsequent motions are stated to be the combined effect of weight and velocity (*vega*) which arises from the first or initial motion.

An interesting aspect of the Vaiśeṣika system is its exposition of different types of actions or motion in the context of elements. The motion in respect of Earth is stated as resulting from impulse (*nodana*), impact (*abhighāta*) and the conjunction with the conjunct (*saṃyukta-saṃyoga*).[51] The impulse itself is to be understood as a type of conjunction resulting from weight, velocity, and effort either cumulatively or from any one or two of them. Impact is the cause of that movement which produces disjunction, depending upon the intensity like a falling of an object on a hard stone. Other types of movement like earthquake, are said to be due to the unseen or invisible factor (*adṛṣṭa*).[52]

The upward movement of the flames, the first transversal movement of air and, as will be seen in the next chapter, the first motion imparted to the atoms as a result of which two like atoms enter into combination to form a dyad, and the first motion imparted to the mind itself are explained to be due to *adṛṣṭa*. Umesh Mishra has rightly stated : 'As regards the motion due to *adṛṣṭa*, it should be pointed out that the systems of Nyāya and Vaiśeṣika, following very closely the common-sense view, have to confine themselves within certain limitations. Hence, sometimes even in such cases, where one can easily, with a little insight, find out some definite cause of the motion, as for instance for earthquake etc., these systems pretend to be ignorant of the reality and attribute the causality to some unseen force (*adṛṣṭa*)'.[53]

It would seem, therefore, that the Nyāya-Vaiśeṣika with its own framework of qualities and causality as well as a sort of an obsession with the attributes of conjunction, disjunction, *saṃskāra* and the like, for the explanation of motion, has found it difficult to explain certain types of natural motion on the basis of these attributes, but deemed it convenient to refer them to the unseen as an escape from the demands of their own causal rigour.

One of the six categories of Nyāya-Vaiśeṣika is *karman* or action (not to be confused with the doctrine of *karma* that is associated with birth–death–rebirth). Action is thought of mainly in terms of five kinds of motion: (i) throwing upwards (*utkṣepaṇa*); (ii) throwing downwards (*apakṣepaṇa*); (iii) contraction (*ākuñcana*); (iv) expansion (*prasāraṇa*) and going (*gamana*).[54] Obviously what distinguishes the one from the other is the direction in which the movement takes place. Throwing upwards and downwards are naturally vertical motions brought about by effort (a quality) in opposite directions; contraction and expansion too are regarded as motion, but explained in terms of conjunction and disjunction (opposite qualities). But *gamana* is considered as motion in general in any direction. It is also explained in terms of conjunction and disjunction with points of space in diverse directions. In any case, motion has not been thought of both in space and time in a measurable manner. It may be noted that it was the measurement of motion in the context of space, among others, that heralded the dawn of early modern science in Europe.

It is true that the Nyāya-Vaiśeṣika admitted the free motion of atoms, but believed that it was caused by *adṛṣṭa* as noted before. At the same time, the free motion was conceived as being of two types: creative and non-creative, the former causing conjunction (a quality) of atoms leading to dyads etc., while the latter was presumed by the Jainas and the Bauddhas, to bring about occasional grouping of atoms like the *skandha*.

In the Nyāya-Vaiśeṣika approach to the cause of motion, it would appear that the qualities that reside in a substance or associated with it, have a major role to play. Otherwise the view is that matter in its gross state is by itself static. The quality of gravity (*gurutva*) present is responsible for the falling motion and this quality, according to Nyāya-Vaiśeṣika, resides only in earth (*pṛthivī*) and water (*ap*) elements, but not in others.[55] The quality of fluidity is the cause of flowing. This quality is stated to be present in earth, water and fire only.[56] Perhaps it could explain the flow (motion) of objects included under these elements depending upon their states—solid, liquid, moist and molten.

The motion involved in the phenomenon of flowing has been dealt with by Praśastapāda and Śrīdhara in considerable detail[57] as an explanation of the *Vaiśeṣika sūtra* in a cryptic way that fluidity (*dravatva*) is the cause of the motion of flowing (V.1.4). Fluidity is stated to be natural to water, but extrinsic to the two other elements, namely, earth and fire. A significant explanation is that in the liquids like honey, melted butter, and lac, the movement in them is regarded as being due to the contact of the fire element and the *vega* of their atoms. Fluidity is also recognized as a causal factor in respect of the downward flow of water in the form of current, as also in the case of drops of water falling from clouds and their uniting together to come down in the form of rain water.

The inner movement of water in plants or trees is, however, believed to be due to *adṛṣṭa*. The unseen then is the cause of such a motion. The absorption of water by the roots of a plant or tree is not caused by impulsion of any type, but by *adṛṣṭa*, which is regarded to be the instrumental cause, while water is considered to be the material cause, although it has been stated that it is water that causes the growth of a plant or tree.

In general a causal explanation by the Nyāya-Vaiśeṣika is conspicuous by its absence in respect of the upward rise of sap in plants, flow or movement of air and the attraction of an iron object by a magnet. While the first cause of motion, say in atoms, could be *adṛṣṭa* it is hard to reconcile with the position of Nyāya-Vaiśeṣika in its explanation of certain types of natural movements caused by natural forces.

However, in one respect, i.e., the continued motion of a body, the Nyāya-Vaiśeṣika explanation is indeed refreshing. Its conclusion that perceptual motion is impossible is equally refreshing. As for the continued motion, it is explained again in terms of an attribute called (*saṃskāra*), which is explained to be of three types—*vega* or impetus, the other two being *bhāvanā* (mental impression) and *sthitisthāpaka* (elasticity).[58] *Vega*, as Praśastapāda explains, has the connotation of momentum and is stated to be not only caused by applied motion but also can be causative of further motion.[59] According to Vyomaśivācārya and Śrīdhara, the able exponents of Nyāya-Vaiśeṣika, *vega* is caused by *nodana* or impelling push, *abhigāta* or impact and *saṃyukta saṃyoga* or forces that set in compounded conjunction.[60] These imply that *vega* or impetus is produced by force or an effort and, in turn, becomes the cause of continued motion in a particular direction unless it is counteracted by ambient opposite forces.

The explanation offered by Praśastapāda regarding continued motion is as follows: when a body experiences the first unit of motion caused by impelling push or impact, *vega* or impetus is also possessed by it. As a result, the body continues to be in motion in the same direction.[61] The impetus is capable of producing the effect in the same direction as the cause by which the impetus itself is produced, and because of it, the direction of motion is not changed. Nevertheless, if it is acted upon by any other moving body or that which is at rest, the direction may be changed or it would cease its motion.[62] Depending upon the other body that encounters it, the body may continue to move, of course, with diminished speed. An impetus theory for the explanation of continued motion had been put forward by John Philopanos of Alexandria in the sixth century A.D. But such a postulate by Praśastapāda is not only earlier but also more detailed in its elucidation.

There is a broader vision of the cause of motion. This relates to *prayatna* or effort on the part of a living being. Apart from explaining in terms of one's own effort such movements as the motion of hand during the cultivation of land, performance of sacrifice, etc., and the evident role in it of *ātman*, the upward and downward movements of a pestle, have been dealt with in considerable detail specially by Praśastapāda and Śrīdhara: When a man, having a *musala* in his hand, desires to throw up the *musala* with the help of the hand, an effort is produced in the *ātman*. With the aid of that effort as the instrumental cause, an upward motion is produced in the hand and simultaneously with the help of the same effort, from the hand–*musala* contact, a motion is produced even in the *musala* itself.

Similarly, we have downward motion of hand and *musala*. Thus when the *musala* has been thrown up, the desire to throw it up further ceases, and another desire to throw it down is produced followed by an effort. With the help of this effort as the instrumental cause and the *ātman* and *manas* contact as well as the contact of the hand and the *musala* as the respective non-material cause, there are simultaneously downward motions in hand as well as in *musala*.

'The motion of the *musala* produces forcible conjunction between a wooden mortar (*ulūkhala*) and the *musala* which, in its turn, is the cause of the upward motion of the *musala* as a result of the velocity belonging to it, without being produced by any effort. Here the velocity is the instrumental cause and the *musala*, is the material cause'.

'This upward motion of the *musala*, in its turn, with the help of the forcible contact produces velocity in the *musala*. With the help of this velocity, again, the *musala* and the hand contact, without depending upon any effort, produces an upward motion in the hand also'.

'As to the question: that the previous velocity produced in the *musala* by the downward motion being now destroyed how can the upward motion of the *musala*, without depending upon any effort, produces another velocity as explained above? It is said that although the previous velocity is destroyed the contact of the *musala* and the mortar is capable of producing a forcible (*paṭu*) motion productive of velocity. It appears to be simultaneous because of the swiftness of motion. . .' (U. Mishra discussing the elucidations given by Praśastapāda and Śrīdhara; *Conception of Matter According to Nyāya-Vaiśeṣika*, pp. 209-210). It will be observed from the above elucidations that what is of fundamental importance to the Nyāya-Vaiśeṣika for an understanding of motion, is the causal approach in terms of the instrumental, non-material and material courses. The objections, if any, were to be set aside if they did not conform to this approach.

Praśastapāda in his commentary has also explained the motion of an arrow shot from a bow,[63] more or less in similar manner. Śrīdhara in his *Nyāya-kandalī* has given details of motion of a javelin thrown by hand.[64] According to him, the volition and the associated effort of a person in the act of throwing results in the conjunction of his hand with the javelin as well as the impelling push and impetus. When the javelin leaves its hand, there is disjunction and the impelling throw or push ceases while the impetus continues as a result of which the javelin continues to move to a distance depending upon the degree of the volitional effort. But the manner by which the javelin experiences or its trajectory before it naturally falls to the ground has not been explained in detail, expect assuming that its weight would be causative of its falling to the ground pointing out the importance of *nodana* for continued motion.[65]

As mentioned earlier, the quality *saṃskāra* includes elasticity. This had been made use of by Praśastapāda while explaining the motion of an arrow. Besides the desire and the effort to shoot an arrow, leading to the conjunction among the fingers, arrow and the bow string, disjunction among them also takes place so that the arrow can move out, but at the same time the elasticity of the bowstring brings about the restoration of the original form of the bow. It is pointed out that elasticity also aids the motion of the arrow leading to the arrow being shot (expelling push) along with an impetus. When the impetus is exhausted, the arrow falls to the ground because of the quality of weight (*gurutva*) residing in the ground. In all such cases, the desire, effort, conjunction and disjunction which, according to the classification of the Nyāya-Vaiśeṣika, are qualities that would be involved in motion.[66] The movement of a potter's wheel is also explained in a similar manner. The change with reference to space is regarded as motion; but the rate of such a change with reference to time was not thought of. In any case the explanations for the observed motion of different types have not been in quantitative or measurable terms involving space and time.

REFERENCES

(The English translations of all the Upaniṣadic references are taken from *The Thirteen Principal Upaniṣads* by R. E. Hume.)
(All references to the *Praśastapādabhāṣya* (PPB) are taken from *Kiraṇāvalī* (ed) Jitendra S. Jetley, including the numbers of the Sūtras mentioned).

1. द्रव्य, गुण, कर्म, सामान्य, विशेष, समवायानां पदार्थानां साधर्म्य-वैधर्म्य-तत्त्वज्ञानं निःश्रेयसहेतुः । PPB.2
   The knowledge of the truth about the similarities and dissimilarities of the categories, viz. *dravya* (substance), *guṇa* (quality), *karma* (action), *sāmānya* (generality), *viśeṣa* (particularity) and *samavāya* (inherence) leads one to the highest good.

2. सामयिकः शब्दादर्थप्रत्ययः । VS. 7-2-20
   The recognition of a meaning from a word is conventional.
   यः शब्दो यस्मिन्नर्थे भगवता सङ्केतितः स तमर्थं प्रतिपादयति । (*Upaskāra* on VS. 2.2.8)
   Whatever word is assigned by the Supreme Being to any meaning, conveys that meaning.

3. The notion of abhāva is novel to the Vaiśeṣika.

4. षण्णामपि पदार्थानां अस्तित्वाभिधेयत्वज्ञेयत्वानि ।

   All the six categories have the characteristics of (i) existence (*astitva*) (ii) nameability (*abhidheyatva*) and (iii) *knowability* (jñeyatva). PPB.11

5. क्रियागुणवत् समवायिकारणमिति द्रव्यलक्षणम् । (VS. 1.1.15)

   The definition of substance is that it is possessed of actions and qualities and is a coinherent cause.

6. पृथिव्यादीनां नवानामपि द्रव्यत्वयोग: । PPB. 16

   All the nine substances such as earth and others are inherent in substanceness.

   पृथिवीत्वाभिसंबन्धात् पृथिवी । PPB. 27

   अस्त्वाभिसंबन्धात् आप: । PPB. 34

   Earth is inherently related to generic differentia of earthness.

   Water is inherently related to the generic differentia of waterness.

7. Eddington, A.S.: *Nature of the Physical World*, pp. 264-265.

8. Sreekantan B.V.: 'Scientific Explanations and Consciousness', *Scientific and Philosophical Studies in Consciousness*, National Institute of Advanced Studies, Bangalore, 1999, p. 13.

9. न हि शरीरं मानसप्रत्यक्षं मानसश्चायमहमिति

   प्रत्यय: बहिरिन्द्रियव्यापारमन्तरेणापि जायमान-

   त्वात् अहं दु:खी, अहं सुखी, जाने, यते, इच्छामि

   अहमिति योग्यविशेषगुणोपहितस्यात्मनो

   मनसा विषयीकरणत्वात् नाहं लैङ्गिको लिङ्गानु-

   सन्धानमन्तरेणापि जायमानत्वात् न शब्द:

   शब्दाकलनमन्तरेणापि जायमानत्वात् तस्मात्

   मनसश्च बहिरस्वातन्त्र्ये शरीरादावप्रवृत्ते: इति भाव: । *Upaskāra*, III. ii. 14

10. Singer, C: *A Short History of Science*, p. 32.

11. *op. cit.* p. 36.

12. *op. cit.* p. 53.

13. रूप-रस-गन्ध-स्पर्शा: सङ्ख्या: परिमाणानि पृथक्त्वं संयोगविभागौ परत्वापरत्वे बुद्धय: सुखदु:खे इच्छाद्वेषौ प्रयत्नाश्च

    गुणा: । VS. 1.1.6

14. च शब्दसमुच्चिताश्च गुरुत्वद्रवत्वास्नेहसंस्काराटदृष्टशब्दा: इत्येव चतुर्विंशतिर्गुणा: । PPB. 5

15. एवं कण्ठोक्त्या समुच्चयेन चैकतया चतुर्दशगुणा व्यवहर्तव्या: । Udayana's *Kiraṇāvalī* on the above.

16. रूपरसो गन्धस्तत: परम्–

    स्पर्श: सङ्ख्या परिमिति: पृथक्त्वं च तत: परम् ।

    संयोगश्च विभागश्च परत्वं चापरत्वकम् ॥

    बुद्धि: सुखं दु:खमिच्छा द्वेषो यत्नो गुरुत्वकम् ।

    द्रवत्वं स्नेहसंस्कारौ अदृष्टं शब्द एव च ॥ *Bhāṣāpariccheda*; 3.5

17. (i) रूपम्‌: Colour

    तत्र रूपं चक्षुर्ग्राह्यं पृथिव्युदकज्वलनवृत्ति द्रव्याद्युपलम्भकं नयनसहकारि शुक्लाद्यनेकप्रकारं ... नित्यं पार्थिवपरमाणुष्व‌–
    त्रिसंयोगविरोधि सर्वकार्येषु कारणगुणपूर्वकं आश्रयविनाशादेव विनश्यति इति । PPB. 118

18. तस्मात्पूर्वं द्रव्यस्य विनाश: तदनु रूपस्य । *Śrīdhara* on PPB. 118

19. (ii) रस: Taste

    रसो रसनाग्राह्य: पृथिव्युदकवृत्ति:, जीवनपुष्टिबलारोग्यनिमित्तं, रसनसहकारी, मधुराम्ललवणतिक्तकटुकषाय-
    भेदभिन्न: । अस्यापि नित्यानित्यत्वनिष्पत्तयो रूपवत्‌ । PPB. 119-120

20. गन्ध: Smell

    (iii) गन्धो घ्राणग्राह्य: पृथिवीवृत्ति: घ्राणसहकारी सुरभि: असुरभिश्च । अस्यापि पूर्ववत्‌ उत्पत्त्यादयो व्याख्याता: ।
    PPB. 121

21. स्पर्श: Touch

    (iv) स्पर्शस्त्वगिन्द्रियग्राह्य: क्षित्युदकज्वलनपवनवृत्ति: त्वक् सहकारी रूपानुविधायी शीतोष्ण-अनुष्णाशीतभेदात्‌
    त्रिविध: । अस्यापि नित्यानित्यत्वनिष्पत्तय: पूर्ववत्‌ । PPB. 122

22. (v) सङ्ख्या: Number

    एकादिव्यवहारहेतु: संख्या । सा पुनरेकद्रव्या अनेकद्रव्या च । तत्र एकद्रव्याया: सलिलादिपरमाणुरूपादीनामिव
    नित्यानित्यत्वनिष्पत्तय: । अनेकद्रव्या तु द्वित्वादिका परार्धपर्यन्ता । PPB. 130

23. (v) परिमाणम्‌ : Volume/extension

    परिमाणं मानव्यवहारकारणम्‌ । तच्चतुर्विधम्‌ । अणु महत्‌ दीर्घं ह्रस्वं चेति । PPB. 148, 149
    तत्र महत्‌ द्विविधं–नित्यं अनित्यं च । नित्यं आकाशकालदिगात्मसु परममहत्त्वम्‌ । अनित्यं त्र्यणुकादावेव । तथा
    अण्वपि द्विविधं नित्यं अनित्यं च । नित्यं परमाणुमनस्सु तत्‌ परिमाण्डल्यम्‌ । अनित्यं द्व्रचणुके एव । PPB. 150- 151

24. पृथक्त्वं अपोद्धारव्यवहारकारणम्‌ । तत्पुनरेकद्रव्यमनेकद्रव्यं च ।

    तस्य तु नित्यानित्यत्वनिष्पत्तय: संख्यया व्याख्याता: एतावांस्तु विशेष:, एकत्वादिवदेकपृथक्त्वाद्यपरसामान्याभाव:
    संख्यया तु विशिष्यते, तद्विशिष्टव्यवहारदर्शनादिति । PPB. 161-164

25. संयोग: Conjunction

    अप्राप्तयो: प्राप्ति: संयोग: । द्रव्यगुणकर्महेतु: ।
    अवयवसंयोगा द्रव्यहेतव: । शब्दस्य भेर्याकाशसंयोग: । कर्मणो नोदनाभिधात: *Kiraṇāvalī*, PPB. 166

26. विभाग: Disjunction

    स च त्रिविध: । अन्यतरकर्मज: । उभयकर्मज: । विभागजश्च विभाग इति । PPB. 183

27. तद्‌ द्विविधं दिक्कृतं कालकृतं च । PPB. 201

28. बुद्धि: Intellect

    संयोग: संयुक्तप्रत्ययनिमित्तम्‌ । स च द्रव्यगुणकर्महेतु: । PPB. 165-168

29. अक्षाणि इन्द्रियाणि, घ्राणरसनचक्षुत्वक् श्रोत्रमनांसि । PPB. 234

30. सुखम् : Pleasure

    अनुग्रहलक्षणं सुखम् । PPB. 290

31. दु:खम् : Pain

    उपघातलक्षणं दु:खम् । PPB. 291

32. इच्छा: Desire

    स्वार्थं परार्थं वाप्राप्तप्रार्थनेच्छा । PPB. 292

33. द्वेष: Aversion

    प्रज्वलनात्मको द्वेष: । PPB. 294

34. प्रयत्न: Effort

    प्रयत्न: संरम्भ उत्साह इति पर्याया: । स द्विविध: जीवनपूर्वक: इच्छाद्वेषपूर्वकश्च । PPB. 295

35. गुरुत्वम्: Gravity

    गुरुत्वं जलभूम्यो: पतनकर्मकारणम् । अप्रत्यक्षं पतनकर्गानुगेयं रांयोगप्रयत्नरांरकारविरोधि ।

    अस्य च अबादिपरमाणुरूपादिवत् नित्यानित्यत्वनिष्पत्तय: । PPB. 297

36. वेगेन प्रतिबन्धात् अपततं बहि: क्षिप्तस्य शरशकलादे: । *NK on the above*

37. द्रवत्वं: Fluidity

    द्रवत्वं स्यन्दनकर्मकारणम् । त्रिद्रव्यवृत्ति । तत्तु द्विविधं, सांसिद्धिकं नैमित्तिकं च । सांसिद्धिकं अपां विशेषगुण: ।

    नैमित्तिकं पृथिवीतेजसो: सामान्यगुण: ।

    सांसिद्धिकस्य गुरुत्ववत् नित्यानित्यत्वनिष्पत्तय: ।... नैमित्तिकं च पृथिवीतेजसोरग्निसंयोगजम् । PPB. 298-

    299, 300

38. स्नेह: Viscidity

    स्नेह: अपां विशेषगुण: । सङ्ग्रहमृजादिहेतु: अस्यापि गुरुत्ववत् नित्यानित्यादिनिष्पत्तय: । PPB. 301

39. संस्कार: Saṃskāra

    संस्कारस्त्रिविध: – वेगो भावना स्थितिस्थापकश्च । PPB. 302

40. धर्म: Dharma

    धर्म: पुरुषगुण: । PPB. 308

41. अधर्म: Adharma

    अधर्मोऽप्यात्मगुण: । PPB. 317

42. शब्द: Sound

    शब्द: अम्बरगुण: श्रोत्रग्राह्म:, क्षणिक:, कार्यकारणोभयविरोधी, संयोगविभागशब्दज:, प्रदेशवृत्ति:,

    समानासमानजातीयकारण: । PPB. 320

43. द्रव्यगुणकर्मणां द्रव्यं कारणं सामान्यम् । VS.1.1.18

44. संयोगविभागवेगानां कर्म सामान्यम् । VS.1.1.20

45. एकस्मिन्नेव द्रव्ये समवायिकारणे द्रव्यगुणकर्माणि वर्तन्ते इत्यर्थः । Upaskāra on VS.1.1.18

The meaning is that substance, quality and action exist in one substance as their inherent cause.

46. तथा गुणः । VS.1.1.19

47. न द्रव्याणां कर्म । VS.1.1.21

48. गुरुत्वप्रयत्नसंयोगानामुत्क्षेपणम् । VS 1. 1.29

49. मणिगमनं सूच्यभिसर्पणमदृष्टकारणम् । VS.5.1.15.

50. नोदनादाद्यमिषोः कर्म तत्कर्मकारिताच्च

संस्कारादुत्तरं तथोत्तरमुत्तरं च । VS.1.1.17.

51. नोदनापीडनात् संयुक्तसंयोगाच्च पृथिव्यां कर्म । VS.5.2.1

52. तद्विशेषेणादृष्टकारितम् । VS.5.2.2

53. Umesh Mishra, *op. cit*, pp. 218-223.

54. उत्क्षेपणावक्षेपणाकुञ्चनप्रसारणगमनानि पञ्चैव कर्माणि । VS. 1.1.7; PPB. 6

There are only five kinds of motion : (i) *utkṣepaṇa* (throwing upwards); (ii) *avakṣepaṇa*; (throwing downwards) (iii) *ākuñcana* (contraction); (iv) *prasāraṇa* (expansion); and (v) *gamana* (going).

55. गुरुत्वं जलभूम्योः पतनकर्मकारणम् । PPB. 297

Gravity is the cause of downward motion of water and earth.

56. द्रवत्वं स्यन्दनकर्मकारणम्, त्रिद्रव्यवृत्ति । P.P.B. 298

The quality of fluidity is the cause of flowing. This quality is present in the three elements, viz. earth, water and fire.

57. द्रवत्वं स्यन्दनकर्मकारणम् । त्रिद्रव्यवृत्ति ।

तत्तु द्विविधं सांसिद्धिकं नैमित्तिकं च ।

सांसिद्धिकम् अपां विशेषगुणः । नैमित्तिकं

पृथिवीतेजसोः सामान्यगुणः । PPB. 298

निमित्तं च वह्निसंयोगः, तस्येदं कार्यमिति

नैमित्तिकम् । सांसिद्धिकं च स्वभावसिद्धम्,

वह्निसंयोगानपेक्षमिति यावत् । सांसिद्धिकम् अपां

विशेषगुणः, अन्यत्राभावात् । नैमित्तिकं च पृथिवीतेजसोः सामान्यगुणः,

साधारणत्त्वात् । *NK* on PPB. 298

तथात्मसंयोगो हस्तकर्मणि । VS. 5. 1.4

58. संस्कारस्त्रिविधः—वेगो, भावना, स्थितिस्थापकश्च । PPB. 302

Tendency or impression is three-fold: impetus (*vega*), mental impression (*bhāvanā*), elasticity (*sthitisthāpakatva*).

59. नियतदिक्क्रियाप्रबन्धहेतुः । PPB. 303

(The impetus) causes motion in a specific direction.

60. नोदनाभिघातादिनिमित्तविशेषापेक्षं न केवलं, मन्दगतौ वेगाभावात् । Śrīdhara on PPB. 303

Impetus needs impelling push (*nodana*), or impact (*abhighāta*)—because motion can not happen independently, when the motion is too slow there is the absence of impetus.

61. कचित्कारणगुणपूर्वक्रमेणोत्पद्यते । PPB. 303

Sometimes (however) the impetus is generated due to the impetus already existing in the substance by inherence.

62. स्पर्शवद्द्रव्यसंयोगविशेषविरोधी । PPB. 303

(The impetus) ceases (विरोधी) when a particular object of contact (is encountered).

63. संस्कारात्कर्म इष्वादिषु उक्तम् । PPB. 354

The enduring action (of motion) is shown by the movement of an arrow.

64. तोमरस्य पतनं यावत् संस्कारात् तदनुरूपाणि कर्माणि भवन्तीत्यर्थः । Śrīdhara on PPB.p.345

As long as the javelin does not fall down there is motion in the javelin according to the impact due to impetus.

65. दूरक्षेपणेच्छायां महान् प्रयत्नः, आसन्नक्षेपणेच्छायां च शिथिलः प्रयत्नः जायत इति तदनुरूपशब्दार्थः । तमपेक्षमाणस्तोमरहस्तसंयोगो नोदनाख्यो नोद्यस्य तोमरस्य नोदकस्य च हस्तस्य सहगमनहेतुत्वात् । तस्मान्नोदनाख्यात् यथोक्तादिच्छानुरूपप्रयत्नापेक्षात् तोमरे कर्मोत्पन्नम् । तत्कर्म नोदनापेक्षं, तस्मिंस्तोमरे संस्कारमारभते । Śrīdhara on PPB. 345

When there is a desire to throw at a distance there is stronger volition, and for a shorter distance it is lesser. Keeping that in view, there is a contact between the hand and the javelin known as '*nodana*'. This happens to determine the movement due to the combination of the two i.e., the javelin (*nodya*) and the hand (*nodaka*). Then there happens motion in the javelin according to the volition due to what is called *nodana*. The motion depends on the *nodana*, and there arises an enduring action.

66. एवमाकर्णादाकृष्टे धनुषि नातः परम् अनेन गन्तव्यमिति यज्ज्ञानं ततस्तदाकर्षणार्थस्य प्रयत्नस्य विनाशः ततः पुनः मोक्षणेच्छा सञ्जायते, तदनन्तरं प्रयत्नस्तमपेक्षमाणाद् आत्माङ्गुलिसंयोगात् अङ्गुलिकर्म, तस्माज्ज्याङ्गुलिविभागः, ततो विभागात् संयोगविनाशः, तस्मिन्विनष्टे प्रतिबन्धकाभावात् यदा धनुषि वर्तमानः स्थितिस्थापकः संस्कारो मण्डलीभूतं धनुर्यथावस्थितं स्थापयति । PPB. 347

Now, when the cord of the bow is drawn up to the ear there arises a thought that this cord should not be drawn any further. This leads to the cessation of the effort to draw the cord further. Then arises the desire to shoot the arrow. As a consequence of the soul and the finger combination, motion starts in the fingers. Then efforts result in doing as desired. Due to the combination of soul and finger motion starts where the role of effort is involved also. Then due to the movement of the finger there will be disjunction between finger and the cord. Consequently the conjunction between the finger and cord ceases. As a result, the bow gets back into its original form being liberated from the hold due to elasticity.

CHAPTER 5

Atomism

Indian atomism encompasses that of the Vaiśeṣika and the syncrectic Nyāya-Vaiśeṣika* schools on the one hand and, on the other, of the Jaina and the Vaibhāṣika as well as the Sautrāntika of the Hīnayāna schools of Buddhism. Each school developed atomism in the matrix of its philosophical ideas and to some degree in a logically-structured presentation of the nature and the attributes of atoms.

A firm belief in the reality of the external world independent of a knower and in the principle that experience through the senses alone should be the sole criterion of our acceptance of the reality of external objects has marked Indian realism as elsewhere. As for the phenomenal matter, there is an irreducible limit to the division of matter and a point will be reached at which further division cannot take place. The concept that the ultimate indivisible particles that would also be indestructible and invisible, are the building units of the observed matter lies behind the concept of atom, as evidenced by the Vaiśeṣika and Greek atomism alike.

In Indian texts, the two words that are generally used for 'atom' are *aṇu* and *paramāṇu*, although the word *aṇu* has been used in some of the Upaniṣads, in the sense of 'very minute' or extremely small'.[1]

In the *Vaiśeṣika sūtra-s*, the word, *aṇu*[2] is consciously used for denoting an atom. The *sūtra-s*, deal with the proof of atoms, though indirectly, as well as their qualities. These and other related ideas have been dealt with in greater detail in the later texts. More importantly, that the atoms are all globular (*pārimāṇḍalya*) has been emphasised in the *sūtra*.[3] Besides, the Vaiśeṣika points out that an atom is partless.

The word, *maṇḍala,* has the connotation of circular shape of an atom. From a common and plausible point of view, an atom is to be spherical and without any parts, although the term, *maṇḍala* might suggest the idea of having parts. 'Thus *parimaṇḍala* here means the attribute of possessing *prakṛṣṭa-aṇutva*, the smallest possible dimension.[4] While the Nyāya-Vaiśeṣika's exposition is that a *paramāṇu* is partless and also eternal, this has not found favour with several opponents, specially the nihilist school of Buddhism which firmly believes in void as a real entity.

Vātsyāyana in his *Nyāya-bhāṣya*[5] has not only examined the Buddhist's objections but also responded to them in keeping with the Nyāya-Vaiśeṣika position that *paramāṇu* is not only the ultimate and indivisible particle of an element but also partless and eternal. The opposing Buddhist view is that since *ākāśa* is an ubiquitous element, it should permeate an atom both 'in' and 'out', and hence an atom must have parts. The Nyāya-Vaiśeṣika does accept that *ākāśa* is one and all-pervasive. In view of this, the Buddhist's argue that the Nyāya-Vaiśeṣika should either discard their postulate that *ākāśa* is all-pervasive or accept that atoms possess parts. The idea of 'in' and 'out' in respect of an atom is rejected by Vātsyāyana by saying that conceptually an atom is regarded as partless. In other words, the 'in' and 'outside' of an atom do not exist at all and *ākāśa*, though all-pervading, cannot extend its all-pervasiveness to some things that do not exist at all.

An altogether different argument against the Nyāya-Vaiśeṣika concept that an atom is partless came from a different standpoint even in the seventeenth century A.D., by a mathematician, astronomer, Kamalākara. This reveals that in subtle debate how a geometrical theorem could be made use of to prove a point, albeit its misconceived nature. Kamalākara tried to prove geometrically with the help of the Baudhāyana (so-called Pythogorean) theorem which states that the square on the hypotenuse is equal to the sum of the squares of the two other sides of a right-angle triangle. If it is assumed that each of the other two sides consists of 2 *paramāṇu-s*, the sum of their 2 squares would be $2^2+2^2= 8$ and hence the square on the hypotenuse would be equivalent to 8; but the square root 8 would be more than 2 and less than 3 and hence, an atom can be split into parts. This type of argument, needless to state, has its contradictions in the context, of the definition of a geometrical straight line. Whatever might be the arguments of its opponents, the Nyāya-Vaiśeṣika stuck to its position that an atom is spherical and partless.[6]

It is only Praśastapāda, the author of the *Padārthadharma saṃgraha*, who first elaborated upon the nature and structure of the Vaiśeṣika atomism that was further developed by the later Vaiśeṣikas with the epistemic support from the Naiyāyikas. The *Nyāya-bhāṣya* (of Vātsyāyana), *Nyāya-kusumāñjali* of (Uddyotakara), *Vyomavatī* (of *Vyomaśivācārya*), *Nyāya-Kandalī* (of Śrīdhara) and Kiraṇāvalī (of Udayana) are of special importance from the point of view of what may be generally called the Nyāya-Vaiśeṣika atomism to which Uddyotakara specially made significant contributions in his exposition of the concerned *Nyāya-sūtra-s*[7].

The followers of the Sāṃkhya, it needs to be emphasised, were not atomists in the accepted sense of the term, though there is a reference to the atom in the *Sāṃkhya-sūtra* ascribed to the sage Kapila.[8] But this is a much later work belonging perhaps to the fifteenth century A.D., and its reference to atom is in the context of contradicting the atomic views. There is a view that the concept of *tanmātra*[9] of the Sāṃkhya system is equivalent to the *aṇu* or *paramāṇu* of the Nyāya-Vaiśeṣika and this view was put forward by Vijñāna Bhikṣu, an able exponent of the Sāṃkhya, while commenting upon the concerned *Sāṃkhya-sūtra*. This is hardly tenable if one critically examines the Sāṃkhya evolutes of which *tanmātra-s* are a part and they are associated with *ahaṅkāra* (ego). It is true that the Sāṃkhya as well as the Nyāya-Vaiśeṣika had a firm faith in the reality of the external world; but their foundational ideas were different. If the Sāṃkhya traced the evolution or manifestation to one unmanifested (*avyakta*) entity that was supposed to be constituted of the three *guṇa-s* (*sattva, rajas* and *tamas*), and also known as *Prakṛti* or *Pradhāna,* the Nyāya-Vaiśeṣika had a pluralistic approach in terms of six or seven categories (*padārtha-s*). If the Nyāya-Vaiśeṣika atoms were regarded as partless and indestructible, the *tanmātra-s* were assumed to share the characteristics of the three *guṇa-s.* And they were not regarded as the ultimate material causes of the world just as the atoms were, as conceived by the Nyāya-Vaiśeṣika. As will be seen later, while the Sāṃkhya believes in the *satkāryavāda* (the effect resides in the cause), the Nyāya-Vaiśeṣika follows the *asatkāryavāda* (the effect comes out of the cause).

Nyāya-Vaiśeṣika Atomism

The Nyāya-Vaiśeṣika concept of the composite (*avayavin*) and the constituent parts (*avayava-s*) as well as their belief in the eternal reality have shaped their atomic theory. The relation between the composite and its constituent parts is that of cause (the latter) and effect (the former). The composite is stated to inhere in constituents. Nevertheless they are regarded as two distinct entities having different qualities and functions. It is this approach that has led the Nyāya-Vaiśeṣika to postulate *Ārambhavāda* or the Theory of Origination (see also Ch.6). According to Nyāya-Vaiśeṣika, what they call the ultimate substances are eternal, and are either infinite or infinitesimal. On the other hand, all compound substances (*avayavi dravya*) are impermanent or non-eternal and hence undergo production and destruction. But the destruction would not be total or endless, but ultimately to a supra-sensible and partless or atomic stage.[10] Of the five elements, the four (earth, water, fire and air) in their produced forms are regarded as non-eternal because they are subject to production and destruction. But in their atomic states, they are eternal.[11] Such a postulate was necessary for the Nyāya-Vaiśeṣika as that alone would be in tune with their philosophic realism.

The basic tenets of their atomism are briefly as follows: Each element has its own class of atoms with specific attributes, namely, earth atom-*odour*;[12] water atom-*taste*; fire atom-*colour*; and air atom-*touch*. It is significant to note that these attributes are also of the elements themselves. Thus the atoms and the respective products have common specific qualities, no distinction being made in this respect between the gross substance and its atomic state—a consistent way of looking at the problem of matter in its totality. Atoms are indestructible (hence eternal), indivisible and without any magnitude; but all atoms, as noted before, are spherical (*parimāṇḍalya*). They can, however, be differentiated by their specific qualities, i.e., qualitatively. Besides, atoms being partless, the Nyāya-Vaiśeṣika position is that atoms have neither exterior nor interior, nor hollow-inside.

The problem of the production of gross matter from the atoms engaged the attention of the Nyāya-Vaiśeṣika exponents. They have painstakingly provided a solution to it in a logical manner, albeit its incongruities here and there. The Nyāya-Vaiśeṣika postulate is that in the beginning atoms are in eternal motion. Hence, there always exists a possibility of the combination of some of them; but to start with, only two atoms of the same element enter into combination, although during such a combination the atoms of the other elements could also be present. Two like atoms are the material cause while those of the other elements could possibly play a supportive role. In any case, two unlike atoms, i.e., an atom of earth and that of air would not enter into combination, according to the Nyāya-Vaiśeṣika.[13]

The term *dvyaṇuka* (dyad) is used for the effect of the combination of two atoms.[14] But the dyad is also regarded as supra-sensible and infinitesimal even though it is formed out of two atoms. An argument advanced for this situation is that the magnitude of a dyad is derived from the number *two* only; for, an atom is so minute that it cannot be a causative agency for contributing any magnitude to the product (effect). Minuteness, in other words, cannot cause grossness and further, atoms have no magnitude. This means that a dyad is not superior in magnitude to the two atoms that give rise to it. Hence it should be concluded that the magnitude of a dyad must be derived from the *number* of atoms giving rise to it. Logically the minimum number of atoms that can be causative is two and therefore, only two atoms combine in the beginning and the first product is a dyad.[15] Like the constituent atoms, the dyad is also invisible or supra-sensible.[16] The minimum visible is designated as *tryaṇuka* (see below) or *trasareṇu* (triad) which, according to the followers of Nyāya-Vaiśeṣika, is of the size of a mote in a sunbeam.[17]

The postulate of the formation of a triad is intriguing and interesting alike. It has been stated that three dyads cause the coming into being of a triad and not six atoms directly. The reason adduced is that a thing of gross magnitude like a triad can only be formed by the first products like dyads. Atoms are eternal and if they were to produce directly a gross material, the process would go on and the resulting product, say earth or water, would also be eternal. But the experience is to the contrary as they are destructible. Hence it is only from the dyads that a triad could be formed.[18]

Later exponents of the Nyāya-Vaiśeṣika atomism, however, have argued that a *tryaṇuka* could be produced directly from three atoms.[19] A *tryaṇuka* being produced from three *paramāṇu-s*, would not remain atomic, as the opponents to this view point out, since it would possess some magnitude, unlike the atoms. There are also differing ideas regarding the number of atoms that constitute a *tryaṇuka* varying from 6/8 to as many as 30. But the generally accepted position was that three dyads would form one triad or *trasareṇu*, stated to be of the dimension of a mote in sun beam.

Atoms and dyads are considered as having no extension in themselves, besides not possessing magnitude on a gross scale. These two concepts mean that the gross magnitude of a triad is not due to atoms nor even the inter-dyadic space. Likewise, a tetrad owes its emergence or formation to four triads and so on. The minimum standard of plurality of dyads is logically three. Hence at least three dyads are required for the formation of a triad. However, it is admitted that triads of different elements could also enter into combination to form a tetrad and the like. Since the atoms of the different elements have their own specific properties and there would be structural arrangement in the triads, tetrads and so on, it is possible to explain the different qualities observed in different substances– a refreshing concept even from the modern scientific point of view. The term used significantly for the structural arrangement is *vyūha*.[20]

Speculative though, the Nyāya-Vaiśeṣika atomism is not devoid of any principle of causality. On the other hand, its postulate is that the effect, a new event, has always a cause. Atoms are the material cause of a dyad, and dyads are the material cause of a triad. The cause in each case brings about an effect, and is immediately absorbed or inheres in the effect which in turn performs the functions of a cause to continue the sequence. The Nyāya-Vaiśeṣika causality is thus known as *ārambhavāda* or *asatkāryavāda* (see next chapter), in which the effect is non-existent antecedently.[21]

Adṛṣṭa: There are two notable questions addressed by the Nyāya-Vaiśeṣika: (i) why do the primordial atoms enter into combination; and (ii) what causes the union of two atoms to begin with? The explanation of the Nyāya-Vaiśeṣika for the former is no doubt the motion of atoms, but in respect of the initial motion, it is explained in terms of an unforeseen force or power (*adṛṣṭa*) that would set off the process. In other words, the unseen force or divine dispensation is held to be the efficient cause, while atoms are the material cause for the formation of dyads and so on.

Praśastapāda, while adding seven more qualities, includes *adṛṣṭa* instead of *dharma* and *adharma* and this has been explained in the *Kiraṇāvalī*.[22] This concept, however, is not fully explained in the *Vaiśeṣika sūtra-s*, although the terms *dṛṣṭa* and *adṛṣṭa* have been used in them. It would appear that Kaṇāda might have preferred to use the word *adṛṣṭa* in the case of such aspects that could not be causally explained. But, a firm adherent to the cause-effect relationship, he used the word *adṛṣṭakārita* in such situations. He sought to explain the attraction of an iron needle to a magnet, the rise of water (sprinkled at the root of a plant) through its branches and leaves, the zig-zag course of wind, the first motion of the atoms, the first movement of mind, the association and dissociation of the body in relation to the soul, nourishment of the body with food and the like, in terms of *adṛṣṭa*, i.e., these are caused by conditions that are invisible.[23] Kaṇāda, however, also refers to supernatural powers, but does not use the word *adṛṣṭa* in some cases.

It would appear that neither the Nyāya nor the Vaiśeṣika in the early stages thought of *adṛṣṭa* in a theistic framework. Whether they denied the existence of God in their dialectics or categorization to begin with is also a moot point. Perhaps they might not have done so. In the *Vaiśeṣika sūtra-s* nowhere is named God or Īśvara,[24] although the later commentators like Śaṅkara Miśra (17th cent. A.D.) point out that there is a reference to Īśvara in a *Vaiśeṣika sūtra*. Vaiśeṣika and the Nyāya have accepted the authority of the Vedas; but this seems to be a later development so far as the *Vaiśeṣika sūtra-s* are concerned.[25] Praśastapāda (4th cent. A.D.) opens his *bhāṣya* (*Padārtha-dharmasaṃgraha*), by paying homage to Īśvara and he also believed in the Vedic scriptures. Nevertheless, his view was that it was the knowledge of the six categories that would eventually lead to liberation., although, according to him, this knowledge itself would result from *dharma* prescribed by Īśvara.[26] He also points out that the periodic processes of creation (*sṛṣṭi*) and dissolution (*saṃhāra*) are caused by Īśvara's design. Further, he explains that the duality (as in dyads) and plurality (as in triads) are contingent upon the intellect of Īśvara[27]—a view that was further developed by Udayana in a theistic manner.[28] Vyomaśivācārya and Śrīdhara have dealt with the theistic impress in connection[29] with the process of creation.

As for the Nyāya, the concept of Īśvara or theism also appears to be a later thinking. In his examination of the sixteen topics, Gautama, regarded as the propounder of the *Nyāya-sūtra-s* in their present form, deals with the production of perceptible things, giving an analogy for it.[30] However, in the *sūtra-s* 19-21,[31] there is a reference to Īśvara as the cause of all things. In the *sūtra-s*,[32] it has been stated that the world has come into being not as a result of any efficient cause, but all things must be evanescent. It is possible that Gautama was inclined to theism perhaps as his personal viewpoint. Even so, Īśvara is mentioned only once in the entire gamut of the *Nyāya-sūtra-s*. But Gautama does not seem to be merely seized with the problem of the existence of God, but is also concerned with causative dimensions of *karma* as *nimitta kāraṇa* in connection with the relation between the soul and the body. The commentators, Vātsyāyana and Uddyotakara have thrown much light on God as the efficient or operative cause of the world.[33]

There is another significant aspect of the Nyāya-Vaiśeṣika atomism, which is concerned with mind (*manas*),[34] an internal sense organ (*antaḥkaraṇa*), the attributes of which, include number and dimensions. The Nyāya-Vaiśeṣika admits that the presence and active participation of mind are necessary for the production of any cognition even when the ātman and the sense organs are in contact with an object. More importantly, mind is regarded as being atomic and endowed with enormous motion, since it cognizes its objects with the quickest possible motion (PPB. 89). The *Yoga-Vāsiṣtha* (*c.* 8th cent.) by an unknown author (in the form of conversations between Rāma and his preceptor, Vasiṣṭha) presents the view that atoms are an essential part of living systems including mind and consciousness (**3**, 50.6; 61.35).

Jaina Atomism

The Jainas have categorized knowledge into mediate (*parokṣa*) and immediate (*aparokṣa*). The former is further classified into *mati* and *śruta*. The perceptible knowledge or the one gained through the mediation of senses is generally included under the mediate one, under *mati*, which encompasses both the perceptual and inferential knowledge, while *śruta* relates to that derived from authority.[35] (see the Chapter on Epistemology).

The Jaina metaphysics, called the *Anekāntavāda*, or the Doctrine of the Many, regards matter (*pudgala*) and spirit (*jīva*) as independent realities, under its two basic categorization of the Universe into *Jīva* (living) and *Ajīva* (non-living), the Universe being considered as beginningless and endless. Ajīva comprises five entities: *dharma, adharma, ākāśa, pudgala* and *kāla*.[36] Each of them, excepting *kāla* or time, is known as *astikāya* i.e., that which exists, has pervasiveness and occupies space (*pradeśa*), space being considered as an integral part of *ākāśa*. In Jaina metaphysics, matter is conceived as an eternal substance (*dravya*) which is undetermined by any processes of transformation of its quality or quantity.

One of the noted Jaina thinkers, Kundakundācārya (*c.* first cent. B.C.), has dealt with atomism in considerable detail in his work called the *Pañcāstikāyasāra*. He enumerates four forms of material bodies (*pudgala-kāya*) which in the Jaina parlance are: *skandha, skandha-deśa, skandha pradeśa* and *paramāṇu*.[37] These are related to one another in the sense that the first three are regarded as the aggregates in one way or the other of *paramāṇus* or atoms.[38] Of them, the atom (*sūkṣma paramāṇu*) alone is held to be indivisible. A *skandha-deśa* is stated to be half of a *skandha* and the latter's half is a *skandha-pradeśa*.

A *skandha* (several aggregates denote *pudgala*) may be either a gross or subtle one. The former exists in six forms: earth, water, shadow, the objects of the four senses (except the visual ones), the kārmic matter, and the aggregates that do not constitute Kārmic matter[39] because the kārmic matter is also regarded as being atomic or minute. The subtle (*sūkṣma*) ones are atomic. But, if a *skandha* is made of two atoms, it is also exceedingly minute similar to the dyads of the Vaiśeṣika, while the atom is the ultimate, eternal indivisible and the minutest particle. A notable characteristic of Jaina atomism is the positional relationship between an atom and space it occupies. It is postulated that an atom occupies a single space point and also corporeal. The space-points of material objects are held to be both numerable and innumerable[40] i.e., countable and countless. Atoms are also the prime cause of the four elements—earth, water, fire and air—and also of their qualities except sound which is the quality of *ākāśa*. But as an element, *ākāśa* does not figure in the Jaina thinking; instead the first four elements are recognized.[41] However, Umāsvāti suggests that the quality of sound can accrue during the formation of an aggregate of atoms. It has been emphasized that sound could be a quality of only the aggregates and that sound is produced when the atoms touch one another.[42] The aggregates themselves are distinguished through their space-points.[43] According to Jaina thinkers, an atom possesses one kind of taste, colour and smell, but two kinds of touch. Although an atom does not by itself have the quality of sound, it could cause sound.[44]

The aggregates are stated to be formed, according to Umāsvāti,[45] either by union (of atoms), or by division (splitting of larger aggregates) or by both union and division. But an atom is produced by division alone.[46] He explains the combination of atoms as being due to two opposing qualities, namely, greasiness or attraction (*snigdhatva*) and dryness or repulsion (*rūkṣatva*).[47] No combination, however, can take place if the atoms have the lowest (one) degree of these qualities, or equal degrees of the same quality.

It has been pointed out that the quality present in an atom to a certain degree could be increased or decreased. It is for this reason, atoms are also called *pudgala* or inanimate matter, the word, *pudgala,* meaning that which can fill up (*pur*) and dissolve (*gala*).[48] A subtle distinction is, therefore, made between the eternality of atoms as material particles and the qualitative changes that they could undergo. The word, *pudgala,* has also the connotation of things for enjoyment by living beings. The Jaina's supposition is that all things are aggregates of atoms and hence atoms are in the nature of *pudgala*. Thus all matter is divided into two categories, the aggregates and atoms.

The *pudgala* also encompasses what is known as *rūpa*, the quality of colour or form.[49]

Jaina atomism, unlike that of the Nyāya-Vaiśeṣika, admits the combination between atoms of the same kind (in terms of the difference in degrees of quality) and those of the opposite kind, provided there is a difference of *two* degrees only. For example, if an atom has three degrees of greasiness, it can enter into combination with an atom that has five degrees of this quality, but not with the one that has either 2 degrees or 4 degrees. Likewise, such an atom can also combine with the one that has five degrees of dryness. The difference in degrees of the two types of properties, one being higher and the other lower, is an important characteristic of Jaina atomism, although the quantitative aspect of a degree has not been spelt out by Umāsvāti and others.

Jaina atomism differs from that of the Nyāya-Vaiśeṣika in several ways. It does not accept the latter's concept of the composite and the *parts* (*avayavin-avayava*) that has a bearing on the Nyāya-Vaiśeṣika atomism. Nor does it accept the special qualities associated with each class of atoms, viz., of earth, water, fire and air. Jaina postulate of atoms is in tune with its own premises for understanding the world of matter and motion in the context of the Jaina *Āgama-s* and the later texts. It is, however, interesting to note that Jainas use the word *dravya* (substance) more or less in the same manner as the Nyāya-Vaiśeṣika in their approach to atomism.

The Jaina *Āgama-s* have conceived that *paramāṇu-s* (ultimate atoms) are infinite in number in respect of *dravya*.[50] The characteristics of an atom are that it is the minutest particle from the point of view of locus or field (*kṣetra*), momentary in relation to time (*kāla*), and is also capable of undergoing changes depending upon the condition (*bhāva*).[51] In any case, in Jaina atomism, all atoms are alike without any classification or label in terms of those of earth, water, fire and air. The Jaina concept of atom is thus totally at variance with that of the Nyāya-Vaiśeṣika. Further, Jaina atomism regards atoms as being both cause and effect, the latter in the nature of transformations which the atoms are stated to undergo owing to both internal and external causes. The Nyāya-Vaiśeṣika, on the other hand, believes that atoms are the material causes of the world and the effect is a new event. Jaina atomism also makes another distinction between what is called *sūkṣma paramāṇu* (the minutest and the finest) and *vyavahāra paramāṇu* (*lit.* the practical ones) and regards that it is only the former that is indivisible while the latter with its qualities (not specific to each atom) of colour, taste, smell and touch, could undergo infinite divisions—a view totally different from that of the Nyāya-Vaiśeṣika. Thus in Jaina atomism, both indivisibility and divisibility as well as eternality and non-eternality are equally real in the context of the eternality of substance and the practical mode respectively. Thus the Jaina atoms, infinite in number, of the *sūkṣma* type are indivisible, impassable (*abhedya*), indestructible, incombustible (*adāhya*) and non-receivable (*agrāhya*); but they have no qualitative differences at all. The atoms, nevertheless, could undergo transformation into gross materials like earth, water, fire and air depending upon the nature and extent of qualities like colour, taste, smell, touch and the like.

According to *Bhagavatīsūtra*,[52] an atom is endowed with one colour, one taste, one smell and two touches. The colour could be either black, blue, red, yellow or white; the taste could be either sour, bitter, astringent, acidic or sweetish; the smell could be either pleasant or unpleasant, and the touches could be either cold and cohesive, warm and cohesive, cold and dry, or warm and dry. This text stresses that there cannot be any matter lighter than atom.

The general Jaina position is that these qualities exist equally in each of the infinite number of atoms, but their varied *degrees* of transformation would give rise to different materials of differing qualities. The atoms combine to form an aggregate called *skandha,* which, according to the Jaina standpoint, is not a new material, but a particular form of the aggregation of atoms. Nevertheless, it has been pointed out that, in view of the appearance of different qualities, modes and actions, a *skandha* can also be different from the atoms that constitute it.

Motion of atoms

As for the motion of atoms, the Jaina thought is that they are in motion and active but *may not* be so always. Such motion is a sequel to what has been termed as *pudgalagati* or the motion of matter itself. Some kind of movements of an atom have also been conceived, viz., vibrations of different forms that will lead to the transformation of atoms into gross materials. In such a state, the atoms have been regarded as being in a state of flux. An atom can also, it is believed, move from one point of space to another (*deśāntaragāmikriyā*). At the same time sometimes it can also have a revolving motion about its own axis. Besides, the movement of an atom can be regular (*niyamita*) and irregular (*aniyamita*), depending upon the conditions prevailing in the ambience of space and time conditions. It is pointed out that the motion of an atom can be natural and also due to its combination or an encounter with the other atoms or even a *skandha* (the aggregation of other atoms).

Even the rate or speed of motion of an atom has been speculated upon by the Jaina thinkers. According to them, an atom has a maximum speed when it travels from one border of the universe to another, and a minimum speed when it moves from one space-point to the adjacent space-point. Although it is stated that the motion of an atom occurs in straight line in one unit of time called *samaya,* it could also be curvi-linear (*vigrahagati*), if during its motion, it is acted upon by others. Jaina atomism does not think of motion in an atom as being due to *adṛṣṭa* like the Nyāya-Vaiśeṣika.

Another aspect of Jaina atomism relates to what is called *pratighāta* or resistance experienced by an atom(s) which may be due to (i) the physical contact with another atom; (ii) a combination with another atom or atoms i.e., *skandha* when its loses its character; and (iii) the motion at the so-called border of the universe! While the first two are to some extent understandable, the last one seems to be unintelligible—perhaps a projection of the Jaina religio-philosophy.

How do the atoms combine? This question naturally engaged the attention of Jaina metaphysicians. That the aggregation of atoms is called *skandha* has been noted already. It has been stated that some *skandha-s* are formed directly from the atomic combination, some others by the dissociation of larger *skandhas,* and yet others by both combinations and dissociations. In other words, Jainas do no think of a linear process involving, atoms to begin with. Nevertheless, like the dyads of the Nyāya-Vaiśeṣika, the Jainas enumerate a *dvipradeśika skandha* etc., (formed out of two atoms), *tripradeśika skandha* (as well as the infinite-fold formed out of infinite number of atoms).

With regard to the process of atomic combination, the Jaina thinkers have postulated that the combination of atoms takes place as a result of the qualities but of unequal degree, but not due to their inherent motion as the Nyāya-Vaiśeṣika has conceived. These qualities, according to Jaina, are in the nature of forces—cohesiveness or attractive force (*snigdhatva*); roughness or dryness or repulsive force (*rūkṣatva*); and (iii) even their combination i.e., cohesiveness–dryness or attractive–repulsive forces that are presumed to be present in atoms as well as in *skandha-s*. Two atoms, it has been stated, combine to form a binary *skandha* because of attractive force. The combinations could be of cohesive and dry components (dissimilar). But cohesive and cohesive, or repulsive and non-repulsive ones (similar). But it is pointed out that an atom cannot enter into combination if the atoms have the same degree of cohesion or repulsion.. It is stated that there should be at least a difference of two units, among each of them. Nevertheless, there does not appear to be any type of quantitative definition of what a unit is. Though Jaina atomism thinks of only one type of atoms, it tries to explain the process of combination in terms of attraction and repulsion intrinsic to atoms as well as their potentiality, the higher and the lower ones only entering into combination. The ideas of space and time are also interwoven into Jaina atomism (see the Chapter on Space and Time).

Bauddha Atomism

The four recognized Buddhist schools are: the Vaibhāṣika and Sautrāntika (of the Hīnayāna (lower order sect), the Yogācāra or Vijñānavāda and the Mādhyamika doctrine (Mahāyāna); the latter is also referred to as *śūnyavāda* or nihilism. These two were the main components of the Mahāyāna Sect, not subscribing to the absolute reality of matter as they believe that the manifold phenomena are relative and ultimately are not real. Reality, according to them, is above all categories and is to be realized through spiritual experience, transcending the duality of subject and object as well as the plurality of phenomena. The followers of Yogācāra or Vijñānavāda, have stressed the pathway of Yoga for the realization of pure knowledge in order to become a *Buddha* after passing through the stages of what is termed as Bodhisattvahood. They have also emphasized that the imposed subject–object duality needs to be sublimated and unity with Pure Consciousness attained. They believe that reality is *dharmakāya*, meaning eventually pure consciousness that is none other than the Buddha's Body of Pure Existence. Somewhat bound by their philosophical positions, both the Mādhyamika and Yogācāra schools never thought of an atomism; on the contrary, they were opposed to such a postulate to explain the reality of the knowable world. The Vaibhāṣika and the Sautrāntika schools, on the other hand, were regarded as realists (*Sarvāstivādin-s*) and in that context they admitted the atomic state of matter, but within their philosophical frame. To the Vaibhāṣika, external objects meant their directly being known through perception (*bāhya-pratyakṣa-vāda*) while the Sautrāntika subscribed to the view that external objects were not directly perceived, but inferred indirectly, since, according to them, we do not know the thing-in-itself (*svalakṣaṇa*).[53]

These two schools, however, have presented an atomic view of matter, but as part of their concept of *rūpa*.[54] They consider that matter is a collocation of the four-fold substratum of colour, taste, odour and touch, and regard an atom as the minutest unit of *rūpa* (that which has the capacity to affect sense organ), thus relating it to an observational entity, indirectly though. According to the followers of these two schools of thought, an atom is indivisible, invisible, inaudible, unassailable or untestable and intangible. They are momentary in the sense they continually undergo phase-changes, in consonance with the philosophical position of these two schools of Buddhism.

Two types of atoms, viz., simple (*dravya paramāṇu*) and compounded (*saṃghāta paramāṇu*) have been postulated. As for the compounded or the aggregation of atoms, some believe that it is a direct combination, while some others think that even so there always remains an intervening space between or among atoms. This is in contradistinction to the postulate among the Nyāya-Vaiśeṣika. However, some Buddhists view that the aggregation of atoms would be too close to be permissive of any such space. It is, nevertheless, pointed out that gross matter is a conglomeration of a cluster of atoms having one atom at the center and the others around it, without any type of interaction or interpenetration—all in a speculative way.

According to the aforesaid Hīnayāna schools, there are eight types of atoms—four fundamental [of earth (solid), water (fluid), fire (hot) and of air (moving)] and four secondary (of colour, odour, taste, and touch). In any case, the Bauddha atomism regards the specific qualities also as being atomic. This is somewhat in consonance with the Jaina atomism although it differs conceptually. Even the organs of sense are regarded as modifications of atomic matter, in a way similar to the Nyāya-Vaiśeṣika. There is also an attempt at quantification: each secondary atom requires four fundamental atoms for its support, the resulting aggregate consisting of $4 \times 4 + 4 = 20$ atoms if the body does not sound; if it is to sound, the aggregate consists of $(5 \times 4 + 5)$ 25 atoms, taking into consideration the attribute, namely, sound.[55]

It should be noted that the two Hīnayāna schools do not regard atoms in terms of particles of some matter. Instead they think of them as force or energy like the repulsive force of earth atom or the kinetic energy of water atom. They also point out that these forces are present in all things and in the same proportion. Different states of bodies like liquid or solid are perceived because of the variation in the force-content of different elements, even though the proportionality of the elements could remain unchanged. The Hīnayāna Buddhist view of atoms as dynamic forces is by and large in tune with their doctrine of momentariness.

Some Reflections

A summary of the foregoing reveals that, like the Vaiśeṣika atomism, Jaina atomism also had an independent origin in the early centuries before the Chirstian era, as evidenced by its exposition in the *Bhagavatī vyākhyāprajñapti*, in the Jaina Āgamic manuals. Perhaps in the second century A.D., Umāsvāti, an able exponent of Jaina metaphysical foundations, developed it to some extent in his own way, but within the framework of the Jaina Āgamas. But later Ācāryas like Kundakunda, Pūjyapāda, Akalaṅka, Vidyānanda and others added new dimensions to it in their own way and in contradistinction to the atomism of Nyāya-Vaiśeṣika as well as the evolutionary scheme of the Sāṃkhya (classical) with its conception of the five *tanmātra-s* or subtle essence through which was supposed to be the formation of the gross five elements. The Jaina atomism has its own characteristics when one tries to understand it in the context of the atomic postulates of Nyāya-Vaiśeṣika as well as its *ārambhavāda* and also of the Hīnayāna Buddhists whose *kṣaṇika-paramāṇuvāda* (doctrine of momentariness of atom). The Jaina thinkers chose to retain the word *skandha* of Buddhists instead of *dvyaṇuka* (dyad), *tryaṇuka* (three dyads) *caturaṇuka* (four dyads) and so on of the Nyāya-Vaiśeṣika. The problem of the possible material constituents of the world and the limit to which matter can undergo destruction loomed large in the minds of the Nyāya-Vaiśeṣika, the Jaina and certain sects of Buddhism. Though each of them conceived of an atomic or an indestructible or indivisible state, they differed from one another in the manner of the formation of gross bodies from atoms. Such differences were governed by their philosophical or metaphysical persuasions. The Jainas thought of it, unlike the Nyāya-Vaiśeṣika, in terms of the transformations (qualitative) that would take place encompassing the atoms. They did not accept the Nyāya-Vaiśeṣika postulate of the whole and its parts. An atom of Jainas is *anantabhāga* (infinite part). 'The doctrine of permanence (in respect of atoms) had to be refuted by certain Buddhists, so that their concept of *paramāṇu* was in the matrix of flux or momentariness. The Jaina theory of *paramāṇu* comes nearer to the Buddhist concept of *paramāṇu* from the Modal point of view; for, according to Jaina metaphysics, *paramāṇu* is eternal from the substantial standpoint, while it is non-eternal from the modal point of view".[56]

The two Buddhist schools, as noted before, accept *rūpa* (material) in its twin aspects, viz. the primary four elements and secondary qualities as being atomic. They may in a way correspond to the *dravya* (substance) and *guṇa* (qualities) of Nyāya-Vaiśeṣika, while the Jaina atomism thinks of the qualities of atoms from the point of view of their differentiation. In Jaina atomism there is also the distinction between that which is the minutest and indivisible (*sūkṣma paramāṇu*) and the practical one (*vyavahāra paramāṇu*). But this idea is noted for its absence either in that of Nyāya-Vaiśeṣika or that of the two Buddhist sects. Besides, while the Jaina atomism accepts that even one *paramāṇu* (*sūkṣma* type) could have the status of *skandha*, neither the Vaiśeṣika nor the Buddhist schools subscribe to such a view. Perhaps a common ground appears to be the characteristics of an atom, its indivisibility and indestructibility among the Nyāya-Vaiśeṣika, Jaina and the two Buddhists sects, despite their philosophical positions. It is significant to note that the structural details of atomism as delineated by the Nyāya-Vaiśeṣika as well as of the Jaina are far more than those of the two Buddhists sects. The reason for this may be the flexibility of the former's approach to the physical world when compared with the doctrinaire position of the Buddhists in their interpretation of the world of phenomena. The conception of substance of the Nyāya-Vaiśeṣika , as noted before, is far more meaningful than that of the Jainas as well as of the Buddhist sects, although all of them use the same word, *dravya* for matter or substance. However, the word, *'paramāṇu'*, means differently among the three systems of thought.

Greek Atomism

In the West, the Greeks were well known for their atomism. The Miletian Leucippus (fl. *c.* 475 B.C.), an younger contemporary of Heracleitus (who thought, as noted before, that everything was in a state of flux), speculated in an entirely different way and become the founder of the atomic doctrine of matter. However, we know very little about the background which stimulated him to formulate an atomism. His pupil, perhaps also of Miletus, was Democritus (*c.* 470-400 B.C.), a contemporary of Socrates, who developed an atomic theory that was not only different from the Heracleitan conception that change alone was real but was also totally at discordance with the outlook of Socrates. In a way Leucippus carried forward the new mood generated by Thales and Anaximander, also of Miletus, concerning the primordial stuff of the world. He expounded that all substances were made up of solid concrete atoms with the void or space between them. He emphasized that both void and atoms were a primary reality. The use of the word, 'atom', signified that it would be indivisible, eternal and invisibly minute. Democritus also viewed the atoms as incompressible and homogeneous, differing from one another in form and size, i.e., *quantitatively* and not *qualitatively* in contradistinction to the Nyāya-Vaiśeṣika approach. Further, according to him, atoms were eternal and uncaused, so also was motion which by its nature would originate from the preceding motion—a continuous process. He sought to explain the qualities of different substances as being due to the movement or rearrangement of atoms. Even the living beings were regarded as a temporary arrangement of atoms and, what is more, the soul was also believed to be composed of atoms. The atomic postulate of Democritus was propagated but with some elaboration or extension of his ideas by Epicurus of Samos (342-270 B.C.) and his followers known as Epicureans.

The greatest exponent among the Epicureans was the Roman Lucretius (*c.* 95-55 B.C.). He explained the origin of the entire world as being due to the interaction of atoms, and thought that behind such an interaction there was no Creator or creative intelligence. He emphasized that even mental phenomena were of atomic origin and that everything would spring forth from atoms or determinate units (*semina certa*). He held that material objects were of two kinds—atomic and compounds of atoms—and that "atoms themselves could not be swamped by any force, for they preserved indefinitely by their absolute solidarity and where there is empty space (what we call vacuity) there matter is not; where matter exists, there can not be a vacuum. Therefore the primary units of matter are solid and free from vacuity".[57] It may be noted that neither the Nyāya-Vaiśeṣika nor Jaina nor Bauddha atomism has taken cognizance of both atom and void as the Greeks did.

As for the motion or movement of atoms, according to Lucretius, they do not move or travel generally as isolated or individual units, but massed together. Thus their pace is retarded by the one dragging back the other as well as by the opposing external objects. But when separate atoms travel through empty space, they encounter no obstruction from without and move as units on the course on which they have embarked. "Obviously, therefore, they must far outstrip the sunlight in speed of movement and traverse an extent of space many times as great in time it takes for the sun's rays to flash across the sky". A somewhat similar idea can be seen in Jaina atomism with regard to its postulate of the maximum and minimum speed of atoms. Likewise the Jaina view that atoms move generally in straight course and also curvilinear sometimes, finds an echo in Lucretius: He says: "When the atoms are travelling straight down through empty space by their own weight, at quite indeterminate times and places, they swerve ever so little from their course, just so much that you can call it a change of direction".[58] His argument was that, if it were not for this swerve, everything would fall downwards like raindrops through the abyss of space. Besides there would be no collision among them, nor an impact of one atom on another atom so necessary for a natural creation or production of substances. Lucretius even explained that empty space would offer no resistance and all bodies must travel at the same speed though they are impelled by unequal weights. The heavier ones would never be able to fall on the lighter ones from above and produce impacts leading to varied motion out of which nature could be productive.[59] Such views as these are not found in Indian atomism relating to the aggregates.

In the history of science, as we now know, it was Greek atomism and the exposition of Lucretius that have found a place. On the other hand, Indian atomism, a part of the Indian doctrine of five elements, perhaps because of its religio–philosophical affiliations and other compulsions of spiritual nature, has not received due attention. Nevertheless, Indian atomism was a favourite proposition among its exponents and opponents alike till about the 13th cent. A.D. until the Navya-Nyāya came up with its own nuances surpassing the general framework of Nyāya-Vaiśeṣika. The Jaina and the Buddha atomism too did not make much headway from their original atomic ideas. Among the opponents of atomism was the great Śaṅkarācārya whose advaitic exposition was so penetrating and his antagonism against the Nyāya-Vaiśeṣika was so powerful that atomism, though it did not take a back seat, could no longer enjoy the status that it had earlier. Even so, the commentators of the both Nyāya and Vaiśeṣika continued to be the torch-bearers of atomism.

In Europe, on the other hand, Greek atomism lay dormant till about the 17th cent. A.D. Even at the time of Galileo, the Greek atomic views had come to the fore, but more in the nature of philosophical ideas. But they stimulated a curiosity specially among the biologists who posed for themselves the questions like: are atoms alive? And are they tiny beings? Among the early exponents of the atomic views were Pierre Gassendi (1592-1655) and Robert Boyle (1627-91). Huygens, who was known for his wave theory of light also supported it. As noted already, in Greek atomism both atoms void were real. Newton, in his computations concerning the motion of planets, found it necessary to assume interstellar space to be a vacuum. As he pointed out in his *Principia*, the conception of atom arose when he tried to extend the idea of vacuum to terrestrial matter. His corpuscular theory of light not withstanding, it is very difficult to know the exact nature of his 'corpuscles' or 'particles'. However, Lucretius had stated that the heat and the bright light which the Sun emits would travel through empty space and, therefore, they would be forced to move more slowly, cleaving their way as it were through waves of air. He postulated that the atoms that compose this radiance would not travel as isolated individual units but linked and massed together' (p. 64). Perhaps these ideas of Lucretius might have influenced the thinking of Newton in formulating his corpuscular theory of light.

Newton's contemporary and opponent (as regards the priority concerning calculus), the German, Leibniz (1646-1716) was opposed to atomism. But in France Voltaire (1694-1778) was an able exponent of atomism which he tried to popularize in his own way. In any case, the physical investigators of the eighteenth century generally considered the constitution of matter as atomic. Early in the nineteenth century John Dalton (1766-1844) put forward his atomic theory (1808) both in quantitative and qualitative terms, placing it on solid foundation.

Greek atomism had one advantage. It did not make any distinction like the atoms of different elements, but considered them as being only different in form and size, and thus they could be the building blocks of any type of substance. The Jaina atomism also projected the idea that atoms were of only one class. Even so it thought of qualities of an atom like colour, smell, taste and touch indirectly in the context of the four elements earth, water, fire and air. Buddhists also thought of atoms in terms of these qualities. This type of circumscribed thinking was not permissive of a broader vision of atoms as the possible building units of the universe. Moreover, the other dimension of Greek atomism, namely, void or vacuum became important in the physical investigations that came up later in Europe. In the Indian context, the idea of void never came down from its philosophical position to the physical plane. As it happened, Indian atomism remained within the Indian philosophical or metaphysical confines and did not stimulate any type of new thinking on the physical world.

There is some evidence to indicate that the Nyāya-Vaiśeṣika atomism was known to Arabic savants in the 9th-10th century A.D., as contained in the works of al-Ashari and al-Rāzi. While the Indian astronomical and medical texts, in their Arabic translations, were rendered into Latin in the 12th-13th centuries and thus were available to the European savants then, Indian atomism did not experience such a pathway because of the 'selectivity of translators from Arabic to Latin', as explained by Needham. Some of the Nyāya-Vaiśeṣika texts were known to the Chinese culture-area through the Buddhist refutations. But any type of atomism did not appeal to either the Taoists or Confucians. In any case there is no denying that Indian atomism has a distinct place in the history of scientific ideas, although, by and large, it remained within the philosophical or metaphysical confines in India.

REFERENCES

(All references to the *Praśastapadabhāṣya* (PPB) are taken from *Kiraṇāvalī* (ed) Jitendra S. Jetley including the numbers of the *Sūtra-s* mentioned. Translation of the *Vaiśeṣika Sūtra-s* are taken from A.E. Gough; *The Vaiśeṣika Aphorisms of Kaṇāda*).

1. किमत्र पश्यसीति अण्व्य इवेमा धाना भगव इति । Ch.up. 6.12.1

2. अणोर्महतश्रोपलब्ध्यनुपलब्धी नित्ये व्याख्याते । VS.7.1.8

   The perception or non-perception of the atomic and that of which has magnitude have been explained to be constant.

3. नित्यं परिमण्डलम् । VS.7.1.20

   (Atomic) globular is eternal.

4. Umesh Mishra, *op. cit.* p. 67

5. तस्याणो: निरवयवस्य नित्यस्यानुपपत्ति: । कस्मात्?

   आकाशव्यतिभेदात् । अन्तर्बहिश्राणुराकाशेन

   समाविष्टो व्यतिभिन्न:, व्यतिभेदात्सावयव:

   सावयवत्त्वादनित्य इति ।

   अत्र उच्यते–परमाणोरन्तनर्नास्त्याकाशमिति

   असर्वगतत्वं प्रसज्यत इति ।

   अन्तरिति पिहितं कारणान्तरै: कारणमुच्यते ।

   बहिरिति च व्यवधायकमव्यवहितं कार्यमेवोच्यते ।

   तदेतत्कार्यद्रव्यस्य संभवति । नाणोरकार्यत्वात् ।

   अकार्ये हि परमाणावन्तर्बहिरिति अस्याभाव: ।

   यत्र चास्य भावोऽणुकार्यं तत्, न परमाणु:

   ततो हि अल्पतरमस्ति स परमाणुरिति । *Nyā.Bhā.* IV. 2. 18-20

6. Umesh Mishra, op. cit. p. 72.

7. NS.4.2.17-25; See G. N. Jha's edition, Vol. IV, pp. 1607-1628; The *Bhāṣya* and the *Vārtika* deals with the division of matter, indivisibility of atom, ākāśa versus atom; eternality of atom which cannot be regarded as a product etc.

8. *Kapila.Sū.*5.87-88 is generally referred to in this connection.

9. See under *tanmatra*, Chapter 3, pp. 77-78 of this Volume.

10. न प्रलयोऽणुसद्भावात् । NS. 4.2.16

    An absolute non-existence is not possible because an atom remains (in the end).

    महत्त्वे सति रूपवत्त्वात् कर्मवत्त्वात् ते सावयवाश्च कार्याश्च । *Kiraṇāvalī*, on PPB 33

    Since they (the objects) have magnitude, colour and motion they are constituents and products.

एकस्य अवयवस्य विभागानुपपत्तौ तत्कार्यस्य विनाशासम्भवे नित्यत्वप्रसङ्गादिति ।

As the ultimate individual part is indivisible and as also can not be destroyed (the ultimate part) remains eternal (ibid).

अवयविविभागमाश्रित्य वृत्तिप्रतिषेधादभाव: प्रसज्यमानो निरवयवात्परमाणोर्निवर्तते, न सर्वप्रलयाय कल्पते ।

निरवयवत्वं परमाणोर्विभागैरल्पतरप्रसङ्गस्य यत: नाल्पीयस्तत्रावस्थानात् ।

The alleged non-existence on the ground of the unjustifiability of residence comes to an end after arriving at an atom which is partless and thus (because of the existence of the atoms) does not lead ultimately to an absolute non-existence of all things. Due to the partlessness of an atom (which represents) an entity, nothing can be smaller in which case the possibility of getting smaller and smaller due to division ends. (Vātsyāyana's *Bhāṣya* on the above NS.)

11. सा तु द्विविधा । नित्या चानित्या च । परमाणुलक्षणा नित्या । कार्यलक्षणा चानित्या ।

The earth is of two kinds, viz. eternal and non-eternal. Earth characterised by its atomic form is eternal and that characterised as a constituent (of atoms) is non-eternal. PPB. 30

(Similarly the water element (37), (तास्तु पूर्ववद् द्विविधा: नित्यानित्यभावात्) the elements of fire (तदपि द्विविधमणुकार्यभावात्) 44; and Air (स चायं द्विविधोऽणुकार्यभावात् ।) 49

The element (earth etc.) is eternal in its atomic form.

अणुसंयोगस्त्वप्रतिषिद्ध: । VS. 4.2.4

A conjunction of atoms is not denied.

तथा अण्वपि द्विविधम् । अनित्यं द्वयणुकके एव । PPB. 151

Atoms are of two kinds viz. eternal and non-eternal. The non-eternal (atomic form) lies in a dyad.

12. क्षितावेव गन्ध: । PPB. 29

Smell is the specific quality of earth alone.

13. पार्थिवाप्ययो: अण्वो: संयोगे सति अन्येन पार्थिवेन पार्थिवस्य आप्येन चाप्यस्य युगपत्संयोगौ भवत:। PPB.175

14. परमाणुभ्यामारब्धं द्वयणुकं परमाणुद्वयणुकमित्युच्यते । (NK. on *Parimāṇa*)

A dyad or *paramāṇudvyaṇuka* is so called when two atoms combine.

15. For further details see Subbarayappa, B.V.: 'The Physical World: Views and Concepts' in *A Concise History of Science* in India, pp. 463-69.

16. अणुत्ववत् द्वयणुके द्वित्वसङ्ख्याचातो ह्रस्वत्वोपपत्ति: । PPB. 158

Like the atomic dimension, the dyad also is invisible when two atoms combine (being small).

अणुत्वह्रस्वत्वयोस्तु परस्परतो विशेषस्तद्दर्शिनां प्रत्यक्ष इति ।

The difference between atomic and short form (of the dyad) is visible only to those who are gifted to see it (the yogins).

17. तैरारब्धे कार्यद्रव्ये त्र्यणुकादिलक्षणे रूपाद्युत्पत्तिसमकालं महत्त्वं दीर्घत्वं च करोति । PPB. 156

The product produced by the dyads characterised as triad or tryaṇuka gets magnitude and length along with other qualities like colour soon after it is produced.

18. तच्च द्वाभ्यां परमाणुभ्यां आरब्धं कार्यं न महत् स्यात् । तथात्वे सति तस्य कारणाभावात् तदपि च द्वयणुकं यदि नारभेत; यदि हि द्वित्वसंख्यायुक्तमेवारभेत । उभयथापि तदुत्पादनं वैयर्थ्यं स्यात् । तस्मात्तेन महद्द्रव्यमारभ्यमाणं बहुत्वसंख्यायोगिनैव इति नियमः । न च द्वयणुकपरमाणवोऽपि बहुसंख्यामाश्रित्य महत्कार्यमारप्स्यन्त इति युक्तम्; अनियमारम्भस्य निषिद्धत्वात् । (*Kiranāvali* on PPB. 33)

A product of two dyads can not have any magnitude. In that case there will be no effect caused; when two dyads conjunct, again the two numbers of each dyad remains. Either way there will be futility of conjunction. Hence, as a rule, there should be higher numbers for conjunction in order to produce an object of magnitude. Any violation of such a rule has to be prohibited (i.e. त्रसरेणोः कस्यचिद् द्वयणुकेन कस्यचिच्च परमाणुभिरारम्भे नियतहेतुत्वं न स्यादित्यर्थः । (*Kiranāvali ṭīkā* on the above).

The rule should not be construed as having conjunction of a triad with a dyad or atom in the production of a product.)

19. Umesh Mishra, *op. cit.* pp. 114-116

20. ईदृशो हि तेजसो लाघवातिशयेन वेगातिशयः स्पर्शातिशयश्च यत् तज्जन्यं कर्म, कर्मद्रव्यं पूर्वव्यूहात् प्रच्यावयति । तदवयवांश्च व्यूहान्तरं प्रापयति । *Kiranāvali* on PPB. 128

Due to volatility of fire there arises action on account of quickness and close touch. The constitute body gets disintegrated. Then again another structural arrangement takes place.

21. क्रियागुणव्यपदेशाभावात् प्रागसत् । VS. 9.1.1

(An effect) is antecedently non-existent, inasmuch as there is non-existence of assertion of actions and qualities.

22. च शब्दसमुच्चिताश्च गुरुत्वद्रवत्वस्नेहसंस्कार अदृष्टशब्दाः इत्येव चतुर्विंशतिर्गुणाः ।
अदृष्टशब्देन धर्माधर्मयोः संक्षेपेणाभिधानम् । *Kiranāvali* on PPB. 5

23. तद्विशेषेणादृष्टकारितम् । VS.5.2.2

That action which is produced in a different manner from these is caused by destiny.

24. Faddegon, *The Vaiśeṣika Aphorisms*, p. 309.

25. तद्वचनादाम्नायस्य प्रामाण्यम् । VS. 1.1.3

Authoritativeness belongs to revelation because it is a declaration of that.
तदित्यनुपक्रान्तमपि प्रसिद्धिसिद्धतया ईश्वरं परामृशति यथा तद्प्रामाण्यमनृतव्याघातपुनरुक्तदोषेभ्य इति गौतमीयसूत्रे तच्छब्देनानुपक्रान्तोऽपि वेदः परामृश्यते ।

The word that (*tat*) signifies God, though it has not been previously mentioned, it being inferred from being universally known, just as in the aphorism of Gautama. Śaṅkaramiśra's *Upaskāra* on VS. 1.1.3.

26. प्रणम्य हेतुमीश्वरं मुनिं कणादमन्वतः । पदार्थधर्मसङ्ग्रहः प्रवक्ष्यते महोदयः ॥ PPB. 1

Salutation to the Lord, the cause of (all that is produced). Salutations then to Kaṇāda, the sage. I now tell 'Mahodaya', that which yields liberation, namely, *Padārthadharma saṅgraha*, a compilation of the attributes of all categories.

27. तत: पुन: प्राणिनां भोगभूतये महेश्वरस्य सिसृक्षानन्तरं सर्वात्मगतवृत्तिलब्ध-अदृष्टापेक्षेभ्य: तत्संयोगेभ्य: पवनपरमाणुषु कर्मोत्पत्तौ तेषां परस्परसंयोगेभ्यो द्व्रणुकादिक्रमेण महान् वायु: समुत्पन्न: । PPB. 58

Then the Lord desires to create the word so that the beings may experience life. Then the power of *adṛṣṭa* existing in all the souls begin the act of conjunction. Motion is generated among the atoms due to the conjunction of souls and atoms caused by *adṛṣṭa*. Due to the motion in the atoms air element (to begin with) is produced on account of the conjunction of dyads.

(The creation of the other elements viz water, earth and fire, is described in the same manner).

28. परमेश्वराधिष्ठानेन अचैतन्यप्रवृत्तिचैतन्यप्रवृत्तिनियमौ च समासयेदिति । Udayana on PPB. 59

One should consider the propriety of the activities of sentient and insentient beings are based on the Supreme Being.

29. ईश्वरमिति विशिष्टदेवताया अभिधानं, लोके तद्विषयत्वेन एव अस्य पदस्य प्रसिद्धे: । Śrīdhara's NK on PPB. p.1

The word Īśvara represents a special deity as this word is well known as signifying such a meaning only in the world.

30. व्यक्ताव्यक्तानां प्रत्यक्षप्रामाण्यम् । NS. 4.1.11

न घटाद् घटानिष्पत्ते: । 4.1.12

व्यक्ताद् घटनिष्पत्तेरप्रतिषेध: । 4.1.13

4.1.11 The (production) of perceptible things is from perceptible things; as is clearly provided by perception. 4.1.12 What is asserted is not true; As the jar is not produced from jar. 4-1-13 In as much as the jar is actually produced out of a 'perceptible' substance, the objection has no force.

31. ईश्वर: कारणं पुरुषकर्माफल्यदर्शनात् । 4.1.19

न, पुरुषकर्माभावे फलनिष्पत्ते: । 4.1.20

तत्कारितत्वादहेतु: । 4.1.21

Īśvara (God) is the cause; because we find fruitlessness in the actions of men. 4.1.19
It is not so; because as a matter of fact no fruit appears without man's action. 4.1.20
In as much as it is influenced by Him, There is no force in the reason (put forward). 4.1.21

32. अनिमित्ततो भवोत्पत्ति: कण्टकतैक्ष्ण्यादिदिदर्शनात् । NS. 4.1.22

अनिमित्तिनिमित्तत्वाच्चानिमित्तत: । NS. 4.1.23

निमित्तानिमित्तयोरर्थान्तरभावाद् प्रतिषेध: । NS. 4.1.24

The production of entities must be without an efficient cause; as we see such things as the sharpness of a thorn and the like. (4.1.22)
Since the non-cause is (spoken of as) the cause the said production of entities is not 'without cause.'
Nimitta (cause) and *animitta* (non-cause), being two distinct things, the answer is no answer at all.

33. Bulcke: *The Theism of Nyāya-Vaiśeṣika*, Motilal Banarasidass, Delhi, 1947, pp. 27-37.

34. मनस्त्वयोगान्मनः । सत्यपि आत्मेन्द्रियार्थसान्निध्ये
ज्ञानसुखादीनामभूत्वोत्पत्तिदर्शनात् करणान्तरं
अनुमीयते । श्रोत्राद्यव्यापारे स्मृत्युत्पत्तिदर्शनात्
बाह्येन्द्रियैरगृहीतसुखादिग्राह्यान्तराभावात् ।
प्रयत्नादृष्टपरिग्रहवशादाशुसञ्चारि च । PPB. 81-82

35. Tatia, Nathumal : *Studies in Jaina Philosophy*, pp. 55-58.

36. अजीवकाया धर्माधर्माकाशपुद्गलाः । *Tat. Sū.* 5.1
The non-soul extensives are *dharma, adharma, ākāśa* and *Pudgala*.

37. खन्धा य खन्ददेसा खन्दपदेसा य होंति परमाणू ।
इति ते चतुवियप्पा पुग्गलकाया मुणेयव्वा ॥ Pañcāstikāya. 4

38. स्कन्धाश्च स्कन्धदेशाः स्कन्धप्रदेशाश्च भवन्ति परमाणवः ।
इति ते चतुर्विकल्पाः पुद्गलकाया ज्ञातव्याः ॥ *Pañcāstikāyasāra*. 80

39. वादरसौक्ष्म्यगतानां स्कन्धानां पुल इति व्यवहारः ।
ते भवन्ति षट्प्रकारास्त्रैलोक्यं यैर्निष्पन्नम् ॥
पुढवि जलं च छाया चउरिं दियविसयकम्पया ओग्गा ।
कम्मातीदा येवं छव्भेदा पोग्गला होन्ति ॥ *Pañcāstikāyasāra*, 82-83

40. संख्येयासंख्येयाश्च पुलानाम् । *Tat.Sū.*5.10
The atoms of matter (are) numerable, innumerable and infinite according to their molecular compositions.

41. सर्वेषां स्कन्धानां योऽन्त्यस्तं विजानीहि परमाणुम् ।
स शाश्वतोऽशब्दः एकोऽविभागी मूर्तिभवः ।
अदेशमात्रमूर्तो धातुचतुष्कस्य कारणं वस्तु ।
स ज्ञेयः परमाणुः परिणामगुणः स्वयमशब्दः ॥

42. शब्दः स्कन्धप्रभवः स्कन्धः परमाणुसंघसंघातः ।
स्फुटेषु तेषु जायते शब्द उत्पादको नियतः ॥

43. नित्यो नानवकाशो न सावकाशः प्रदेशतो भेत्ता ।
स्कन्धानामपि च कर्ता प्रविभक्ता कालसंख्यायाः ॥

44. एकरसवर्णगन्धं द्विस्पर्शं शब्दकारणमशब्दम् ।
स्कन्धान्तरितं द्रव्यं परमाणुं तं विजानीहि ॥ *Pañcāstikāyasāra*, 84-88

45. सङ्घातभेदेभ्यः उत्पद्यन्ते । (*Tat.Sū.* 5.26)
Clusters of matter are produced in three ways: by integration, dis-integration and by a combination of integration and disintegration.

46. भेदाद् अणुः । (*Tat.Sū.* 5.27)
An atom is produced by disintegration.

  Indian Perspectives on the Physical World

47. (i) अर्पितनार्पितसिद्धे: । *Tat.Sū.* 5.32

The ungrasped aspect of an object is attested by the grasped one.

(ii) स्निग्धरूक्षत्वाद् बन्ध: । Ibid.5.33

The integration of atoms is due to their tactile quality of greasiness and dryness.

(iii) न जघन्यगुणानाम् । Ibid. 5.34

There cannot be integration of atoms that possess the minimum one degree of greasiness or dryness.

(iv) गुणसाम्ये सदृशानाम् । Ibid. 5.35

Atoms which have the same degree of greasiness or same degree of dryness cannot integrate.

48. वर्णगन्धरसस्पर्शयोगिन: पुला मता: ।

पूरणात् गलनाच्चैव संप्राप्तान्वर्थनामका: ॥ *Ādipurāṇa,* 24.1.5

49. रूपिण: पुला: । *Tat.Sū.* 5.5

The cluster of matter and single atom have material qualities.

50. नाणो: । *Tat.Sū.*5.11;

There is no additional unit in an atom of matter
(explained by commentators as being infinite in number).

51. For details, see Sikdar, J. N. 'Jaina Atomism' *Indian Journal of History of Science,* **2**, 5, 1969.

52. *Bhagavatīsūtra,* Sections 20 and 25.

53. C. Sharma, *op. cit.* pp. 80-81.

54. Das Gupta, S. N.: *History of Indian Philosophy,* I. (reprint) pp. 121 ff.

55. Stcherbasty, Th: *Buddhist Logic,* I. pp. 190 ff

56. Sikdar J. N.: *Indian Journal of History of Science,* **2**, 5, pp. 202-203.

57. Lucretius: *The Nature of the Universe* (Tr. R. E. Latham), The Penguin Books, Hammondsworth, 1951, pp. 41-42, 63 ff.

58. *op. cit.* p. 66.

59. *op. cit.* p. 64.

CHAPTER 6

Indian Epistemological Concerns

INDIAN PERSPECTIVES ON the physical world need to be understood in relation to their epistemological concerns that were recognized and fostered over a long period, but within the respective philosophical or metaphysical seed-ideas. The nature and structure of how a knowledge of the phenomenal world is acquired and whether such knowledge is right or fallacious have engaged the attention of Indian thinkers over a long period. Therefore, a brief discussion of Indian epistemology would be necessary, here, with a view to understanding their approach to knowledge itself. In the Vedic period, the general attitude as pointed out earlier was a part of the triple-stranded man–spirit–cosmos view that was considerably mixed up with mythological elements. Gradually the mythological shackles were discarded and in the process *logos* gained some ascendancy over *mythos*. It needs to be recognised that the major Indian systems of thought, both orthodox and heterodox, have paid adequate attention to the knowledge of the physical world as an integral component of the means of attaining valid knowledge, setting aside myths and other weird aspects. Nevertheless, the knowledge gained through the senses and even the knowledge of the Vedic literature have been regarded as something inferior (*aparāvidyā*) while that of the highest knowledge, the knowledge of the Absolute, has been accorded an exalted status as the superior one (*parāvidyā*).[1] In any case the totality as well as the nuances of knowledge itself engaged the attention of the propounders of various schools or systems notwithstanding some basic differences among them in their approach. The realistic school of the Nyāya-Vaiśeṣika has enunciated its own methodology and categorization that reveal its considered view of the components of the sensorial knowledge as well as the means for gaining the right or valid knowledge. The most notable dimension of this school or system is its succinct exposition of practically all aspects of the nature of the knowledge obtainable through senses and, more importantly, the terminology associated with the precise knowledge-process itself.

The Upaniṣadic approach in the form of dialogues as well as discussions, albeit in the realm of higher knowledge, had in them the proto-layers of questioning or debating coupled with reasoning. One may even say that there was an enquiring mind-set which in course of time stimulated what is called *ānvikṣīkī* (the method of enquiry) and *hetu-vidyā* (the science of reasoning). The *Maitrāyaṇī upaniṣad*[2] emphasized the importance of an epistemic approach by pointing out that the existence of an object could be established only by a valid mode of cognition, using the words, *pramāṇa* and *prameya* in this connection. The then emerging challenges to the Vedic including the Upaniṣadic tradition specially from Buddhism, Cārvākas and others led in due course to the development of *pramāṇaśāstra*, strengthened by what was known as *vākovākya* referred to in the *Chāndogya upaniṣad*[3] or a thesis to be refuted or established evidently by reasoning and debate. This was interpreted by Śaṅkara as *Tarkaśāstra* (science of logic). The term *Ānvīkṣikī* occurs in the *Arthāśāstra* of Kauṭilya as one of the four branches of study. *Ānvīkṣikī* in general was concerned with critical and rational assessment of all types of theoretical and practical issues. It was rightly given a high position as the science of logic, a rationalistic thinking in contrast to the then surrounding dogmatic ensemble. It was also given a distinct place along with *Tarkaśāstra* in the *Mahābhārata*. *Ānvikṣikī* was also referred to as *tantra-yukti* (forms of argumentation). Caraka in his *Saṃhitā*, mentions in some detail, thirty four *tantra-yukti-s* (*Siddhi-sthāna*, XII) as well as the means of acquiring or substantiating knowledge (perception, inference and *āpta-vākya* or the knowledge of the experts). The importance as well as the art of debate which one finds in the medical classics reveals the high level of rational thinking even in the sixth or fifth century before the Christian era. It may be noted that though these classics were redacted in the early centuries after the Christian era, their foundational ideas in a rational manner were at least six or seven centuries earlier.

The *Nyāya-sūtra* (I. 1.1.2) enumerates as many as sixteen entities, pointing out that it is the knowledge of the real essence or true character (*tattva*) of the sixteen categories that will lead to the attainment of the highest good (*niḥśreyas* or *apavarga*). The sixteen entities or categories (*tattva-s* or *padārtha-s*) are: (i) the means of right cognition or instruments of knowledge (*pramāṇa*); (ii) the objects of right cognition (*prameya*); (iii) doubt (*saṃśaya*); (iv) motive (*prayojana*); (v) example (*dṛṣṭānta*) (vi) theory (*siddhānta*); (vii) factors of inference (*avayava*); (viii) hypothetical reasoning (*tarka*); (ix) demonstrated truth (*nirṇaya*); (x) discussion (*vāda*); (xi) disputation (*jalpa*); (xii) wrangling (*vitaṇḍa*); (xiii) fallacious reason (*hetvābhāsa*); (xiv) perversion (*chala*); (xv) casuistry (*jāti*); and (xvi) clinchers (*nigrahasthānam*).[4]

The commentators, *Vātsyāyana* (*Nyāya-bhāṣya*) and *Uddyotakara* (*Vārttika*) have tried to throw some light on the word, *tattva*,[5] and *niḥśreyasa*.[6] According to Vātsyāyana, the highest good is attained by the knowledge of the real nature (*tattva*) of such entities as the self and the others. Udayana further says: 'That which forms the basis of a certain thing being cognized in its true form constitutes the real nature of that thing; that is to say, in the case of every thing it is found that there is something in it by virtue of which the thing comes to be known as what it is, and it is this something that forms the real nature of that thing. As regards the highest good, it is of two kinds: (i) Seen or perceptible and (ii) Unseen or imperceptible. That which follows from the knowledge of the real nature of *pramāna* and other categories is seen or the perceptible good. . . . The fact of the matter is that (while some sort of perceptible good might follow from the knowledge of each of the categories), the imperceptible highest good follows only from the knowledge of the soul and the other objects of cognition'.[7] The sixteen entities of the Nyāya have been critically examined by various commentators and logicians from different points of view. It is not possible here to delineate and discuss all of them in great detail. What follows is their brief presentation that would provide a general insight into the thought-processes involved in them.

Pramāna (Instrument of knowledge)

(i) Perception

The instrument or the means that would lead to the acquisition of valid or right knowledge are: (i) Perception; (ii) Inference; (iii) Analogy; and (iv) Testimony.[8] As for perception, Gautama's (the author of the *Nyāya-sūtra-s*) concept includes (a) the instrument of perceptual awareness; (b) the perceptual awareness itself; and (iii) the object of perceptual awareness. Vātsyāyana explains the concerned *sūtra* (1.1.3) that perception consists of the functioning or action of each sense organ upon an object, and such action would be in the nature of contact or cognition. In the case of contact, it results in cognition, i.e., right knowledge, '. . . . If the action is in the form of cognition, when it would result in an idea of the object, that could be discarded or accepted or even treated with indifference'.[9] Perception is duly recognized to be the most important one and is defined by Gautama in terms of cognition which is a result of the contact of the object with the concerned sense organ and such a perception is not only well defined but also exact though it cannot be expressed in words.[10] As Vātsyāyana explains, sense-perception is the cognition which is produced as a result of the sense organ with the cognised object.[11] The question regarding the inexpressible nature of perception by words is answered by pointing out that, at the time of the sensorial perception of the object, it is never expressed by means of any name, and the name of the object is an additional factor added on to the perception for purposes of communication. The role of mind or its related interplay with sense organs during cognition has been described by the commentators. But the *Nyāya-sūtra* does not specifically mention this aspect. But it is assumed (and the explanation offered) is that when perceptual cognition is distinguished from the other forms of cognition, there is no need for the inclusion of others like the part played by mind and the like.[12] Moreover, mind is regarded as an internal sense organ. As a result, it is pointed out that the cognition would be erroneous if the object is apprehended as what it is not, and the perception itself would not be erroneous, if the object is perceived as it presents itself. The *Nyāya-bhāsya* makes a significant declaration with regard to mind. '. . . Even though the *sūtra* does not mention the *Mind* among the 'sense organs', the fact that the *mind* is a sense-organ can be learnt from another philosophical system (the *Vaiśesika,* for instance); and it is a *rule* with all systems that those theories of other systems which are not directly negatived are meant to be accepted as true'.[13] Such a declaration is vehemently opposed by Diṅnāga, the Buddhist logician.

The relationship between sense organ and the object is of prime importance to a Naiyāyika. The question as to what is the nature of contact of the sense-organ with the object? has been posed and answered as well, albeit the latter's inadequacies. Six types of contact have been envisaged by Uddyotakara in his *Vārttika* (i) Conjunction; (ii) Inherence in which that is in conjunction; (iii) Inherence in that which itself inheres in that which is in conjunction; (iv) Inherence in general; (v) Inherence in that which is itself inheres; and (vi) the relation of qualification.[14] The Naiyāyika has shown his discernible knowledge in this regard since the six types which have subtle differences, have been explained clearly by giving an example. 'When a jar which is coloured is seen, there ensues a contact between it, the 'object' and the, the sense organ, (the eyes) and such a contact is in the nature of conjunction between the two substances (*dravya-s*) But the colour of the jar is not a substance (but an attribute) and inheres in that which is in conjunction; because the colour also inheres in the jar.[15] Thus it follows that in the perception of the genus subsisting in the colour, the 'contact' is one of inherence in that which inheres in that which is in conjunction. Likewise, in the perception by means of the olfactory organ (nose), there is conjunction with the substance that is as well as odorous, inherence of the odour in the substance, and at the same time the inherence of the odour itself in that substance which is in conjunction with the sense organ. As for sound, it inheres in the substance, *ākāśa* of the auditory organ which apprehends it. The same type of argument is advanced by way of inherence of the inherent. The Nyāya-Vaiśesika has rather a protracted approach to explain the direct perception in the conceptual framework of substance and inherence. But its concept of inference is refreshing and meaningful alike.

(ii) *Inference*

Kaṇāda has dealt with inferences emanating from the cause and effect in their inherent relationship (VS 9.18).

But he uses the term *laiṅgika* (derived from *liṅga* or mark) for inference. Praśastapāda does not appear to carry forward this view, though he tries to throw some light on its characteristics.[16] The inferential mark, according to him, is related to probandum and does not exist in the absence of any probandum. Śrīdhara, on the other hand seeks to elucidate it in his own way.[17] The three kinds of inference—*anvayin, vyatirekin* and *anvaya-vyatirekin*—marks have been discussed in detail by Uddyotakara in his *Nyāyavārttika*.

Praśastapāda, has also thought of inference as being of two varieties: *dṛsta* and *sāmanyatodṛsta*,[18] the former being the one that is already known to have been associated with the mark; the latter, on the other hand, being concerned with that which is to be proved or inferred, i.e., the particularity as well as the generality, each being different from the other.

In the Vaiśeṣika approach, both the effect and non-eternality belong only to those that have causes and are related to the first three categories, namely, substance, quality and action; but these do not belong to the atomic state. In this process of thinking, dyad, the ubiquitous *ākāśa*, time, space, soul, and mind and qualities like posteriority and priority have been excluded.

Apart from the perception which has been rightly given the first place in the Nyāya scheme of the acquisition of knowledge, it has accorded an equally important place to inference. According to the *Nyāya-sūtra*;[19] 'after perception comes inferential cognition which is led by perception'.[20] It is of three kinds: (i) the *pūrvavat* (in which the effect is inferred from the cause); (ii) *śeṣavat* (the cause is inferred from the effect); and (iii) *sāmānyatodṛsta* (inference based on general observation)'. Thus the Nyāya has meaningfully recognized the salient differences between perception and inference. The former pertains to the objects present and to the role of senses, while the latter is related to objects either present or not present, the past and the future. In other words, inference is applicable to the present, the past and the future. The *Nyāya-bhāsya* and the *Nyāyavārttika* have explained the nature of these three types of inferences and commented upon the words used for these types.[21]

The general approach to inference (*anumāna*) specially by Uddyotakara merits some attention. His comments on Vātsyāyana's statement that 'inference is preceded by perception' are indeed worthy of note. With a view to distinguishing inference from the other forms of valid cognition, he makes a distinction between *anumāna* as a form of cognition and that as a *means* of cognition, adhering by and large to the latter position. He states: "The perception of the relation (of concomitance) between the *probans* and the *probandum* is the first, and that of the probans itself is the second. What happens in the case of inference is as follows: when a man who is desirous of getting at inferential cognitions, perceives the *probans* a second time (i.e., after *probandum*), this perception arouses in his mind the impression left in his mind by the former perception, which leads him to remember that relation between the *probans* and the *probandum*; and after this remembrance, when he again perceives the *probans*, this last perception, led up to by the former two perceptions, and the subsequent remembrance, becomes the *anumāna* or means of inferential cognition, which is known by the name of *parāmarśa*".[22] According to Uddyotakara, there are two constituents of *parāmarśa* as its contents, namely, *vyāpti*—the relation of concomittance between the probans and the probandum, and *pakṣadharmatā*—the presence of the probans in the *pakṣa*, the subject. He has discussed the assertion made by Vātsyāyana in his *Bhāṣya* that 'Perception pertains to things present, while inference pertains to things present as well as not present'. He is opposed to the definition of inference given by the Sāṃkhyavādins, according to whom, inference is a type of relationship between one perception of the probans and the cognition that arises of the other, or the cognition that arises of the subject out of one perceptible relationship.[23]

(iii) *Analogy*

The *Nyāya-sūtra*[24] states that analogy is that which accomplishes its purposes by shedding light through an examination of the noticeable similarity to a known object. As explained in the *Nyāya-sūtra bhāṣya*, analogy is that which makes known that which is to be made known through similarity to an object that is already well known. The example given is the assertion 'as the cow, so the *gavaya* (i.e., the animal called *gavaya* is like the cow).[25] If one who has heard or known this analogy, perceives an object similar to cow, his remembrance of *gavaya* as the name of this object leads to the cognition of this particular name with the perceived object. Uddyotakara and others argue that it is the similarity that is actually observed when the animal is seen to resemble a cow. The Buddhists-Diṅnāga and others do not accept analogy as a separate instrument of cognition, and include it under perception itself.[26]

(iv) *Verbal testimony*

The fourth and the last instrument of right cognition relates to the word of a reliable (*āpta*) person.[27] An *āpta* is explained as not only the one who possesses the direct and right knowledge of objects but also has the desire to impart it to others as he has known it. The word *āpti* means the direct and right knowledge of things. It is also recognized that an *āpta* could be a sage or a venerable person or even any other person, provided he has direct and valid knowledge of the concerned situation and that he has no motive to give incorrect information.[28] The Vedas which are regarded as infallible the revealed knowledge are believed to be the unassailable *āptavākya*. A distinction is made between the reliable assertion and assertion of a reliable person. It is only the latter that is to be considered as an instrument of right cognition, and this is stated to be of two types: (i) that which the thing spoken of is perceived (*dṛṣṭārtha*) and that of which the thing is not perceived (*adṛṣṭārtha*).[29] Uddyotakara has sought to clarify this issue by saying that, though a reliable assertion may be of several kinds, this is meant to be restricted to such assertions as refer to the objects that are amenable to perception and inference.

Although Kaṇāda has not advanced any argument against verbal testimony but has emphasized the two *pramāṇa-s* (perception and inference), Praśastapāda and Śrīdhara have thrown sufficient light on this aspect. In general, the position of the Vaiśeṣikas as well as of the Naiyāyikas seems to be that the Vedas or *śrutis* as also *smṛtis* are by themselves not the authority or the sources of ascertainment, but their authority is dependent upon how great an authority the speaker or Vedic savant is. Śrīdhara in his *Nyāya-Kandalī*[19] has dealt with this aspect in great detail *vis-à-vis* the strict acceptance of verbal testimony or the *śrutis* by the mīmāmsakas as well as the Naiyāyikas. It would appear that to the Vaiśeṣikas the trustworthiness of the speaker well versed in the scriptures was more important than the words of the scriptures themselves. Nevertheless, to the Vaiśeṣikas, verbal testimony is not an independent means of cognition.

Objects of Right Cognition (Prameya-s)

In the ambience of the four instruments of cognition noted above, the following, according to Gautama, constitute the objects of cognition: self or soul, body, sense organs, objects, awareness or apprehension, mind, activity, defect, re-birth, fruition, pain and release.[30] The *self* or *the soul* is the perceiver and experiencer of pleasure, pain and their causes; the *body* is the receptacle of the experiences of the self; sense organs are the instruments of different experiences of the *senses*; objects are those to be experienced and enjoyed; *awareness* is the experience itself; *mind* is that internal organ capable of bringing about the apprehension of all objects, specially those which the sense organs cannot do; *activity* is stated to be the cause of the propagation or manifestation of the body, the sense organs, objects, the experience of pleasure and pain, etc; *re-birth* means that the body which belongs to the self in one's life is neither its first nor its last, but it is that which constitutes rebirth; fruition is regarded as meaning the experience of the pleasure and pain as well as the causes for them; *pain* is interpreted as a disagreeable one and even pleasure is also stated to be a form of pain, being never free from the latter; and lastly, the *release* means the complete cessation of births and deaths, and the eventual disappearance of pain.[31] The inclusion under the *prameya-s*, such categories as re-birth, fruition, pain and release, as objects of cognition reveals that, besides the valid knowledge of the physical world, the right cognition or understanding of pleasure, pain and the like as also the release from their bondage, are regarded as being equally important—an integrated approach towards the known and the knower with his multilevel experiences, in the context of the material and the non-material aspects. Indian thought in general and that of the Nyāya-Vaiśeṣika in particular have been developed in such a way that the ultimate aim of real knowledge is to obtain the release from the bondage of ignorance and the cycle of births and deaths.

The parameters of self have been delineated in a comprehensive manner. They are: desire, aversion, effort, pleasure, pain and cognition.[32] But the Vaiśeṣika, as noted earlier, has added some more including the five generic attributes (number, distinctness, dimension, conjunction and disjunction) as well as virtue, vice and faculty. The existence of self is sought to be proved on the basis of the re-cognition process involved in desire, aversion and the like. The *Nyāya–Vārttikatīkā* projects the idea that desire, aversion etc, are qualities which do not have a separate existence apart from their inherence in a substance (*dravya*), and, that the related substance is not body but *self*, that has been derived by 'inference per residue.'[33]

As for the body, it is regarded as the vehicle of action or motion for the purpose of obtaining what is beneficial and discarding what is injurious. Body is also stated to be the vehicle of sense organs inasmuch as the latter follow or tuned to the changes that occur in the body.[33a]

Doubt (*Saṁśaya*)

It has been rightly pointed out that doubt is the wavering judgement in which the specific character of any one object is wanting. Differing views, however, have been expressed on the kinds of doubt. It is important to note the place of doubt in the acquisition of right knowledge, immediately after the instruments and objects of knowledge. As the *Nyāya-sūtra* emphasizes, doubt is the first to be examined because it is the principal accessory of all examinations. In any case, it has been accepted that doubt may not be a necessary factor in all cases of ascertainment or definitive cognition, but is surely a necessary component of all inquiry or hypothetical reasoning. Even though definitive cognition may or may not be preceded by doubt, the process of enquiry must always be preceded by doubt. Doubt would never cease as long as the property whose cognition gives rise to doubt continues to exist. The entertainment of doubt leads to sharpening of intellectual edge, so necessary for a meaningful understanding of the object in question or the opponent's point of view. The *Nyāya-sūtra* has a succinct definition of doubt namely, doubt is a wavering judgement which arises: (i) from the cognition of the characters common to the objects concerned; (ii) from the cognition of characters that would enable one to distinguish an object from the other diverse objects; and (iii) from the presence of contradictory or opposing opinions; and the appearance of diverse or wavering judgements due to the uncertainty associated with perceptions as well as even non-perceptions.[34] Kaṇāda in his *sūtra*[35] defines that doubt arises when there is perception of an object possessed of common characters (*sāmānya pratyakṣa*) and the non-perception of the specific characters (*viśeṣāpratyakṣa*). The followers of the Nyāya-Vaiśeṣika have examined several dimensions of doubt and have accorded the rightful place to it either while examining a treatise of scientific importance or a perplexing controversy.

Purpose (*prayojana*)

Purpose is defined in the *Nyāya-sūtra* 'as that object, aiming at which one acts'.[36] This is obviously concerned with a person's determination or *will* either to acquire an objective or discard it. That object is called purpose or motive and it would be in the nature of the causation of the related actions. The difference between doubt and purpose lies in the fact that doubt, if it has no motivation, cannot act as an incentive to reasoning, while an internally well defined purpose always leads to investigation on the basis of sound reasoning.

Example (*dṛṣṭānta*)

According to *Nyāya-sūtra*[37] and the *bhāṣya*, the three-in-one purpose served by an example are: (i) to discard or overthrow contrary opinions by showing that they are contradictory to or not in consonance with the example adduced; (ii) to vindicate one's own point of view by demonstrating the compatibility or near identity with the known or widely accepted example; and (iii) to make use of it as an illustration among the members of a syllogism. An *example*, therefore, relates to the parties i.e., the common man (*laukika*) and the trained investigator (*parīkṣaka*) both entertaining similar ideas,[38] the former being not well versed or intelligent, and the latter being capable of examination by means of reasoning and adducing proofs. The *Vārttika* makes a difference between analogy and example, by stating that analogy does not give rise to any notion of similarity, while an appropriate example does so.[39] However, it has been recognized that an example does not serve the purpose of proving what is *not* or incapable of being proved.

Doctrine (*siddhānta*)

Siddhānta or doctrine is defined as a theory or conviction about 'the exact nature of a thing dealt with in philosophy'.[40] The word *siddha*, means accomplished, but in this context it connotes the opinion held by one regarding the exact nature of an object or the opinion (*anta*) that people have about the particular character of the concerned objects, according to *Vātsyāyana*.[41] The *Nyāya-sūtra* thinks of a doctrine being of four kinds in terms of (i) that which is common to all philosophies; (ii) peculiar to one philosophy; (iii) resting on implication (*adhikaraṇa*); and (iv) hypothetical doctrine.[42] The first one relates to the philosophical conviction that is compatible with any philosophy,[43] the second to the position taken only by one of the parties.[44] The *Nyāya-bhāṣya* adds that an author takes to the hypothetical doctrine with a view to showing off cleverness of his own intellect with utter disregard for the intellect of others', although Uddyotakara does not appear to subscribe to this view.[45]

Factors of inference (*avayava*)

The *Nyāya-sūtra-s*, 1.1.32-39, throw light on reasoning and the factors of inference. The latter is thought of in its five aspects: (a) statement of proposition; (ii) statement of the *probans*; (iii) example; (iv) reaffirmation; and (v) final conclusion.[46] The first one consists in the assertion of what is to be proved, the probandum;[47] demonstration of the probandum;[48] the example shows the relation between the probandum and the probans.[49] In respect of the fourth factor called reaffirmation, the object functioning as reason is compared with a definitive example.[50] The fifth one or the final conclusion is eventually a reiteration of the proposition on the strength of the probans.[51] The Nyāya thus presents five members of a syllogism.

Argument (*tarka*)

Argument (this is also called hypothetical reasoning)[52] is not considered as a means of knowledge or knowledge itself. But its purpose is to ascertain the real character of an object, when it is not well known, and it confirms the real character of an object, i.e., the character that is free from all misconceptions or contrary conclusion about the object.[52] There have been divergent views on the part played by argument, as if it is a separate entity. Some hold the view that it does not in any way differ from doubt as well as definitive cognition; others think that argument is only a form of inference; yet others believe that argumentation is a particular kind of inference which is dependent upon corroborative proof in the form of establishing the absurdity or inconsistency of contrary conclusion.

Ascertainment (*nirṇaya*)

The *Vārttika* has clearly brought out the distinction between inference and ascertainment or definitive cognition, saying that inference is a cause or an instrument while ascertainment is the effect or the result.[53] The *Nyāya-sūtra*[54] points out that definitive cognition results when two sides of the concerned question are critically examined or discussed and both the arguments, one in favour of a certain conclusion and the other against it, are also deliberated upon. If in a debate that would obviously have opposing views, if one has to establish one's own position (in favour of a conclusion) one will have to examine in detail the opponent's position. The *nirṇaya,* therefore, would have a strong data-base(s) to win over the other side, if it is to carry forward the winner's philosophical or other ideas which, in turn, would have a large number of followers. It is significant to note that, whether in the Upaniṣadic texts or in the religio-philosophical texts, such debates have had an important place, the opponent's questions being examined in a meaningful manner. However, as regards the position or ideas of scriptures, the *Nyāya-bhāṣya*[55] says that there should not be any deliberation or doubt about them. The *Vārttika* asserts that the ascertainment is to be sought or obtained entirely with the help of Scriptures, and there could be no room for any other type of data or sources of information.[56] Further, there could not at all be two sets of arguments, one for and another against, about scriptural matters. Thus the scriptures have been accorded the high status of unquestionable authority. This is in tune with the tacitly accepted position of the Nyāya system, namely, *Śabda* as a *pramāṇa*.

Discussion, Sophistry and Cavil (*vāda, jalpa and vitaṇḍa*)

The Nyāya is naturally concerned with the conception (*pakṣa*) and counter-conception (*pratipakṣa*) along with the associated controversy. It regards such controversies as being of three kinds—Discussion, Disputation and Wrangling.

The *Nyāya-sūtra*[57] explains the meaning of discussion as follows: In discussion, two scholars put forth their ideas, a conception and a counter-conception, adducing proofs or valid reasons either in supporting or opposing them, but they are not totally at variance with the main thesis. At the same time, the discussion is carried on with reasoning through the five factors; as noted already. In other words, what characterises a discussion is that the supporting or condemning of an idea is carried out by proofs as well as sound reasoning, while disputation is that in which the supporting and condemning exercises are done by means of futile rejoinders (*jāti*), according to the *Nyāya-bhāsya*.[58] Such means that are intended only to demolish the arguments put forward do not result in a meaningful discussion. Cavil or wrangling is a sort of disputation in which no counter-conception is established by the other person, but he becomes a wrangler, a person who does not establish his own view but goes on to criticize the concepts as well as proofs of the first person.[59]

Fallacious probans (*hetvābhāsa*)

Fallacious probans or fallacies of reasoning do not possess all the characteristics of the real or true probans, but *appear* to have such characteristics.[60] Further, the fallacies of reason are stated to be of five kinds: (i) a reason which is not decisive; (ii) one that is contradictory; (iii) one that is apparently established, but leading to suspense; (iv) a reason that is not definite or what ever it establishes is as much in need of proof as the idea to be proved; or (v) a reason that is mistimed.[61] The *Nyāya sūtra-s* have discussed in considerable detail, the nature of quibble as well as its possible forms.

Casuistry or futile rejoinder (*jāti*)

According to *Nyāya-sūtra*, casuistry consists in opposing a proposition by ascribing or assigning to it a meaning not originally intended. Such an attempt is in the nature of an objection which is taken on the basis of mere similarity or dissimilarity.[62] When a certain reasoning has been put forward by one, naturally an objection to it takes birth or is put forth by an opponent, and such an objection is called *jāti,* or an attempt to oppose the original meaning. A defective answer, in such a situation, refutes itself. Different forms of defective replies have been examined in sufficient detail in the Nyāya texts.

Clinchers (*nigrahasthānam*)

This is a significant aspect of the Nyāya-approach towards knowledge. According to *Vārttika,* when a thing really exists or is described as different from a person's own idea of it, there could be either incomprehension or misapprehension, or no comprehension at all of the soundness or the strength of his own arguments.

Several ways of losing an argument have been described and discussed in the *Nyāya-bhāṣya* and the *Vārttika*.[63]

As noted before the *Nyāya-sutra* posits the idea of *apavarga* as one of the objects of knowledge. A question arises: Does the highest good (*nihśreyasa*) or *apavarga* result immediately due to true knowledge.[64] Answering this, *Vātsyāyana* emphatically says that the highest good accrues only *after* obtaining true knowledge. The very process of acquiring error-free or true knowledge is the pathway towards the attainment of the highest good. He avers that, as a result, there would be cessation of birth, pain, activity, defect and erroneous ideas as well as that which causes the irrational ones, eventually leading one to the final release.[65]

Nature of God

For a critical appreciation of the epistemic position of the Nyāya-Vaiśeṣika relating to the physical world, it would be desirable to understand this system's approach to God either as the First cause or the immanent principle. The Vaiśeṣika system was originally not theistic, so too was Nyāya, although there are indications to the effect that the propounder of this system, Gautama could have been a theist on his own. The *sūtra* (4.1.19),[66] states that Iśvara (God) is the cause (of the world) and we find fruitlessness in the action of human beings. Vātsyāyana's commentary on this *sūtra,* though simple and direct, is mundane. He says that, since a human being does not always get the desired fruits of his actions, his acquisition of them is dependent upon some other person and that Person is God who is the cause of the world. And this type of conclusion has been debated upon by Uddyotakara and others, in rather a circumscribed manner. Another *Nyāya-sūtra* (4.1.21), points[67] out that actions or efforts of man are actuated by Iśvara, leading to the view that God in this context is not the Creator but an omnipresent *Controller* or a Ruler. What is God? According to *Nyāya-bhāṣya*, 'God is a distinct Soul endowed with certain qualities, such as the absence of demerits, wrong knowledge and negligence on the one hand and, on the other, the presence of merit, knowledge and intuition. He possesses the eight-fold power (*aṇimādi aṣṭasiddhi-s*). It is rather strange that the Nyāya has perceived God in the form of a Siddha or the Perfect human being. However, it is stated that He controls the activities of merit and demerit that subsist in each individual soul at the organic level and at the inorganic level, that of the Earth and other material substances. True to the concept of God, the Nyāya projects him as omnipresent with regard to His creation, "just as the father acts for his children, so does God act as father-like for all living beings". It has, nevertheless, been emphasized that there is no other category except that of soul to which God could belong. From scriptures also we learn that 'God is the Seer, the Cogniser and the Knower of all things'.[68] Uddyotakara has an interesting observation in this context when he affirms that the very argument that proves God's causality also proves His existence because a cause should exist if it is to function as a cause.[69]

Uddyotakara has also examined three diverse opinions, namely, whether 'God' or 'Time' or primordial matter like atoms, could be the efficient cause. The right view, as he says, is that God is the efficient cause of the world.[70] According to him; 'Primordial matter', atoms and *karma* can act only when they are controlled by an intelligent or conscious cause, because they are themselves unconscious'.[71] A notable aspect of Uddyotakara's concept of God is that by reason of His nature, He creates things: 'Just as the Earth upholds things, because that is its very nature, exactly in the same manner God acts because that is His very nature; for as a matter of fact the very nature of God consists of activity. If God's activity is due to its nature, He should act constantly, without cessation.[72] According to Vyomaśivācārya, the efficient cause is the will of *Maheśvara*. Śrīdhara, Bhāsarvajña and Jayanta Bhaṭṭa also accept God as the intelligent cause. Jayanta even attributes the five qualities of self, namely, knowledge, pleasure, desire, volition and merit to God.

Causality

Generally one comes across four kinds of major *vāda-s* in Indian philosophical systems; *Ārambhavāda* (Nyāya-Vaiśeṣika) *Pariṇāmavāda* (Sāṃkhya); *Vivartavāda* (Śaṅkara-Vedānta); and *Śūnyavāda* (Buddhists). The Nyāya-Vaiśeṣika has endeavoured in its own way to throw light on the relationship between cause and effect. It distinguishes three kinds of causes:[73] (i) The inherent cause (*samavāyīkāraṇa*), and expounds it as a substance. Either it could be the material out of which a product is made (e.g. threads and the cloth), or a substance in which a quality or a movement inheres (e.g. carpet as the inherent cause of its colour). (ii) The non-inherent cause (*asamavāyīkāraṇa*), on the other hand, is the one which is either a quality or movement that inheres in the inherent cause or inheres in the inherent cause of the inherent cause of the product. The conjunction of the threads that produce the cloth is an example of the first type. The colour of the threads producing the colour of the carpet is an example of the second kind.[74] and (iii) The efficient or the instrumental cause (*nimittakāraṇa*) which is of two types: (a) efficient cause of general nature (*sādhāraṇa nimittakāraṇa*) that includes God, space and time, *adṛṣṭa* and the like; and (b) *asādhāraṇa nimittakāraṇa* causes of particular types that are innumerable, encompassing all kinds of operations that would produce the effect.[75]

It may be noted that, while some of the other Indian systems regard a positive one as being due to two sets of causes, namely, the material (*upādāna kāraṇa*) and the efficient cause (*nimitta kāraṇa*), in the Nyāya-Vaiśeṣika, the material cause is replaced by two, i.e., the inherent and the non-inherent cause because these would be in accordance with the Nyāya-Vaiśeṣika postulate that a substance is different from its attributes, but the attributes inhere in a substance and have no separate existence apart from the latter. But, if the effect is negative, e.g. a stick breaking a pot, it is stated that these two causes would not be operative.

The notable characteristic of the Nyāya-Vaiśeṣika is its firm belief that whatever exists is knowable and also its basic postulate that there exists a reality even outside of our knowledge, but it too can be known and that knowledge is the means of the attainment of reality or truth. Hiriyanna writes: 'It may be asked how the correspondence with reality which is said to constitute truth, can be known. There can obviously be no direct testing of correspondence, for we cannot get outside of our knowledge. Hence, the Nyāya-Vaiśeṣika proposes an objective or indirect test through putting the knowledge in question to practice. If we doubt whether a thing we cognize as water is really water or not, we have to see whether it will quench our thirst. The proof of the pudding is in the eating of it. This is what is known as *samvādi-pravrtti* or fruitful activity. The verification is pragmatic; but the definition of truth, it should be remembered, is not so. Truth is not what 'works'; it is what conforms to reality. Knowledge is for its own sake, and it need not necessarily have a practical end in view. Unlike the Buddhists, the followers of the Nyāya-Vaiśeṣika lay stress on the cognitive significance of knowledge'.[76]

The theory of causation as developed by the Nyāya-Vaiśeṣika is known as *asatkārya vāda* or *ārambhavāda*, because the effect is a new product having its own distinguishing features. The effect (*kārya*) is non-existent (*asat*)[77] and is a new beginning (*ārambha*). It is pointed out that the cause precedes the effect as an invariable antecedent and is necessary for the effect. Further, cause and effect are never simultaneous. The Nyāya-Vaiśeṣika argues further that the effect is not existent before its production; neither does it pre-exist in its cause.[78] In other words, the effect is not a transformation of the cause.

Sāṃkhya

The Sāṃkhya (as well as the allied system Yoga) is realistic like the Nyāya-Vaiśeṣika since it also regards the external world of objects as existing independently of the mind. It also postulates a plurality of the selves similar to the Nyāya-Vaiśeṣika. But there is a basic difference between the two, namely, the Sāṃkhya, unlike the Nyāya-Vaiśeṣika, thinks that *Prakṛti* or the unmanifested nature, undergoes *evolution* or certain modifications as a result of the interaction of *Puruṣa*, the changeless, eternal and passive sentient being. In this dualistic approach, *Prakṛti* is the first cause of the universe but *puruṣa* is uncaused. The main Sāṃkhya doctrine is known as *pariṇāmavāda*[79] (theory of change or evolution) which encompasses even space and time. It may be noted that, in Sāṃkhya there is no clear distinction between cause and effect since *Prakṛti*, as the material cause of all things, must contain in it all that pertains to the universe or knowable world of matter,[80] hence the effect would not be different from the material cause.

Prakṛti is conceived as being an intertwining of three *guṇas* (like three strands of a rope): *sattva, rajas* and *tamas* that are thought of not in terms of qualities like the Nyāya-Vaiśeṣika, but the abstract ones. *Sattva* represents whatever is fine or light; *rajas* active; and *tamas,* heavy and inert,[81] According to the Sāṃkhya, each of these is manifold and thus the infinite character of *Prakṛti* is a result of the multiplicity of the three *guṇas*. Sāṃkhya believes in the indestructibility of matter and emphasizes that something cannot come out of nothing or whatever is non-existent. Naturally this process of thinking has led the Sāṃkhyavādins to the view that production is not a new creation but is only a manifestation of that which is already there in a latent form. The Sāṃkhya exposition, therefore, comes under the category of *satkāryavāda*. Sāṃkhya also believes that there cannot be absolute destruction, and that evolution and dissolution would be periodically alternating.

According to the *Sāṃkhya-kārikā* of Īśvarakṛṣṇa, there are five reasons in support of the *satkāryavāda:* (i) if the effect does not exist already in its cause, it would become a non-entity like the sky-flower or hare's horn; (*asad akaraṇāt*) (ii) the effect is only a manifestation of its material cause (*upādānagrahaṇāt*); (iii) everything cannot be produced out of everything, thus emphasizing the fact that the effect is implicit in its material cause (*sarvasambhavābhāvat*); (iv) it is only an efficient potential (*śaktasya śakyakaraṇāt*); and lastly (v) the cause and the effect are thus the *implicit* and the *explicit* stages and, therefore, the effect pre-exists in its material cause.[82] (*kāraṇabhāvat*).

There are several words in the Sāṃkhya for the potential nature: *Prakṛti* (the uncaused root-cause), namely, *pradhāna* (first and the foremost principle of the Universe); and *avyakta* (unmanifested state); *jaḍa* (unintelligent and unconscious principle); *Śakti* (unlimited power); *anumāna* (that which is inferred from its products). Since it is also constituted of *rajas*, besides *sattva* and *tamas* as noted above, motion, associated as it is with *rajas,* is believed to be inherent in Prakṛti.

Mīmāṃsā Position

While the Nyāya-Vaiśeṣika and the Sāṃkhya developed an epistemological frame, each in its own way in consonance with its metaphysical approach, the Pūrva-Mīmāṃsā[83] has followed a different path. It accords a prime position to the Vedas, specially the *Brāhmaṇas* or the ritualistic compendia, and holds them as eternal and infallible. Even so, it has not only accepted the position of the Nyāya-Vaiśeṣika in several ways, but also rejected it in some respects. Between the two schools of Pūrva-Mīmāṃsā, one of Prabhākara and the other of Kumārila Bhaṭṭa, there are some differences with regard to what constitutes valid knowledge. To Prabhākara, memory that arises from the stored sensorial impressions of a prior cognition is not valid knowledge.[84] All apprehension (*anubhūti*) is direct and therefore valid. On the other hand, Kumārila regards valid knowledge as being produced from defect or error-free causes and its validity consists in not being uncontradicted by subsequent knowledge. Besides, a Mīmāṃsaka considers that cognition leading to valid knowledge, apart from the aforesaid two conditions, should also apprehend a thing or an object that has not been already apprehended, i.e., the cognition should be a new one and, in any case, it should be consistent.[85] Like Prabhākara, Kumārila does not recognize memory as constituting valid knowledge.[86]

The followers of Mīmāṃsā regard self (*ātman*) as being distinct for every body and in this respect they accept the pluralistic position of the Nyāya-Vaiśeṣika.[87] But, unlike the latter which does not think of any action associated with the self, nor a change of form, the former postulates the change of form of the self. In fact knowledge is considered as a mode of the self'.[88] However, the knowledge itself is regarded as being attained or gained not directly but through inference. The Nyāya-Vaiśeṣika, on the other hand, believes that cognition of a thing or an object arises when three entities are in operation—self combines with the mind, mind with the senses, and the latter with the objects.[89]

As for the *pramāṇa-s*, Jaimini, the propounder of *Pūrva-Mīmāṃsā*, recognizes three pathways, namely, perception, inference and verbal testimony. Prabhākara introduces, in addition, comparison and also implication, while Kumārlia includes the sixth one, i.e., non-apprehension also. Perception is explained as immediate knowledge arising from the contact of the sense organ(s) with an external object, but it should be free from defects. But the auditory organ, according to Mīmāṃsā, proceeds from *dik* (space) and not from *ākāśa*, as the Nyāya-Vaiśeṣika has postulated. Further, the Nyāya-Vaiśeṣika holds that all perception is determinate, and the indeterminate perception is inferred at an earlier stage in the process, while the Mīmāṃsā considers this as a normal experience. With regard to inference, the Mimāṃsā, however, accepts only three members of syllogism. It also makes a distinction between comparison and inference.

Verbal Testimony: As could be expected, verbal testimony (*śabda-pramāṇa*) has an exalted position in the *Pūrva-Mīmāṃsā* which, as noted earlier, has accepted the Vedas (*śabda*) as infallible. Kumārila explains that verbal testimony consists of personal authority of trustworthy savants (*āptavākya*) as well as the impersonal ones or the Vedas since the Vedas are regarded as being *apauruṣeya*. If the former could be contradicted or doubted in certain cases, the latter (the Vedas) would not have any contradictions whatsoever. For this reason, Prabhākara unequivocally emphasizes the importance of Vedic testimony as a perfectly valid one. Such a view or an implicit belief in the Vedas was its own undoing so far as the rational approach of the Mīmāṃsā was concerned. The Mīmāṃsā's unquestioned faith in the Vedas not only as the repository of all that is knowable but also they are an unblemished source of knowledge is sought to be substantiated by a theory that words and their meanings are not only natural but also permanent. Hiriyanna rightly observes: 'Thus the Mīmāṃsā doctrine of the fixity of the Vedic text rests upon a certain view of language it takes upon and the supposed absence of all references in long standing tradition to its having been by one or more authors. In neither case, it is clear, is the premise adequate to support the important conclusion drawn from it. The 'idolatry of scripture' appears comparatively late and seems to have been arrived at by extending to the form of the Veda what was once taken to hold good of its content'.[90]

Be that as it may, Kumārila holds in a way rightly that knowledge also extends beyond an object itself in the context of truth and error. He has thrown light on what error is and how it can be distinguished easily from truth. Prabhākara, on the other hand, does not admit the existence of error. The so-called error, according to him, is a combination of two cognitions. Thus, the well-known example of mistaking a shining shell as silver is the combination of two cognitions, namely, the perception of the shell without grouping its extraordinary features, and the memory of silver. The perception of certain features (shining etc.) of a shell that are common with silver and the stored impression about silver in memory thus lead to an erroneous understanding of shell *vis-à-vis* silver. He admits that direct perception leads to the knowledge about the object itself and hence, valid, but considers that memory cannot have such claims. The error, according to him, lies in not recognizing the separateness of these two aspects and thus it leads to an incomplete knowledge. Another example relates to a white (reflecting) crystal placed side by side with a red flower. The crystal may look like a red one because of its reflecting capacity. In this situation, there are two types of perceptions: one of the crystal without its true colour, and the other, the sensation of only the red colour of the flower. Each conveys a partial knowledge in that context, without any clear distinction being made between the two types of partial knowledge and, therefore, such a knowledge would be erroneous. In other words, error can also arise due to the wrong synthesis of two types of perceptions.[90a]

Though the Mīmāṃsaka is as much a realist as the Nyāya-Vaiśeṣika is, he does not admit the production of a new *dravya* or substance, but accepts only the changes in its forms or attributes, as represented by the Bhāṭṭa school. It has been postulated that things are not self-identical units, but have differences through their changes that go on continuously without any beginning or end. In other words, the Mīmāṃsā rejects the doctrine of creation or dissolution. This is substantiated by Kumārila's statement: 'There was never a time when the world was otherwise than now'. As for the individuals, a Mimāṃsaka believes that the changes that take place emanate from the past *karma* of the selves. The doctrine of *Karma* is as much a part of the Mīmāṃsā as it is with the Jainas.

It would appear that Pūrva-Mīmāṃsā in its earlier stages was materialistic in its approach. In course of time, it began to recognize a supernatural entity and throughout it owed allegiance, as mentioned earlier, to the revealed authority of the Vedas—an incoherent mixture of some rational and dogmatic approaches.

The Nyāya epistemology has postulated a theory called the *Parataḥ prāmāṇyavāda*,[91] i.e., knowledge having a validity known by external means. But, if the knowledge involves or leads to a fruitful or meaningful activity, it becomes valid; otherwise it would be invalid. In other words, the validity of knowledge is conditional. The Mīmāṃsā, on the other hand, views all knowledge as basically valid and thus does not subscribe to the *paratastva* character of knowledge, and stresses that even such a knowledge would be an impossibility. If the knowledge is without defect or contradiction, it should be regarded as valid knowledge in itself. However, like the Nyāya, the Mīmāṃsā admits that the correspondence with the external object would be determinative of the validity of knowledge.

There is another aspect that needs some consideration at this stage. According to Prabhākara, knowledge is self-luminous (*svaprakāśa*) and hence it manifests itself. It is, however, not eternal because it emanates in a particular situation and also could vanish. Further, as it reveals itself, it also reveals at the same time, the subject as well as its object. Thus there are triple revelations: *jñātṛ or mātṛ* (the self or the knower); *jñeya or meya* (the object) and *jñāna or mati* (knowledge through cognition).[92] Kumārila on the other hand, differs from Prabhākara by saying categorically that knowledge is not self-luminous, incapable of perception directly or indirectly. In his view, knowledge is a mode of the self and a process (*kriya*) or action (*vyāpāra*) and this can be inferred because even in the absence of its knowledge, an object could become known.[93]

Buddhist Logic

The *Laṅkāvatāra sūtra* (3rd or 4th cent. A.D.) is an important work of *Vijñānavāda*. It points out that the world is only a knowledge (*vijñāna*) or consciousness (*citta*), but at the same time it regards them as illusory as the perceived objects, thus accepting the doctrine of void (*śunyatā*). This text regards that all forms of knowledge arise out of the basic consciousness (*ālaya-vijñāna*), but they do not disappear in the absence of consciousness. Ālaya-vijñāna is stated to be of two forms. *Khyāti-vijñāna* and *Vastu prativikalpa vijñāna*, the former being the effect of innate impressions, and the latter, the effect of sense-impressions.[94]

Buddhist thinkers, within the framework of Buddhism which denies the existence of God, the soul as well as eternity but expounds a transient flow or flux of events characterized by their evanescence, have endeavoured to examine critically the nature and structure of human knowledge. The Sarvāstivāda of Hīnayāna encompasses a theory of Momentariness (*Kṣaṇabhaṅgavāda*), also known as *Santānavāda* (theory of Ceaseless Flow or Flux). The soul is regarded as an aggregate of the *skandha-s*, and matter in general is considered as a conglomeration of momentary atoms. Reality is explained in terms of a continuous flow of becoming, and subject to production and destruction in an impermanent manner. It is well known that the doctrine of momentariness was strongly opposed by the orthodox Hindu as well as Jaina thinkers.

Nāgārjuna in his *Mādhyamika kārikā* has dealt with the Buddha's postulate of dependent-origination (*pratītya-samutpāda*), i.e., the production is contingent upon certain conditions. He proclaims also *No-origination* view. "Never and no-where can anything be produced. A thing can originate neither out of itself, nor out of a not-self, nor out of both, nor out of neither. A thing cannot arise out of itself. If the effect is already existing in its cause, it is already an existing fact requiring no further production; if the effect does not exist in its cause, nothing can produce it; for, nothing can produce a hare's horn or a barren women's son. And if a thing cannot arise of itself, how can it arise out of a not-self'.[95] Nāgārjuna declares that both cause and effect are relative and causality is just an appearance. Even the five elements—earth, water, fire, air and *ākāśa*—are held to be equally unreal. Likewise, the attributes of these elements are relative and hence they too are not real. According to Nāgārjuna, reality or *tattva* can only be realized not through intellect but in spiritual experience in which state all plurality and intellectual categories are obliterated. He thus points out that the empirical reality is itself relative and not the ultimate. The Buddhist concept of *śunyatā* is not strictly one of absolute negation of everything, void or nihilism, although the two great ācāryas, Śaṅkara and Madhva, tried to counteract Buddhism from the standpoint that it is nihilistic. The *Mādhyamika*, recognizes through a process of intellect that there are several contradictory dimensions inherent in an understanding of the world of matter and motion. These by their nature are only passing appearances resulting in ignorance which needs to be set aside, and the self has to transcend these barriers to identify itself with spiritual experience. There are differing views about Nagārajuna's philosophy, whether he was a monist or a transcendentalist.

Buddhist logic in several ways was a rejoinder or an attempt to repudiate the position of the Nyāya-Vaiśeṣika *vis-à-vis* the external world and its cognition. Nāgārjuna's ideas on the external world and its relative reality for a time receded to the background as the brothers, Asaṅga and Vasubandhu came on the scene. They studied the logical expositions of the Nyāya and tried to adopt them in furtherance of Buddhist idealistic approaches. Vasubandhu followed the five-membered syllogism of the Nyāya, although sometimes he adopted the three membered syllogism. It was Diṅnāga, a pupil of Vasubandhu, who blazed new trails in Buddhist logic. Another luminary was Dharmakīrti, a disciple of Diṅnāga's own pupil, Īśvarasena. It may be noted that both Diṅnāga and Dharmakīrti came from a Brāhmaṇa parentage and later embraced Buddhism.

According to Buddhist approach to knowledge, right or valid knowledge is the experience without any contradiction and it would be the cause of successful action by means of which it becomes efficacious knowledge. But this is the experience of common men and their sense perceptions, an understandable logic that cannot be ignored. However, Diṅnāga makes a distinction between the first instant or moment of cognition and a re-cognition that endures but only as a fleet of moments of cognition without a limit. He further explains that every cognition cannot be regarded as a source of knowledge and adds that it is the intellect that constructs the image of the object cognized, and such a construction is produced by what he thinks productive imagination. He points out that it is not a source of cognition, it is re-cognition and not cognition',[96] a view shared by the Mīmāṃsaka-s and to some extent by the Naiyāyika-s who think of a source of right knowledge as the one that is predominant among all those that result in cognition, like sense perception as well as inference that involves intellectual processing. In the Buddhist approach there is a distinction between the role of senses and that of intellect. The senses receive the raw stimuli while the intellect processes and constructs them. Thus they hold that the first moment of awareness is the source of right knowledge.

The Nyāya-Vaiśeṣika exponent, Śrīdhara[97] has criticized the Buddhist approach to knowledge. According to him, the Buddhists do not think of a succinct definition of sense perception in relation to an object perceived. For, if the thing is known, its definition is useless and if it is not known, it is still more useless, because it is inexpressible. Buddhists were more concerned with the relations and relativistic aspects of the observed objects than with the *thing-in-itself* which does not exist and hence inexpressible. Even their approach to knowledge appears to be rather negative inasmuch as that it is regarded as indistinct or mysterious and that 'sensibility is not the understanding, and understanding is not sensibility'.[98] Uddyotakara in his *Vārttika,*[99] with reference to the Buddhist (Diṅnāga and others) position that 'perception is that which is free from determination (*kalpanāpoḍha*) or connections with name and class, comments: '..... *Kalpanāpoḍha* may be regarded as a conventional name for the specific form of 'perception' (without having any literal meaning of its own). But even then the contradiction does not cease; the specific form of anything cannot be spoken of by means of any word; and yet, the specific form of perception would be sought to be spoken of by means of the word *kalpanāpoḍha*. If (with a view to escaping from this, it be held that) the word expresses nothing, then what is the use of introducing the word at all in the definition, *kalpanāpoḍham pratyakṣam*? Not expressing anything at all, it is exactly like the dream of a dumb person. Thus it is found that the more we examine the definition proposed by Diṅnāga and others, the more incapable it is found to bear the scrutiny of reasons'. Dharmakīrti and Dharmottara have discussed the illusive aspect of sense perception and these discussions are more polemical and hair-splitting. Diṅnāga sought to omit the non-illusiveness and also rejected *Vasubandhu's* definition that sense-perception is that knowledge which is produced by the (pure) object, although he did not deny the possibilities of illusive or wrong perceptions'.[100]

Inference: Inference that has the pride of place in Nyāya logic, has two aspects in the Buddhist (Sautrāntika) logical scheme, *svārthānumāna* and *parārthānumāna*. Distinguished from perception, *svārthānumana* is thought of as an indirect one; e.g., if there is smoke cognized, it is direct, and if the causative fire is not observed but is inferred, it is indirect. In other words, the cognition of what is not perceived through the perceived one is inference for judgement. Even so there should be an interrelation between the perceived and the non-perceived ones like smoke and fire. Buddhist logic admits of three terms—the subject, the logical predicate and between them, the reason.

Dharmottara follows the same line of argument and thinks of inference as a combination of a part perceived directly and a part not actually perceived also. He believes that the subject of an inference is in the nature of a substratum and elaborates upon it in terms of the logical predicate or the probandum. 'Diṅnāga emphasizes that 'all inferential relation is based upon a substance-to-quality relation. It is constructed by our understanding and it does not represent the ultimate reality'. The most important component of the inference is the third term which is a logical mark of the reason. It is also a quality of mark of the subject and is itself marked off by the predicate'.[101]

It will thus be observed that inference has been explained in Buddhist logic as the cognition of an object through its concomitant mark which, according to Dharmottara, is its origin and not its essence. Inference is also the cognition of that which is inferred (hidden object), besides its being an inseparable link that unites the mark with the object inferred. Buddhist's position, by and large, in respect of inference is that it cognizes the general or the universal in contradistinction to the sense perception that cognizes a particular object. While Diṅnāga expounds this aspect, Dharmottara states that the inferred object is an imagined one (smoke-fire). The Buddhists, however, have not preferred inference in terms of a deduction of a proposition like the Naiyāyika, but have tried to indulge in subtleties relating to perceptual judgement, illusion *vis-à-vis* reality, momentariness, the nuances of cognition, reason and associated matters. Causality, it is stated, is in the nature of an interpretation of reality, but not reality itself, while the point-instant which is also a cause, an ultimate one, is the reality. The validity of inference in Buddhist logic, it may be noted, is confined only to the observed phenomena.

In tune with their heterodoxical attitude and the doctrine of momentariness, Buddhist thinkers do not at all accept verbal authority or the Vedas as a *pramāṇa*. Dharmakīrti says that if the truth of things can be proved by perception and inference, there will be no harm even if we ignore the Śāstras. He wonders as to who made a rule that every time one should consult the Śāstras, and without their authority one should not infer fire from the observed smoke[102]—a bold assertion citing a common but convincing example.

Jaina Approach

Although perceptual knowledge is generally recognized as an immediate one, it is regarded as relative and hence is included in *mati* or mediate knowledge. Jainas believe that mere perception does not give rise to knowledge unless it is fortified and arranged by concepts or associated thoughts. In other words, perceptual knowledge emanates from the thinking process and thus is mediate. Hence both perceptual and inferential knowledge comprise *mati*. Besides these two *pramāṇas*, Jainism has accepted *śruti* or the verbal authority, but not of the Vedas obviously. In Jainism, knowledge is constituted of (i) *pramāṇa* which is that of an object as it exists, and (ii) *naya*, the knowledge of a thing in its relativistic aspects, that is concerned with a standpoint from which a statement about a thing is made.[103]

Perhaps the most significant aspect of Jaina approach to knowledge is their exposition that all truth is relative to our standpoints. Even partial knowledge and judgement are included in *naya*. The seven *nayas* are: (i) examination of an object by looking at it as having both universal and particular qualities, but without making any distinction between them; (*naigama naya*); (ii) consideration of universal qualities, but not the particulars (*saṃgraha naya*); (iii) a common or general view based on empirical knowledge (*vyavahara naya*); (iv) identification of the real with the momentary (*ṛjusūtra naya*) by reducing the particulars to a series of moments; (v) relation between word and the meaning it signifies (*śabda-naya*); (vi) distinguishing terms according to their roots (*samabhirūḍha naya*); and (vii) a special type of the proceeding one (*evambhūta naya*). It has been stated that each of the above as a standpoint provides only a partial view of one of the many aspects of an object. According to Jaina thinkers, if a partial approach alone is adopted or taken into consideration without keeping in view the whole truth or the totality of reality, it would result in a fallacious position (*nayābhāsa*).

There does not appear to be any systematic logical postulates in the early Jaina teachings of Mahāvīra until the time of Umāsvāti (2nd cent. A.D.).

The *Tattvārthādhigama sūtra* of Umāsvāti emphasizes in its very first *sūtra* that the path of liberation consists of acquiring right insight (*samyag-darśana*), right knowledge (*samyag-jñāna*) and right conduct (*samyag-caritra*). It classifies knowledge under terms that are not found in the other schools. The means of knowledge are stated to be *mati, śruta, avadhi, manaḥ-paryāya and kevala.*[104] The first two are called indirect (*parokṣa*)and the rest direct (*pratyakṣa*). *Mati* is either the sensorial or non-sensorial knowledge (reflective or undifferentiated one). Several synonyms for *mati* are used including *smṛti* and *saṃjñā* with further subdivisions into *yathā-svam* (by means of sense organs), *īhā* (desire to know more about the object), *apāyā* (reflection on the nature of the perceived object) and *dhāraṇā* (final cognition of the object).

Śruta, it is pointed out, follows *mati* knowledge.[105] The main difference between *mati* knowledge and the *śruta* one is that *mati* is related to the objects existing at the present time, while *śruta*, to those of all the three times past, present and future. Besides, it is said to be purer form of knowledge, and it is also of the type of communication from some reliable authority, more or less similar to *āpta-vākya* or verbal testimony. The term, *manaḥ-paryāya*, has not been defined succinctly; perhaps it represents mental knowledge. Another term, *avadhi*, is also in the same situation. Nevertheless, the difference between the former and the latter is that *manaḥ-paryāya* is stated to be a knowledge of the world of human beings, while *avadhi* relates to a much larger field and is concerned with that of the whole universe. More importantly, Jainism attaches the greatest importance to *kevala*—a knowledge of the perfect absolute, pure and all-comprehensive and infinite. "It constitutes the essence of the soul in its pure and undefiled condition".[106]

Anekāntavāda

One of the dimensions of Jaina thought is called *Anekāntavāda* or the doctrine of the manifold aspects of reality. This is also related to Jaina atomism (see pp. 136-140) that has its own nuances differing in some respects from the Nyāya- Vaiśeṣika and the Bauddha atomism. The *Anekāntavāda* posits the idea that a thing has innumerable characteristics, both positive and negative. Ordinarily, only certain attributes or qualities of some objects are known because of the limitations of human knowledge as well as the associated judgements that are only of relative nature. Jainas, like the Nyāya-Vaiśeṣika, use the word *dravya* for a substance and also accept that it possesses qualities. But with an addition, namely, they add the concept of *mode* or modifications to it. The qualities are called *guṇa* like the Nyāya-Vaiśeṣika, but the mode is called *paryāya*. While the Nyāya-Vaiśeṣika thinks of qualities as inhering in a substance, Jainas believe that both the *dravya* and *guṇa* are inseparable, emphasizing that the qualities are the very essence of the related substance. As for the modes, they are regarded as changing as well as accidental. Jaina approach to the conception of a substance is both a thesis and an antithesis in some ways. For, a substance could be one that is permanent and thus real. But it could also be many, momentary and unreal. It has been rightly remarked: 'Jainism here becomes a theological mean between Brāhmanism and Early Buddhism'.[107] According to Jainism, both are the two aspects of the same substance and these point to the fact that a substance could have the characteristics of production, destruction as well as permanence. But each presents itself as a partial view and such a view is fallacious because Jainas do not believe in what is called the *ekāntavāda*, but emphasise that the universe is to be examined from many points of view (*anekāntavāda*), since each partial view-point would lead to a different conclusion.

Syādvāda

This type of approach to knowledge naturally has led the Jaina savants to think of the indeterminate nature of reality. They have, therefore, put forward a postulate which goes by the name of *Syādvāda,* the doctrine of *may be* (this literal translation in English does not do full justice to the Sanskrit word). In tune with their abhorrence of partial standpoints, the *Syādvāda* perhaps arose to serve as a bridge between the Upaniṣadic affirmation that Being alone is real on the one hand and, on the other, that the Undifferentiated Being or Non-Being is the ultimate truth.[108] Jaina thinkers visualized that each of the above two would be partially true and, moreover, each would become a dogma if it is to be recognized as the whole truth about reality.[109] In the *Muṇḍaka upaniṣad* there is also a view that neither Being nor Non-Being is the truth and reality must, therefore, have the characteristics of both or neither of them. This would mean that reality would be 'is' or 'is not', both 'is' and 'is not' and neither 'is' nor 'is not'. Jaina savants have examined these upaniṣadic aspects and, holding that these are partially true statements, expounded a series of seven steps (*sapta-bhaṅgīnaya*) that could cumulatively represent or encompass the ultimate reality. This is the *Syād-vāda*, the word *syād* meaning 'may be' or 'relatively speaking'. The *syādvāda* points to the inestimably indeterminate nature of reality. Our judgements according to Jainism relate to different aspects of reality and hence partial truth.

The seven components of the *syād-vāda* are:

(i) May be (*Syād asti*)

(ii) May be is not (*Syāt nāsti*)

(iii) May be is and is not (*Syāt asti nāsti*)

(iv) May be is inexpressible (*Syāt avaktavyaḥ*)

(v) May be is and is inexpressible (*Syāt asti ca avaktavyaḥ*)

(vi) May be is not and is inexpressible (*Syāt nāsti ca avaktavyaḥ*).

(vii) May be is, is not and is inexpressible (*Syāt asti ca nāsti ca avaktavyaḥ*).

Jainism thus emphasises that the knowledge of reality, which itself is very complex, may be partial and possibly erroneous, if the particular (partial) view of it is preferred to be taken.

The *Syādvāda*, or the *saptabhaṅigi* though good in itself aiming at the non-recognition or the discarding of partial knowledge, does not appear to shed any light on its full implications in the context of the observed world of matter, motion, space and time. In fact "the primary aim of Jainism is the perfection of the soul, rather than the interpretation of the Universe—a fact which may be supported by the old statement that *āsrava* and *saṃvara* constitute the whole of Jaina teaching, the rest being only an amplification of them'.[110] The Buddhists and the Vedāntins were highly critical of the *Syādvāda*, taking the word *syāt* to mean probability. Śāntarakṣita ridicules this Jaina doctrine by saying that 'Syādvāda which combines the real and the unreal, the existent and the non-existent, the one and the many, the identity and the difference, the universal and the particular is like a mad man's cry'.[111] The Vedāntin criticizes it by saying that if everything is probable, the doctrine itself becomes probable. However, *Syādvāda*, cannot be summarily set aside. In this respect it may be desirable to note that even in modern physics, there is the theory of probability or the principle of indeterminacy that has its own nuances in the context of the interpretation of the world of fundamental particles, the building blocks of the universe, although *Syādvāda* cannot be equated with the modern scientific concepts.

Among the basic tenets of Jainism, there is no conception of God as Creator of the World. In fact, Jainism thinks of the divinity in man himself and regards the liberated soul as divine. The eventual aim of Jainism is liberation. Nevertheless, Jainism accepts both matter and spirit (*jīva*), both being infinite in number. It regards that the entire physical world is one kind of *pudgala* and which is in intimate relation with spirit. *Karma* is also explained as a form of matter.

It is important to note that the orthodox and the heterodox schools have influenced one another in the field of epistemology. It is rather difficult to determine precisely the priority or otherwise of the noted exponents in presenting a new edge to an old idea specially in the early centuries of the Christian era. The Buddhist and Jaina epistemologies have their characteristics developed in such a way that some aspects of them could be earlier than what has been generally admitted now. Such aspects or propositions could well have stimulated new thinking on the part of those of the orthodox school in their refutations of the opponent's views and the substantiation of their own standpoint. The debates in terms of justifying one's own viewpoint or counteracting the opponent's approach are a fascinating aspect of the respective epistemic positions, though sometimes they bordered on dogmatic approach.

REFERENCES

(The English translations of all the Upaniṣadic references are taken from *The Thirteen Principal Upaniṣads* by R. E. Hume; those of the *Nyāya-sūtra* as well as the *bhāṣya* of Vātsyāyana and the *Vārttika* of Uddyotakara are from Ganganath Jha's edition on *The Nyāya-Sūtra-s* of Gautama (see Bibliography).
(All references to the *Praśastapādabhāṣya* (PPB) are taken from *Kiraṇāvalī*, (ed) Jetley J. S, including the numbers of *sūtra-s* mentioned).

1. तत्रापरा ऋग्वेदो यजुर्वेदः सामवेदोऽथर्ववेदः शिक्षा कल्पो व्याकरणं निरुक्तं छन्दो ज्यौतिषमिति अथ परा यया

   तदक्षरमधिगम्यते । *Muṇḍaka.* 1.4.5
   Of these the lower (knowledge) is Ṛgveda, Yajurveda, Sāmaveda, Atharvaveda, Phonetics (*Śikṣā*), Ritual (*Kalpa*), Grammar (*Vyākaraṇa*), Etymology (*Nirukta*), Metrics (*Chandas*) and Astronomy (*Jyotiṣa*).
   Now, the higher is that whereby that imperishable (*akṣara*) is apprehended.

2. न विना प्रमाणेन प्रमेयस्योपलब्धिः

   प्रमेयोऽपि प्रमाणतां पृथक्त्वादुपैति

   आत्मसंबोधनार्थमित्येवं ह्याह । *Maitrāyaṇī. up.* VI. 14

3. स होवाचर्ग्वेदं भगवोऽध्येमि यजुर्वेदं सामवेद-

   मथर्वणं चतुर्थमितिहासपुराणं पञ्चमं वेदानां

   वेदं पित्र्यं राशिं दैवं निधिं वाकोवाक्यमेकायनं

   देवविद्यां ब्रह्मविद्यां क्षत्रविद्यां नक्षत्रविद्यां

   सर्प-देवजन-विद्यामेतद्भगवोऽध्येमि । *Ch. up.* VII.1.2

4. प्रमाण–प्रमेय–संशय–प्रयोजन–दृष्टान्त–सिद्धान्त–अवयव–तर्क–निर्णय–वाद–जल्प–वितण्ड–हेत्वाभास–च्छल–

   जाति–निग्रहस्थानानां तत्त्वज्ञानानि:श्रेयसाधिगमः । NS.1.1.1

   It is the knowledge of the real essence (of true character) of the following sixteen categories that leads to the attainment of the Highest Good—(i) The means of right cognition (ii) The objects of right cognition (iii) Doubt (iv) Motive (v) Example; (vi) Theory; (vii) Factors of inference; (viii) Hypothetical Reasoning; (ix) Demonstrated truth; (x) Discussion; (xi) Disputation; (xii) Wrangling; (xiii) Fallacious Reason; (xiv) Perversion; (xv) Casuistry; and (xvi) Clinchers.

5. तदिदं तत्त्वज्ञानं निःश्रेयसाधिगमार्थं यथाविद्यं वेदितव्यम् । इह तु अध्यात्मविद्यायां आत्मादितत्त्वज्ञानं तत्त्वज्ञानम् ।

निःश्रेयसाधिगमोऽपवर्गप्राप्तिः । *Bhāṣya* on 1.1.1

As regards the knowledge of truth (*tattvajñāna*) and 'attainment of good', it must be borne in mind that there is such 'knowledge' and much 'attainment' dealt with (pertaining specially to) each of the four sciences (or branches of knowledge) in its own peculiar manner. In the science we are dealing with here the science of soul which forms the 'knowledge of truth', which is the knowledge of the soul and other objects of cognition and the attainment of good is the obtaining of release.

6. आत्मादेः खलु प्रमेयस्य तत्त्वज्ञानात् निःश्रेयसाधिगमः । *Bhāṣya* on 1.1.1

The highest good is attained by the knowledge of the real nature (of such things as the soul and the rest).

यत्तावदपरं निःश्रेयसं तत् तत्त्वज्ञानानान्तरमेव भवति । तथा चोक्तम्– जीवन्नेव हि विद्वान् संहर्षायासाभ्यां विमुच्यत

इति । अयं शास्त्रार्थ इति । परं च निःश्रेयसं तत्त्वज्ञानात्क्रमेण भवति ।

Nyāyavārttika: Introductory.

It is with reference to this lower 'Release' that we have the declaration—'the man with true knowledge, while he still lives, becomes freed from pleasure and pain; and it is this lower Release (following immediately after the true knowledge) which becomes the cause or the basis of scientific instruction.

The higher kind of release, on the other hand, comes gradually by degrees.

7. तत्त्वज्ञानान्निःश्रेयसाधिगमः इति तत्त्वं ज्ञायमानं कर्म सम्पद्यते निःश्रेयसाधिगम्यमानं भवति इति । किं पुनस्तत्त्वं, किं

वा निःश्रेयसमिति ? तत्त्वं पदार्थानां यथावस्थितात्मप्रत्ययोत्पत्तिनिमित्तत्वं, यो यथावस्थितः पदार्थः, स तथाभूत

प्रत्ययोत्पत्तिनिमित्तं भवति यत्, तत् तत्त्वम् । निःश्रेयसं पुनः दृष्टादृष्टभेदाद् द्विधा भवति। तत्र प्रमाणादिपदार्थ-

तत्त्वज्ञानात् निःश्रेयसं दृष्टम् ।

दृष्टं प्रमाणादिपरिज्ञानात्, अदृष्टं पुनरात्मादेः प्रमेयस्य तत्त्वज्ञानान्निःश्रेयसम् अधिगम्यते ।

(*Nyāyavārttika*: Introductory)

Says the *Bhāṣya*, 'the highest good is attained by the knowledge of the real nature (of such things as the soul and the rest)'. In this clause, the word *tattva* (real nature) becomes the objective, by being that which is known; *niḥśreyasa* (highest good) also becomes the objective, by being that which is attained.

What is the nature of *tattva* and what is the highest good?

That which forms the basis of a certain thing being cognised in its true form constitutes the real nature of that thing; that is to say, in the case of everything it is found that there is something in it in virtue of which the thing comes to be known as what it is and it is this something that forms the real nature of that thing.

As regards *niḥśreyas* or good, it is of two kinds, seen or perceptible and unseen or imperceptible; that which follows from the knowledge of the real nature of *Pramāṇa* and other categories is the seen or perceptible good.

The fact of the matter is that (while some sort or perceptible good might follow from the knowledge of every one of the categories) the highest good (which is imperceptible) follows only from the knowledge of soul and the other objects of cognition (G N. Jha, 41-43).

8. प्रत्यक्षानुमानोपमानशब्दाः प्रमाणानि । NS. 1.1.3

   Perception, inference, analogy and word are the *pramāna-s*.

9. अक्षस्य अक्षस्य प्रतिविषयं वृत्तिः प्रत्यक्षम् । वृत्तिस्तु सन्निकर्षः ज्ञानं वा । यदा सन्निकर्षः तदा ज्ञानं प्रमितिः, यदा ज्ञानं, तदा हानोपादानोपेक्षाबुद्धयः फलम् । *Bhāṣya* on NS 1.1.3

   Perception consists in the functioning or action of each sense organ upon a particular object; this 'action' being in the form either of contact or of cognition; when it is in the form of contact then the result is in the form of cognition or right knowledge; and when 'action' is in the form of cognition, the result is in the form of the idea of the thing being discarded or selected or treated with indifference (G. N. Jha, p. 100).

10. इन्द्रियार्थसन्निकर्षोत्पन्नं ज्ञानमव्यपदेश्यमव्यभिचारि व्यवसायात्मकं प्रत्यक्षम् । NS. 1.1.4

    Sense perception is that cognition (a) which is produced by the contact of the object with the sense organ (b) which is not expressible (by words) (c) which is not erroneous (d) and which is well-defined (G N. Jha, p. 111).

11. इन्द्रियस्यार्थेन संनिकर्षादुत्पद्यते यज्ज्ञानं तत् प्रत्यक्षम् । Bhāṣya on NS.1.1.4

    That cognition which is produced by the contact of the sense organ with the object cognised is sense-perception.

12. यदिदम् अनुपयुक्ते शब्दार्थसम्बन्धेऽर्थज्ञानं, न तत् नामधेयशब्देन व्यपदिश्येत गृहीतेऽपि च शब्दार्थसंबन्धे अस्यार्थस्यायं शब्दः नामधेयमिति । यदा तु सोऽर्थो गृह्यते, तदा पूर्वस्मादर्थज्ञानात् न विशिष्यते, तदर्थज्ञानं ताद्गेव भवति । *Bhāṣya* on 1.1.4

    In a case where the relation of the object with a word is not known, the apprehension of the object that there is, is certainly not spoken of by any name and even when the relation is known, it is known in the form that, 'such is the name of the thing I perceive'.

    Even when the fact that 'such is the name of the thing', is known, what happens is that (this notion) is an additional factor super-added to the apprehension, of the thing, this apprehension, by itself, remaining as before; also G. N. Jha, p. 113.

13. G N. Jha, p. 117.

14. सन्निकर्षः पुनः षोढा भिद्यते । संयोगः, संयुक्तसमवायः, संयुक्तसमवेतसमवायः, समवायः, समवेतसमवायः, विशेषणविशेष्यभावश्चेति । Uddyotakara, *Nyāyavārttika*

    As for the contact, this is of six different kinds, viz. (i) conjunction (ii) inherence in that which is in conjunction (iii) inherence in that which inheres in that which is in conjunction (iv) inherence (v) inherence in that which inheres and (vi) the relation of qualification (G. N. Jha, p.118).

15. तत्र चक्षुरिन्द्रियं, रूपवान् घटादिरर्थः । तेन सन्निकर्षः संयोगः, तयोः द्रव्यस्वभावत्वात् । अद्रव्येण च तत् रूपादिना संयुक्तसमवायः, यस्माच्चक्षुषा संयुक्ते द्रव्ये रूपादि वर्तत इति । वृत्तिस्तु समवायः । रूपादिवृत्तिना सामान्येन संयुक्तसमवेतसमवायः सन्निकर्षः । Uddyotakara, *Nyāyavārttika*

    To exemplify these when a certain thing, the jar, for instance, is seen, the jar which has colour is the 'object' and the eye, the sense-organ, and in this case, the contact of these two is of the form of conjunction; because both are substances. In the perception of the colour of the jar the contact of the eye with the colour, which is not a substance, is of the nature of 'inherence in that which is in conjunction'; because the colour (which is in contact) subsists in the jar which is in conjunction with the eye—the substance being in the nature of inherence. In the perception of the gems subsisting in the colour, the contact is in the form of, 'inherence in that which inheres in that which is in conjunction' (the gems inhering in the colour, which inheres in, which is in conjunction with the eye).

शब्दे समवायः । अयं खलुशब्दः संयोगविभागयोनिराद्यः ।

In the case of the perception of sound, the contact is in the form of inherence (G. N. Jha, p. 119).

ततेषु च सामान्येषु समवेतसमवायात् ।

In the case of the perception of the genus or class-character belonging to the sounds, the contact is in the form of 'inherence' of the 'inherent' (the genus inhering in sound which inheres in the *ākāśa* of the auditory organ).

समवाये चाभावे च विशेषणविशेष्यभावादिति ।

In the perception of inherence and non-existence, the contact bringing about the perception is in the form of the relation of the qualification. (Inherence being the qualification of that which is inherent, and non-existence, the qualification of the spot on earth which is perceived (G. N. Jha, p. 121).

16. लिङ्गदर्शनात्सञ्जायमानं लैङ्गिकम् । PPB. 246

17. तत्रान्वयी विशेषोऽभिधेयः, प्रमेयत्वात् सामान्यत्वात् । व्यतिरेकी च सात्मकं जीवच्छरीरं प्राणादिमत्त्वादिति । समस्तं लक्षणमन्वयव्यतिरेकिणः । साध्यसाधनत्वं सामान्यलक्षणं त्रयाणाम् । NK. on PPB. 246

18. तच्च द्विविधम्, दृष्टं, सामान्यतोदृष्टं च । PPB. 252

(*Laiṅgika*) is two fold; *dṛṣṭa* and *sāmānyatodṛṣṭa*.

19. NS. 1.1.5

20. अथ तत्पूर्वकं त्रिविधमनुमानम् – पूर्ववत् शेषवत् सामान्यतोदृष्टं च ।

After perception comes inferential cognition led up to by perception. It is of three kinds (i) *pūrvavat* (ii) *śeṣavat* and (iii) *sāmānyatodṛṣṭa*.

21. पूर्ववदिति–यत्र कारणेन कार्यमनुमीयते–यथा मेघोन्नत्या भवति वृष्टिरिति ।

शेषवत्–यत्र कारणेन कार्यमनुमीयते, पूर्वोदकविपरीतमुदकं नद्याः पूर्णत्वं शीघ्रत्वं च दृष्ट्वा स्रोतसोऽनुमीयते भूता वृष्टिरिति ।

सामान्यतोदृष्टं, प्रज्ञापूर्वकं अन्यत्र दृष्टस्यान्यत्र दर्शनमिति, तथा चादित्यस्य, तस्मादस्ति अप्रत्यक्षा आदित्यस्य व्रज्या इति । *Bhāṣya* on NS. 1.1.5

The *pūrvavat* inference is that in which the effect is inferred from the cause, eg. when we see the clouds rising, we infer that there will be rain.

The *śeṣavat* inference is that in which we see the cause is inferred from the effect, e.g. when we see that the water of the river is like what it used to be, and that the stream is full and the current is swifter, we infer that there has been rain.

The *sāmānyato dṛṣṭa* inference (is that in which the inference is based upon a general observation) e.g. we have observed in all classes that we see a thing in a place different from where we saw it before only when it was moved, and from this fact of general observation we infer that the Sun must be moving, even though we cannot perceive it. Also see *Vārttika* (G. N. Jha, pp. 163-179).

22. G. N. Jha, pp. 156 ff.

23. idem, p. 194.

24. प्रसिद्धसाधर्म्यात् साध्यसाधनमुपमानम् । NS.1.1.6

Analogy is that which accomplishes its purpose through similarity to a known object.

25. प्रज्ञातेन सामान्यात् प्रज्ञापनीयस्य प्रज्ञापनमुपमानम् । यथा गौरेव गवय इति । *Bhāṣya* on NS. 1.1.5

That is, analogy is that which makes known what is to be made known, through similarity to an object that is already known, e.g. the assertion, 'as the cow so the *gavaya* (an animal similar to cow).

26. G. N. Jha, p. 194.

27. आप्तोपदेश: शब्द: । NS. 1.1.7

The assertion of a reliable person is word, verbal testimony.

28. आप्त: खलु साक्षात्कृतधर्मा यथाट्टष्टस्यार्थस्य चिख्यापयिषया प्रयुक्त उपदेष्टा । Bhāṣya on 1.1.7

That person is called '*āpta*,' 'reliable,' who possesses right knowledge of things, a desire to make known (to others) the things as he knows it; and who is capable of speaking of it.

साक्षात्कृतधर्मा अस्य आप्ति: । तया प्रवर्तत इति आप्त: । ऋष्यार्यम्लेच्छानां समानं लक्षणम् । तथा च सर्वेषां

व्यवहारा: प्रवर्तन्त इति ।

The word *āpta* is explained denoting one who acts or proceeds, through *āpti*, i.e. through the direct knowledge of things. This definition applies to sages as well as to Āryas and Mlecchas.

29. स द्विविधो दृष्टादृष्टार्थत्वात् । NS. 1.1.8

Verbal Testimony is of two kinds—the *dṛṣṭārtha* i.e. that of which the thing spoken of is perceived and *adṛṣṭārtha*, that of which the thing is not perceived.

यस्येह दृष्टोऽर्थ: स दृष्टार्थ: । यस्यामुत्र प्रतीयते सोऽदृष्टार्थ: । एवमृषिलौकिकवाक्यानां विभाग इति । *Bhāṣya* on 1.1.8

The 'word' of which the thing spoken of is perceived in this world, is called *dṛṣṭārtha*, while that of which the thing spoken of is only believed to exist in the other world, is called *adṛṣṭārtha*. These are the two divisions under which are included all the assertions of the sages and ordinary men. Uddyotakara, *Vārttika*, G. N. Jha, pp. 209-10.

30. आत्म, शरीर, इन्द्रिय, अर्थ, बुद्धि, मन:, प्रवृत्ति, दोष, प्रेत्यभाव, फल, दु:ख, अपवर्गास्तु प्रमेयम् । NS.1.1.9

Soul, body, sense, organs, things, apprehension, mind, activity, defect, rebirth, fruition, pain and release really constitute the objects of cognition.

31. तत्र आत्मा सर्वस्य द्रष्टा, सर्वस्य भोक्ता, सर्वानुभावी । तस्य भोगायतनं शरीरम् । भोगसाधनानि इन्द्रियाणि। भोगो बुद्धि: । सर्वार्थोपलब्धौ नेन्द्रियाणि प्रभवन्तीति सर्वविषयान्त:करणं मन: । शरीरेन्द्रिय-बुद्धिसुखदु:खवेदनानां निवृत्तिकारणं प्रवृत्ति:, दोषाश्च । नास्येदं शरीरम् अपूर्वमनुत्तरं च, पूर्वशरीराणामादिनास्ति, उत्तरेषाम् अपवर्गो अन्त: इति प्रेत्यभाव: । ससाधनसुखदु:खोपभोग: फलम् । दु:खमिति नेदमनुकूलवेदनीयस्य सुखस्य प्रतीते: प्रत्याख्यानम् । समाहितो भावयति, भावयन्निर्विद्यते, निर्विण्णस्य वैराग्यं, विरक्तस्यापवर्ग: इति । *Bhāṣya* on 1.1.9.

The perceiver (of all that brings about pain and pleasure), the experiencer of all (pains and pleasures and their causes), who gets at all things is the soul.

The body is the receptacle of the soul's experiences.

The sense organs are the instruments of the experiences.

The things are the objects to be enjoyed and experienced.

Apprehension consists of the experience itself.

The mind is that internal organ which is capable of bringing about the apprehension of all things—which the sense organs can not do.

Activity is the cause of the propagation of the body, sense organs, the things and the sensing of pleasure and pain.

So also are the defects.

The body that belongs to the soul in one life is not the first that the soul has had nor is it the last. In fact, there can be no first in the previous bodies that the soul has had and as we cannot trace any beginning of the worldly process as for its subsequent bodies, there can be an end to those only when release is attained and it is this that constitutes re-birth.

By the special mention of pain, it is not meant that there is no pleasure at all—which is what is felt as agreeable... when one is thoughtful and contemplates (on pain) he becomes disgusted; this disgust makes him free from all attachment; and brings dispassion, and having become dispassionate, he attains release.

32. जन्ममरणप्रबन्धोच्छेद: सर्वदु:खप्रहाणम् अपवर्ग: इति । *Bhāṣya* on 1.1.10

Release consists in the cessation of the series of births and deaths, and the consequent disappearance of all pain.

33. इच्छाद्वेषप्रयत्नसुखदु:खज्ञानान्यात्मनो लिङ्गानि । NS.1.1.10

सर्वपुरुषसाधारणत्वप्रसङ्गाच्च न पृथिव्यादिगुणा:, तदुत्पत्तौ करणत्वेन कल्पनाच्च नाकर्तुर्मनस:, तस्मादष्टद्रव्यातिरिक्तं द्रव्यान्तरं, स चात्मेति सिद्धं इत्याह । *Nyāyavārttika* on 1.1.10

Desire etc. cannot be qualities of the five elementary substances, earth etc.; as if they were so, they would be common to all men; just as the odour of the earth is received by all men—they can not be the qualities of mind; as the mind is the instrument which produces them, Therefore it lies beyond all the eight *dravyas*, then it is Ātman is an established fact.

33a. चेष्टेन्द्रियार्थाश्रय: शरीरम् । NS. 1.1.11

34. समानानेकधर्मोपपत्ते:, विप्रतिपत्ते:, उपलब्ध्यनुपलब्धिव्यवस्थातश्च विशेषापेक्षो विमर्श: संशय: । 1.1.23

Doubt is that wavering judgement in which the definite cognition of the specific character of any one object is wanting and which arises either (i) from the cognition of the characters common to the other objects concerned, (ii) from the common characters that serve to distinguish an object from diverse objects or (iii) from the presence of contradictory opinions—and the appearing of such wavering judgements is due to the uncertainty attaching to perceptions and non-perceptions.

Accepting the above, the *Bhāsya* adds two more:

(a) समानधर्मोपपत्तेर्विशेषापेक्षो विमर्श: संशय इति; ... अनेकधर्मोपपत्ते:; ... विप्रतिपत्ते:; ... उपलब्ध्यवस्थात:; ... अनुपलब्ध्यवस्थात: । *Bhāsya* on 1.1.23

Uddyotakara, however, adds: तस्मात् पञ्चविध: संशय इति न सूत्रार्थ: । (*Vārttika* on 1.1.23)

Therefore the *sūtra* does not mean that doubt is of five kinds.

35. सामान्यप्रत्यक्षाद्विशेषाप्रत्यक्षाद्विशेषस्मृतेश्च संशयः । Vai.sū. 2.2.17

Doubt arises from perception of a general, non-perception of a particular and remembrance of particularity.

36. यमर्थमधिकृत्य प्रवर्तते तत्प्रयोजनम् । NS. 1.1.24

That object aiming at which one acts is 'motive' or purpose.

37. लौकिकपरीक्षकाणां यस्मिन्नर्थे बुद्धिसाम्यं स दृष्टान्तः । NS. 1.1.25

That is example with regard to which both parties—the ordinary man and the trained investigator—entertain similar ideas.

38. दृष्टान्तविरोधेन हि प्रतिपक्षाः प्रतिषेद्धव्या भवन्तीति, दृष्टान्तसमाधिना च सपक्षाः स्थापनीया भवन्तीति, अवयवेषु च उदाहरणाय कल्पत इति । Bhāṣya on NS. 1.1.25

The purposes served by the example are :
(i) The contrary opinions are overthrown by being shown to be contradictory to, incompatible with, the example.
(ii) One's own opinions are established by being shown to be compatible with, supported by, the example, and
(iii) The example is utilised as the corroborative instance or illustration, which is one of the inferential processes.

39. सारूप्यव्युत्पत्त्यर्थं तावदुपमानं न भवतीति वर्णितम्, दृष्टान्तः सारूप्यव्युत्पत्त्यर्थः, असिद्धसाधनार्थो वेति दृष्टान्तो न भवति । (*Vārttika* on NS.1.1.25)

We have already explained that analogy does not afford any notion of similarity. As regards the examples it does serve the purpose of affording the notion of similarity. As to whether or not the example serves the purpose of proving what is not proved, our reply is that it does not serve that purpose. G.N. Jha, p. 343.

40. तन्त्राधिकरणाभ्युपगमसंस्थितिः सिद्धान्तः । NS. 1.1.26

Doctrine is a theory or conviction in regard to the exact nature of a thing dealt with in philosophy.

41. अधिकरणानुषक्तार्थसंस्थितिः अधिकरणसंस्थितिः अभ्युपगमसंस्थितिरनवधारितार्थपरिग्रहः । *Bhāṣya* on 1.1.26

'AdhikaraLa saṃsthiti' is the conviction resting on implication, not on direct assertion. 'Abhyupagama saṃsthiti' is the hypothetical acceptance of an opinion not duly ascertained.

42. स चतुर्विधः सर्वतन्त्रप्रतितन्त्राधिकरणाभ्युपगमसंस्थित्यर्थान्तरभावात् । NS.1.1.27.

Doctrine is of four distinct kinds:- (i) Doctrine common to all philosophers; (ii) Doctrine peculiar to one philosophy; (iii) Doctrine resting on implication; and (iv) Hypothetical doctrine.

43. सर्वतन्त्राविरुद्धस्तन्त्रेऽधिकृतोऽर्थः सर्वतन्त्रसिद्धान्तः । NS. 1.1.28

The 'Doctrine common to all philosophies' is that philosophical conviction or theory which is not incompatible with any philosophy.

44. समानतन्त्रसिद्धः परतन्त्रासिद्धः प्रतितन्त्रसिद्धान्तः । NS. 1.1.29

That which is accepted by only one philosophy, and is not accepted by any other philosophy, is called the Doctrine peculiar to one philosophy.

45. सोऽभ्युपगमसिद्धान्तः स्वबुद्धिचिरख्यापविषया परबुद्ध्यवज्ञानाच्च प्रवर्तत इति । *Bhāṣya* on 1.1.31

    An author has recourse to this kind of doctrine with a view to show off the cleverness of his own intellect and through utter disregard for the intellect of the others (G. N. Jha, p. 351).

46. प्रतिज्ञा हेतूदाहरणोपनयनिगमनानि अवयवाः । NS.1.1.32

    (i) Statement of proposition; (ii) reason; (iii) example; (iv) application; and (v) final conclusion.

47. साध्यनिर्देशः प्रतिज्ञा । NS. 1.1.33

    The statement of proposition consists in the assertion of what is to be proved, The Probandum. NS. 1.1.33.

48. उदाहरणसाधर्म्यात्साध्यसाधनं हेतुः ।

    The 'statement of the probans' is that which demonstrates the probandum, through its similarity to the example. NS. 1.1.34.

49. साधर्म्यसावैधर्म्याद्धर्मभावी दृष्टान्त उदाहरणम् । NS. 1.1.36

    The familiar instance— which, through similarity to what is to be proved, is possessed of a property of that, constitutes the statement of the example.

50. उदाहरणापेक्षस्तथेत्युपसंहारः न तथेति वा साध्यत्वोपनयः । NS. 1.1.38

    The statement of reaffirmation is that which, on the strength of the example, reasserts the subject as being, 'so' or as being 'not so'.

51. हेत्वपदेशात् प्रतिज्ञायाः पुनर्वचनं निगमनम् । NS. 1.1.39

    The final conclusion is a restatement of the proposition on the basis of the statement of the Probans.

52. अविज्ञाततत्त्वेऽर्थे कारणोपपत्तितस्तत्त्वज्ञानार्थं ऊहः तर्कः । NS. 1.1.40

    When the real character of a thing is not well-known, there is put forward, for the purpose of ascertaining that real character, a reasoning (in support of a certain conclusion) which indicates the presence of proof (showing the undesirability or absurdity of a contrary conclusion) and this is called 'hypothetical reasoning'.

53. निर्णयः स्वविषय एव, अनुमानं तु स्वविषयेऽन्यत्र च । *Vārttika* on NS. 1.1.41

    Definitive cognition pertains to its own subject matter, while inference pertains to its own subject matter, as well as to others.

54. विमृश्य पक्षप्रतिपक्षाभ्याम् अर्थावधारणं निर्णयः । NS. 1.1.41

    When there is an ascertainment of the real character of the thing after duly deliberating over the two sides of the question an argument in favour of a certain conclusion and also that in its consultation, we have 'Definitive Cognition' (*nirṇaya*).

55. G. N. Jha, p. 464.

56. न शास्त्रे वादे वा विमर्शोऽस्ति उभयोर्निश्चितत्वात् शास्त्राभ्युपगतपदार्थस्य निश्चितत्वात् च । *Vārttika on NS.* 1.1.41

    Neither in the case of discussions nor in the case of scriptural matters, is there room for deliberation or doubt; because so far as discussions are concerned, both parties to it are equally certain as to their conclusions; as regards scriptural matters, the definitive cognition is obtained entirely with the help of the scriptures themselves.

57. प्रमाणतर्कसाधनोपलम्भः सिद्धान्ताविरुद्धः पक्षप्रत्यवयवोपपन्नः पक्षप्रतिपक्षपरिग्रहो वादः । NS. 1.2.1

Discussion consists in the putting forward of a conception and counter conception, in which there is supporting and condemning by means of proofs and reasonings—neither of which is quite opposed to the main doctrine, and both of which are carried on in full accordance with the method of reasoning through the five factors.

58. सोऽयं पक्षप्रतिपक्षपरिग्रहो वादः ।.... छलजातिनिग्रहस्थानोपलम्भ एव जल्पः प्रमाणतर्कसाधनोपलम्भः वादः एव ।
Bhāṣya on NS.1.2.1

Discussion is that in which supporting and condemning are done by proofs and reasoning; where the supporting and condemning are done by casuistry etc. it is disputation or wrangling.

59. स प्रतिपक्षस्थापनाहीनो वितण्डा । NS. 1.2.3

The same disputation is wrangling when there is no establishing of the counter conception. G.N. Jha, p. 522.

60. सव्यभिचार-विरुद्ध-प्रकरणसम-साध्यसम-कालातीता हेत्वाभासाः । 1.2.4

Inconclusive (*savyabhicāra*), contradictory (*viruddha*), Neutralised (*prakaraṇasama*) unknown (*sadhyasama*) and mistimed (*kālātīta*) are fallacious probans.

61. अनैकान्तिकः सव्यभिचारः । NS. 1.2.5

सिद्धान्तमभ्युपेत्य तद्विरोधी विरुद्धः । NS.1.2.6

यस्मात् प्रकरणचिन्ता स निर्णयार्थमपदिष्टः प्रकरणसमः । NS.1.2.7

साध्याविशिष्टः साध्यत्वात् साध्यसमः । NS.1.2.8

कालात्ययापदिष्टः कालातीतः । NS.1.2.9

Inconclusive (probans) is that which is tainted by indecision.
A certain doctrine having been accepted, the Probans that is contradictory to it is called the contradictory.
Neutralised probans is that which is put forward to establish a definite conclusion while it is one that only gives rise to suspense in regard to the point at issue.
The unknown probans is that which being still to be proved, is not different from probandum.
Mistimed probans is that which, as adduced, is behind time.

62. साधर्म्यवैधर्म्याभ्यां प्रत्यवस्थानं जातिः । NS.1.2.18

Futile rejoinder is that objection which is taken on the basis of mere similarity and dissimilarity.

प्रयुक्ते हि हेतौ यः प्रसङ्गो ज्ञायते स जातिः । *Bhāṣya* on 1.2.18

When a certain reasoning has been put forward, the objection to it that follows takes birth is called *jāti*-futile rejoinder. G.N. Jha, p. 579.

63. विप्रतिपत्तिरप्रतिपत्तिश्च निग्रहस्थानम् । NS. 1.2.19

It is a case of clincher when there is misapprehension as also there is incomprehension.
समर्थे साधने निग्रहस्थानप्राप्तौ कथमप्रतिपत्तिः? विप्रतिपत्तिः? यदायं साधयिता साधनेन उपात्तेन परेण जात्यादिभिराकुलीकृतः उत्तरं न प्रतिपद्यते तदा कथमप्रतिपत्तिः कथं वा विप्रतिपत्तिः? तदापि साधनस्यैव सामर्थ्यापरिज्ञानादसमर्थ एतत् साधनमिति अप्रतिपत्तिः विप्रतिपत्तिः इति ।

Nyāyavārttikā on NS. 1.2.18

It is possible for a clincher to be urged even where the man has put forward a sound argument; how then can clincher be said to be indicative of misapprehension or incomprehension?

That is to say, it may so happen that a man supports his contention by a perfectly sound argument and yet when his opponent meets him with a futile rejoinder, he becomes confounded and fails to find the proper answer to that rejoinder—how can this be said to be a case of either misapprehension or incomprehension?

Even in such cases there would be (a) incomprehension and (b) mis-comprehension consisting in the man; (c) not comprehending the soundness and strength of his own arguments; and (d) in his regarding his own sound arguments as unsound.

64. तत् खलु निःश्रेयसं किं तत्त्वज्ञानानन्तरमेव भवति? नेत्युच्यते । किं तर्हि? तत्त्वज्ञानात् ।

Bhāṣya on NS. 1.1.1

Does the highest good appear immediately after the 'true knowledge?'

No! after true knowledge. *Bhāṣya* (preceding NS. 1.1.2)

65. दुःख-जन्म-प्रवृत्ति-दोष-मिथ्याज्ञानानाम् उत्तरोत्तरापाये तदनन्तरापायादपवर्गः । NS. 1.1.2

There is a cessation of each member of the following series, pain, birth, activity, defect and wrong notion—the cessation of that which follows bringing annihilation of that which precedes; and this ultimately leads to 'Final Release.' G. N. Jha. p. 83.

66. ईश्वरः कारणं पुरुषकर्माफल्यदर्शनात् । NS.4.1.19

God is the cause because we find fruitlessness in the actions of men.

पुरुषोऽयं समीहमानो नावश्यं समीहाफलं

प्राप्नोति तेनानुमीयते पराधीनं पुरुषस्य कर्मफला-

राधनमिति, यदधीनं स ईश्वरः । तस्मादीश्वरः

कारणमिति । *Nyā. Bha.* on NS.4.1.19

67. तत्कारितत्वादहेतुः । NS.4.1.21

Inasmuch as it is influenced by Him, there is no force in the reason (forwarded).

Answer to the objection.

न, पुरुषकर्माभावे फलानिष्पत्तेः । NS. 4.1.20

It is not so, because, as a matter of fact, no fruit arises without man's action.

68. गुणविशिष्टात्मान्तरमीश्वरः । तस्य आत्मकल्पात् कल्पान्तरानुपपत्तिः, अधर्ममिथ्याज्ञानप्रमादहान्या धर्मज्ञान-समाधिसम्पदा च विशिष्टात्मान्तरमीश्वरः, तस्य च धर्मसमाधिफलम् अणिमादि अष्टविधम् ऐश्वर्यम् । सङ्कल्पचानुविधायी नास्य धर्मः प्रत्यात्मवृत्तीन् धर्माधर्मसञ्चयान् पृथिव्यादीनि च भूतानि प्रवर्तयन्ति ।

युक्तं च स्वकृताभ्यागमस्यालोपेन निर्माणप्राकाम्यम् ईश्वरस्य स्वकृतकर्मफलं वेदितव्यम् । आप्तकल्पश्चायम्, यथा पितापत्यानां तथा पितृभूत ईश्वरो भूतानाम् । न चात्मकल्पादन्यः कल्पः सम्भवति । न तावदस्य वृद्धिं विना कश्चिद्धर्मो लिङ्गभूतः शक्यं उपपादयितुम् । आगमाच्च द्रष्टा, बोद्धा, सर्वज्ञाता ईश्वर इति । *Bhāṣya* on 4.1.21

God is a distinct soul endowed with certain qualities; for as being of the same kind as 'soul'. He can not be put under any category; hence god is defined as a particular soul endowed with such qualities as, (i) absence of demerit, wrong knowledge and negligence and (ii) presence of merit, knowledge and intuition, and to Him also belongs, the eight-fold power consisting of minuteness and the rest, as the result of His merit and knowledge—His merit follows the bent of His volition—He controls the activity of the residuum of Merit and Demerit subsisting in each individual soul, as also that of the earth and other material substances; and He is omnipotent in regard to His creation, not however, failing to be influenced by the results of acts, done by the beings He creates; He has obtained all the results of His deeds. Just as a father acts for his children, so does god also act father-like for living beings. There is no other category except the category of soul to which god could belong; for in the case of God, no other property, save *buddhi*, cognition can be pointed out as being indicative of His existence. From scriptures also we learn that God is the seer, the cognizer and the knower of all things.

69. G. N. Jha, pp. 1400 ff.

70. तदकारितत्वात् इत्येवं ब्रुवता निमित्तकारणम् ईश्वर इत्युपगतं भवति । *Vārttika* on 4.1.21

When the author of the *sutra* declares that things are influenced by God, he admits that God is the efficient cause (of things).

71. G. N. Jha, pp. 1462-63.

सति निमित्तविशेषप्रतिपत्तौ ईश्वरप्रक्रिया, यस्मिन्निमित्तकारणे विप्रतिपद्यन्ते । केचित् कालं केचिदीश्वरं केचित्प्रकृतिमिति । *Vārttika,* p. 461.

Having admitted that the perceptible substances are the constituent cause of the world—and there being a difference of opinion in regard to the constituent cause—there is a treatment on the subject of God, people have different views in regard to the efficient cause of the world — some people holding Time as the cause, some others, God, while others again put forward Primordial matter.

ईश्वर इति न्याय्यम्, तत्र हि प्रमाणानि अविघातेन प्रवर्तन्त इति । Ibid

The right view is that God is the efficient cause of the world; for, in support of this view proofs come forward unimpeded.

72. यथावास्यादि बुद्धिमता तक्ष्णा अधिष्ठितमचेतनत्वात् प्रवर्तते इति प्रवृत्तिस्वभाविकं तत्त्वत्वमिति । *Vārttika,* p. 467, G. N. Jha, p. 1473.

Just as the earth upholds things, because such is its very nature and similarly with the other things, exactly in the same manner God acts because such as His very nature; for as a matter of fact, the very nature of God consists in activity.

73. कारणं त्रिविधम्, समवायि-असमवायि-निमित्तभेदात् ।

यत्समवेतं कार्यमुत्पद्यते तत्समवायिकारणम् । यथा तन्तवः पटस्य, पटश्च स्वगतरूपादेः । -तर्कसङ्ग्रहः

Causes are of three kinds : inherent cause, non-inherent cause and efficient cause.

If the material in which the product is produced by the relation of inherence it is called inherent cause of the product, *samavāyi kāraṇa*, like the yarns to the cloth and the cloth to its colour.

74. कार्येण कारणेन वा सह एकस्मिन्नर्थे समवेतं सत् कारणम् असमवायिकारणं यथा तन्तुसंयोगः पटस्य, तन्तुरूपं पटस्य । Ibid

The non-inherent cause is the one which is either a quality or movement that inheres in the inherent cause itself. The conjunction of the threads is an example for the first kind. It inheres in the threads which are the inherent cause of the cloth and produces the cloth.

The colour of the threads is an example for the second type. It inheres in the threads which are the inherent cause of the inherent cause of the product, namely, the colour of the cloth, the colour of the threads which inheres the cloth or the colour itself or the conjunction of threads.

75. तदुभयभिन्नं कारणं निमित्तकारणम् यथा तुरीवेमादिकं पटस्य । Ibid

The efficient cause is different from the other two namely, the inherent and the non-inherent cause, eg. the shuttle and the loom etc., in the production of cloth.

निमित्तकारणं तु साधारणासाधारणभेदेन द्विविधमस्ति । तत्र साधारणनिमित्तकारणानि अष्टविधानि । ईश्वर:, तज्ज्ञानेच्छाकृतय:, दिक्कालौ, अदृष्टं, प्रागभावश्चेति ।

Nimittakāraṇa, efficient cause is of two kinds, *sādhāraṇa* and *asādhāraṇa*. The former is of eight kinds, viz. *Īśvara* and his *Jñāna*, *Icchā*, action, Time, Space, *Adṛṣṭa* and Prior non-existence.

असाधारणनिमित्तकारणानि तु कार्यभेदेन अनेकविधानि । (न्यायकोश: P.226)

The *asādhāraṇa* efficient causes depending on the product, are innumerable.

76. Hiriyanna, M, *Outlines of Indian Philosophy,* p. 253.

77. क्रियागुणव्यपदेशाभावात् प्रागसत् । *VS.* 9.1.1

An effect is antecendentally non-existent, inasmuch as there is non-existence of assertion of actions and qualities.

यस्य प्रयत्नानन्तरम् आत्मलाभ: तत्खलु अभूत्वा भवति, यथा घटादिकार्यम् । Bhāsya on NS. 5-1.37

Now, that which is the outcome of the effort is such as, not having previous existence comes into existence; as found to be the case with such products as the jar and the like.

78. प्रागभाववत् कार्यम् । *Saptapadārthī,120*

A product is one that has antecedent non-existence.

Jayanta Bhaṭṭa discusses *satkāryavāda* at length and refutes it by asserting:

न च कार्यकारणयोरभेदात् सत्कार्यमिति वक्तव्यम्, तयो: प्रत्यक्षसिद्धभिन्नस्वरूपत्वात् ।

Nyāyamañjarī, āhnika 8

One cannot say that cause and effect are the same; perception of cause and effect shows that each is different from the other.

79. कारणमस्त्यव्यक्तं प्रवर्तते त्रिगुणत: समुदायाच्च ।

परिणामत: सलिलवत् प्रतिगुणाश्रयविशेषात् ॥ SK.16

It (the unevolved) functions in respect of three constituents both (individually) and in their combination, being modified like water, by the specific nature abiding in the respective constituents.

80. सोऽयं कारणात् परमाव्यक्तात् साक्षात् परिणाम: पारम्पर्येणान्वितस्य विश्वस्य कार्यस्य विभाग: । *Sāṃkhya tattva Kaumudī* on SK.16

This universe is a product manifesting itself gradually as a change directly from the Primordial Prakṛti which itself is the cause.

81. सत्त्वं लघु प्रकाशकमिष्टमुपष्टम्भकं चलं च रज: । गुरु वरणकमेव तम:, प्रदीपवच्चार्थतो वृत्ति: । SK.13

Sattva is considered to be buoyant and illuminating, *Rajas* to be stimulating and mobile; *Tamas* alone is heavy and enveloping; their functioning for the goal (of spirit) is like (the flame of) a lamp.

82. असदकरणादुपादानग्रहणात् सर्वसम्भवाभावात् ।

शक्तस्य शक्यकरणात्कारणभावाच्च सत्कार्यम् ॥ SK.9

The effect subsists (even prior to the operation of the cause) since what is non-existent cannot be brought into existence by the operation of a cause, since there is recourse to the (appropriate) material cause, since there is not production at all (by all), since the potent (cause) effects only that or which it is capable, and since (the effect) is non-different from the cause.

83. Hiriyanna, M.: *op.cit.*, pp. 298 ff.; Sharma, C., *op.cit.*, pp. 211 ff.

84. अनुभूति: प्रमाणम् । स्मृतिव्यतिरिक्ता च संविदनुभूति: । इति प्राभाकरा: । *Mānameyodaya, Upodghāta*
Experience is valid knowledge. And cognition other than recollection is experience.

85. पूर्वपूर्वज्ञानजनितानां प्राकट्यानामुत्तरोत्तरज्ञानपर्यन्तमवस्थानात् तदवच्छिन्नानां कालांशानां तत्र तत्र अवगम इति ।
Since the manifestedness that is produced by each of the preceding cognitions lasts right upto the succeeding cognition, the cognition there is the element of time defined by that.

तत्त्वपदेन भ्रमसंशयादीनां अयथार्थज्ञानानां निरास: ।

By the word real (*tattva*), there is the exclusion of knowledge like delusion, doubt etc.

86. अज्ञातपदेन अत्र ज्ञातविषययो: स्मृत्यनुवादयो: निरास: ।

By the word 'unknown' there is the exclusion of recollection and restatement.

87. तत्सिद्धमात्मा प्रतिक्षेत्रं भिन्न इति । *Mānameyodaya*, p. 111

Therefore it is established that the soul is distinct for every body.

88. Hiriyanna M., *Outlines of Indian Philosophy*, p. 303.

89. तत्र बाह्ये रूपादौ विषये चतुष्टयसन्निकर्षाज् ज्ञानमुत्पद्यते, आत्मा मनसा संयुज्यते । मन इन्द्रियेण, इन्द्रियमर्थेनेति ।
(*Nyāyamañjarī*, p.115) (Part-I)
In regard to external objects like colour etc. cognition arises when three things come together, i.e. the self combines with mind, mind with senses, senses with the objects.

90. Hiriyanna M: Outlines of Indian Philosophy, p. 312.

90a.*op.cit.* pp. 314-17.

91. *Parataḥprāmāṇya*

प्रमाणाप्रमाणत्वे स्वत: सांख्या: समाश्रिता: ।

नैयायिकास्ते परत: सौगताश्रमं स्वत: ॥

प्रथमं परत: प्राहु: प्रामाण्यं वेदान्तिन: ।

प्रमाणत्वं स्वत: प्राह परतश्चाप्रमाणताम् ॥

See, S.C. Chatterji: 'The Nyāya Doctrine of Pramāṇa', Journal of the *Department of Letters*, Vol. XVI, 1927, p. 160.

तस्माद् दृढं यदुत्पन्नं नापि संवादमृच्छति । ज्ञानान्तरेण विज्ञानं तत् प्रज्ञानान्तरं प्रतीयताम् ॥ Śl.vā. 2.80

So let that knowledge be accepted as Pramāṇa which is produced with a sense of certitude; and which does not seek verification by another knowledge.

92. गुरुमते घटत्वेन घटमहं जानामीत्याद्याकारकं व्यवसायात्मकमेष सर्वं ज्ञानम् । तच्च स्वप्रकाशकम् । मितिमातृमेयत्वात्
त्रिपुटीत्युच्यते । न्यायकोश: p.562

According to the '*guru*' i.e. Prabhākara, the knowledge that arises from the conceptualisation of the object, say a pot, that I know the pot from the genus potness presented before. This knowledge is self-luminous. There is the trio involved here, viz., the knowledge, the knower and the known.

93. भाट्टमते अयं घट: इति ज्ञानानन्तरं घटे ज्ञाततानामकं फलं भवति । ततो ज्ञातो घट इति प्रत्यक्षम् । पश्चात्तया ज्ञाततया ज्ञानमात्रस्यातीन्दियत्वात् ज्ञातं तन्निष्ठाप्रामाण्यं चानुमीयते । Ibid

In the opinion of Bhaṭṭa (Kumārila), the quality of cognizedness results after one gets the knowledge, 'this is pot'. Then the perception arises that 'the pot is known'. Then, by means of the state of cognition one can infer the knowledge and the validity that lies in it because knowledge, per se, transcends all the sensibilities.

94. Prasad, Jwala: *Indian Epistemology*, p. 97 ff.
95. C. Sharma, *op. cit.* pp. 90-91.
96. Sctherbatsky: *Buddhist Logic*, p. 64.
97. *Nyāya kandalī*, p. 22, p. 28.
98. Sctherbatsky, *op. cit.*, p. 147.
99. कल्पनापोढशब्देनापि यदि प्रत्यक्षमुच्यते तदा व्याघात: । अथ नोच्यते, तथापि कल्पनापोढवचनं व्यर्थम् । प्रत्यक्षं कल्पनापोढमिति वाक्यम् । अथास्य वाक्यस्य कोऽर्थ: ? यदि प्रत्यक्षं व्याघात: । कथम् । प्रत्यक्षं कल्पनापोढमिति चानेन वाक्येनाभिधीयते । न च अभिधेयमिति कोऽन्यो भदन्ताद्रुकुमर्हति । अथ न प्रत्यक्षमस्यार्थ: वर्णोच्चारणमात्रं तर्ह्येतद्वाक्यं प्रत्यक्षं कल्पनापोढमिति । अनित्यादि शब्दविषयत्वाच्च न सर्वथा अवाच्यम् । अनित्यं प्रत्यक्षं दु:खभूम्यमनात्मकं च प्रत्यक्षमित्येषां चेच्छब्दानां विषयतामुपयाति, कथमवाच्यम् । अथ नोपैति? सर्वं संस्कृतं अनित्यमित्येत्तथागतेन नाख्यातव्यम् । अथ कल्पनापोढशब्देन प्रत्यक्षस्य स्वरूपम् अभिधीयते? एवमपि अनिवृत्तौ व्याघात: स्वरूपं चानभिधेयं इत्यनेन शब्देनाभिधीयते किमस्य शब्दस्योच्चारणसामर्थ्यं प्रत्यक्षं कल्पनापोढमिति? अप्रतिपादकत्वात् मूकस्वप्नसदृशमेतत् । एवं यथा यथा इदं लक्षणं विचार्यते, तथा तथा न्यायं न सहते इति । *Vārttika* on N. S. 1.1.4; G.N. Jha, pp. 148-151.

100. Stcherbatsky, *op. cit.*, pp. 160-180.
101. Ibid. pp. 234-35.
102. Sharma, Chandradhar: *A Critical Survey of Indian Philosophy*, p. 134.
103. Ibid. pp. 49-50.
104. मतिश्रुतावधिमन:पर्यायकेवलानि ज्ञानम् । *Tat. Sū.* 1.9

The means of knowledge are *mati, śruta, avadhi, manahparyāya* and *kevala*.

105. श्रुतं मतिपूर्वं द्वयनेकद्वादशभेदम् । *Tat.Sū.* 1.20

Śruta follows *mati* knowledge. It can be two, many or twelve kinds.

106. सर्वद्रव्यपर्यायेषु केवलस्य । *Tat.Sū.*1.30; C. Sharma, p. 59.

Direct knowledge has for its object all objects (worldly, non-worldly and infinite).

107. C. Sharma, *op. cit.*, p. 51.
108. कुतस्तु खलु सोम्यैवं स्यादिति होवाच कथमसत: सज्जायेतेति । सदेव सोम्येदमग्र आसीदेकमेवाद्वितीयम् । *Ch.up.*6.2.2

109. आवि: सन्निहितं गुहाचरं नाम महत्पदमत्रैतत्समर्पितम् । एजत्प्राण्न्निमिषच्च यदेतज्ज्ञानथ सदसद्वरेण्यं परं विज्ञानाद्वरिष्ठं प्रजानाम् ॥ *Muṇḍ. up.* 2.2.1

110. M. Hiriyanna, *op.cit.*, p. 173.
111. *Tattvasaṅgraha* 311-327 (quoted by C. Sharma, *op. cit.*, p. 54).

CHAPTER 7

Space and Time

SPACE AND TIME are intimately involved in our daily life and perceptions of every event or occurrence. Even so they seem to be the two enigmatic entities which continue to defy succinct definitions of their true states. That there are two aspects of them, namely, the absolute and the practical, have been more or less accepted by philosophers and other thinkers alike. Modern scientists too are concerned with their nature as well as mutual relationship. But, their primordial origin is still an elusive one even among modern scientists who admit the real existence of both space and time either separately or a space–time continuum [see Chapter 10 in this Volume: *Modern Perspective on the Physical World*].

There are statements like 'tensed time' (i.e., past, present and future) and 'tenseless space' as well as the flow of time or the 'arrow' of time. There is a dynamic view of time (see below); but such a view does not seem to be commensurate with all that the word, space, stands for as a real entity, notwithstanding its relevance in the context of matter and motion.

We speak of limited and unlimited space, the abstract space being conceived as boundless. The word, *ākāśa*, literally means that which provides space and the concept of *ākāśa* in Indian thought is different from that of space (*dik*) although sometimes it is used to denote the sky, the vast expanse of space. Both *ākāśa* and *dik*, as noted before, have been regarded as reals in the Nyāya-Vaiśeṣika scheme; likewise time.

What is time? Is it real or relative ? Are the man-made divisions of time merely pragmatic or is there any underlying unitary principle behind them? Is the tensed time—past, present and future—a mental construct so as to be in tune with the human perceptions? Questions such as these have engaged the attention of Indian thinkers of all shades, just as they have done so in the West over a long period. In the Indian context, the concept of time was to a great extent evolved not independently by itself, but in the matrix of ontology and also some sort of epistemology. The importance of the idea of time was such that the savants who pondered over it were called *Kālacintaka-s, Kālakāraṇavādin-s or Kālavādin-s*. The *Gauḍapāda (Māṇḍūkya) kārikā*[1] says that 'all beings are born of Time', thus pointing out that without time, phenomenal or otherwise, the objects and experiences would not be properly understood. In general, time has been given the same status as that of reality, in a way intimately associating it with the seminal concept of *Being* and *Becoming* as well as the dynamic relations between them.

Early Ideas

The *Ṛgveda*, the earliest literary compendium, that projects an array of gods invoking them through a spectrum of hymns, does not appear to have dealt with the concept of time (*kāla*), in any meaningful way. However, it has given an account of the divisions of time based on the lunar and solar movements. The *Atharvaveda*, on the other hand, has described time as the manifestation of divinity. Commenting on one of the enigmatic *mantra-s*, Yāska has interpreted it as having the implication that every being exists in time. The *Atharvaveda* has several hymns devoted to the deified *Kāla*, and it even proclaims that everything is created by it and the entire universe is positioned in it.

The *Kālasūkta* of the *Atharvaveda* is entirely devoted to the glorification of time, as the Creator as well as the sustainer of the universe is regarded as Brahman itself.[2] The ontological aspect of time appears again in the *Atharvaveda* which presents the view that Time is the Creator, and from time was born the creative heat or fervour generated by sacrifice. It is likened to a steed with seven reins (rays), thousand-eyed like the Ṛgvedic cosmic person (*Puruṣa*) and all the worldly beings are his wheels. It was conceived too in terms of its seven wheels, seven navels and more significantly, it's axle being immortal. It was also considered to be the primeval Lord.[3] The Creation of earth, space, heaven, the fervour of creation (*tapas*), mind and breath are all stated to be the creations of time.

The *Maitrāyaṇīya upaniṣad*,[4] refers to time as a purifier of all beings through self-awareness, and states that the knowledge of the Vedas requires a proper understanding of time. Thus an exalted place has been accorded to time even in the early Indian thinking.

The Upaniṣads, however, describe Brahman as transcending time, although one of the Upaniṣads (the *Śvetāśvatara*) hails time as the originator of the Universe. The Upaniṣads do not, however, accord such an exalted status to time. Even the deistic *Śvetāśvatara*,[5] while suggesting a series of seminal factors of the universe, starts with time and ends with soul. the intermediate factors are: the inherent nature (*svabhāva*), necessity (*niyati*), chance (*yadṛcchā*), the elements (*bhūtāni*), womb (*yoni*) and male (*puruṣa*). But the Upaniṣad does not think of time as the first cause; instead speaks of the self-will (*ātma-śakti*) of god. Two forms of Brahman have been conceived—*time* and *not-time* and that which existed before Sun was regarded as *not-time*, and that which began with the Sun was duly considered as *time* and divisible.[6] In any case, the upaniṣadic Brahman is projected as being beyond both space and time. The *Bṛhadāraṇyaka*, expatiates that whatever is above the heaven, beneath the earth, or across the space, is imperishable Brahman,[7] Further, time is stated to be indivisible which implies that Brahman is independent of space too. The *Kāṭhaka* stresses symbolically that there is no divisibility or plurality of time.[8] According to *Maitrāyaṇīya upaniṣad*, the creation is manifested in time, and grows as well as decays. It also reiterates that the course of the Sun is in the nature of a proof of time.[9] Likewise, Brahman is also regarded as being independent of the past, the present and future, and 'at his feet time rolls'. The *Māṇḍūkya* thinks of *Oum,* the sacred syllable, as the past, the present and the future[10]. *Maitrāyaṇīya upaniṣad* thinks of Brahman as the soul of the Sun itself.[11]

The Upaniṣadic approach to space and time is in tune with its concept of Brahman and its idealistic elucidation. To know or experience Brahman, one has to discard the categories of space and time that are after all sensorially determined. There was the Vedic view that time was the Creator as a temporal cosmic principle and Prajāpati, the primordial creator God[12] was related to it, and thus time was integrated into the concept of eternity. The view of time and eternity runs in one form or the other in various shades of Indian thinking process. In any case the Vedic approach to time and space was not only in the matrix of ONE becoming MANY but also in the cyclic notion of *Kāla* and *Karma,* a belief that was a dominant one, then as now.

Time in the Purāṇa-s

The deification of time, the origins of which can be traced to the Vedic period, assumed significant dimensions specially in the Purāṇa-s. The *Bhāgavata purāṇa,* for instance, calls time, Īśvara who exists from the minutest period (atomic) to the full day of Brahmā,[13] while the *Viṣṇu purāṇa* describes time as a supreme form of Brahmā.[14] The Purāṇa-s speak of huge durations of time in a linear as well as cyclic manner as will be seen later. The *Bhagavadgītā* also refers to time. The Lord (Kṛṣṇa) states that He is time eternal and also He is the divisions of time.[15]

It is well known that the Purāṇa-s are specially noted for their five characteristics (*pañca-lakṣaṇa-s*). Of them, the idea of Manvantara has an important place in the Purāṇic matrix, in which space has also been given its due consideration, although time is regarded as more abstract than space.

In general, the Purāṇic approach is to consider time both as indivisible (*akhaṇḍa*) and divisible (*khaṇḍa*) or transcendental time and empirical time. At the same time, the Purāṇas have thought of time as the ultimate principle, as the embodiment of God or even a particular phase of the Universal spirit itself[16] in the very process of creation and dissolution of the universe. One of the Purāṇa-s speaks of time as the power of God which creates disturbance in the three *guna-s* of *Avyakta* so that it manifests itself as the visible universe.[17] The *Visnu purāna* avers that time (a form of Purusa),[18] is the Creator, sustainer and destroyer of the universe[19] and time (a form of *Visnu*) establishes intimate union or disunion between *purusa* and *pradhāna*.[20] This Purāna also stresses the dynamic aspect of time in its own way.

Space and Time in the Vaiśesika

Time and space are the substances (*dravya-s*) in the scheme of the Vaiśesika categories of reals. Time is recognized as one, all-pervading and eternal like space and *ākāśa*. But unlike *ākāśa*, which has a specific quality of sound (ears), both space and time have no specific sensorial attributes. Each, however, has five common qualities: number, dimension, distinctness, conjunction and disjunction and regarded as the efficient causes of all products.[21] It may be noted that these attributes are also common to all the other seven substances, namely, the five elements, self and mind which in addition have some other attributes. According to Kanāda, the knowledge of time is inferential and is associated with priority (*paratva*), posteriority (*aparatva*), succession (*ayaugapadya*), and simultaneity (*yaugapadya*) as well as quickness (*ksipratva*) and slowness (*ciratva*). And these would be the *linga* or ground for the inference of time.[22]

Praśastapāda, in a practical manner, has tried to explain that these notions as well as the various common usages like *ksana, lava, nimeśa, kāsthā, kalā, muhūrta* and the like do not relate in any manner to the other *dravya-s* or substances like the five elements, space, *ātman* and mind. But these notions need a substratum and that is Time.[23]

The Vaiśesika regards *kāla* as an instrumental (*nimittakārana*) cause of every produced object.[24] The observations or judgements like moving at *present* and the like indicate that time is also a substrate (*ādhāramātra*) of motion, according to Praśastapāda who also states that time is the cause of the production, existence and destruction of every product. The *Kiranāvalī*, however, thinks of time as an auxiliary (*upanāyaka*) of motion.[25]

The words of practical usage like priority and posteriority are of considerable importance in this respect. The Vaiśesika has thought of these, strange it may seem, as being independent of time itself and as attributes possessed by every produced and observed substance. What is specially notable is that they are supposed to be in relation to a large or small numbers of solar revolutions (*ādityaparivartanāni*). An interesting example adduced by the Vaiśesika (or Nyāya-Vaiśesika) is that if one person is prior to another person or the other person is posterior to the first person, though both of them are contemporary, the other person obviously has been connected with a larger number of solar revolutions than the first person. In other words, in terms of the age of a person relative to that of another, this example has validity, the time being conceived in such a manner.[26] Thus the solar days could be regarded, from the practical point of view, as the yardstick of the passage or arrow of time. However, associated with the notions of priority and priority there is rather a circumlocutory idea, called *saṃyukta saṃyukta samavāya*. According to this, although there is no direct relationship between a person and the solar motion, the motion inheres in the Sun and it would be logical to think that there should be a conjunction with some substance that itself is in conjunction with the Sun in which the motion inheres. This approach is in conformity with the general model of the Nyāya-Vaiśeṣika according to which the attributes have no existence by themselves, apart from the substances in which they inhere.

Vyomaśivācārya has a different viewpoint with regard to the notions of simultaneity and the others *vis-á-vis* the solar movements. Posing the question as to whether the movements of the Sun themselves could be accepted as the cause of the aforesaid notions, his reply is in the negative and he stresses that even the objects of the universe are not expressed in terms of the movements of the Sun alone. According to Vyomaśivācārya, if the motion by itself is the time, then there would have been hardly any notion of simultaneity and the like.[27]

The *Kiraṇāvalī's* argument in this context is worthy of note. Since there should be a conjunction both with the individual and with the Sun, there should be some substance that cannot be of limited magnitude, but ubiquitous and connected with all finite substances.[28] *Ākāśa* is one such ubiquitous nature, but it cannot serve this purpose since it is a substratum for sound, its specific quality. Moreover, it has no capacity to bring one finite substance into relation with the other substance. The example given is that, if a drum is struck, the sound produced cannot be transferred to another drum. Though *ākāśa* is connected simulataneously with the other drum or all drums, ubiquitously,[29] it is unable to effect transmission from one substance to another. The *Kiraṇāvalī* has also examined in the same manner the self or *ātman* and its limitations or incapacity for transmitting the attribute of one object to another.[30] In the case of the notions of priority and posteriority, wherein a direct relation with the object and solar motion is impossible, and if *ākāśa* and self cannot play any role in generating or accommodating this relation, there should, of necessity, be another special substance which can encompass this relation and this particular substance is Time, asserts the Nyāya-Vaiśeṣika. According to *Upaskāra* of Śaṅkara Miśra, the revolutions of the Sun which have not yet taken place as well as the ones that have not occurred cannot be the determinants of time.[31] Therefore, the substance that determines notions (of priority, posteriority etc.) is evidently Time which is one[32] and related to a cause.[33] Thus, the approach of the Nyāya-Vaiśeṣika towards time is based on its perceived logical necessity within its own basic premises. The existence of time is sought to be established by *reductio ad absurdum* of the other causes, time having been considered as a cause of an indirect relation between an individual substance and solar motion. Implicit in this logical necessity, however, is (i) the recognition of the fact that solar motion and time are two-in-one, and (ii) the conviction that time is one of the nine substances governed by the other five categories (*padārtha-s*) namely, in terms of the attributes that inhere in a substance, action, generality, particularity and inherence.

The Nyāya-Vaiśeṣika has also thought it wise to explain the notions or occurrences of simultaneity, quickness and slowness in relation to the solar motion only, and it does not appear to swerve in any other way to explain these perceptible occurrences. These are, like priority and posteriority, only the logical grounds to infer time as a substance. In any case, the Nyāya-Vaiśeṣika does not seem to have endeavoured to explain the true nature of time as well as its nuances, but clings to the view that time is an entity of relation and that there is an inter-relatedness between the object and the solar motion on the one hand and, on the other, that it would give rise to the notions of priority, posteriority, etc. Time is also thought of as the cause of these subjective notions and it is to be *inferred*[34] but not directly perceived. Nevertheless, the changes that objects undergo in succession or otherwise, are supposed to be connected with time. The notion of time vis-à-vis, the origin and destruction of all objects in the context of their experience is presented as their cause.[35] In such a restricted frame of thinking, the orthodox Nyāya-Vaiśeṣika was unable to comprehend time in all of its details.

However, Vallabhācārya in his *Nyāya-līlāvatī*, has presented an idea that the basis of the notion of time is the knowledge or perception that an object actually exists at *present* and the existence has in it a temporal character.[36] He also points out that existence or *existent-ness* is the same as present or *present-ness*, and time is *one* in all of its innumerable happenings because the existence is perceived as being common to all of them.[37]

Three divisions of time: If time, as a substance is indivisible, in practical life its three components have been recognized—the present, the past and the future, besides its other divisions into smaller units, day, months and year (see below). The Nyāya-Vaiśeṣika, however, does not believe that these are natural, but thinks that these are man-made and, therefore, they are not integral to time as a substance. For, according to the Nyāya-Vaiśeṣika, each of them (the past, the present and the future) would be essentially and even numerically different from the two others. Since the definite time-span would always have intrinsically the element of *presentness*, it cannot be cognized either as the past or the future. Also, a unit of time cannot have as its qualities neither the pastness, nor the presentness nor the futurity. A close examination of this would reveal, the Nyāya-Vaiśeṣika avers, the contradiction if it were to have these three aspects together because that which is experienced as present cannot be of the past or the future.[38] Obviously this would mean that when an object is cognized *as* and *at* present, it would be erroneous to associate with this cognition either the past or the future or both. The Nyāya-Vaiśeṣika also thinks that these distinctions of time-series are to be in relation to something outside of them. It further asserts that such distinctions are the derivatives of the already generated events of finite duration as a result of their association with what it calls *upādhi* (adjuncts of limiting character). The main thrust of the Nyāya-Vaiśeṣika seems to be that time as a substance is independent of all of these, although time spoken of as *present* is dependent upon its relation to an event that is occurring, but not ended. In view of this, the past would be the time associated with an event that has ended and not perceived, while the future would be the time associated with an event that has yet to happen, again unperceived.[39] Time, therefore, is beyond the distinctions of the past, present and future as well as its divisions for practical purposes. Time is thus a real substance and eternal for the Nyāya-Vaiśeṣika. Yet, the Nyāya-Vaiśeṣika admits the distinguishable features of the past, the present and the future sometimes on the basis of external determinants like the solar motion.

In the context that inference (*anumāna*) is applicable to the three divisions of time, there is an interesting discussion centering round the *Nyāya-Sūtra* (2.1.39) which refers to the Bauddha view, namely : '...There is no *present* time; for when an object falls, the only possible points of time are that which has been fallen through, and that which has to be fallen through'. Interestingly, in this view, time is also thought of in relation to space, citing the example of a fruit falling from the stalk: '...When the fruit becomes detached from the stalk, it falls and comes gradually nearer and nearer to the ground; while it is so nearing the ground, the space above the fruit (and below the tree) is *space traversed;* and the time related to that traversed space is '*that which has been fallen through*' (the past); and the space below the fruit and above the ground is the *space to be traversed,* and the time related to this latter space is 'that which has to be fallen through' (the future)—and apart from these two there is no third space, in relation to which there could be the notion of *being traversed,* which would give rise to the conception of the *Present Time.* From this we (Buddhists's view) conclude that there is no such a thing as Present Time' (G. N. Jha, p. 805).

The *Nyāya-Sūtra*, 2.1.40 categorically states that if there is no present, the other two, namely, the Past and the Future also would be inconceivable, as these are relative to the present time.

Time and Action

Vātsyāyana, in his commentary on this *sutra*, emphatically denies the manifestation of time in relation to space as conceived by the Buddhists, and asserts that it is manifested by action (*kriyā*). He explains: 'We have the conception of time that *has been fallen through* (i.e., past time) when the *action* of falling—which is expressed by the phrase 'its fall has ceased; and when that some *action* is going to happen, we have the conception of time *that has to be fallen through* (i.e., future time); and lastly, when the action of thing is perceived as *going on* at the time, we have the conception of *Present Time*. Under the circumstances, if a person were never to perceive the *action* as 'going on' at the time, what (or how) could he conceive of as 'having ceased' or as 'going to happen'. For, as a matter of fact, what is meant by time, having fallen through is that the *action* of falling is over, has ceased; and what is meant by 'time to be fallen through' is that the action is going to happen so that at both these points of time (Past and Future), the object is devoid of the *action*; when we have the idea that the 'thing is falling down', the object is actually imbued with *action*; and it is only on the basis of this that we could have the conception of the other two points of Time (Past and Future) which, for this reason, would not be conceivable if the Present did not exist'.[40] Vātsyāyana's explanation was in connection with the applicability of inference to the Present, the Past and the Future. In any case, the Nyāya-Vaiśeṣika exposition is that Time becomes conceivable *not* by *space* as the Buddhist advocate, but by *action* with which an object is connected. Uddyotakara adds that space being the same throughout, it is the *action* that renders Time to be meaningful.

The Nyāya-sūtra-s[41] clearly state that the conception of Past and Future cannot be merely relative to each other and that 'there being no present, there could be no cognition of anything and the Present means the existence'.

The "tenseless" space has been explained by the Nyāya-Vaiśeṣika as One, all-pervasive, formless and is the substratum of conjunction. Like Time, Space also has no special quality (*Kiraṇāvalī*, pp. 33-34). The usage of words like 'priority' and 'posteriority' in respect of space is in terms of the conjunction existing between two points, greater or smaller. In fact, it is stated that which makes these conjunction possible is *dik* (*Kiraṇāvalī*, p. 123). There are, however, some basic points of difference between time and space, which establish their separate existence. Time and its three divisions, as noted before, are determined by the *action* with which an object is connected, while space and its practical directions are attributed to the conjunctions between points. Both of them are, totally different from *ākāśa*, which is one of the five elements, with sound as its specific quality.

Such a view is not without its contradictions and untenability as Śrīdhara has pointed out.[42] The notions of the past, the present and the future, are also related to the solar motion which is common to all of them. But the nature of this type of relation in the three events does not appear to have been examined by the Nyāya-Vaiśeṣika satisfactorily. But there is a tangential explanation that time determined by action, is the *present*, that of the pre-non-existence of action, is the *past*, and that of the cessation of the action, is *future*. Even this approach is more in the nature of jugglery than a rational explanation of time and its three dimensions.

In conclusion it may be stated that the Nyāya-Vaiśeṣika position with regard to time is at best metaphysical. It regards time as an ever-present entity and holds that all empirical division of time have the character of presentness. In the context of the perceived present, the unperceived past as well as the future would be meaningful and the latter are relatively associated with the former i.e., the *present*. Viewed in this light, even the 'present', like the past and the future, is also externally determined, and is a part of the eternality of time. The Nyāya-Vaiśeṣika, however, believes that eternal substances like the atoms of the four elements, *ākāśa* and space do not exist in time, i.e., time is not applicable to them. But the qualities and action or motion as well as the produced ones are stated to exist in time. A significant aspect, nevertheless, is that the Nyāya-Vaiśeṣika does not accord the status of cosmic power to time like the *Atharvaveda* or the *Śvetāśvatara upaniṣad.* Nor does it think of time as a power that would be involved in motion either at the atomic level or in the produced things. In the causal scheme of the Nyāya-Vaiśeṣika, time is in the nature of a cause[43] and, as noted before, a substance that is real, being one of the *dravya-s*. Though space and time have several attributes in common, in the Nyāya-Vaiśeṣika frame, they are distinctly separate substances, the main difference being that time is conceived and interpreted on the basis of *action* unlike space.[44] But both are viewed as an infinite continuum.

Yogabhāṣya

The *Yogabhāṣya*, attributed to Vyāsa, does not, however, accept such a continuum of time. It even argues that time has no real existence apart from an uninterrupted succession of particulate (atomic) moments (*kṣaṇa*). It regards that each of these moments as an independent entity or an indivisible unit of time and as the measure of the irreducible minimum positional change like the movement of an atom from one position to another. It is refreshing to note that here the space-time relationship has been somewhat anticipated. For, it is pointed out that each moment exists only by superseding the one that precedes it. This would mean that there cannot exist two moments simultaneously, nor do they exist in a linear arrangement.[45] Following this thought process, the *Yoga-bhāṣya* inclines to the view that the continuity of time is an ideal series of moments in the matrix of the present, the past and the future. But it regards every moment or the *present one* as an independent one, while that of either the past or the future would be non-existent as independent entities.[46]

The Nyāya-Vaiśeṣika does not subscribe to the idea that time is merely a summation of momentary reals; nor has it postulated an atomic state of time. Its concept of atomism has been limited, as stated earlier, to the four elements—earth, water, fire and air—and to some extent mind which is regarded as being corporeal. The position of the Nyāya-Vaiśeṣika is that time is *one* or unitary, and the divisions or distinctions like *ghaṭī*, and so on are for practical or pragmatic purposes. It unequivocally emphasises that time cannot but be *one* and the *one* only, on logical grounds, relating the cognition with moment.[47] The *Nyāya–bhāṣya* of Vātsyāyana, also affirms that the future and the past have meaning and content only in relation to the present, which is in agreement with the statement of the related *Nyāya-sūtra*.[48] The *bhāṣya* adds that the present could also be mixed with the past and the future as a sort of continuum.

There is an interesting discussion on whether or not time can be directly perceived. A question is raised: since time has no colour how could it be an object of perception through the eyes? It is argued that the possession of colour is not the only cause of perception through the eyes and whatever is apprehended through the eyes like time is perceptible.[49] Further, there is also a view that the movement could be known as time since all the notions about time could be explained by this very movement. However, such a movement or motion would be related to the celestial bodies like planets and stars.[50] But this view did not find the acceptance of all the Nyāya-Vaiśeṣika exponents. Yet another interesting view about time relates to the causal notion of posteriority and priority,[51] a view advocated by Śivāditya. Raghunāthaśiromaṇi included space and time in Īśvara—a culmination of all the analytic-synthetic intellectual exercises of the elusive ensemble of space and time by the exponents of the Nyāya-Vaiśeṣika.

Sāṃkhya-Yoga

The followers of the Sāṃkhya do not accept the independent reality of time. To them there is no all-pervasive infinite time (*Yuktidīpikā*, pp. 88, 158).[52] They even hold an extreme view that time is just an intellectual process, and the time-distinctions like the past, the present or the future are a practical part of such a process. Our notions of time and its divisions, according to the followers of Sāṃkhya, would arise because of our experiencing either the limited or the persistence of events.[53] Their view of time is in keeping with the basic structure of the Sāṃkhya system itself inasmuch as they have also explained it as a peculiar product of the three *guṇa-s* (*sattva*, *rajas* and *tamas*) that are intertwined in

Prakṛti, and hence time would be a modification of *Prakṛti* itself. The Sāṃkhyavādins have even gone to the extent of identifying time with *ākāśa* (one of the five elements in the evolutionary scheme of Sāṃkhya).

Yoga: Yoga, though regarded as a system allied to the Sāṃkhya, has a different approach to time. According to the *Yogasūtra* of *Patañjali,* 'concentration (*saṃyama*) over what it calls the *moment* and its *succession,* gives rise to discriminative knowledge'.[54] A commentary on this *sūtra*[55] states that the minutest time which a moving atom takes to reach the next position in space from its previous one is *kṣaṇa* or a moment and the flow of such moments is succession. However, it has been pointed out that a moment and its succession are not together, and that the practical computations like *muhūrta* (modern equivalent: 48 minutes), day, night, etc., are just aggregates of conceptual character, or mental constructs and not substantial, although an ordinary person may consider them as objectively real. The moment, however, pertains to what is real, though determined by its succession. Further, it is argued that two moments cannot coexist which means that there cannot be a succession of two co-existing moments. According to the Yogic view, the present is only one moment. Since earlier or later moments do not have any separate existence, what are normally called the past and the future moments should be interpreted in terms of fleeting changes that take place. The entire universe should be regarded as undergoing change in that one moment.[56]

Yoga system appears to take an extreme view, discarding not only the conception of time as infinite but even the practical time divisions, as noted above. Advocating, however, that time is both dynamic and static, Yoga inclines to the view that instead of accepting that there is the all-pervading, eternal entity of time, one should realize or experience the *moment,* the minutest division of time. Following the Sāṃkhya explanation, Yoga too thinks of this minutest division of time, as being equivalent to the time taken by a moving atom from one position to another. In any case, neither the Sāṃkhya nor the Yoga has thrown any meaningful light on the distance traversed by an atom and the time taken by it in a quantitative manner. In fact Yoga appears to hold that both the magnitude and dimension of time are unreal. Such questions as—what is a moment? What are its characteristics? Why should an atom move? Is it due to *adṛṣṭa* as pointed out by the Nyāya-Vaiśeṣika?—have not been faced and answered at all, except taking shelter under the postulate that a moment is beyond ordinary experience, but perceptible only through Yogic meditation and associated intuition.[57] Though the Yogic approach to time appears to be atomistic, it does not elaborate it further; nor does it explain that there would be transformations or changes *vis-á-vis* the moment. It seems to identify what it calls the 'succession' with the changes,[58] while the common experience is that time is an entity that makes changes intelligible. A curious view is that all the manifestations or changes are potential at the present moment, and that through self-control (*samyama*) and concentration on the one moment and its succession, the omniscience of time is apprehended and experienced. In other words, the Yogic mind has its own perception of time and since the emphasis is on concentration, it has to be one moment and the experience itself is its succession.[59] Eventually in the heightened Yogic state of mind, even this moment is stated to fade away when all changes would come to an end.

The Sāṃkhya-Yoga believes that temporal being and activity are not the characteristics of *Prakṛti* and *Puruṣa*. But it gives importance to consciousness or Mahat (the first evolute of the Sāṃkhya system of thinking) as the determinant of the notion of time. It regards that in a state of experience it would be what may be called 'timeless existence', the 'timelessness' meaning a state of 'actionlessness'. It is difficult to understand the Yoga view of time; for, it generally aims at a state of mind that has its own vision, inexpressible or incommunicable, of both space and time.

There is, however, one strand of thinking that merits some consideration. It is true that an ordinary human being perceives time and understands it from the point of view of his pragramtic living till his death. But, a *jīvan-mukta* who is liberated in his life, according to Indian thinking, transcends time in his exalted experience, For him, even the Sun is stated to remain motionless, as the *Chāndogya upaniṣad* declares;[60] and for him who knows Brahman, the Sun is in the heavens once and for all without rising or setting. A Siddha who is stated to possess supernatural powers (*siddhi-s*) is believed to have attained material immortality, his body and mind being an everlasting one. One of the Tamil siddhas, Yogimunivar, says that breathing 21,600 times a day in a rhythmic manner is the secret of being ever young.[61] Here the idea of change associated with time does not have any significance, but becomes extrapolated to what may be called Cosmic Time. A yogi is believed to transcend the time that governs the Universe as well as the Universe itself. In other words, through intense meditation and the rhythmic *prāṇāyāma*, time assumes no dimension and it either becomes an irrelevant entity or no entity at all!

Advaitins

The Advaitins have different views about time among themselves just as they differ even with regard to the approach to their doctrine of Brahman, and the non-duality of Ātman (individual self) and Brahman (Universal Self). Śaṅkara, the main exponent of Advaita, has discussed with some detail his concept of time in his commentary on the *Vedānta sūtra*.[62] In tune with his exposition of Māyā, he regards time as an effect (*kārya*) of *avidyā* (ignorance) or *Māyā*. In the same vein, even space too is considered as an effect of *avidyā,* thus pointing out that both space and time are not primary entities, but are in the nature of effects due to ignorance. Nevertheless, time is believed to be 'objective' in the same manner as the other products of ignorance are. The commonly perceived temporal relations as well as divisions of time, according to advaita, have no relevance to Brahman, and even *avidyā* is just an empirical reality, an appearance like the others.

An advaitic concept somewhat of a different but contradictory character, is that time is not an effect of *avidyā,* but is a relation between time and Brahman. But Brahman is not a product, while time has a beginning and Brahman is beginningless.[63] Since time is in an intimate relation with Brahman, it follows that time has a beginning. It is, nevertheless, not regarded as having an end, but existing along with *avidyā.* As soon as the right knowledge is gained, obliterating *avidyā,* time would also be *mithyā.*

Yet another advaitic view is that time is a differential aspect (*rūpa-bheda*) of Brahman itself, and as such is eternal. The overall approach of advaitins to time is that the changes perceived in time are transcended in Brahman or the ultimate Reality. Of the three states of experience *jāgrat* (waking), *svapna* (dream) and *suṣupti* (deep sleep), the first two are stated to be governed by time.[64] Understandably a distinction is made between the physical time in the waking state and the mental time in the dream state. In contrast, the state of deep sleep is regarded as the timeless experience. The main reason adduced is that there is no experience at all in this state, nor any duality in that state. But, according to some advaitins, since Māyā persists even in sleep as evidenced by the duality of the subject and object that surfaces immediately in the waking stage, there is a temporary suspension of time, only to rise again in the waking state.

The fourth, called the *turīyā,* is the one that transcends or beyond the three states; an experience of non-duality and is therefore timeless. Gauḍapāda in his *Māṇḍūkya kārikā*[65] says that '*turīyā* is all-seeing always', and Śaṅkara states that in *turīyā,* there is no ignorance and there is nothing other than eternality, giving an analogy that when the ever-brilliant Sun shines, there can be neither darkness, nor erroneous appearance. The *Maitrāyaṇīya upaniṣad* thinks, as noted before, of two forms of Brahman—Time and Timeless—pointing out that timeless is what is prior to the Sun and is one without any parts, while that which begins with the Sun is time which has parts. According to this Upaniṣad, time 'cooks' because it makes everything 'mature' and dissolves it in Brahman and is one of the principal forms of Brahman, the ultimate Reality.[66] It points out that time is a form of Brahman and is to be meditated upon to experience through *sādhana* the timeless Brahman. It asserts that, 'time itself withdraws from him, who worships time as Brahman'.[67]

The Advaita does, however, recognize that time is the 'gateway' to Reality— a channel for all the created objects to get back to the Creator, Brahman. Even so it has been stated that time also returns to Brahman. The physical aspect of time is thus relegated to the background.

The Bauddha Views

The Sarvāstivādins of the Hīnayāna school of Buddhism uphold the three divisions of time—past, present and future from their own point of view, in fact, because they accept the existence of things in three divisions of time, they are referred to as sarvāstivādins. Among them, the Sautrāntikas maintain that only the present exists—a view endorsed by Vasubandhu, and subscribed to also by the Vaibhāṣikas. Another school called the *Vibhājyavādins,* have tried a sort of reconciliation between the Sautrāntikas and the Vaibhāṣikas. Accepting the reality of the present, this school considers that part of the past which has not already lost its force, but denies the reality of the future.

The Vaibhāṣikas appear to favour the idea that both space and time are uncaused and eternal. The Mādhyamikas, on the other hand, have rejected this idea, holding that all things are related as cause and effect and any entity that is not thus related is non-existent. The *Mādhyamika Kārikā*[68] says that space and time do not have any type of objective existence even from the empirical stand point, but are in the nature of mental constructs. In general, the Mādhyamikas discard the three divisions of time as well as the notion that time exists apart from the objects. They assert that time exists in relation to objects which undergo continual changes (hence unreal) and consequently time also is unreal.

Buddhists use the word, *ākāśa*, for denoting space, and define its main characteristic as having freedom from any type of obstruction (*anāvaranatva*), is permanent and all-pervasive. Its innumerable contents are either produced or destroyed at a time, but *ākāśa* itself remains unchanged. In the Hīnayāna view, *ākāśa* should not be considered as void or non-existent. A negative element can never render possible the activity of other elements as *ākāśa* does, and hence it is a positive entity. On the other hand, the Mādhyāmikas reject this view and emphasise that space is also a composite made of parts with epithets, 'here'; 'there' and 'elsewhere' and hence space is also impermanent and mutable.[69]

In general, Buddhists discarded any idea of *being* as permanent and instead held that everything that existed had to undergo change. With this approach to the phenomenal world, they could not but reject the oneness and all-pervasiveness of time. But the concept that time is something instantaneous or point-instant and also impermanent fitted well their doctrine of momentariness (*kṣaṇikavāda*) as well as the associated logical postulates (see pp. 333-335).

The Jaina Postulates

While the Vedāntins, the Sāṃkhyavādins and the Buddhists do not admit the absolute reality of time, the Jainas regard in a definitive manner that time is a real substance in the same way as its other real categories, namely, *dharma, adharma, pudgala* and *ākāśa*. Like the Nyāya-Vaiśeṣika,[70] the Jainas also view time as a *nimitta kāraṇa* of the transformation of or change in objects, and this view is sought to be substantiated by the ordinary experience and the associated common notions of time. As mentioned before (p. 139) there is the Jaina concept of *samaya* (a duration or a time measure) which is described as the time taken by an atom in moving across from one *pradeśa* (space-point) of *ākāśa* at the micro-level, and at the macro-level, *samaya* is also the time involved in 'crossing' the whole universe! The *samaya*, therefore, in the Jaina Āgamic thought, refers to the differing speed. It does not, however, represent the reality of time even as the Jaina concept of *dharma* accounts for motion with which time is naturally associated. Time, a reality like *dharma*, is stated to be the accompanying condition of motion or the observed change. The other Jaina views on time include: (i) time is within *ākāśa* and brings about modifications in any part of it (just as the potter's stick moves the entire wheel by sticking or rotating at one point; or a pleasant object when it comes in contact with a particular point of body giving rise to the feeling of pleasure in the body as a *whole*); (ii) time has three aspects: *utpāda* (origination), *vyaya* (annihilation) and *dhrauvya* (persistence).[71] When the present time arises (*utpāda*) and cognized, the time that preceded it is at an end (*vyaya*). Both these are called *paryāyakāla* (time in modification) or *vyavahāra kāla* (time in common usage); (iii) the divisions of time, like hour, day, month, etc., are empirical time coming under this category since they have the beginning as well as the end. They are temporary too, denoting the changes or modifications that are ordinarily experienced. Discarding the general idea that an hour is the effect of a water—clock, or the day as the effect of the solar movement, the Jaina view is that time is a reality and is distinct from matter; and (iv) the persistent aspect of time, called the *niścaya paramārtha kāla*, that is noumenal, and hence called *paramārtha kāla*.[72] It is explained that when a material thing undergoes changes, there is something real that persists throughout these moments of change, and that permanence is noumenal time as the accompanying cause of the changes of modifications of the material thing. The example cited is the base-stone in a potter's wheel which acts as an accompanying cause. Thus, real time does not cause the changes in things, but is an invariably accompanying condition in respect of the observed changes.

In the Jaina view, the functions of time are (i) the process of becoming change; (ii) action; and (iii) the notion of *before* and *after vis-à-vis* consciousness.

It is the instrumental or efficient cause of the modifications that occur in entities in the form of *jīva, pudgala, dharma, adharma* and *ākāśa* which are classed under *astikāya-s* or extended substances, while *kāla* is regarded as an unextended one.[73] The minutest part of substance is called *aṇu* (atom) by Jainas. In the case of substances other than time, atoms are supposed to be in a state of inseparable combinations. But in respect of time, its minutest parts are called *kālāṇu-s* or instants of time. An interesting Jaina postulate is that *lokākāśa* is pervaded by time-atoms in each space-point.[74] They are distinctly separate from one another, i.e., they are individual entities and do not thus come under the notion of *astikāya* or extension. Time atom, it is stated, may have one *pradeśa* (space-point) or none at all. It is significant to note that Jaina thinkers do not accept that time is *one*, but try to explain that, since time-units are separate, the simultaneity, the present, the past and the future could be understood as variations of time-units without any reference to the *present* itself. This Jaina approach is a marked departure from that of the Nyāya-Vaiśeṣika.

Ākāśa in the Jaina thought-structure does not mean the same substance as in the Nyāya-Vaiśeṣika. It generally stands for space and the existence of *pudgala-s* (matter) depend on the spatial accommodation. Space is supposed to be infinite, formless and inactive[75] as well as constituted of innumerable *pradeśa-s;* hence an *astikāya* or extended body. Jainas do not accept the view of the Nyāya-Vaiśeṣikas that sound is a specific quality of the auditory organ. A strange argument advanced is that *ākāśa* is formless while the auditory organ has form, and therefore the two are incompatible!

The Jainas think of two forms of *ākāśa*: the *Lokākāśa* and the *Alokākāśa*. The former is regarded as mundane space and as the one that provides room for *dharma, adharma, kāla, and pudgala-s,*[76] having innumerable *pradeśa-s*. Even so *ākāśa* is considered as a limited one. Beyond the *Lokākāśa* is said to exist the *Alokākāśa* which is devoid of any type of material objects. It is stated to be infinite and indestructible.

Mahābhāṣya

The linguistic interpretation of time is indeed fascinating and has a new and rather curious dimension. The author of the *Mahābhāṣya*, Patañjali, has stated that both time and stars are eternal or permanent[77] and regards time as the ultimate substratum of the universe itself. Time is defined as that by which the growth and decay of all material things are perceived, and which is the cause of qualitative and quantitative changes in an object Patañjali[78,79]. Also subscribes to the view that the time-divisions like day and night, months and years, are artificial and have relation only with solar movement.[80] However, time is conceived as being eternal and all-pervading. The tensed-time in terms of the present, the past and the future is of great relevance to the *Mahābhāṣya*.

Kaiyaṭa, in his *Pradīpa* on the *Mahābhāṣya*, has discussed the nature of existence (*sattā*) as to whether it could be qualified as the past or the future one, since it has generally the connotation of the present. Patañjali has pointed out that there are two types: (i) of actions of the senses; and (ii) of the mind. The actions of the senses relate to the past and the future tenses, while those of the mind are concerned with the present tense.[81] The question of an ever-existing object like a mountain has been examined and a view is expressed that the notions of the past, the future and the present are applicable only to objects that have an origin with a definite limit, though the exact quantitative aspect of that limit has not been explained succinctly. There is, however, a new definition of the past, the present and the future. According to Kaiyaṭa, in respect of the objects or events when their production or *origination is expected*, it is the *future*; after their origination if they persist, it is the *present*; and if after their origination, they have perished, it is the *past*. If there is no past or future, it may be argued, there is no present. In any case it has been recognized that action is a process which is the determinant of time.[82] But, the *Mahābhāṣya* points out that even in the case of the ever lasting mountains, the past, the future and the present are the 'sub-strata' of mountains and hence all the three tenses are applicable to them—a geological approach perhaps.[83] Bhartṛhari, the grammarian and philosopher, has given a succinct explanation of time.[84] He himself appeared to accept that time was *śakti* i.e., *Śakti* of Brahman.

Other Ideas

There were some other ideas of time also. It would appear that there was a special school of Indian philosophy (*Time in Indian Philosophy*, 301 ff.) called *kālavāda* which receded to the background as its basic ideas were absorbed by the other well known systems. It has been mentioned already that in the *Atharvaveda, kāla* was elevated to the status of a deity conceiving it as the highest principle or the Creator of Prajāpati as well as the Universe. Significantly, the *Atharvaveda*[85] thinks of *kāla* or time as a horse with seven reins and a thousand eyes. It also speaks of a solar deity, Rohita, in terms of *Kāla* and Prajāpati. Prajāpati is characterized as *saṃvatsara* (year) itself, i.e., an astronomical time. There is a view that the seven reins would correspond to the seven planets and the 'thousand eyes', with the stars. But there is one ambiguity here because if the Sun were to be the horse with seven reins, the number of other planets would be seven.

Time was also regarded in terms of fate or what is called *karma*. The *Mahābhārata* posits the idea of time as fate.[86] It is well known that Yama, the god of death, is identified with, Kāla, and Śiva is referred to as *Mahākāla* or the Great Time. In the *Bhāgavatapurāṇa,* Viṣṇu is related to *Kāla,* sometimes called *Kāla* itself.[87]

Astronomical Elements

In Indian ethos, man's intimate relationship with time has been inseparable. The astronomical-cum-astrological elements with their firm base in time-reckoning and religious acts are intimately woven. At the beginning of each ritual, an individual 'resolves' (*saṃkalpa*) to realize the goal of his religious performance. During such a resolution, the time or the instant of the performance is recited, starting with *Kalpa* (aeon), the *Yuga* (extant Cosmic Age like Kaliyuga), the year, the part of the year (southern *dakṣiṇāyana* or the northern or *uttarāyaṇa* course of the Sun), the month, the bright or dark half (*pakṣa*) of the month, the week days, the *tithi* of the day as well as the *muhūrta.* In so doing, the individual's terrestrial and the celestial relationship is sought to be established, or identified, at the same time recognizing the wheel of time (*kālacakra*). The spectrum of Hindu festivals includes those of astronomical elements such as full-moons, new-moons, solstices and the like. Other festivals too are celebrated on the astronomically determined days/nights. But, in essence, year after year the festivals and other rituals are performed in a cyclic way with the notion that the wheel of time moves on perpetually and time is eternal. Nevertheless, these rituals are also in the nature of propitiations of one's own *karma* (deeds of the present or of the past) in the belief that one's future life would be a happy one. The past, the present and the future time connote a purpose in Indian cultural life. These are also supposed to be the pathways for those who perform them with intense devotion, leading to deliverance from the world of temptations and attendant sorrow, ultimately to the attainment of salvation away from the confinement or the shackles of time.

Time in Āyurveda: There is no gainsaying the fact that man's very life biologically is temporal or has a limited span in time. Even within the body, the physiological processes have their own time-rhythm in a normal healthy person. Āyurveda has recognized the importance of time both in its diagnostic methods and curative practices. Medical astrology in the context of what is perceived as good or bad time of a patient based on a reading of his horoscope is also an element to reckon with in Āyurvedic and the Siddha medical practices. Āyurveda has developed a postulate of *ṛtu-sandhi*[88] as representing the period of transition between the outgoing and the incoming or the onset of seasons, seven days on either side (i.e., 14 days in all) that would be required by the organism to adapt itself gradually to the possible stresses of the incoming season—a biological adaptation governed by time. There is also an Āyurvedic concept known as *Kriyākāla*, relating to the mode as well as the developmental stages of a disease, which emphasizes the importance of time for the determination and dispensation of both the preventive and curative measures.

Time and History: It is often said that Indians lack a sense of history. It is even alleged that their chronological frame of historical events is clouded by an unhistorical, uncritical and Indo-centric approach, specially in the ancient period when mythology held the scales. While this may be true to some extent, it needs to be recognized that history is invariably on the canvas of time. Human history even in the civilisational milieu is not only a chronological record of events but also of the rise and fall of civilisations mainly because of human greed, wars, killing man by fellowman, diseases of devastating dimensions—all contributing to human suffering. In Indian thought, the Vedāntic, the Jaina, the Buddhists' approach to the world of human beings and their sufferings, the emphasis is more on liberation and the cessation of suffering. Practically all systems of thought in India have a lukewarm attitude towards the phenomenal world. Although it is not viewed with disdain, the physical world perceived by the senses is not regarded as the ultimate reality. The Advaitins and the Mahāyāna Buddhists viewed time, like Kant, not only as an *a priori* of our sensible intuition but also as the one which has no independent reality. Besides, philosophical pursuits engaged the attention of thinkers and writers more than the historical events. For, history or historical episodes, it was believed, did not have the potential of liberating man from bondage and suffering.

Even so, it cannot be stated, that there is no Indian history. India's religio-philosophical history has as much validity, may not be as events in time like the later chronological, political history. The two had mutual influences and some of the kings either patronised religio-philosophy or were philosophers themselves. *Rājadharma* or the righteousness of kings was an important component of the royal polity, deriving inspiration from one or the other religio-philosophy. It would be wrong to think that Indians considered the events of the world as not worth understanding or the act of recording unreal or regarded time as an entity of no consequence. Indian thinkers and writers did not deliberately relegate history to the background. In several ways they have bequeathed to us important records of their thoughts that are historically significant.

IDEAS OF TIME AND SPACE IN THE WEST: SOME REFLECTIONS

The problem of space and time has over a long time seized the western thinkers too.[89] Among the Greeks and the Greco-Romans whose conceptions of time deserve special mention, are Aristotle and Archimedes. To Aristotle, every change needed a cause and, as he says in his *Physics*: 'Everything that is in motion must be moved by something'.

Aristotle's preceptor, Plato, was seriously engrossed in his doctrine of *Ideas* and he did not appear to have paid adequate attention to the very nature of *Ideas* which at one stage or the other would pass on to memory and stored in it. Even the *Ideas* become objects of memory, i.e., the tensed past, but recalled in the present with their implications for the future. The past, the present and the future, therefore, cannot be divorced from them, although the present would be the perceived past. Apart from this dimension of time, the remembrance has also in it the space in which the object was present and the event that happened. There is thus mental space and time event in respect of an *Idea*. Plato, however, in his *Timaeus*, distinguishes between eternity and time, and regards the former as a basic unity, its image moving according to what he thought in terms of numbers in the world of appearance, i.e., a change but within the frame of timelessness. This was also a Pythagorean concept. In other words, Plato thought of time as belonging to the world of appearances, not a real one. The Greek thinkers, in general, thought that time was brought about by the revolutions of the celestial luminaries.

Aristotle thought of the universe as being limited in *space* but contained within an outer sphere that was unlimited in *time*, i.e., it was neither created nor destroyed as a whole. His view of the universe was that it was finite both in space and time. He sought to explain the motion in space and time, but he had a different view of the movements of stars and planets in terms of uniform circular velocity in crystalline spheres (a view that had been already put forward by Pythagoreans) centered round the earth, each sphere being subjected to the influence of those outside it. He also pointed out that the circular movement would be the perfect one, representing the unchanging eternal order of the heavens, while on what he described as imperfect Earth, the motion would be rectilinear. Aristotelian approach to time was, by and large, in relation to the movement and attendant changes. Alongside Aristotle was also concerned with such questions as whether time would exist without consciousness and the like, as he points out in his *Physics*.

Aristotle also projected the idea that without 'soul' there would be no time at all. Further, he regarded time as an attribute of motion, and wondered whether it would be possible to imagine any type of motion existing without a 'soul' as its motive force. In his view all types of motion coupled with their time factor related ultimately to the uniform circular motion of the heavens. He pointed out that our minds must necessarily conform to the world order which would therefore control both our perception of time and the process by which we calculate or measure it.

Archimedes did not try to explain motion in space and time, holding the view that temporal concepts had no part in it. He held the view that natural laws were those of what he called equilibrium. Space, however, was considered by him to have some relevance because it would present itself to us in one entity whereas time would be discontinuous and in succession.

Centuries later, St. Augustine was deeply concerned with the enigmatic character of time and stated: 'who can readily and briefly explain this (time)? Who can even in thought comprehend it so as to utter a word about it? But what in discourse do we mention more familiarly and knowingly than time? And we understand when we speak of it; we understand also when we hear it spoken of by another. What, then, is Time? If no one asks me, I know; if I wish to explain it to one that asketh, I know not'.[90]

Motion, Space and Time: During the 13th–14th centuries, the problem of motion in space became an important field of enquiry and the concept of time and its measurement in space, of necessity, had to play an important role. Time was treated as a homogeneous ordered continuum, capable of measurement. Measurement needed a standard unit that must remain constant. From such devices as the time taken to burn a candle of determined length and thickness, the operation of the sand-vessel, gnomon or the shadow of a sundial, water-clocks, mechanical clocks and chronometers—all intended for the fixation of an accurate standard time, it has been a long story in which the importance of a reference time that is measurable has become seminal. The recent devices, electronic or otherwise, aiming at precision have only emphasized the imperative need of the science of measurement. Poincare has stated that, 'there is not one way of measuring time more true any another; that which is generally adopted is only more convenient. Of two watches, we have no right to say that the one goes true, and the other wrong. We can only say that it is advantageous to conform to the indications of the first'.[91]

When Galileo laid the scientific foundations for dynamics or mechanics, the concept of measurable time was built into it. Speed or velocity and acceleration involved the measurement of time. Newton's laws of motion encompassed mass, space (measurable) and time (also measurable). However, Newton also conceived the idea of real time as being Absolute that flows on its own without any relation to the external ones, distinguishing it from the apparent time—measures like hour, month, year, etc. In Newton's view, 'all motions could be accelerated or retarded, but the true or equable progress of Absolute time would be liable to no change. In other words, the duration can undergo change, but the true progress of Absolute time is not liable to any change. The duration or perseverance of the existence of things would remain the same (whether the motions are swift or slow or none at all), and therefore it ought to be distinguished from what are only sensible measures thereof'. According to Newton who enunciated clearly the three laws of motion, that still bear his name as well as the law of universal gravity, space is a three-dimensional substratum in which material objects are located and events like motion take place. But space itself remains unaffected by such events; in other words, space is dynamically independent of all the dynamics. Newton also thought that like space, time too had its own independence, thus pointing to the absolute character of both space and time. Newton in his *magnum opus*, the *Principles of Natural Philosophy* (briefly called *Principia*, 1687) put forward the view that 'space is an absolute, infinite, three dimensional and an eternally fixed, uniform receptacle into which, 'God' placed the universe at the moment of creation'. Likewise, in his view, Time was one dimensional uniform framework. Newton's ideas were opposed by his German contemporary, Gofffried Liebniz (of calculus fame). He advocated the relational aspects of space and time.[92]

In the West, alongside, what may be called the 'psychological time' has also been examined. If in the relativity physicist's understating and interpretation of space–time, his position or the frame of reference is important, in respect of the psychological time obviously mind has a distinct place. In a way, a relativity physicist's time is his thought-model, while mental time is an experienced one for an awareness in terms of the past, the present and the future. William James[93] describes the 'specious present' that it is 'no knife-edge, but a saddle back, with a certain breadth of its own on which we sit perched, and from which we look in two directions in time. The unit of composition of our perception of time is a duration, with a bow and a stern as it were, a rearward and a forward looking end. It is only as parts of this duration-block that the relation of succession of one end to the other end perceived'. Thus the psychological present is a duration or a stretch of time and not at all a point of time. Dewey has viewed the knowledge of the past as no knowledge at all (*Creative Intelligence*, Henry Hold and Co, New York, 1917; p.13) saying that 'anticipation is more primary than recollection; projection than summoning of the past; the prospective than retrospective'. He thinks that the knowledge of the past is unreal, just a reminiscence and not an intelligence. According to Collingwood[94] the future is one of hopes and fears and not of knowledge. Such views as these and other ideas about time point out that the concept of time continues to be enigmatic, while its practical dimensions are an integral part of human thought and actions.

T.M.P. Mahadevan,[95] while pointing to the broad categorization of philosophers put forward by William James as 'tough-minded' and 'tender-minded' (identifying the former with the realists, and the latter with the idealists), states; 'It is usual to say that every man is born either a Platonist or an Aristotelian, indicating thereby that there are two contrasted natures among human beings, the in-turned and the out-turned. For, the idealist, mind is the creative principle and ultimate form of reality, while for the realist, mind is merely one in a democracy of things. Time for the idealist is subjective, whereas for the realist it is objective in character. Idealism has, on the whole, tended to minimize the importance of time, while the different forms of Realism have been vying with one another in glorifying it'.

Immanuel Kant, the Königsberger philosopher who was also a man of science, has examined the two attitudes and pointed out that these two are not irreconcilable. He regarded time as a form of our sensorial intuition and not an object of perception, time being in *a priori* form. He did not accept the view that time belongs to objects *per se*, but only to the subject that perceives them. Time, therefore, would be real only empirically as a condition of subjective experience. Nevertheless, it would be transcendental identity in the sense that it would be unreal when it was devoid of subjective conditions of sensorial perception. Kant's exposition of time was based on his tacit assumption that time was not something that would either exist by itself or 'inhere in things as an objective determination'. Kant believed that our thoughts must be distinguished from our experience. His approach to time was in tune with his exposition and explanation of 'thing' and 'thing-in-itself', the phenomena and noumena, as well as *part* as a mechanism, and the *whole* as purpose.

Early in the eighteenth century Bishop George Berkeley in his approach to motion rejected the notions of absolute space and time and his argument was the familiar one, namely, that space and time had no corroboration in our sense experience. Nearly two centuries later Earnest Mach of the Positivist school, supported this argument emphasizing that direct sense experience should be the main criterion since it has a role in matters scientific. Further, he pointed out that considerations of the relativistic aspects of space and time would also provide the much needed simplicity in understanding the physical world.

Till the middle of the 19th century, the three-dimensional space was more important than the one-dimensional time for the understanding of any type of motion. However, Lagrange, the great mathematician, saw time as a fourth dimension of space. An elaboration of the foregoing views as also those of Husserl, Heidegger, Sartre and other Western thinkers on the temporality, consciousness and associated ideas is beyond the scope of this Volume.

A reference has been made to the Big Bang theory, which indicates that what we now know as the Universe is about 13 billion years old. The exponents of this theory aver that time became an inseparable part at the very beginning of the Universe and when its 'age' was around a billion billion billion billionth part of a second. Even at such an acutely micro-measure of time, the Universe underwent a rapid phase of expansion. Thereafter it grew in age and size—an expanding Universe. In the History of Science, the conceptual as well as experimental vicissitude through which the problem of space and time have passed and have been passing, is a fascinating story.

TIME IN INDIAN ASTRONOMY

The *Vedāṅga jyotiṣa*, one of the six auxiliaries of the Vedas, has unequivocally described the relationship of the performance of sacrifices with astronomy thus: 'The Vedas have indeed been revealed for the sake of the performance of sacrifices; these sacrifices have been set out (to be performed) according to the sequence of time. Therefore, only he who knows astronomy, the science of time, understands (the importance) of sacrifices'.[96] One of the well known traditional astronomers of the early tenth century, Vaṭeśvara, in his *Vaṭeśvara siddhānta*, says that astronomy has been regarded as the crown of the Vedas since Vedic sacrifices have to be performed at the specified times so that they effectively lead to the desired objective. He stresses that astronomy stands greatly honoured among the Vedic scholars.[97]

The terrestrial and the celestial correlation or correspondence through the mediation of sacrifice (*yajña*) was a seminal idea of the Vedic people, fortified by the belief that microcosm (man) is a recapitulation or an epitome of the macrocosm (heavens). This belief in several ways has also played an important role in the origins and ramifications of various shades of Indian thought. In this respect astronomy and the associated calendrical computations had a distinct position not only among the Vedic priests, then as now, but also among Indian (traditional) astronomers.

Right from the Vedic period till the advent and growth of what is known as the Siddhāntic astronomy, it was mainly the sacerdotal class that was the custodian of astronomical observations and the associated calendrical computations. The priests were indeed careful observers of the sky, of the movements of the Sun, the Moon and other celestial bodies (planetary observations came up later). They were skilled in time-reckoning based principally upon the paths of the Moon and the Sun in the backdrop of 27 or 28 *nakṣatra-s* or asterisms. In the beginning, both 'day' and 'night were obviously the natural units of time, the 'day' being taken as the time period from the observed dawn to the observed sunset, i.e., in relation to the observed movement of the Sun. The Moon and its movements also received due attention, its bright half and the dark half broadly giving a measure of time.

Division of Time

The *Atharvaveda*[98] and the *Taittirīya Brāhmaṇa* have dealt with five parts of a 'day', namely, rising sun (*udayan sūryaḥ*), time for gathering cows (*saṅgava*), midday (*madhyandina*), *aparāhna* (afternoon) and sunset (*astamaya*). It was not long before a 'day' was thought of in terms of the now familiar *muhūrtas*, and was divided into 30 of them. The *Śatapatha Brāhmaṇa*[99] has given a progressive scale of divisions and their relations in terms of what are known as *muhūrta-s, kṣipru-s, etarhi, and idāni.* In a year: 1800 *muhūrta-s;* 15 times as many *kṣipru-s* as there are *muhūrta-s;* 15 times as many *idāni* as there are *etarhi;* and 15 times as many breathings as there are *idāni,* one day being divided into or composed of 30 *muhūrta-s.* The *Ṛgveda* symbolically refers to 'days' and 'nights' as being 720 in a year of 360 days.[100] Both solar and lunar months as well as the corresponding lunar days, called *tithi* were recognized, a *tithi,* being the 30th part of one lunation—a period in which the Moon's elongation increases by 12 degrees. The *tithi,* it may be noted, is not much of astronomical significance, but a calendrical device for time-reckoning that came up later. Fifteen *tithi-s* constitute half lunation or *pakṣa* named by Sanskrit ordinals *prathamā* (first), *dvitīyā* (second), *tṛtīyā* (third) and so on up to fourteen. Likewise, fourteen *tithis* are reckoned for the other half lunation, the last or the fifteenth one being named *pūrṇimā* (full moon) and *amāvāsyā* (dark) in accordance with the fact whether it is bright half (*śuklapakṣa*) or dark half (*kṛṣṇapakṣa*).

Months and Seasons

The Moon was the obvious choice for the determination of time. The *Ṛgveda* describes the Moon as the one that shapes the year.[101] It is also referred to as *māsakṛt* or the maker or marker of the month in the same way as the modern month is derived from the word 'mooneth'. There were two systems of month-reckoning: one ending with the New Moon day, and the other with the Full Moon day. The names of the lunar months were derived from the *nakṣatra-s* (asterisms) in which the full moon occurred. The naming of months was also adopted after the seasonal ones or the solar months. In the beginning it would appear that only three seasons (*ṛtu*) were recognized, each season encompassing four months as evidenced by four-monthly (*cāturmāsya*) sacrifices in a year, corresponding to the warm, rainy and cold seasons. Such sacrifices were called *ṛtu mukhāni.* In course of time, two more seasons were added, the autumn and the spring, and further on, the dewy season was included.[102] Differing views apart, there was some sort of a relationship or correspondence of the lunar and solar months as well as the seasons (mainly six) in the Vedic period as follows.

Lunar Months	**Solar Months**	**Seasons**
Caitra	Madhu	
Vaiśākha	Mādhava	Vasanta ṛtu (spring)
Jyeṣṭha	Śukra	
Āṣāḍha	Śuci	Grīṣma ṛtu (summer)
Śrāvaṇa	Nabha	
Bhādrapada	Nabhasya	Varṣa ṛtu (rainy)
Āśvina	Īṣa	
Kārttika	Ūrja	Śarad ṛtu (autumn)
Mārgaśira	Saha	
Pauṣa	Sahasya	Hemanta ṛtu (dewy)
Māgha	Tapa	
Phālguna	Tapasya	Śiśira ṛtu (winter)

Intercalation

To bring about luni-solar adjustments by taking into account also the durational differences between the lunar and solar months so that they are in tune with the seasons, it became necessary to add at regular intervals 5 or 6 days to one or more months. The *Ṛgveda* symbolically refers to an additional or the thirteenth month in a particular year.[103] The *Atharvaveda* speaks of the measurement of the thirteenth month of 30 days.[104] The *Kṛṣṇa Yajurvedā* calls the thirteenth month, *saṃsarpa* (lit: a creeping one), while the *Atharvaveda* and the *Kāṭhaka saṃhitā* call it *sanisrasa* and *malimluca* respectively. Generally there was the practice of adding 12 days to each lunar year, or a thirteenth month of 30 days every 2 1/2 years. It may be noted that this practice in a somewhat modified form has continued even to this day in traditional almanacs (*pañcāṅga*). The additional lunar month is called *adhikamāsa*.

Year

According to Shama Sastry, there were five kinds of reckoning the time period of a year: (i) the sidereal lunar year of 324 days, the length of each of the twelve months being 27 days; (ii) the sidereal lunar year of 351 days consisting of 13 months, each month having a span of 27 days; (iii) the synodic lunar year of 354 days comprising 6 months of 30 days each and 6 months of 29 days each; (iv) the civil (*sāvana*) year of 360 days having 12 months of 30 days each; and (v) a type of solsticial but a long year of 378 days by adding 18 days to the third year after two civil years of 360 days each. The first one used to be brought in agreement with the civil and the sidereal year by the addition (intercalation) of 9 and 15 days respectively. The sidereal lunar year was also intercalated with 12 days to bring it on par with the sidereal solar year, the period of which was reckoned to be 366 days. Whether the Vedic astronomer–priests had calculated the period of a year as being 365 1/4 days or not is a moot point, although there is a veiled reference to such a calculation in the *Taittirīya saṃhitā*.[105]

The *Vedāṅga jyotiṣa*, a concise respository of Vedic astronomical computations, has described a five year luni-solar cycle called *yuga*, stating that at the beginning of the cycle, both the Sun and the Moon would lie at the starting point of the asterism, Dhaniṣṭhā. Of interest to us are the astronomical time-periods in a five-year cycle as given in this text as follows:

The number of revolutions or the days have been given in brackets. The Sun's revolutions (5); the Moon's sidereal revolutions or months (67); The Moon's synodic revolutions or months (62); civil (*sāvana*) days (1830); sidereal days (1835); solar days (1800); and lunar days or *tithis* (1860). The *Vedāṅga jyotiṣa* has also given the shortest and the longest day as being 12 and 18 *muhūrta-s*, the former being at winter solstice, and the latter at the summer solstice. The text has even provided details of time-division as follows: a civil day into 30 *muhūrta-s*; 1 *muhūrta* into 2 *nāḍikā-s*; 1 *nāḍikā* into 10 1/20 *kalā-s*; 1 *kalā* into 124 *kāṣṭhā-s* and 1 *kāṣṭhā* into 5 *akṣara-s*. Further each *nakṣatra* space has also been subdivided into 124 parts and the length of the day between two solstice has been calculated. In the two or three centuries preceding the Christian era, the length of year was refined, as observed in the *siddhānta-s* of this period. The *Romaka Siddhānta* has given the length of one solar year as 365 days 5h. 55' 12" and the *Pauliśa*, 365.2583 days, while the *Vasiṣṭha* has recorded it as 365.36 days.[106]

Cyclic (Periodic) time

The idea of the *yuga* of *Vedāṅga jyotiṣa* in course of time was developed into a huge cyclic period of 4,320,000 years (each year being equivalent to 360 days). It would appear that the Purāṇas, in their mythological lore, had already thought of cyclic time in terms of four yugas: *Kṛta, Tretā, Dvāpara* and *Kali,* attributing to each of them certain characteristics. The epic hero Srī Rāma was supposed to have been born in the *Treta*, while Sri Kṛṣṇa of the *Mahābhārata*, in the *Dvāpara Yuga*. The 'Great War' between the Kauravas and the Pāṇḍavas is stated to have been the dividing line between the *Dvāpara* and *Kali yugas*. Be that as it may, the nomenclature of these four yugas also entered Indian astronomy which, however, presumed their solar year lengths as follows: *Kṛta*, 1,728,000; *Treta*, 1,296,000; *Dvāpara*: 864,000; and *Kali,* 432,000 projecting them as being in the ratio of 4:3:2:1, i.e., in the descending order.

The *Sūryasiddhānta,* one of the important basic texts of Indian astronomy, follows this order, but apportions 1000 divine years (1 divine year = 360 years) to *Kali,* 2000 to *Dvāpara,* 3000, to *Treta,* to *Kṛta,* 4000 and 1/10 of duration to the dawn and twilight in each case, thus amounting to 12,000 divine years or 12,000 × 360 = 4,320,000 years. Indian astronomy, in any case, has adopted this cyclic time inasmuch as the planets are supposed to be in conjunction at the beginning, of this period and, after their performance of integral numbers of revolutions round the Earth, they would again be in conjunction at the end of this period. Indian astronomers have designated this period of 4,320,000 years as the *mahāyuga* (or *caturyuga*). French astronomer, Biot, has shown that if the length of the year is 365 days 6h, 12′35.56″, the least number of years containing a whole number of civil days is 1,080,000 and four times this number is 4,320,000 years. The Indian approach towards the determination of the *mahāyuga* is thus partly paurāṇic and partly mathematical. That the Kali epoch started at midnight at the meridian of Ujjayinī between February 17 and 18, 3102 B.C. (computed from modern standpoint) has been the premise for determining astronomical parameters in Indian astronomy.

The *Yuga* concept does not end with the notion of *mahāyuga*. It extends further by postulating that 1000 *mahāyuga-s* constitute what is called one *Kalpa* i.e., 432,000,000 years and this has been stated to be the 'day' part of Brahmā, twice that being Brahmā's whole day. The end of *Kalpa* is believed to be the dissolution of all that exists, and the beginning of a new one—all in a cyclic manner. There are other dimensions of such ideas which need not be dealt with here.

Time-reckoning

A notable aspect of time-reckoning in Indian astronomy is the relation established between the minutest unit of time and the life of Brahmā, the Creator. Vateśvara who has stressed the imperishable character of time, has succinctly provided this relation in the following way:[107]

    Lotus pricking time called *truṭi*
    (time taken by a sharp needle
    to pierce a petal of lotus flower)
    100 *truṭi-s* = 1 *lava*
    100 *lava-s* = 1 *nimeṣa* (twinkling of cyclid)
    4 *nimeṣa-s* = 1 long syllable

4 long syllables = *kāsthā*

2 1/2 *kāsthā-s* = 1 *asu* (respiration) or *prāna* (equivalent to modern 4 seconds)

6 *asu-s* = 1 *pala* also called casaka, vinādī or vighatikā

60 *pala-s* = 1 *ghatikā* (modern 24 minutes)

60 *ghatikā-s* = 1 day

30 days = one month

12 months = 1 year

43,20000 years = 1 *yuga* or *mahāyuga*

72 *yuga-s* = 1 *manu*

14 *manu-s* = 1 *kalpa*

2 *kalpa-s* = 1 day of Brahmā (including night)

30 days of Brahmā = 1 month of Brahmā

12 months of Brahmā = 1 year of Brahmā (72 × 14 × 2 × 30 × 12 *yuga-s* or 725,760 *yuga-s*)

100 years of Brahmā = *mahākalpa*

The foregoing relations indicate symbolically the Indian view that time is indeed eternal and, Brahmā being the Creator, time is also associated with his first act of creation. Although the Indian astronomical texts do not make use of the huge periods of time beyond a *mahāyuga,* the linkages of the minutest to the beginning of creation and the Creator himself, are in the nature of holistic approach, emphasizing that time is one of which the divisions are an integral part.

The *Bhāgavata* and the *Vārāha purāna-s* have provided the division of time as follows:[108]

3 *paramānu-s* (make)	=	1 *anu*
3 *trasarenu-s*	=	1 *vedhas*
3 *vedha-s*	=	1 *lava*
3 *lava-s*	=	1 *nimesa*
3 *nimesa-s*	=	1 *ksana*
5 *ksana-s*	=	1 *kāsthā*
15 *kāsthā-s*	=	1 *laghu*
15 *laghu-s*	=	1 *nādikā*
2 *nādikā-s*	=	1 *muhūrta*
6 or 7 *nādika-s*	=	1 *prahara* or *yāma*
4 *yāma-s*	=	1 day or night
15 days and nights	=	1 *paksa*
2 *paksa-s*	=	1 *māsa* (a day and night for ancestors)
2 *māsa-s*	=	1 *rtu* (season)
6 *māsa-s*	=	1 *ayanam*
2 *ayana-s*	=	1 year

1 day of Brahmā	=	1 period of Manu
1 night of Brahmā	=	1 period of *pralaya*
1 yuga	=	5 years

The *Manusmṛti's* divisions of time comprise: 18 *nimeṣa-s* make 1*kāṣṭhā*; 30 *kāṣṭhā-s* = 1 *kalā*; 30 *kalā-s* = 1 *muhūrta*; and 30 *muhūrta-s* = make 1 day and night. There are variations in the enumeration of the relationships of the smaller units like *nimeṣa* and *kāṣṭhā*. But from the unit *muhūrta* upwards, there does not seem to be any significant difference among the various authors. The *yuga* of five years appears in the *Vedāṅga jyotiṣa* for astronomical purposes. Later Kauṭilya also adopted it in his practical division of time. In some astronomical texts the word *yuga* is also sometimes used to indicate a *mahāyuga*. In any case both *yuga* and *mahāyuga* are concepts of cyclic time.

The Indian seminal idea of *dharma* is intimately woven into that of yuga too, called the *Yugadharma*, it is said to be at the highest level in the *Kṛtayuga*, gradually declining through the *Tretā*, *Dvāpara* and *Kali* in which it is believed to be in its decadent state largely because of human degeneration and the practice of *adharma* or ignoble acts proceeding from human greed and evil ridden mind.

Associated with the *yuga-s* are the *Manvantara-s,* 14 in number, viz., Svāyambhuva, Svarociṣa, Auttama, Raivata or Cariṣnava, Tāmasa, Cākṣuṣa, Vaivasvata, Sāvarṇi, Dakṣa-Sāvarṇi, Brahma-Sāvarṇi, Dharma-Sāvarṇi, Rudra-Sāvarṇi, *Raucya* and *Bhautya* (*Vāyu Purāṇa* 140.3.118).

Śaṅkaravarman in his *Sadratnamālā*[109] has given another type of time-relationship: time to utter a long syllable = *gurvakṣara;* 10 *gurvakṣara-s* = 1 *prāṇa* or respiration; 6 *prāṇa-s* (i.e., 60 *gurvakṣaras*) = 1 *vighaṭikā;* 60 *vighaṭikā-s* = 1 *ghaṭikā*; 60 *ghaṭikā-s* = 1 day; 30 days = 1 month; and 12 months = 1 year.

The importance of time in astronomical calculations was well recognized and significantly an astronomer was also called *gaṇaka* (calculator). Varāhamihira in his *Bṛhatsaṃhitā*[110] has given details of time as well as the four systems of the measurement of time, namely, The *Saura* (relating to the motion of the Sun); *Sāvana* (terrestrial time or the time intervening the first rising of any given planet or star and its next rising); *Nakṣatra* (sidereal); and *Cāndra* (lunar). An astronomer was also expected to be proficient in the calculation of the beginning and ending times of the Jovian cycle of sixty years and the quinquennial (5 years) cycle as well as the time of commencement, progress and the end of an eclipse. Vaṭeśvara[111] has prescribed various other qualifications of an astronomer, some of which relate to time-calculation with great care.

Several types of instruments[112] were devised for the determination of time, like a shadow contrivance or gnomon (*chāyāyantra*) and water instrument or clepsydra (*toyayantra*); the former was used for determining the *ghaṭi-s* and the degrees elapsed since sunrise on a particular day. There were as many as 365 such contrivances, one for each day of the year. Daily time-reckoning was an accomplished expertise.

In the Vedic period, the indigenous *nakṣatra vidyā* with its nuances of auspicious and inauspicious stars, the propitiation of the inauspicious ones and the performance of sacrifices during auspicious stars, needed a methodology for determining time in an exact manner. With the advent and assimilation of planetary astrology that derived its inspiration from the Hellenistic influences during the two or three centuries before and after the Christian era, the computation of time as exactly as possible coupled with the determination of planetary positions became a felt necessity. In all of these, the concept of time assumed a new dimension. Apart from the divisions of the day into *ghaṭikā-s* and *vighaṭikā-s*, certain durations of time were regarded as inauspicious like what is now known as Rāhukāla—a tradition that continues even to this day. Time was thus interwoven into daily life along with the specific lunar or solar days on which festivals, worship of several god- forms and *vratas* had to be performed, then as now, based on the traditional calendar which came later to be called the *pañcāṅga-s*.

Calendrical Computation

A brief reference to the calendrical computation that had its origin in the Vedic period may not be out of place here, since in all of its dimensions the time factor looms large. The *pañcāṅga* has its five constituents: *tithi* (lunar position); *vāra* (week-day); *nakṣatra* (asterism); *karaṇa* and *yoga*. There is an unshakeable belief among the Hindus that the usage and even its hearing on the New year's day (this differs in some ways from one region to the other) are beneficial and hence *pañcāṅga* is regarded as a sacred compendium. It is stated that *tithi* leads to wealth, *vāra* to longevity, *nakṣatra* to the eradication of sins, *karaṇa* to the cure of diseases and *yoga* to the fruition of one's efforts. It would, however, appear that the *pañcāṅga* as a compendium is not very old, while the two of its components, *tithi* and *nakṣatra* can be traced to the Vedic times when the concepts of week and its days named after the Sun and the other planets were noted for its absence. The division of a month was in terms of *tithi* and *pakṣa* (14 or 15 days). The week as a time period of seven days, was in practice in the Greco-Roman world around 200 B.C. if not earlier. Indian culture-area appears to have absorbed the idea of week (seven days) soon after, as a result of Greco-Roman trade and other influences when planetary astrology of the *Yavanas* also made its debut.

Social Aspects: Time is an integral part of Indian culture and in this respect the *pañcāṅga* plays a pivotal role. Various rites and rituals, celebration of birth, marriage and others on the one hand and, on the other, the festivals at regular intervals year after year are performed in appropriate time, strictly in accordance with the computations found in a *pañcāṅga*. Generally such computations are done by a traditional almanac-maker on the basis of the formulae given in the texts like the *Sūryasiddhānta* and *Āryabhaṭīya* as well as the observed data. There are several families all over India who have been assiduously fostering the tradition of preparing *pañcāṅga* annually, both lunar and lunī-solar.

Tradition dies hard, more so in an ancient culture that India is. It is the traditionally determined time for festivals and others that holds the fort even today, in contradistinction to modern astronomical parameters relating to the planetary motions. However, in the matter of calculating the exact time of the occurrence of eclipses and its duration as well as its end, traditional alamanac-makers prefer to adopt the modern astronomical data, although certain traditional astronomical texts have given details as to how the planetary motions could be calculated accurately from time to time. That the calculation of planetary motions need corrections in view of the very nature or character of their revolutions was recognized by Indian astronomers. Some of the *Karaṇa* texts have attempted to take this into account, despite their desire to start with an epoch of their choice. *Parameśvara* (a Kerala astonomer of the 15th centrury A.D.) has in his *Dṛggaṇita* pointed out that one second (*liptikā*) should be subtracted for every 200 years from the mean position of the Sun to get its accurate mean position; one second to be added in the case of the Moon for every 41 years, and an addition of one second in the case of the node for every 135 years, while one minute (*kalā*) should be subtracted in respect of the higher apsis for every three years. Accurate time–reckoning was an important vocation of Indian astronomers not only for making the *pañcāṅga* precise but also for astrological purposes.

In pursuance of its basic premise that happenings on the Earth and the life of man would be influenced by the movements of the Sun and planets in the matrix of time, astrology is inexorably concerned with the time of one's birth and the disposition of the Sun and planets at the time of birth besides their moments over time. There is no denying that planetary astrology in India owes its inspiration to the Greeks. Varāhamihira (6th cent. A.D.) in his *Bṛhajjātaka,* has duly acknowledged the Greek expertise in this field. It is significant to note that there are several Greek words still in use in Indian astrology.

Indian astrology is a fusion of the Vedic *nakṣatra vidyā* and planetary movements both in space and time. The twelve signs of the zodiac (each of 30°) and 27 *nakṣatras* (each of 13°20') in the celestial sphere are taken into consideration along with the time-periods associated with them during the planetary movements for making predictions. The accuracy or otherwise of the predictions apart, the notion of time and its exact determination are an inseparable part of astrology that has become, controversies notwithstanding, a factor to reckon with practically in all cultures, more so in India. The word, *jyotiṣa* (relating to the luminaries in the sky) that connotes astronomy is also used to denote astrology since astrology is dependent upon the astronomical computations of time.

REFERENCES

(The English translations of all the Upaniṣadic references are taken from The Thirteen Principal Upaniṣads by R. E. Hume.)

(All references to the *Praśastapādabhāṣya* (PPB) are taken from *Kiraṇāvalī* (ed) Jitendra Jetley J. S; including the numbers mentioned and related to each commentary/discussion).

1. इच्छामात्रं प्रभो: सृष्टिरिति सृष्टौ विनिश्चिता: ।

   कालात्प्रसूतिं भूतानां मन्यन्ते कालचिन्तका: । *Māṇḍūkya kārikā*.1.8

   The creation occurred as a mere desire of the Lord according to some. Those who hold Time as supreme believe that all the beings are born of Time.

2. कालो हि ब्रह्म भूत्वा बिभर्ति परमेष्ठिनम् । (AV. XIX-53-9)

   The very *Kāla*, being Brahman, the mighty one, sustains the vast universe, the greatest sacrifice of His.

3. सप्त चक्रान्वहति काल एष सप्तास्य नाभिरमृतं न्वक्ष: ।

   स इमा विश्वा भुवना न्यञ्जत्काल: स ईयते प्रथमो नु देव: ॥ AV.XIX.53.2

   Kāla carries along seven wheels, seven are its navels, and immortality its axle; the self-same Kāla, revealing all the three worlds, is truly known to be primeval Lord.

4. काल: पचति भूतानि सर्वाण्येव महात्मनि ।

   यस्मिंस्तु पच्यते कालो यस्तं वेद स वेदवित् ॥ -Mai.up. 6.16

   Time purifies all beings by means of self-awareness. He by whom even time is known, knows the Vedas.

5. काल: स्वभावो नियतिर्यदृच्छा

   भूतानि योनि: पुरुष इति चिन्त्या ।

   संयोग एषां नत्वात्मभावात्

   आत्माप्यनीश: सुखदु:खहेतो: ॥ *Śvet.up.* 1.2

   Time, or inherent nature, or necessity or chance or the elements, or a womb or a (male) person are to be considered as the cause. Not a combination of these, because of the existence of the soul. The soul certainly is impotent over the cause of pleasure and pain.

6. द्वे वाव ब्रह्मणो रूपे, कालश्चाकालश्च अथ य: प्रागादित्यात् सोऽकालोऽकल: । अथ च आदित्याद्य: स काल: स कल: । *Mai.up.*6.15

   In truth there are two forms of Brahman, time and not-time. That is, that which existed before the Sun is not-time and that which began with the Sun as time, is divisible (Mai.up.6.15) (Tr. Paul Deussen p.153).

7. स होवाच यदूर्ध्वं गार्गि दिवो यदवाक्पृथिव्या यदन्तरा द्यावापृथिवी इमे यद्भूतं च भवच्च भविष्यच्चेत्याचक्षत आकाश
एव तदोतं च प्रोतं चेति कस्मिन्नु खल्वाकाश ओतश्च प्रोतश्चेति । *Br.up.* 3.8.7

He said, 'That O Gārgi, which is above the sky, that which is beneath the earth, that which
is between the two, sky and earth, that which people call the past and the present and the
future, across space alone is that woven, warp and woof!

8. यदेवेह तदमुत्र यदमुत्र तदन्विह ।

मृत्योः स मृत्युमाप्नोति य इह नानेव पश्यति ।

मनसैवेदमाप्तव्यं नेह नानास्ति किञ्चन ।

मृत्योः स मृत्युं गच्छति य इह नानेव पश्यति ॥ *Katha.* 2.1.10,11

Whatever is here, that is there
What is there, that again is here.
He obtains death after death
Who seems to see a difference here.
By the mind indeed, is this to be attained
There is no difference here at all
He goes from death to death
Who seems to see a difference here.

9. यावन्त्यो वै कालस्य कालस्तावतीषु चरत्यसौ यः कालं
ब्रह्मेत्युपासीत कालस्त्यातिदूरमपसरति इत्येवं ह्याह
कालात्स्रवन्ति भूतानि कालाद् वृद्धिं प्रयान्ति च ।
काले चास्तं नियच्छन्ति कालो मूर्तिरमूर्तिमान् ॥ *Mai.up.* 6.14

6-14 On account of the subtlety (of time) this (course of the Sun) is the proof, for only
in this way time is proved.
However many parts of time— Though all of them runs yonder (Sun).
Whoever reverences Time as Brahma, from him time with draws afar.
For thus has it been said—
From time flow forth created things
From time, too, they advance to growth.
In Time, to they disappear
Time is a form and formless too.

10. आदिः स संयोगनिमित्तहेतुः परस्त्रिकालादकलोऽपि दृष्टः । *Śvet.up.* 6.5
ओमित्येतदक्षरमिदं सर्वं तस्योपव्याख्यानं भूतं भवद्भविष्यदिति सर्वमोङ्कार एव । यच्चान्यत्त्रिकालातीतं तदपि ओंकार
एव । *Māṇḍ.up.* 1

The beginning, the efficient cause of combination,
He is to be seen far beyond the three times, without parts too.
Om! This syllable is the whole world. It is further explained.
Past, present and future—everything is just the word Om.
And whatever else that transcends three-fold time, that too just the word Om!

11. विग्रहवानेष काल: सिन्धुराज: प्रजानाम् ।

एष तत्स्थ: सवितारूयो यस्मादेनेमे चन्द्रर्क्षग्रहसंवत्सरादय: ॥

सूयन्तेऽडथैभ्य: सर्वमिदमत्र वा यत्किञ्चिच्छुभाशुभं दृश्यते लोके

तदेभ्यस्तदादित्यात्मा ब्रह्माथकालसंज्ञाम् आदित्यमुपासीत ब्रह्येत्येकेऽथैव प्राह । *Mai.up.* 6.16

This embodied time is the great ocean of creatures. In it abides he who is called Savitṛ, from whom, indeed, are begotten moon, stars, planets, the year and these other things. And from them comes this whole world here, and whatever thing, good or evil, may be seen in the world. Therefore Brahma is the soul of the Sun. So one should reverence the Sun as a name of time.

Some say Brahma is the Sun.

12. काले तप: काले ज्येष्ठं काले ब्रह्म समाहितम् ।

कालो ह सर्वस्येश्वरो य: पितासीत्प्रजापते: । AV.XIX-53.8

In the self-same *kāla* are fully established austerity, grandeur, the vast universe and the Vedic lore. He is the Lord of all; He is the father or the protector or Prajāpati.

13. कालोऽयं परमाण्वादिद्विपरार्धान्त ईश्वर: ।

नैवेशितुं प्रभुभूँडग्र ईश्वरो धाममानिनाम् ॥ *Bhāg.pu.* 3.11.38

Īsvara exists in the form of time from the minutest period to the full day of Brahman. Therefore O Agni, do not aspire to become the Lord of those who give light.

14. व्यक्ताव्यक्ते तथैवान्ये रूपे कालस्तथा परम् ॥ *Viṣṇu pu.* 1.2.14

The other two, manifest and un-manifest, forms are Time and Supreme Form of Brahman.

15. अहमेवाक्षय: काल: । *Bhagavadgītā* 10.33

I am Time Eternal.

कालोऽस्मि लोकक्षयकृत्प्रवृद्ध: । *op.cit.* 11.32

I am Time, Ever-extending to bring an end to the world.

काल: कलयतामहम् । *op.cit.* 10.30

I am Time for those who count (the division of time).

16. प्राकल्पविषयामेतां स्मृतिं च सुरसत्तम ।

न ह्येष व्यवधात्काल एष सर्वनिराकृति: ॥ *Bhāg.pu.* 1.6.4

17. कालवृत्त्या तु मायायां गुणमय्यामधोक्षज: ।

पुरुषेणात्मभूतेन वीर्यमाधत्त वीर्यवान् ॥

ततोऽभवन्महत्तत्वं अव्यक्तात्कालचोदितात् ।

विज्ञानात्माऽऽत्मदेहस्थं विश्वं व्यञ्जस्तगोनुद: ॥

सोऽप्यंशगुणकालात्मा भगवद्दृष्टिगोचर: ।

आत्मानं व्यकरोदात्मा विश्वस्यास्य सिसृक्षया ॥ *Bhāg.pu.* 3.5.26-28

18. परस्य ब्रह्मणो रूपं पुरुष: प्रथमं द्विज । *Viṣṇu pu.* 1.2.14

19. अनादिर्भगवान्कालो नान्तोऽस्य द्विज उच्यते ।

   अव्युच्छिन्नास्ततस्त्वेते सर्गस्थित्यन्तसंयमाः ॥ *Viṣṇu pu.* 1.2.26

20. विष्णोः स्वरूपात्परतो हिते द्वे रूपे प्रधानं पुरुषश्च विप्र ।

   तस्यैव तेऽन्येन धृते वियुक्ते रूपान्तरं तद् द्विज कालसंज्ञम् ॥ *Viṣṇu pu.* 1.2.24

21 दिक्कालयोः पञ्चगुणवत्त्वं सर्वोत्पत्तिमतां निमित्तकारणत्वं च । PPB. 24

   The space and time have five qualities, they are also the efficient causes of all products.
   तस्य गुणाः सङ्ख्याचापरिमाणपृथक्त्वसंयोगविभागाः । PPB. 69

   The qualities of Time are number, dimension, distinctness, conjunction and interjuction.

22. अपरस्मिन्नपरं युगपत् चिरं क्षिप्रमिति काललिङ्गानि । VS. 2.2.6

   The notions of posteriority in relation to posteriority of simultaneity, of slowness, and quickness are the marks of existence of the time.

   बहुतरतपनपरिस्पन्दनान्तरितजन्मनि स्थविरे युवानम् अवधिं कृत्वा परत्वमुत्पद्यते तच्च परत्वसमवायिकारणसापेक्षम् ।

   एवं स्थविरमवधिं कृत्वा यूनि अपरत्वोत्पत्तिर्निरूपणीया ।

   If in relation to an old man, between whose birth and the present time there is an interval of many revolutions of the Sun, we make a youth in term of relation, a notion of priority is evolved, and this must have some no-coinherent cause. In like manner if the old man be made the term of comparison with reference to the youth, we shall find that a notion of posteriority is evolved.
   —Śaṅkara Miśra on VS 2.2.6

23. कालः परापरव्यतिकरयौगपद्यायौगपद्यचिरक्षिप्रप्रत्ययलिङ्गः ।

   तेषां विषयेषु पूर्वप्रत्ययविलक्षणानामुत्पत्तावन्यनिमित्ताभावाद् यद्यत्र निमित्तं स कालः ।

   सर्वकार्याणां चोत्पत्तिस्थितिविनाशहेतुः तद्व्यपदेशात् ।

   क्षणलवनिमेषकाष्ठाकलामुहूर्तयामाहोरात्रार्धमासर्त्वयनसंवत्सरयुगकल्पमन्वन्तर

   प्रलयमहाप्रलयव्यवहारहेतुश्च । PPB. 67-68

24. नित्येष्वभावात् अनित्येषु भावात् कारणे कालाख्येति । VS. 2. 2.9

   कारणे कालः । VS. 1. 2.5.

25. Umesh Mishra, *op.cit.* p. 179.

26. एवं परत्वापरत्वे अपि कालपिण्डसंयोगनिबन्धने गृहीत्वा कालः अनुमीयते । NVTT, II.1.39

   Thus time is inferred in relation to the relative age keeping oneself in the relative time.
   अत्र कालशब्देन कालोपाधयः सूर्यगत्यादयः उच्यन्ते, तेषां प्रत्ययैः कालोऽनुमीयते । (*Kiraṇāvalī,* p.77)
   (In relation to young and old) the attributes of time such as the movement of the Sun are indicated by the word time. By such understandings time is inferred.

27. Umesh Mishra, p. 178.

28. न च सूर्यगतिः साक्षात्पिण्डसम्बन्धा, नापि संयुक्तसमवायः सम्भवति पिण्डसूर्ययोः संयोगाभावात् । पृथिव्यादिषु

   यत्पिण्डप्राप्तौ तच्च सूर्यसंबद्धम् । यत्सूर्यसंबद्धं तच्च पिण्डप्राप्तम् इत्याप्तिः किञ्चित्सौरं तेजः पिण्डसूर्यसंबद्धम्

अस्तीति चेन्न । कचित् पिण्डे तथा भावेऽपि भूनिखातादौ व्यभिचारात् ।

The movement of the Sun can not have direct contact with the mass of an object; neither can there be any conjunction in inherence because there is no conjunction between the mass of the object and the Sun. What is obtained as a mass of object on the earth cannot have any relation with the Sun.

What is related to the Sun cannot be had in a mass of object; but the rays of the Sun have contact with the mass of the object; this point cannot be accepted. The rays would not be able to contact with the objects existing inside the earth.

(*Kiraṇāvalī Bhāskara* quoted by Umesh Miśra, p. 177.)

29. न, आकाशस्य स्वप्रत्यासत्तिमात्रेण संयुक्तसमवायिनं धर्ममन्यत्र सङ्क्रामयितुम् असमर्थत्वात् । तथात्वे च एकत्र भेर्यामभिहतायां सर्वभेरीषु शब्दोत्पत्तिप्रसङ्गात् । (*Kiraṇāvalī*, p.77)

Ākāśa cannot transmit the attribute of an object with which the former is in relation of *saṃyuktasamavāya* to another. If it were so, then when one particular drum is beaten, sound ought to have been produced in all the drums.

30. आत्मनोऽपि द्रव्यान्तरधर्मेषु द्रव्यान्तरावच्छेदाय

स्वप्रत्यासत्ति-अतिरिक्त-सन्निकर्षापेक्षत्वात् । Ibid, p.77

Ātman is not capable of transmitting the attribute of one object to the other and therefore cannot be a connecting link.

31. न च अप्राप्ता एव सूर्यगतयो विशेषणताम् अनुभजन्ति न च स्वरूपप्रत्यासन्ना एव ताः एतादृशविशिष्टप्रत्ययान्यथानुपपत्त्या

विशेषणप्रापकं यद्द्रव्यं स कालः । *Upaskāra* on VS 2.2.6.

Revolutions of the Sun which have not yet taken place are not thus determinant nor are those resolutions actually presented. The substance then, which determines such particular notions, because otherwise they could not be produced, is time.

32. तत्त्वं भावेन । (VS 2.2.9)

Its unity is explained by existence.

33. कारणे कालः । (VS 7.1.25)

Time relates to a cause.

34. अत्र कालशब्देन कालोपाधयः सूर्यगत्यादयः उच्यन्ते, तेषां प्रत्ययैः कालोऽनुमीयते । *Kiraṇāvalī*, p.77

Here the word time (*Kāla*) indicates only the attributes of time such as the rise and setting of the Sun. By such conceptions time is inferred.

35. तेन कालेनोत्पत्त्यादीनां व्यपदेशात् उत्पत्तिकालो विनाशकाल इत्यादिविशेषात् कालस्य तत्र हेतुत्वम् इत्यर्थः ।

The point is: 'this is the time of the origin of an object,' 'this is the time of its destruction; for such experiences the conception of time is the cause. NK.p.159

36. एवं कालोऽपि सर्वत्राभिन्नाकारवर्तमानप्रत्ययवेद्यः । *Nyāyalīlāvatī*, p. 310.

Thus even time should be known as being present in the same form every where.

37. अस्तित्वं वर्तमानत्वमिति चेन्न । तद् हि वस्तूनां वा सत्तासामान्यं वा । नाद्यः । भिन्नेष्वभिन्नावभासानुपपत्तेः ।

नेतरः । अभावे सामान्येऽपि वर्तमानप्रत्ययात् । *Nyāyalīlāvatī*, p. 310.

(Time) is it 'is-ness' or 'existenceness?'

'A thing is' implies that the thing has a unique intrinsic nature. It can also be existence-universal.

It is not the former; because it conveys different meanings to different propositions.
It is not the other too.
The conception of existence-ness remains in non-existence as well as generality.
(It can be predicated to all kinds of existenceness.)

38. य एव च कालो वर्तमान इति प्रतीयते स एव पूर्वभावीति पश्चाद्भूत इति च न प्रतीयेत ।

Khaṇḍanakhaṇḍakhādyam. p. 682

Whatever is experience as 'present' cannot be experienced as what is going to happen or happened already.

39. तेन कालेन उत्पत्त्यादीनां व्यपदेशात् 'अद्योत्पन्न: श्व: परश्वो वा' इति, 'इदानीमत्रास्ति अद्य नष्ट: श्व: परश्वो वा'

इति व्यपदेश्यते । *Kiraṇāvalī,* pp.78-79

Because birth etc., are indicated with reference to time, 'Today it is born, tomorrow or day after tomorrow it is being born,' or 'now it is here, today it is destroyed, may be it will be destroyed tomorrow or the day after tomorrow, such statements are made (with reference to time.)

40. G. N. Jha, pp. 805-806.

41. NS. 2.1.41-42

42. कालस्य लिङ्गानां युगपदादिप्रत्ययानाम् अविशेषाद् एकत्वं कालस्य भेदे प्रमाणान्तराभावादित्यर्थ: । *Nyāyakandalī,*
p. 78

Since there is no specificity with reference to 'simultaneous' etc. relating to its mark time there lies no proof to determine the divisibility of time.

43. तेषां विषयेषु पूर्वप्रत्ययविलक्षणानाम् उत्पत्तौ अन्यनिमित्ताभावात् यदत्र निमित्तं स काल: । PPB.76

Among these (objects of apprehension) each of the apprehension has a uniqueness which is different from the other.
The uniqueness in each of the apprehension must certainly have a cause and that cause is called 'Time.'

44. दिक् व्यवहारम् अन्तर्भाव्या, न तु वर्तमानादि: तथा, वर्तमानस्य सर्वत्र वर्तमानत्वात् । *Kiraṇāvalī,* p.82

The use of space is for internal things (like east, west etc) but present etc are not so, because present time is present every where.

कालस्य क्रियामात्रोपाधिनिबन्धनहेतुत्वात् । *op.cit.,* p.82

Time is the cause restricted to the adjunct of action only.

45. क्षणतत्क्रमयो: संयमाद्विवेकजं ज्ञानम् । *Yogasūtra,* III-52

Knowledge born of discernment appears when there is concentration on the moments (of time) and their continuity.

क्षणस्तु वस्तुपतित: क्रमावलम्बी । क्रमश्च क्षणानन्तर्यात्मा । तं कालविद: काल इत्याचक्षते योगिन: । न च द्वौ क्षणौ

सह भवत: । क्रमश्च न द्वयो: सह भुवो: असंभवात् । *Vyāsabhāṣya* on the above

A moment exists in relation to the object only and depends on its continuity. A continuity is an event of one moment coming after another. The yogins who know the truth of time call it Time. Two moments cannot exist simultaneously together.

46. पूर्वस्मादुत्तरभाविनो यदानन्तर्यं क्षणस्य स क्रम: । तस्माद्वर्तमान एव एक: क्षणो न पूर्वोत्तरक्षणा: सन्तीति ।

तस्मान्नास्ति तत्समाहार: । ये तु भूतभाविन: क्षणास्ते परिणामान्विता: व्याख्येया: । Ibid

A series (क्रम) is that where one moment occurs after the previous one expires. In a given moment the previous or successive moment does not exist. Therefore there can not be any conjunction (of moments). It should be noted that the previous moment and the successive moment are included under evolution (pariṇāma).

47. कर्मरूपं तज्जनितविभागप्रागभावादिरूपश्च उपाधिः । *Nyāyalīlāvatī*, p.45

'The cognition (*jñānaviśeṣa*) which apprehends the motion of datum and the pre-non-existence of disjunction (born of it) together, is the determinant of motion'.

Vallabha maintains that the datum is a particular motion and the pre non-existence of the disjunction (*vibhāgaprāgabhāva*) caused by it as determinant (*upādhi*) of that motion.. .. . . . . A cognition does not arise except when its own conditions are fulfilled, the datum of this cognition must be a unique fact called moment, quoted by Sadānanda Bhāduri, *Time in Indian Philosophy,* p.206

48. कृतताकर्तव्यतोपपत्तेस्तूभयथा ग्रहणम् । NS. 2.1.43

We have the conceptions of 'has been done' 'to be done' — it follows that the idea (of the present) is established in both ways.

सोयमुभयथा वर्तमानो गृह्यते अपवृक्तो व्यपवृक्तश्च अतीतानगताभ्याम् । (Vātsyāyana's *bhāṣya* on *Ny.Sū.* 2.1.4)

The present is conceived of both ways— (i) as not mixed up with past and future; and (ii) as mixed up with them.

49. अरूपो नन्वयं कालः कथं गृह्येत चक्षुषा ? – *Nyāya mañjarī,* p.199

Time has no colour; then how it can be known through the eyes?

तस्मात् स्वतन्त्रभावेन विशेषणतयापि वा ।

चाक्षुषज्ञानगम्यं यत् तत्प्रत्यक्षमुपेयताम् ॥

अत एव प्रत्यक्षः कालः । *op.cit.* p. 200

Whether an object is cognized independently or through its attributes, whatever is apprehended through the sense organ, eye, is to be considered as perception. Therefore, time is perceptible.

50. तस्मात् ग्रहादिपरिस्पन्द एव तैस्तैर्निमित्तैः उपलक्ष्यमाणप्रमाणः काल इति । कालविदश्च ज्योतिर्गणकाश्च एनं बुध्यन्ते । *op.cit.,* p. 200

By the observation of the movement of the planets in their respective order it is proved that time exists. The knowers of time and the followers of astronomy consider this (phenomenon) as time.

51. आदित्यपरिवर्तनोत्पाद्यपरत्वापरत्वसमवायिकारणाधारः परत्वापरत्वानधिकरणं कालः । *Saptapadārthī,* Ed. Gurumurthy, p.66

Time is that substance which is the abode of the non-intimate cause of posteriority and priority produced by the motion of the Sun and which is not, at the same time, the abode of posteriority or priority by themselves.

Padārthatattvanirūpaṇa of Raghunātha Śiromaṇi (Tr. and Ed), K. Potter, Harvard-Yenching Institute, Cambridge, Mass, 1957.

52. न हि नः कालो नाम कश्चित्पदार्थोऽस्ति । *Yuktidīpikā* quoted by Sanatkumara Sen in *Indian Philosophical Quarterly*, 1968, p. 411

There is no substance called Time at all.

53. क्रियाणां विशिष्ट-अवधि-स्वरूप-प्रत्यय-निमित्तत्वम् । Ibid. p.412

Time is the means of conceiving limited existence or persistence of events.

54. क्षणतत्क्रमयोः संयमाद्विवेकजं ज्ञानम् । *Yoga.sū.* 3-52

'By concentration over the moment and its succession, comes discriminative knowledge'.

55. Sen S. K : In *Time in Indian Philosophy*, pp. 515-516.

56. यथापकर्षपर्यन्तं द्रव्यं परमाणुरेवं परमापकर्षपर्यन्तः कालः क्षणः । यावता वा समयेन चलितः परमाणुः पूर्वदेशं जह्यादुत्तरदेशम् उपसंपद्येत स कालः क्षणः । तत्प्रवाहाविच्छेदस्तु क्रमः । क्षणतत्क्रमयोर्नास्ति वस्तुसमाहारो इति बुद्धिसमाहारो मुहूर्ताहोरात्रादयः । स खल्वयं कालः वस्तुशून्योऽपि बुद्धिनिर्माणः । शब्दज्ञानानुपाती-लौकिकानां व्युत्थितदर्शनात् वस्तुस्वरूप इव अवभासते ।

क्षणस्तु वस्तुपतितः क्रमावलम्बी । क्रमश्च क्षणानन्तर्यात्मा । तं कालविदः काल इत्याचक्षते योगिनः । न च द्वौ क्षणौ सह भवतः । क्रमश्च न द्वयोः सहभुवोरसम्भवात् । पूर्वस्मादुत्तरभाविनो यदानन्तर्यं क्षणस्य स क्रमः ।

तस्माद्वर्तमानैक एव क्षणः न पूर्वोत्तरक्षणाः सन्तीति । तस्मिन्नास्ति तत्समाहारः । ये तु भूतभाविनः क्षणाः ते परिणामान्विता व्याख्येयाः । तेनैकेन क्षणेन कृत्स्नः लोकः परिणामम् अनुभवति । तत्क्षणोपारूढाः खल्वमी सर्वे धर्माः । । Vyāsa on *Yoga sū.* 3.52

A moment or *kṣaṇa* is the minutest time or the minutest duration which a moving atom takes to reach the next position in space from its previous one. The uninterrupted flow of these is succession (*krama*). However, there is no real togetherness of a moment and its succession. *Muhūrta* (modern equivalent : 48 minutes), day, night etc. are conceptual or imaginary aggregates. Being a mental construct such time is unsubstantial, and a mere verbal idea, although to ordinary persons it seems to be an objective reality. The moment, however, pertains to what is real (*vastupatita*) and is determined by 'succession' and the succession consists in sequence of moments. The yogis who experience call this by name time. Further, two moments do not co-exist. Nor can there be any 'succession' of two co-existing moments. For, that is impossible. The sequence of a posterior moment from the one that precedes it is succession. Therefore, only one moment is present. Its antecedent as well as the later moments do not exist, and hence there is no combination of them. The so-called past and the future moments should be explained as connected only by change. For this reason, the whole universe undergoes change in that one moment; all the characteristics (*dharma*) are installed in that moment.

जातिलक्षणदेशैरन्यतानवच्छेदात् तुल्ययोस्ततः प्रतिपत्तिः ।

Although distinction among generality, characteristics and place is not apprehended there arises knowledge of similar objects.

57. अपरे (अवशेषिकाः) तु वर्णयन्ति येऽन्त्या विशेषाः तेऽन्यताप्रत्ययं कुर्वन्तीति । तत्रापि देशलक्षणभेदो मूर्तिव्यवधिजातिभेदश्चान्यत्वे हेतुः । Vyasa's com. on *Yoga sū.* 3. 53

58. क्षणानन्तर्यात्मा परिणामस्यापरान्तेन अवसानेन गृह्यते क्रमः । न हि अननुभूतक्रमक्षणान्नवस्य पुराणता वक्तव्यस्यान्ते भवति । नित्येषु च क्रमो दृष्टः । Vyasa's com. On *Yoga sū.* 4.33

59. क्षणभेदस्तु योगिबुद्धिगम्य एव । Ibid.

The difference in the moments is accessible to yogic intuition only.

60. असौ वा आदित्यो देवमधु तस्य द्यौरेव तिरश्चीनवंशोऽन्तरिक्षमपूपो मरीचयः पुत्राः । *Ch.up.* 3.1

Verily yonder Sun is the honey of the gods. The cross-beam for it is the sky. The honey comb is the atmosphere. The brood are the particles of light.

61. Yogimunivar; *Vaidyacintāmaṇi*: Pt. I, 1973, p81

62. (यावद्विकारं तु विभागो लोकवत् ।) अहमेवेदानीं जानामि वर्तमानं वस्त्वहमेवातीतमतीततरं चाज्ञासिषमहमेवानागतमनागततरं च ज्ञास्यामि इति अतीतानागत-वर्तमानभावेनान्यथा भवति अपि ज्ञातव्ये तु ज्ञातुरन्यथाभावोऽस्ति सर्वदा वर्तमानस्वभावत्त्वात् । तथा भस्मीभवत्यपि देहे नात्मन उच्छेदो वर्तमानस्वभावादन्यथास्वभावत्वं वा न संभावयितुं शक्यम् । (Śaṅkara on *Vedānta Sūtra* 2-3-7)

(Trans) Thus it is that when a man says, 'It is I myself who know the present object now, it is I who know the past and the remote past, and it is I who shall know the future and the remote future, it is seen that though the object to be known has different modes varying with the past, present and future, the knower remains un-changed; for he has the nature of being ever present. Similarly even when the body is reduced to ashes, the self is not reduced to nothing, its nature being such that it is even present.

63. कार्यं हि वस्तु कालेन परिच्छिद्यते । अकार्यं च ब्रह्म । तस्मात् कालतोऽपि अनन्तम् । Śaṅkara on *Tai.up.* 21

An object which is produced is measured in terms of time. But Brahman is not a product. Therefore he is infinite compared to time. (In other words, time has a beginning.)

64. Mahadevan T. M. P.: *Time in Indian Philosophy*, pp. 543 ff

65. नात्मानं न परं चैव न सत्यं नापि चानृतम् । प्राज्ञः किञ्चन संवेत्ति तुर्यं तत्सर्वदृक्सदा ॥ *Māṇḍ. kār*, 1.12

The self of the sleep state knows neither itself nor another, neither truth nor untruth; *turīyā* is all-seeing always.

66. ब्रह्मणो वावेता अग्र्यास्तनवः परस्यामृतस्य अशरीरस्य । *Mait.up.* 4-6

Time is one of the principal forms of the Supreme, immortal, unembodied Brahman.

67. यः कालं ब्रह्म इत्युपासीत कालस्तस्य अतिदूरमपसरति । *Mait.up.* 6-14

He who worships time as Brahman, from him time withdraws afar (Mai.up. 6.14).

68. *Mādhyamika Kārikā.* IX. 5

69. Mandal, K. K: A Comparative Study of the Concepts of Space and Time in Indian Thought Chowkhamba Sanskrit Series, Banaras.

70. न निमित्तमन्तरेण कार्यस्योत्पत्तिरस्ति । तस्माद् यदत्र निमित्तं स काल इति । NK, p. 156 (Ed. D. Jha)

There can be no production without an efficient cause and therefore such an efficient cause is time.

71. Harisatya Bhattacharya: 'The Theory of Time in Jaina Philosophy' in *Time in Indian Philosophy*, pp. 531-39

72. कालो हि द्विविधः परमार्थकालो व्यवहारकालश्च । *Jaina Siddhāntā kośa* स.सि. 5.22.263.2.

73. वर्तनापरिणामः क्रिया परत्वापरत्वे च कालस्य । *Tat.sū.* 5.22

The functions of time are, becoming, change, motion and the sequence of before and after.

74. सब्भावसहावणं जीवाणं सह य पाग्गलाणं च ।

परिचट्टणसंभूओ कालो णियमेण पण्णत्तो ॥ *Jaina Siddhānta kośa* 4.1.5.1.3.315

75. आ आकाशादेकद्रव्याणि । *Tat.sū.* 5.6
Up to space (i.e. *dharma, adharma,* and *ākāśa*) are substances (indivisible wholes).
आकाशस्यावराह: । Tat.sū. 5.18
The function of space (is to give) place (to all the other substances).

76. आकाशस्यानन्ता: । *Tat.sū.* 59
The (*pradeśas*) of *ākāśa* are infinite.
लोकाकाशस्य यावन्त: प्रदेशास्तावन्त: कालाणवो निष्क्रिया एव एकैकाशप्रदेशे एकैकवृत्त्या लोकं व्याप्य व्यवस्थिता: ।
स.सि. 5.39.312.11

77. (*Pāṇini sūtra* — नक्षत्रेण युक्त: काल: । (4.2-3)

नित्ये हि कालनक्षत्रे । (on *Pāṇ.* 4.2.3)
Both time and stars are permanent.

78. मूर्तीनां तेन भिन्नानाम् उपयापचया: पृथक् । लक्ष्यन्ते परिणामेन सर्वेषां भेदयोनिना ॥ *Mahābhāṣya* (कालसमुदेश:)
Kārikā 13
Among various corporeal beings different kinds of changes are observed but originating from (time) they are different from all the others.

79. तरुतृणलताप्रभृतीनां कदाचिदुपचय: अन्यदा तु अपचय: स: प्रत्ययान्तराविशेषेऽपि यत्कृत: स काल: । Kaiyata
(प्रदीप) on *Kārikā* 13
Sometimes the growth and sometimes the decay are seen among such things as trees, grass or creepers and although the cause remains the same what brings change is Time.

80. Patañjali on *Pāṇini Sūtra*, 2.2.5

81. Ibid.

क्षिप्रवचने ल्युट् । (3.3.133)

इह हि किंश्चिदिन्द्रियकर्म किंश्चिदुबुद्धिकर्म । इन्द्रियकर्म समासादनम् । बुद्धिकर्म व्यवसाय: । तद्यदा इन्द्रियकर्म तदा
एता विभक्तय: । यदा हि बुद्धिकर्म तदा वर्तमाना भविष्यति ।

There are two different actions, one of the senses, another of the mind. The action of senses is approach and that of the mind is conceiving..... when we have the action of senses we have the past and the future tenses; when, however, we have the action of the mind, we have the present tense.

82. पर्वतास्तिष्ठन्तीत्यादौ स्थानादे: सर्वदा सञ्चावात् साध्यत्वाभावात्तद्धर्मस्य वर्तमानस्यापि अभाव
इति भाव: । साध्यस्यार्थस्यानित्यत्वादवश्यं भविष्यत्वेन भाव्यम् । उत्पन्नस्यापि नाशाद् भूतत्वेन,
भूतभविष्यत्प्रतिद्वन्द्वे । वर्तमानो धात्वर्थो, नित्यप्रवृत्तस्य भूतभविष्यत्त्वाभावाद् वर्तमानत्वाभाव: क्रियारूपत्वाभावश्च
इत्यर्थ: ।

When we say "mountains stand" since it exists always, it is neither produced nor has it any action and therefore there is also the absence of present. Things have future when the means are there and production is expected as the object is non-eternal. They are past they have perished. The appellation present stands between past and future. As far as those which are constant, since there is the absence of past or future there is, consequently, absence of present and absence also of action (Kaiyaṭa on Pāṇ. 3.2.123).

83. तिष्ठन्ति पर्वता:, स्रवन्ति नद्य इति । किं पुन: कारणं न सिध्यति? कालविभागात् । इह भूतभविष्यत्प्रतिद्वन्द्वो

वर्तमान: काल: । न च भूतभविष्यन्तौ कालौ स्त: । *Mahābhāṣya* on Pāṇ, 3.2.123, वर्तमाने लट्

'The mountains stand,' 'the rivers flow'. In these sentences why does not present occur? Here present becomes opposite of past and future; neither do past and future exist. (Bhartṛhari, *Vākyapadīya kāṇḍa*, III, Sec.9)

84. (i) उत्पत्तौ च स्थितौ चापि विनाशे चापि तद्वताम् ।

निमित्तै: कालमेवाहुर्विभक्तानात्मना स्थितम् ॥ ३ ॥

तमस्य लोकयन्त्रस्य सूत्रधारं प्रचक्षते ।

प्रतिबन्धाभ्यनुज्ञाभ्यां तेन विश्वं विभज्यते ॥ ४ ॥

यदि न प्रतिबध्नीयात्प्रतिबद्धं च नोत्सृजेत् ।

अवस्था व्यतिकीर्येरन् पौर्वापर्यविनाकृता: ॥ ५ ॥

तस्यात्मा बहुधा भिन्नो भेदैर्धर्मान्तराश्रयै: ।

न हि भिन्नमभिन्नं वा वस्तु किञ्चन विद्यते ॥ ६ ॥

नैको न चाप्यनेकोऽस्ति न शुक्लो नापि चासित: ।

द्रव्यात्मा स तु संसर्गादिवं रूप: प्रकाशते ॥ ७ ॥

संसर्गिणां तु ये भेदा विशेषास्तस्य ते मता: ।

स भिन्नस्तैर्व्यवस्थानां कालो भेदाय कल्पते ॥ ८ ॥ (quoted in *Time in Indian Philosophy*, p.222)

It is said that Time is the cause of the creation, persistence and destruction of all things and exists in diverse forms.

It is also said that Time is the controller of the World in all its activities. The world is found in two aspects of true viz. its preventive power and permissive power.

If Time does not prevent or release what is prevented, then there will be chaos every where the objects being not discriminated as earlier and later.

Time appears in manifold forms as the objects are different with different characteristics. There can not be any object without being either one or different.

But, Time is neither single nor many, It is neither white nor black. As a substance Time appears in its (divided) form only in relation to the objects.

Time has that characteristic which the object has, and thus its differences are accounted for according to the object which has relation with it, Time is considered therefore as different according to temporal conditions of the objects.

85. कालो अश्वो वहति सप्तरश्मि: सहस्राक्षे अजरो भूरिरेता: ।

तमा रोहन्ति कवयो विपश्चितस्तस्य चक्रा भुवनानि विश्वा ॥ *Atharvaveda*, XIX.53.1

Just as a fast horse, with seven-roped reins carries a chariot, similarly the All-stirring, Omnipresent, Omniscient, All-potent god of thousand fold powers of vigilance time. Indestructible, the Almighty carries on this universe under His sway. The seers, possess-ing all kinds of knowledge and powers of action reach up to him. All the worlds are sheer wheels of His machine of creation (Tr. Devi Chand, Munshiram Manoharlal, p. 782) (Note : *Kāla* is all-pervading God.)

86. इति कालेन सर्वार्थानीप्सितानीप्सितानिह ।

  स्पृशन्ति सर्वभूतानि निमित्तं नोपलभ्यते ॥ *MBh.* xii.28-32

Thus all beings acquire good or bad things due to Time (or Fate). The good or bad can happen to the beings caused by Time only as there can not be any other cause.

87. एते देवाः कला विष्णोः कालमायांशलिङ्गिनः ।

  नानात्वात्स्वक्रियानीशाः प्रोचुः प्राञ्जलयो विभुम् ॥ *Bhāg.pu.* 3.6.37

88. नित्यं सर्वरससाभ्यासः स्वस्वाधिक्यमृतावृतौ

  ऋत्वोरन्त्वादिसप्ताहावृतुसन्धिरिति स्मृतः ।

  तत्र पूर्वो विधिस्त्याज्यः सेवनीयोऽपरः क्रमात् ॥ *Aṣṭāṅga Hṛdaya*, 3-57,58

In every season substantial amount of 'rasas' should be taken always. (But during 'ṛtusandhis' a transition is taking place and rasas should be adopted in such a way as to avoid diseases due to seasonal changes.) A 'ṛtusandhi' is the last week of present season and the first week of the arriving season. One should give up gradually the old practices and adopt new practices conforming to the seasons.

89. Whitrow, J. G: *The Natural Philosophy of Time*, Clarendon Press, Oxford, 1963, pp.1-55; *The Physics* of Aristotle. (Eng. Tr) P. H. Wicksteed and Francis M. Cornford, Harvard Univ. Press, Cambridge, Mss, 1957; W.T. Stace: *A Critical History of Greek Philosophy*, McMillan, London, 1960.

90. Augustine: *Confessions*, BK XI-6, in J. A. Gunn, *The Problem of Time*, George Allen & Unwin, London, 1929, p. 33.

91. Cleugh, M.F.: *Time and Its Importance in Modern Thought*, Methuen & Co. London, 1937, p. 40.

92. Paul Davies: *About Time*, Touchstone, New York, 1995.

93. James, William: *Principles of Psychology*, McMillan, London, 1890, vol. I, p. 609.

94. Colingwood: *The Idea of History*, Oxford University Press, Oxford, 1946.

95. Mahadevan T. M. P.: *Time in Indian Philosophy*, pp. 595 ff.

96. *Vedāṅga Jyotiṣa*, verse 36

  वेदा हि यज्ञार्थमभिप्रवृत्ताः

  कालानुपूर्व्या विहिताश्च यज्ञाः ।

  तस्मादिदं कालविधानशास्त्रं

  यो ज्योतिषं वेद स वेद यज्ञान् ॥

97. *Vaṭeśvara siddhānta* 1.1.4

  श्रुत्युत्तमाङ्गमिदमेव यतो नियोगः

  कालेऽयनर्तुतिथिपर्वदिनादिपूर्वे ।

  वेदीककुब्भवनकुण्डतदन्तरादि

  ज्ञेयं स्फुटं श्रुतिविदां बहुमान्यमस्मात् ॥

98. तस्मा उदन्त्सूर्यो हिङ्कृणोति सञ्जवः प्रस्तौति । मध्यं दिन उद्गायति अपराह्णः प्रति हरत्यस्तं यंनिधनम् ।

Atharvaveda, 9.6.5.4,

For the house-holder who knows how to honour a guest, the rising Sun brings the message or joy early in the morning. Sun filled with rays sings praise; the mid-day Sun chants virtues; the afternoon Sun grants nourishment; the setting Sun grants shelter.

99. S. N. Sen: 'Astronomy' in *A Concise History of Science in India*, p. 68.

100. द्वादशारं न हि तज्जराय वर्वति चक्रं परि द्यामृतस्य ।

आ पुत्रा अग्रे मिथुनासो अत्र सप्त शतानि विंशतिश्च तस्थुः ॥ RV.I.164.11

द्वादश प्रधयश्चक्रमेकं त्रीणि नाभ्यानि क उ तच्चिकेत ।

तस्मिंत्साकं त्रिंशता न शङ्कवोऽर्पिताः षष्टिर्न चलाचलासः ॥ RV.I.164.48

Formed with twelve spokes, by length of time, unweakened rolls round the heaven. This wheel of during order. Herein established, joined in pairs together, seven hundred sons and twenty stand, O Agni.

Twelve are the fellies and the wheel is single; three are its naves. What man hath understood it? Therein are set together spokes three hundred and sixty, which in nowise can be loosened.

101. यत त्वा देव प्रपिबन्ति तत आप्यायसे पुनः ।

वायुः सोमस्य रक्षिता समानां मास आकृतिः ॥ RV.X.85.5

When they begin to drink thee then, O God, thou swellest out again.
Vāyu is Soma's guardian God. The Moon is that which shapes the years.

102. Śat.Br. 3.1.3.17; 3.1.4.20; 2.1.1.13; 5.2.1.4; 7.1.3.35

103. वेद मासो धृतवतो द्वादश प्रजावतः । वेदा य उपजायते । RV.I.25.8

True to his holy Law, he knows the twelve Moons with their progeny.
He knows the Moon of later birth.

104. AV. XIII. 3.8.

105. Sen, S. N: 'Astronomy' in *A Concise History of Science in India*, p. 75.

106. Idem, pp. 78-79; 82-87.

107. *Vaṭeśvara Siddhānta*. I.17.9.

कमलदलनतुल्यः काल उक्तस्त्रुटिस्त-

च्छतमिह लवसंज्ञस्तच्छतं स्यान्निमेषः ।

सदल'जलधि'भिस्तैर्गुर्विहैवाक्षरं तत्-

'कृत'परिमिति काष्ठा त'च्छरार्धे'न चासुः ॥

आर्क्षं पलं षडसवो घटिका पलानां

षष्ट्या दिनं च घटिकां खलु षष्टिमहाम् ।

मासं 'खवह्नि'भिरथाब्द'मिना'हृतं तं

क्षेत्रे च कालसदृशावयवं विनासुम् ॥

‘दन्ताब्धयो’ऽयुतहता युगमर्कवर्षाः
‘दस्राद्रयो’ युगगणा मनुरेक उक्तः ।
कल्पश्चतुर्दश‘मनु’द्युनिशं च तौ द्वौ
कस्य स्ववर्षशतमत्र तदायुरुक्तम् ॥

108. *Bhāgavata pu.* 3.11.5-15
109. *Saḍratnamālā* of Śaṅkaravarman, 2.1; quoted in *Indian Astronomy: A Source-Book* (see below)

गुर्वक्षरं विघटिका घटिका दिनं च
पूर्वाणि षष्टिगुणितानि निजोत्तराणि ।
त्रिंशद्गुणं दिवसमत्र च माससंज्ञः
मासो ‘दिवाकर’गुणः खलु सावनाब्दः ॥

110. सममण्डललेखासंप्रवेशवेलाः करोति योऽर्कस्य ।
तत्रत्ययं च जनयति जानाति स भास्करं सम्यक् ॥३६॥ *Pañcasiddhāntikā,* 4.36.

111. आनयति यो द्युराशिं विनाधिमासैस्तथा तिथिप्रलयैः ।
रविदिवसेभ्योऽस्माद् वा द्युचरार्धं यः स तन्त्रज्ञः ॥ २ ॥
कुदिनैः शशिदिवसान् तैः खरांशुदिवसान् करोति तैर्भाहान् ।
अधिकैरवमानवमैरधिकान् वा यः स तन्त्रज्ञः ॥ ४ ॥ *Vateśvara Siddhānta,* 1.9.2 and 4

112. Subbarayappa B.V. and Sarma K. V.: *Indian Astronomy: A Source Book,* Nehru Centre, Bombay, 1985, pp. 84-99.

CHAPTER 8

Heat, Light and Sound*

THE PHYSICAL CHARACTERISTICS of heat, light and sound, the three sensorial experiences ever since the animal life appeared on the Earth, were not properly understood in all cultures for a very long time. It was only in the middle of the last millennium, about 500 years ago, that a clear picture of their nature, both qualitative and quantitative, began to emerge and their inter-relatedness in terms of energy was established by scientific investigations. It is strange but true that, although the phenomenon of combustion or the burning of an object like wood, or the lighting of an oil lamp, was a daily occurrence, the cause for combustion remained practically uninvestigated or pondered over till the middle of the eighteenth century. It was indeed an incredibly very long period between—the Paleolithic man who observed fires in the forests and bushes, and the various settlements, primitive or advanced, which constantly made use of fire that proved to be an important promoter of human life on the earth. In course of time, fire was raised to the divine level and the concept of fire-god was assiduously fostered with certain rites and rituals in all ancient cultures in one form or the other. The offering of oblations to fire as well as the performance of sacrifices associated with it was an important cultural trait in Mesopotamia, but more so India.

The Indian fire-god, Agni, had a distinct place in the Vedic life. The *Ṛgveda* has many hymns in praise of Agni. The *Yajurveda* invokes Agni in the context of the performance of sacrifices and other rituals. The *Atharvaveda* speaks of the fire-cult. In fact, the fire-cult had established itself among all the Indo-European communities particularly Indo-Iranians. Agni was considered as Aṅgiras and the fire-worshippers were called Aṅgirasas, the term, *aṅgelos*, meaning a messenger. The *Taittirīya saṃhitā* explicitly states that Aṅgirasas were the originators of fire-cult in India. Both in the Mesopotamian texts and in the *Ṛgveda*, the fire-god is hailed as a messenger. Agni, in the Vedic sacrifice, was regarded as an envoy or a medium between the sacrificer and the heavens. The term, *Atharvan*, has the connotation of 'one who has Agni', a priest or a follower of Agni-cult. In any case the exact nature of *agni* or fire remained unknown, although the priests used to produce *agni* through friction by rubbing hard and fast certain types of wooden sticks or

---

*This Chapter is largely based on 'The Physical World: Views and Concepts' by this author published in *A Concise History of Science in India*, pp. 478-483.

stones. But no correlation between the friction and the fire produced was attempted to understand the production of heat and fire.

The story is more or less the same in the case of light. The celestial luminaries—the Sun, the Moon, and the stars—were viewed with wonder and a divine status was accorded to them. In the *Ṛgveda*, the celestial sphere is called *dyaus,* which implies light or the illumined one. The light rays and the effulgence of the Sun or the exhilarating light of a full moon, though were common, the nature of light or its propagation was still regarded as mysterious.

In the middle of the eighteenth century, the problem of combustion or what happens when a combustible substance is subjected to the action of heat took a new turn with the experiments of quantitative nature on the gases. Although it was known that air would be essential for combustion or the production of fire, the exact manner in which such a combustion would take place was still an unresolved one.

Early in the eighteenth century, George Ernst Stahl had introduced a hypothetical idea of 'phlogiston' which was supposed to exist in all combustible substances as the matter of fire, perhaps influenced by the element 'Fire' of the Hellenic doctrine of four elements. The old view of the four elements was still current at that time.

More importantly, a phenomenon that was observed for a very long time was the increase in weight when a metal was heated in air and the process was called calcination. A series of experiments conducted on gases, the discovery of hydrogen then called 'inflammable air', and those on the calcinations and other chemical reactions by Joseph Black, Wilhelm Scheele, Joseph Priestly and A. L. Lavoisier led to the discovery of a gaseous element, the prime agent involved in combustion. Lavoisier's careful experiments specially on mercuric oxide dealt a serious blow to the phlogiston postulate by way of demonstrating experimentally, and quantitatively too, that there was something, taken from the air that played an active role in combustion. This was called oxygen, the discovery of which was an important milestone in the history of chemistry. In India such experiments were never pushed even by the rasavādins or the exponents of the *rasaśāstra* who were known for their experimental skills involving metals and minerals as well as their oxides. The nature of heat and light remained as a speculative exercise, centering round *tejas,* one of the *pañcamahābhūta-s* (five elements).

The Vaiśeṣika view*

The Vaiśeṣika sūtra (2.1.4) clearly says that heat belongs to *tejas.* As stated before, according to the Nyāya-Vaiśeṣika school, the element *tejas* or fire is material and

---

*The relevant original Sanskrit passages are given at the end of the chapter.

eternal in the form of atoms and non-eternal in the form of its products. The atomic view of *tejas* is generally maintained in the case of heat, while the atomic as well as the wave nature of this element is advanced in the case of light.

What happens when a body is heated? The Vaiśeṣika and the Nyāya schools have considered this problem, each in its own way and in considerable detail. The example given is the heating of an earthen pot. It is well known that when a fresh earthly pot is subjected to the action of heat, its colour changes, generally into red, and the body of the pot hardens. The Vaiśeṣika believes that these changes or fresh attributes take place at the atomic or the particulate level. The Naiyayikas, on the other hand, hold the view that they occur in the body as a whole. The former is known as *pīlupākavāda* (argumentation concerning the heating of *pīlus* or particles) and the latter, *piṭharapākavāda* (argumentation concerning the heating of the body as a whole). In either case, during heating what happens is that the fire element is regarded as playing an active role. The element is considered to be in high motion, producing forcible contact (*abhighāta*) with the object being heated.

Pīlupākavāda

The *pīlupākavāda* envisages the action of heat at various stages. According to the Vaiśeṣika, when an earthly body (pot) is heated, the fire element enters into it with great force, thus setting into motion the earth-atoms. Udayanācārya says that the impact is so strong that the motion produced by the fire element results in the destruction of the previous structure (*vyūha*). As a result, disjunction of atoms takes place, i.e. the dyads are split and atoms become isolated. At this stage, fire destroys the original colour of the earth-atoms which, as a result, attain a native state. Fire now produces in them the red colour. Afterwards, the unseen force (*adṛṣṭa*) causes conjunction of atoms into dyads which ultimately form, through triads, the pot once again. This is evidenced by the fact that before the action of heat the constituent parts of the pot are not hard, while they do become hard after heating. Though a series of events take place, the Vaiśeṣika holds that the original shape of the pot remains the same.

Another interesting aspect of the *pīlupākavāda* is that the whole process is enumerated in terms of distinct stages, and the time necessary for attaining each stage is reckoned in terms of moments—five to eleven, according to the different opinions concerning the acceptance or otherwise of the concept of *Vibhāgīyavibhāga*. If one does not believe in it, the process is said to be complete even in nine moments. As an example, heating process involving ten moments, broadly, is as follows: (i) motion produced in the atoms, and isolation of atoms; (ii) destruction of the original colour; (iii) production of the red colour; (iv) destruction of the motion of the atoms produced earlier; (v) production of the creative motion between the atoms; (vi) disjunction between the atoms and *ākāśa*; (vii) destruction of the conjunction produced earlier; (viii) coming into being of productive conjunction; (ix) production of the dyad; and (x) production of the red colour in it, and the formation of triad. Likewise, details are also given of processes involving nine or eleven movements. There are even processes involving six, five, four or three moments, in consonance with the different stages of the process reckoned. What is of importance in this scheme is that the colour of the pot is produced by the colour of the triads which owe their colour to the constituent dyads which, in turn, owe it to the colour of the atoms themselves. It is very difficult to understand the exact connotation of a moment indicated by the Nyāya-Vaiśeṣika. Sometimes, it indicates the steps or stages involved;

Piṭharapākavāda

The *piṭharapākavāda* of the Naiyāyikas, sets forth the view that the colour change takes place in the entire body of the pot, i.e. the pot in the oven or the furnace, remains structurally intact. It does not undergo any change in size or shape, and the invisible process of disintegration at the level of atoms is wholly untenable, according to this argumentation.

These two views obviously try to explain a common phenomenon on logical grounds without going into the quality or quantity of heat itself. The ideas relating to the differences in the sources of heat is also not thought of, and different types of fuels are stated to be different forms of fire. There is a view held by Vijñāna Bhikṣu that heat is latent in the fuel and under favourable conditions it breaks forth. Udayanācārya has given expression to a more rational view that the solar heat is the source of all forms of heat manifested.

Another aspect of the element fire *vis-à-vis* what is known as *pāka* deserves consideration. *Pāka,* in general, seems to connote conjunction of the element fire in different ways with earthly substances. For example, when a mango fruit is kept surrounded with straw, the heat produced changes its colour from green to yellow without affecting the taste of the fruit. This is a case of conjunction involving the fire element. Similar types of conjunctions are possible resulting in the change of taste, smell and touch. The Nyāya-Vaiśeṣika tries to explain different transformations such as the production of milk from grass, formation of curd, cream, etc., on the basis of conjunction involving fire atoms.

LIGHT

In respect of light, the concept in the *Nyāya sūtra* of Gautama and elaborated upon by Vātsyāyana in the *Nyāyabhāsya* deserves special mention. How is the object perceived by the eye or the visual organ? As noted before, the element fire is the principle of the visual (sensory) organ supposed to be at the tip of the pupil. The prominent attributes of the visual (sense) organ are colour and touch, while its special quality is colour. It is pointed out that the light rays emanate or issue forth from the eye and get into contact with the objects, large or small, in the same way as there occurs the contact between the light ray (going out from the lamp) and the object. The rays which issue forth from the eye, if obstructed by an intervening object, cannot have the direct contact with the object. Hence the latter cannot be perceived in such a situation. (Vātsyāyana in his *bhāsya* on the Nyāya-sūtra 3.1.42)

Then how is the colour perceived? Perception of colour is stated to be the result of the presence of several components and also their characteristic manifested, in order that it be perceived. The light rays coming out from the eye have their colour *unmanifested*. Hence they are not perceived. Light, in general, is stated to possess a diversity of character, viz. (i) both colour and touch manifested (Sun's rays perceived by eye and skin); (ii) colour manifested but touch unmanifested (light from the lamp or Moon seen by eye only); (iii) touch manifested but colour unmanifested (as in hot water); and (iv) both colour and touch unmanifested (rays from the eye itself).

The view regarding the perception of objects larger than the size of the eye is very interesting. According to the Nyāya-Vaiśesika, just as *tejas* of the burning wick of a lamp gradually spreads out in ever increasing circles and illumines the objects of various sizes, so also the *tejas* in the eye goes out and spreads in wider circles apprehending the objects of different sizes. It is also held by the Mīmāmsakas, according to Vātsyāyana, that, like a ray of light, the stretch of vision also goes on expanding gradually, the range of vision depending upon the extent of the stretch. The extent of this stretch itself is said to terminate at the object, perhaps encompassing it. It is even stated that the vision of the rays emanating from the eye would not proceed beyond the object in view.

The Mīmāmsakas also think that a flame is the collection of a large quantity of light particles at the burning zone, say wick, and that the light particles are in a state of high motion. Further, the Mīmāmsakas even recognize a sort of radiation diffused by the flame, proceeding away from the burning wick. These are in the nature of explanations of commonly observed phenomena.

As regards reflection, a curious view is expressed by the followers of the Nyāya school. The mirror is believed to be possessed of a particular colour as an intrinsic part of its very nature. When a man stands before it, the light rays emanating from the eyes strike the mirror and are turned back. Again they establish contact with his own face. The reflected image is perceived as a result of the peculiar colour of the mirror's own surface.

It will be seen from the foregoing observations that the speculation concerning light revolves round the fact that the rays issue forth form the eye itself to establish contact with the object. The contact-theory, as it may be called, seems to derive its sanction from (i) the fact that the principle of visual organ is *tejas* (fire), and (ii) an observation that the light rays appear to emanate from the eyes of 'night-walkers', i.e. cats and other feline animals. The *Nyāyabhāṣya* asserts that there is no justification for the assumption that there is a difference of character between the eye of the cat and the human eye.

Of particular interest are the different views on the characteristics of the visual sense organ itself. The Nyāya-Vaiśeṣika holds that the eyes are produced mainly from the ultimate particles of *tejas* so that they apprehend colour alone. It is pointed out that this particular type of production is rendered possible by *adṛṣṭa*. The Buddhists, however, believe that the eyeballs represent the visual organ. These eyeballs, which are material, perceive the external objects because of external light and the past deeds of the observer. Buddhists do not subscribe to the idea that the visual organ moves up to the object of perception at a distance. In respect of the number of visual organs, too, there are differing views. The author of the *Nyāyabhāṣya*, Vātsyāyana, states that there are two independent eyes and hence two sense organs of sight. Uddyotakara, in his *Nyāyavārttika*, asserts that there is only one organ of sight. This view is supported by the later exponents of the Nyāya-Vaiśeṣika like Vācaspati Miśra and Viśvanātha as well as by the Buddhist, Vasubandhu.

SOUND

There are divergent views about the production and propagation of sound. The followers of the *Nyāya-Vaiśeṣika* school consider sound as a quality. The substance in which sound subsists as a special quality corresponding to the auditory sense organ, is *ākāśa*. In the *Nyāya-Vaiśeṣika* view sound is a produced phenomenon having a beginning as well as an end. Even so, it is not believed to be coeval with the substance in which or by which it is produced, because experience reveals that sound moves out of the substance.

Two types of sound are recognized: (i) articulate; and (ii) noise in general. The first is considered as the one that proceeds from mind and self. An effort on the part of the subject brings about the conjunction of the self with air. This conjunction produces in air a certain movement. The air then strikes the region of throat to produce letter-sound, i.e. the articulate one, in contact with *ākāśa*.

The noted exponent of the *Vaiśeṣika* school, Praśastapāda, is of the view that sound is produced always in series which may be likened to the series of water ripples. It has been stated that these wave motions, ripple-like as they are, occupy successive points in *ākāśa*. The first sound causes the second one. As soon as the latter is formed, the former (as the cause) gets destroyed. This kind of production and destruction goes on in a chain, and what is perceived by the ear is the last of the series. In other words, the first sound so produced and, for that matter, the intervening ripples of sound, are not heard. Yet in this way the auditory organ is said to be connected with the source of sound through the successive movements. The latter are indeed a result of the cause and effect relationship. The first movement is the cause with the second as the effect, the second is the cause with the third as the effect and so forth.

When a drum is struck by a stick the impact is believed to set up vibrations as a consequence of which sound is produced in all directions. The mechanical impact is held by the *Nyāya-Vaiśeṣika* to be the efficient cause while *ākāśa* alone is the true substratum of sound. Further, while *ākāśa* is an eternal substance, sound is transient quality because it is related to the notion of being produced and destroyed.

The position of the followers of the *Mīmāṃsā* school is entirely different in this respect. They believe that sound is eternal and not a produced phenomenon. The movement of the air and the perception of sound appear to have been linked together by the *Mīmāṃsakas*. Owing to an effort, say when one speaks, the internal air is said to acquire a certain forceful moment and reach the *ākāśa* of the ear, thus imparting to the auditory organ a faculty or potency. It is only when this faculty, imperceptible as it is, occurs that sound is heard. The changes perceived with reference to the intensities of sound are believed to be due to the fluctuations in the air-current itself. In this way the *Mīmāṃsakas* explain the propagation of sound while strictly maintaining the eternality of sound. This is in line with their philosophical position, viz. that *śabda* or word (Veda included) is real and eternal.

The Jainas believe that sound is neither a substance nor an attribute of *ākāśa*, but is a sort of a modification of matter. When the *skandhas* or aggregates of atoms come in contact with one another, sound is said to become manifest and travel as such to the ears. The *Sāṃkhya* view is that the auditory organ as a part of the all-pervading *ākāśa* expands imperceptibly into the region where sound is produced. And *ākāśa* itself is formed out of the *tanmātrā-s* (subtle states) of sound.

It will be observed from what has been stated above that the *Nyāya-Vaiśeṣika* school alone tries to explain the phenomenon of sound in a causal sequence. The other schools attempt to accommodate the phenomenon into their philosophical views.

ORIGINAL PASSAGES

The first *sūkta* of the *Ṛgveda* is dedicated to Agni and its first *mantra* glorifies Agni.

अग्निमीळे पुरोहितं यज्ञस्य देवमृत्विजम् । होतारं रत्नधातमम् । RV.1.1.1

I propitiate Agni, the chief priest of sacrifice. (He is) a shining god, the invoking priest and the greatest giver of valuable gifts.

अग्निः पूर्वेभि ऋषिभिरीड्यो नूतनैरुत ।

स देवाँ एह वक्षति । RV.1.1.2

Agni has been propitiated by the ancient sages as well as the modern. May he bring the gods here (to receive the offerings made in the sacrifice).

इध्मेनाग्र इच्छमानो घृतेन जुहोमि हव्यं तरसे बलाय ।

यावदीशे ब्रह्मणा वन्दमान इमां धियं शतसेयाय देवीम् । AV.3.15.3

O Agni, with fuel and butter longing for profit, mine offering I present for strength and conquest. So far as I have strength, adoring the fine intellect with Vedic knowledge, may I become competent to gain a hundred treasures.

उदेनमुत्तरं न याग्रे घृतेनाहुत । समेनं वर्चसा सृज प्रजया च बहुं कृधि । AV. VI.5.1

O fire, ablaze with the butter oblation, lift up this man to a high position; endow him with full store of strength, and make him rich with progeny.

पीलवः परमाणवः । त एव स्वतन्त्राः पच्यन्ते । *Nyāyakośa,* p. 500

Pīlu means atoms. They are heated separately (in a constituent object). (Hence the name *Pīlupākavādinaḥ*).

पिठरं कार्यकारणसमुदायः (अवयवावयविसमुदायः) घटपटादिः । यथा पिठरपाकवादिनो नैयायिकाः इत्यादौ । *Nyāyakośa,* p.500

Piṭhara is the collection of cause and effect or constituent whole and constituting parts. The followers of Nyāya system are called *piṭharapākavādinaḥ.*

कारणगुणपूर्वकाः पृथिव्यां पाकजाः । *VS.* 7.1.6

(Colour, taste, smell and touch) produced by combustion in earth, have for their antecedents the qualities of their causes.

पिठरपाकवादिनस्तु अवयविनां सच्छिद्रतया विजातीयाग्निसंयोगात् तेषामपि रूपादिपरावृत्तिः भवति न तु तत्र

अवयविनां नाशः प्रत्यभिज्ञाविरोधादित्याहुः । *Vivṛti* (on the *sūtra*) quoted in *The Vaiśeṣika Aphorisms of Kaṇāda:* (Tr) A. E. Gough, p. 194

Those who maintain the combustion of wholes such as the pot, teach that, the whole being porous, it is in them that the change of colour etc. takes place as a consequence of conjunction with the particular kind of fire and that there is in this case no destruction of the wholes, for this would be contrary to observation.

घटादेः आमद्रव्यस्य अग्निना सम्बद्धस्य अभिघातात् नोदनात् वा तदारम्भकेषु अणुषु कर्माणि उत्पद्यन्ते । PPB.p.125

There happens due to heat, in a constituent product like jar, collision and pushing among the atoms which constitute it, due to heat.

तस्मिन् विनष्टे स्वतन्त्रेषु परमाणुषु अग्निसंयोगाद् औष्ण्यापेक्षात् श्यामादीनां विनाशः । PPB. 126

Due to loss (of conjunction) the atoms get separated and as a result of fire and heat energy the black colour of the jar is lost.

तदनन्तरं योगिनो अदृष्टापेक्षात् आत्माणुसंयोगात् उत्पन्नपाकजेषु अणुषु कर्मोत्पत्तौ तेषां परस्परसंयोगात् द्व्यणुकादिक्रमेण कार्यद्रव्यमुत्पद्यते । PPB. 127

Later, due to unseen force, there happens the conjunction of soul and atom. As a result chemical action ensues and action in the atoms follows. Then the substance is produced commencing from the dyads formed by the conjunction of atoms.

The ten moments are given by Udayana as follows: *Kiraṇāvalī* on PPB.122-23 (see also Umesh Mishra, pp. 84-89).

  (i)   द्व्यणुकनाशविभागजविभागोत्पत्ती

  (ii) पूर्वसंयोगनाशश्यामादिनिवृत्ती

 (iii) उत्तरसंयोगरक्ताद्युत्पत्ती

 (iv) विभागजविभागक्रिययोर्निवृत्तिः

  (v) द्रव्यारम्भणाय परमाणौ क्रिया

 (vi) क्रियया विभागः

 (vii) तेन पूर्वसंयोगनिवृत्तिः

(viii) परमाण्वन्तरसंयोगः

 (ix) द्रव्योत्पत्तिः

  (x) गुणोत्पत्तिः

पुनरन्यस्मादग्निसंयोगात् औष्ण्यापेक्षात् पाकजा जायन्ते ।

Subsequently as a result of contact with the other fire and heat energy, chemical actions happen.

ईदृशो हि तेजसो लाघवातिशयेन वेगातिशयः स्पर्शातिशयश्च यत् तज्जन्यं कर्म, कार्यद्रव्यं पूर्वव्यूहात् प्रच्यावयति ।

The fire is very light, very fast spreading and very closely touching and therefore action follows. This results in the loss of earlier structure.

तदवयवांश्च व्यूहान्तरं प्रापयति ।

(The fire) then causes a new structure of the constituent parts.

इन्द्रियस्य अर्थेन संनिकर्षाद् उत्पद्यते यद् ज्ञानं तत् प्रत्यक्षम् । and other passages. Vātsyāyana, *Nyāya bhāṣya* on NS. 3.1.38-70

प्राप्यकारि तेज एव चक्षुरिति सिद्धम् । *Nyāyamañjarī*, pp. 201-2

It is proved that the eye is the light which reaches the object (of perception).

तैजसं हि प्रदीपादि द्रव्यं रूपमेव प्रकाशयद् दृश्यते न तेजोवृत्त्येव रूपम् ।

Tejas is a substance like a lamp and it illuminates (objects) and not in the function of light only. (It extends to the object to illuminate it.)

रश्म्यर्थसन्निकर्षविशेषात्तद्ग्रहणम् । *Nyāyabhāsya*, on NS. 3.1.32

तयोः महदण्वयोः ग्रहणं चक्षूरश्मेरर्थस्य च सन्निकर्षविशेषात् भवति यथा, प्रदीपरश्मेः अर्थस्य चेति ।

रश्म्यर्थसन्निकर्षश्चावरणलिङ्गः । चाक्षुषो हि रश्मिः कुण्डादिभिरावृतम् अर्थं न प्रकाशयति यथाप्रदीपरश्मिरिति ।

The apprehension of large and small things is brought about by the peculiarity of contact between the light rays emanating from the visual organs and the object perceived just as there is by contact between the light rays from the lamp and the object. That there is such contact between the light rays and the object perceived is proved by the phenomenon of obstruction. i.e. when the rays of light emanating from the eye are obstructed by such things as the wall and the eye intervening between the eye and the object they do not illumine the object; this is exactly what happens in the case of light emanating from a lamp.

अनेकद्रव्यसमवायाद् रूपविशेषाच्च रूपोपलब्धि: । *Nyāya bhāṣya*, on NS. 3.1.36

दृष्टश्च तेजसो धर्मभेद: । उद्भूतरूपस्पर्शं प्रत्यक्षं तेज: यथा आदित्यरश्मय: । उद्भूतरूपमनुद्भूतस्पर्शं च प्रत्यक्षं यथा प्रदीपरश्मय: । उद्भूतस्पर्शमनुद्भूतरूपं अप्रत्यक्षं यथा अबादिसंयुक्तं तेज: । अनुद्भूतरूपस्पर्शो अप्रत्यक्षश्च चाक्षुषो रश्मिरिति ।

With regard to light we find that it possesses a diversity of character:

(i)   Sometimes it has both colour and touch manifested, as in the Sun's rays.
(ii) Sometimes its colour is manifested, but touch unmanifested, as in the rays of a lamp.
(iii) Sometimes its colour is unmanifested but touch manifested as light in contact with heated water.
(iv) Sometimes its both colour and touch unmanifested as in the case of light rays emanating from the eye.

नक्तंचरनयनरश्मिदर्शनाय । दृश्यन्ते हि नक्तं नयनरश्मय: नक्तंचराणां वृषदंशप्रभृतीनां, तेन शेषस्यानुमानमिति ।

जातिभेद: इन्द्रियभेद इति चेत् धर्मभेदमात्रं नानुपश्यन्नावरणस्य प्राप्तिप्रतिषेधार्थस्य दर्शनादिति । *Nyāyabhāṣya*, on NS. 3.1.42

We see rays of light in the eyes of night walkers, i.e. the cat and other animals; and from this we infer the existence of light in the eyes of other living beings. But just as the genus is different so would their sense organs be of different characters. There is no justification for the assumption that there is such difference of character (between the eye of the cat and the eye of the man).

आदर्शोदकयो: प्रसादस्वाभाव्याद् रूपोपलब्धिवत् तदुपलब्धि: ।

यथा आदर्शप्रतिहतस्य परावृत्तस्य नयनरश्मे: स्वेन मुखेन सन्निकर्षे सति स्वमुखोपलम्भनं प्रतिबिम्बग्रहणाख्यं आदर्शरूपानुग्रहात् तन्निमित्तं भवति, आदर्शरूपोपघाते तदभावात् । *Nyāyabhāṣya*, on NS. 3.1.48

In the case of mirror, we find that when a man puts his face before it, the light rays emanating from his eyes strike the mirror and are turned back, and thereby come in contact with man's own face, whose colour and form thus become perceived; this perception being called the reflected image; and it is brought about by the peculiar colour of the mirror's surface; that it is so is proved by the fact that any such reflection fails to appear whenever there is a deterioration in the brightness of the mirror's surface.

CHAPTER 9

Weights and Measures

IN THE HISTORY of human civilisation, the conception as well as the adoption of weights and measures as physical entities, has added a quantitative veneer to the practicalities of daily life, then as now. In the past, they differed in some ways from one culture to another, but such variations had similar basic approaches, though empirical, to the somewhat standardized ratios of weights and measures. In all of these, the number-reckoning was of prime importance; for, without the numbers and their association with the weights and measures, these physical quantities would not have acquired any meaning of quantitative values.

Numbers

There is no denying that language and number-system, each being articulative and communicative in its own way for a purposive community living, are the warp and weft of any civilisational fabric, the socio-economic compulsions being the hues and designs of that fabric. The numbers and numerical forms have played a pivotal role in strengthening as well as augmenting the civilisational matrix. If god is supposed to have created man, in a way man could be regarded as the creator of numbers, since numbers or numerical forms do not exist as such or have not remained in nature covered for man to discover them. It is desirable, indeed necessary, to ponder briefly over the numbers and their forms that were adopted in the Indian subcontinent over a long period; for, they governed the usage of weights and measures of the region in the same way as they did elsewhere.

On the basis of the available archaeological evidence, the earliest numerical forms, the proto-Elamite, Egyptian and Mesopotamian ones apart, are those found on what are called the Indus seals and other inscribed objects around 2500 B.C. They are in the form of vertical strokes up to 12. Whether all the script forms found on these objects represent numbers on the decimal additive-multiplicative system is still a moot point, since the so-called Indus script has not been deciphered satisfactorily yet. But surely that the people of the Indus Valley civilisation (or the Harappans as the archaeologists choose to call them) should have had a number system and also the associated weights and measures needs no emphasis. A substantive number of the latter in cherts and others sometimes in the ratio of 1:2:4 and so on, have been found in some Harappan sites.

Archaeologically again, it was not before the time of Aśokan edicts (*c.* 3rd cent. B.C.) that we come across the numerical forms known as Brāhmī numerals. Around that time came up also what is now called the Kharoṣṭhī inscriptions in which certain numerical forms have been included. Both the Brāhmī and the Kharoṣṭhī differed considerably from one another in presenting the numbers (see Tables I and II). While the Kharoṣṭhī numerals appeared to have receded to the background in the early centuries of the Christian era, the Brāhmī numerals continued to be adopted for a long time and became acceptable not only in India but also in the West as well as south-east Asia and China. With the advent of the decimal place-value system, using nine digits and zero for the first time in India (*c.* 4th-5th cent. A.D.) this system as well as the associated Brāhmī numerical forms began to spread far and wide by about the 9th or 10th cent. A.D. and have since become universal, with some modifications (Table III), through the adoption of Brāhmī numerals by the Arabs. Al-Khwārizmī was the noted exponent of these numerals in the Caliphate at Baghdad. Al-Bīrūnī and Al-Kindi also played their role in this endeavour. The doyen of historians of science, George Sarton, has recorded as follows: 'Our numerals and the use of Zero were invented by the Hindus and transmitted to us by the Arabs, hence the name Arabic numerals which we often give them'.[1] At home, the Brāhmī numerals gradually underwent changes in their forms in different regions of India along with their decimal place-value (Table IV). In Europe, the printed ones assumed elegant forms (Table V) by about the fifteenth century.

In the Vedic Period

Vedic Indians had adopted ten (decimal) as the base and evolved appropriate terminology for expressing large numbers on the ascending decimal scale (*daśaguṇottara*). The *Yajurveda* has an enumeration as follows: *eka* (one); *daśa* (ten), *śata* (10^2); *sahasra* (10^3); *ayuta* (10^4); *niyuta* (10^5); *prayuta* (10^6); *arbuda* (10^7); *nyarbuda* (10^8); *samudra* (10^9); *madhya* (10^{10}); *anta* (10^{11}); and *parārdha* (10^{12})[2]. Even much larger numbers were expressed by the Bauddhas and the Jainas. These reckonings, however, were more in the nature of past-time exercises than for practical purposes. There does not appear to be much information about the weights and measures used except a weight called *niṣka* and a measure called *droṇa* in the Vedas. The term, *niṣka*, means necklace in the Vedic parlance, and whether it represented a gold piece of definite weight or not is debatable. However, in the early medical period, the term, *niṣka,* was sometimes used to denote a coin, hence of a definite weight about which little is known so far.

The *Śulbasūtra-s*, which are a part of one of the six auxiliaries (*Vedāṅgas*) of the Veda called the *Kalpa,* are known for their prescription of accurate

Table I

KHAROṢṬI NUMERALS

ONE	/
TWO	//
THREE	///
FOUR	X ////
FIVE	I X /////
SIX	// X
SEVEN	/// X
EIGHT	X X
NINE	၅
TEN	⊃
TWENTY	3
FORTY	33
SIXTY	333
EIGHTY	3333
HUNDRED	𐨅 𐨅I
TWO HUNDRED	𐨅II

Source: Corpus Inscriptionum Indicarum, Vols II and VI Pls, VI XII XIII XIV and XXVIII Ojha, Pl LXXVI; Meninger, p. 62.

Table II

BRĀHMĪ NUMERALS

Number	Aśokan	Nānāghāt	Nāsik	Āndra Kuśān Mathura	Gupta	Pallava	Place-value Notation: copper plates and Gwalior
ONE	[glyph]	[glyph]	[glyph]	[glyph]	[glyph]	[glyph]	[glyph]
TWO	[glyph]	[glyph]	[glyph]	[glyph]	[glyph]	[glyph]	[glyph]
THREE		[glyph]	[glyph]	[glyph]	[glyph]	[glyph]	[glyph]
FOUR	[glyph]	[glyph]	[glyph]	[glyph]	[glyph]	[glyph]	[glyph]
FIVE			[glyph]	[glyph]	[glyph]	[glyph]	[glyph]
SIX	[glyph]	[glyph]	[glyph]	[glyph]	[glyph]	[glyph]	[glyph]
SEVEN		[glyph]	[glyph]	[glyph]	[glyph]	[glyph]	[glyph]
EIGHT			[glyph]	[glyph]	[glyph]	[glyph]	[glyph]
NINE		[glyph]	[glyph]	[glyph]	[glyph]	[glyph]	[glyph]
TEN		[glyph]	[glyph]	[glyph]			[glyph]
TWENTY		[glyph]	[glyph]	[glyph]	[glyph]		[glyph]
THIRTY				[glyph]	[glyph]		[glyph]
FORTY			[glyph]	[glyph]			[glyph]
FIFTY	[glyph]			[glyph]			[glyph]
SIXTY		[glyph]		[glyph]	[glyph]		[glyph]
SEVENTY			[glyph]	[glyph]			[glyph]
EIGHTY		[glyph]		[glyph]	[glyph]		[glyph]
NINETY				[glyph]	[glyph]		[glyph]
HUNDRED	[glyph]	[glyph]	[glyph]		[glyph]		[glyph]
TWO HUNDRED	[glyph]	[glyph]	[glyph]		[glyph]		[glyph]
FOUR HUNDRED		[glyph]	[glyph]		[glyph]		[glyph]
THOUSAND		[glyph]	[glyph]				[glyph]
FOUR THOUSAND		[glyph]	[glyph]				[glyph]
TWENTY THOUSAND		[glyph]	[glyph]				[glyph]

Source: Georges Ifrah, *From One to Zero: A Universal History of Numbers,* New York, 1985, pp. 454-5.

Table III

Brāhmī numerals and their modifications in West Asia and Europe

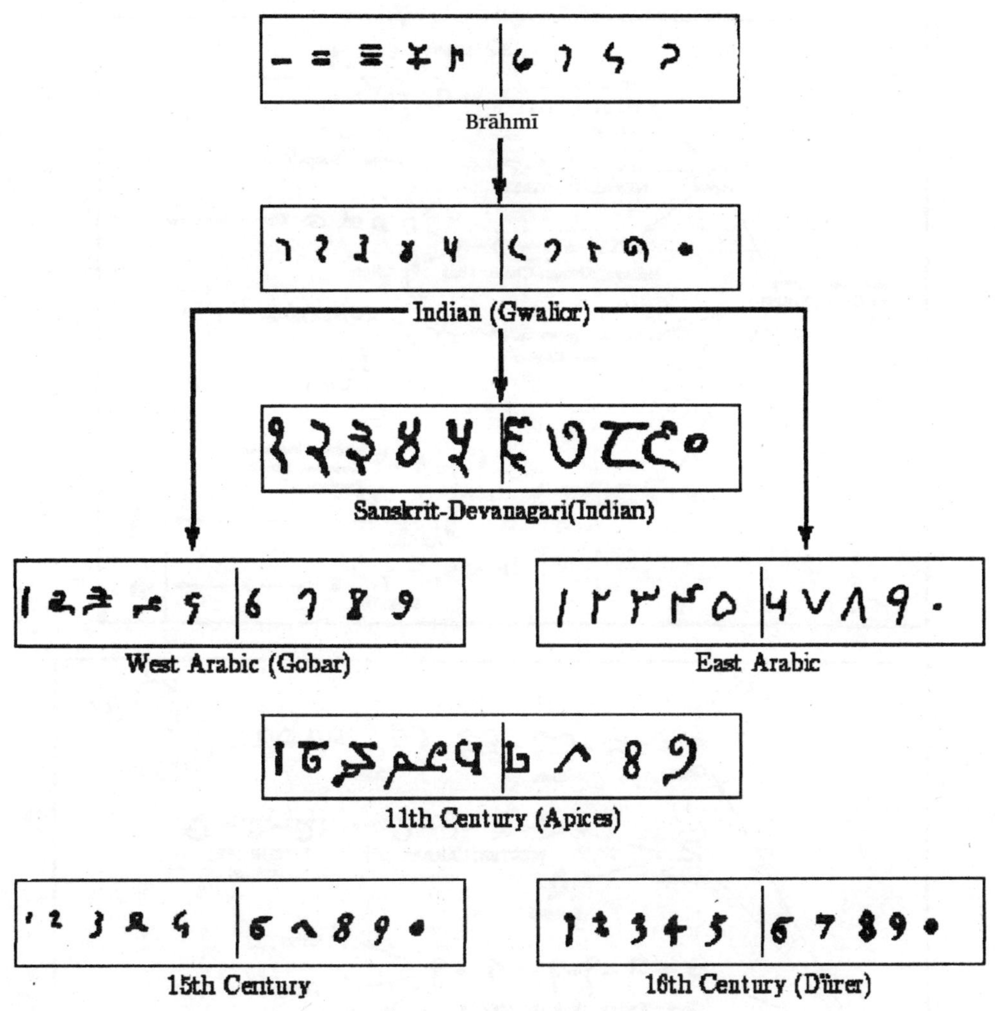

Source: Menninger, Part II, p. 233.

Table IV

Transformation of Numerals: Inscriptional Sources

Source: Georges Ifrah: *One to Zero: A Universal History of Numbers*, pp. 485-89.

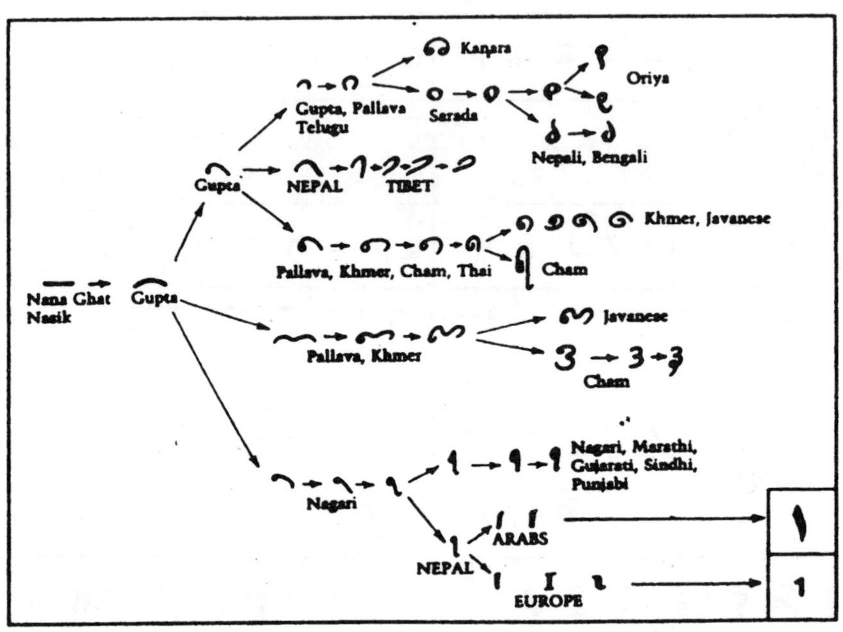

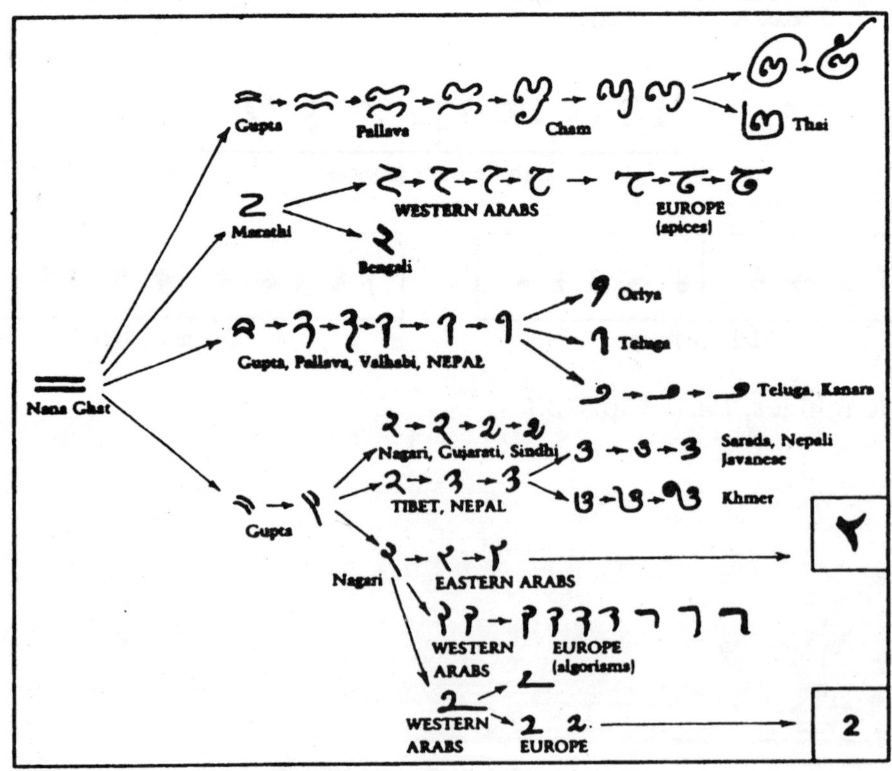

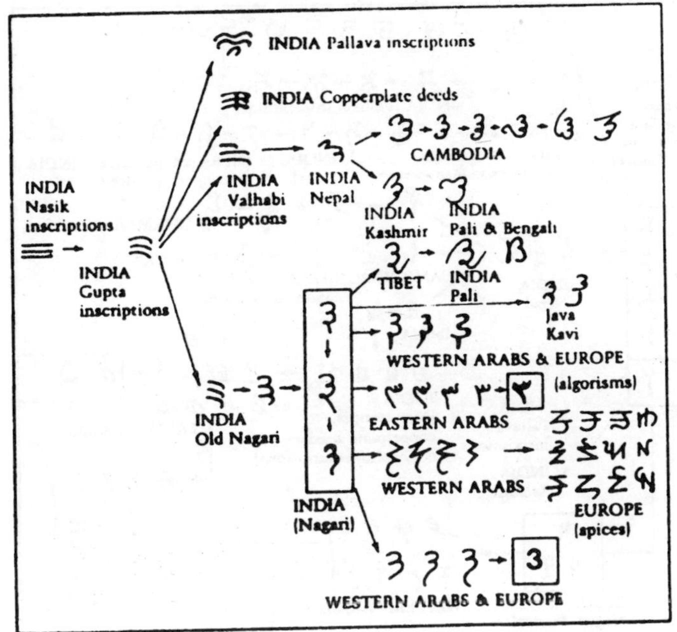
INDIA Pallava inscriptions
INDIA Copperplate deeds
CAMBODIA
INDIA Nasik inscriptions
INDIA Valhabi inscriptions
INDIA Nepal
INDIA Kashmir
INDIA Pali & Bengali
INDIA Gupta inscriptions
TIBET
INDIA Pali
Java Kavi
WESTERN ARABS & EUROPE
INDIA Old Nagari
(algorisms)
EASTERN ARABS
WESTERN ARABS
EUROPE (apices)
INDIA (Nagari)
WESTERN ARABS & EUROPE

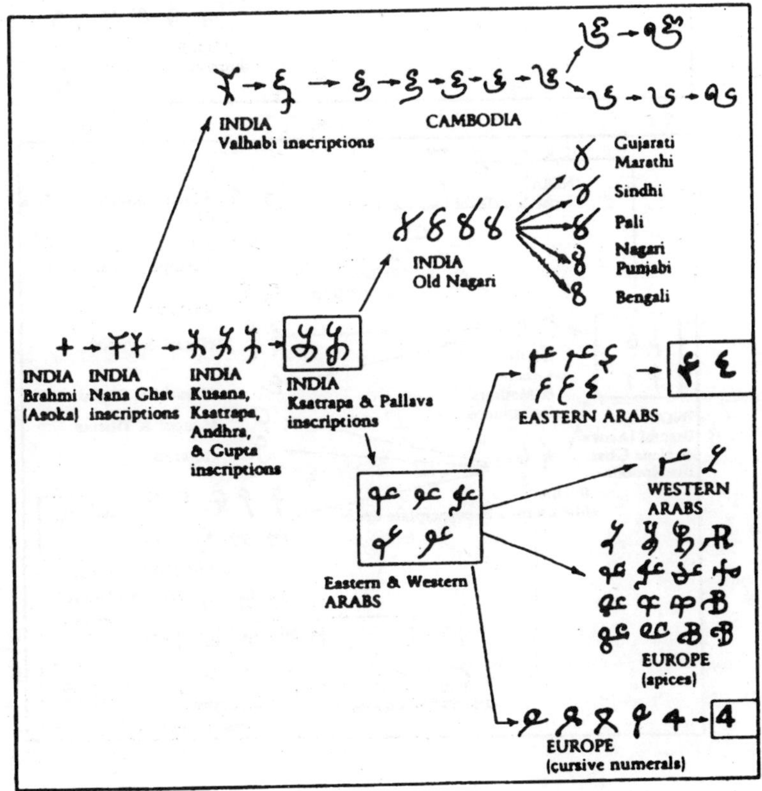
INDIA Valhabi inscriptions
CAMBODIA
Gujarati Marathi
Sindhi
Pali
Nagari Punjabi
Bengali
INDIA Old Nagari
INDIA Brahmi (Asoka)
INDIA Nana Ghat inscriptions
INDIA Kusana, Ksatrapa, Andhra, & Gupta inscriptions
INDIA Ksatrapa & Pallava inscriptions
EASTERN ARABS
WESTERN ARABS
Eastern & Western ARABS
EUROPE (apices)
EUROPE (cursive numerals)

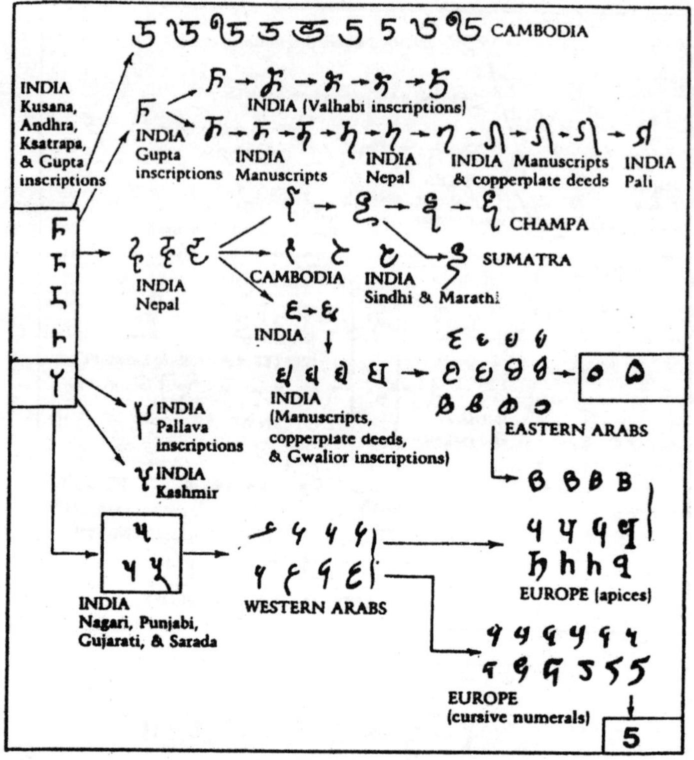

CAMBODIA
INDIA Kusana, Andhra, Ksatrapa, & Gupta inscriptions
INDIA (Valhabi inscriptions)
INDIA Gupta inscriptions
INDIA Manuscripts
INDIA Nepal
INDIA Manuscripts & copperplate deeds
INDIA Pali
CHAMPA
INDIA Nepal
CAMBODIA
INDIA Sindhi & Marathi
SUMATRA
INDIA
INDIA (Manuscripts, copperplate deeds, & Gwalior inscriptions)
EASTERN ARABS
INDIA Pallava inscriptions
INDIA Kashmir
INDIA Nagari, Punjabi, Gujarati, & Sarada
WESTERN ARABS
EUROPE (apices)
EUROPE (cursive numerals)
5

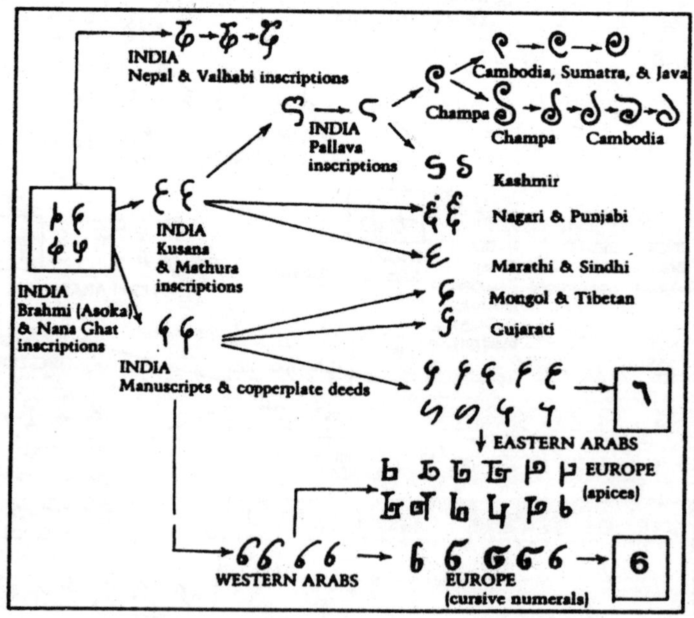

INDIA Nepal & Valhabi inscriptions
Cambodia, Sumatra, & Java
Champa
Champa   Cambodia
INDIA Pallava inscriptions
Kashmir
INDIA Kusana & Mathura inscriptions
Nagari & Punjabi
Marathi & Sindhi
Mongol & Tibetan
Gujarati
INDIA Brahmi (Asoka) & Nana Ghat inscriptions
INDIA Manuscripts & copperplate deeds
EASTERN ARABS
EUROPE (apices)
WESTERN ARABS
EUROPE (cursive numerals)
6

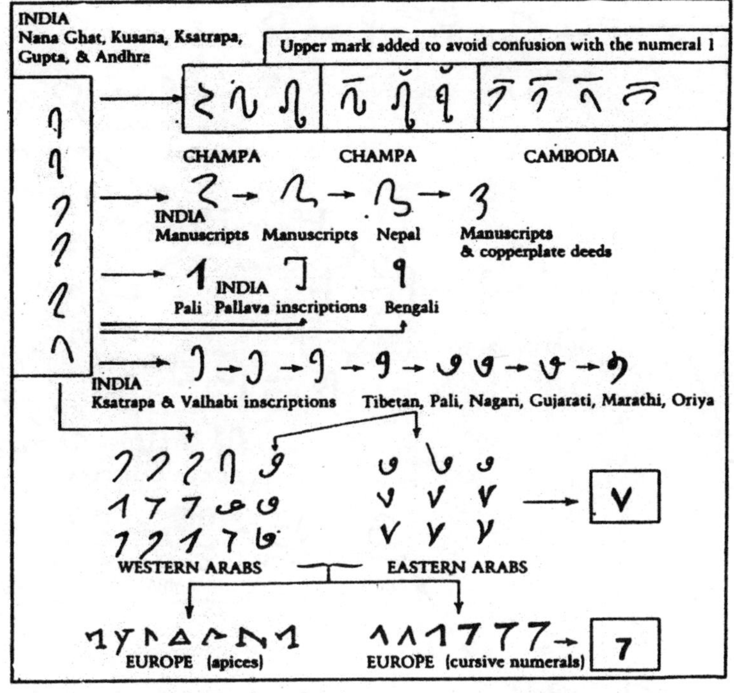

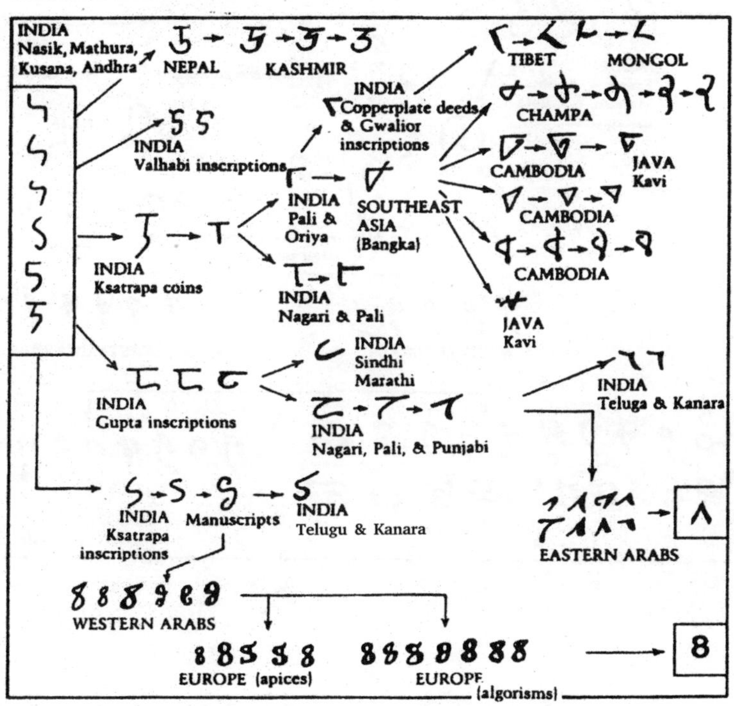

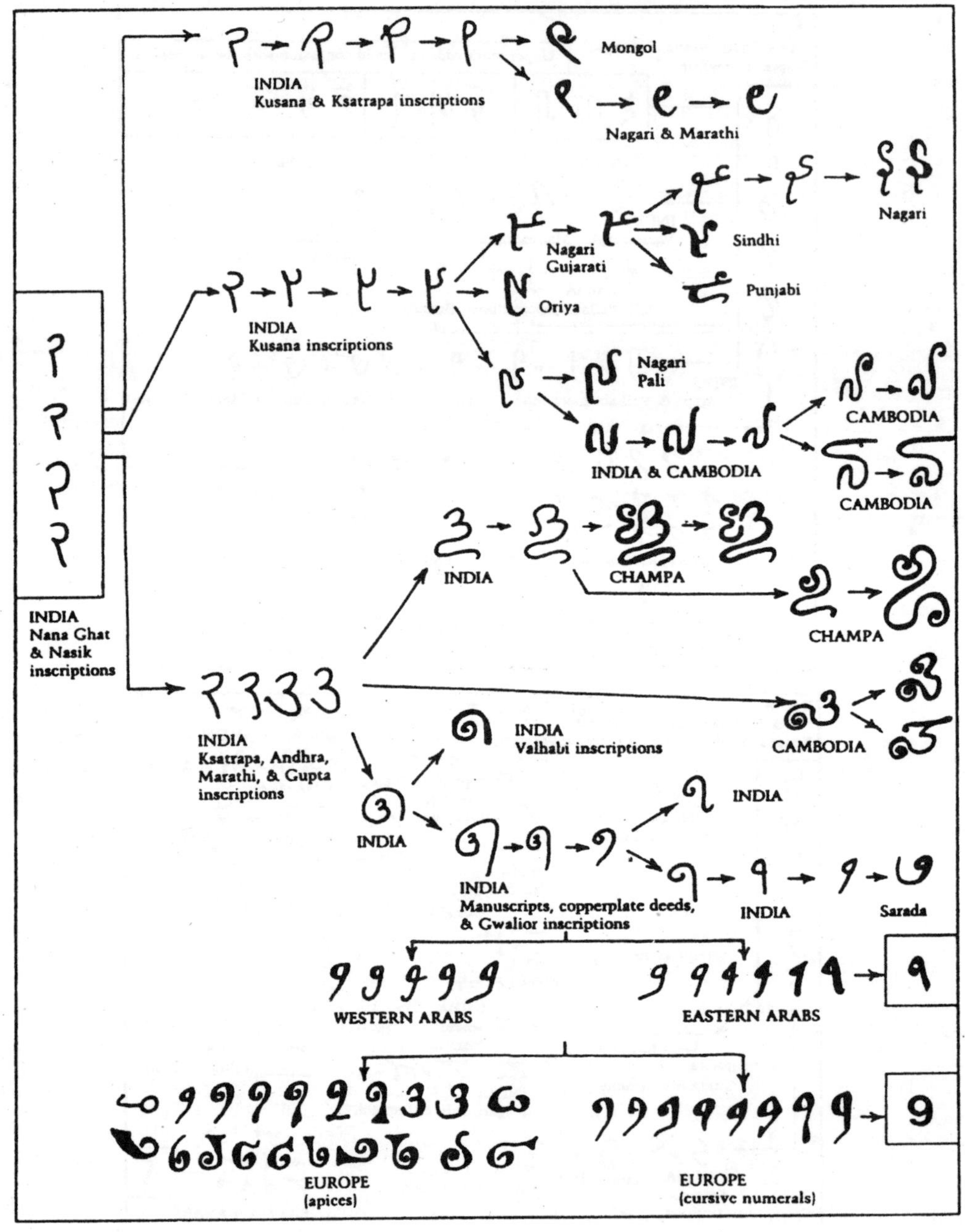

Mongol
INDIA
Kusana & Ksatrapa inscriptions
Nagari & Marathi
Nagari
Sindhi
Nagari
Gujarati
Oriya
Punjabi
INDIA
Kusana inscriptions
Nagari
Pali
CAMBODIA
INDIA & CAMBODIA
CAMBODIA
INDIA
CHAMPA
CHAMPA
INDIA
Nana Ghat
& Nasik
inscriptions
INDIA
Ksatrapa, Andhra,
Marathi, & Gupta
inscriptions
INDIA
Valhabi inscriptions
CAMBODIA
INDIA
INDIA
INDIA
Manuscripts, copperplate deeds,
& Gwalior inscriptions
INDIA
Sarada
WESTERN ARABS
EASTERN ARABS
EUROPE
(apices)
EUROPE
(cursive numerals)

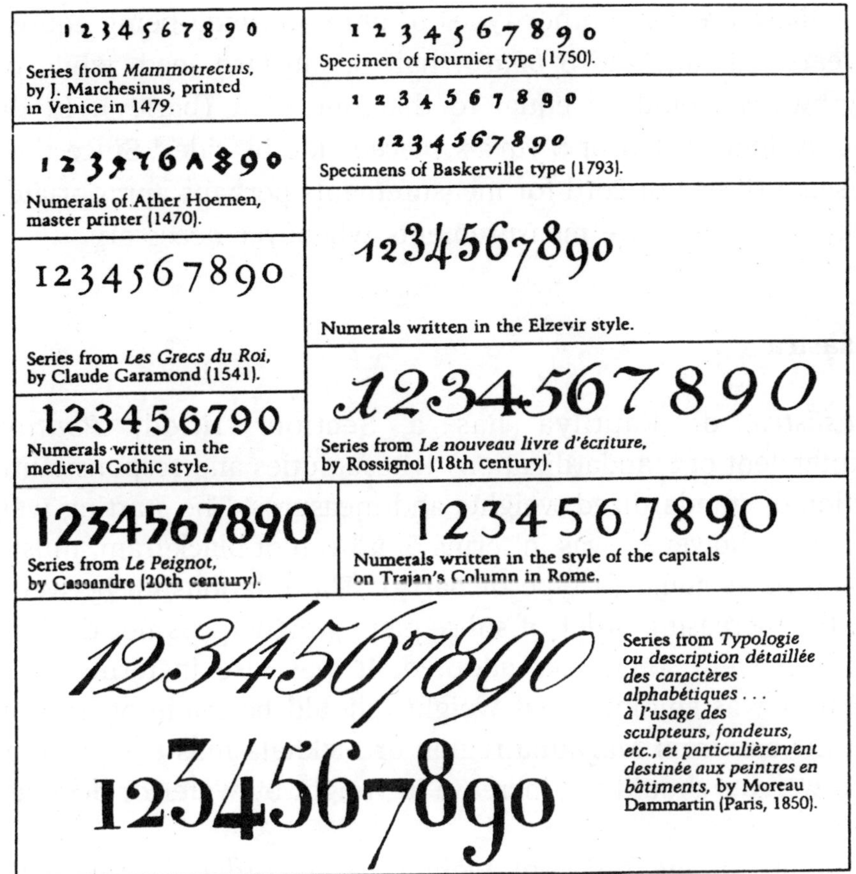

measurements for the construction of sacrificial altars. The *Baudhāyana śulbasūtra* enumerates the measurements as follows:[3]

'The measure of an *aṅgula* is 14 *aṇu-s* (one *aṇu* supposed to be one grain of *Panicum millicaceum*); according to others, (it is) 34 *tila-s* (*Sesamum indicum*) placed broad side on. One small *pāda* is 10 *aṅgula-s*; one *pradeśa*: 12 *aṅgulas*; one *pṛtha* and one *uttarayuga*: 13 *aṅgula-s each*; one (big) *pāda*: 15 *aṅgula-s*; one *īṣa measures 188 aṅgulas*; one *akṣa 104 aṅgulas*; one *yuga*: 86 *aṅgulas*; one *jānu*: 32 *aṅgula-s*; one *śamyā* and one *bāhu 36 aṅgulas* each; one *prakrama* equals 2 pādas (30 *aṅgula-s*); one *aratni*: 2 *pradeśa-s* (24 *aṅgulas*). But there are also instances of *pada, yuga, prakrama, aratni and śamyā* having different measures when these (words) are used as units of measrurment 5 *aratni-s* (120 *aṅgulas* make one *puruṣa*; one *vyāma* has also the same measures (5 *aratni-s*); and 4 *aratni-s* (96 *aṅgula-s*) one *vyāyāma*.

The *Āpastamba-śulba sūtra* has the same values of Baudhāyana for *pradeśa, īṣa, akṣa, yuga, aratni, puruṣa and vyāyāma*; likewise, the *Kātyāyana* and the *Mānava-śulba-sūtras*, but with the difference that these two use the term *vitasti* in the place of *pradeśa*. Kauṭilya's *Arthaśāstra* has also used *vitasti*. In the *Mānava śulba-sutra-s* there are some other types of units: 6 *tuṇḍa* being equivalent to one *bāla* of 3 years old calf; and 3 *bāla-s*, half of mustard seed, while two mustard seeds (lengthwise) would be equal to that one *yava* (barley). In this text one *aṅgula* is equivalent to that of 6 *yava-s* placed side by side.[4] Since the *Śulba-sūtra* generally used a thread or cord for measurements perhaps appropriate knots were tied in relation to the above measurements whenever necessary.

The Arthaśāstra

The *Arthaśāstra* of Kauṭilya has a Section[5] titled, *Poutavādhyakṣaḥ* (the Superintendent of Standardization) whose duties and responsibilities included the production of standardized weights and measures. The starting weight of such a standardisation, however, was in terms of a bean of blackgram, mustard seed, or what was known as *guñja* (a type of berry). The relationship between one small weight and the increasing order of subsequent weights was not decimal, although multiples of ten were sometimes adopted. It was also in terms of four and its multiples. But it was enjoined that weights should be made of iron or stone, the latter being the one from Magadha region or Mekhala hills (?) and the stipulation was that the weights should *not* increase in weight by water or decrease in weight by heat.

The relation among different weights as recorded in the *Arthaśāstra*, as follows:

Ten *māṣa* (blackgram bean) = one *māsaka* of gold = 5 guñja-berries
16 *māsaka-s* of gold = one *suvarṇa* or *karṣa*
4 *karṣa-s* = one *pala*

There was also another enumeration:
88 *mustard* (white) seeds = one *māsaka* of silver
16 *māsaka-s* = one *dharaṇa;* in respect of diamond, it was indicated that a *dharaṇa* of a diamond would be equivalent to the weight of 20 rice-grains. There were also weights of half—*māsaka*, 2, 4, 8 units as well as 10, 20, 30, 40 and even 100 *suvarṇa-s* as different denominations.

Balance: The *Arthaśāstra* has given details of the construction of a huge balance: 'He (The Superintendent of Standardisation) should cause the *Samavṛtta* (balance) to be made of metal (perhaps iron or brass) of thirty-five *palas* in weight and seventy two *aṅgula-s* (slightly less than an English inch) in length. Fixing a ball (of metal) five *pala-s* in weight (at one end), he should cause the level to be secured (on the beam). From that point onwards, he should cause markings to indicate one *karṣa* (each) increasingly up to the weight of one *pala*, then increased by a *pala* up to ten *pala-s,* then for 12, 15 and 20 *pala-s*. Thus, he should, cause markings (to be made) increased by ten, up to 100 *pala-s*. Even a much bigger balance was constructed. It was called *parimāṇī* to be made with double the amount of the metal used in the earlier one with 96 *aṅgula-s* in length. This had the markings beyond one hundred viz., 120, 150 and 200 *palas* for weighing. In Kauṭilya's time, one revenue measure comprised one hundred *palas* or ten *dharaṇa-s*. There was also another revenue measure, namely, a *droṇa* which was equivalent to two hundred *palas* of blackgram beans. But, for trading purposes, a *droṇa* would be 187 1/2 *pala-s,* and for making payments in kind, it would be 175 *palas'*. Strangely, the *Arthaśāstra* says that measurements for the palace or the royal household, a *droṇa* would be much less, i.e., 162 1/2 *pala-s.*

There were smaller measures too, known as *āḍhaka, prastha* and *kuḍuva,* each being 1/4 of the proceeding. A measure comprising 16 *dronas* was called one *khari* and 20 *droṇa-s* was also a cumulative measure under the name of one *kumbha, and* ten *kumbha-s* constituted one *vaha.* The measures, *kuḍuba* had also its 1/4 and 1/8 parts as smaller measures; there was also a measure known as *vāraka* specially for measuring clarified butter (*ghṛta*) equivalent to 84 *kuḍuba-s;* for oil, the equivalent was 64 *kuḍuba-s.*

It would thus appear that in Kauṭilya's time, there were both small and big units in a somewhat standardized manner, despite the basic small units being rather indeterminate in the sense they were in terms of beans, seeds or stone.

In Medicine

In medicine with the advent of the second urbanization and the emergent standardization of medicinal formulations atoms from about the sixth century B.C. and later, there was a new compulsion for fairly accurate weights and measures not only for the preparation of medicines but also for their administration.

In addition to their nomenclature as indicated in the *Arthaśāstra,* one finds in the two Āyurvedic classics the *Caraka* and the *Suśruta saṃhitā,* systematically related units of weight.[6] Caraka presents a system starting with what is known as *dhvaṃsī* as follows: (synonyms in brackets): (P.V. Sharma, pp. 87-97).

6 *dhvamsī-s*	=	1 *marīci*
6 *marīci-s*	=	1 *sarṣapa*
8 *sarṣapa-s*	=	1 *rakta-sarṣapa*
2 *rakta-sarṣapa-s*	=	1 *taṇḍula*
2 *taṇḍula-s*	=	1 *yava*
4 *yava-s*	=	1 *aṇḍikā*
4 *aṇḍikā-s*	=	1 *māṣaka* (*hema, dhānyaka*)
3 *maṣaka-s*	=	1 *śāṇa*
2 *śāṇa-s*	=	1 *drankṣaṇa* (*kola, badara*)

2 *draṅksaṇa-s*	=	1 *karṣa* (*suvarṇa, ākṣa, biḍālapadaka, picu, pāṇitala, kavalagraha*)
2 *karṣa*	=	1 *palārdha* (*śukti, astamika*)
2 *palārdha-s*	=	1 *pala* (*muṣṭi, prakuñca, caturthikā, bilva, ṣoḍaśika, āmra*)
2 *pala-s*	=	1 *prasṛta* (*aṣṭamāna*)
2 *prasṛta-s*	=	1 *kuḍava* (*caturguṇa, pala, añjali, maṇikā*)
4 *kuḍava-s*	=	1 *prastha*
4 *prastha-s*	=	1 *āḍhaka* (*patra, kamsa, prasthāṣṭaka*)
4 *āḍhaka-s*	=	1 *droṇa* (*armaṇa, nalvana, kalaśa, ghaṭa, unmāna*)
2 *droṇa-s*	=	1 *śurpa* (*kumbha*)
2 *śurpa-s*	=	1 *goṇi* (*khāri, bhāra*)
32 *śūrpa-s*	=	1 *vaha*
100 *pala-s*	=	1 *tulā*

These weights are prescribed or adopted in relation to the dry substances.

The *Suśruta saṃhitā,* on the other hand, has a different enumeration, in the following manner[7] for the dry substance, stating that these should be doubled and adopted in the case of liquid substances.

According to Suśruta, 'twelve *dhānya-māṣa-s* of medium size make one *suvarṇa-māṣaka;* these (i.e., *suvarṇa-māṣaka*) sixteen constitute one *suvarṇa;* or according to other scheme of measures, nineteen *niṣpāvas* (a kind of pulse, *Dolichos sinensis*) as medium size, makes one *dharaṇa;* two and half *dharaṇa-s* are one *karṣa;* by increase of four (*karṣa-s*) at every unit of measure, results (the weights, like) *pala, kuḍava, prastha, āḍhaka, droṇa.* Again one hundred *pala-s* make one *tulā;* twenty *tulās* make one *bhāra*'. These are the measures of weights for dry substances, and then become double in the case of liquid substances.

There are also other terms like *akṣa pāṇi-śukti* and *prakuñca.*[8] It would appear that some of these weights and measures might be equivalent to the modern reckonings[9] (according to P. Ray) as follows:

Suvarṇa-māṣaka	=	180 grains troy
Dhāraṇa	=	18 gm
Karṣa	=	about 23 gm
Pala	=	about 93 gm
Kuḍava (*kuḍuba*)	=	about 370 gm
Prastha	=	About 1.5 kg
Tulā	=	About 11.66 kg
Āḍhaka	=	About 6 kg
Droṇa	=	About 12 litres (in later practice *droṇa* is equal to 16 seers, i.e., weight of 15 litre of water approx.)

Rasaśāstra: The iatro (medicinal) chemical or the *Rasaśāstra* texts are noted for the adoption of appropriate weights and measures in their experiments for the preparation specially of metallic and mineral medicines. The *Rasaratnasamuccaya*, probably of the 14th cent. A.D., has given in sufficient detail,[10] the whole set of weights and measures along with their relations, starting with mustard seed (see below), six of which being equivalent to the weight of one barley seed. The heaviest unit mentioned in this text is *tulā* which is equal to one hundred *palas*, like the *Caraka saṃhitā*. According to Kauṭilya, on the other hand, the heaviest unit is one *bhāra* equivalent to 20 *tulā* weights.

'Six white mustard seeds make one *yava;* three *yavas* are equal to one *guñjā* (*Abrus precatorius*) which is also called *raktikā*. Ten *raktikā-s* make one *māṣaka*, also known as *hema* and *dhāmaka* (the other reading is *dhānyaka*). Four *māṣas* compose one *śāṇa*, also *dhāraṇa* and *taṅka*. Two *śāṇas* are one *kṣudra* (*morata* and *dramkṣaṇa* are the different names of this measurement). Two *kola-s* make one *karṣa*, also called *pāṇimānika, akṣa, picu, pāṇitala, pāṇi, tiṇḍuka, bidāalapadaka, ṣoḍaśika, karmadhya, hamsapāda, suvarṇa, kavalagraha,* and *udumbara*; (these are all the synonyms of *karṣa*). Two *karṣa-s* are equal to *ardha-pala* (half *pala*), called also *śukti* and *aṣṭamikā*. Two *śukti-s* are one *pala*, known also as *muṣṭimātra, caturthikā, parakuñca, ṣoḍaśī and bilva*. Two *pala-s* make one *prasṛti*, also called *prasṛta. Two prasṛta-s* compose one *añjali,* known also as *kuḍava, ardhaśarāvaka* and *aṣṭamāna*. Two *kuḍava-s* make one *māṇikā.,* which is considered as being equal to one *śarāva*, or eight *palas* by the experts (in weights and measures). Two *śarāvas* are one *prastha;* four *prastha-s* make one *āḍhakam,* known by the terms, like *bhājana, kaṃsa-pātra,* and equal to 64 *pala-s*. One *droṇa* is made of four *āḍhaka-s*. The synonyms indicating one *droṇa* are *kalaśa, nalvaṇa, armmaṇa, unmāna, ghaṭa and rāśi*. Two *droṇa-s* are equal to one *śūrpa*, or one *kumbha* or 64 *śarāvaka*. Two *śūrpa-s* make one *droṇi,* also called *vāhi* and *goṇi*. The practitioners, in minute details, count four *droṇi-s* as one *khārī,* which is also equal to four thousand *palikā-s* (*pala-s*) increased by ninety-six. Two thousand *pala-s* are one *bhāra*. In all units of measures, *tulā* is equal to one hundred *pala-s*'.

The *Śārṅgadhara saṃhitā*, a medieval medical text, starts with atoms, saying that thirty of them constitute one *trasareṇu* or *truṭi*. As noted earlier, *trasareṇu* in the Nyāya-Vaiśeṣika parlance is a triad (*tryaṇuka*) made of three dyads or six atoms, the minimum visible entity like a mote in a sun beam. But Śārṅgadhara thought of 30 atoms, constituting minute particle that is visible in such a beam. His enumeration of weights and their relationships are as follows:[11]

Thirty *paramāṇu-s* constitute what is called *trasareṇu,* also known as *dhvamsī*. (Sun rays coming through the passage of a lattice making visible some minute particles of dust). One thirtieth part of this dust is called *paramāṇu. Dhvamsī* is visible in sun rays coming through the lattice. Six *dhvamsī-s* constitute one *marīcī* and six such *marīcīs* make one *rājikā* (white mustard seed). Eight *sarṣapa-s* (mustard seeds) make one *yava* and four *yava-s* form one *guñjā*. Six *raktikā-s* make one *māṣaka*, the synonyms of which are *hema* and *dhānyaka*. Four *māṣaka-s* compose one *śāṇa*, also called *dharaṇa* and *taṅka*. Two *śāṇas* are one *kola; kṣudra*, *morata* and *draṅkṣaṇa* are the different names (of this measurement). Two *kolas* make one *karṣa*, also called *pāṇimānika*, *akṣa*, *picu*, *pāṇitala*, *pāṇi*, *tiṇḍuka*, *biḍāla-pādaka ṣoḍaśikā*, *karamadhya*, *haṃsapāda*, *suvarṇa*, *kavalagraha* and *udumbara*, (these form different synonyms of *karṣa*). Two *karṣa-s* are equal to half *pala*, called also *śukti and aṣṭamika*. Two *śukti-s* are one *pala*, known also as *muṣṭi-mātra*, *caturthikā*, *prakuñca*, *ṣoḍaśi*, and *bilva*. Two *pala-s* make one *prasṛti*, also called *prasṛta*. Two *prasṛtas* compose one *añjali*, also known as *kuḍava*, *ardha-śarāvaka* and *aṣṭamāna*. Two *kuḍavas* make one *mānikā* which is considered equal to one *śarāva* and eight *palas* by the experts (in weights and measures). Two *śarāvas* are one *prastha*; four *prastha-s* make one *āḍhaka* known by other synonymous terms like *bhājana*, *kaṃsapātra* and equal to 64 *pala-s*. One *droṇa* is made of four *āḍhaka-s*; other synonymous terms are *kalaśa*, *nalvaṇa*, *armmaṇa*, *unmāna*, *ghaṭa* and *rāśi*. Two *droṇas* are equal to one *śūrpa*, one *kumbha* or 64 *śarāvaka*. Two *śūrpas* make one *droṇī*, also called *vāhī and goṇī*. The practitioners in minute details reckon four *droṇīs* as one *khārī*, also equal to four thousand *palikā-s* (or *pala-s*) increased by ninety-six. Two thousand *pala-s* make one *bhāra*. In all units of measurement, *tulā* is equal to one hundred *pala-s*".

The *Rasaratnasamuccaya* clarifies[12] that two *śukti-s* make one *pala* and, according to others, three of the former are equivalent to one of the latter. It also gives alternative names for *pala-muṣṭi*, *prakuñca* and *bilva*. The *pala-s* are stated to be equal to one *prasṛta*, the twice of which constitutes one *kuḍava*, also known as *añjali*. Another weight, *maṇikā* is also mentioned being equal to two *kuḍavas*, double the weight of which becomes equal to one *prastha*. Yet another weight is thought of and its nomenclature is *śubha*[13] being equivalent to two *prasthas*. There is also weight named *ghaṭaka*, equal to four *āḍhaka-s* or *pātraka-s*, and its synonyms are *unmāna*, *lavaṇa* and *kumbhaka*. It may be noted that *ghaṭaka or kumbhaka* means a measuring pot. The weight *niṣka* is defined to be equal to the weight of four *māṣa-s* (blackgram beans), four *niṣka-s* constituting one *tala*.[14] The texts also *provides* alternate names for *karṣa* – *udumbara*, *pāṇitala*, *suvarṇa*, *kavaḍa-graha*, *akṣa*, *viḍālapadaka* and *śukti*.

The *Rasārṇava*, another iatro-chemical text, has almost a different approach to the weights and measures.[15] It equates 6 *truṭi-s* to one *likṣā*; six of the latter being equal in weight to one *rajaḥ*. The weight of six *rajaḥ-s* would be the same as that of one mustard seed, which is called *siddhārtha*. One *yava* (barley grain) is stated to be composed of six *siddhārtha-s*, while six *yava-s* make the weight of one *guñjā* (about 1/2 g. in modern terms). Six *guñjā-s* make one *māsaka* and twelve *māsaka-s* constitute one *tola*, while eight *tola-s* make one *pala*.

The *Śārṅgadhara saṁhitā*,[16] has another enumeration starting with 12 white mustard seeds being equivalent in weight to one *yava*, the weight of two of which would be equal to that of what it calls one *valla*. Eight (or even seven) *guñjās* make one *māṣa*, while six of them would make one *gadyāna*, and ten of them, one *karṣa*. It also speaks of *śāna* being equivalent to the weight of four *māṣa-s* and four *karṣa-s* make one *pala* equivalent to ten *śāna-s*, according to some scholars.

It may be noted that *truṭi, likṣā, rajaḥ, sarṣapa and yava* are indeed extremely small weights and their weights from the point of view of modern metrology are impossible of determination. However, according to the History of Indian Pharmacy,[17] a *truṭi* or *trasareṇu* could be about 1/16 mg, and *likṣā* about 1/162 of a *guñjā*. For smaller weights, *guñjā* seed(s) seem to have been preferred possibly because of their practically uniform size and therefore weight.

Architectural Measures

Temple architecture in India, apart from its artistic and religious dimensions is noted not only for its geometrical excellence but also certain types of measurements that govern the former. According to the *Samārāṅgaṇa sūtradhāra* and the *Īśānaśiva gurudeva paddhati,* there are three principal styles or types of temple architecture namely, *Nāgara, Drāviḍa, and Vesara* (in the latter text) and *Vārāṭa* in the former text, differentiated probably by the precise plans of the temples as well as by regions. The *Nāgara* temples are found mostly in the northern region between the Himālayas and the Vindhyas, the *Vesara* ones, between the Vindhyas and the river Kṛṣṇā while the Drāviḍa types, in the south of the river *Kṛṣṇā*. There are also other styles like *Sārvadeśika* (for all places), and *Kaliṅga* (of Orissa). Nevertheless, it should be noted that these are not strict regionally characterized styles since some of them are found in the other regions too.

The plans of temples and the measurements have influenced each other in the construction of temples, and both are governed by the *Śāstric* injunctions. A close examination of the existing temples reveals that they are either circular or square on plan. There are, however, certain temples built on a rectangular and elliptical plans which are *mutatis-mutandis* the modifications of a square and circle respectively. The other variations of a square plan are eight-angled, sixteen-angled (polygonal) and the like. There are also some temples of apsidal plan. Suffice it, for our purpose, to have some insight into the types of measurements that were adopted in the process of construction, specially the south Indian temples which are associated with what is called *Vimāna*. This name itself signifies a structure that is made up of a variety of measures. There is also a term *prāsāda* broadly divided into *alpaprāsāda* and *mahāprāsāda*. The mahā-*prāsādas* include four varieties, namely, *Jāti, Chandas, Vikalpa* and *Ābhāsa,* each being different from the other in its measurement and the number of storeys. The worshipper (or builder of a temple; *Yajamāna*) approaches the *guru* who arranges to get a temple of appropriate measurements built and which is worthy of the deity to be installed in it. 'There is a group of formulae which governs the measurement of any architectural worth. These are *āya, vyaya, yoni, tithi, vāra* etc. Each formula which is meticulously worked out is a *śāstraic* technicality and is known after the division in each case or group. Regarding the multiplying number nothing is known. The invention of the *Āyādivarga* is an architectural device, the intention of which is to find out a proper orientation to the structure with a proper dimension. Among the architectural conventions of India, *Āyādivarga* occupies an important place. Every measurement, before it is accepted, is required to satisfy these six fundamental requisites based on the auspiciousness, property and orientation'.[18]

The height of a temple from the lowest part of its basement to the topmost point (*stūpikā*) is of four kinds. If b is the breadth of the basement, the height could be 1 1/3 b; 1 1/2 b; and 2b. According to *Mānasāra*, there could be an additional one, namely, the height being the same as the breadth of the basement itself. The *Mayamata* has, however, described fourteen types of basements, while the *Kāśyapa* has dealt with twenty two. But the *Mānasāra* has descriptions of as many as 64 types–all in terms of the related measurements.

The four types of *mahāprāsāda-s* have their own measurements. Of them *Jāti-prāsāda* is stated to have 3 to 12 *tāla-s* encompassing a measure ranging from 11 to 70 cubits (*hasta-s*) with 30 measures being odd and the other 30 even. The *Chandas-prāsādas* have 4 to 12 *tāla-s*, each class of the *tālas* possessing 6 different types of measures—3 odd, and 3 even. The odd measures begin with thirteen cubits and end with 65, while the even ones begin with 14 and end with 66. Likewise, the *Vikalpa,* and the *Ābhāsa-prāsāda-s* have their own measurements for different types.

It is significant to note that Indian temples are not similar to those in the West since the concept of a large prayer hall or congregational structure that characterizes the Western ones, is nearly absent specially in the construction of Hindu temples. The whole temple architecture is worship oriented, all eyes concentrated on the consecrated deity in the small sanctum sanctorum. However, the adjoining proportionate areas provide space for the performance of dance and music as temple art forms.

The size of the temple depends upon the size of the deity (*mūla-bhera*) mostly carved out in stone of suitable variety, but sometimes of bronze. While the Jainas and the Bauddhas prefer to use brass for the icons, Hindus prefer bronze for their icons with appropriate iconography and iconometry.

Iconology[19] was an accomplished, aesthetic craft engendered by two methodologies: (i) the exactness of the proportion of the limbs (both of the male and female body) in relation to the eight-fold vertical anatomical units; and (ii) delineation of the idealized stature. In the sculpting tradition measuration starts with *aṅgula* (less than the British inch) which is the 24th part of a *hasta*, measured from the tip of the middle finger to the end of the elbow point. The word *aṅgula* is related to the digit of the middle finger of a person. There are three types of *aṅgula*; (i) *mānāṅgula*: equivalent to the total length of 8 standard barley grains placed side by side; (ii) *mātrāṅgula*: reckoned in terms of the length of the middle digit of the middle finger of the right hand of the chosen preceptor or *ācārya*; and (ii) *dehalabdhāṅgula* as calculated by taking the total height of the intended icon divided into ten parts, and further dividing each part into twelve units. In general, the word *tāla* is used to denote 24 *aṅgula-s* and the whole iconometry revolves round the *tālamāna* or measurements in relation to *tāla*.

The *Manusmṛti*[20] has given the following weights and their relationships:

4 *trasareṇu-s*	= 1 *likṣā*
3 *likṣā-s*	= 1 *rājasarṣapa*
3 *rājasarṣapa-s*	= 1 *gaurasarṣapa*
6 *gaurasarṣapa-s*	= 1 *madhyayava*
3 *madhyayava-s*	= 1 *kṛṣṇala*
5 *kṛṣṇala-s*	= 1 *māṣa*
16 *māṣa-s*	= 1 *suvarṇa* or *karṣa*
4 *Suvarṇa-s*	= 1 *pala*
10 *pala-s*	= 1 *dharaṇa*
2 *kṛṣṇla-s*	= 1 *raupyamāṣaka*
16 *raupyamāṣaka-s*	= 1 *raupyadharaṇa*
10 *raupyadharaṇa-s*	= 1 *raupyaśatamāna*

Trasareṇu: *Jālāntaragate bhanau yat sūkṣmaṃ dṛśyate rajaḥ|*
Prathamaṃ yat pramāṇam tat trasareṇum pracakṣate ||

REFERENCES

1. Sarton, G, *An Appreciation of Ancient and Medieval Science during the Renaissance (1450-1600)*, Univ. of Pennsylvania, Pennsylvania, 1955, p.151.

2. *Taitt.sam.* 4.4.11.4; 7.2.20.1

3. बौधायनशुल्बसूत्र १-३

अथाङ्गुलप्रमाणम् । (१-३), चतुर्दशाणवः (१-४)

चतुस्त्रिंशत्तिलाः पृथुसंश्लिष्टा इत्यपरम् (१-५), दशाङ्गुलं क्षुद्रपदम् (१-६), द्वादशप्रदेशाः (१-७), पृथिवुत्तरयुगे

त्रयोदशिके (१-८) पदां पञ्चदश (१-९), अष्टाशीति शतमीशा (१-१०), चतुःशतमक्षः (१-११),

षडशीतियुगम् (१-१२), द्वात्रिंशज्जानुः (१-१३), षट्त्रिंशच्छम्याबाहू (१-१४), द्विपदः प्रक्रमः (१-१५), द्वौ

प्रादेशावरत्निः (१-१६), अथाप्युदाहरन्ति (१-१७), पदे युगे, प्रक्रमेऽरत्नाविपयति शाम्यायाम् च मानार्थेषु यथाकामीनि (१-१८) पञ्चरत्निः पुरुषो (१-१९), व्यामश्च (१-२०), चतुररत्निर्व्यायामः (१-२०)

4. Sen, S. N.: *The Śulba sūtras*, Indian National Science Academy, New Delhi, 1983. pp. 147-148.

   Kauṭilya's *Arthaśāstra*: 2.19, section 37

5. पौतवाध्यक्षः पौतवकर्मान्तान् कारयेत् ।

   धान्यमाषा दश सुवर्णमाषकः पञ्च वा गुञ्जाः ।

   ते षोडश सुवर्णः कर्षो वा ।

   चतुष्कर्ष पलम् ।

   अष्टाशीतिगौरसर्षपा रूप्यमाषकः ।

   ते षोडश धरणम् शैम्ब्यानि वा विंशतिः ।

   विंशतितण्डुलं वज्रधरणम् ।

   अर्धमाषकः माषकः द्वौ चत्वारः अष्टौ माषकाः सुवर्णौ द्वौ चत्वारः अष्टौ सुवर्णाः

   दश विंशतिः त्रिंशत् चत्वारिंशत् शतमिति ।

   तेन धरणानि व्याख्यातानि ।

   प्रतिमानान्ययोमयानि मागधमेकलशैलमयानि यानि वा नोदकप्रदेहाभ्यां वृद्धिं गच्छेयुरुष्णेन वा ह्रासम् ।

   षडङ्गुलादूर्ध्वमष्टाङ्गुलोत्तरा दश तुलाः कारयेत् लोहपलात् ऊर्ध्वमेकपलोत्तराः यन्त्रमुभयतः शिक्यं वा ।

   पञ्चत्रिंशत्पललोहां द्विसप्तत्यङ्गुलायामां समवृत्तां कारयेत् ।

   तस्याः पञ्चपलिकं मण्डलं बध्वा समकरणं कारयेत् ।

   ततः कर्षोत्तरं पलः पलोत्तरं दशपलं द्वादशपञ्चदश

   विंशतिरिति पदानि कारयेत् ।

   तत आशताद्दशोत्तरं कारयेत् ।

   अक्षेषु नद्धीपिनद्धं कारयेत् ।

   द्विगुणलोहां तुलामतः षण्णवत्यङ्गुलायामां परिमाणीं कारयेत् ।

   तस्याः शतपदादूर्ध्वं विंशतिः पञ्चाशत् शतमिति पदानि कारयेत् ।

   विंशतितौलिको भारः ।

   दशधरणिकं पलम् ।

   तत्पलशतमायमानी ।

   पञ्चपलावरा व्यावहारिकी भाजन्यन्तःपुरभाजनी च ।

   तासामर्धधरणावरं पलम्, द्विपलावरमुत्तरलोहम् ।

   षडङ्गुलावराश्चायामाः ।

   पूर्व्योः पञ्चपलिकः प्रयामो मांसलोहलवणमणिवर्जम् ।

   काष्ठतुला अष्टहस्ता पदवती प्रतिमानवती मयूरपदाधिष्ठिता ।

काष्ठपञ्चविंशतिपलं तण्डुलप्रस्थसाधनम् ।

एष प्रदेशो बहुलपयोः ।

इति तुलाप्रतिमानं व्याख्यातम् ।

अथ धान्यमाषद्विपलशतं द्रोणमायमानम्, सप्ताशीति-
पलशतमर्धपलं च व्यावहारिकं पञ्च सप्ततिपलशतं
भाजनीयं द्विषष्टिपलशतमर्धपलं चान्तःपुरभाजनीयम् ।

तेषामाढकप्रस्थकुडुबाश्चतुर्भागावराः ।

षोडशद्रोणी च खारी ।

विंशतिद्रोणिकः कुम्भः ।

कुम्भैर्दशभिर्वहः ।

शुष्कसारदारुमयं समं चतुर्भागशिखं मानं

कारगेदन्तःशिखं वा ।

रसस्य तु सुरायाः पुष्पफलयोस्तुषाङ्गाराणां
सुधायाश्च शिखामानं द्विगुणोत्तरा वृद्धिः ।

सपादपणो द्रोणमूल्यं आढकस्य पादोनः षण्माषकाः

प्रस्थस्य माषकः कुडुबस्य ।

द्विगुणं रसादीनां मानमूल्यम् ।

विंशतिपणाः प्रतिमानस्य ।

तुलामूल्यं त्रिभागः चतुर्मासिकं प्रतिवेधनिकं कारयेत् ।

अप्रतिविद्धस्यात्ययः सपादः सप्तविंशतिपणः ।

प्रतिवेधनिकं काकणीकमहरहः पौतवाध्यक्षाय दद्युः ।

द्वात्रिंशद्भागस्तत्सव्याजी सर्पिषः चतुःषष्टिभागस्तैलस्य ।

पञ्चाशद्भागो मानस्त्रावो द्रवाणाम् ।

कुडुबार्धचतुरष्टभागानि मानानि कारयेत् ।

कुडुबाश्चतुरशीतिर्वारकः सर्पिषो मतः ।

चतुःषष्टिस्तु तैलस्य पादश्च घटिकानयोः ॥ *Arthaśāstra*, 2.19. Section 37

6. षड्ध्वंश्यस्तु मरीचिः स्यात् षण्मरीच्यस्तु सर्षपः ।

अष्टौ ते सर्षपा रक्तास्तण्डुलश्चापि तद्द्वयम् ॥

धान्यमाषो भवेत्ताभ्यां धान्यमाषद्वयं यवः ।

अण्डिका ते तु चत्वारस्ताश्चतस्रस्तु माषकः ॥

हेम च धान्यकाश्रोत्ता भवेच्छाणस्तु ते त्रयः ।

शाणौ द्वौ द्रङ्क्षणं विद्यात् कोलं बदरमेव च ॥

विद्याद् द्रौ द्रंक्षणौ कर्षं सुवर्णं चाक्षमेव ।

बिडालपदकं चैव पिचुं पाणितलं तथा ॥

तिन्दुकं च विजानीयात् कवलग्रहमेव च ।

द्वे सुवर्णे पलार्धं स्याच्छुक्तिरष्टमिका तथा ॥

द्वे पलार्धे पलं मुष्टि: प्रकुञ्चोऽथ चतुर्थिका ।

बिल्वं षोडशिका चाम्रं द्वे फले प्रसृतं विदु: ॥

अष्टमानं तु विज्ञेयं प्रसृतौ द्वौ तु मानिका ।

चतुर्गुणफलं विद्यादञ्जलिं कुडवं तथा ॥

चत्वार: कुडवा: प्रस्थश्चतुप्रस्थमथाढकम् ।

पात्रं तदेव विज्ञेयं कंस: प्रस्थाष्टकं तथा ॥

कंसश्चतुर्गुणो द्रोणश्चार्मणं नल्वणं च तत् ।

स एव कलश: ख्यातो घटमुन्मानमेव च ।

द्रोणस्तु द्विगुण: शूर्पा विज्ञेय: कुम्भ एव च ।

गोणी शूर्पद्वयं विद्यात् खारीं भारं तथैव च ॥

द्वात्रिंशतं विजानीयाद्भारं शूर्पाणि बुद्धिमान् ।

तुलां शतपलं विद्यात् परिमाणविशारद: ॥

Ca.saṃ, Kalpa, XII. 87-97   P. V. Sharma, Chowkhamba Oreintalia, Varanasi, 1987.

7. पलकुडवादिनामतो मानं तु व्याख्यास्याम: । तत्र द्वादश

धान्यमाषा मध्यमा: सुवर्णमाषक: ते षोडश सुवर्णम् ।

अथवा मध्यमनिष्पावा एकोनविंशतिर्धरणम् ।

तान्यर्धतृतीयानि कर्ष: ततश्चोर्ध्वं चतुर्गुणमभिवर्धयन्त:

पलकुडवप्रस्थाढकद्रोणा इत्यभिनिष्पाद्यन्ते, तुला

पुन: पलशतम्, ता: पुनर्विंशतिभिर्भार:, शुष्काणाम्

इदं मानम् ।

8. आर्द्रद्रव्याणां च द्विगुणमिति ॥

ततो यथायोगं शुक्तिं प्रकुञ्चं वोपयुञ्जीत ।

पाणिशुक्तिमात्रं क्षौद्रेण प्रजिसंगृह्योपयुञ्जीत ।

Suś.saṃ. Ci 31.11 and 10.12; 10.15

Thereafter, as required one *śukti* or one *prakuñca* weight (of the prescribed substance) is to be added.

9. *Suśruta saṃhitā : A Scientific Synopsis* : P.Ray, H.N. Gupta and Mira Roy, Indian National Science Academy, New Delhi, 1984, pp. 445-447.

10. षड्भिस्तु सर्षपैर्गौरैर्यवस्त्वेक: प्रकीर्तित: ।

त्रिभिर्यवैश्च गुञ्जैका मता सैवेह रक्तिका ॥

दशभिस्तु रक्तिकाभिः स्यान्माषको हेमधामकैः ॥

माषैश्चतुर्भिः शाणः स्याद्धरणं तन्निगद्यते ॥

टङ्कः स एव कथितस्तद्द्वयं कोल उच्यते ।

क्षुद्रमोरटकश्चापि द्रंक्षणं स निगद्यते ॥

कोलद्वयं च कर्षः स्यात् स प्रोक्तः पाणिमानिकः ।

अक्षः पिचुः पाणितलं किञ्चित्पाणिश्च तिन्दुकम् ॥

बिडालपदकं चैव तथा षोडशिका मता ।

करमध्यं हंसपादं सुवर्णं कवलग्रहम् ॥

उडुम्बरश्च पयायैः कर्ष एव निगद्यते ।

स्यात्कर्षाभ्यामर्धपलं शुक्तिरष्टमिका तथा ॥

शुक्तिभ्यां च पलं ज्ञेयं मुष्टिमात्रैश्चतुर्थिकाः ।

प्रकुञ्चः षोडशी बिल्वं पलमेवात्र कीर्त्यते ॥

पलाभ्यां प्रसृतिर्ज्ञेया प्रसृतं च निगद्यते ।

प्रसृतिभ्यामञ्जलिः स्यात्कुडवार्धशरावकः ॥

अष्टमानं च स ज्ञेयः कुडवाभ्यां च मानिका ।

शरावोऽष्टपलं तद्वत् ज्ञेयमत्र विचक्षणैः ॥

शरावाभ्यां भवेत्रस्थश्चतुः प्रस्थैस्तथाढकम् ।

भाजनं कंसपात्रं च चतुःषष्टिपलं च तत् ॥

चतुर्भिराढकैर्द्रोणः कलशो नल्वणोऽर्म्मणः ।

उन्मानश्च घटो राशिर्द्रोणपर्यायसंज्ञकाः ॥

द्रोणाभ्यां शूर्पकुम्भौ च चतुःषष्टिशरावकाः ।

शूर्पाभ्यां च भवेद् द्रोणी बृहद्द्रोणी च सा स्मृता ॥

द्रोणीचतुष्टयं खारी कथिता सूक्ष्मबुद्धिभिः ।

चतुःसहस्रपलिका षण्णवत्यधिका च सा ॥

पलानां द्विसहस्रं च भार एकः प्रकीर्तिता ।

तुला पलशतं ज्ञेयं सर्वैत्रैव विनिश्चयः ॥

(*Rasaratnasamuccaya*, Pariśiṣṭa, Māna-Paribhāṣā, verses. 2-15)

11. त्रसरेणुबुधैः प्रोक्तस्त्रिंशता परमाणुभिः ।

त्रसरेणुस्तु पर्यायनाम्ना ध्वंसी (वंशी) निगद्यते ॥

(जालान्तरगते भानौ यत् सूक्ष्मं दृश्यते रजः ।

तस्य त्रिंशत्तमो भागः परमाणुः स कथ्यते ॥

जालान्तरगतैः सूर्यकरैर्ध्वंसी विलोक्यते ।)

षड्ध्वंसीभिर्मरीचिः स्यात् ताभिः षड्भिस्तु राजिका ।

तिसृभी राजिकाभिश्र सर्षपः प्रोच्यते बुधैः ॥

यवोऽष्टसर्षपैः प्रोक्तो गुञ्जा स्यातचतुष्टयम् ।

षड्भिस्तु रक्तिकाभिः स्यान्माषको हेमधान्यकौ ॥

माषैश्चतुर्भिः शाणः स्यात् धरणः स निगद्यते ।

टङ्कः स एव कथितः तद्द्वयं कोल उच्यते ॥

क्षुद्रमोरटकश्चैव द्रंक्षणं तन्निगद्यते ।

कोलद्वयं च कर्षः स्यात् स प्रोक्तः पाणिमानिका ॥

अक्षः पिचुः पाणितलं किञ्चिद्पाणिश्च तिन्दुकम् ।

विडालपदकं चैव तथा षोडशिका मता ॥

करमध्यो हंसपदं सुवर्णं कवलग्रहः ।

उडुम्बरं च पयायैः कर्ष एव निगद्यते ॥

स्यात् कर्षाभ्यामर्धपलं शुक्तिरष्टमिका तथा ।

शुक्तिभ्यां च पलं ज्ञेयं मुष्टिराम्रं चतुर्थिका ॥

प्रकुश्च षोडशी बिल्वं पलमेवात्र कीर्त्यते ।

पलाभ्यां प्रसृतिर्ज्ञेया प्रसृतं च निगद्यते ॥

प्रसृतिभ्यामञ्जलिः स्यात् कुडवोऽर्धशरावकः ।

अष्टमानं च स ज्ञेयः कुडवाभ्यां च मानिका ॥

शरावोऽष्टपलं तद्वत् ज्ञेयमत्र विचक्षणैः ।

शरावाभ्यां भवेत् प्रस्थश्चतुः प्रस्थैस्तथाढकम् ॥

भाजनं कंसपात्रं च चतुः षष्टिपलं च तत् ।

चतुर्भिराढकैर्द्रोणः कलशो नल्वणोऽर्मणः ॥

उन्मानं च घटो राशिर्द्रोणपर्यायसंज्ञकाः ।

द्रोणाभ्यां शूर्पकुम्भौ च चतुः षष्टिशरावकः ॥

शूर्पभ्यां च भवेद्द्रोणी वाही गोणी च सा स्मृता ।

द्रोणीचतुष्टयं खारी कथिता सूक्ष्मबुद्धिभिः ॥

चतुःसहस्रपलिका षण्णवत्यधिका च सा ।

पलानां द्विसहस्रं च भार एकः प्रकीर्तितः ॥

तुलापलशतं ज्ञेया सर्वैरेवैष निश्चयः ॥

Śār.saṃ. Pūrvakhaṇḍa i.14.28

12. शुक्तिद्वयं पलं केचिदन्ये शुक्तित्रयं विदुः ।

तदेव कथितं मुष्टिः प्रकुश्चौ बिल्वमित्यपि ॥

पलद्वयं तु प्रसृतं तद्द्वयं कुडवोऽञ्जलिः ।

कुडवो माणिका तौ स्यात् प्रस्थो द्वे मणिके स्मृतः ॥ *Rasaratnasamuccaya*, XI, 6-7

13. op.cit. 8-9

14. स्यादुञ्जात्रितयं वल्लो द्वौ वल्लौ माष उच्यते ।

द्वौ माषौ धरणं ते द्वे शाणनिष्ककलाः स्मृताः ॥

निष्कद्वयं तु वढकः स च कोल इतीरितः ।

स्यात् कोलद्वितयं तोलः कर्षो निष्कचतुष्टयम् ॥

उदुम्बरः पाणितलं सुवर्णं कवडग्रहः ।

अक्षं बिडालपदकः शुक्तिः पाणितलद्वयम् ॥

op.cit., XI, 3-5

15. षट्त्रुत्यश्रैकलिक्षा स्यात् षड्लिक्षा यूक एव च ।

षड्यूकास्तु रजः संज्ञाः कथितास्तव सुव्रते ॥

षड्रजः सर्षपः साक्षात् सिद्धार्थः स च कीर्तितः ।

षट् सिद्धार्थाश्च देवेशि यवस्त्वेकः प्रकीर्तितः ॥

षड्यवश्चैकगुञ्जा स्यात् षड्गुञ्जाश्चैकमाषकः ।

माषा द्वादश तोलः स्यात् अष्टौ तोलाः पलं भवेत् ॥

Rasārṇava 10.32

16. यवो द्वादशभिर्गौरसर्षपैः प्रोच्यते बुधैः ।

यवद्वयेन गुञ्जा स्यात् त्रिगुञ्जो वल्ल उच्यते ॥

माषो गुञ्जाभिरष्टाभिः सप्तभिर्वा भवेत् क्वचित् ।

स्याच्चतुर्माषकैः शाणः स निष्कटङ्क एव च ॥

गद्याणो माषकैः षड्भिः कर्षः स्यादशमाषकः ।

चतुःकर्षैः पलं प्रोक्तं दशशाणमितं बुधैः ॥

चतुःपलैश्च कुडवः प्रस्थाद्यः पूर्ववन्मता ॥

Śār.Sam. Pūrvakhaṇḍa, I, 36-38

17. *History of Indian Pharmacy*, p. 165.

18. Srinivasan, P.: *Indian Temple, Art and Architecture*, Mysore, 1982, pp. 33 ff.

19. Soundararajan K. V.: 'Copper Bronze Technology in India', *Chemistry and Chemical Techniques* (Ed). B. V. Subbarayappa, Centre for Studies in Civilizations, New Delhi, 1999, pp. 54-105.

20. *Manusmṛti* 8.132-138.

CHAPTER 10

Modern Perspective on the Physical World

B.V. Sreekantan

National Institute of Advanced Studies, Bangalore 560 012

Einstein: *"The most incomprehensible thing is that
the universe is comprehensible"*

COMPREHENSIBILITY (or the lack of it) is the power of human mind which has its own limitations. However science and technology have made it possible to expand the horizon of the knowable to a very large extent. But as John Wheeler has said, "as the island of our knowledge grows so does the shore of our ignorance". Thus it has happened that we do know a great deal about the physical world, but there is certainly very much more we do not know.

Let us first understand where we are in the scheme of the Universe. Each one of us is one among about six billion people on the earth. The earth itself is one among nine planets circling round the star called the Sun. The Sun is one among a hundred billion stars in the galaxy called the Milky Way and there are two hundred billion galaxies in the Universe.

The most fantastic achievement of modern science, developed over the past four hundred years, is to establish that the entire universe is the play of just three entities—matter, radiation and force. But these three by themselves are complex entities which we have to understand in detail before being able to form a modern perspective on the physical world.

Matter and its Ramifications

The first thing that we recognize about matter around us is that it exists in three states—solid, liquid and gas and some of the substances like water exist in all three states depending on the environmental temperature. The chemists have been able to establish that the matter around us and as we shall see later, all the matter in the entire universe, is ultimately made out of ninety-two elements—hydrogen to uranium. Each element is reducible to its characteristic molecules and it is the combination of the different elements at the molecular level that leads to the formation of different substances. The molecule of each element in turn is made of atoms of that substance, which is the ultimate level up to which the identity of the element is retained. Each atom has a nucleus which is positively charged and is surrounded by a shell of electrons, which carry negative charge with the result that atom as a whole is always electrically neutral. The nucleus which is at least a thousand times smaller in radius compared to the atom, carries practically all the mass of the atom. The nucleus itself is composed of two types of fundamental particles called the Protons and Neutrons. They both have roughly the same mass, about 1800 times the mass of the electron. While the proton is positively charged the neutron is electrically neutral. The positive charge of the proton is identical in magnitude to the negative charge of the electron. Thus to make the atom neutral, the number of electrons in the atom has to be equal to the number of protons in the nucleus which is so. This number designated 'Z' is called the atomic charge number and is the same as the atomic number is in the Mendeleev Periodic Table of elements. The total number of protons and neutrons in the nucleus determines its atomic weight called the mass number and designated as A. If we denote the number of neutrons by n, then among the light elements n equals Z. But as we go to heavier elements the number of neutrons can be far in excess of the number of protons. Those that have the same nuclear charge but different number of neutrons are called isotopes, and those that have the same mass number but different nuclear charges are called isobars. While originally one started with only 92 elements found in nature, several transuranic elements have been produced at accelerators and have also been recognized in stellar explosions. These are extremely unstable. As of now there are about 300 stable and 1000 unstable (radioactive) isotopes. Stable isobars occur mostly in pairs. Fifty-nine isobaric pairs have been discovered and there are 5 isobaric triads.

Even though one cannot define an exact radius for the nucleus, the order of magnitude of this radius which has a weak dependence on the Atomic Number A is given by $R = R_0 A^{1/3}$ where $R_0 \sim 1.3\text{--}1.7 \times 10^{-13}$ cms. One of the important parameters concerning the structure of a nucleus is "the binding energy" which is the difference between the energy of the protons and neutrons in the nucleus and their energy in the free state; and the magnitude of this binding energy determines its stability against disintegration into other elements. The protons and neutrons in the nuclei are held together by nuclear forces the nature of which we shall discuss later on.

Even before these structural details of nuclei were figured out, the spontaneous disintegration phenomena of elements like Uranium had been discovered towards the end of the 19th century, through the detection of the emission of three different kinds of radiations—α-particles, β-particles and Υ-rays. It turned out that the α-particles were the nuclei of Helium, the β-particles were electrons and the Υ-rays were high frequency electromagnetic waves. While Radioactivity itself was discovered by Becquerel, detailed investigations on the nature of these emitted particles and their identity were all established by Rutherford. The puzzling feature was that even though the α-particle inside the nucleus did not have sufficient energy to overcome the potential barrier of the nucleus, occasionally the particle did leak out. This particular feature was explainable only in terms of quantum mechanical theory, which we shall discuss later on.

The α-particles became an important tool in the hands of Rutherford in establishing the fact that inside the atom, there was the nucleus much smaller in size and carried all the mass of the atom.

Radiations

Heat and Light are the two most familiar radiations we encounter in everyday life. The idea of hot and cold and of temperature as a measure of these features and the expansion and the contraction of bodies as a function of temperature and the general explanations of these in terms of molecular structure and motion and vibrations of molecules, the varying specific heats of materials and conduction and convection of heat are all features that have all been well accounted for, quantitatively explained as part of thermodynamics and statistical mechanics. In these contexts certain very important principles followed rigorously by nature are recognized which form the foundations of physics—the law of conservation of energy, the natural direction of energy transformation (from mechanical to heat energy) as determined by entropy increase, entropy being a measure of disorder. These ideas have considerable influence on engineering designs of transport, locomotion, and the recognition of the impossibility of perpetual machines. The most important philosophical fall out is that the entropy of the universe as a whole is increasing—moving towards more and more disorder. This means that as we go backwards in time there was increasing order. The idea of heat energy being transferred by a third mode, namely radiation is also quite old. This is the mode by which heat energy comes to us from the Sun—from a distance of 93,000,000 miles across practically vacuum. All the substances that we are familiar on the earth turn into gaseous state at a temperature of 6000°C. Since the solar material is the same, all the matter in the sun is in a gaseous form.

Light—Particle or Wave?

Light is what enables us to see things around us and to admire those twinkling bright stars that fill the horizon of our view in the sky. Great names are associated with systematic study of light—Newton, Huygens, Fresnel, Young, Maxwell and Einstein. These great scientists and others made experimental studies and offered theoretical explanations for the most significant properties of light like rectilinear propagation, reflection, refraction, polarization, interference, diffraction and velocity of propagation in different media. Newton famous for his dynamics also made pioneering contributions in the field of optics. He believed, on the basis of the beautiful experiments he carried out, that light consists of swarms of particles emitted by a source, that move away at a very high speed. This corpuscular theory of light was opposed by his contemporary Christian Huygens the proponent of the wave theory of light. These two theories predicted exactly opposite results on the velocity of light in substances, and since during their time there was no capability for measuring such high velocities, the nature of light remained an open question. The phenomenon of interference and diffraction went in favour of the wave theory of light. However with the advent of quantum mechanics and the explanation of photoelectric effect in terms of the 'photon' theory of light by Einstein, the corpuscular theory was revived but in a very different sense as we shall see later.

An important development that goes back to the time of Newton himself is the Prism Spectroscope followed by the Spectrometers with Diffraction gratings. These opened up the whole field of Spectroscopy which provided much insight into our knowledge regarding the structure of atoms. Each chemical element emits a set of spectral lines characteristic of that particular element. Helium, was first discovered by the spectral analysis of the light from the Sun. The study of spectral lines characteristic of different elements led to the discovery of certain regularities in the emissions of light by the atoms and pointed to the possible mechanism behind these line emissions based on Bohr's theory of the atom which we will discuss after becoming familiar with the quantum hypothesis of Max Planck.

In the wave picture, light of different colours corresponds to different wave lengths of the associated wave. The shortest wave length visible to the eye is 4×10^{-5} cms and is beyond the blue colour—namely violet shade. An important relation between the wave length of maximum intensity emitted by a hot body and its temperature is known as the Wien's Law which states that the wave length of maximum intensity is inversely proportional to the absolute temperature. Stefan and Boltzman came up with another important relation that the total intensity of the emitted radiation is proportional to the fourth power of the emitter's absolute temperature.

Beyond the range of human eye perception we have on the longer wave length side infrared radiation which is essentially the 'heat radiation' that we talked about earlier and on the shorter wave length side the ultraviolet radiation.

The Quantum Hypothesis

When James Jeans made an attempt to determine the distribution of energy between the different wave lengths on lines similar to what Maxwell had done to calculate the distribution of energy between different molecules of gas (the famous Maxwell-Boltzman distribution of velocities), he ended up with a paradoxical result which came to be known as the "ultraviolet catastrophe". The calculations showed that all the available energy will be redistributed in such a way that it will be all at the shortest wave length. This exposed the inadequacy of the classical theories present till then. Radically new ideas and concepts were required and this came in the form of quantum theory—which was a development on the quantum hypothesis made by Max Planck in the Christmas week of 1899.

Planck made the hypothesis that for each kind of radiation there corresponds a definite amount of energy which he called "the quantum". Light of different types carry different amounts of energy and the amount of energy in the corresponding "quantum" is inversely proportional to the wave length of light or directly proportional to the frequency. He wrote down $E = h\upsilon$ where E is the energy of the quantum and υ is the frequency of light. The proportionality constant, known as the Planck Constant has the value of 6.6×10^{-27} erg seconds.

On the basis of this hypothesis Planck was able to rework the relation between wave length and energy distribution and showed that the problem of ultraviolet catastrophe had disappeared. Planck also derived the Wien and Stefan-Boltzman laws on the basis of his new hypothesis.

This new hypothesis of Planck, was soon very strongly supported by Albert Einstein which he adopted for explaining the photo-electric effect. It had been found that some materials like copper plates when irradiated with visible or ultraviolet light emit electrons—the particles responsible for conduction of electricity in metals. The anomaly that had remained unexplained before Einstein was, that the energy of the electron was not proportional to the intensity of light that shone on the substance.

Einstein explained the phenomenon on the basis of quantum hypothesis that the electron absorbs the entire energy of the quantum (which he called the photon) in one bite and not fraction of it, and the energy of the outgoing electron will depend on the energy of the photon incident in it. This explained why the number of electrons emitted depends on the intensity of light, but not the energy of the outgoing electron. These considerations led Arthur Compton to study the scattering of x-rays (photons of energy much higher than the optical photons) and establish that the photons did behave like particles in the collisions very similar to the collisions of billiard balls.

The Bohr Atom

Rutherford's experiments on the scattering of α-particles hitting metal targets, had clearly established the existence of nuclei inside atom, the nuclei carrying all the mass and being very much smaller in size (a factor of 1000 in radius) compared to the atoms. He came up with the planetary model of the atom in which the electrons revolved round the central nucleus in very much the same fashion as planets revolve round the sun. The problem however with this model was that in going round the nucleus, the electrons emit electromagnetic waves and lose energy and finally spiral into the nucleus and the atomic configuration will not be stable. Bohr, who had joined Rutherford as a student calculated that in a hundred-millionth of a second, the orbiting electron would lose all its energy. This was certainly against what had been observed in nature. Bohr came up with rather revolutionary ideas and made some bold assumptions. Bohr's postulates were:

(i) From all the mechanically possible circular and elliptical orbits of electrons around the atomic nucleus, only a few highly restricted orbits are "permitted" and selection of these "permitted orbits" is to be carried out according to specially established rules.

(ii) Circling along these orbits around the nucleus, the electrons are "prohibited" from emitting any electromagnetic waves, even though conventional electrodynamics says they should.

(iii) Electrons may "jump" from one orbit to another, in which case the energy difference between the two states of motion is emitted in the form of a single Planck-Einstein light quantum.

Clearly all these were arbitrary assumptions that were made just to fit the experimental observations. There were no logical arguments in favour of them. These hypotheses, however, did permit Bohr to interpret the regularities (the Balmer series), that had been observed in the analysis of spectral lines of hydrogen. In fact the constants in Bohr's theory were adjusted to fit the Balmer series. The success came with the verification of the predictions that were made for other atoms. While Bohr had assumed circular orbits, Sommerfeld added an elliptical orbit to Bohr's second orbit and two elliptical orbits to the third Bohr orbit and so on and these extensions helped in understanding the fine structure of spectral lines. Wolfgang Pauli came up with his famous principle that two electrons moving in the same orbit have to have opposite spins. This was an important development since it explained the periodic elements of the chemicals that had been arranged by Dmitri Mendeleev and also to fill the gaps in the elements that had been left out and which were discovered later.

Matter Waves: Particle/Wave duality

Bohr's hypotheses of stationary orbits of electrons in atoms, which did not radiate electromagnetic waves, led de Broglie to take a cue from the concept of standing waves in mechanical vibrations (violin strings, organ pipes etc.) and consider the possibility that the motion of electrons within an atomic orbit may be guided by some kind of waves which he called "pilot waves". Further de Broglie postulated that for stationary waves to be established, the wave length of the associated wave must be such that there are an integral multiple of them to fit exactly into the circumference of the orbit. De Broglie figured out that for the nth orbit, this relation would lead to

$$\lambda_n = \frac{nh^2}{2\pi m_e^2}$$

based upon Bohr's theory for the hydrogen atom that gave the relation

$$r_n = \frac{n^2 h^2}{4\pi^2 m_e^2}$$

for the radius of the nth orbit, h is the Planck constant, which had crept in from the restriction that Bohr had made that the angular momentum of the electron should be an integral multiple of $h/2\pi$, (Quantization rule assumed by Bohr). This gives for the velocity of the electron in the nth orbit the relation

$$\left(V = \frac{2\pi e^2}{nh} \right)$$

With these considerations, de Broglie deduced the relation $1 = h/m_e v$ as the wave length of pilot wave associated with an electron of mass m_e and velocity v and generalized it to all particles of mass m by stating $\lambda = h/mv$.

Through a study of the scattering of electron beams in a crystal, Davisson and Germrer obtained a diffraction pattern of the electrons and established that electrons also behave like waves and the wave length corresponds to what de Broglie had calculated. Later Stern showed that Sodium atoms too behave in a similar manner.

This was another major revision of classical ideas of material particles and raised the question about what "reality" is? How can an entity be both—a particle and a wave?

In this context, Gamow and Cleveland say "Modern Physics extends its horizons far beyond everyday experience upon which all the "common sense" ideas of classical physics were based, and we are thus bound to find striking deviations from our conventional way of thinking and must be prepared to encounter facts that sound quite paradoxical to our ordinary common sense. In the case of the theory of relativity, the revolution of thought was brought about by the realization that Space and Time are not the independent entities they were always believed to be, but are the parts of a unified space-time continuum. In quantum theory we encounter a non-conventional concept of the minimum amount of energy, which although of no importance in the large scale phenomena of everyday life, leads to revolutionary changes in our basic ideas concerning motion of tiny atomic mechanisms".

Elementary Particles and their Interactions

We have already talked about four elementary particles—the proton, the neutron, the electron and the photon. The protons and the electrons were discovered as elementary particles in the study of electrical discharge phenomena in gases. The analysis of the streams of particles that moved from the cathode to the anode, originally called Cathode rays, and the discovery that the individual particles carried the same charge as the hydrogen ions in electrolysis and that they had a mass about 1800 times smaller than the hydrogen atom, all led J.J. Thomson to conclude that these particles were the carriers of electricity everywhere and the name 'electron' was given to them. Around the same time in late 1890's, it was also discovered that there were also streams of particles of opposite charge in the discharge tubes which moved in the opposite directions from anode to cathode of discharge tubes. These were called Positive Rays. In 1898 Wien measured the charges and masses of these carriers by the method of electric and magnetic deflections. Each particle was found to carry a positive charge equivalent to the negative charge on the electron and had the mass of the hydrogen atom. Stripped of one electron the hydrogen atom had become a positive ion. The name 'Proton' was given by Rutherford much later in the early 1920's.

The second constituent of the nucleus, the neutron was discovered by Chadwick in 1932 at the Cavendish Laboratory. Bothe and Becker had observed in 1931, that when Beryllium was bombarded by a-particles, a highly penetrating radiation was produced. They had thought that this radiation comprised gamma rays. The very next year, Chadwick proved that this radiation emitted by beryllium consisted of material particles of the same mass as the hydrogen atom, and he gave the name neutron to these particles.

Discovery of Mesons and Meson Theory

With the protons and the neutrons as the constituents of nuclei, the question arose as to how these are held together so closely despite the Coulomb repulsive force between the protons, compounded further by lack of any electrical force between protons and neutrons and neutrons and neutrons. In the early 1930's, Hideki

Yukawa of Japan proposed that the nuclear forces that held these particles in the nucleus were due to the exchange of heavy mass particles between them. These exchange particles were initially called Yukons and later the word Meson which meant a particle of mass intermediate between that of the proton and electron, became more popular and has stuck on.

Around the time Yukawa's theory was gaining ground, it so happened that a particle of mass intermediate between proton and electron was discovered in Cosmic rays in a cloud chamber by Carl Anderson, the discoverer of the 'positron' the anti-particle of the electron. Yukawa had persuaded in the light of his theory, his Japanese colleague Nishina to design an experiment to look for the Yukon. Despite being the second world war period, and facing acute shortage of electrical power for his magnet, Nishina did set up a cloud chamber experiment and recorded the existence of a particle of mass 200 m_e. By this time, the papers by Anderson and his collaborator Neddermayer and also by another group at Harvard, Street and Stevenson were published in the Physical Review.

Apart from the suggestion of Yukawa, the existence of a particle of intermediate mass had also been necessitated by the presence of a penetrating component in cosmic rays at mountain altitudes and sea level. From a systematic analysis of all cosmic ray data on the soft and penetrating components and from a critical assessment of quantum-electro-dynamics Homi Bhabha had in mid 1930's come to the conclusion that either quantum-electrodynamics breaks down at high energies or there should exist a particle of mass intermediate between proton and electron. The discovery of Anderson seemed to fit well with the requirement of Yukawa. However, the rather hasty identification of the Anderson meson with the Yukon created serious problems and confusion. It was found that the Anderson particle was very weakly interacting with nuclei, while Yukon had to be a strongly interacting particle. The spontaneous disintegration of the meson was theoretically predicted by Bhabha and others and the measured lifetime of the particle was about two micro seconds, however did not fit well with Yukawa's requirements of the nuclear force particle in terms of lifetime. The Yukon was to have a lifetime of the order of 10^{-8} seconds. These contradictions were resolved by the discovery by Powell and his collaborators of another meson heavier than what Anderson had discovered and which spontaneously decayed into the Anderson meson with a lifetime of 2×10^{-8} seconds as required by Yukawa for the Yukon. It turned out that the meson of Powell was strongly interacting and agreed well the requirements of the particle responsible for nuclear forces. The heavier meson was called the 'pi-meson' and the lighter one the 'mu-meson'. Clearly the era of particle physics had begun. Very soon in cosmic rays several new types of mesons, and particles heavier than nucleon called hyperons were discovered. These were extremely short lived but they played an important role in focussing attention on the microworld of elementary particles and their interactions which, though not very much in the limelight of everyday experiences, have important controlling effects behind many natural phenomena. The list of elementary particles discovered in Cosmic rays is given in Table I. The particles discovered in cosmic rays range in their mass values from one electron mass to 2586 electron masses and the lifetimes of those which are unstable range from 2×10^{-6} seconds to 10^{-17} seconds. They are all singly charged particles, some of them have half integral spin like the electron and the proton, and some '0' spin and some +1 and –1. The K-mesons which were the mesons to be discovered immediately after the Pi-meson, had a very strange property. They were always produced in association with another K-meson or a $\wedge$-particle which was a hyperon, a particle of mass higher than nucleon. This led Gell-Mann to postulate that there is a new conservation principle operating in the production of these particles and for this purpose he introduced a new parameter

TABLE I
Properties of elementary particles discovered in Cosmic Rays 1930-1955.
(Some of the properties listed—spin, lifetime, anti-particle, decay modes were determined later in accelerator experiments.)

Name of Particle	Symbol	Strangeness no.	Anti-Particle Symbol	Anti-Particle Strangeness no.	Mass in terms of (m_e)	Spin	Charge	Lifetime in Seconds	Decay Modes
Positron	e^+	0	e^-	0	1	1/2	1	–	–
Muon	μ^-	0	μ^+	0	207	1/2	1	2.2×10^{-6}	$(e^-\, \nu_\mu\, \nu_e)$
Pion	π^-	0	π^+	0	273	0	–1	2.6×10^{-8}	$(\mu^-\, \nu_\mu)$
	π^0	0	π^0	0	264	0	0	8.0×10^{-17}	$(\gamma\, \gamma)$
Kaon	K^+	+1	K^-	–1	966	0	+1	1.2×10^{-8}	$(\pi^+\, \pi^0)$, $(\mu^+\, \nu_\mu o)$, $(e^+\, \pi^0\, \nu_e)$
	K^0	+1	$\overline{K}_0$	–1	974	0	0	K_S: 9×10^{-11} K_L: 5.4×10^{-8}	$(\pi^+\, \pi^-)$, $(\pi^0\, \pi^0)$ $(\pi^0\, \pi^0\, \pi^0)$, $(\pi^0\, \pi^+\, \pi^-)$, $(\pi^-\, e^+\, \nu_e)$
Lambda Hyperon	λ^0	–1	$\wedge_0$	+1	2183	1/2	0	2.5×10^{-10}	$(P\, \pi^-)$, $(n\, \pi^0)$
Sigma	Σ^+	–1	$\overline{\Sigma}^+$	+1	2328	1/2	+1	8.0×10^{-11}	$(P\, \pi^0)$, $(n\, \pi^+)$
Hyperon	Σ^0	–1	$\overline{\Sigma}^0$	+1	2334	1/2	0	10^{-14}	$(\wedge^0\, \gamma)$
	Σ^-	–1	$\overline{\Sigma}^-$	+1	2343	1/2	–1	1.5×10^{-10}	$(n\, \pi^-)$
Cascade	$\equiv^0$	–2	$\equiv^0$	+2	2573	1/2	0	3.0×10^{-10}	$(\wedge^0_0\, \pi^0)$
	$\equiv^-$	–2	$\equiv^-$	+2	2586	1/2	–1	1.7×10^{-10}	$(\wedge^0\, \pi^-)$

called "strangeness quantum" number and as can be seen from the table excepting the electrons, μ-mesons and pions, all the others have strangeness quantum numbers associated with them. While the strangeness quantum number is conserved in production (in strong interaction) as can be seen from the table itself, this is not so in the case of spontaneous decay (weak interaction).

Meson and Baryon Production

The various particles discovered in cosmic rays were all produced in the nuclear collisions of the very high energy incoming cosmic rays (protons, α-particles and other nuclei) with the nuclei of air. Depending on the energy of the incoming cosmic ray, the number of secondaries produced could be anywhere from a few to several hundred in a single collision.

Among the secondaries produced the most abundant were the Pi-mesons. Next in abundance were the K-meson and hyperons. A new feature that was discovered was that in addition to the particles, their anti-particles (see the table) were also produced, but the strange aspect was that in these collisions electrons, Mu-mesons, and photons were not produced. Nucleon-Anti-nucleon pairs were produced in large numbers at higher energies. The lighter particles, the electrons and Mu-mesons were produced in the decay of the π-mesons and K-mesons. The decay of the neutral π^0 mesons gave rise to Υ-rays. A very interesting development followed the observation of two types of decay of the K-meson. Sometimes the K-meson would decay into two particles and sometimes into three particles. This created complication for a feature known as parity conservation. The violation of this parity meant that the laws of physics were not the same when the observation was made in a mirrored system. This was a very strange result, and two Chinese-American theoretical physicists Lee and Young made the bold hypothesis that in weak interactions i.e., the spontaneous decay of particles, 'parity' is not conserved. The violation of parity was confirmed experimentally by a Chinese-American Scientist madam Wu at the Columbia University, New York.

The Mysterious Neutrino

The neutron, one of the constituents of all nuclei, when free decays into a proton and electron and another neutral particle. The existence of this neutral particle called the neutrino was proposed by Wolfgang Pauli to save the principle of Conservation of Energy in the decay of the neutron. The detailed theory of β-decay of the neutron based on Pauli's proposal was worked out by Fermi, who gave this neutral particle the name 'neutrino'. Apart from the fact that the particle had no charge, the neutrino had to have either 0 mass or a very small mass compared to the lightest of all material particles, the electron. Though the neutrino was predicted in the 1930's, it was only in the early 1950's, after the advent of nuclear reactors that the particle was experimentally detected, by Reines and Cowan. It turns out that the neutrinos like the μ-mesons are produced only in the decays of fundamental particles, as can be seen from the table. The neutrino which has half-integral spin, also serves the other important purpose of spin conservation. The neutrino has also, like all other particles, an anti-particle called the anti-neutrino, whose spin direction is always anti-parallel to the direction of motion. As we shall see later, accelerator experiments have revealed that there are three different types of neutrinos—the electron neutrino υ_e, the muon neutrino υ_μ and the Tau neutrino υ_τ and corresponding anti-neutrinos. The υ_μ's were produced in the decay in mu-mesons and υ_τ in the decay of τ-mesons. Being the decay products of so many particles, the neutrinos are in abundance in cosmic rays. Since they are very weakly interacting, they can go through the earth without suffering any interaction and energy loss. The first detection of Cosmic ray muon neutrinos was done in India in the Kolar Gold Mines at a depth of 8000 ft. below ground in 1965 with a very large scale set up. The neutrinos have a great astrophysical significance too. The Sun is an abundant source of neutrinos produced in the fusion reaction—conversion of hydrogen to helium in the core of the sun. A serious anomaly has cropped up with regard to the recorded flux of solar neutrinos (υ_e's) on the earth. Measurements carried out in a mine in the US revealed that the observed flux is lower by a factor of 3 compound to the calculated flux. The solar physicists are quite confident that their calculations cannot be wrong. To resolve this discrepancy one of the proposals is that there could be an oscillation of one flavour of neutrino say the υ_e to another flavour $\upsilon_{\mu,\tau}$. Such an oscillation with favourable oscillation length would remove the discrepancy by a factor of 2. However, this would demand that one of the flavours has to have a finite mass. While there is some indication from some cosmic ray experiments carried out underground in Japan that such an oscillation is taking place, the question is not fully settled. There is another context in which the neutrino mass problem has become very crucial. This is in connection with the so called 'missing mass' problem of the universe which we will come to later on.

Particle Physics at Accelerators

The discovery of so many new particles in cosmic rays particularly during the period 1945-55 motivated the construction of higher and higher energy accelerators; this paid off rich dividends through the discovery of many more new particles and high energy processes and served to delve deep into the structure of matter at the most fundamental levels, and understand the nature of the forces operative at the subatomic levels and finally to formulate a grand theory of particle physics known as the Standard Model. This model has evolved out of the close collaboration between theoretical physicists and experimentalists.

A very large number of elementary particles, running into several hundreds have been discovered over the past fifty years. Many of them belonged to the class of mesons and many were baryons and the rest called "resonances", had all fundamental particle identities like mass, spin, change strangeness number etc, but decayed away into other particles in times of the order of 10^{-23} seconds or less. A vast majority of them belonged to the class of strongly interacting particles given the general name hadrons. With such large number of particles with varying properties, all qualifying to be fundamental, it became necessary to classify them in some order. We have seen that the first classification was according to whether their mass is higher or lower than the nucleons. The higher mass particle were called hyperons and those of lower mass mesons among strongly interacting particles—the hadrons. A parameter called isotopic spin was introduced by Heisenberg to distinguish between particles that had the same mass, but different charge-states like proton and neutron, p^+ , p^0 and p^- etc. The number of charge states was $2I+1$ where I was the Isotopic spin. The notation Z-component of I was introduced to distinguish between the different charge components. We have

TABLE II

Isotopic Spin, Z-component of Isotopic Spin and Strangeness number
for Mesons and Baryons.

Particles	Isotopic Spin	Z-component of Isotopic Spin	Strangeness
π^+, π^0 and π^-	1	1, 0, –1	0
K^+, K^-	½	½, –½	+1
K^+, K^0	½	–½, ½	–1
P, n	½	½ –½	0
P, ñ	½	–½, ½	0
Λ^0	0	0	+1
Σ^+, Σ^0, Σ^-	1	1,0, –1	–1
Σ^+, Σ^0, Σ^-	1	–1, 0, 1	+1
Ξ^-, Ξ^+	½	–½, ½	–2
Ξ^-, Ξ^+	½	½, –½	+2
Ω^-	0	0	–3
Ω^+	0	0	+3

already seen that some particles were always produced in pairs though they belonged to different category. The strangeness quantum number was introduced by Gell-Mann for this purpose and the Conservation of strangeness quantum number was strict in strong interactions i.e. production of particles, while it was not necessary in weak interactions.

Table II gives the values of these parameters for some of the mesons and baryons.

Ω^- was predicted by Gell-Mann and was discovered later at the accelerators in the interaction $K^- + P = \Omega^- + K^+ + K^0$ involving the production of three strange particles and requiring conservation of strangeness. Since K^- has strangeness -1, and K^+ and K^0 have strangeness of K^+ is $+1$ and K^0 also $+1$, the Ω^- disintegrates in three stages as follows:-

$$K^- + P = \Omega^- + K^+ + K^0$$

$$\equiv^0 + \pi^-$$

$$L^0 + \pi^0$$

$$P + \pi^-$$

The identification of Ω^- required this three cascade decay to be registered and was achieved.

Quarks

One of the anomalies that had been noticed, particularly after the discovery of a large number of hadrons among the elementary particles, was the lack of proliferation of light weight particles called the Leptons. The only particles discovered among the non-interacting leptons were e^-, e^+, μ^+, μ^-, $v_{e,}\, v_{\mu}$, $v_{e,}\, v_{\mu}$. To resolve this discrepancy, Gell-Mann put forward in 1964, the "quark hypothesis" which assumed that all hadrons consist of few elementary "building blocks" called quarks and the number of quarks should be equal to the number of leptons, thus ensuring quark-lepton symmetry.

In 1964, when the quark hypothesis was first proposed by Gell-Mann and Zweig, they had thought that three quarks (u, d, s) and three antiquarks (u, d, s) standing for up-quark, down-quark, and strange-quark and their corresponding anti-particles would be sufficient to build all the known particles and anti-particles among the hadrons. The quarks and antiquarks had to have special properties which are given in the following table.

TABLE III

Quarks and Anti-quarks.

		Electric Charge	Baryon Number	Z Component of Isospin	Strangeness
Quark	u	+2/3	+1/3	+ 1/2	0
	d	–1/3	+1/3	– 1/2	0
	s	–1/3	+1/3	0	–1
Anti-quark	$\bar{u}$	–2/3	–1/3	– 1/2	0
	$\bar{d}$	+1/3	–1/3	+ 1/2	0
	$\bar{s}$	+1/3	–1/3	0	+1

Quark Structure of Baryons and Mesons

P	N	Λ°	Σ^+	Σ°	Σ^-	$\equiv^\circ$	$\equiv^-$	Ω^-	π^+	π^-	K^+	K°
uud	udd	uds	uvs	uds	dds	uss	dss	sss	ud	ud	us	ds

u = up-quark, d=down-quark, s=strange-quark

The interesting facts to note are that the quarks and antiquarks have fractional charges and fractional baryon numbers. There are also strange quarks and antiquarks. All the quarks are fermions with spin 1/2. The s-quark has strangeness quantum number –1.

Later experiments showed that there has to be a further elaboration of the quarks. Each quark (and antiquark) has attached with it another parameter that has been given the name colour—thus there is red u-quark, a yellow u-quark and a blue u-quark. Similarly the other d and s have the three colours. Each baryon is made of 3 quarks of different colours, the baryons by themselves having no colour attached to them. A surprising feature is that despite considerable effort, free individual quarks have not been recorded in any experiment so far. The signature of fractional change which they possess is one that makes detection of free quarks easy. While no free quarks were observed, scattering experiments with high energy electrons on nucleons somewhat reminiscent of the way Rutherford established the existence of nuclei with-in atoms, conclusively proved that there are three scattering centres in each nucleon as required in the quark theory. Confirmation also came from another direction—from the discovery of yet another type of new particles called "Charm Particles".

Towards the end of 1974, a new particle of mass about 6000 m_e with a lifetime for decay of 10^{-20}s was discovered almost simultaneously at two American accelerator centres, Brookhaven in the east coast and in Stanford in the west coast.

The east coast discoverers called it J and the west coast scientists called it ψ for no particular reason. Hence the name J/ψ has stuck on. J/ψ is a neutral particle. To account for the properties of particles a new quark called Charm quark c had to be introduced in addition to the prevalent three quarks u, d and s. It was necessary also to assume that like parity and strangeness, charm also had to be conserved in particle production interactions, and also in electromagnetic interactions, but not in weak interactions. The electric charge of the new c-quark is +2/3. The quark structure of the J/ψ was $c\bar{c}$ and is naturally given the name Charmonium. Charmonium has higher level energy states called ψ, χ_0, χ_1, χ_2 etc.

In 1976, another meson the D^0 meson was discovered with the quark structure (cu) and later in 1977 $F^{\pm}$ meson which had the quark structure (cs). A long time after the discovery of the three leptons electron, muon and neutrino, yet another called τ-meson was discovered in 1975. It had a mass around 3500 m_e. Still it belongs to the class of leptons because of other properties. The assumption had to be made in the light of the existing theories that there must be a corresponding τ-neutrino. Experimentally, τ_u has not been directly discovered yet.

Further experiments at accelerators have shown that there are two more very heavy mass quarks—one called the beauty quark (also called bottom quark) b and the other true quark (or top quark) called t. The beauty quark b has a mass ~10,000 m_e and charge – 1/3, The $b\bar{b}$ meson has a mass of ~20,000 m_e.

SPACE, TIME, MATTER AND FORCE UNDER THEORIES OF RELATIVITY

(a) Special Theory of Relativity

In the previous sections, we have seen how the scientific efforts of the 19th and 20th centuries to understand the properties of the structure and properties of matter and radiation, gradually led to the discovery of the microworld of molecules, atoms and elementary particles as technological abilities enabled the probing of smaller and smaller entities. We also saw that this reductionistic drive led us finally to recognise that the ultimate concept of all matter are two species of particles quarks and leptons with specific well identified intrinsic properties like mass charge, spin and interaction characteristics. In dealing with these particles, we have accessed regions of space smaller than 10^{-16} cms and intervals of the order of 10^{-23} seconds. Four very different types of interactions have been identified which account for most of the phenomena which we encounter in everyday life and also in some of the specially created laboratory conditions and also many celestial phenomena. The four forces are Gravitational force, Electro-magnetic Force, Weak force and Strong force. Of these the gravitation and electro-magnetic forces are long range forces and the weak and strong forces are extremely short range. What is most interesting is that the very concept of force and the way it is mediated has totally changed over the past hundred years, especially with the advent of relativity and quantum mechanics and a closer link has been established with happenings in space and time.

While the concept of force is an anthropomorphic one, which probably arose with the muscular strain experienced while lifting a heavy weight or pushing a loaded cart, the scientific quantification concept of force was introduced by Newton through the two relations

(i) $F = ma$,

where F is the force, m the mass and a is the acceleration of the particle

$$\text{(ii)} \quad F = G\frac{m_1 m_2}{r^2}$$

where m_1 and m_2 are the masses of two particles and r is the distance of separation and G is the constant of proportionity. While Newton's gravitation equation stipulated the distance dependence of the force, there was no indication from his theory how this force was mediated between the two objects. In the case of the astronomical objects, say the Sun and the Earth held together by the gravitation force between them the distance will be as large as 89,280,000 miles.

Regarding this action at a distance and the mechanism of gravity, Newton's views have been stated by Sir Edward Whittaker in his book "From Euclid to Eddington", as follows: Newton's views as to the mechanism of gravity have been preserved in Query 21 of his "optics" and his letters to Bentley and Boyle.

Having postulated an ether pervading all bodies and all space, he proceeds: "Is not this Medium much rarer within the dense bodies of the *Sun, Stars, Planets, and Comets,* than in the empty celestial spaces between them? And in passing from them to great distances, doth it not grow denser and denser perpetually, and thereby cause the gravity of those Bodies towards one another and of their parts towards the Bodies; every Body endeavouring to go from denser parts of the Medium towards the rarer?" Whether this might be true explanation or not, at any rate he says, 'to suppose that one body must act on another at a distance through vacuum without the mediation of anything else ... is to me so great an absurdity, that I believe that no man who has in philosophical matters a competent faculty of thinking can ever fall into'.

Even in subsequent years no one succeeded in formulating a mechanical picture of action of gravity.

This mysterious Medium ether turned up again and again in several contexts. Leibnitz introduced the idea of Kinetic Energy, visvive the quantity obtained by multiplying the mass of the particle by the square of the velocity of the particle, followed by John Bernouli with the principle of conservation of energy (conservatio virium vivarum) and Rankine the concept of potential energy. The conservation principle was extended to the field of optics by Fresnel who had supposed that light consists of vibrations of 'aether', though the nature of aether itself was not clear. The vibrations of aether helped him to formulate equations similar to ordinary dynamics for the case of light rays, in dealing with reflection and refraction properties. While tackling the problem of the potential energy associated with electric and magnate charges, Thomson showed that the energy was not in the magnets or electrified bodies, but in the fields surrounding them and this led Maxwell to propose the electromagnetic theory of light. To explain the propagation of electromagnetic waves, Maxwell tried very hard to invoke the mechanical properties of aether—the elastic deformities, but was unsuccessful.

The concept of aether despite so many negative aspects was not given up since it had provided the possibility of a mechanical model for all physical phenomena and also served as a fixed frame of reference for all motion. It had not been possible, however, to provide experimental proof of its existence. A.A. Michelson and Morley carried out a classic experiment at Cleveland, USA, in the year 1881. The experiment was based on the sample principle; if all space is simply motionless aether, then the earth's motion through this aether should be measurable in the same way as one can determine the velocity of a ship sailing in water. The velocity of the earth in its orbit around the Sun is about 20 miles per second. If a light beam is sent against the aether stream, then its velocity would be reduced from 186,284 miles per second to 186,264 miles per second while a light beam sent with the aether stream would be 186,304 miles per second. Setting up a light interferometer with a system of mirrors, Michelson and Morley tried to measure the expected difference in the light velocities on this assumption of a stationary ether (for the source of light they used a distant star). The experimental results conclusively showed that the light beam travelled with the same velocity regardless of the directions.

The negative results could be interpreted on the basis of two alternatives. One was that the earth itself was stationery and did not move which was against the well established Copernican theory of the motion of planets and the other was to give up the aether theory.

The results also meant that light, as an electro magnetic wave had a peculiar feature; its velocity did not follow the theory of addition of velocities which had been the basis of Newtonian Dynamics.

It is in this context that Einstein formulated his special theory of relativity; completely transforming the concepts of space and time that had been prevalent till that time. Space and time are concepts that are drawn into the field of scientific explanation on the basis of everyday experience of phenomena occurring around us. In our minds, space is characterized by emptiness and is essentially regarded as plenum for matter to occupy. Time is an entirely different kind of experience and the flow of time is considered to be independent of us. In Newtonian Dynamics, space and time are independent of each other. Time is universal and rate of flow of time is the same everywhere, wherever we go in the universe. All these ideas had to be changed to account for just one observed fact that velocity of light is independent of the motion of the source or the observer as revealed by the Michelson and Morley experiment and those that followed.

Einstein said, "We can do away with the aether, velocity of light may be regarded as a constant of nature independent of the motion of the source or the observer. But, we have to give up our conventional ideas of space and time". According to Einstein "The laws of science should be the same for all freely moving observers no matter what their speed" Formulating the special theory of relativity, he stated:

(1) There is no absolute time; space and time have to be fused into four-dimensional space-time continuum.

(2) Space contracts and time dilates in a moving medium—the extent depends on the velocity.

(3) Idea of simultaneity has no longer any meaning.

These new ideas themselves were revolutionary and contrary to common sense and daily experience. However, they were all verified to be true by a set of beautiful experiments in the following years. They also led to other important consequences—Mass and Energy, though distinctly different concepts till then, were shown to be equivalent and the famous relation $E=mc^2$ was given by Einstein connecting these entities. As is well known, it is this equation that enabled the realization of the Atom Bomb and all the peaceful uses of atomic energy. This equivalence of mass and energy also meant that the two principles, conservation of mass and conservation of energy as two distinct and separate laws of nature, had to be combined into one principle of conservation of mass and energy.

This principle of equivalence of mass and energy and the possibility of transformation of one to the other gave an insight into the mechanism of stellar energies and to the physical possess going on in the interior of stars.

It is extremely interesting and instructive for us to familiarize ourselves with the novel methodology by which a concept like time dilation due to motion could be verified. We saw in the previous section that the penetrating charged component of cosmic radiation is a particle called the μ-meson, which is the spontaneous decay product of the Pi-meson produced in high energy nuclear collisions of the primary cosmic rays with air nuclei. The m-meson itself is an unstable particle and decays into an electron and neutrino and an antineutrino. In its own rest system, the Mu-meson has a half-life of 2.2 microseconds. This can be measured by bringing the meson to rest in the laboratory in a medium like carbon. Even though its life time is 2.2 microseconds, it is found that in the atmosphere it is able to travel the entire length of more than 10 kms from the point of production to the point of decay, moving almost with the velocity of light the time taken is of the order of 33 microseconds. How does it do it? This happens because of relativistic time dilatation. It is shown in the theory of relativity that the dilatation factor is given by $E_\mu/m_\mu c^2$ where $E\mu$ is the energy of the µ-meson and m_μ is the rest mass of the m-meson. In the case we are considering, if the µ-meson has to live for more than 30 microseconds, then its energy must be more than 300 mev.

Another important consequence of relativity theory was that the mass of a particle increases with velocity and as velocity approaches the velocity of light, the mass becomes infinite. This fact ensures that no particle can travel with a velocity faster than that of light.

In the context of the finiteness of the velocity of light and its independence of the motion of the observer, the meaninglessness of simultaneity may be explained in the following way: Suppose you are standing in a railway platform and you notice with the help of a system of 45° inclined mirror right in front of you, two lightning flashes occurring at the same time, and you make a note of the exact time. Let us further suppose that the lightning flashes have occurred exactly on the railway lines and at the same distance from you. Next suppose there is another observer, perched on the top of a fast moving train and he crosses you at the same instant when you saw the two simultaneous flashes. The question is whether the moving observer on the train equipped with a similar mirror device will observe the flashes at the same instant as you. The answer is No, since the train is moving with a velocity it is moving away from one flash and towards the other. Naturally the meeting point of the lights from the two flashes for him will be closer to the point the train is approaching and away from the other.

The flashes meet for the moving observer at a different location and time. In the extreme case of the train moving with the velocity of light, the light from hind direction will never reach the observer on the train, and he will maintain that he saw only one flash the one from the front. For any other lower velocity of the train, the observer will say that the flash from the direction ahead of him struck first and the one from behind later. Consequently in relativity, we have the strange concept of 'relativity of simultaneity'!

If phenomena of nature have to be accounted for in terms of uniform and consistent laws, then according to the special theory of relativity, the measures of distance and time are variable quantities. The relations that connect these variable quantities are known as the Lorentz transformations, in which the unchanging quantity is the velocity of light c.

Table IV
Lorentz Transformation

$$x^1 = \dfrac{x - vt}{\sqrt{1 - v^2/c^2}}$$ $$y^1 = y$$ $$z^1 = z$$	$x^1 y^1 z^1, t^t$ coordinates in moving frame with a velocity v
$$t^q = \dfrac{t - (v/c^2)}{\sqrt{1 - v^2/c^2}}$$ $$m^1 = m^0 \Big/ \sqrt{1 - \dfrac{v^2}{c^2}}\ .$$	x,y,z,t coordinates in the system at rest. c = velocity of light. m^1 = mass at velocity v m^0 = rest mass

The Lorentz transformation equations show that when the velocity v is very small compared to the velocity of light, the transformation equations reduce to those earlier equations based on the principle of addition of velocities. On the other hand, when the velocity is comparable to that of c, radical transformations take place in the distance and time intervals.

Another interesting consequence of the theory of relativity is the variation of the mass of a particle with velocity. It can be seen that as the velocity approaches c, the mass become large and larger and at c, any particle with finite rest mass, becomes one with infinite mass. This naturally sets the limit to the velocity of any particle to the value c.

Interestingly this increased mass with velocity is what led Einstein to deduce the equation $E=mc^2$. The increased mass could only be attributed to the increase in energy at higher velocities.

All the consequence of the special theory of relativity have been beautifully confirmed by ingenious experiments. What this theory highlights is that the old Newtonian Dynamics based on ideas of absolute space and absolute time is not adequate to describe phenomena at high velocities which is necessarily the case in the atomic world and in the realm of elementary particles. The velocities of electrons in the atomic orbits and of the protons and neutrons inside the nuclei are very high and comparable to the velocity of light.

(b) The General Theory of Relativity

While the special theory of relativity brought about radical transformation of our concepts of space, time and matter, established the equivalence of mass and energy and had profound relevance to phenomena associated with very high velocity particles, the general theory of relativity by Einstein completed by 1917, went deeper into the structure of space, time, matter and force and gave insights that had significant implications to the origin of the universe and the large scale phenomena in the universe filled with celestial objects and environments very different from those encountered in our daily experience, on earth and its immediate surroundings.

It is known from the time of Galileo and Newton that all objects fall to the earth when thrown up, at the same rate, regardless of their inertial mass. It is also known from Newton's second law that the force acting on a body is proportional to the mass. Since all the bodies fall at the same time and have therefore the same acceleration, it is obvious that Gravitation and Inertia are at perfect balance in the case of falling bodies. How can this be explained? For almost three hundred years this had remained a puzzle. Einstein did not believe that this coincidence was just an accident, nor did he like the idea of instantaneous gravitational interaction between bodies separated by such large distances as the Earth and the Sun. He developed a new ingenious theory of gravitation instead. Einstein did this again with recourse to a gedanken experiment—an imaginary experiment, as he did in the case of special theory.

Imagine that you are inside a completely closed, freely falling elevator which is coming down under the action of the earth's gravity. Now you start dropping things from your pocket—say a kerchief, a key bunch, a fountain pen, a coin, etc. You find that none of them would fall to the ground of the lift and stay wherever you released them. You feel that you have moved out into outer space, for away from domain of the gravitation of the earth. If you try to push things horizontally, then you find that they are obeying the usual Newton's laws in an inertial frame. What is a freely falling elevator under the action of gravity for an observer on the earth outside the lift, behaves exactly like an inertial system for the observer inside. The reverse situation can also be imagined. If in an outer space environment where there is no action of gravity, the same elevator with you inside is pulled up with an acceleration equal to the gravitation as acceleration of a freely falling body, you start feeling that gravity has appeared. Things start falling down, there is upward pressure on your feet, and so on.

From such simple considerations, Einstein demonstrated the equivalence of gravitation and inertia in the case of accelerating systems.

The gravitation force of Newton was based on the assumption that material bodies attract each other under the influence of this force. According to Einstein gravitation is not a force. The movement of material bodies stems from their inertia and their path is determined by the properties of space and time around the bodies—more appropriately of the space-time continuum. Unlike that of Newton the law of gravitation that Einstein formulated contains nothing about the force, but gives a quantitative description of the gravitational field at various locations, analogous to the magnetic and electric forces in the terms of the fields around magnets and electrically charged bodies. The characterisation of the field is nothing but the characterisation of the space in all these cases. According to the general theory of relativity, it is not that matter is housed in a space-time continuum which in turn is influenced by the matter itself in its surroundings. On the contrary, matter itself is regarded as equivalent to curvature of space—the substratum is space-time continuum. While curvature of space gives rise to matter, what about its effect on time? Einstein showed that the gravitation field has an effect on time too. He showed that the time interval also varies with the gravitational field. A terrestrial clock transported to the Sun runs at a slightly lower rhythm than on earth. This would also mean that the frequency of light emitted by an atom say of hydrogen, in the neighbourhood of the Sun would be lower than the frequency emitted by a hydrogen atom on the earth. This shift in frequency is quite small and may be difficult to measure. However, if you consider say the companion star of Sirus (the brightest star in the sky), then the gravitational red shift can be quite appreciable and measurable. This is because of the very high density of the star (white dwarf) which is as much as a ton per cubic centimetre, while its diameter is only three times that of the earth.

The concept of the universe as matter floating in the infinite sea of space had to be modified in the light of Einstein's general theory of relativity. Unlike his predecessors, Einstein did not believe that the universe was infinite and the geometry that defined space was Euclidean. He had shown that the geometry was not Euclidean in a gravitational field and the predicted bending of light in the gravitational field of the sum had been confirmed by experiments carried out at the time of solar eclipse. According to the new ideas of Einstein, the gravitating bodies like the earth, the Sun, the planets, the stars, the galaxies, determined the geometrical structure of space—the local irregularities in space-time—and this resulted in an overall curvature of space-time continuum. All this resulted in a curved universe of finite dimension. But the curved universe though finite is unbounded. The emerging picture of such a universe is described by Sir James Jeans as follows:

> A Soap-bubble with corrugations on its surface is perhaps the best representation, in terms of simple and familiar materials of the universe revealed to us by the theory of

Relativity. The universe is not the interior of the soap bubble but its surface and we must remember that while the surface of a soap bubble has only two dimensions, the universe bubble has four- three dimensions of space and one of time. And the substance out of which this bubble is blown, the soap film, is empty space welded onto empty space.

It is extremely difficult, nay impossible to visualize this modern concept of space. However it can be represented mathematically and the consequences on natural physical phenomena in the universe tested. This situation is not different from the difficulty we have in envisaging the fundamental particles and their interactions. There also we can only observe their effects in large scale phenomena. We can never even imagine how they really are.

The Dirac Vacuum—anti-particles

In the section on elementary particles, we have made a reference to antiparticles without considering in detail how they arise and in what way they are different from normal particles. Considerations on antiparticles is extremely important from the point of view of understanding the structure of empty space—the quantum mechanical vacuum.

In the late 1920's, Dirac formulated the quantum mechanical equation for relativistic electrons and found to his surprise that the solution of the equation gave both positive and negative energy states for the electrons. Without disposing off the negative energy states as unphysical and therefore not to be considered further, Dirac tried to find a meaning to these legitimate mathematical solutions. He made the bold assumption that what we regard as normal vacuum is not empty, but is filled with these negative energy electrons without any vacancy in the allowed states according to his equation and there could be infinite number of them. Normally they are not observable. They become observable only when a vacancy arises which can happen either by spontaneous fluctuation or by deposition of sufficient positive energy in an extremely small region of space. When a vacancy does arise by the removal of a negative energy electron to a positive energy state— to that of a normal electron, something very strange happens. The vacancy will behave like a positively charged particle with a positive energy and this should become detectable. Thus in this process a pair of electrons—one the normal negatively charged electron and the other a positively charged electron the 'hole' in the Dirac sea—the 'positron' as it came to be known later are produced. This is the phenomenon of pair creation. The positron as a positively charged equivalent of the electron and the phenomenon of pair creation were almost simultaneously observed in the studies on cosmic rays. It also became clear in subsequent years that corresponding to every known fundamental particle there is an antiparticle. So the Dirac Vacuum was filled with not only negative energy electrons, but also with the negative energy states of all the fundamental particles discovered so far. Further, with the concept of exchange of particles, the bosons namely the photons, the $W^{\pm}$ and the gluons as the mediators of the electromagnetic, weak and strong forces created as virtual particles in the vacuum between the particles on which the forces are acting, the material constituents of the universe and the forces all reduced to the activity of this substratum—the quantum mechanical vacuum—or empty space in the normal parlance. While the need for identifying the four-dimensional space-time continuum of relativity with the Dirac Sea of fundamental particles is obvious there are still some technical difficulties connected with quantization of gravity. Also experimental detection of gravitons , the particles that have been postulated to mediate gravitational force has not been feasible yet, though there are considerable international collaboration efforts towards this. The connection between elementary particles, quantum mechanics and gravitation will become obvious in the next section.

THE FIRST MOMENTS OF THE UNIVERSE*

Does the Universe have a beginning? If so, When? And How did this happen?—are the questions that have engaged the consideration of mankind for thousands of years. The concept of the Universe itself has undergone radical changes with the passage of time, especially after discovery of telescope and the applications of spectroscopy for the analysis of the light received from different celestial objects. Developments in the field of Astronomy since the beginning of this century especially after the commissioning of the large telescopes, and the advent of radio and space astronomies, have made us realise the vast dimensions of the Universe and the existence of totally new environments very different from our experiences on the earth. The recent astronomical observations together with advances in the field of High energy and Elementary Particle Physics, have led to plausible theories on the origin of the Universe and its probable evolutionary course. The two most important astronomical discoveries of relevance in this context are:

    (1) the discovery of the general expansion of the Universe, and

    (2) the discovery of the Universal Microwave Radiation.

While the first led to the postulation of the Big Bang theory of origin, the second provided the strongest support for this theory. When we talk of the "the first moments of the Universe", it is with reference to the Big Bang.

---

*Reproduced from the article by the author in *Trans. Bose. Res. Inst.*, Vol 50(1) pp. 1-12, 1987.

2. The Structure and Composition of the Universe

Figure-1 summarizes in a way our current knowledge regarding the composition, the distance scale, and the relation between the size and mass of the different constituents of the Universe.

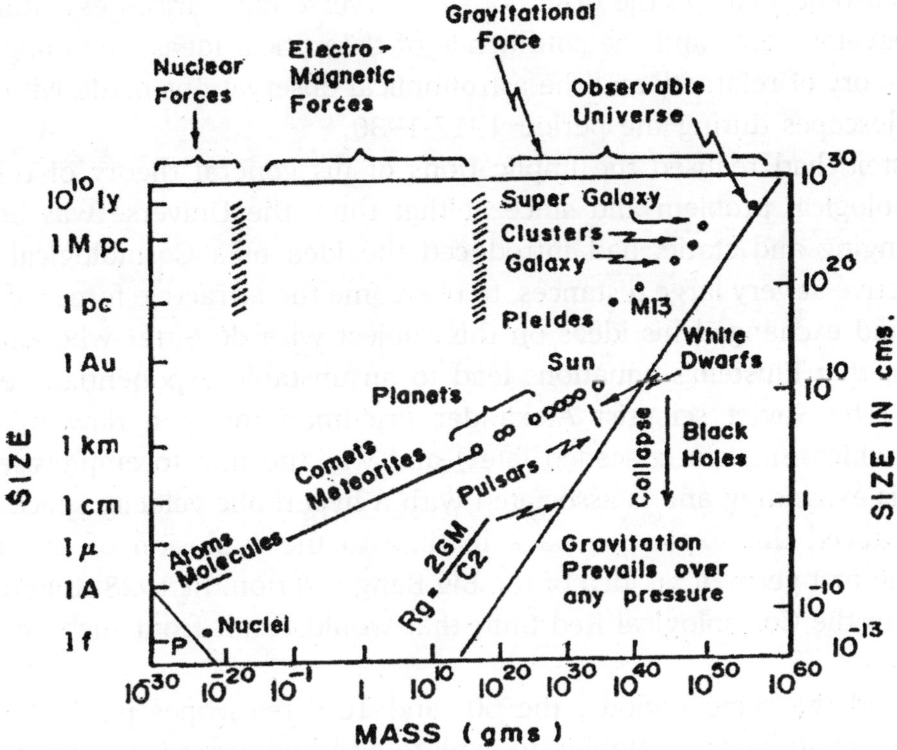

Fig. 1. Mass and size of the structural units of the universe
(From Kleczek—*The Universe*).

The mass range of the structural units extends from 10^{-24} gms (mass of the nucleon) to 10^{56} gms, which is the total mass of the observable Universe. The corresponding size range is 10^{-13} to 10^{20} cms, with the hierarchy of celestial objects like Comets, Meteorites, Planets, Stars, Cluster of Stars, Galaxies and Cluster of Galaxies falling in between in terms of size and mass. It is also to be noted from the figure that majority of the objects populating the Universe satisfy the relation

$$Rg > \frac{2GM}{c^2}$$

It is only in recent years that the evidence has started accumulating on collapsed objects like Neutron Stars and Black Holes which fall in the category

$$Rg \leq \frac{2GM}{c^2}$$

The Universe in addition is also filled with photons, neutrinos, antineutrinos, electrons and positrons, which also play a major role in the history of the Universe.

3. The Expanding Universe

Our current ideas on the origin of the Universe have arisen essentially out of parallel developments and the confluence of theoretical ideas stemming from the general theory of relativity and the astronomical observations made with the giant optical telescopes during the period 1917-1930.

Einstein had realised the implications of his general theory of relativity to the Cosmological problem and since at that time, the Universe was believed to be unchanging and static, had introduced the idea of a Cosmological repulsive force effective at very large distances, to overcome the attractive forces of gravity— Einstein had exchanged his ideas on this subject with de Sitter who came to the conclusion that Einstein's equations lead to an unstable exponentially expanding Universe. The Soviet scientist Alexander Friedman found a flaw in Einstein's solution (which Einstein conceded later) and was the first to emphasise that the Universe is expanding and is associated with a hyperbolic velocity space. In 1925, Lemaitre traced this expansion back in time to the explosion of a "superdense atom"—the first germ of an idea of the Big Bang creation. In 1928 Robertson drew attention to the Cosmological Red Shift that would result from such an Universal expansion.

Around the same period , the 60" and 100" telescopes in California were being used by Slipher and Hubble to explore and understand the structure of the bright patches in the sky—the Nebulae. They arrived at the unexpected and fascinating result that these are discrete galaxies composed of large number of Stars, similar to our own galaxy. Their observations led to another fundamental aspect of the Universe that these galaxies are receding from us—the greater the distance of a galaxy from us, the greater is its velocity of recession as revealed by the red shift of the spectral lines $\nabla \lambda/\lambda = Z = kr..$ Assuming that the observed red shift is due to Doppler effect, Hubble deduced the famous relation $v=Hr$ where H is the Hubble's constant and v is the velocity of recession.

Figure-2 shows the current status of this relation between the red shift and the distance of the galaxy expressed in terms of brightness magnitude. Hubble's original data corresponded to a very small range of distances. The Validity of Hubble's relations is now established over a wide range of distances by Sandage.

It is most important to realise that this general expansion of the Universe is discernible only over distance scales of 100 to 300 megaparsecs (1 megaparsec $\sim$ 10^{24} cms). On this scale the number of Stars, and Galaxies is the same, in any

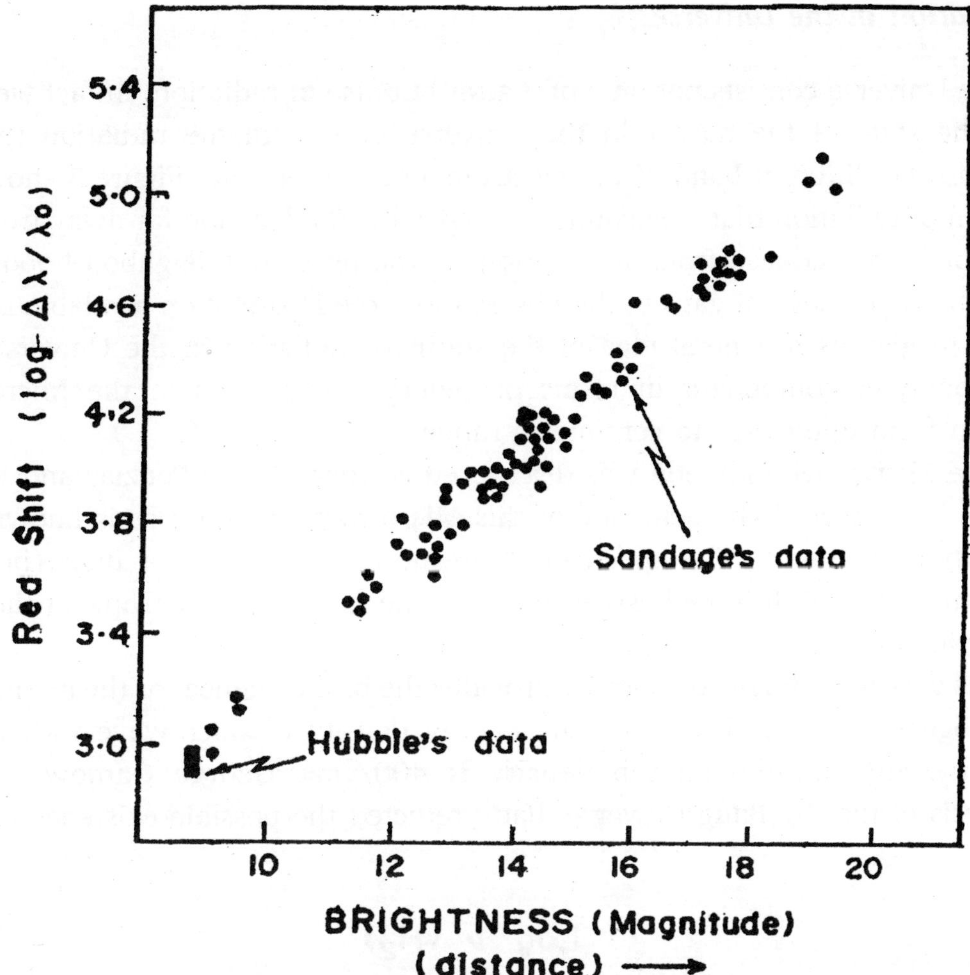

Fig. 2. Expansion of the universe.

region of space and on these scales we can talk about an average density of the Universe and also of homogeneity of the Universe.

The implications of such a universal expansion for Cosmology were first realised by Abbe Georges Lemaire. Such a picture meant that as we go back in time any region of the Universe would have been in a highly squeezed state with much higher density, and this density would continuously go up as the Universe contracts more and more and will ultimately result in infinite density and therefore in a singularity. Thus the universe starts with the Big Bang singularity, and as some scientists believe, "time" also started with this Big Bang explosion. The laws of Physics as are familiar to us, will not determine the initial state of this singularity. We can only use the physical laws to work out the evolution after the lapse of some finite time. The crucial question is how close in "time", an we get to the Big Bang Singularity? Surprisingly as close as 10^{-43} seconds.

4. Radiation in the Universe

The Universe consists not only of matter but also of radiation. In fact we learn about the state of the matter in the Universe only from the radiation that we receive in the different band of the electromagnetic spectrum. Figure-3 shows the spectrum of radiation that is encountered typically in a location far away from any single source as deduced from observations in the terrestrial neighbourhood. Even though there are several gaps in the observation, the information available is good enough to give us a general idea of the status of radiation in the Universe. The most dominant component in terms of "energy density" is in the Microwave radiation from millimetre to centimetre range.

The Microwave radiation was discovered accidentally by Penzias and Wilson in 1965. The spectral characteristic of this Microwave radiation as is known now is shown in Figure-4. The spectrum corresponds to that of a black body of temperature $2.96°K$. It is well established that the radiation is isotropic at the level of one part in 10^4.

This very high degree of isotropy provides the best evidence for the assumption of homogeneity of the Universe. The energy density of microwave radiation is ~ 0.27 ev/cm^3 and the Photon density is 400/cm^3. George Gamow, on the hypothesis of the Big Bang Universe, had predicted the possible existence of such

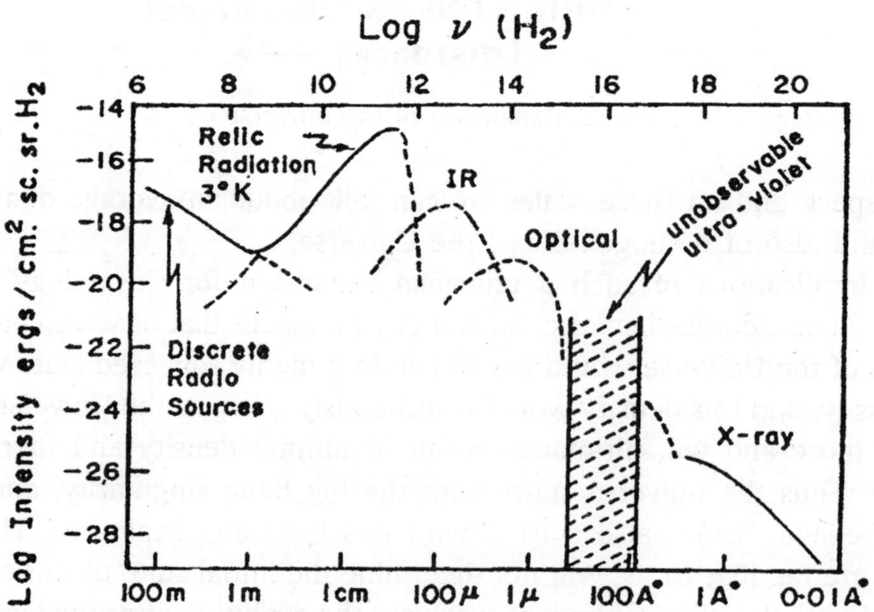

Fig. 3. Spectrum of the Isotropic Background Radiation: Full lines—observation, Dashed lines—theoretical estimates.

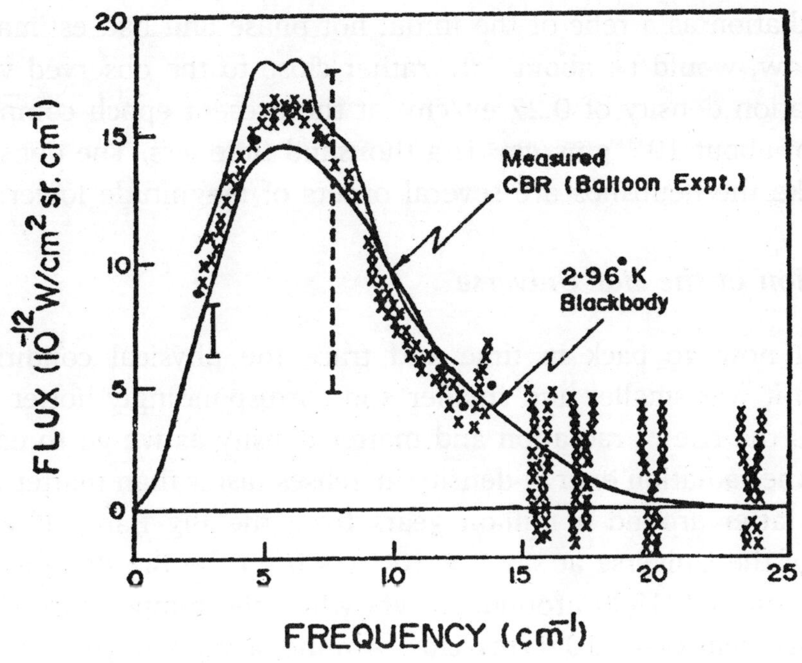

Fig. 4 Spectrum of Microwave Radiation.

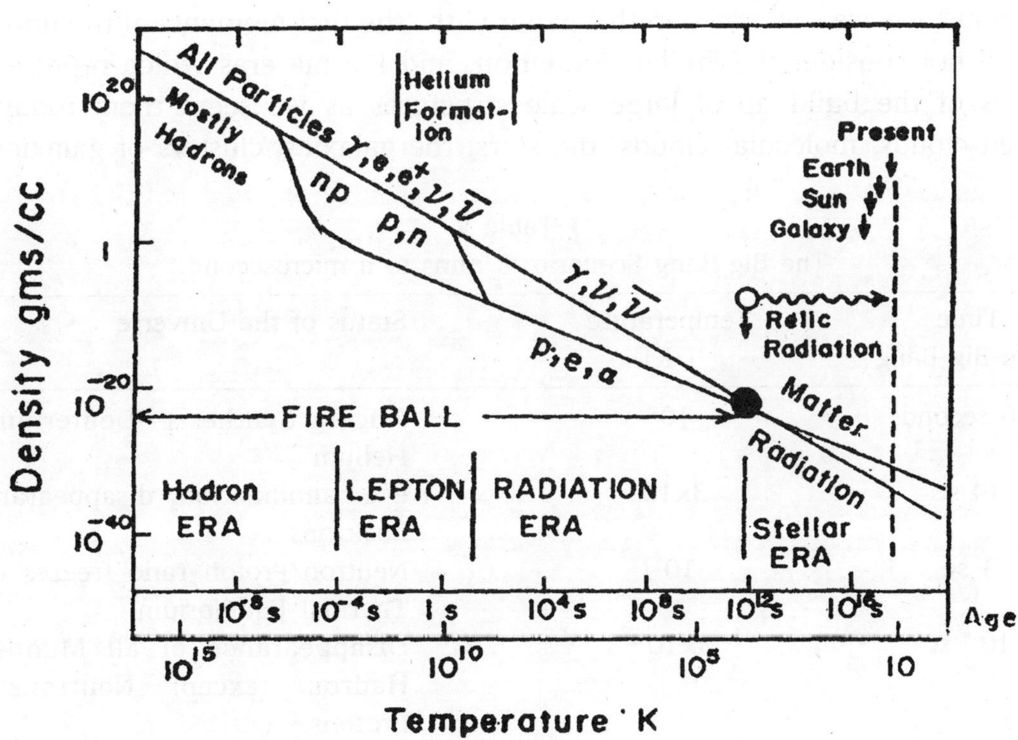

Fig. 5 Plausible Scenario of Evolution of the universe (10^{-9}–10^{-15} s)
[From Kleczek—*The Universe*].

a universal radiation as a relic of the initial hot phase and had estimated that its temperature now, would be about 5°K, rather close to the observed value.

The radiation density of 0.27 ev/cm^3 at the present epoch compared to the mass density of about 10^{-34} gms/cm^3 is a thousand time less. The density of other components like the neutrinos are several orders of magnitude lower.

5. *The Evolution of the Hot Universe*

We shall now go back in time and trace the physical conditions of the Universe when it was smaller and smaller and correspondingly hotter and hotter. Figure-5 shows the rise of radiation and matter density as we go to earlier times. It is seen that the radiation energy density increases faster than matter density and overtakes the latter around a million years from the Big Bang. If we take the present scale of the Universe at say 2×10^{10} yrs from the Big Bang as I, then the scale factor becomes 1/1500 around 10^7 yrs when the temperature shoots up to 4000°K and the density to 10^{-20} gms/cm^3. Around a million years from the Big Bang, the scale factor would be 1/20,000 and the temperature close to 60,000°K. As we get to still earlier times, around a few minutes, the temperature would exceed the billion mark.

Since we are concerned in this paper with "the first moments of the universe", we will not consider the Stellar, Radiation, and Plasma eras which represent the periods of the build up of large scale structures as we seem them today—the ionized clouds, molecular clouds, the stars, the galaxies, clusters of galaxies, etc.

Table V

The Big Bang Scenario: 3 mins to a microsecond.

Time from Big Bang	Temperature (°K)	Status of the Universe
180 seconds	10°	Nucleo Synthesis—Deuterium and Helium
14 sc	3×10^9	e$^+$e- annihilation, disappearance of Positrons
1 sc	10^{10}	Neutron/Proton ratio freezes out of Thermal Equilibrium
10^{-3} sc	3×10^{10}	Disappearance of all Muons and Hadrons except Neutrons and Protons
10^{-6} sc	10^{13}	Quark-Gluon plasma in thermal equilibrium with Photons and Leptons

We shall proceed straight to a consideration of the happenings earlier than a few minutes from the Big Bang.

6. *Happenings in the Universe earlier than a few minutes*

As the temperature of the Universe goes beyond 10^9 K and the density higher than 10^9 gms/cm^3, the application of our knowledge from the field of high energy physics on elementary particle production becomes necessary and relevant. The threshold for the production of electron-positron pairs is 5.93×10^9 K, for the production of Pi-mesons 1.56×10^{12} K and for Nucleon-Antinucleon production 1.1×10^{13} K. Table I shows the processes that take place from a microsecond when the temperature of the Universe was 10^{13} K, to a few minutes, when the temperature dropped to 10^9 K. An important feature of this period is the production of Helium-4, which carries almost 24% of the mass of the Universe today and was all produced during this very early phase of the Universe. This is also the phase when all the fundamental particles produced (see table II) earlier than a microsecond disappear due to annihilations except protons, neutrons, electrons and neutrinos and antineutrinos which form the constituents of the present Universe. By this time the dominance in the number of photons over nucleons by a factor of 10^9—a feature that persists up to the present time was also decided. This radiation dominance is one of the very challenging aspects of the Universe for which an answer has been found in the happenings earlier than a microsecond.

Table VI

The Big Bang Scenario: 10^{-6} to 10^{-43}.

Time from Big Bang	Temperature	Status of the Universe
10^{-6}	10^{13} K	Pronounced changes in the non-gravitational properties of matter. Weak interactions have the same strength.
	(10^9ev)	
10^{-12} sc	10^{16} K	Spontaneous Symmetry breaking;
	(10^{12}ev)	Higgs mechanism operates to generate masses of W$^{\pm}$, Z^0 from mass-less boson state.
10^{-43} sc	10^{23} K	Unification of Strong and Electro-Weak forces; Production of the lepto-quarks (X, X), Massive Magnetic Monopoles ($\sim 10^{36}$ Gev/c^2) Barrier
10^{-43} sc (PLANCK TIME)	10^{32} K (10^{28}ev)	Quantum gravity becomes important. No good theories yet to make any predictions

7. The very early Universe: 10^{-6} to 10^{-43} seconds

As we move to a time less than a microsecond from the Big Bang, the temperature rises from $10^{13}\,^0K$ to $10^{29}\,^0K$ at 10^{-36} seconds. Here the crucial question comes up—Can the temperature rise very much beyond the thermodynamical Hagedorn limit of $2 \times 10^{12}\,^0K$, that was set on the basis of production of large numbers of mesons at these temperatures? We also move to a distance scale very much less than the nuclear size of $\sim 10^{-13}$ cm. How is this possible? These questions find answers from comparatively recent developments in physics, in particular the discovery that the elementary particles—the hadrons like the protons, neutrons, pi-mesons, etc., are themselves composite particles. They are made of more fundamental units—"the quarks" which have rather strange properties like fractional charge, fractional Baryon number, but are Fermions and have spin 1/2. They are point particles whose dimensions are deduced to be less than 10^{-18} cm. Though free quarks with their characteristic properties have not been seen in the accelerator experiments, or in cosmic rays, there are good reasons to believe in their existence. The new theory of Quantum Chromodynamics (QCD) is concerned with the question of "quark confinement" and "quark-quark" forces mediated by the mass-less bosons called 'gluons'. A large number of experimental features discovered at the accelerators are beautifully explained by the quark theory. From the point of view of the very early Universe the most important consequences of the quark theory are the temperature limit of few times $10^{12}\,^0K$ can be exceeded by orders of magnitude and one can proceed to dimensions much smaller than 10^{-13} cms.

Another important development in high energy physics that is particularly relevant to this very early phase of the Universe is the "trend" that has been discerned towards the "unification" of the four fundamental forces—Strong, Weak, Electromagnetic and Gravitational. The discovery of the intermediate Vector Bosons $W^\pm$ and Z^0, has put the final stamp on the success of the Electro-Weak theory—the unification of the electromagnetic and weak forces. Further extension of the Gauge Theories which brought about this electro-weak unification in the framework of Quantum Chromodynamics, lead to possibilities of the unification of the Strong and Electro-Weak interactions, to the so called Grand Unification Theory (GUT). This predicts the existence of particles, the lepto-quarks $(X, \overline{X})$, in the mass range of 10^{15} Gev/c^2 — which mediate quark-quark interactions at extremely close range, and also lead to their production. It is clear that the production of such particles which requires energies greater than 10^{24} ev, in any terrestrial accelerator is beyond the realm of feasibility. However, the same GUT theories lead to the possibility that the Protons, the stablest of all particles in the Universe, undergo spontaneous decay—of course with a life time in excess of 10^{29} years. The three quarks that compose the proton, because of the fact that they are confined to a volume less than 10^{-29} cm^3, move around with very high velocities; If two of them come very close to each other then they will exchange a massive lepto-quark and lead to the production of a lepton and an antiquark which immediately interacts with the remaining quark to give a meson. Thus the proton will decay into a lepton and a meson. There are many other decay modes possible. There are quite a few experiments in the world including the one at the Kolar Gold Fields in India, which are specially designed to look for this very rare phenomenon of Proton Decay.

These grand unification ideas have important implications to the very early Universe. Figure-6, shows the variation of the coupling strengths of the electro weak and strong interactions as a function of energy. The corresponding temperatures of the Universe at the respective times are also shown in the figure. What this trend means is that before 10^{-36} s, all the three forces were one and the same, and the temperature high enough to produce the lepto-quarks—which are the very first species of particles to be produced in this hierarchy of particle production. The lepto-quarks give rise to leptons and quarks as the Universe cools. It is important to point out that at the limiting time of 10^{-43} seconds, the size of the Universe is around 10^{-33} cms and the density 10^{94} gms/cm^3. During this phase of Universe, massive magnetic monopoles of mass $\sim 10^{16}$ Gev/c^2 could be produced, in addition to $X, \bar{X}$.

The Planckian Era

Why do we stop our considerations at 10^{-43} seconds? Why not go to still smaller interval of time?

It turns out that the smallest time interval that can be constructed out of the three familiar constants G, h and c is the Planck time $= \left[\dfrac{Gh}{c^5}\right]^{1/2} \approx 1.3 \times 10^{-43}$ seconds

and the smallest space interval, the Planck Length $= \left[\dfrac{Gh}{c^3}\right]^{1/2} \approx 1.6 \times 10^{-33}$ cm.

At these lengths, it is surmised that "quantum gravity" effects will start dominating. There is no good quantum gravity theory yet which can help us to proceed further. There are theoretical efforts based on Super Symmetry, Super Gravity and String Theories to explore this domain. These are still in their early stages.

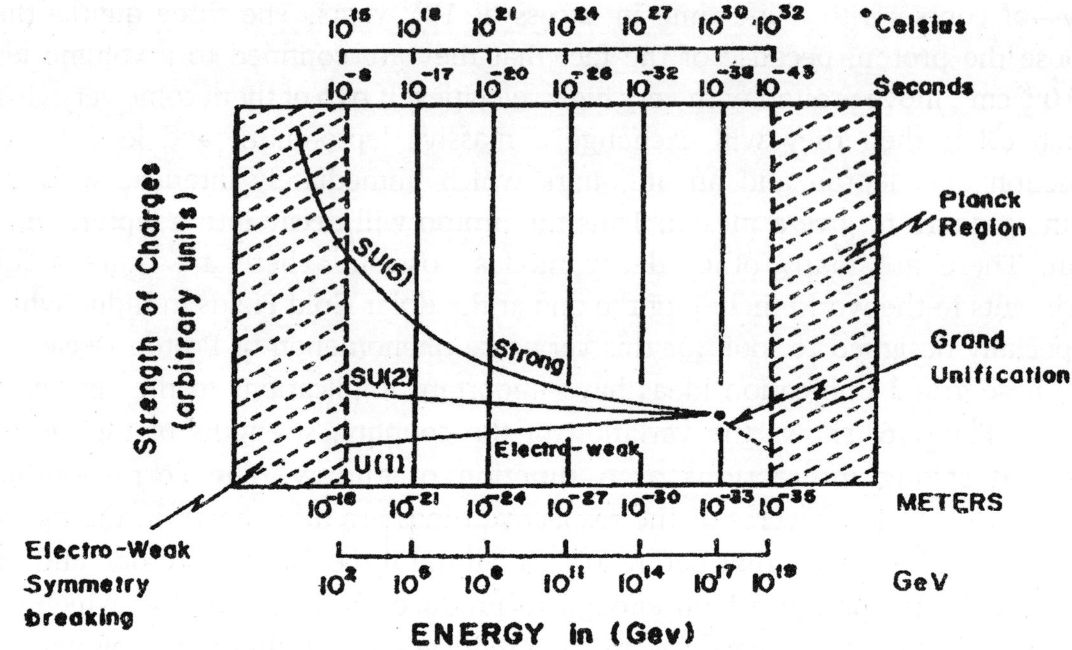

The very early Universe and Grand Unification
[From M. Green, 'Superstrings', *Scientific American*, Sept. 1986]

8. The Big Bang Scenario

We cannot say anything from 0 to 10^{-43} seconds. Immediately after the Planck Era ($\sim 10^{-43}$ seconds) the Universe was at a temperature of $\sim 10^{32}$ °K, density $\sim 10^{94}$ gms/cm³ and dimension $\sim 10^{-33}$ cms. At this temperature the Super heavy particles, the lepto-quarks were produced as also the magnetic monopoles. As the Universe cools the lepto-quarks lead to the formation of the quark-lepton soup. By about a microsecond the Universe consisted of nucleons, antinucleons, electrons, muons, pions, neutrinos, photons and gravitons. By about a millisecond, many of these annihilated leaving the proton, neutrons, photons, electrons and neutrinos and antineutrinos. Deuterium and Helium formed as the Universe cooled further. This was followed by the formation of ionized gases, Stars, Galaxies, etc. The dominance of matter over antimatter, and of radiation over matter can be adequately accounted for on the basis of this scenario.

What is amazing is, that we are able to extrapolate over almost 60 decades of time from 5×10^{17} seconds (Now) to 10^{-43} seconds, over 128 decades of density from 10^{-34} gms/cm³ and over a temperature scale of 3 K to 10^{32} K, and come to some quantitative understanding of the early Universe; and its evolutionary course. This has been the combined achievement of astronomy, astrophysics and high energy physics and a synthesis of our knowledge of the micro and macrocosms based on a unification of the forces of nature.

9. The Inflationary Universe

Some outstanding problems remains the understanding of which require further ramifications of the very early phase of the Big Bang expanding Universe. The outstanding problems are:

(a) *The Horizon Problem:*

The experimentally well established isotropy of the microwave radiation at a level better than 1 in 10^4, implies that very distant parts of the Universe, which are beyond each other's horizon (defined as the distance ct, where c is the velocity of light and t is the time from Big Bang) are at the same temperature. Since no physical process that can bring about such an equalisation of temperature can progress faster than light, this feature is one of the unsolved riddle's of Cosmology. The same situation would have persisted at earlier and earlier epochs in the kind of picture that we have presented above. The 3 radiation that we receive from the horizon today decoupled from the hot plasma around 10^5 years after the Big Bang. If we consider two locations on opposite sides of us in the horizon today, they would be 10^7 years apart when this decoupling took place and could not have had a causal connection at that time. How then do we understand the situation that the temperature is identical at these locations now?

(b) *The Flatness Problem:*

Will the Universe expand for ever? This depends on whether the average density of the Universe is higher or lower than a critical density which is calculated as 10^{-29} gms/cm^3 in the Friedman Universe models. We have already seen that the estimated matter density is close to this critical value—around 10^{-29} to 5, 10^{-30} gms/cm^3. The radiation density at the present time is however much lower. But there are reasons to believe that there could be considerable amount of 'hidden mass' in the Universe which is so cold that it is not perceived through the electromagnetic radiation. Also if the neutrinos which are abundant in terms of numbers, do have even a small mass, say of the order of ~ 10 ev, their contribution to mass density may even exceed the ordinary matter density.
In the Friedman theory, the average density varies as $t^{-3/2}$ in the matter dominated era and as t^{-2} in the radiation dominated era (earlier than a million years from cosmic explosion) where 't' is the Cosmological time. But the "critical density" in the same theoretical model varies only as t^{-1}. This means that near to the Planck time (10^{-43} s) the energy density is

"fine tuned" to an accuracy of the order of 10^{-59}. If this was not so the Universe would recollapse immediately after the Planck era. You can imagine how very exceptional our Universe is.

(c) *The Monopole Problem:*

In the era before 10^{-36} seconds, the possibility exists of profuse super massive ($\sim 10^{16}$ Gev/c^2) monopole production. Their numbers could be as large as that of Nucleons. The monopoles cannot be easily destroyed. There is no evidence for such high intensity of monopoles (also they would upset completely the mass densities. The Universe would have collapsed within 10,000 years of Big Bang). How did the Universe get rid of these monopoles or were they not produced at all?

(d) *Fluctuations:*

The large scale structure in the Universe arose out of fluctuations in density. How did these fluctuations take place in an otherwise highly homogeneous, isotropic Universe expanding uniformly.

All these questions find an answer in a new scenario first proposed by Alan Guth, which has similarity to be Sitter's solutions of Einstein's equation, without the Cosmological constant term. According to Guth, the Universe, beginning in a hot highly symmetric state with all the forces united (GUT), undergoes a phase transition and expands exponentially by a large factor in a short time ($\sim 10^{-30}$ s).

During this phase transition the temperature falls. The conditions that prevail after this transition provide answers to the questions raised above. There is of course a further complication—How to stop this exponential expansion?

There are many Cosmological theories. In fact there are many solutions even to the Cosmological Equations of Einstein, and each one of them leads to a different Cosmology. The Big Bang Cosmology is perhaps the one that explains most of the astronomical observations, especially with the modifications of 'inflation' introduced into it.

- -

The Living Universe

Thus far we have discussed the current status of our knowledge regarding the non-living or inanimate part of the Universe. We have seen how insignificant the planet earth is, in the vast scheme of the Universe. However, when it comes to a question of the living Universe, so far at least the definitive evidence for life and its activities is confined only to the planet earth. Efforts to look for evidence of even rudimentary form of life on the planet Mars have not so far yielded positive results. Even our nearest neighbour, the Moon, has no evidence of any form of life. Elaborate searches for signals from advanced extraterrestrial civilizations have proved negative. This uniqueness is attributed to the requirement of very special conditions for the emergence of life from inanimate matter.

According to the Big Bang picture of the evolutionary events, the interstellar clouds which led to the formation of the solar system are dated to be about 4–8 billion years, and the formation of solidified rocky planets to about 3.8 billion years ago. The earliest known forms of life date back to 3 billion years. How did this formation of life from non-living inanimate matter occur as has become the belief of the scientist from the time of Pasteur? It was the Soviet scientist Oparin who proposed that to be able to answer this question, one should simulate in the laboratory the conditions that must have prevailed on the earth 3 billion years ago—the "primal soup" consisting of the chemical molecules—hydrogen, ammonia, methane etc—in an atmosphere free from nitrogen and oxygen. This suggestion was made by Oparin in the late 1920's. The experimental efforts of Stanley Miller and others since 1950's using ultraviolet light or electric sparks resulted only in producing some of the organic chemicals—several amino acids and sugar. However no evidence of the emergence of life has been recorded.

While the fundamental question of the origin of life remains, considerable progress has been made in life sciences especially after the formulation of the theory of evolution by Darwin in the mid 19th century. The two publications of Darwin the *Origin of Species* in 1859 and *Descent of Man* in 1871 are certainly important landmarks in the history of life sciences. Mendel's discovery of the units of heredity—later identified as chromosomes and genes, gave a boost to Darwin's evolutionary theory.

In the middle of the 20th century came yet another landmark, the determination of the double helix structure of the DNA molecule by Crick and Watson. This brought life sciences closer to physical sciences and the new discipline of Molecular Biology was born and has been prospering since then leading to the currently most exciting field of Biotechnology.

The 'Cell' has been recognized as the "unit" of life for a long time now. The human body starts of as a single fertilized cell and multiplies into ten million billion cells (10^{16}). There are about 260 types of cells in a man or woman and 100,000 different genes. What is amazing is that each cell has the same DNA molecule in its nucleus. The cells however differ in their functions—blood cells make blood, bone cells make bones, liver cells make lever etc.

George Wald a renowned biologist raises the question "How could it be that a collection of molecules come together, in just the right way to form a living cell?" and addresses it by saying "with very many trials—the unthinkably improbable becomes virtually assured. Time is the hero of the plot. Two billion years (present estimate 4 billion)—given so much time the impossible becomes possible, the possible becomes probable and the probable virtually certain".

Though, not all share this optimistic view, it is undoubtedly the most popular one among biologists. While the reductionistic approach has paid rich dividends in understanding many aspects of both inanimate and animate matter, it is increasingly becoming apparent that for the resolution of some of the key issues like the appearance of "life", of "consciousness" etc., one has to take recourse to a "systemic approach" which is a radical shift from reduction to holism. In this, one looks for organizational principles that lead to the emergence of wholly new properties which are not there in the constituents. In fact the emergent properties are destroyed when the system is broken up into parts. As the Nobel Laureate P.N. Anderson has said "I believe that at each level of organization on scale, types of behaviour open up which are entirely new and basically unpredictable from a concentration on more and more detailed analysis of entities which made up the objects of these higher level studies".

Another very important realisation that has come about in recent decades is that in nature in the inanimate and animate systems, there is a certain amount of feed back from the output to the input which guides the long term behaviour, and even systems obeying deterministic laws become unpredictable because of the uncertainty in the initial conditions. However such chaotic system occasionally lead to very creative outcomes. These are some of the realizations that have come about because of the ability to carry out large scale computer simulations.

The advent of a variety of non-invasive tomographic instruments like fNMR, PET, LASER, Microelectrodes coupled to on-line computers has led to remarkable developments in neurosciences engaged in understanding the most intricate organ of the human body, namely the brain. This enabled Francis Crick, the discoverer of the structure of DNA in the early 1950's to say in the mid 90's that "your joys, your sorrows, your memories, your ambitions, your personal identity and your free will are in fact no more than the behaviour of the vast assembly of nerve cells and their associated molecules" This, Crick calls the most "Astonishing Hypothesis" and tries to justify it (though not to his entire satisfaction), on the basis of neuronal processes that have been mapped out and examined in minute detail. On the other hand Marvin Minsky, expert on Artificial Intelligence says "Many scientists look to Chemistry and Physics as ideal models of what psychology should be like. After all, atoms in the brain are subject to the same inclusive laws that govern other forms of matter. Then can we explain what our brains actually do entirely in terms of these basic principles? The answer is "No" simply because even if we understand how our billions of brain cells work separately, this would not tell us how the brain works as an agency. The laws of thought depend not only on particles of brain cells, but also on how they are connected. All these connections are established not only by the basic general laws of physics, but by the particular arrangement of millions of bits of information in our inherited genes". In dealing with problems of consciousness the relevance of quantum processes in the brain and its accessories is also under active discussion now-a-days.

To summarise, the current knowledge of the physical world with regard to both the animate and inanimate parts, is certainly very different from what it was even a hundred years ago. Despite increasing awareness of the multi-layered microscopic/macroscopic activities in both fields, the general tendency is towards recognizing a unification of the ultimate constituents and forces at the deepest substratum levels which are now accessible for detailed study thanks to the availability of a variety of instruments which in turn are products of advances in basic sciences. Thus the science—technology spiral is enabling us to march ahead in our quest for ultimate knowledge.

Epilogue

"Matter is made of atoms and void" was the view held by the early Indian and Greek philosophers—Kaṇāda of the Vaiśeṣika school (who envisaged ākāsa in place of void) in India going back to 600 *B.C.* and Leucippus, and his student Democritus in Greece around 550 *B.C.* followed by Epicurus of Samos in 300 *B.C.* The atom which meant "uncuttable" in Greek was the ultimate indivisible unit and Kaṇāda spoke of 'Paramāṇu' which also had the same connotation. Much later Newton (1642-1727) stated:

> It seems probable to me that God in the beginning formed matter in solid, massy hard impenetrable, movable particles of such size and figures and with such other properties ....., so very hard as never to wear and break in pieces, no ordinary power being able to divide what God himself made one in the first creation.

The British Scientist John Dalton (1766-1844) who started his career in meteorology and did extensive studies on the atmosphere by collecting air samples from very many difference places is generally regarded as the father of modern 'atomic theory'. What led him to the atomic theory was the discovery that all the air samples had the same chemical composition and the various gases wherever collected were thoroughly mixed—the heavier and lighter ones. He came to the conclusion: *"All materials are made of small uncuttable particles called atoms. Atoms of different elements have different properties, but all atoms of the same element are exactly same. The whole atom takes part in chemical changes. Atoms are not changed as they enter into chemical compounds. Atoms cannot be created or destroyed".*

This atomic theory of Dalton propounded in the early years of the 19th century became one of the foundations of modern physics and chemistry, though in the later part of 19th century and in the early decades of the 20th, the indestructibility of the atom was disproved experimentally. As we saw in the earlier sections, the atoms were smashed, the nuclei split and many new particles created by the bombardment of high energy particles. While radioactivity and collisions by low energy accelerated particles led to the understanding of the atom structure and the nuclear structure, the collisions at very high energies opened up the thoroughly unexpected world of elementary particles. Many of these were extremely unstable and decayed away into other particles in very short intervals of time. The developments in the field of astronomy and the discovery of the expanding nature of the universe and of the universal microwave radiation led to the Big Bang theory of creation of the universe—creation characterized by unbelievably high temperatures in its first moments. This focussed attention on the connection between high energy physics and cosmology, portraying the special significance of the role played by those extremely short lived particles. The most exciting realization that has come about is that very early universe is the highest energy accelerator laboratory through the study of the happenings of which one could test, if at all, the grand unification of all the forces of nature—the gravitation, the strong, weak and electromagnetic. These forces normally behave so differently and are responsible for so much of variety in the universe. Do they converge in the very early moments of the universe to just one type of force? This is the expectation. Will it be established? At the moment only the unification of electromagnetic and weak forces is established unambiguously. The lack of confirmation of Proton Decay has been a fly in the ointment.

Another important consequence of the developments in physical sciences in the 20th century is the unification of matter and energy, time and space leading to the idea that in the ultimate analysis, everything arises out of fluctuations of just one entity—just one all pervading substratum. What modern science has been endeavouring to do is to determine what all this substratum should contain in a potential form, and establish the natural laws by which the products that come out of the substratum—space, time, particles, radiations, etc., by spontaneous fluctuation and with passage of time to give rise to the universe that we are cognizing and attempting to understand. Most importantly this whole process should result in the emergence of life and of man. As stated in the opening sentences of this article, man has progressed a lot in this direction and but there is much more to be learnt. As Frost has said "miles to go before I sleep".

BIBLIOGRAPHY

Barnett, Lincoln: *Universe and Dr. Einstein,* Mentor Book, New York, 1952.

Barrow, John and Silk, Joseph: *The Left Hand of Creation,* Counter Point, London, 1985.

Danin, Daniel: *Probabilities of the Quantum World,* Mir Publishers, Moscow, 1983.

Davies, Paul: *Accidental Universe,* Cambridge University Press, 1982; *About Time,* Touchstone, New York, 1995.

Eddington, Arthur: *New Pathways in Science,* Cambridge University Press, 1944.

Gamow, George and Cleveland, John: *Physics: Foundations and Frontiers,* Prentice-Hall of India, New Delhi, 1963.

Gurevich, L.E.and Cherin, A.D.: *Magic of Galaxies and Stars,* Mir Publishing, Moscow, 1987.

Hawking, Stephen: *Brief History of Time,* Bantom Books, New York, 1988.

Kragh, Helge *: A History of Physics in the Twentieth Century,* University Press of India, 2001.

Kleczek, Joseph: *The Universe,* Reidel Publishing House, Boston, 1976.

Resnik, Robert: *Introduction to Special Relativity,* Wiley Eastern Ltd, New Delhi, 1968.

Schram, David N.: 'The Early Universe and High Energy Physics', *Physics To-day*, April, 1983.

Sreekantan B. V.: 'The First Moments of the Universe', *Transactions of Bose Research Institute,* Vol.**50**, 1987.

Weinberg, Steven: *First Three Minutes,* Bantom, London, 1979.

Whittaker, Edmund: *From Euclid to Eddington,* Dover Books on Science, New York, 1958.

APPENDICES

APPENDIX 1

Time and Eternity in Indian Thought

Mircea Eliade

(Reproduced with permission from the book *Man and Time,* Routledge and
Kegan Paul, London, 1958, pp. 173-200)

Indian myths are *myths* before they are *Indian—that* is to say, they belong to a particular category of archaic man's spiritual creations; consequently, they can be compared to any other groups of traditional myths. Before presenting the Indian mythology of time, we might say a word about the close connection between myth, as an original form of culture, and time. For, aside from its specific functions in archaic society, which need not concern us here, myth is significant for the light it throws on the structure of time. As most modern thinkers agree, myth relates events which took place in *principio,* at the beginnings, in a primordial, atemporal moment, a *sacred time.* This mythical or sacred time is qualitatively different from profane time, from the continuous and irreversible time of our everyday, desacralized existence. In narrating a myth, we reactualize, as it were, the sacred time in which occurred the events of which we are speaking. (And that is why, in traditional societies, myths cannot be related at any time or in any manner one chooses: one can recount them only during holy seasons, in the woods at night, or around the fire before or after the rituals, etc.) In a word, myth is supposed to take place in an intemporal time, if we may be pardoned the term, in a moment without duration, as certain mystics and philosophers conceive of eternity.

This observation is important, for it follows that the narration of myths has profound consequences both for him who narrates and for them who listen. By the simple fact of a myth's narration, profane time is—symbolically at least-abolished: narrator and audience are projected into a sacred, mythical time. We have elsewhere attempted to show that the abolition of profane time by the imitation of exemplary models and the reactualization of mythical events constitutes a specific mark of all traditional societies, and that this in itself suffices to distinguish the archaic world from our modern societies.[1] In the traditional societies men endeavored consciously and voluntarily to abolish time at periodic intervals, to efface the past and to regenerate time by a series of rituals which in a sense reactualize the cosmogony. Here we need not go into details which would take us too far from our subject. It may suffice to recall that a myth tears man away from his own time, from his individual, chronological, "historical" time-and projects him, symbolically at least, into the Great Time, into a paradoxical moment that cannot be measured because it has no duration. Which amounts to saying that myth implies a breach in time and the surrounding world; it opens up a passage to the sacred Great Time.

Merely by listening to a myth, man forgets his profane condition, his "historical situation," as it is nowadays called. A man need not necessarily belong to a historical civilization to justify us in saying that he is in a "historical situation." The Australian who feeds on insects and roots is also in a "historical situation"—that is to say, in a situation that is delimited, expressed in a certain ideology, and sustained by a certain type of social and economic organization; specifically, the existence of the Australian very probably represents a variant of the historical situation of paleolithic man. For "historical situation" does not necessarily imply "history" in the major sense of the term: it implies only the human condition as such-that is to say, a condition governed by a certain set of attitudes. And in listening to a myth an Australian, as well as an individual belonging to a far more highly developed civilization—a Chinese, for example, or a Hindu or a European peasant—forgets, as it were, his particular situation and is projected into another world, into a universe which is no longer his poor little every-day universe.

It must be recalled that for all these individuals, for the Australian as well as the Chinese, the Hindu, and the European peasant, myths are true, because they are *sacred*—they speak of sacred beings and events. Consequently, in narrating or listening to a myth, one resumes contact with the sacred and with reality and in so doing transcends the profane condition, the historical situation. In other words, one transcends the temporal and the obtuse self-sufficiency which is the lot of all men because all men are "ignorant"—that is, because they identify the real with their own particular situation. For ignorance is primarily that false identification of the real with what each one among us seems to be or seems to possess. A politician believes that the sole and true reality is political power, a millionaire is convinced that wealth alone is real, a scholar has the same belief with regard to his studies, his books, his laboratories, and so on. The same tendency is also found among the less civilized, among primitive peoples and savages, but with this difference: here myths are still alive to prevent them from identifying themselves—fully and continuously with nonreality. The periodic recitation of myths breaks through the walls erected by the illusions of profane existence. Myth continuously reactualizes the Great Time and in so doing transfers its audience to a superhuman and suprahistorical plane, which, among other things, enables it to approach a reality that is inaccessible on the plane of individual, profane existence.

Indian Myths of Time

This capital function of "breaking through" individual, historical time and of actualizing the mythical Great Time is strikingly illustrated by certain Indian myths. We shall give a famous example, drawn from the *Brahmavaivarta Purāṇa,* which the late Heinrich Zimmer summed up and commented upon in his book *Myths and Symbols in Indian Art and Civilization.*[2] This text has the particular advantage of starting right in with Great Time as an instrument of knowledge and hence of deliverance from the bonds of Māyā.

After his victory over the dragon Vṛtra, Indra decides to rebuild and embellish the residence of the gods. Viśvakarman, the divine architect, labors for a year and succeeds in constructing a magnificent palace. But Indra is not satisfied. He wishes to make it still larger and more splendid without its equal in the world. Exhausted with his effort, Viśvakarman complains to Brahmā, the Creator God. Brahmā promises to help him and intervenes with Viṣṇu, the Supreme Being, of whom Brahmā himself is only a simple instrument. Viṣṇu undertakes to bring Indra back to his senses.

One fine day Indra in his palace receives the visit of a ragged boy. It is Viṣṇu himself, who has assumed this aspect to humiliate the King of the Gods. Without immediately revealing his identity, he calls Indra "my child" and speaks to him of the innumerable Indras who have inhabited innumerable universes up to this time.

'The life and kingship of an Indra endure seventy-one eons [a cycle, a *mahāyuga,* consists of 12,000 divine years or 4,320,000 years, and when twenty-eight Indras have expired, one day and night of Brahmā have elapsed. But the existence of one Brahmā, measured in such Brahmā days and nights, is only one hundred and eight years. Brahmā follows Brahmā; one sinks, the next arises; the endless series cannot be told. There is no end to the number of those Brahmās—to say nothing of Indras.

But the universes side by side at any given moment, each harboring a Brahmā and an Indra: who will estimate the number of these? Beyond the farthest vision, crowding outer space, the universes come and go, an innumerable host. Like delicate boats they float on the fathomless, pure waters that form the body of Viṣṇu. Out of every hair-pore of that body a universe bubbles and breaks. Will you presume to count them? Will you number the gods in all those worlds—the worlds present and the worlds past?'

As the boy speaks, a procession of ants has made its appearance in the great hall of the palace. Drawn up in a column four yards wide, they parade across the floor. The boy perceives them, pauses, and then, seized with amazement, breaks out in a sudden laugh. "Why do you laugh?" Indra asks him.

And the boy replies: "I saw the ants, Oh! Indra, filing in long parade. Each was once an Indra. Like you, each by virtue of pious deeds once ascended to the rank of a king of gods. But now, through many rebirths, each has become again an ant. This army is an army of former Indras..."

This revelation brings home to Indra the vanity of his pride and ambitions. He recalls the admirable architect Viśvakarman, rewards him royally, and abandons forever his project of enlarging the palace of the gods.

The intention of this myth is transparent. The dizzy evocation of the innumerable universes rising and vanishing from the body of Viṣṇu suffices to awaken Indra; it compels him to transcend the limited and strictly contingent horizon of his situation as King of the Gods, we might even be tempted to add, of his *historical* situation, for Indra happens to be the Great Warrior Chieftain of the gods in a certain historical moment, at a certain stage of the grandiose cosmic drama. And from Viṣṇu's very mouth Indra hears a *true story:* the true story of the eternal creation and destruction of the worlds, beside which his own history, his own innumerable heroic adventures culminating in his victory over Vṛtra, seem indeed to be "false," that is, events without transcendent significance. The *true story* reveals to him Great Time, mythical time, which is the true source of all cosmic beings and events. It is because he is enabled to transcend his historically conditioned situation and to rend the illusory veil created by profane time—that is to say, by his own "history"—that Indra is cured of, his pride and ignorance; in Christian terms, he is "saved." And this redeeming function of myth operates not only for Indra but also for every human being who hears the story of his adventure. To transcend profane time, to recover the mythical Great Time, is equivalent to a revelation of ultimate reality. And this is a strictly metaphysical reality, accessible only through myths and symbols.

This myth has a sequel, to which we shall return. For the moment it needs only be remarked that the conception of a cyclical, infinite Time, presented so strikingly by Viṣṇu, is the pan-Indian conception of cosmic cycles. The belief in the periodic creation and destruction of the universe is already as early as the *Atharva-Veda* (X, 8, 39-40). And as a matter of fact it belongs to the *Weltanschauung* of all archaic societies.

The Doctrine of the Yugas

India developed a doctrine *of* cosmic cycles which expands the periodic creations and destructions of the universe into staggering proportions. The smallest unit of measurement is the *"yuga"* or "age". Each yuga is preceded by a "dawn" and followed by a "dusk," which constitute the transition between them. A complete cycle, or *mahāyuga,* consists of four "ages", of unequal length, the longest occurring at the beginning of the cycle and the shortest at its end. The names of these yugas are borrowed from the names for the "throws" in the game of dice. Kṛta Yuga (from that verb *kṛ,* "to make, accomplish") means the "perfect age," from four, the winning throw in the game of dice. For in the Indian tradition, the number four symbolizes totality, plenitude, and perfection. The Kṛta Yuga is also called Satya Yuga, that is, the "real," true, authentic age. From every point of view, it is the golden age, the beatific epoch of justice, happiness, prosperity. During the Kṛta Yuga the moral order of the universe, the Dharma, is respected in its entirety. Moreover, it is observed by all men spontaneously and without constraint; for during the Kṛta Yuga, the Dharma is in a sense identified with human existence. The perfect man of the Kṛta Yuga incarnates the cosmic and consequently the moral norm. His existence is exemplary, archetypal. In other non-Indian traditions, this golden age is equivalent to the primordial, paradisiacal epoch.

The following age, the Tretā Yuga, the triad, so named from the three-pointed die, marks a regression. Now men observe only three-quarters of the Dharma. Labour, suffering, and death are now the human lot. Duty is no longer spontaneous, but must be learnt. The modes of life pertaining to the four castes begin to be vitiated. With the Dvāpara Yuga (the "age" characterized by "two") only half of the Dharma subsists on earth. The vices and evil increase, human life becomes still shorter. In the Kali Yuga, the "evil age," only one quarter of the Dharma remains. The term *kali* signifies the die marked by a single point, consequently the losing throw (personified moreover by an evil genius); *kali* also signifies dispute, discord, and in general the worst of a group of men or objects. In the Kali Yuga man and society attain the supreme point of disintegration. According to the *Viṣṇu Purāṇa* (IV, 24) the syndrome of the Kali Yuga is recognized by the fact that during this epoch property alone confers social rank, wealth becomes the sole criterion of virtue, passion and lewdness the sole bonds between mates, falsehood the sole condition of success in life, sexuality the sole means of enjoyment, and an outward, purely ritualistic religion is confounded with spirituality. For several thousand years, it goes without saying, we have been living in the Kali Yuga.

The figures 4, 3, 2, and 1 denote both the decreasing length of the yugas and the progressive diminution of the Dharma prevailing in them. Correspondingly the span of human life grows shorter, morality becomes increasingly lax, and human intelligence declines. Certain Hindu schools, the Pāñcarātra for example, establish a connection between the "decline of knowledge" (*jñāna bhraṃśa*) and the theory of cycles.

The relative duration of each of these four yugas may be reckoned in various ways: everything depends on the value accorded to the years, which may be considered as human years or as divine years, each of which embraces

360 human years. According to certain sources,[3] the Kṛta Yuga measures 4,000 years plus 400 years each of dawn and of dusk; then follow the Tretā Yuga, measuring 3,000 years, the Dvāpara, measuring 2,000 years, and the Kali Yuga, of 1,000 (plus the corresponding dawns and dusks, of course). A complete cycle, a mahāyuga, consequently comprises 12,000 years. The passage from one yuga to another occurs in the course of a dusk, marking a decrescendo within each yuga, which always ends with a stage of darkness. As we approach the end of the cycle—that is, the fourth and last yuga—the darkness thickens. The last yuga, in which we now find ourselves, is regarded as the "age of darkness" par excellence, for by a play on words it is associated with the goddess Kālī, the "Black." Kālī is one of the numerous names of the Great Goddess of Śakti, consort of the god Śiva. This name for the Great Goddess has been related to the Sanskrit word *kāla,* "time": Kālī according to this etymology is not only "the Black One" but also the personification of Time.[4] But regardless of the etymology, the association of *kāla,* Time, with the goddess Kālī and Kali Yuga is structurally justified: Time is black because it is irrational, hard, pitiless; and Kālī, like all the other Great Goddesses, is the mistress of Time, of the destinies she forges and accomplishes.

A complete cycle, a mahāyuga, ends in a "dissolution," a *pralaya,* which is repeated more radically (*mahāpralaya,* the "Great Dissolution") at the end of the thousandth cycle. For later speculation has amplified the primordial rhythm of "creation-destruction-creation" *ad infinitum,* projecting the unity of measure, the yuga, into vaster and vaster cycles. The 12,000 years of a mahāyuga have been considered as "divine years," each comprising 360 years; this would yield a total of 4,320,000 years for a single cosmic cycle. A thousand such mahāyugas constitute a *kalpa* ("form"); 14 kalpas make up a *manvantara* (so called because each manvantara is held to be governed by a Manu, or mythical ancestor-king). One kalpa is equivalent to a day in the life of Brahma; another kalpa to a night. A hundred of these "years" of Brahma, or 311,000 billion human years, constitute the life of the god. But even this considerable life-span of Brahmā does not exhaust Time, for the gods themselves are not eternal and the cosmic creations and destructions go on forever.

The essential element in this avalanche of figures is the cyclical character of cosmic Time. The same phenomenon (creation-destruction-new creation), foreshadowed in each yuga (dawn and dusk) but fully realized in a mahāyuga, is repeated over and over. The life of Brahmā comprises 2,560,000 of these mahāyugas, each one consisting of the same stages (Kṛta, Tretā, Dvāpara, Kali), and ending in a *pralaya,* a *ragnarök.* (A "definitive" destruction, or total dissolution of the cosmic Egg occurs in *the mahāpralaya* at the end of each kalpa. The *mahāpralaya* implies a regression of all the "forms," the modes of existences, into the original undifferentiated *prakṛti*. On the mythical plane nothing subsists but the primordial Ocean, on the surface of which sleeps the Great God Viṣṇu.)

The ideas that stand out from this orgy of figures are: (1) a metaphysical depreciation of *human history,* which by the mere fact of its duration provokes an erosion of all *forms,* exhausting their ontological substance;[5] (2) the notion of the *perfection of beginnings,* a universal tradition which is here exemplified in the myth of a paradise which is gradually lost by the simple fact that it is realized, takes form, and exists in time; and above all (3) the eternal repetition of the fundamental *cosmic rhythm,* the periodic destruction and re-creation of the universe. From this cycle without beginning and end, which is the cosmic manifestation of *māyā,* man can save himself only by an act of spiritual freedom (for, all Indian stereological solutions reduce themselves to a previous deliverance from the cosmic illusion, and to spiritual freedom).

The two great heterodoxies, Buddhism and Jainism, accept this same pan-Indian doctrine of cyclical time in its broad outlines and liken it to a wheel with twelve spokes (this image occurs also in the Vedic texts).[6] Buddhism measures the cosmic cycles by the unit of the *kalpa* (Pāli: *kappa),* which is divided into a variable number of what the texts call "incalculables," *asaṃkhyeya* (Pāli: *asaṅkheyya).* The Pāli sources in general speak of 4 asaṅkheyas and 100,000 kalpas.[7] In the Mahāyānic literature the number of incalculables varies between 3, 7, and 33, and they are related to the career of the Bodhisattva in the diverse cosmoses. The progressive decadence of man is marked in the Buddhist tradition by a continuous diminution in his life span. Thus, according to the *Dīgha-Nikāya* (II, 2-7), the length of man's life was 80,000 years at the epoch of the first Buddha, Vipassi, who appeared 91 kappas ago; it was 70,000 years at the epoch of the second, Buddha, Sikhi (31 kappas ago), and so on. The seventh Buddha, Gautama, makes his appearance when the human life span amounts to only 100 years, the absolute minimum. (We find the same motif in the Iranian apocalypses.) Yet for Buddhism as for all Indian speculation, time is unlimited; and the Bodhisattva is incarnated in order to announce the glad tidings of salvation to all men, for ever and ever. The sole possibility of escaping from time, of breaking through the iron ring of existences, is to abolish the human condition and attain to Nīrvāṇa. All these innumerable "incalculables" and eons also have a steriological function: the mere contemplation of them terrorizes man and compels him to realize that he must begin this same evanescent existence over and over again, billions of times, always enduring the same endless sufferings. And the effect of this is to exacerbate his will to escape, to impel him to transcend his condition as an "existent" once and for all.

Cosmic Time and History

Let us for a moment consider this vision of infinite Time, of the endless cycle of creation and destruction, this myth of the eternal return, as an instrument of knowledge and means of liberation. In the perspective of Great Time, all existence is precarious, evanescent, illusory. Considered in the light of the major cosmic rhythms—that is, of the mahāyugas, kalpas, manvantaras—not only do human existence and history, with all their empires, dynasties, revolutions, and counterrevolutions without number, prove to be ephemeral and in a sense unreal, but the universe itself is bereft of reality, for as we have seen, universes are born continuously from the innumerable pores of Viṣṇu and vanish as rapidly as air bubbles bursting on the surface of the waters. 'Existence *in* Time is ontologically nonexistence, unreality. It is in, this sense that we must understand the belief of Indian idealism, and first and foremost of the Vedānta, that the world is illusory, that it lacks reality because its duration is 'limited, for, seen in the perspective of eternal recurrence, it is non-duration. This table is unreal not because it does not exist in the strict sense of the term, not because it is an illusion of our senses, for it is not an illusion: at this precise moment it exists—rather, this table is illusory because it will no longer exist in ten thousand or one hundred thousand years. The historical world, the societies and civilizations arduously built by the effort of thousands of generations, all this is illusory because, from the standpoint of the cosmic rhythms, the historical world endures for only the space of an instant. In drawing the logical conclusions from the lesson of infinite Time and the Eternal Return, the Vedāntist, the Buddhist, the Ṛṣi, the Yogi, the Sādhu, etc. renounce the world and seek absolute Reality; for only knowledge of the Absolute helps them to deliver themselves from illusion, to rend the veil of Māyā.

But renunciation of the world is not the only consequence which an Indian is justified in drawing from the discovery of infinite, cyclical Time. As we begin to understand today, India has not only known negation and total rejection of the world. Starting from this same dogma of the fundamental unreality of the cosmos, Indian thought also mapped out a road that does not necessarily lead to asceticism and abandonment of the world. An example is the *phalatṛṣṇāvairāgya* preached by Kṛṣṇa in the *Bhagavad Gītā,* which is to say, "renunciation of the fruits of one's actions," of the profits one might derive from action, but not of action itself.[8] The sequel to the myth of Viṣṇu and Indra recounted above throws light on this principle.

Humiliated by Viṣṇu's revelation, Indra renounces his vocation as warrior god and withdraws to the mountains to practice the harshest asceticism. In other words, he prepares to draw what seems to him the only logical consequence of his discovery of the world's unreality and vanity. He finds himself in the same situation as Prince Siddhārtha immediately after abandoning his palace and his wives at Kapilavastu and undertaking his arduous mortifications. But it may be asked whether a king of the gods and a husband had the right to draw such conclusions from a metaphysical revelation, whether his renunciation and asceticism did not imperil the balance of the world. And indeed, his wife, Queen Śacī, desolate at having been forsaken, soon implores the help of their spiritual guide, Bṛhaspati. Bṛhaspati takes her by the hand and leads her to Indra. He speaks to Indra at length, lauding the merits not only of the contemplative life, but also of the active life, the life which finds its fulfillment in this world. Thus Indra receives a second revelation: he now understands that each individual must follow his own path and vocation, or, in the last analysis, do his duty. But since his vocation and duty are to remain Indra, he resumes his identity and pursues his heroic adventures, but without pride and self-conceit, for he has perceived the vanity of all "situations," even that of a king of the gods.

This sequel to the myth restores the balance: the essential is not to renounce one's historical situation, seeking vainly to attain to universal being, but to keep constantly in mind the perspectives of the Great Time while continuing to fulfill one's duty in historical time. This is precisely the lesson which Kṛṣṇa teaches Arjuna in the *Bhagavad-Gītā*. India, as elsewhere in the archaic world, this access to Great Time gained by the periodic recitation of myths makes possible the indefinite prolongation of a fixed *order* which is at once metaphysical, ethical, and social. This order does not encourage an idolization of history; for the perspective of mythical Time makes any segment of historical time illusory.

As we have just seen, the myth of cyclical Time, by shattering the illusions spun by the minor rhythms of time—that is, by historical time—reveals to us the precariousness and ontological unreality of the universe, and also points a way of deliverance. Actually, we may save ourselves from the trammels of Māyā, either by the contemplative way, by renouncing the world and practicing asceticism and related mystical techniques—or by an active way, by remaining in the worm, but ceasing to enjoy the "fruits of our actions" (*phalatṛṣṇāvairāgya*). In both cases, the essential is not to believe *exclusively* in the reality of the forms that arise and unfold in time: we must never forget that such forms are "true" only on their own plane of reference, and are ontologically devoid of substance. As we have said, time can become an instrument of knowledge, in the sense that we need only project a thing or an individual upon the plane of cosmic Time in order to become aware of its unreality. The gnoseological and soteriological function of such a change of perspective obtained through access to the major rhythms of time is admirably elucidated by certain myths relating to Viṣṇu's Māyā.

Let us examine one of these myths in the modern, popular variant recorded by Śrī Ramakrishna.[9] A famous ascetic named Nārada has gained the favour of Viṣṇu by his innumerable austerities. The god appears to him and promises to grant a wish. "Show me the magical power of thy *māyā*," Nārada asks of him. Viṣṇu consents and beckons the ascetic to follow him. A little later, they find themselves on a deserted path in the blazing sun. Viṣṇu is thirsty and asks Nārada to go on *for* another few hundred yards, where a village may be seen, and to bring him back some water. Nārada hastens to the village and knocks at the door of the first house. A beautiful girl opens the door. The ascetic gazes upon her at length and forgets why he has come. He enters the house and the girl's parents receive him with the respect due to a saint. Time passes. At length Nārada marries the girl and learns to know the joys of marriage and the hardships of a peasant's life. Twelve years pass: now Nārada has three children and at the death of his father-in-law, he has inherited the farm. But in the course of the twelfth year the region is flooded by torrential rains. In one night the herds are drowned and the house collapses. Supporting his wife with one hand, holding his two children with the other, and carrying the smallest child on his shoulder, he struggles through the water. But the burden is too much *for* him. The smallest child slips into the water. Nārada leaves the other two and tries to recover him, but it is too late, the torrent has swept him away. While he is looking *for* the little one, the torrent swallows up the two other children and not long after, his wife. Nārada himself falls, and the torrent carries him along unconscious and inert as a piece of wood. When he awakens, he has been cast up on a rock. Remembering his sorrows, he bursts out sobbing. But suddenly he hears a familiar voice: "My child! Where is the water *you* were to bring? I have been waiting *for* more than half an hour!" Nārada turns his head and looks. In place of the torrent that had destroyed everything, he sees the deserted sun-baked fields. "And now do *you* understand the secret of my Māyā?" the God asks him.

Obviously Nārada cannot claim to understand it entirely; but he has learned one essential thing: he knows now that Viṣṇu's cosmic Māyā is manifested through time.

The "Terror of Time"

The myth of cyclical Time—of the cosmic cycles that repeat themselves *ad infinitum*—is not an innovation of Indian speculations. As we have elsewhere shown,[10] the traditional societies—whose representations of time are so difficult to grasp precisely because they are expressed in symbols and rituals whose profound meaning sometimes remains inaccessible to us—the traditional societies conceive of man's temporal existence not only as an infinite repetition of certain archetypes and exemplary gestures but also as an *eternal renewal*. In symbols and rituals, the world is recreated periodically. The cosmogony is repeated at least once a year—and the cosmogonic myth serves also as a model for a great number of actions: marriage, for example, or healing.

What is the meaning of all these myths and rites? Their central meaning is that the world is born, grows weary, perishes, and is born anew in a precipitate rhythm. Chaos and the cosmogonic act that puts an end to chaos by a new creation are periodically reactualized. The year—or what is understood by this term—corresponds to the creation, duration, and destruction of a world, a cosmos. It is highly probable that this conception of the periodic creation and destruction of the world, although reinforced by the spectacle of the periodic death and resurrection of vegetation, is not a creation of agricultural societies. It is found in the myths of pre-agricultural societies and is in all likelihood a lunar conception. For the most evident periodicity is that of the moon, and it was terms relating to the moon which first served to express the measurement of time. The lunar rhythms always mark a "creation" (the new moon) followed by a "growth" (the full moon), and a diminution and "death" (the three moonless nights). It is most probably that; image of this eternal birth and death of the moon that helped to crystallize early man's intuitions concerning the periodicity of life and death; and subsequently gave rise to the myth of the periodic creation and destruction of the world. The most ancient myths of the deluge reveal a lunar structure and origin. After each deluge a mythical ancestor gives birth to a new mankind. And most frequently this mythical ancestor takes the form of a lunar animal. (In ethnology, this name is applied to those animals whose life reveals a certain alternation and particularly a periodic appearance and disappearance.)

Thus for "primitive" man, Time is cyclic, the world is periodically created and destroyed, and the lunar symbolism of "birth–death–rebirth" is manifested in a great number of myths and rites. It was on the basis of such an immemorial heritage that the pan-Indian doctrine of the ages of the world and of the cosmic cycles developed. Of course, the archetypal image of the eternal birth, death, and resurrection of the moon was appreciably modified by Indian thought. As for the astronomical aspect of the yugas, it was probably influenced by the cosmological and astrological speculations of the Babylonians. But these possible historical influences of Mesopotamia on India need not concern us her. What we wish to bring out at this point is that with their headlong multiplication of cosmic cycles, the Indians had in mind a soteriological aim. Terrified by the endless births and rebirths of universes, accompanied by an equal number of human births and rebirths governed by the law of karma; the Indian was obliged, as it were, to seek, an issue from this cosmic wheel and from these infinite transmigrations. The mystical doctrines and techniques aimed at the deliverance of man from the pain of the infernal cycle of "life–death–rebirth" take over the mythical images of the cosmic cycles, amplify them, and utilize them for purposes of proselytism. For the Indians of the post-Vedic period—that is, for those Indians who had discovered the "suffering of existence"—the eternal return is equivalent to the infinite cycle of transmigration governed by karma. This illusory, ephemeral world, the world of *saṃsāra,* the world of suffering and ignorance, is the world that unfolds in time—Deliverance from this world and attachment of salvation are tantamount to a deliverance from cosmic Time.

Indian Symbolism of the Abolition of Time

In Sanskrit the term *kāla* is employed both for indefinite periods of time and for definite moments—as in the European languages. For example: "What *time* is it *now?*" The most ancient texts stress the temporal character of all possible universes and existences: "Time has engendered everything that has been and will be."[11] In the Upaniṣads, Brahman, the Universal Spirit, the Absolute Being, is conceived both as transcending time and as the source and foundation of everything that is manifested in time: "Lord of what has been and will be, he is both today and tomorrow."[12] And Kṛṣṇa, manifesting himself to Arjuna as a cosmic God, declares: "I am the Time which, in progressing, destroys the world."[13]

As we know, the Upaniṣads distinguish two aspects of Brahman, of universal being: "the corporeal and the incorporeal, the mortal and the immortal, the fixed (*sthita*) and the mobile, etc.,"[14] which amounts to saying that both the universe in its manifest and nonmanifest aspects and the spirit in its conditioned and nonconditioned modalities repose in the one, in the Brahman which unites all opposites and all oppositions. And the *Maitri Upaniṣad* (VII, II, 8), ill establishing this bipolarity of universal being on the plane of time, distinguishes two forms (*dve rūpe*) of Brahman (that is, the aspects of the "two natures" of a single essence [*tad ekam*]), as "Time and Without-Time" (*kālaś-cākalaś-ca*). In other words, Time and eternity are the two aspects of the same principle: in Brahman" the *nunc fluens* and the *nunc stans* (a term by which Boethius defined eternity) coincide. The *Maitri Upaniṣad* continues: "What precedes the Sun is Without-Time (*akāla*) and undivided (*akāla*); but what begins with the Sun is Time which has parts (*sakala*) and its form is the Year. . ."

The expression "What precedes the Sun" may be interpreted cosmologically as relating to the epoch which preceded the Creation-for in the intervals between the mahāyugas or kalpas, during the Great Cosmic Nights, time no longer exists—but its application is 'above all metaphysical and soteriological: it refers to the paradoxical situation of him who obtains illumination, who becomes a *jivan-mukta,* who is "delivered in this life," and thereby transcends time in the sense that he no longer participates in it. Thus the *Chāndogya Upaniṣad* (Ill, 11) declares that for the sage, the illumined, one, the sun remains motionless. "But after having risen to the zenith it (the Sun) will never rise or set again. It will remain alone in the Center (*ekala eva madhye sthitātā*).' Whence this verse: 'There (in the transcendent world of *Brahman*) it has never set and never risen. . .' It neither rises nor sets; for him who knows the doctrine of *brahman* it is in the heavens once and for all (*sakṛt*)."

Here, of course, we have a concrete image of transcendence: at the zenith, that is, at the summit of the celestial vault, at the "center of the world"—where a cutting-across the planes, a communication between the three cosmic zones, is possible—the sun (= time) remains immobile for "him who 'knows"; the *nunc fluens* is paradoxically transformed into a *nunc stans*. Illumination, understanding, accomplishes the miracle of an escape from time. In the Vedic texts and Upaniṣads the paradoxical instant of illumination is likened to the lightning flash. Brahman is understood suddenly, like a lightning flash.[15] "In a lightning flash the truth."[16] (In both Greek metaphysics and Christian mysticism we find the same image used to denote spiritual illumination.)

Let us pause for a moment to consider this mythical image: the zenith which is at once the summit of the world and the "center" par excellence, the infinitesimal point through which passes the cosmic axis (*Axis Mundi*). In our last year's lecture we showed the importance of this symbolism for archaic thought.[17] A "center" represents an ideal point belonging not to profane, geometric space, but to sacred space, a point in which communication with heaven or hell may be realized; in other words, a center is the paradoxical place that cuts across the planes; it is a place where the sensuous world may be transcended. But by transcending the Universe, the created world, one also transcends time and achieves stasis, the eternal intemporal present.

The relation between the acts of transcending space and of transcending the temporal flux is elucidated by a myth relating to the nativity of the Buddha. The *Majjhima-Nikāya* (III, p. 123) relates that "as soon as he was born, the Bodhisattva set his feet flat on the ground and turning toward the north, took seven steps, sheltered by a white parasol. He contemplated all the regions round about him and said with the voice of a bull: 'I am the highest in the world, I am the best in the world, I am the oldest in the world; this is my last birth; for me there will never again be a new existence.' This mythical picture of the Buddha's birth is carried over with certain variations into the subsequent literature of the *Nikāya-Āgamas*, the *Vinaya*, and the biographies of the Buddha.[18] The *sapta padāni*, seven steps which carry the Buddha to the summit of the world, also play a part in Buddhist art and iconography. The symbolism of these seven steps is quite transparent.[19] The phrase "I am the highest in the world" (*aggo'ham asmi lokassa*) signifies the spatial transcendence of the Buddha. For he attained to the "summit of the world" (*lokkagge*) by traversing the seven cosmic stories, which, as we know, correspond to the seven planetary heavens. But in so doing he likewise transcends Time, for in the Indian cosmology, the creation begins at the summit, which is therefore the "oldest" point. That is why the Buddha cries out: "I am the oldest in the world" (*jettho'ham asmi lokassa*). For in attaining to the cosmic summit, the Buddha becomes contemporaneous with the beginning of the world. He has magically abolished time and creation, and finds himself in the atemporal instant preceding the cosmogony. The irreversibility of cosmic time, a terrible law for all those who live in illusion, no longer counts for the Buddha. For him time is reversible, and can even be anticipated: for he knows not only the past but also the future. In addition to abolishing time, the Buddha can pass through it backward (*patiloman,* Skr. *pratiloman,* "against the fur"), and this will be equally true for the Buddhist monks and the yogis who, before obtaining their Nirvāṇa or their *samādhi,* effect a "return backward," which enables them to know their previous existences.

The "Broken Egg"

Side by side with this image of the Buddha transcending space and time by rutting across the seven cosmic plans to the "center" of the world and simultaneously returning to the atemporal moment which precedes the creation of the world, we have another image which felicitously combines the symbolisms of space and time. In a remarkable article, Paul Mus calls attention to this text from the *Suttavibhaṅga.*[20]

'When a hen has laid eggs, says the Buddha, eight or ten or twelve of them, and she has sat upon them and kept them warm for a sufficient time; and when the first chick breaks through the shell with his toe or beak and issues happily from the egg, what shall we call this chick, the oldest or the youngest?—We shall call him the oldest, venerable Gautama, for he is the firstborn among them.—So likewise, O Brāhman, I alone among the men who live in ignorance and are as though enclosed and imprisoned in an egg have burst this shell of ignorance, and I alone in all the world have obtained the beatific universal dignity of the Buddha. Thus, Oh Brāhman, I am the oldest, the noblest among men.'

As Paul Mus says, this imagery is "deceptively simple. To understand it correctly, we must remember that the Brāhmanic initiation was regarded as a second birth. The most common name for the initiates was *dvija:* 'twice-born.' But the birds, snakes, etc. were also given this name, inasmuch as they were born of eggs. The laying of the egg was likened to the 'first birth that is, the natural birth of man. The hatching out corresponded to the supernatural birth of initiation. Moreover, the Brāhmanic codes establish the principle that the initiate is socially superior, 'older' than the uninitiated, whatever may be their relations of physical age or kinship."[21]

But this is not all. "It was scarcely possible to liken the supernatural birth of the Buddha to the breaking of the egg containing in germ the 'firstborn' (*jyeṣṭha*) of the universe without reminding the listeners of the 'cosmic egg' of Brāhmanic traditions, whence at the dawn of time there issued the primordial God of creation, variously named the Golden Embryo (Hiraṇyagarbha), the father or Master of Creatures (Prajāpati), Agni (God of the fire, and ritual Fire), or *brahman* (sacrificial principle, 'prayer,' deified text of the hymns, etc.)."[22] And the "cosmic egg" was "definitely identified with the year, the symbolic expression for cosmic Time: so that *saṃsāra,* another image of cyclical Time reduced to its causes, corresponds exactly to the mythical egg."[23]

Thus the action of transcending time is formulated in a symbolism that is both cosmological and spatial. To break the envelope of the egg is equivalent in the Buddha's parable to breaking through *saṃsāra,* the wheel of existences-in other words, to *transcending both cosmic Space and cyclical Time.* In this case, too, the Buddha makes use of images similar to those of the Vedas and Upaniṣads. The motionless sun at the zenith in the *Chāndogya Upaniṣad* is a spatial symbol which expresses the paradoxical act of escape from the cosmos with the same force as the Buddhist image of the broken egg. In describing certain aspects of Tantric Yoga, we shall encounter further archetypal images of this sort, employed to symbolic transcendence.

The Philosophy of Time in Buddhism

The symbolism of the seven steps of Buddha and of the cosmic egg implies the *reversibility of time,* and we shall have occasion to say more of this paradoxical process. But first we must present the broad outlines of the philosophy of time elaborated by Buddhism and particularly Mahāyāna Buddhism.[24] For the Buddhist, too, time consists of a continuous flux (*santāna*), and this fluidity of time suffices to make every "form" that is manifested in time not only perishable but also ontologically unreal. The philosophers of the Mahāyāna have written copiously on what might be called the instantaneity of time—that is, the fluidity and hence unreality of the present instant which is continuously transformed into past and nonbeing. For the Buddhist philosopher, says Stcherbatsky, "existence and non-existence are not different appurtenances of a thing, they are the thing itself." As Śāntarakṣita writes, "the nature of anything is its own momentary stasis and destruction."[25] The destruction to which Śāntarakṣita alludes is not empirical destruction—for example, that of a vase which breaks when it falls to the ground—

but the intrinsic and continuous annihilation of every existent that is involved in time. It is in this sense that Vasubandhu writes: "Because of immediate destruction, there is no (real) motion."[26] Movement and consequently time as such are pragmatic postulates, just as for Buddhism the ego is a pragmatic postulate; but the concept of motion corresponds to no outward reality, for it is "something" constructed by ourselves. Mahāyāna Buddhism expresses the unreality of the temporal world chiefly in terms of its fluidity and instantaneity, its continuous annihilation. From the Mahāyānic conception of time some writers have concluded that for the philosophers of the Greater Vehicle motion is discontinuous, that "motion consists of a series of immobilities" (Stcherbatsky). But as Coomaraswamy remarks, a line is not made up of an infinite series of points but presents itself as a continuum.[27] Vasubandhu himself said as much: "The arising of instants is uninterrupted" (*nirantara–kṣaṇa–utpāda*). Etymologically the term *santāna*, which Stcherbatsky translated by "series," means "continuum."

There is nothing new in all this. The logicians and metaphysicians of the Greater Vehicle did no more than derive the ultimate conclusion from the pan-Indian intuitions concerning the ontological unreality of everything existing in time. Fluidity conceals unreality. The only hope and path of salvation is the Buddha, who has revealed the Dharma (absolute reality) and disclosed the road to Nirvāṇa. Indefatigably he repeats the central theme of his message: all that is contingent is unreal; but he never forgets to add: "this is not I" (*na me so attā*). For he, the Buddha, is identical with the Dharma, and consequently he is "simple, noncomposite" (*asaṃghata*) and "atemporal, timeless" (*ākaliko*, as the *Aṅguttara–Nikāya* puts it, IV, *35–406*). Over and over the Buddha repeats that he "transcends the cons" (*kappātito. . . vipamutto*), that he "is not a man of the eons" (*akkapiyo*), which is to say that he is not really involved in the cyclical flux of time, that he has transcended cosmic Time.[28] For him, according to the *Saṃyutta–Nikāya* (I, 141) "there exists neither past nor future" (*na tassa paccha na purattam atthi*). For the Buddha all times are made present (*Viśuddhi Magga*, 411); in other words, he has abolished the irreversibility of time:

The total present, the eternal present of the mystics, is stasis, nonduration. Translated into spatial symbolism: nonduration, the eternal present, is immobility. And indeed, to indicate the unconditioned state of the Buddha or the *jīvan-mukta*, Buddhism-like Yoga-makes use of terms relating to immobility, stasis. "He whose thought is stable" (*thita-citto*)[29] "he whose spirit is stable" (*thit'attā*), etc.[30] It should not be forgotten that the first and simplest definition of Yoga is given by Patañjali himself at the beginning of his *Yoga-Sūtras* (I, 2): *yogaḥ cittavṛttinirodhaḥ*, "yoga is the suppression of the states of consciousness." But this suppression is only the final goal. The yogi begins by "halting," by "immobilizing" his states of consciousness, his psychomental flux. (The most usual sense of *nirodha* is "restriction or obstruction," the act of enclosing, etc.). We shall come back to the consequences of this "stoppage," this "immobilization" of the states of consciousness, for the yogi's experience of time.

He "whose thought is stable" and for whom time no longer flows lives in an eternal present, in the *nunc stalls*. The present moment, the *nunc,* is called *kṣaṇa* in Sanskrit and *khaṇa* in Pali.[31] It is by the *kṣaṇa,* the "'moment," that time is measured. But this term also has the meaning of "favorable moment, opportunity," and for the Buddha it is through the mediation of such a moment that one can escape from time. The Buddha exhorts his adepts "not to lose the moment," for "those who lose the moment will lament." He congratulates those monks who have "seized the moment" (*khaṇo vo paṭiladdho*)*;* and he pities those "for whom the moment is passed" (*khaṇātīta*).[32] This means that after the long road travelled in cosmic Time, through innumerable existences" the illumination is instantaneous (*ekakṣaṇa*). "The instantaneous illumination" (*ekakṣaṇābhisambodhi*), as the Mahayanic authors call it, means that the comprehension of reality occurs suddenly, like a lightning flash—a metaphor which we have already encountered in the Upaniṣads. Any moment, any *kṣaṇa,* may become the "favorable moment," the paradoxical instant which suspends time and projects the Buddhist monk into the *nunc stans,* an eternal present. This eternal present is no longer part of time; it is qualitatively different from our profane "present," from this precarious present which stands out feebly between two nonentities—the past and the future—and which will cease with our death. The "favorable moment" of illumination may be compared to the lightning flash which communicates revelation, or to the mystical ecstasy which is paradoxically prolonged beyond time.

Images and Paradoxes

It should be noted that all these images through which the Indians endeavoured to express the paradoxical act of escape from time also serve to express *the passage from ignorance to illumination* (or, in other words, from "death" to "life," from the contingent to the absolute, etc.). We may group them roughly into three classes: (1) the images which suggest the abolition of time and hence illumination by a cutting across the planes (the "broken egg," the lightning flash, the seven steps of the Buddha); (2) those which refer to an inconceivable situation (the immobility of the sun at the zenith, the cessation of the flux of the states of consciousness, total cessation of respiration in the practice of Yoga, etc.); and (3) the contradictory image of the "favorable moment," a temporal fragment transfigured into an "instant of illumination." The two last images also suggest a cutting across the planes, for they denote a paradoxical passage from a normal state in the profane sense (the movement of the sun, the flux of consciousness, etc.) to a paradoxical state (the immobility of the sun etc.), or imply the transubstantiation which takes place within the temporal moment itself. (As we know, the passage from profane time to sacred Time provoked by a ritual also implies a "cutting across planes": liturgical Time does not prolong the profane time in which it is situated, but, paradoxically, continues the time of the last ritual accomplished).[33]

The structure of these images should not surprise us. All symbolism of transcendence is paradoxical and impossible to conceive in profane terms. The most common symbol to express the cutting across the planes and penetration into the "other world," the transcendent world (of the dead or of the gods), is the "difficult passage," the razor edge. "It is hard to pass over the whetted blade of the razor," say the poets to express the arduousness of the road (leading to supreme knowledge).[34] We are reminded of the Gospel passage: "Strait is the gate and narrow the way, which leadeth unto life, and few there be that find it" (Matthew 7:14). The "strait gate," the razor edge, and the narrow, dangerous bridge by no means exhaust the wealth of this symbolism. Other images represent a seemingly hopeless situation. The hero of a tale of initiation must go "where night and day meet"; or find a gate in a wall that discloses none; or ascend to heaven by a passage which half opens for the barest instant; or pass between two millstones in continual movement, between two cliffs that touch continuously, or between the jaws of a monster, etc.[35] All these mythical images express the necessity of transcending the contraries, of abolishing the polarity which characterizes the human state, in order to accede to ultimate reality. As Coomaraswamy says, "whoever would transfer from this to the Otherworld, or return, must do so through the undimensioned and timeless 'interval' that divides related but contrary forces, between which, if one is to pass at all, It must be 'instantly.'"[36]

For Indian thought, the human state is defined by the existence of the contraries; deliverance (that is, abolition of the human condition) is equivalent to an unconditional state which transcends the contraries, or, what amounts to the same thing, a state in which the contraries coincide. We are reminded that the *Maitri Upaniṣad,* in speaking of the manifest and unmanifest aspects of being, distinguishes two forms of *brahman* as "Time and Timeless." For the sage, *brahman* plays the part of an exemplary model; deliverance is an "imitation of *brahman.*" Thus for "him who knows" there ceases to be an opposition between "time" and the "timeless"; they cease to be distinct from each other; the pairs of opposites are done away with. To illustrate this paradoxical situation Indian thought, like that of other archaic peoples, makes use of images which contain contradiction in their very structure (images such as finding a door in a wall which reveals none).

The coincidence of opposites is still better elucidated by the image of the "instant" (*kṣaṇa*) which is transformed into a "favourable moment." Apparently nothing distinguishes any fragment of profane time from the intemporal instant obtained by illumination. To understand fully the structure and function of such an image, we must recall the dialectic of the holy: any object at all may paradoxically become a hierophany, a receptacle of the sacred, while still continuing to participate in its cosmic environment. (A holy stone for all its holiness still remains a *stone* along with other stones, etc.[37] From this point of view the image of the "favorable moment" expresses the paradox of the coincidence of opposites even more forcefully than do the images of contradictory situations, immobility of the Sun, etc.)

Techniques of Escape from Time

Instantaneous illumination, the paradoxical leap outside or time, is obtained in consequence of a long discipline which implies a philosophy as well as a mystical technique. Let us consider a few techniques aimed at halting the temporal flux. The most common of them, which is truly pan-Indian, is the *prāṇāyāma,* the rhythmization of breathing. In this connection it should be noted that although its ultimate aim is to transcend the human state, the practice of Yoga starts out by ameliorating this same human state, by giving it a fullness and a majesty which seem inaccessible to the profane. We are not thinking immediately of Haṭha Yoga, whose express aim is an absolute mastery of the human body and psyche. All forms of Yoga imply a previous transformation of profane man—this feeble, dispersed slave of his body, incapable of a true mental effort—into a glorious Man: possessed of perfect physical health, absolute master of his body and his psychomental life, capable of concentration' conscious of himself. What Yoga seeks ultimately to transcend is a perfect man of this sort, and not merely a profane, everyday man.

In cosmological terms (and to penetrate Indian thought we must always use this key), Yoga starts from a *perfect cosmos* 'in order to transcend the *Cosmic condition as such—it* does not start from a chaos. The physiology and psychomental life of the profane man resemble a chaos. Yoga practice begins by organizing this chaos, by "cosmifying" it. Little by little *prāṇāyāma,* the rhythmization of breathing, forms the yogi into a cosmos: breathing is no longer arrhythmic, thought is no longer dispersed, the circulation of the psychomental forces is no longer anarchic.[38] But in thus working on the respiration, the yogi works directly on lived time. And there is no adept of Yoga who, in the course of these breathing exercises, has not experienced another quality of time. Attempts have been made to describe this experience of lived time during the *prāṇāyāma;* it has been compared to the beatific time of one listening to good music, to the raptures of love, to the serenity or plenitude of prayer. But all these comparisons are inadequate. What is certain is that in progressively decelerating the rhythm of breathing in prolonging the expiration and inspiration, and increasing the interval between these two elements of respiration, the yogi experiences a time different from ours.[39]

It seems to us that the practice of *prāṇāyāma* presents two essential points: (1) the yogi starts out by "cosmifying" his body and psychomental life; (2) by *prāṇāyāma* the yogi succeeds in integrating himself at will with the diverse rhythms of lived time. In his extremely concise manner, Patañjali recommends "the control of the moments and of their continuity.[40] The later Yogic–Tantric treatises give more details regarding this "control" of time. The *Kālacakra Tantra,* for example, goes so far as to relate inspiration and expiration with day and night, then with fortnights, months, years; arriving finally at the great cosmic cycles.[41]

In other words the yogi by his own respiratory rhythm may be said to repeat Great Cosmic Time, the periodic creations and destructions of the universe. The purpose of this exercise is twofold: on the one hand the yogi is led to identify his own respiratory moments with the rhythms of Great Cosmic Time, and in so doing realizes the relativity and ultimate unreality of time. But, on the other hand, he obtains the reversibility of the temporal flux (*sāra*): he returns backward, relives his previous existences and, as the texts put it, "burns" the consequences of his former acts; he annuls these acts in order to escape from their karmic consequences.

In such an exercise of *prāṇāyāma* we discern a will to relive the rhythms of the Great Cosmic Time: the experience is similar to that of Nārada related above; but here it is obtained voluntarily and consciously. Proof that this is so may be found in the assimilation of the two "mystical veins," *iḍā* and *piṅgalā,* to the moon and the sun.[42] In the mystical physiology of Yoga, *iḍā* and *piṅgalā* are, as we know, the two canals through which psychovital energy circulates within the human body. The assimilation of these two mystical veins to the sun and the moon completes the operation that we have called the cosmification of the yogi. His mystical body becomes a microcosm. His inspiration corresponds to the course of the sun—that is, to the day; and his expiration to the moon—that is, the night. Thus the breathing rhythm of the yogi ultimately enters into the rhythm of Great Cosmic Time.

But this entrance into Great Cosmic Time does not abolish time as such; only its rhythms have changed. The yogi lives a cosmic Time, but he nevertheless continues to live in time. Yet his ultimate purpose is to issue from time. And this is what happens when the yogi succeeds in unifying the two currents of psychic energy that circulate through *iḍā* and *piṅgalā.* By a process that is too difficult to explain in a few words, the yogi stops his respiration and, by unifying the two currents, concentrates them and forces them to circulate through the third "vein," *suṣumnā,* the vein situated at the "center." And according to the *Haṭhayoga-pradīpikā* (IV, 16–17), "*Suṣumnā* devours Time." This paradoxical unification of the two mystical veins *iḍā* and *piṅgalā,* the two polar currents is equivalent to the unification of the sun and the moon—that is, the abolition of the cosmos, the reunion of contraries, which amounts to saying that the yogi transcends both the created universe and the time that governs it. We recall the mythical image of the egg whose shell is broken by the Buddha. Thus it happens to the yogi who "concentrates" his breath in *suṣumnā:* he breaks the shell of his microcosm, he transcends the contingent world which exists in time. A considerable number of Tantric texts allude to this absolute, intemporal state in which there exists neither day nor night, "in which there is neither sickness nor old age"—naive and approximate formulas for the "escape from time." To transcend day and night means to *transcend the contraries,* which corresponds on the temporal plane to the passage through the "strait gate" on the spatial plane. This experience of Tantric Yoga prepares the way for *samādhi,* the state which is usually translated as "ecstasy" but which we prefer to call "enstasis." The yogi ultimately becomes a *jīvan-mukta,* one who is "delivered in this life." We cannot conceive of his existence, for it is paradoxical. The *jīvan-mukta* is said to live no longer in time, in our time— but in an eternal present, in the *nunc stans.*

But these processes of Tantric Yoga do not exhaust the Indian techniques of "escape from time." From a certain point of view one might even say that Yoga as such aims at deliverance from temporal servitude. All Yoga exercises of concentration or meditation isolate the adept, remove him from the flux of psychomental life, and consequently reduce the pressure of time. Moreover, the yogi aims at a destruction of the subconscious, at a combustion of the *vāsanās.* Yoga, as we know, attaches a considerable importance to the subliminal life designated by the term *vāsanās.* "The *vāsanās* have their origin in memory," writes Vyāsa in his commentary on *Yoga–Sūtra* IV, 9. But more is involved than the individual memory, which for the Hindu includes not only the recollection of actual existence but the karmic residues of innumerable previous existences. The *vāsanās* also represent the entire collective memory transmitted through language and traditions: in a sense, they are equivalent to Professor Jung's collective unconscious.

In seeking to modify the subconscious and finally to "purify," to "burn" and to "destroy" it,[43] the yogi endeavors to deliver himself from memory that is, to abolish the work of time. And this is no specialty of the Indian techniques. A mystic of the stature of Meister Eckhart never ceases to repeat that "there is no greater obstacle to union with God than time," that time prevents man from knowing God, etc. And in this connection it is not without interest to recall that archaic societies periodically "destroy" the world in order to remake it and consequently to live in a new universe without "sin"—that is, without history, without memory. A great number of periodic rituals also aim at a collective wiping away of sin, public confessions, the scapegoat, etc., amounting ultimately to an abolition of the past.

All this, it seems to me, proves that there is no breach in continuity between the man of the archaic societies and the mystic belonging to the great historic religions: both fight with the same energy, though with different means, against memory and time.

But this metaphysical deprecation of time and this struggle against "memory" do not exhaust the attitude of Indian spirituality toward time and history. Let us recall the lesson of the myths of Indra and Nārada: Māyā is manifested through time, but Māyā itself is only the creative force and above all the cosmogonic force of the absolute Being (Śiva, Viṣṇu); and that means that the *Great Cosmic Illusion is ultimately a hierophany.* This truth, revealed in myths by a series of images and stories, is expounded more systematically by the Upaniṣads,[44] and the later philosophers who state explicitly that the ultimate foundation of things, the *Ground,* is constituted *both by Māyā and by the Absolute Spirit,* by Illusion and Reality, by Time and Eternity. In placing all the contraries in one and the same universal void (*Śūnya*), certain Mahāyānic philosophers (for example, Nāgārjuna), and above all the various Tāntric schools both Buddhist (Vajrayāna) and Hindu, have come to similar conclusions. In all this there is nothing to surprise us, for we know the eagerness of Indian spirituality to transcend the contraries and polar tensions, to unify the, real, to return to the primordial One. If time as Māyā is also a manifestation of the godhead, to live in time is not in itself a "bad action"; *the bad action consists in believing that there exists nothing else, nothing outside of time.* One is devoured by time, *not* because one lives in time, but because one believes in the *reality* of time and hence forgets or despises eternity.

This conclusion is not without importance; we tend too much to reduce Indian spirituality to its extreme positions, which are intensely specialized and hence accessible only to the sages and mystics, and to forget the pan-Indian attitudes, illustrated above all by the myths. Indeed, the "escape from time" obtained by the *jīvan-mukta* amounts to an enstasis or an ecstasy inaccessible to most men. But if the escape from time remains the royal road of deliverance (let us recall the symbols of instantaneous illumination etc.), this does not mean that all those who have not obtained it are inexorably condemned to ignorance' and servitude. As the myths of Indra and Nārada show, to be delivered from illusion, it is sufficient to achieve consciousness of the ontological unreality of time and to "realize" the rhythms of Great Cosmic Time.

Thus, to recapitulate, India is not limited to two possible situations with respect to time: that of the ignorant who live solely in time and illusion and that of the sage or yogi who endeavors to "issue from time"; there is also a third, intermediate, situation: the situation of him who, while continuing *to* live in his own time (historic time), preserves an opening toward Great Time, never losing his awareness of the unreality of historic time. This, situation, illustrated by Indra after his second revelation, is amply elucidated in the *Bhagavad-Gītā*. It is expounded above all in the Indian spiritual literature for the use of laymen, and by the spiritual masters of modern India. It is not without interest to observe that this last Indian position is in a certain sense a continuation of primitive man's attitude toward time.

REFERENCES

1. Cf. Eliade, *The Myth of the Eternal Return, tr.* W. R. Trask (New York and London 1954), pp. 51ff.
2. Ed. Joseph Campbell (New York and London, 1946), pp. 3ff.
3. *Manu,* I, 69ff.; Mahābhārata, III, 12, 826.
4. Cf. J. Przluski, "From the Great Goddess to Kāla," *Indian Historical Quarterly* (Calcutta), XIV (1938), 267-74.
5. On all this see *The Myth of the Eternal Return,* pp. 130ff and passim.
6. Cf., for example, *Atharva–Veda,* X-, 8, 4; Ṛg-Veda, I, 164, 115.
7. Cf., for example, jātaka, I, p. 2.
8. Cf. for example, *Bhagavad-Gīta,* IV, 20, see Eliade, *Techniques du Yoga* (Paris, 1948), pp.141ff.
9. *The Sayings of Sri Ramakrishna* (Madras edn., 1938), IV, 22. Cf. another version of this myth according to the *Matsya Purāṇa,* related by Zimmer, *Myths* and Symbols, pp. 27ff.
10. Cf. *The Myth of the Eternal Return,* passim.
11. *Atharva-Veda,* XIX, 54, 3.
12. *Kena Upaniṣad,* IV. 13.
13. *Bhagavad-Gītā,* XI, 32.
14. *Bṛhadāraṇyaka Upaniṣad,* II, 3. 1.
15. *Kena Upaniṣad,* IV, 4.5.
16. *Kauṣītakī Upaniṣad,* IV. 2.
17. Cf. Eliade, "Psychologie et historie des religions: apropos du symbolisme du 'centre'", EJ 1950, pp. 247-82.
18. In a long note to his translation of the *Mahāprajnāpāramitasūstra* of Nāgārjuna, Etienne Lamotte has collected and arranged the most important of these; cf. Le *Traite de la grande vertu de sagesse de Nāgārjuna,* Book I (Louvain, 1944). pp. 6ff.
19. Cl. Eliade, "Les Sept Pas du Bouddha," in *Pro Regno, pro Sallduario, Hotnmage Van der Leeuw",'* (Nijkerk, 1950), pp. 160-75.
20. *Suttavibhaṅga, Pārājika* I, 1,4; cf. H. Oldenberg, *The Buddha,* tr. Wm. Hoey (London,1928), p. 325; Paul Mus, *La Notion du temps reversible dans la mythologie bouddhique* (Extrait de l'Annaire de l'Ecole Pratique de l'Ecole Pratique des Hautes Etudes, section des sciences religieuses, 1938-39; Melun, 1939), p. 13.
21. Mus, pp. 13-14.
22. Ibid, p.14.
23. Ibid, p. 14, n. 1
24. The elements of this philosophy will be found in the two volumes of T. Stcherbatsky's *Buddhist Logic* (Bibliotheca Buddhica, XXVI; Leningrad, 1930-32), and in Louis de la

Vallee Poussin's valuable *Documents d'Ablridarma: La Col/traverse du temps* (Melanlges chinoiset houddhiqucs, V; Brussels, 1937), 1-158. See also S. Schayer, *Contributions to Problem of Time Indian Philosophy* (Cracow, *1938*) and Ananda K. Coomaraswamy, *Time and Eternity* (Ascona, 1947), pp. 30ff.

25. Stcherbatsky, *Buddhist Logic*, I, pp. 94ff.; *Tattvasaṅgraha*, p. 137.

26. *Abhidharmokośa*, IV, T, quoted by Coomaraswamy, p. *58*. Cf. the translation with commentary by Louis de la Vallee Poussin, *L'Abhidlzarmako, de r Vasabandhu* (5 vols., Paris, 1923-31).

27. Coomaraswamy, p. 60.

28. Sutta Nipāta, 373, 860ff.; and other texts collected by Coomaraswamy, pp. 40ff.

29. Dīgha-Nikāya, II, 157.

30. Ibid., I. 57.

31. See Louis de la Vallee Poussin, "Notes sur le 'moment' ou *kṣaṇa des bouddhistes,*" *Rocznik Orientalistczny* (Lwow), VIII (1931), 1-13, Coomaraswamy, pp. 56ff.

32. Saṃyutta-Nikāya, IV, 126.

33. Cf. Eliade, *Traite d'historire des religions* (Paris, 1949), pp. 332ff.

34. *Kaṭha Upaniṣad*, III, 14.

35. On these motifs see A. B. Cook, *Ze14s* (Cambridge, 1940), Ill, 2, appendix P: "Floating Islands," pp. 975-1016; Coomaraswamy, "Symplegades," *Studies and Essays in the History of Science and Learning Offered in Homage to George Sarton* (New York, 1947), pp. 46J-88; Eliade, *Chaanismc et les leclmiqlles archaiqles de l'exttase* (Paris, 1951), pp. 419ff. and passim.

36. Coomaraswamy, "Symplegades," p. 486.

37. On the dialectic of the holy, see Eliade, *Traite d'histoire des eligions,* pp. 15ff.

38. Cf. Eliade, "Cosmical Homology and Yoga," *Journal of the Indian Society of Oriental* Art' (Calcutta), V (1937), pp. 188-203. On the *prāṇāyāma*, see Eliade, *Tuhniques dll Yoga,* pp. 75ff.; *Yoga: Immortality and Liberty* (New York, in press), passim.

39. It is even possible that the rhythmization of breathing has considerable effects on the physiology of the yogi. I have no competence in this field; but I was struck, at Rishikesh and elsewhere in the Himalayas, by the admirable physical condition of the yogis, although they took scarcely any food. One of the neighbours of my *kutir* at Rishikesh was a *nāga,* a naked ascetic who spent nearly the whole night in practicing the *prāṇāyāma* and never ate anything more than a handful of rice. He had the body of a perfect athlete, showed no signs of undernourishment or fatigue. I wondered how it came about that he was never hungry. "I live only in the daytime," he replied. "At night I reduce the number of my respirations by one-tenth." I am not entirely sure of having understood what he meant, but perhaps it was simply that since vital time is measured by the number of inspirations and expirations, he lived in ten hours only a tenth part of our time, namely one hour, by virtue of the fact that during the night he reduced his breathings to one-tenth of the normal rhythm. Counted in respiratory hours, a day of twenty-four solar hours only had a length of twelve to thirteen hours for him: thus he ate a handful of rice not every twenty-four hours, but every twelve or thirteen hours. This is only a hypothesis and I do not insist. But, as far as I know, there has still been no satisfactory explanation for the surprising youthfulness of the yogis.

40. Yoga-Sūtra, III, 52.

41. *Kālacakra Tantra,* quoted by Mario E. Carelli in his edition of Sekoddeśatikā: *Sekoddeśatikā of Nadopāda (Nāropā), Being a Commentary of the Sekoddeśa Section of the Kālacakra Tantra* (Gaekwad Oriental Series, XC; Baroda, 1941), preface, pp. 16 ff.

42. See the texts collected by P. C. Bagchi, "Some Technical Terms of the Tantras," *Calcutta Oriental Journal,* **1.** 2 (November, 1934), 75-78, especially pp. *82ff.;* and Shashibhusan Dasgupta, *Obscure Religious Texts* (Calcutta, 1946), pp. 274ff.

43. Such a presumption will probably seem vain if not dangerous to the Western psychologist. Though claiming no right to intervene in this debate, I should like to remind the reader of the extraordinary psychological science of the yogis and the Hindu ascetics, and on the other hand, of the ignorance of Western scientists in regard to the psycho-logical reality of the Yogic experiences.

44. See above, pp. r86f.

APPENDIX 2

Geographical Knowledge

Sashibhushan Chaudhuri

(Reproduced with permission from *The Cultural Heritage of India,* Vol. VI,
Ramakrishna Mission Institute of Culture, Calcutta, reprint, 2001, pp. 5-17)

Geography as branch of scientific study has developed as a consequence of man's immediate need for functioning in the world around him. Familiarity with the surrounding terrain, its lakes and rivers, the climatic conditions, and the neighboring tribes—matters of daily experience—was the rudimentary beginning of geographical study.

In India the earliest references to geographical data are found in the *Ṛg-Veda.* Casual references to tribes, rivers, and other geographical landmarks indicate that geographical knowledge was not lacking during the Vedic period. The subject may be studied with reference to the (i) Vedic and (ii) Post-Vedic periods.

Vedic Period

The Ancient Indians' conceptions of the universe and the earth determined to a great extent their understanding of the earth's physical properties and conditions. In Vedic literature the universe is sometimes conceived as consisting of the earth and sky (heaven), and sometimes of the earth, air (atmosphere), and sky.[1] Solar bodies are understood as belonging to the realm of the sky, and atmospheric phenomena such as lightning to that of the air. The semispherical shape of the sky as seen by the eye led to the comparison in the *Ṛg-Veda* of the sky and earth to two great bowls (*canvā*) turned towards the other (III.55.20). The *Śatapatha Brāhmaṇa* (IV.6.5.1) uses the term *graha,* which later came to mean 'planet', but in this text the word seems to signify a sort of power. The question whether the Vedic Indian used the word to denote 'planet' is not free from doubt. Some scholars like Oldenberg identify the *grahas* with the *ādityas,* numbering seven—the sun, moon, and the five planets.[2] Hillebrandt thinks that the planets are the *adhvaryus* referred to in the *Ṛg-Veda* (III.7.7).[3]

The earth is denoted in the *Ṛg-Veda* by such words as *pṛthivī* (the expansive or large), *pṛthvī* or *urvī* (the broad), *mahī* (the great), *apāra* (the limitless) and *uttānā* (the stretched out). The *Ṛg-Veda* contains references suggesting the spherical shape of the earth. It says, for instance, that every sacrificial altar or ground on the surface of the earth is its centre (III.5.9; IX.86.8).

This has been interpreted as implying the earth's sphericity. Elsewhere the earth is compared to a wheel (X.89.4) and the dawn is stated to precede the sunrise (I.123.1). In the *Śatapatha Brāhmaṇa* the earth is expressly mentioned as being circular (*parimaṇḍala*).[4] In the cosmogonic and theosophic hymns of the *Atharva-Veda* the earth and the heavens have been imagined as constituting two hemispheres (XI.5.8-11). The Vedic Hindus had clear ideas about the four directions (*diś*), further elaborated in connection with the placement of sacrificial altars (*vedi, citi*).

The term *dvīpa* (island) occurs in the *Ṛg-Veda* (I.169.3) and other Vedic texts. But it is unlikely that the word refers to any island, continent, or major land-area as it does in the Epics and Purāṇas. Sandbanks are perhaps indicated by the term.[5] It appears likely that no major geographical divisions of the earth are mentioned in Vedic literature. Use of the expression *sapta sindhavaḥ* (VIII.24.27), i.e., 'seven rivers', however, has led some scholars to think that the Ṛg-Vedic Indians conceived of a definite territory covering the basin of some of the existing rivers.[6] The names of a large number of rivers occur in the *Ṛg-Veda* (X.75.5-6). Some among these are the Sindhu, Gaṅgā, Yamunā, Sarasvatī, Śatadru, Vitastā, Sarayū, and Gomatī. The *Ṛg-Veda* also refers to mountains, e.g. the Himavant (X.121.4) and Mōjavat (X.34.1). The Himavant may reasonably be identified with the Himalayas, though it is possible that it included hills of the Suleiman range. The ancient lexicographer Yāska suggests that Mōjavant is equivalent to Muñjavant which figures in the *Mahābhārata* (X.785; XIV.180) as the name of a mountain in the Himalayan range. The *Kauṣītakī Upaniṣad* (II.13) speaks of the Dakṣiṇa-parvata, which is probably to be identified with the Vindhyan range. The names of many places also figure in Vedic texts.

In the Vedic period a kind of zonal geographical conception evolved. The *Śatapatha Brāhmaṇa* (I.7.3.8) calls the people of eastern Indian the Prācyas, and those of western India, the Bāhlīkas. The expression *madhyamā pratiṣṭhā diś* (the middle fixed region) occurs in the *Aitareya Brāhmaṇa* (VIII.14.3). The inhabitants of this region are stated to be the Kurus, Pāñcālas, Vaśas, and Uśīnaras. This middle zone is called Āryāvarta in the *Baudhāyana Dharmasūtra* (I.2.10) and is described as the area north of the Pāriyātra or Pāripātra (western Vindyas), east of Adarśana (near Kurukṣetra), south of the Himavat (Himālaya), and west of Kālakavana (probably near Allahabad).[7]

Abundant evidence of the geographical knowledge of the Indian people is available in post-Vedic literature. The Epics contain numerous incidental geographical references about the earth in general and Bhāratvarṣa in particular, the latter being especially dealt with in the *Kiṣkindhā-kāṇḍa* of the *Rāmāyaṇa* and the *Bhīṣma-parvan* of the *Mahābhārata*. Pāṇini's *Aṣṭādhyāyī* and Patañjali's *Mahābhāṣya* allude to some of the then prevailing conceptions of the earth and provide considerable details relating to the geography of the subcontinent. Buddhist works like the *Vinaya Piṭaka, Mahāvastu,* and the *Nikāyas,* particularly the *Aṅguttara Nikāya,* are important sources of geographical information. Indeed, from about the time of the Buddha to that of Aśoka, Buddhist canonical literature constituted the principle source of geographical information about contemporary India. Even for later periods, the works of Buddhaghoṣa and the Ceylonese chronicles *Dīpavaṃsa* and *Mahāvaṃsa* provide valuable references. The Buddhist Jātaka stories mention various places and add to our geographical knowledge of the country. Chinese Buddhist accounts also throw considerable light on the geography of India. Among the accounts left by Chinese travellers, particular importance is given to those of I-tsing, Fa Hien, and Hiuen Tsang. The Jaina canonical texts and Apabhraṃśa literature together with the Prabandhas furnish valuable geographical data and supplement the information given by the Buddhist texts.

The Purāṇas constitute the most detailed and comprehensive source of geographical knowledge of the post-Vedic period. They seem to have originated prior to the fifth or fourth century B.C., but in their present form they cannot be dated earlier than the seventh century A.D. The Purāṇas draw much of their material from the Epics, but they expand the concepts and furnish greater details. According to Ali, the range of their treatment of the subject covers the 'geography of practically the whole of the old world, the surrounding oceans and observation of some of the atmospheric phenomena'.[8] The treatment of geographical information is not uniform in all the Purāṇas; some go into greater detail than others. The *Vāyu, Brahmāṇḍa, Vāmana,* and *Mārkaṇḍeya,* for instance, contain sections entitled *Bhuvana-koṣa, Bhuvana-vinyāsa, Jambūdvīpavarṇana,* and so on, which deal primarily with geographical information.

Kauṭilya's *Arthaśāstra* and medical works like the *Caraka* and *Suśruta* provide additional details by way of mentioning the natural products of different regions. The astronomical works of Varāhamihira, Parāśara and others contribute topographical data regarding the regions of the subcontinent and are valuable sources of the knowledge of mathematical geography which developed in the post-Vedic period. Literary works of Kālidāsa, Bāṇa, Kalhaṇa, Rājaśekhara, and others also contain geographical material relating to India and her colonies. In addition to the accounts of Chinese travellers, the reports of foreigners like Megasthenes,

Al-Bīrūnī, and Abū'l-Fazl are important eye-witness records of the regions of the subcontinent.

The Earth and its Dvīpas: The concept of the earth comprising a number of *dvīpas*, meaning continents, seems to have emerged in the post-Vedic period. The *Mahābhārata* gives the number of such continents variously in its different sections. In the *Bhīṣma-parvan* (6.13) four major *dvīpas* are mentioned; elsewhere seven, eleven, and thirteen have been spoken of. The earliest references to the seven-continent theory occur in the *Rāmāyaṇa*, *Mahābhārata*, and Patañjali's *Mahābhāṣya*. The Pāli Buddhist literature mentions four *mahādvīpas* (great islands), namely, Uttara-Kuru or Kuru in the north, Jambūdvīpa in the south, Pūrva-Videha in the east, and Apara-Godāna in the west, as constituting the earth. The *Mahābhārata* gives a description of these four regions, Jambūdvīpa in particular. Use of the term *cakravāla-rājya* to mean the whole world is also found in Pāli literature. The *cakravāla* is conceived as 'a vast circular plane covered with water with Mount Meru or Mahāmeru standing at the centre'.[9] Seven *Kulācalas* or concentric circles of rock surround Meru. Beyond these are the four great *dvīpas*, one in each of the cardinal directions. The post-Gupta Jaina work *Tiloyapaṇṇatti* (V.11-26) speaks of the earth being constituted of sixteen inner and sixteen outer islands, each having an ocean beyond it.

According to most Purāṇas, the earth (*pṛthivī*) consists of seven *dvīpas*. These are said to be seven concentric circles of land, like seven rings, one inside the other. The names of the *dvīpas* beginning from the innermost are Jambu, Plakṣa, Śālmali(a), Kuśa, Krauñca, Śāka, and Puṣkara.[10] Each of these *dvīpas* is said to be surrounded by a particular sea. Beginning from the innermost, these are named Lavaṇa (salt-water), Ikṣu (sugar-cane juice), Surā (wine), Sarpi (ghee), Dadhi (curd), Kṣīra or Dugdha (milk), and Svādūdaka or Jala (fresh-water).[11] The question which arises is: What is really meant by the Purāṇic *dvīpas*[12] and seas? The Purāṇas appear to imply by the term *dvīpa* 'any land which was ordinarily inaccessible or detached by virtue of its being surrounded by water, sand, swamp or even high mountains or thick forests'.[13] Thus the term may indicate an island, a peninsula, or a doab, or even a specific area of land, large or small, which is distinguished by particular geographical features. It may also stand for tribal or national territories. The Purāṇic *dvīpa* therefore signified 'all types of natural or human regions—big or small'.[14] The descriptions of the seven seas as consisting of sugar-cane juice, wine, etc., should not be taken too literally. They may indicate that these seas had special characteristics which distinguished them from each other. Similar names—the Red Sea, Black Sea, and White Sea, for instance—are found even today, but they are not taken in their literal sense. One of the Jātaka stories lends credence to the idea that the seas were named after certain characteristics found to be present in them. The story narrates how a ship which was carried off its course by a storm passed in turn through seas named Aggimāla (blazing like fire), Dadhimāla (the colour of curd), Nīlavaṇṇa–Kusamāla (the color of *Poa cynsuroides grass*), and Nalamāla (red like coral).[15] The Epic and Purāṇic periods are marked by predominance of mythology, albeit not entirely devoid of factual elements. The theory of seven concentric *dvīpas* and seas seems to have developed out of this mythological conception of the world. The Purāṇic writers apparently tried to fit geographical data based on tradition and report of over-imaginative travellers into a mythological concept.

Most of the Purāṇas give details of the vegetation, rivers, mountains, climates, etc. of the *dvīpas*. Some scholars have, on studying these details, tried to identify specific geographical regions with the *dvīpas* spoken of. Even though one may not fully agree with such specific identification, it cannot be denied that the Purāṇic details of the seven *dvīpas*, whether based on concrete information (the chain of which has been lost in the course of time) or on limited data of the existing land and water masses on the earth's surface. Reference may be made in this connection

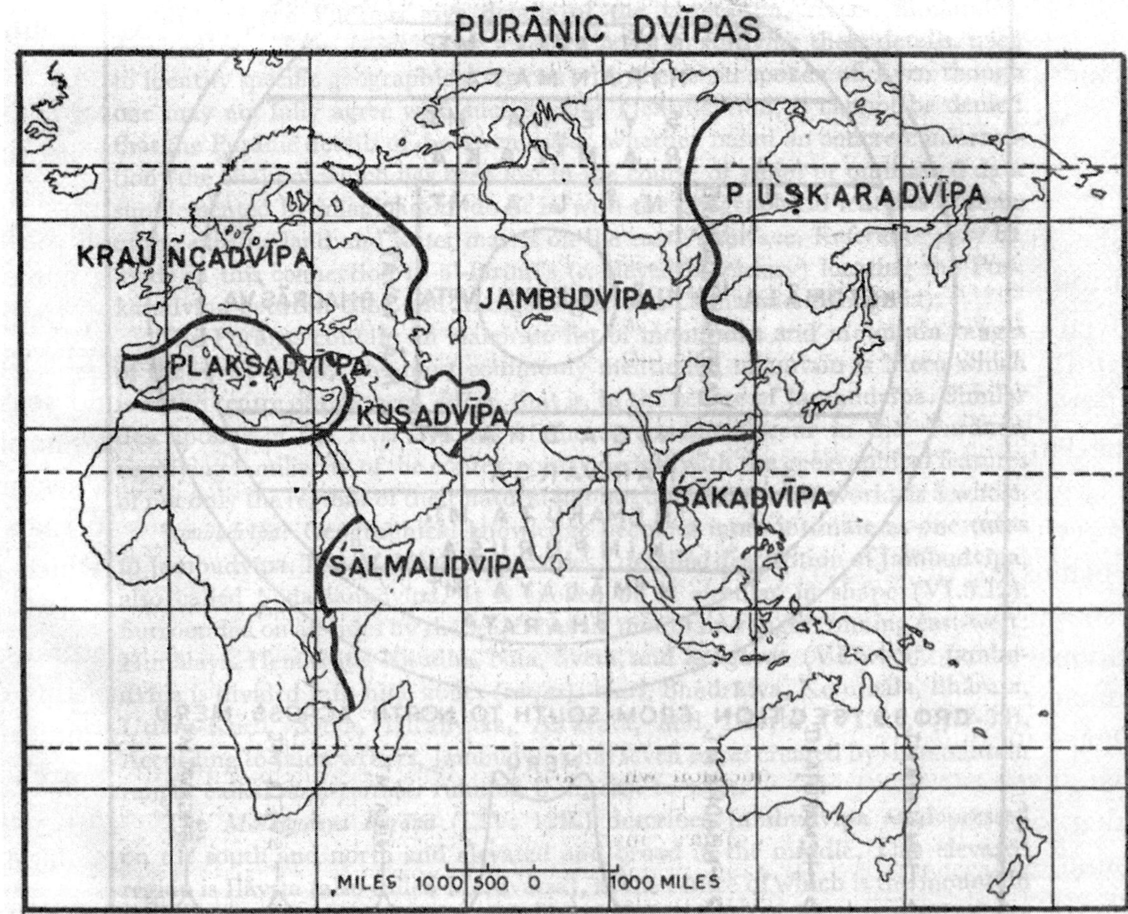

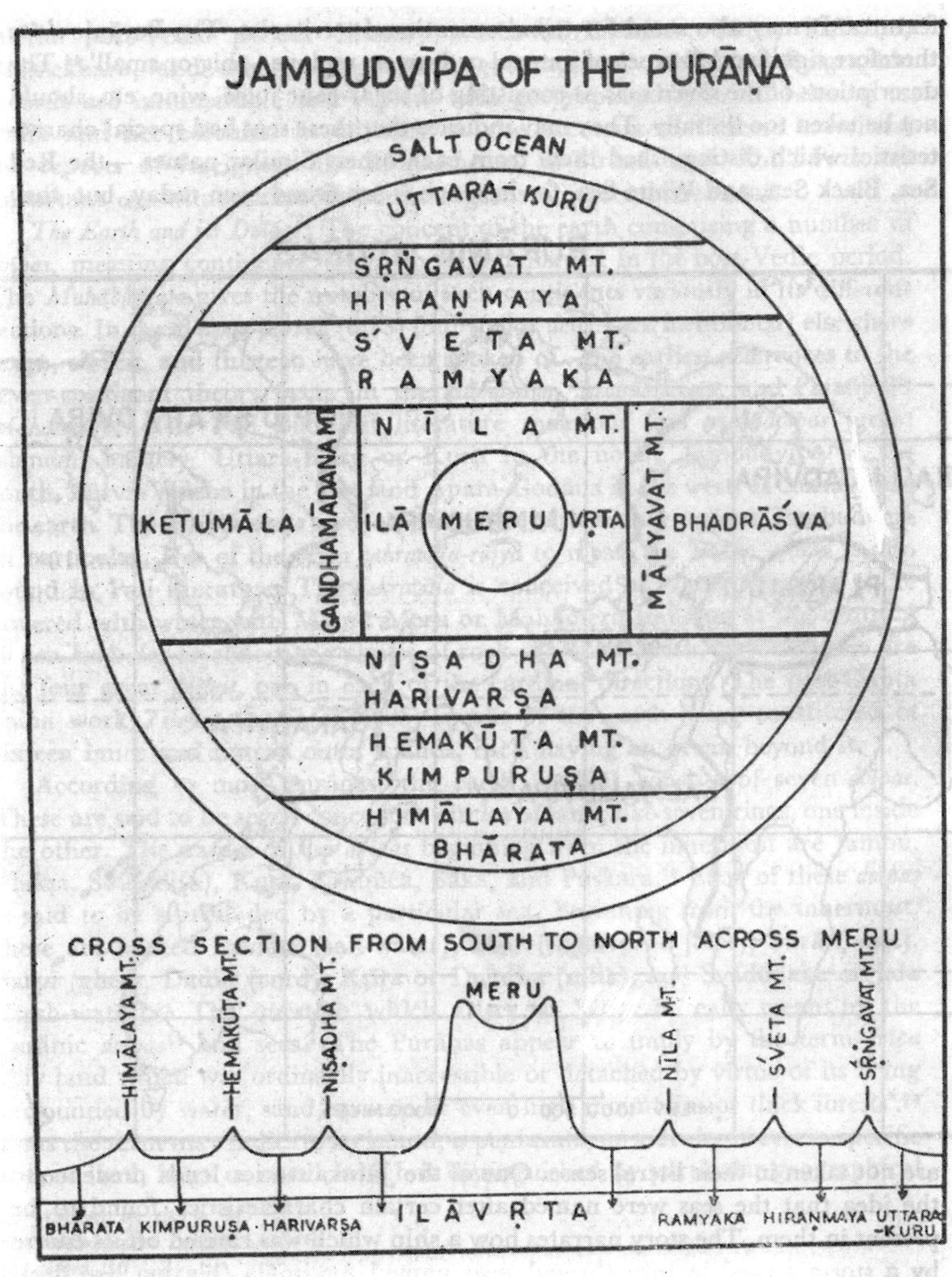

to Al-Bīrūnī's (*c.* eleventh century) locating the Puṣkaradvīpa between Cīna and Maṅgala (perhaps China and Mongolia).

The Purāṇas contain an elaborate list of mountains and mountain ranges of the seven *dvīpas*. The most commonly mentioned mountain is Meru which is at the centre of the seven *dvīpas*, that is, in the centre of Jambūdvīpa. Similar descriptions of the river systems of the seven *dvīpas* occur in the Purāṇas, signifying familiarity of the contemporary people with the geographical features of not only the regions of their natural habitat but also the old world as a whole.

Jambūdvīpa: Geographical knowledge becomes more intimate as one turns to Jambūdvīpa. The *Mahābhārata* provides a detailed description of *Jambūdvīpa*, also called Sudarśanadvīpa. It is spoken of as circular in shape (VI.5.12). Surrounded on all sides by the sea, it has six mountain ranges running east-west: Himālaya, Hemakūta, Niṣadha, Nīla, Śveta, and Śṛṅgavat (VI.6.4-5). Jambūdvīpa is divided into nine zones (*varṣas*): Hari, Bhadrāśva, Ketumāla, Bhārata, Uttar-Kuru, Śveta, Hiraṇyaka, Airāvata, and Ilāvṛta (VI.6.8,13,37-38). According to Jaina writers, Jambudvīpa has seven *varṣas* created by six mountain ranges called *varṣa-parvatas* running from east to west.

The *Mārkaṇḍeya Purāṇa* (LIV. 12ff.) describes Jambūdvīpa as depressed on the south, and north elevated, and broad in the middle. This elevated region is Ilāvṛta (also called Meruvarṣa), at the centre of which is mountain Meru. In different Purāṇic texts Jambūdvīpa is said to be composed of the following nine divisions: (i) Ilāvṛta, (ii) Ramyaka or Ramaṇaka, (iii) Hiraṇmaya or Hiraṇyaka, (iv) Uttara-Kuru or Śṛṅgaśaka, (v) Bhadrāśva, (vi) Ketumāla, (vii) Hari, (viii) Kimpuruṣa, and (ix) Bhārata.[16] Relative to the central *varṣa*, Ilāvṛta, the next three figure in the north, the last three in the south while Bhadrāśva and Ketumāla are to the east and west respectively. Four rivers are stated to flow from Meru—Bhadrā to the north, Sītā to the east, Gaṅga to the south, and Cakṣu to the west. There are three mountain ranges north of Ilāvṛta—Nīla, Śveta, and Śṛṅgavat—each consecutive range occurring after each successive *varṣa*. similarly, three ranges stand south of Ilāvṛta; Niṣadha, Hemakūta, and Himālaya. To the east and west of Ilāvṛta running north-south are the Mālyavat and Gandhamādana ranges respectively. The descriptions of three *varṣas* to the north of Meru, some of which are also mentioned in the *Mahābhārata* (*Bhīṣma-parvan*), are rather sketchy in the Purāṇas. Neverthelss, the details of three latitudinal ranges—Nīla, Śveta, and Śṛṅgavat—of this region, their valleys, river systems, and other information as available in the *Vāyu Purāṇa*, make it possible to identify quite a few of their important geographical features. According to Ali, the description of the northern regions of Jambūdvīpa 'covers a very vast area, from the Urasls and the Caspian to the Yenisei and from the Turkestan, Tien-Shan ranges to the Arctic. It describes the topography of the whole land very accurately and in some cases picturesquely. . .'[17] Turning east, Bhadrāśva is 'identical with the basins of the Tarim and Hwangho rivers, i.e., the whole of Sinkiang and Northern China'.[18] Ketumāla, located to the west of Meru, is irrigated by the river Cakṣu which is probably the Oxus. This region corresponds to western Turkestan.[19] Ketumāla is believed to cover 'practically the whole of the ancient Bactria which included the whole of the present Afghan

Turkistan (north of Hindukush), the lower Hari Rud Valley, the basin of Murghab Kashka system (all south of the old bed of Āmū Darya) and the basins of the Surkhan, Kafirnigan, Vakhsh and Yaksu rivers. . . .' [20] Hari appears to have been western Tibet;[21] Kimpuruṣa was presumably Nepal;[22] and Bhārata probably means greater India.

Bhāratavarṣa: The concept of Bhāratavarṣa as we know it did not emerge apparently before the fourth century B.C., for Pāṇini's *Aṣṭādhyāyī* (*c.* fifth century B.C.) makes no mention of the southern and extreme eastern regions of the subcontinent.[23] In the third century B.C. however, reference to the South Indian peoples like the Colas and Pāṇḍyas occur in Kātyāyana's *vārttikas* and in the accounts of Megasthenes. This indicates a growing awareness of the extent of the subcontinent and of the peoples who inhabited it.

The Buddhist and Jaina canonical works of the fourth-second centuries B.C. mention sixteen *mahājanapadas* (great states) comprising much of the area of the subcontinent. The nomenclature of the *mahājanapadas* differs in the two traditions. The regions noted in each are mostly confined to the northern and western parts of the subcontinent with occasional reference to the east and south. Aśoka's (269-232 B.C.) empire comprised almost the whole of the Indian subcontinent and parts of Afghanistan. This area, which practically corresponds to what subsequently came to be known as Bhāratavarṣa, is referred to in his inscriptions as *pṛthivī* and *Jambūdvīpa*. The earliest epigraphic reference to the name 'Bhāratavarṣa' is found in the Hāthigumphā inscription of Khāravela (first century B.C.).[24]

The term 'Bhāratavarṣa' occurring in the Mahabhārata (VI.9.10ff) stands for a vast area comprising numerous rivers, mountains, and territories which are described in some detail. It is not possible, however, to construct a precise geographical outline of this area because the boundaries are not clearly defined. Seven major mountains and ranges are named (VI.9.11): (i) Mahendra (Eastern Ghats), (ii) Malaya (Travancore Hills and the southernmost portion of the Western Ghats), (iii) Sahya (Western Ghats to the north of Malaya), (iv) Śuktimat (parts of the Vindhyan range including the Sakti Hills in Easter M.E.); (v) Ṛkṣavat (parts of the Vindhyan range to the south of Malwa), (vi) Vindhya (the Vindhyan range from Gujarat to Bihar excluding portions covered by Śuktimat, Ṛkṣavat, and Pāripātra), and (vii) Pāripātra or Pāriyātra (the Western Vindhyan range including the Aravallis).[25] Among the important rivers mentioned are the Gaṅgā, Sindhu, Sarasvatī, Godāvarī, Narmadā, Śatadru, Candrabhāgā, Irāvatī, Vipāśā, and Yamunā. A list of more than seventy major territorial units (*janapadas*) other than those in the south is given. Among these are Sindhu, Videha, Magadha, Aṅga, Vaṅga, Kaliṅga, Gāndhāra and Kāśmīra. The southern part of Bhāratavarṣa is said to include territories like Drāviḍa, Kerala, Mālava, Karṇāṭaka, and Cola.

Some geographical information about Bhāratavarṣa, particularly the south, also occurs in the Rāmāyaṇa. Rāma's journey from Ayodhyā to Kanyākumārī, the gateway to Laṅkā (Ceylon), provides the context for describing the forests, rivers, and *janapadas* on the way (IV.42-43).

Bhārata or Bhāratavarṣa is described in the Purāṇas as semi-circular[26] and lying between the Himavat in the north and the sea in the south.[27] The *Mārkaṇḍeya Purāṇa* (LVII. 58-59) depicts this region as having the Himavat like the string of a bow in the north and the sea in the south, east, and west. The same text gives its shape as conforming to that of a tortoise lying outspread and facing eastward (L VIII.4), and also refers to Bhārata as being constituted with a fourfold conformation (L VII.58-59).

Bhāratavarṣa has been spoken of in ancient texts variously as comprising five, seven, and nine divisions. The *Mahābhārata,* a few of the Purāṇas[28] Buddhist writers like Hiuen Tsang (seventh century), and Rājaśekhara (*c.* 900) in his *Kāvyamīmāṁsā* speak of five regions. These are named (i) Madhyadeśa (central), (ii) Udīcya (northern), (iii) Prācya (eastern), (iv) Dakṣiṇāpatha (southern), and (v) Aparānta (western). Madhyadeśa has been defined as the land bounded by the Himalayas in the north, the Vindhyas in the south, Vinaśana (in Ambala district) in the west, and Prayāga (Allahabad) in the east.[29] Udīcya covers eastern Punjab and the Oxus valley including the Himalayas. Its southern boundary may be taken as the river Sutlej. Prācya extends from the eastern end of Madhyadeśa to the Assam hills and from the Himalayas to the eastern coastal plain. This region may have included Kāśi, Kośala, Videha, and Magadha. Dakṣiṇāpatha includes the entire area of South India to the south of the Vindhyas. Aparānta is the area lying to the west of Madhyadeśa and seems to have comprised Sind, western Rajasthan, Gujarat, and a part of the adjoining coast on the lower course of the Narmadā.

Reference to a division into seven zones is also found in the *Mahābhārata* and most of the Purāṇas. This classification is not essentially different from that consisting of five regions. In addition to the five already mentioned, the Himalayan region and the Vindhyan range are included as the sixth and seventh divisions.

A third classification which divides Bhāratavarṣa into nine regions, current in several of the Purāṇas and the *Kāvyamīmāṁsā* has probably been borrowed from the astronomical works of Parāśara and Varāhamihira, although it is likely to be of earlier origin.[30] The *Mārkaṇḍeya Purāṇa* (LVII.6-7) specifies eight of these regions or *khaṇḍas* as Indradvīpa, Kaśerumat, Tāmravarṇa, Gabhastimat, Nāgadvīpa, Saumya, Gāndharva, and Vāruṇa.[31] Regarding the ninth *khaṇḍa* it simply says: 'It is this one which is girdled by the sea (*sāgarasaṁvṛta*)'. The *Kāvyamīmāṁsā* names this ninth *khaṇḍa* as Kumārī; the *Vāmana Purāṇa* calls it Kumāra; and the *Skanda Purāṇa* designates it as Kumārikā.

Opinions differ about the identification of these nine divisions. Abū'l-Fazl and Al-Bīrūnī have identified the nine regions within the area of the subcontinent itself.[32] Abū'l-Fazl names seven mountain ranges running east to west between Laṅkā and Himācala: Mahendra, Śukti, Malaya, Rikṣa; Pāriyātra, Sahya and Vindhya. The region between Laṅkā and Mahendra he calls Indradvīpa; between Mahendra and Śukti, Kaśerumat; between Śukti and Malaya, Tāmravarṇa; between Malaya and Rikṣa, Gabhastimat; between Rikṣa and Pāriyātra, Nāgadvīpa; and between Pāriyātra and Sahya, Saumya. He divides the area between Sahya and Vindhya into two parts, Kumāradvīpa being the eastern section and Vāruṇadvīpa, the western.[33] Al-Bīrūnī describes Indradvīpa as central India; Kaśerumat as eastern-central; Tāmravarṇa as south-eastern; Gabhastimat as southern; and Gāndharva as north-western. Ali also locates the nine *khaṇḍas* within the area of the subcontinent. Basing his view on relevant passages of the *Vāyu Purāṇa,* he maintains that Indradvīpa is a region east *of* the Brahmaputra; Kaśerumat is the eastern coastal plain; Tāmravarṇa is the peninsula south of Kāverī; Gabhastimat is the hilly region between the Narmadā and the Godāvarī; Nāgadvīpa is possibly the area of the Vindhyan and Sātpura ranges; Saumya is the coastal belt west of the Indus; Gāndharva is the trans-Indus region; and Vāruṇa is the western coast. He does not offer any identification of the ninth *khaṇḍa,* unnamed in the *Vāyu Purāṇa.*[34]

Majumdar Sastri, on the other hand, considers that the Purāṇic conception of Bhāratavarṣa implies greater India, i.e. India proper plus eight *khaṇḍas* outside the area of the subcontinent. He identifies Indradvīpa with Burma; Kaśerumat with the Malay Peninsula; Tāmravarṇa (Tamraparṇa) with Ceylon; Gabhastimat with Laccadive, Maldive, or Ernaculam in the southwest; Nāgadvīpa with Salsette, Elephanta, and Kathiawar in the west; and Saumya with Kutch in the north-west. Other identifications include Gāndhara with the Kabul valley; Vāruṇa with the Indian colony in Central Asia; and the ninth division called Kumārī with practically the whole of the Indian subcontinent.[35] Support is lent to this view *by* the *Kāvyamīmāṃsā* which, in course of describing the mountain ranges of the subcontinent, specifically states: 'This is Kumārīdvīpa'.[36] Similarly, the *Vāmana Purāṇa* (XIII.59), after enumerating the peoples of the respective divisions of India proper, concludes *by* saying that the detailed narration of the countries of Kumāradvīpa is now complete. Further, the list of the *Varāha Purāṇa* replaces the ninth *dvīpa,* Kumāra with the word 'Bhārata', suggesting the identity of the two. It seems likely, therefore, that the term 'Bhāratavarṣa' had both a wider and a narrower connotation and that in the narrower sense it meant India proper. It is well substantiated that Indian colonies were established in the Far East before the Christian era. 'For nearly fifteen hundred years, and down to a period when the

Hindus had lost their independence in their own home, Hindu kings were ruling over Indo–China and the numerous islands of the Indian Archipelago, from Sumatra to New Guinea'.[37] Reference may be made in this connection to four inscriptions of King Mūlavarman (*c.* fourth or fifth century A.D.) found in East Borneo, showing that the area was under Indian rule. It is not unreasonable to suppose that these territories were considered a part of greater India and that they might have been included as divisions of Bhāratavarṣa in the Purāṇic scheme.

The Indian subcontinent has been from the dim past the home of many races and peoples. Throughout the ancient period this movement of peoples presented a changing panorama. The impact of these tribes and ethnic groups on the soil of India and their efforts to adjust themselves to the opportunities which the geographical environment afforded provides the background of ancient Indian geography. This is perhaps why the Purāṇas and the astronomical works emphasize the regional conception of geography and take particular note of the *janapadas* and major geographical landmarks. The Purāṇas follow the tradition dating back to the Vedas of using tribal names to indicate the region which particular tribes inhabited. It is clear that such names are ethnographical in character although territorial or place names are by no means few. In fact, the people of Bhāratavarṣa appear in the Purāṇic texts only in their relevant geographical setting, which indicates that in ancient India the different human groups were regarded as so many essential units of a comprehensive geographical system. The lists of *janapadas* occurring in the various Purāṇas are arranged in an almost identical manner, but there are indications that the lists were altered to receive later additions and were brought up to date from time to time by the inclusion of the names of foreign invaders. Thus there is mention of the Yavanas, Śakas, and Pahlavas of the second and first centuries B.C., as well as of the Hūṇas of the fifth century A.D. and the Turuṣkas of the Muslim period. The lists received further alteration with the introduction of the names of *janapadas* and geographical landmarks of newly-explored regions or areas of colonization.

Considerable geographical information about Bhāratavarṣa and its neighborhood is contained in some texts of medieval Indian literature. Rājaśekhara's *Kāvyamīmāṃsā,* as we have seen, supports the view that the Indian subcontinent (designated Kumārīdvīpa) was one of the units of Bhāratavarṣa. Rājaśekhara devotes one chapter of this work to a detailed description of the major mountains and rivers, and various regions of Bhāratavarṣa. Kalhaṇa's *Rājataraṅgiṇī* (twelfth century) provides excellent topographical data about the Kāśmīra region of Uttarāpatha (Udīcya). A few lexicons of the period between the eleventh and sixteenth centuries also give some geographical information. Mention may be made in this connection of the following works: Yādavaprakāśa's *Vaijayantī* (eleventh century), Hemacandra's *Abhidhāna-cintāmaṇi* (twelfth century), Puruṣottama's *Trikāṇḍaśeṣa* (twelfth century), and Keśava's *Kalpadruma* (sixteenth century).

REFERENCES

1. A. A. Macdonell, *The Vedic Mythology* (Indological Book House, Varanasi, 1963), pp. 8-11.
2. H. Oldenberg, *Religion des Veda*, pp. 185 *et sq.; Zeitschrift der Deutschen Morgenlandischen Gesellschaft*, pp. 50, 56 *et seq.*
3. A. Hillebrandt, *Vedische Mythologie,* pp. 3 and 423.
4. Macdonell, *op, cit.,* p. 9.
5. A. A. Macdonell and A. B. Keith, *Vedic Index of Names and Subjects* (John Murray, London, 1912), Vol. I, p. 387.
6. *Ibid.,* Vol. II, p. 424; D. C. Sircar, *Cosmography* and *Geography in Early Indian Literature* (Indian Studics, Calcutta, 1967), p. 14
7. Sircar, *op. cit.,* p. 16
8. S. M. Ali, 'Geography in Ancient India', *Bulletin of the National Institute of Sciences in India*, No. 21 (1963), p. 279.
9. Sircar, *op. cit.,* p. 39.
10. *Mārkaṇḍeya Purāṇa.* LIV. 6
11. *Ibid.,* LIV. 7
12. Pāṇini derives *dvīpa* from *dvi + ap,* meaning 'land between two arms of water' (*Aṣṭādhyāyī,* V.4.74; VI.3.97)
13. S. M. Ali, *The Geography of the Purāṇas* (People's Publishing House, New Delhi, 1966), p. 37.
14. *Ibid.*
15. The *Jataka,* ed. E. B. Cowell, Vol. IV (Luzac and Co. for pali Text Society, London, 1957), Bk. XI, pp. 88-89.
16. *Matsya Purāṇa,* CXIII. 26-31. Another tradition current in the *Markaṇḍeya* (LV. 20ff) and *Brahmāṇḍa* (XXXV.50) *Purāṇas* divides Jambūdvīpa into four regions shaped like four petals of a lotus.
17. Ali, *op. cit.,* p. 87.
18. *Ibid.,* p. 99, H. Raychaudhuri, *Studies in Indian Antiquities* (University of Calcutta, 1932), pp. 75-76.
19. Raychaudhuri, *op. cit.,* p. 75.
20. Ali, *op. cit.,* p. 97.
21. N. L. Dey, *The Geographical Dictionary of Ancient and Medieval India* (Luzac and Co., London, 1927), p. 74.
22. *Ibid.,* p. 100
23. Sircar, *op. cit.,* pp. 34ff.
24. *Ibid.,* p. 34
25. *Ibid.,* p. 70; Ali, *op. cit.,* pp. 111-13.
26. *Matsya Purāṇa,* CXIII. 13; *Brahmāṇḍa Purāṇa,* XXXV. 13.

27. *Uttaram yat samudrasya himavaddakṣiṇañca yat; Varṣam yadbhāratam̐ nāma yatreyam̐ bhāratī prajā. Vāyu Purāṇa, XLV. 75-76.*

28. *Matsya, Vāyu,* and *Viṣṇu purāṇas.*

29. *Manu-smṛti,* II. 21.

30. *Cunningham's Ancient Geography of India,* ed. S. Majumdar Sastri (Chuckervertty, Chatterjee & Co., Calcutta, 1924), p.6.

31. The *Kūrma Purāṇa* substitutes Tāmaraparṇa for Tāmravarṇa, while the Matsya calls it Tāmraparṇī, The *Vāmana* and *Garuḍa Purāṇas* have Kaṭāha and Sim̐hala in place of Saumya and Gāndharva respectively.

32. Sircar, *op. cit.,* p. 55.

33. *Ain-I-Akbari of Abul Fazl-I-'Allami,* trans. H. S. Jarrett, revised and annotated by Jadu Nath Sarkar, Vol. III (Royal Asiatic Society of Bengal, Calcutta, 1948), pp. 36-37.

34. Ali, *op. cit.,* pp. 128.30.

35. *Cunningham's Ancient Geography of India,* ed. S. Majumdar Satri, Appendix I, pp. 751-54.

36. *Atra ca kumārīdvīpa*

37. R. C. Majumdar, H. Rayachadhuri, and K. Datta, *An Advanced History of India* (Macmillan & Co., London, 1960), p. 222.

APPENDIX 3

The Sāṃkhya Concept of Pramāṇa: Dharmakīrti's Critique

D. Prahladachar

Among the various philosophical schools of India, the Sāṃkhya system is not only the oldest but also the one that has attracted the dialectical attention of the widest range of later Indian philosophical systems. The later philosophical schools, whether they were realists or otherwise, have almost uniformly opposed it. The importance that was given to this system can be measured by the attack on it launched by Śrī Śaṅkara, who considered it as his main opponent. Even the realists such as the Nyāya-Vaiśeṣika and others never accepted the views of the Sāṃkhya School, although the latter were realists as well. They opposed the atheism, the theory of causation and also the theory of evolution as expounded by the Sāṃkhya system. Just as the controversial metaphysical stand of the Sāṃkhya has had an impact on these other systems, their views on epistemology also have influenced the epistemological stand taken by the later schools. Though it appears that their view concerns with the view of some Buddhists by holding that the perception of an object is effected by the *ākāra* or the image of the object, they distinguish themselves from the Buddhist stand by maintaining that the objects whose mental images—ākāra, lead to the perceptual cognition of the same, have external existence. Thus a number of epistemological points made by the Sāṃkhya system are very subtle and interesting. This paper intends to make a brief presentation of the Sāṃkhya view of epistemology and discuss the Buddhist objections to it.

Īśvarakṛṣṇa, in his Sāṃkhyakārikā first states the division of the *pramāṇa-s* and then gives the definition of each of the *pramāṇa-s*. However, Vācaspati Miśra[1] suggests that the very word *pramāṇa,* which is used while stating the division of *pramāṇa,* should be taken as the term indicating the general definition of the *pramāṇa-s.* He further states that the same word *pramāṇa* stands for both the definiendum and the definition. When the etymological sense is taken into account,

The author is Vice-Chancellor, Rashtriya Sanskrit Vidyapeetha, Tirupati.

the word conveys the definition; otherwise it just denotes the definiendum—the means of true cognition. Accordingly, by pursuing the etymology—'that by which *pramā*—true cognition is caused', the definition applicable to all the means of true cognition, *viz.,* 'being the instrumental cause of true cognition' is obtained'.

True Cognition

A true cognition, as per the Sāṃkhya school, is *cittavṛtti*—a mode of mind. This *cittavṛtti is* regarded as true cognition when its content is *asandigdha*—not an object of doubt, *aviparīta*—not an object of error and *anadhigata*—not an object already known. In short, a true cognition is a mode of mind, which is not either doubt, illusory cognition or recollection[2].

The Sāṃkhya system holds that a true cognition is of two kinds. One is the mode of mind and another is the cognition that is *pauruṣeya*—related with the self. The true cognition related with the self is considered as the *phala*—the result,[3] while the mode of mind is the *sādhana*—the instrument. When the cognition's relation with the self is stated as the result, it is not meant that it is produced and the mode of mind also is not the instrument in its true sense of being a cause. Similarly, when the true cognition—the result, is considered as *pauruṣeya,* it is not intended that the self is the locus of the cognition. Instead, the self is just reflected in the *vṛtti*—the mode of mind. Hence, it is considered as the *phala,* while the mode of the mind facilitating the reflection is regarded as the instrument. Since the self is not the locus of the true cognition, the Sāṃkhya maintains that it is neither, in the real sense of the term, the knower. The knowership actually belongs to the mind, which is the locus of the knowledge. Thus, the self is likened to the moon, which though motionless, is attributed with motion by being reflected in the water that actually has the motion.

It is interesting to note that, though there are doctrinal differences, Dharmakīrti also more or less agrees with the Sāṃkhya's definition of *pramāṇa*. Dharmakīrti defines a true cognition as *avisaṃvādijñāna*—the cognition that is devoid of *visaṃvāda*—mismatch are lack of consistency with practice. Dharmakīrti himself clarifies the notion of *avisaṃvāda,* explaining it as *arthakriyāsthiti—the* capability of producing a successful effort.[4] Here, the word 'capability' must be noted. A person, even after having the cognition of the thing, may not put his efforts to have it. Sometimes, in spite of his efforts, he may not succeed in getting the object desired due to some obstruction. Even in such cases, in spite of the absence of the successful effort on the part of the person, his cognition of the thing is considered as true, as it has the *capability* of producing the successful efforts.[5]

Again it may be objected that the capability of producing a successful effort itself can be known only after the successful efforts; in the absence of such efforts, we cannot decide about the capability by a single cognition. But, there are cognitions, which due to the repeated dealings, are instantly distinguished from illusory cognitions. In such cases of perceptual cognitions the capability of producing the successful efforts is known, immediately. In the case of inferential cognitions that are based on the relation of concomitance between the thing to be proved and the reason, our common experience tells us that the doubt about the capability of the cognition to produce *the arthakriyā* will never arise.[6]

The above view of Dharmakīrti regarding the definition of a true cognition, as is obvious, comes very close to that of the Sāṃkhyas. A cognition, which is capable of producing a successful effort, has to be different from the cognition of doubtful nature and the erroneous cognition. But Sāṃkhya also insists that a cognition in order to be considered as true, in addition to its being different from *saṃśaya* and *viparyaya,* should also be *anadhigataviṣaya, i.e.,* should be having a content that is unknown. Dharmakīrti concurs with this view also. However, he considers it as an independent definition.[7] Thus, a recollection is, according to Dharmakīrti, not a true cognition. For, it does not lead to an effort, much less to a successful one. Often it is doubted also.[8]

Though thus the above definition of a true cognition appears to be an independent definition, as a matter of fact, it is not so. The two definitions, *viz.,* *avisaṃvāda* and *ajñātārthaprakāśa*—though distinct, are dependent upon each other. The cognition of a yellow conch, though is a cognition of an object hitherto unknown, is not considered as true, as it is unable to produce a successful effort. Thus a cognition, though has an object which is unknown, to be a true one, needs the absence of *visaṃvāda.* Similarly, a recollection, though does not have any *visaṃvāda,* is not considered as a true cognition, for its content is not unknown. Thus, a cognition in order to be a true one, in addition to its being *avisaṃvādi,* has to be *ajñātārthaprakāśa* also.[9]

Buddhi

The above definition of *pramāṇa* offered by Dharmakīrti makes it clear that the Sāṃkhya and the Buddhists do not differ that much in defining *pramāṇa.* But, when we closely examine the views of the two schools about the concept of *pramāṇa,* we come to notice many subtle but significant points which make the two schools absolutely distinct with each other. One such distinct point is made by the term in singular number (ablative case) *'pramāṇāt'* in the Sāṃkhakārikā—*'prameyasiddhiḥ pramāṇāt hi'.*[10] *Pramāṇa*—the means of true cognition, according to the Sāṃkhya is just *one*. For, it is the principle called *buddhi*, which is one, that takes different forms such as *pratyakṣa*, *anumāna* and *śabda* due to various adjuncts.[11] The *buddhi*, which is thus a *pramāṇa*, is also described as *adhyavasāya*.[12] The actual meaning of the term *adhyavasāya is niścaya*—assertive cognition. Thus the cognitions in the form—'this surely is a cow' or 'this, surely, is a person', are *adhyavasāya-s*.[13] As a matter of fact, according to the Sāṃkhya, the principle called *buddhi is* not quite identical with the assertive cognition. Instead, it is, by being the locus of the function, *viz.*, the assertive cognition, the agent of it. However, just as a person selling curds is addressed as 'curds' (when we call out "curds! come here!") the *buddhi* being identified with its function called *adhyavasāya, is* called *adhyavasāya*.[14] Since *buddhi* is a product of *prakṛti* consisting of the three factors, *viz., sattva, rajas* and *tamas,* it also consists of the same three factors. When the *sattva* factor of the *buddhi* dominates the other two factors, it is called true cognition—*pramā*. The significant point made by the Sāṃkhya here is that the *buddhi,* also called as *adhyavasāya, is* eternal as it is a modified form of the eternal principle called *prakṛti*. It is this aspect of the *buddhi, i.e.,* externality that is challenged by Dharmakīrti.

Dharmakīrti holds that the object of a cognition has no existence apart from that of the cognition. In other words, objects exist only in the form of the "grasped" aspect of grasping cognitions. If the objects are different from their cognitions, he contends that it is difficult to explain as to why they are revealed by their cognitions. The only possible explanation, according to him, is that the object of cognition offers its form to the cognition and hence that object is revealed by that cognition. Since a yellow object does not lend its form to the cognition of blue, it is not revealed by the cognition of blue. Had the object been non-momentary, i.e. permanent and imperishable such as a diamond or a stone appears to be, then without depending upon any other factor or object, it would have produced all the cognitions in this world, all at once. But that does not happen. Objects and their cognitions arise inseparably *depending* upon other objects and cognitions.[15] Therefore it should be admitted that the content of a cognition is momentary and the cognition, having the form of the object that it is identical with, is as momentary as that object.

The Buddhist has some more arguments to refute the eternality of the *buddhi.* Since *buddhi* is the cognition of an object, it has to be non-eternal. For, to grasp an object, a cognition has to depend on so many factors such as the presence of the object, contact of the sense organ with the object, absence of obstruction etc. A thing dependent on something else cannot be claimed as eternal. Hence the *buddhi* is not eternal.[16]

In response, the Sāṃkhya may contend that the sense organ, the object etc. do not produce the *buddhi* that already exists. Instead, they only reveal it. Thus the dependence upon the sense organ etc. does not, in any way, contradict the eternality of the *buddhi*. Rejecting the contention, the Buddhist points out that the revelation of the *buddhi* should either be obtaining its own nature or the removal of the obstruction. If the revelation is of the nature of the first, then it is nothing but being produced and again the eternality of the *buddhi is* contradicted. The revelation cannot be of the second type also, as it is again contradictory to hold that the *buddhi* exists along with the obstruction.

The Buddhist further points out that a revealed thing such as a jar will remain the same in spite of the difference in the revealing factors such as the moonlight, sunlight etc. But in the case of the *buddhi* it is not so. As we experience, the *buddhi* differs with the difference in the objects it grasps. We experience that the cognition of the jar is quite different from the cognition of the cloth. The Sāṃkhya may contend here that only the *vṛttis*—the modes of the *buddhi,* which take place with the *buddhi* assuming the shape of the object, will differ with the difference in the object, while *the buddhi* remains the same. However, the Buddhist rejects the contention by pointing out the Sāṃkhya stand that the modes and the possessor of the modes are quite identical.[17]

The Buddhist further draws our attention to the Sāṃkhya view that the *buddhi* has *sattva, rajas* and *tamas* as its constituents and it changes its manifestations due to upheaval and predominance in one or more of the constituents. This change, the Buddhist maintains, involves nothing but origination and destruction. Hence it is absurd to hold that the *buddhi is* eternal.[18]

The above criticism of the Buddhist appears to be very strong. But the Sāṃkhya has the following counter-arguments against the Buddhist:

The Sāṃkhya holds that the criticism that the *buddhi* cannot be eternal is unwarranted, for, non-eternality of the modes of the *buddhi is* actually acceptable to him, without giving up the underlying permanence of the basic principle behind *buddhi*. The Sāṃkhya school maintains that whatever is manifest has a cause and for the same reason is non-eternal also.[19] The *buddhi,* being manifest, has a cause, the cause being *prakṛti* and naturally, is non-eternal also.[20] Therefore, the non-eternality of the *buddhi is* not repugnant to the Sāṃkhya.

The Sāṃkhya also admits that the *buddhi,* being identical with the eternal *prakṛti,* is eternal. A Sāṃkhya philosopher also knows that eternality and non-eternality are contradictories and hence the *buddhi* cannot be claimed as both eternal and non-eternal. However, he maintains that the *buddhi,* which is eternal in its original essence, is non-eternal in the form of its modes. In other words, the modes of the *buddhi* are non-eternal, whereas the *buddhi,* which is the possessor of the modes, is eternal. This, of course, leads to the question whether the Sāṃkhya admits difference between the modes and their possessor. The Sāṃkhya's answer is that though they are identical, there is no contradiction in having the two, *viz.,* eternality and non-eternality, in different states. For instance, a line of soldiers or a circle of them is not different from each individual soldier. But, while the line or the circle of the soldiers is disturbed or broken the individuals could remain undisturbed or unbroken. This shows that one and the same object can have contrary characteristics during different states. Therefore, though the *buddhi is* eternal in its original state, it can be non-eternal in the state of its mode[21].

The other argument of the Buddhist that due to selective upheaval in the *guna-s,* the constituents of the *buddhi* gets both origination and destruction is also rejected by the Sāṃkhya on the same ground. When the *sattva* dominates over *rajas* and *tamas,* the *buddhi* takes the form of *dharma*—righteousness. Thus it is just a case of transformation. Here, neither did a new thing come into existence nor did anything become extinct[22].

Apart from non-eternality, momentariness is also ascribed to *the buddhi* by the Buddhist. His contention is that cognition differs when its object differs. Since objects are momentary according to him, the cognitions grasping those objects should be momentary only. As against this view, the Sāṃkhya maintains that cognition will differ only with the difference in the mode—*vṛtti.* The possessor of the mode—*vṛttimat,* may continue to be the same. There *need* not be any change in *the buddhi*—the *vṛttimat.* If it is still maintained that cognition differs with the difference in momentary objects, then we will not be able to explain the apprehension of different kinds of objects by a single cognition through its different modes, such as *vikalpa* (verbally generated illusions), *bādha* (cancellation), *samuccaya* (awareness of conjoined contents), *saṃśaya* (doubting awareness with two opposite alternative possibilities) etc. Here, though the apprehending factor is experienced as one, the contents such as absolutely non-existent, cancelled, contradictory alternatives etc. are quite different[23]. Therefore, the Sāṃkhya maintains that the Buddhist view that the *buddhi* differs with the difference in the objects, and hence is momentary, is baseless.

The above reply of the Sāṃkhya to the Buddhist's criticism of the eternality of the *buddhi* is based on the Sāṃkhya view that cognitions are modes of the *buddhi,* and in being so they are identical with it. By holding that the cognitions are a state of the *buddhi,* the Sāṃkhya could justify his stand that though the cognitions are non-eternal, the *buddhi in* its original form can be eternal also. But from the Buddhist point of view the principle called *buddhi* does not exist apart from the cognition, and the explanation based on such a concept is quite unconvincing to him.

Nature of Pleasure, Pain, etc.

Dharmakīrti makes some critical observations about the Sāṃkhya view of the nature of cognitions of pleasure, pain, etc. also, which are quite interesting. The

Sāṃkhya holds the theory that the *guṇa-s* like *sattva, rajas* and *tamas* are of the nature of pleasure, pain and delusion respectively and that they are the constituents of the *prakṛti.* Therefore, the objects that are the modified forms of the *prakṛti* are also of the nature of pleasure, pain and delusion. Hence, when the objects are experienced by a person, pleasure etc. will be experienced along with it by him.

The question that would naturally arise here is that if the objects are thus of the nature of pleasure, pain, etc., then all of them should be experienced by all the persons who experience them. The Sāṃkhya has an explanation for this. When the merit earned earlier by a person reaches the state of fruition, then in him, as well as in the objects coming into contact with him, the *sattvaguṇa* predominates and the other two *guṇa-s, viz., rajas* and *tamas* will be suppressed by it. One must remember, however, that a Sāṃkhya "guṇa" if is a "guṇa" in the sense of a string or strand that binds the puruṣa then the person experiencing the object experiences the pleasure also, which is another form of the *sattvaguṇa.* On the other hand, when the demerit acquired earlier reaches the state of fruition, the quality called *rajas* predominates in his mind and so does the object coming into contact with him and consequently the person experiences pain.

Similarly, when *tamas* dominates and suppresses *sattva* and *rajas,* delusion is experienced. Since this domination of a strand is due to a past deed attaining the fruition state, the experience of pleasure, pain etc. which, as already explained, is indirectly related with the domination of a particular strand, is not common to all persons.

As against this Sāṃkhya view, the Buddhist holds that pleasure, pain etc. do not have any existence apart from the subjective mental existence in the form of their cognitions. It is for this reason that they are experienced only by those who have those cognitions and not by the others. Thus, the Buddhist's view of pleasure etc. is absolutely opposite to the view held by the Sāṃkhya on the same.

The main objection of the Buddhist against the Sāṃkhya is that if pleasure etc. are external things, then the apprehension of pleasure etc. invariably along with the object cannot be explained. For no two really distinct things are thus invariably grasped together [24]. The Sāṃkhya might reply that blue etc. objects are not different from pleasure etc. and hence they are always grasped simultaneously. But the pertinent question raised by the Buddhist is as to how the objects such as blue and pleasure etc. can be identical. The point made here is that while blue etc. objects are grasped by an external sense organ, pleasure etc. are grasped by the internal organ. When thus they are cognised differently, how can the two be regarded as identical. Had they been identical, they must have been grasped by the same sense organ[25].

Further if pleasure etc., as maintained by the Sāṃkhya, being identical with the objects, were external, Dharmakīrti points out that it would be difficult to explain the fluctuation in our feelings of pleasure etc. The increase and decrease of the feelings are found to be varying with the subjective differences in the persons who experience them. If, as the Sāṃkhya claims, pleasure etc. are identical with the external objects, then since the objects continue to be the same for a long time and for several different persons, there must not be any change in the pleasure etc. also. As a matter of fact, the change in the feeling of pleasure etc. is found to be due to the change in the moods, i.e., *bhāvanā-s* in the persons. It may even be said that all the objects, whether they are inner or outer, are thus closely connected with the mental states of a person. This shows that the entire world has no existence apart from the moods, and hence is unreal[26].

The Sāṃkhya has an argument to consider pleasure etc. as external things. He is of the view that something that is dissimilar to the grasper, cannot be grasped by it. Therefore, since *buddhi,* the grasper, being a product of *prakṛti* is an external material, pleasure etc. also should be considered as external. Dharmakīrti rejects this argument by pointing out the fact that the rule that the grasper and the grasped should belong to the same class is not valid. If that is the rule, he argues that *puruṣa*—the principle of consciousness cannot be the *bhoktṛ*—either the enjoyer or the sufferer. For, as is obvious, *puruṣa* being *cetana, is* totally dissimilar to the so-called 'external' pleasure and pain,[27] which it is supposed to enjoy.

Another pertinent question raised by the Buddhist about the Sāṃkhya view that pleasure etc. are identical with the objects is as to what is the evidence on the basis of which pleasure etc. can be held as identical with the objects. The Sāṃkhya would reply that since the objects are products of *prakṛti,* which is identical with pleasure etc., on the ground that the cause and effect are of the same nature, objects also are of the nature of pleasure etc. But, as is obvious this leads to the fallacy of mutual dependence. For, the objects can be considered as identical with pleasure etc. only when they are known as the products of *prakṛti.* And when the objects are known as identical with pleasure etc., they can, on that ground, be ascertained as the products of *prakṛti*[28].

The Sāṃkhya has another argument to establish pleasure etc. to be identical with the external objects. According to him, the *buddhi,* i.e., cognition also is a product of its object that is grasped. In other words, *grāhya* and *grāhaka*—the grasper and the grasped are related by the relation of cause and effect. The relation of cause and effect, as a matter of fact, holds good if the two belong to the same class. Therefore, pleasure etc., to have the relation of cause and effect with the *buddhi,* should belong to the same class of *buddhi,* which is identical with pleasure etc. In other words, objects also are identical with pleasure etc. Dharmakīrti rejects this argument on the ground that the rule, *viz., grāhya* and *grāhaka* should belong to the same class. He points out that *puruṣa* also is known as *grāhaka*—the grasper. But, as the Sāṃkhya himself has admitted, *puruṣa* is neither an effect, nor a cause. This shows that to be a grasper, one need not be a product of the grasped. Therefore, without being cause and effect, the objects and the *buddhi* can be *grāhya* and *grāhaka*. Hence, on the ground that, the *buddhi is* the *grāhaka* of the objects, one cannot claim that they are cause and effect and consequently are of the similar nature of being external[29].

With these strong arguments, Dharmakīrti demonstrates that pleasure etc., are, actually, internal things and being the objects of the cognition they are identical with the consciousness. He holds that if *buddhi is* cognition, it is an internal one and pleasure etc. being identical with the cognition are only internal[30].

BIBLIOGRAPHY

1. Sāṅkhyatattvakārikā by Mahāmunīśvarakrṣṇa with the commentary Sāṅkhyatattva-kaumudi by Vācaspati Miśra, published by Bhāratīya Vidya Samsthan, Vārāṇasī, 1991.
2. Pramāṇavārttikam by Dharmakīrti with the commentary Vṛtti by Ācārya Manorathanandi, published by Bauddhabhārati, Vārāṇasī, 1994.
3. Sāṅkhyakārikā by Īśvarakṛṣṇa with the commentary Yuktidīpikā by an unknown author, edited by Dr. Ramāśaṅkara Tripāṭhī, published by Balakṛṣṇa Tripāṭhī, Vārāṇaśi, 1970.
4. Pramāṇavārttikam by Dharmakīrti, part - II with the commentary Vārttikālaṅkāra by Svāmi Yogendrānanda.

REFERENCES

1. *pramīyate'neneti nirvacanāt pramāṃ prati karaṇatvam avagamyate.* Sāṃkhyatattvakaumudī. p. 51.
2. *asandigdhāviparītānadhigataviṣayā cittavṛttiḥ. Ibid.*
3. *bodhaśca pauruṣeyaḥ phalaṃ pramā. Ibid.* p. 52.
4. *arthakriyāsthitiḥ.*
   avisaṃvādanam Pramāṇavārttikam. p. 3.
5. ataśca *yato jñānādarthaṃ paricchidyāpi* na *pravartate, pravṛtto va kutaścit pratibandhāderarthakriyāṃ nādhigacchati, tadapi pramāṇameva; pramāṇayog-yatālakṣaṇasyāvisaṃvādasya sattvāt.* Vṛtti. *Ibid.*
6. saiva *pramāṇayogyatā kathamasatyāmarthakriyāprāptau niścīyata iti cet? yat tāvadasakṛdvyavahārābhyāsād darśanamātreṇopalakṣitabhramaviviktasvarūpaviśeṣaṃ sādhanādhyakṣam, tasya svata eva pramāṇayogyatāniścayaḥ kṛtrimākṛtrimamaṇi-rūpyāditattvaniścayavat. anumānasya ca sādhyapratibaddhajanmano vyabhicārā-śaṅkavirahāt. Ibid.*
7. *ajñātārthaprakāśo vā.* Pramāṇavārttikam. p. 7.
8. *smaraṇaṃ ca pūrvagṛhītārthavikalparūpatvānnādhikagrāhi. gṛhīte ca prāktanameva pramāṇam. idānīṃ tu smaraṇapravartakam; tasyaiva sandehāt.* Vṛtti. *Ibid.*
9. *tasmādubhayamapi parasparasāpekṣameva lakṣaṇaṃ boddhavyam. Ibid.*
10. *dṛṣṭamanumānamāptavacanañca sarvapramāṇasiddhatvāt.*

trividham pramāṇamiṣṭaṁ prameyasiddhiḥ pramāṇāddhi. Sāṁkhyakārikā (with Yuktidīpikā). p. 33.

11. *pramīyate'neneti pramāṇaṁ, karaṇasādhano lyuṭ. tadekameva, buddherekatvābhyupagamāt; upādhivaśāttu bhinnamāśrīyate pratyakṣamanumānamityādi.* Yuktidīpikā. p. 34.

12. *adhyavasāyo buddhidharmo jñānaṁ virāga aiśvaryam.*
    sāttvikametadrūpaṁ tāmasamasmādviparyastam.
    Sāṁkhyakārikā (with Yuktidīpikā). p. 126.

13. *gaurevāyaṁ, puruṣa evāyamiti yaḥ pratyayo niścayo'rthagrahaṇaṁ so' dhyavasāyaḥ.* Yuktidīpikā. p. 128.

14. *yathā dadhivikretā loke dadhiśabdenāpi āhūyate, evamevātrāpi kriyākriyāvatorabhedaviva kṣayā adhyavasāyakartryāḥ buddhyāḥ adhyavasāyaḥ lakṣaṇamuktam.* Ibid. p. 127.

15. *vajropalādirapyarthaḥ sthiraḥ so'nyānapekṣaṇāt.*
    sakṛt sarvasya janayejjñānāni jagataḥ samam.
    Pramāṇavārttikam. p. 187.

16. *yadyarthagrahaṇaṁ buddhiḥ anityā. kasmāt? hetvāpekṣaṇāt. arthagrahaṇaṁ hīndriyādiviṣayasannidhānamāvaraṇādyabhāvaṁ cāpekṣate. na ca nityasya kāraṇāpekṣopapadyate. tasmādanityā buddhiḥ.* Yuktidīpikā. p. 128.

17. *Ibid.*

18. *sattvādīnāmaṅgāṅgibhāvābhyupagamāt vṛddhikṣayāvabhyupagantavyau.tataśca buddhiranityeti prāptam.* Ibid. p. 129.0

19. *hetumadanityamavyāpi sakriyamanekamāśritaṁ liṅgam.*
    sāvayavaṁ paratantraṁ vyaktaṁ viparītamavyaktam.
    Sāṁkhyakārikā (with Yuktidīpikā). p. 72.

20. *yattāvaduktaṁ hetvapekṣaṇādanityā buddhiriti tadayuktam. kasmāt?*
    siddhasādharāt. kasyātra vipratipattiranityā vā buddhiḥ syānnityā veti?
    kiṁ tarhi hetumadanityaṁ vyaktamiti vacanādanityaiva. tasmādiṣṭamevaitat. Yuktidīpikā. p. 129.

21. *tadyathā   senāpaṅktisenākuṇḍalādyuparame   na tatsanniveśināmuparamaḥ kāryabhedaśca, na cānyatvam. evaṁ vṛttitadvatorapi ca syāt.* Ibid.

22. *yadapyuktaṁ guṇavṛddhikṣaye'nityatvamiti tadanupapannam. kasmāt? rūpāntarāpyāyanāt. sattvaṁ hi prakarṣamanubhavadrajastamasī ca nyūnatāṁ dharmādirūpāṁ buddherāpyāyayanti, nārthāntaraṁ kurvanti no khalvapyabhāvam, evaṁ rajastamo vā prakarṣamanubhavatsattvaṁ ca nyūnatādharmādirūpaṁ buddherāpyāyayanti, nārthāntaraṁ kurvanti nābhāvam. evaṁ guṇavṛddhikṣaye' pi rūpāntarāpyāyanānnāsti kṣayo buddheḥ.* Ibid. p. 130.

23. *yadi pratyarthamanyadanyad grahaṇaṁ kalpyate, vikalpabādhasamuccayasaṁśayadvitvātiśayanivāraṇeṣu, tathā kalmāṣaṁ śabalaṁ citramityanekārtharūpamekaṁ grahaṇaṁ na syāt.* Ibid.

24. *kaścid bahiḥsthitāneva sukhādīnapracetanān.*
    grāhyānāha na tasyāpi sakṛd yukto dvyagrahaḥ.
    Pramāṇavārttikam. p. 152.

25. *sukhādyabhinnarūpatvānnīlādeścet sakṛd grahaḥ. bhinnāvabhāsinorgrāhyaṁ cetasostadabhedi kim.* Ibid. p. 153.

26. *tasyāviśeṣe bāhyasya bhāvanātāratamyataḥ.*

tāratamyañca buddhau syānna prītiparitāpayoḥ. Pramāṇavarttikam (with the commentary Vārttikālaṅkāraḥ) p. 783.

bhāvanānvayameva sakalamāntarambāhyañceti bhāvanābalaprabhavamatattvameva sakalaṃ jagadityāpatitam. Vārttikālaṅkāraḥ. p. 784.

27. *agrāhyagrāhakatvācced bhinnajātīyayoḥ pumān.*
agrāhakaḥ syāt sarvasya tato hīyeta bhoktṛta. Ibid. p. 785.

28. *pradhānapariṇāmitve śabdādīnaṃ sukhādyanvayaḥ.*
sukhādita parijñanācchabdādestattva niścayaḥ.
Vārttikālaṅkāra. *Ibid.*

29. *kāryakāraṇatānena prayukta' kāryakāraṇe.*
grāhyagrāhakatābhāvād bhāve'nyatrāpi sā bhavet.
Pramāṇavarttikam. Ibid. p. 786.

30. *tasmāt te āntarā eva saṃvedyatvācca cetanāḥ. saṃvedanaṃ na yadrūpaṃ na hi tat tasya vedanam. Ibid.*

APPENDIX 4

Concept of *Sākṣin* in Dvaita-Advaita Schools of Vedānta (Similarities and Dissimilarities)

D. Prahladachar

*S*āksin—'direct awareness' is a fascinating concept discussed in detail in both the Dvaita and the Advaita Schools of Vedānta. Though this concept is used by these two schools to justify their respective metaphysical standpoints they also provide many interesting insights into the students of epistemology and psychology. It is interesting to note that though Viśiṣṭādvaita School also is a Vedānta School, it does not see any need to envisage a concept of this kind. The other schools of philosophy, including the Nyāya-Vaiśeṣika do not accord any place to the concept of *Sākṣin,* either in their epistemological or metaphysical setup. This paper intends to briefly discuss the concepts of *Sākṣin* on the basis of the presentation made by these two schools and bring out the similarities and dissimilarities in them.

The Advaita view

A perceptual cognition, as a matter of fact, any cognition, as per the Advaita School, cannot be anything other than the *cētana* or the self. For, the capacity to illuminate an object, exclusively lies only with *cetana,* which is of the nature of consciousness. *Acetana*—a non-conscious thing cannot illuminate anything. Hence, a perceptual cognition is the *caitanya* qualified by the *vṛtti*—the modification of inner sense which happens to take place when the faculty of internal organ reaches the object through the external sense organ. Just as the consciousness delimited by the *vṛtti* is perceptual cognition, the Advaita School holds that *Sākṣin* also can be considered as perceptual cognition. This *Sākṣin,* according to the school, is of two kinds—*Jīvasākṣin* and *Īśvarasākṣin.* Though both the *Sākṣin-s* are consciousness only, the consciousness with the adjunct *Māyā* (*antaḥkaraṇōpahitacaitanya*) (some sort of cosmic illusory power) is *Īśvarasākṣin.*

The Advaita school defines '*Jīva*' in '*Jīvasākṣin*' as the consciousness delimited or qualified by the internal organ (*antaḥkaraṇāvacchinnacaitanya*), while the *Sākṣin* in '*Jīvasākṣin*' is the consciousness with the adjunct—inner sense. An adjunct is different from a qualifying property, as it only differentiates the thing with which it is related without getting involved in its functioning. Thus, in the case of *Sākṣin* inner sense just plays the role of an adjunct as it, being a non-sentient thing, is not involved in the functioning of the *Sākṣin*, viz. *prakāśakatva*—illuminating the object. Though thus the inner sense is not involved in the functioning of the consciousness—the *Sākṣin*, it differentiates one *Jīvasākṣin* from the other such *Sākṣin-s*. Thus, for example, Caitra-*Sākṣin* is different from the Maitra-*Sākṣin* as they are related with different internal organs. As a consequence, while the *Caitra-Sākṣin* illuminates the jar only the Caitra-*jīva* becomes aware of it and not the Maitra-*jīva*. For, though purely from the consciousness point of view, Caitra-*jīva* and Maitra-*jīva* are identical, they are different, the difference being super-imposed with the relation of two different adjuncts—the separate internal organs.

The Advaita School also holds that all the things are objects of the *Sākṣin*, either through *jñāna* or *ajñāna*, through awareness or unawareness. While an object is grasped by the *Sākṣin* through *jñāna*, the awareness tends to be in the form 'I am aware of it'. While something is grasped through *ajñāna*, the awareness wants to be in the form 'I am not aware of it'. However, the *Sākṣin* can directly grasp the inner objects such as pleasure, pain, desire, hatred etc. It also grasps the super-imposed objects such as the silver super-imposed on the sea-shell. This silver, as per the Advaita School, is neither non-existent, nor externally existent. It is through *āvidyaka*, i.e. the modification of the ignorance that has enveloped the 'through *śukti-avacchinna-caitanya*' the *caitanya* qualified with the sea-shell. Due to the defect in the sense organ, when the self fails to grasp the sea-shell as sea-shell, there arises the illusory cognition of the super-imposed silver, which being a modified form of the 'positive ignorance', is an inner object. Thus, the *Jīvasākṣin*, as per the Advaita School can also be an erroneous cognition. In the case of an erroneous cognition, the mind's role is thus limited to grasp only the sea-shell as just 'This'.

As already stated, *Jīvasākṣin*, though it is one, appears to be many because of the plurality in the internal organs. However, *Īśvarasākṣin*, unlike *Jīvasākṣin*, is only one. For, the adjunct *Māyā* also is only one. Here again the *Māyā* just differentiates the *Īśvarasākṣin* from *Jīvasākṣin* without getting involved in the functioning of it, namely grasping all the things of the universe.

This, in brief, is the nature of *Sākṣin* as discussed by the Advaita school. We may note here that the nature of *Sākṣin* as detailed above serves the metaphysical purposes of the school.

The Dvaita view of *Sākṣin*

To understand the nature of *Sākṣin* as advocated by the Dualist (Dvaita) Vedantins, it is necessary to know the epistemology that the School advocates. The following is a brief account of the Dvaita epistemology.

The School maintains that there are three *pramāṇa-s*—means of true cognition, namely, perception (pratyakṣa), inference (*anumāna*) and verbal testimony (*āgama*). The cognitions produced by these are perceptual cognition (*pratyakṣa*) inferential cognition (*anumiti*) and verbal cognition (*śabdabōdha*). Cognition again is of two kinds namely *vṛttijñāna* and *svarūpajñāna*. *Vṛttijñāna* is the cognition in the form of *antaḥkaraṇapariṇāma* i.e. a particular transformation of the internal organs or inner sense (*manas*). This *vṛttijñāna* is perceptual cognition, if it is produced by the contact between sense-organ and object. The same is inferential cognition or verbal cognition if it is generated by the instruments of inference or verbal testimony. The other kind of cognition namely *svarūpajñāna* which is identical with the self, is perceptual cognition only. The same is also called *sākṣī* or *Sākṣijñāna*, direct witness.

The sense organs, which coming into contact with the object lead to perceptual cognitions, according to this school, are seven and not six or five as maintained by the other schools. They are *Cakṣus, Śrōtṛ, Tvak, Ghrāṇa, Rasana, Manas* and *Sākṣin*. The first five and the sixth are known as external senses and internal sense (*bāhyēndriya* and *antaḥkaraṇa*), respectively. The seventh sense is designated as *svarūpēndriya* as it is identical with the self. It is also called as *Sākṣin*. Thus the school gives the name *Sākṣin* to both the sense organ and the cognition. For the sake of clarity they are called *sākṣīndriya* and *sākṣijñāna* respectively. The first six sense organs being the products of the principle *Ahaṅkāra*, are indirectly the products of *Prakṛti* and hence are called *prākṛtēndriya-s*. The seventh i.e. *sākṣīndriya*, being identical with the self, is described as *aprākṛtēndriya*. The question as to how the same self can be both the sense organ—the means, and the perceptual cognition—the result, will be discussed later.

The Dvaita school maintains that a cognition called *Sākṣin* has to be admitted by all the schools of philosophy. When we analyse the perceptual cognitions that we obtain, it will be clear that some of them cannot be the products of any of the first six sense organs. It is our common experience that during the state of deep sleep we are aware of ourselves and we also experience a kind of bliss. This awareness of the self and the experience of the peculiar bliss cannot be said as generated by any of the external sense organs or the internal sense *manas*. For, at that time all of them are in the state of rest, without functioning.

The *Nyāya* School which admits only six senses argues that during the state of deep sleep we do not have any awareness. This the Dvaita school rejects on the ground that it is contrary to our common experience. It also draws our attention to the after-sleep experience or rather recollection that, 'all this time I had a blissful sleep' (*ētāvantaṃ kālaṃ sukhamahamasvāpsam*) which nobody can deny. This recollection, as is obvious, has three items as its contents, namely, the self, the bliss and the duration of the deep sleep. Since a recollection of something is possible only with the past experience of the same contents of the recollection, we have to admit the presence of an experience of these three during the deep sleep. The Nyāya School may contend that during the deep sleep there is no pleasure or pain and the absence of pain is later wrongly referred to as bliss. This again is contrary to our experience. Even if we concede that the later recollection is not that of bliss, but only that of the absence of pain, the Naiyāyika has to accept the experience of the absence of pain during the deep sleep, in the absence of which we cannot recollect the same later. Further, since the recollection of the self and the duration of the deep sleep cannot be explained in any other manner, one has to accept the presence of the experience of the self and also the period in which the deep sleep occurred.

An attempt is made by some to explain the after-sleep cognition, 'I had a blissful deep sleep all this time' as an inferential cognition and not a recollection. But, as is well known, an inferential cognition is produced by the cognition of the concomitance between the probans (sign) and the probandum (property to be inferred) and also the cognition of the presence of the probandum in the subject. As we know, the after-sleep cognition takes place without any such cognition. Hence, the said after-sleep cognition has to be accepted as a recollection and consequently we have to accept the presence of an experience during the deep sleep without which such a recollection is impossible. The Dvaita School holds that such an experience during the deep sleep has to be admitted as a perceptual cognition as it cannot be explained in any other manner. This perceptual cognition, again not being a product of any other sense organ, including the inner sense, has to be held as the cognition identical with the self. This contention of the Dvaita School, incidentally rejects the Nyāya view that the self is only the locus of consciousness and not identical with consciousness.

The *Sākṣin*, which is self-luminous according to the Dvaita School, can grasp not only the self, its properties, and the period of the deep-sleep as discussed above, but also several others such as the inner sense and its various modifications, space and time. It is interesting to note that while mind is held as beyond the reach of senses and can only be inferred the Dvaita School holds it as perceptible—i.e. an object of *Sākṣi-Pratyakṣa*. All of us have the experience—'my mind says this'— '*manō me kathayati*', which shows that we are aware of the presence of our mind without taking recourse to any inference. Similarly, all the modifications of mind such as various cognitions, desire, hatred, fear, shame etc., are also grasped by *Sākṣin*.

According to the Nyāya School, cognition etc., are the qualities of *Ātman*. It holds that following the series of contacts such as the contact between the self and the mind, the mind and the sense and finally the sense organ and the object, there arises the perceptual cognition of the object in the self. Similarly, following the cognition of concomitance etc. and the cognitions of the verbal testimony, the self will get as its property, the cognitions—either inferential or verbal, as the case is. These cognitions, the Dvaita school holds as the properties of mind, as they are mental states. When such mental state occurs, immediately the *Sākṣin* will grasp them and thus the self will be aware of them.

The Nyāya view that cognitions are special qualities of the self and that they are grasped by the inner sense is rejected by the school on another ground also. As we know, another peculiar nature of the properties such as cognitions, desire, hatred etc. is that they are *jñātaikasat,* i.e. they exist only insofar as they are known. It is contrary to our experience that we have a cognition or desire etc. and that we are ignorant of it. If, following the Nyāya view, it is held that these are grasped by the internal organ, we will have to accept a situation in which a desire or an awareness exists without being known. For instance, the cognition that arises in the immediately previous moment of deep sleep, cannot be grasped by the internal organ, for from the first moment of the deep sleep, till the end of it, internal organ ceases to function. Since such cognitions etc. perish without being known, there is no possibility of getting an impression of them and recollecting the same after the sleep. If, on the other hand, cognitions etc. are held to be grasped by *Sākṣin*—the self, there will not be any cognition or desire etc. which remains being unknown. For, the moment they arise they are grasped by the *Sākṣin*.

Space and time, according to the Nyāya and some other schools are not perceptible. It is obvious that these two having no colour or touch are not perceptible to the external senses. The inner sense also cannot grasp them as they are external objects. Thus they are held to be known only through inferences. The Dvaita School is of the view that these two also are directly grasped by *Sākṣin.* Even a child, in darkness, stretches its hands to know whether there is anything solid occupying the space. Similarly, even a layman knows the presence of time and is never doubtful or ignorant of it. He may be ignorant or doubtful of only a particular time. This, the Dvaita school holds as the justification of its view that both space and time are grasped by *Sākṣin.*

The Dvaita School which upholds the *pramāṇyasvatastvavāda* i.e. the theory of intrinsic correctness of cognitions, is also of the view that the truth of cognitions also is grasped by the same *Sākṣin.* Generally, when a cognition arises, the *Sākṣin* grasps the cognition along with its truth. In exceptional cases only we are doubtful of the truth of our cognitions and in such cases the *Sākṣin* grasps the cognition and remains silent about its truth. It is our common experience that we resort to test the truth of our cognition only occasionally and generally we accept them as true.

Another interesting characteristic of *Sākṣin* that the Dvaita School recognizes is its *niyatayāthārthya* i.e. its unmistakable character, its necessary truthfulness. In other words, it holds that the *Sākṣin* is always correct and that there is no instance where it is erroneous. This aspect of *Sākṣin* is justifiable when we examine the contents of *Sākṣijñāna*. It is never a case that just as a cognition of a jar—a *manōvṛttijñāna,* can take place. Sometimes even when there is no jar, *a Sākṣijñāna* also can take place without its contents such as cognition, desire, fear, hatred etc. In other words, we are never aware of a cognition, a desire or hatred that does not exist. One can hallucinate water in a dry desert, but one cannot hallucinate pain in oneself, because if one feels a pain it surely exists. As a matter of fact, the very term 'awareness' which stands for *Sākṣin,* indicates the existence of its content. We never use the term 'awareness' when the content is not a fact.

Though this stand of the Dvaita School with regard to the infallible nature of the *Sākṣin* holds good in respect of its other contents, it is argued that it is not applicable in case of the truth of a cognition. The point is that the *Sākṣin* having the nature of grasping the cognitions whenever they arise, grasps not only the true cognitions but also the erroneous cognition. Thus, when the cognition of silver arises on seeing a sea-shell, it immediately grasps it and also the truth in it when, of course, the truth is not there. Here, one cannot argue that the *Sākṣin* stops only with grasping the erroneous cognition without grasping truth in it. For, the person who has the cognition and does not know its falsity, immediately proceeds to get the silver with the same earnestness with which he proceeds to take it when he has a true cognition of silver. Thus, the Dvaitin being a *Prāmāṇyasvatastvavādin* has to admit that the *Sākṣin* grasped the non-existent truth in the erroneous cognition, making itself an erroneous cognition. Thus, the infallibility of *a Sākṣin* seems to be incompatible with its task of witnessing all awareness, true or false.

Here the Dvaitin justifies his view that *Sākṣin* is invariably true in this way: *Sākṣin* has the ability to grasp many things such as the self, its properties, mind, its modifications such as cognitions, desire, volition, hatred, fear, shame etc., and also space and time. When we closely examine, we come to know that in none of the cases the *Sākṣin* is wrong. It never grasps cognition, desire etc, when they do not exist. On the basis of this close examination, we can conclude that the *Sākṣin* is invariably true. However, this stand does not seem to hold good in case of an erroneous cognition which is taken as true. But, instead of discarding the rule which was made on the basis of the critical examination of the nature of *Sākṣin,* his exception can be explained in a different manner. In such circumstances, the *Sākṣin* would just grasp the cognition being silent about the truth or untruth of the cognition. But, the inner sense which has no such restriction of grasping only actual facts, would grasp, i.e., claim the truth that does not exist in the cognition.

In other words, it is the mental cognition of the non-existent truth that persuades the person to proceed to take the silver. Thus *Sākṣin* can maintain its characteristic of never going wrong.

Another unique feature of the Dvaita concept of *Sākṣin* is that it, as already stated, acts as a sense organ also. It may appear to be absurd to hold that one and the same is both the sense organ and the resulting perceptual cognition as well as the knowing self. For, it amounts to admitting one and the same as both the cause and its effect. However, the Dvaita School avoids the absurdity taking recourse to the concept of *Viśeṣa*. *Viśeṣa,* according to the School, is a unique capacity of the objects that acts as the representative of difference even where actually substantially difference does not exist. In the present instance, *Sākṣin* the sense organ and *Sākṣin* the resultant cognition have no difference, but because of the *Viśeṣa* that it has, it can act as both the sense organ and the resulting cognition. But, the question as to how can one and the same be both the cause and effect will still remain. Here the Dvaitin draws our attention to the fact that the *Sākṣin-*cognition being identical with the self, can never be a product like any other Vṛtti-cognition. It will only get revealed by itself. That is its origination. Though there are no instances where one and the same is both cause and effect, there are several instances wherein one and the same is both the revealer and the revealed. So, the *Sākṣin* in its capacity as the revealer, may be considered as a sense organ while the same *Sākṣin* as a revealed one can be regarded as the resulting cognition.

Some Similarities and Dissimilarities between the Dvaita and Advaita Concepts of *Sākṣin*

The striking similarity between the two concepts is that both hold that *Sākṣin* is consciousness itself and identical with the Self. Both the Schools also hold that it is the *Sākṣin* that grasps the inner objects such as cognition, volition, desire etc. But, the similarity ends here. As a matter of fact, dissimilarities are more between them.

While the Advaitin holds the *Jīvasākṣin* as the consciousness with the inner sense and as the adjunct and the inner sense just plays the role of distinguishing one *Sākṣin* from the other, the Dvaitin does not have any such assumptions. For him no such adjuncts are needed. For, the *Sākṣin-s* themselves are naturally different from each other. Apart from this dissimilarity which is metaphysical in nature, there are other differences also that are epistemological. As per the Dvaita school a *Sākṣijñāna* is invariably true, whereas in the Advaita school, as explained, it may be even an erroneous cognition. Consequently, the Advaitin cannot consider the *Sākṣin* as invariably true. It may be noted here that Gaṅgeśa, the celebrated author of Tattvacintāmaṇi, also holds that *anuvyavasāya* which plays the role of *Sākṣin,* is invariably true. The significant difference between the Nyāya view of *anuvyavasāya* and the Vedānta view of *Saksin* is that while according to Nyāya *anuvyavasāya* is a cognition produced by the inner sense, the *Sākṣin* of the Vedantin is identical with the consciousness—the self.

Another unique feature of the *Sākṣin* about which both the Advaitin and the Dvaitin seem to be in argument, is its *svaprakāśatva*—self-luminosity. However, the argument is only in the designation. In reality, the difference is absolute. The Advaitin who thinks that one and the same cannot be both the knowledge and the known explains the self-luminosity in terms of 'not being an object of a cognition other than itself'—*avedyatva*. The Dvaitin who sees no contradiction in accepting both the knowledge and the known being one admits the self-luminosity of the *Sākṣin* in the literary sense of the term.

Yet another interesting point related with the *Sākṣin* on which the Dvaitin and the Advaitin differ is that the opposition between the *Sākṣin* and ignorance. The Advaitin contends that there is no opposition between the *Sākṣin* and ignorance. The Advaitin contends that there is no opposition between the two. One may be having *Sākṣijñāna* and the ignorance of the same. The typical instances, which highlights the peculiar nature of the *Sākṣin* is the awareness—'*māmahaṃ na jānāmi*'—I do not know myself'. If I am not aware of the self how can I express myself as 'I'. At the same time, ignorance of the self is also experienced. The Dvaitin who thinks that it is absurd to hold awareness and ignorance about the same thing existing simultaneously, explains that awareness and ignorance have different objects here. While the awareness is about the general nature of the self, the ignorance is about the specific properties of the same. The Indian Philosophical Schools, particularly the Advaita and the Dvaita Vedānta Schools, have attached much significance to the concept of *Sākṣin*. It is needless to say that the concept demands much deeper investigations.

ABBREVIATIONS, GLOSSARY AND GENERAL BIBLIOGRAPHY

Abbreviations

Ait. Br	Aītareya Brāhmaṇa
Ait. up	Aītareya upaniṣad
AV	Atharvaveda
Bhāg. Pu	Bhāgavata Purāṇa
Br. up	Bṛhadāraṇyaka upaniṣad
Ca. Saṃ	Caraka saṃhitā
Ch. up	Chāndogya upaniṣad
Kaṭha	Katha upaniṣad
Mai. up	Maitrāyaṇīya upaniṣad
Māṇḍ. up	Māṇḍūkya upaniṣad
Mūṇḍ up	Muṇḍaka upaniṣad
Nyā. Bhā	Nyāya Bhāṣya of Vātsyāyana
NK	Nyāya Kandalī of Śrīdhara
Ny.mañ	Nyāya Mañjarī of Jayanta
NS	Nyāya Sūtra of Gautama
NVTT	Nyāya Vārttika tātparyaṭīkā of Vācaspati Miśra
PPB	Praśastapādabhāṣya of Praśastapāda
RV	Ṛgveda
SK	Sāṃkhya Kārikā of Iśvarakṛṣṇa
Śat. Br	Śatapatha Brāhmaṇa
Suś.saṃ	Suśruta saṃhitā
Śvet. up	Śvetāśvatara upaniṣad
Tat. sū	Tattvārthādhigama sūtra of Umāsvāti
Taitt. up	Taittirīya upaniṣad
Var. Pu	Varāha Purāṇa
VS	Vaiśeṣika Sūtra of Kaṇāda
Viṣṇu. Pu	Viṣṇu Purāṇa
Vārttika	Nyāyavārttika of Uddyotakara
YV	Yajurveda (Taittirīya saṃhitā)

Glossary

A

Abādhita	Undoubtedness
Ābhāsa	Appearance
Abhāva	Non-existence
Abheda	Non-difference
Abhibhūta	Suppressed
Abhinibodha	Perceptual cognition
Abhidhammapiṭaka	Basket of Higher subtleties of doctrines
Abhidheyatva	Nameability
Abhighāta	Striking, a kind of contact producing sound
Abhihitānvaya	Relation of what are expressed
Abhinibodha	Inference
Abhinnajātīyatvam	Non-dissident genus cognition
Abhyāsa pratyaya	Repetitional cognition
Abhrānta	Unerring (cognition), non-illusion
Ācāra	Custom
Acit	Non-spirit, matter
Ādhārapratyaya	Regardful cognition
Āḍhaka	A measure
Adharma	Principle of rest (Jaina); Vice
Adhidaiva	Related to gods
Adhikaraṇa kaivalya	Mere existence of the locus (Prābhākara-mīmāṃsā)
Adhyavasāya	Determinate cognition; cognizable entity; judgement
Adhikārī	A qualified person, one to whom the result accrues
Adhiṣṭhāna	Real substratum
Adho-loka	Lower World
Adhyāropa	Super-imposition
Aditi	Infinity, Infinite nature, Mother of gods
Adṛṣṭa	Unseen potentiality of force (God)
Āgama	Revelation; sacred works accepted by some schools
Agnihotra	A sacrifice
Agniṣṭoma	Praise of Agni
Ahaṅkāra	Egotism, empirical ego
Āhāraka	A temporary body (Jaina)
Āhārya	Assumptive
Aitihya	Tradition
Aja	Absolute Brahman

Ajīva	Non-being; material
Ajīvadravyas	Non-soul substances
Ajñāna	Ignorance, nescience
Ākāra	Determinate
Ākāśa	One of the five elements; ubiquitous; the substratum of sound; space (Jaina)
Akhaṇḍadeśa	Invisible space
Akhyāti	Erroneous knowledge (Prābhākara)
Akriyāvāda	Doctrine of non-action
Ākuñcana	Contraction
Alaukika	Supra normal
Ālayavijñāna	Stream of consciousness
Aloka	The world beyond
Alokākāśa	Space beyond
Āmla	Sour, acid
Anāgata	The past
Anaikāntika	A fallacy leading to many conclusions
Anākāra	Indeterminate
Ānandamayakośa	A sheath of bliss
Anantadharmaka	Infinite number of facts
Anātmavāda	Non-soul theory
Anavasthā	Regress ad infinitum
Aṇḍaja	Born of egg
Anekāntavāda	Relativism
Aṅgula	A unit of length
Anindriya-nibandhana	Non-sensuous perception
Anirvacanīya	Inexpressible
Anirvacanīyakhyāti	Indefinable apprehension
Anitya	Non-eternal
Annamayakośa	The sheath of food
Anṛta	Opposed to moral order or natural law
Antarindriya	Internal sense organ (mind)
Antyāḥ	Ultimates
Aṇu	Atom; individual discrete particle; indestructible
Anudbhūta	Sub-perceptional
Anumāna	Inference, instrument of knowledge
Anumiti	Inference
Anupasaṃhārin	Non-conclusive reason
Anusandhāna	Cognition
Anuvāda	Restatement
Anvitābhidhāna	Expression of what are inter-related
Anuvyavasāya	After cognition (when the subject is also presented)
Anuyogin	Correlated substratum
Aṅga	Subsidiary
Antya-viśeṣa	Ultimate particularity

Anupalabdhi	Non-perception
Anupapatti	Indemonstrability of the universal
Anvaya-vyāpti	Affirmative concomitance
Anvayavyatireki	Concomitant in assertion and negation
Ānvikṣikī	Science of logic
Anyatarāsiddha	Non-established for either party
Anyathākhyāti	Mis-apprehension
Anyathānupapatti	Universal pervasion
Anyathāsiddha	Dispensable antecedent
Anyonyābhāva	Reciprocal non-existence
Anyonyāśraya	Reciprocal dependence
Ap	Water (one of the five elements)
Apāna	One of the vital airs
Aparatva	Spatial or temporal proximity
Aparāvidyā	Lower knowledge
Aparigraha	Absence of avarice; non-possession
Aparokṣa	Direct (perception)
Apasiddhaviśeṣaṇa	Having a non-established qualification
Apauruṣeya	Not man-made
Apavarga	Final emancipation
Apekṣābuddhi	Enumerative cognition
Apoha	Common negation
Aprāmāṇya	Invalidity
Aprāpyakāri	The senses as characterised by the Buddhists
Apratyakṣa	Non-perceptibility
Aprayojaka	Non-efficient
Apṛthaksiddhi	Inseparable relation between cit, acit and Īśvara
Āpta	Trustworthy person, scriptural statement
Ārambhavāda	Production theory; cause produces the effect
Aratni	A linear measure
Arhat	Sublime in knowledge
Ārjava	Integrity
Āropa	Super imposition, hypothetical admission,
Āropavāda	Argumentation of superimposition
Artha	Substance
Arthakāra	Content of an object
Arthakriyā	Purposeful action, practical efficiency
Arthakriyājñāna	Volitional experience
Arthakriyākāritā	Efficiency
Arthabhāvanā	Objective productive operation
Arthāpatti	Presumptive testimony
Arthasaṁvṛti	Apprehension of an object
Arthasārūpya	Objective equiformity
Arthavāda	Praise
Arthāvagrāha	Object perception

Arūpajñāna	Four states of elimination
Asādhāraṇadharma	Specific feature
Asādhāraṇa kāraṇa	Special cause
Asambhava	Total inapplicability
Asamavāyikāraṇa	Non-inherent cause
Asat	Non-being
Asatkāryavāda	Doctrine of non-existence of the cause in the effect; the exposition of Nyāya-Vaiśeṣika (ārambhavāda)
Asatkhyāti	A theory of erroneous perception
Asat pratipakṣa	Having no counter probans
Āsrava	Inflow of kārmic particles
Astikāya	Having extension
Astitva	Existence
Atideśavākya	Assimilative proposition
Ativyāpti	Practical in-applicability
Atīndriya pratyakṣa	Extra sensory perception
Ativyāpti	Over-applicability
Ātmā	Soul, spirit, Brahman
Ātmakhyāti	Self-apprehension
Ātmasaṃsthā	Existing in ātman naturally
Ātmāśraya	Self-dependence
Atyantābhāva	Absolute non-existence
Atyantāsat	Complete non-being
Avacchedaka	Delimiting
Avadhi	Visual intuition
Avagraha	Perception of object
Avakṣepaṇa	Downward motion
Avāya	Perceptual judgement
Avayava	Factors of inference; parts
Avayavin	Composite structure, product; whole
Avinābhāva	Non-existence without invariable relation
Avidyā	Nescience
Avisaṃvādi	Which does not fail to accord
Avyabhicāra	Non-inconstancy
Avyākṛta	Unmanifest (cause)
Avyapadeśya	Non-verbal
Avyāpyavṛtti	Non-pervasive
Avyūha	Pattern of structure
Ayutasiddha	Induced relationship

B

Bādha	Sublation
Baddha	Bound
Bādhaka pratīti	Sublating cognition
Bādhita	Stultified reason

Bādhitaviśeṣaṇa	Having a sublated attribute
Bādhitaviṣaya	Having its content sublated
Bhākta	Secondary
Bhāktavedana	Phenomenal knowledge
Bhāvakārya	Positive product
Bhāvanā	Reminiscent impression
Bhāvapadārtha	Existent entities
Bheda	Difference
Bhrama	Delusion
Bhrānti	Illusion
Brahma (n)	Etymologically, prayer (Bṛh- to grow), Conscious substrate (of the world), priest; upaniṣadic monistic principle
Brahmā	One of the Hindu Trinity; Creator
Bheda agraha	Neglect of dissimilarity
Buddhi	Intelligent agent, intellect, cognition, second principle of evolution in Sāṃkhya; also called Mahat

C

Caitanya	Intelligence
Cakṣus	Visual sense, sense of sight
Calana	Motion
Cārvāka	Material philosophy
Cetana	Sentient (opposite of jaḍa)
Chala	Dialectic quibbling, perversion
Cit	Spirit, consciousness, soul
Citta	The mind which apprehends
Cittavṛtti	A mental mode, undifferentiated unity of intelligence
Cintā	Reasoning
Codanā	Injunction

D

Darśana	Philosophy, intuition
Deva	Shining one
Dhāraṇa	Retention
Dharma	Duty, righteousness; merit; motion (Jaina)
Dharmabhūtajñāna	Attributive knowledge
Dharmin	Thing qualified
Dhāraṇā	Retention
Dik	Spatial direction
Dravya	Substance
Dravyārthika dṛṣṭi	Stand-point of substance

Dṛṣṭānta	Typical instance
Draṣṭavyopaśamanam	Cessation of perceivability
Dravatva	Fluidity
Dravyatva	Substance-ness
Dhātu	Verb root, metal; sustaining principle
Dṛṣṭārthāpatti	Presumption from what is seen
Dvaita	Duality
Dvyaṇuka	Dyad
Dyaus	Heaven
Droṇa	A unit of measure

E

Eka	One
Ekāgra	One pointed concentration
Ekatva	Unitary, absolute self-being
Eka pṛthaktva	Unit distinctness
Evaṃ bhūta naya	Such like standpoint

G

Gamana	Going, motion in any direction
Gandha	Smell
Gati	Motion
Ghaṭatva	Potness
Ghrāṇa	Olfactory sense
Gocara	External organs
Golaka	Sphere
Grāhaka	Sense organ
Grāhya	Object
Guṇa	Character, quality
Gurutva	Weight, heaviness; gravity

H

Hetu	Reason, probans, middle term
Hetvābhāsa	Fallacious reason
Hetumantaḥ	Heretical puṇḍits
Hetu phale	Dharma, Adharma and the body, a product of it
Hetu vibhakti	Limitation of reason
Hetuvidyā	The science of reason in inference
Hiraṇyagarbha	Golden germ, the Cosmic Man, Creator

I

Icchā	Desire
Icchāśakti	Power of desire
Īhā	Speculation
Indriya	Sense, sense organ
Indriyārthasannikarṣa	Contact between sense organ and object
Indriya Pṛthaktvam	Natural for being open to the senses
Īṣaṇā	Desire
Īśvara	God
Īśvaravāda	Divine cause of the origin of the universe
Itaretarābhāva	Mutual non-existence

J

Jaḍa	Inert
Jāgaritam	Wakeful stage
Jalpa	Argument for victory, destructive reasoning
Janya	Producible thing
Janyā	Origin of time
Jīvan mukta	Liberated during life
Jarāyuja	Produced from a womb
Jāti	Genus
Jīva	Soul, self
Jīvadravya	Self-substance
Jīvakarma	Conscious karmic particles
Jīveśvarābheda	Identity of soul and god
Jīveśvara bheda	Possessing difference between jīva and Īśvara
Jñāna	Knowledge
Jñātatā	Quality of cognizedness (being an object of knowledge Bhāṭṭa-mīmāṃsā)
Jñānacetanā	Knowing consciousness
Jñānayoga	Discipline of knowledge
Jñānendriya	Sensory organs of knowledge
Jñānakāṇḍa	The Upaniṣadic part of the Vedas
Jñātā	Knower
Jñeya	To know; known

K

Ka	Who?, Prajāpati (Vedic)
Kaivalya	Liberation
Kāla	Time
Kālāṇu	Atom of time (Jaina)
Kālātīta	Mistimed middle, beyond time

Kalpa	A huge cycle of time (4,320,000,000 years each of 360 days)
Kalpanā	Ideation, category, presumptive knowledge
Kalpanāpoḍha	Negation of mental concepts
Kalpita	Imaginary
Karma	Action; instrument; motion; fate
Kāraṇa	Cause
Kāraṇadoṣa	Deficient conditions of knowledge
Kāraṇaguṇa	Efficient conditions of knowledge
Kāraṇasāmagrī	Collocation of conditions for perception
Karmakāṇḍa	Vedic Parts which ordain rituals
Karmamārga	The path of action
Karmamīmāṃsā	Science of discussion on rituals
Karmayoga	The discipline of action
Kārmaṇaśarīra	Kārmic body
Karsa	An unit of weight
Karmendriya	Organ of action
Karmāṇu	Karmic atoms
Kartā	Agent of action
Kāryarūpa	Event-determined entities
Kārya	Effect
Kāryānumāna	Synthetical judgement
Kevalādhikaraṇa	Mere conainer
Kevalajñāna	Absolute apprehension, knowledge
Kevala	Omniscience
Kevalānvayi	Agreement in presence
Kevalavyatireki	Agreement in absence
Kṛtakatva	Producibility
Kṣaṇikavijñāna	Momentary consciousness
Kṣaṇikavāda	Doctrine of momentariness
Kṣetrajña	The self which knows its body

L

Labdhi	Potential
Lāghava	Parsimony
Lakṣaṇa	Definition
Lakṣaṇā	Secondary implication
Laukika	Worldly
Likṣā	A unit of weight
Liṅga	Middle term; mark
Liṅgaparāmarśa	Subsumptive reflection of the probans.
Lokākāśa	Occupation of space points
Lokāyatikas	Cārvākas, those who advocate material enjoyment of life

M

Mahābhūta	Material element
Mahākāla	Undivided time
Mahat	Large, second principle of evolution, also called *buddhi*, finite intelligence (Sāṃkhya)
Mahat tattva	Principle of Mahat
Mahāyuga	A cyclic period of 4,320,000 years (each of 360 days)
Mahāsāmānya	Grand generality
Māna	Measurement, means of knowledge
Manana	Reflective thinking
Manas	Spririt, Mind
Mānasabodha	Conceptual Knowledge
Manomayakośa	The sheath of intellect
Mano-vṛtti	Reflective knowledge
Mārgaṇā	Searching
Māsa	Blackgram; a unit of weight
Mati	Sensorial (or without the aid of senses) knowledge
Matijñāna	Sensuous cognition
Mātṛ	Agent of cognition
Māyā	Illusion
Meya	Object of knowledge
Mithyā	Unreal
Mithyādarśanaṃ	Wrong conception
Mithyājñāna	False cognition
Mokṣa	Liberation, enlightenment
Mukhya	Primary perception
Mūrta	Moving substance
Mūlaprakṛti	The root principle
Mūlāvidyā	Cosmic illusion

N

Naigamanaya	Universal particular
Naimittikakarma	Occasional rite
Nairātmyavāda	Doctrine of no soul.
Nāmarūpa	Name and form
Naya	Potential predication
Nayavāda	Doctrine of relative pluralism
Nidāna	Causal chain binding one to suffering
Nididhyāsana	Constant meditation
Nigamana	Conclusion
Nigrahasthāna	Vulnerable point
Nimittakāraṇa	Instrumental cause
Nirguṇa	Devoid of all attributes

Nirṇaya	Decisive knowledge, demonstration
Nirvacana	Definite predication
Nirvāṇa	Cessation of suffering and desire
Nirūpaka	Correlating
Nirupādhika	Absolute
Nirvikalpaka	Indeterminate
Nirvikalpakajñāna	Primary perception
Niścaya	Determination
Niṣkampaka pravṛtti	Unfaltering effort
Niṣprapañcavāda	A cosmic idea of Reality or Brahman
Nityānityaviveka	Discriminating ability between permanent and ephemeral
Nityaguṇa	Permanent quality
Nityadoṣa	Permanent defect
Niyama	Rule; one of the yogic sādhanas
Niyata	Invariable
Niyatapūrvavṛtti	Invariable antecedent
Niyati	Determinism
Nodana	Pushing
Nyāya	Debate; logic; epistemological inquiry; one of the six orthodox systems of Indian thought

P

Padārtha	Category, word-sense
Pāka	Chemical action
Pala	A unit of measure
Pāramārthikasattā	Unity in pure existence
Pāramarthika	Transcendental
Pakṣa	Locus subject
Pakṣābhāsa	Fallacious subject
Pakṣadharmatā	Being an attribute of subject
Pakṣatā	Having a subject
Para	Comprehensive
Parabrahman	Supreme Being
Paramāṇu	Invisible ultimate atom
Parāmarśa	Subsumptive reflection
Paramātman	Supreme soul
Paramārtha sat	Ultimate existence, Pure and Absolute being
Parārthānumāna	Inference for others
Parataḥ prāmāṇya	Extrinsic validity
Paratva	Temporal or spatial remoteness
Parāvidyā	Higher knowledge
Paricchedaka	Measure of determinate
Paricchitti	Destruction of definition
Parīkṣā	Investigation

Parimāṇa	Size, volume
Pārimāṇḍalya	Spherical (atom)
Pariṇāma	Evolution, modification
Paripūrṇa	Perfect
Parispanda	Simple motion
Parokṣa	Non-perceptual
Paryāya	Modification of modes
Paryāyadṛṣṭi	Standpoint of modes
Pauruṣeya	Man-made
Piṇḍa	Mass
Piṭharapāka(vāda)	Thermal (heat) action in the object without destroying constituent parts
Pīlupāka (vāda)	Chemical action in the atoms only
Pradhāna	The first principle of evolution
Prāgabhāva	Prior non-existence
Prajñā	Third of the four states of existences, intuition (Paññā-Bud); Wisdom (Jaina); self-realization.
Prakāra	Adjunct
Prajāpati	Lord of creatures
Praharṣa	Excellence
Prakaraṇasama	Reason equivalent to proposition
Prakāya	Manifestation
Prakāśa	Luminosity
Prakarṣa	Excellence
Prakṛti	Matter, primordial matter, nature
Pralaya	Dissolution
Pramā	Valid knowledge
Pramāṇa samyakjñāna	Right knowledge
Pramāṇa	Means of valid knowledge, evidence, authority, valid knowledge
Pramātā	The subject
Prāmāṇya	Truth, validity
Prameya	The object
Prāṇa	One of the vital airs
Pratīti	Comprehension
Prāṇamayakośa	The sheath of life (one of the five sheaths mentioned in the Upaniṣads)
Prāpaka	Presentation
Prāpyakāri	Reaching the object
Pratibandha	Mutual relation, Psycho-physical reactions
Prastha	A measure
Prasakti	Logical implication
Prasāraṇa	Expansion
Pratibandhaka	Counteracting agent
Prātibhāsikasattā	Apparent existence

Pratijñā	Challenge, promise, thesis
Pratikūlatarka	Non-favourable counter argument
Pratipādya Pratipādaka	Relation of the treated and the treatise
Pratipatti	Combined cognition; acquisition of knowledge
Pratipatti	Acquisition of knowledge
Pratītya samutpāda	Dependent Origination
Pratiyogitā	Correlativeness
Pratiyogin	Counter correlate
Pratyabhijñāna	Extra sensory perception
Pratyabhijñā	Illusory appearance
Pratyagātmā	The inner self
Pratyakṣa	Perception (direct)
Pratyaya	Conception
Pravṛtti	Involvement in worldly life
Pravṛttimārga	One of the paths for liberation
Pravṛtti sāmarthya	Volitional experience
Pravṛttivijñāna	Knowledge which is real but momentary
Prayatna	Volition
Prayojana	Motive; purpose; aim
Pṛthaktva	Distinctness, separateness
Pṛthvī	Earth, goddess earth; one of the mahābhūtas
Pudgala	Matter (with *rūpa*, form) (Jaina)
Pūrṇaprajña	Omniscient
Puruṣa	Material cause of the universe; embodied spirit; man
Puruṣārtha	Human values
Pūrvavat	From cause to effect

R

Rāddhānta	Final doctrine
Rajas	Passion, resistance to movement, one of the three guṇas
Rajjusarpaviveka	Discretion between rope and serpent
Rasa	Taste, one of the sensorial qualities
Rasanā	Tongue, gustatory sense
Rūḍhi	Convention
Rūpa	Colour
Rūpin	Form
Rūpatva	Colourness
Ṛjusūtranaya	Standpoint of momentariness
Ṛta	Cosmic law or order; moral order

S

Śabda	Sound, verbal experience; one of the sensorial qualities
Śabda pramāṇa	Verbal testimony

Śabda-tanmātra	Sound essence
Śabda-naya	Standpoint of synonyms
Śabdavṛtti	Significative force
Śābdabodha	Verbal cognition
Sādhakatama	Most efficient ground
Sādhanacatuṣṭaya	Four prerequisites in the quest for perfection
Sādhāraṇa	Common
Sādhya	To be established by inference
Sādṛśya	Similarity
Sākṣin	Witness
Sama	Equal, equanimity
Samadhirūdhanaya	Etymological standpoint
Sāmānādhikaraṇya	Co-existence in the same locus
Sāmagrī	The whole causal apparatus
Sāmānya	Generality; one of the six padārthas of Vaiśeṣika
Sāmānyaguṇa	Common quality
Sāmānyaviśeṣa	Generic diffentia
Samavadhāna	Synthesis
Samavāya	Inherent relation
Sāmayīkābhāva	Temporary non-existence
Samavāyikāraṇa	Inhering cause
Saṃjñin	Named
Saṃjñā	Name, recognition
Saṃsāra	The cycle of birth and death
Sandigdha	Doubtful probans
Saṃsarga	Relation
Saṃsargābhāva	Non-existence of relation
Saṃśaya	Doubt
Saṃskāra	Mental impressions, faculty, purification; one of the 24 qualities of Vaiśeṣika
Sāṃsiddhika	Natural
Saṃsthāna	Pattern
Samūhāvalambana	Group cognition
Saṃvitti	Knowledge
Saṃvṛtti	Phenomenal knowledge
Saṃvṛtti satya	Empirical reality
Samyag darśana	Perfect knowledge
Samyajjñāna	Right knowledge, total comprehension
Saṃyoga	Conjunction
Saṃyogaja	Conjunction by contact
Saṅgrahanaya	Class point of view
Sāṃkhya	One of the six systems of Indian thought
Sannikarṣa	Sense relation; contact
Sapakṣa	Similar instance
Sapakṣasattva	Where middle term is present

Saptabhaṅgīnyāya	Seven fold judgement; also syādvāda (Jaina)
Sarṣapa	An unit of weight
Sārūpya	Relation
Sat	Being
Satkāryavāda	The doctrine that cause and effect are the same substance; Sāṅkhya exposition
Satkhyāti	Illusory knowledge as apprehension of real knowledge
Sat pratipakṣa	The subject counter balanced
Sattā	The order of existence
Sattvaguṇa	Light, brightness, goodness
Savikalpa	Resultant judgement
Savikalpaka	Determinate perception
Savyabhicāra	Inconclusive reason
Śeṣavat	Reasoning from effect to a cause
Siddhasādhana	Establishing what is already established
Siddhānta	Theory
Skandha	Aggregate; things which come into being and perish
Smṛti	Memory, sacred works like Purāṇas and Dharmaśāstras
Smṛtipramoṣa	Confused memory
Snigdha	Smooth
Sopādhika	Conditional relation
Sparśa	Touch
Sparśa-tanmātra	Touch essence
Śraddhā	Faith
Śravaṇa	Listening to scriptures
Śruta	Knowledge of objects existing in all the three times
Śrutārthāpatti	Presumption from what is heard
Sthitisthāpakatva	Elasticity
Sūkṣmaparamāṇu	Ultimate atom (Jaina)
Śūnya	Void
Śūnyavāda	Nihilism
Suṣupti	Deep sleep
Suttas	Aphorisms of the Buddha
Svabhāvānumāna	Analytical judgement
Svabhāvapratibandha	Existentially determined
Svabhāvavādin	The naturalist
Svalakṣaṇa	Momentary particular
Svārthānumāna	Inference for oneself
Svarūpalakṣaṇa	Definition with reference to essence
Svarūpa sambandha	Self-relation
Svataḥpramāṇatāvāda	The theory that knowledge carrying its validity and self-revealing
Svasaṃvedana	Introspection
Svatastva	Intrinsicality
Svatogrāhya	Intrinsically brought about

Svato vyāvartaka	Self-differentiated
Svedaja	Born of perspiration
Syādvāda	'May be' theory

T

Tādātmyam	Identity
Tad ekam	That is one
Tajjalān	Causality
Taijasa	Second state of experience; one of the trigunas
Tamas	Darkness, inertia; one of the trigunas
Tanmātra	Subtle matter (Sāmkhya)
Tarka	Indirect argument, reduction ad absurdum
Tarkaśāstra	The science of argument
Tarkavidyā	Science of debating
Tatasthalaksana	Disjunction of the accidentals
Tatorthād vijñānam	Objectively determined
Tejas; Tejobhūta	Fire, heat, light; one of the five elements
Tikta	Bitter
Tithi	Moon's position, time unit
Trīkālātīta	Transcending time
Triputisamvit	Perception
Trutī; Tryanuka; Trasarenu	Triad
Tulā	Balance, equivalent to 100 *pala-s* measure
Tvak	Sense of touch, tactus; one of the five sense organs

U

Ubhayāsiddha	Not established either way
Udāharana	Example
Udbhūta	Perceptible
Udbhijja	Produced from sprouts
Uddeśa	Enumeration
Uddeśya	Subject
Upādānakārana	Material cause
Upadeśa	Direct teaching
Upādhi	Limiting agent; adventitious condition; an attribute which is not a jāti
Upādāna kārana	Material cause
Upalabdhi	Apprehension
Upamāna	Comparison as a means of knowledge
Upamiti	Assimilative cognition or experience
Upanaya	Application
Upānga	Minor, subsidiary, analogy
Upapādaka	That which explains

Upapādya	Fact to be explained
Uparati	Renunciation of formalism
Upasthiti	Thought
Upayoga	Manifest
Utkṣepaṇa	Upward motion
Utpatti	Originating conditions

V

Vācaka	Designation
Vācya	Designatum
Vācyārtha	Expressed meaning
Vāda	Disputation
Vahni	Fire
Vaināśikas	Nihilists
Vaiśeṣika	One of the six orthodox systems of Indian thought
Vākyārthabodha	Verbal judgement
Vāsanā	Psychical dispositions, impression unconsciously left in the mind
Vāyu	Air, one of the five elements
Vega	Velocity
Vibhāga	Division, disjunction
Vibhāgīya	Caused by disjunction
Vibhrama	Illusion
Vibhu	All pervasive; ubiquitous
Vibhudravya	All pervasive substance
Vidhi	Injunction
Vidheya	Predicate
Vijñāna	Consciousness
Vijñānamayakośa	The sheath of discriminative knowledge; one of the five sheaths of upaniṣads
Vikalpa	Inquisitive and constructive activity of the mind, verbal knowledge
Vimarśa	Conflicting notions, enquiry
Vipakṣa	Counter example
Viparītakhyāti	Erroneous knowledge, contrary experience due to distortion of the present with memory
Viparyaya	Erroneous knowledge
Viṣaya viṣayī bhāva	Subject–object relation
Viruddha	Adverse probans, or reason
Viṣaya	Object
Viśeṣa	Particularity
Viśeṣalakṣana	Particular characteristics
Viśeṣya	Substantive
Viśeṣyatā	Substantiveness
Viśiṣṭapratīti	Determinate cognition

Vitaṇḍa	Wrangling
Vivarta	Illusory modification
Vṛtti	Psychical; activity
Vyabhicāra	Inconstancy
Vyāghāta	Practical contradiction
Vyākṛta	Manifested
Vyaktāvyakta	Unfolding of the implicit
Vyañjanā	Suggestion
Vyañjanāvagraha	Contact awareness
Vyāpāra	Function
Vyāpti	Pervasion, concomitance, invariable concomitance
Vyāpyatvāsiddha	Unestablished in respect of its concomitance
Vyāsajyavṛtti	Particularly contained
Vyatireka sahacāra	Concomitance of negation
Vyatirekadṛṣṭānta	Negative example
Vyatireka vyāpti	Negative concomitance
Vyavacchedya	What is to be concluded
Vyāvahārikasattā	The empirical existence
Vyāvartaka	Differentiating feature
Vyāvartya	What is to be excluded
Vyavasthāpanā	Determination of particular object
Vyavahāra paramāṇu	Atom (Jaina)
Vyāvṛtti	Differentiation
Vyūha	Structural arrangement (atoms)
Vyutpatti	Learning, etymology

Y

Yadṛcchāvādi	Supporter of the theory of accidentalism (also called animittavādin)
Yathārtha	Real
Yathārthānubhava	Presentational knowledge
Yathārthaparicchedakatva	Object in its real nature
Yatna	Volitional effort
Yoga	Contemplation; conjunction
Yogyānupalabdhi	Effectual non-cognition
Yuga	A cyclic period of 5 years (generally)

General Bibliography

PRIMARY SOURCES

Abhidhammottarasaṅgraha: (Compendium of Buddhists Philosophy): (Tr) Aung Shwe Zan, Pali Text Society Translation Series, Oxford University Press, London, 1910.

Abhisamayālaṅkāra: (Tr) Edward Conze, Serie Oreintale Roma, Rome, 1954.

Abhidharmakośa with the commentary of Yaśomitra: (Ed) Swami Dvarikadas Sastri, Varanasi, 1910; (Ed) Shrimat Prahalad Pradhan, Kashi Prasad Jayaswal Research Institute, Patna, 1967.

Advaitasiddhi of Madhusūdana Sarasvati: (Tr) Ganganath Jha, *Indian Thought,* Vol. VI, X, 1914-17.

Āgamaśāstra of Gauḍapāda: (Ed) V. Bhattacharya, University of Calcutta, Calcutta, 1933.

Aitareya Āraṇyaka: (Ed) A. B. Keith, Clarendon, Oxford, 1909.

Aitareya Brāhmaṇa: Sacred Books of the Hindus, **IV**, 1922.

Aitareya Upaniṣad: (Ed) Vidyaranya, 2 Vols. Anandashrama Series, Poona, 1889.

Ālambanaparīkṣā and Vṛtti: (Ed) N. A. Sastri, The Adyar Library, Madras, 1942.

Aṅguttaranikāya or More Numbered Sūtras: (Ed) Frank Woodward Lee, Vol. I, 1932, 1951.

Apohasiddhi: (Ed) Govind Chand Pande, Darshana Pratisthana, Jaipur, 1971.

Arthaśāstra of Kauṭilya: (Ed and Tr) R. P. Kangle, 3 parts, Bombay University, Bombay, 1960, 1963 and 1965.

Arthasaṅgraha of Laugākṣi Bhāskara: (Ed) A. B. Gajendragadkar and R. D. Karmarkar, Motilal Banarasidass, Delhi, 1984.

Astāṅgahṛdayam: (Tr) K. R. Srikantha Murthy, 3 Vols., Krishnadas Academy, Varanasi, 1995.

Atharvavedasaṃhitā: (Tr) Maurice Bloomfield, *Hymns of the Atharvaveda,* Sacred Books of the East, Vol. 42; (Tr) R. T. H. Griffith, 2 Vols. Chowkhamba Sanskrit Series, Varanasi, 1968.

Ātmatattvaviveka of Udayana with the commentary of Nārāyana, Raghunātha and Gadādhara: (Ed) Pt. Dhundiraja Sastri, Benares, 1940.

Ātmatattvaviveka and Ātmabodha of Śaṅkarācārya: (Tr) M. Mohini Chatterjee, Bombay Theosophical Publishing House, Bombay, 1932; (Ed) Jayakrishna Haridasa Gupta, Chowkhamba Sanskrit Series, Benares, 1900.

Bāhyārthasiddhi of Śubhagupta: (Ed) N. Aiyaswami Sastri, *Bulletin of Tibetology,* IV. No. 2. Namgyal Insitute of Tibetology, Gangtok, 1967.

Bhāṣāpariccheda of Viśvanātha with commentaries of Dinakara and Ramarudra: (Ed) Atmarama Sarma, Nirnayasagar Press, Bombay, 1933.

Bhāṣāpariccheda with Siddhānta Muktāvali, (Ed) S. Mukherjee, Advaita Ashrama, Calcutta, 1954.

Bhagavadgītā, Gita Press, Gorakhpur, 1953.

Bhagavadgītā with Śaṅkara's Bhāṣya: (Tr) Alladi Mahadeva Sastri, Advaita Ashrama, Mayavati, 1933.

Bhagavadgītābhāṣya of Srī Rāmānuja: (Ed) Alkandavathi Govindācārya, Vaijayanti Press, Madras, 1908.

Bhagavadgītābhāṣya of Sri Madhvācārya: (Tr) S. Subba Rau, Minerva Press, Madras, 1906.

Bhāgavata Purāṇam: Gita Press, Gorakhpur, 1954.

Bhagavatīsūtra (Vols I and II): English translation and notes by K. C. Lalwani, Jain Bhawan, Calcutta, 1947.

Bhagavatīsūtra with commentary of Abhayadeva Sūri: (Ed) Nanak Chandaji, 4 vols. Benares, 1882.

Bhāmatī, Catuḥsūtrī: (Tr) S. S. S. Sastry and C. Kunhan Raja, Theosophical Publishing House, Madras, 1933.

Bhāgavatamahāpurāṇam: (Tr) M. A. Goswami, 3 Vols., Gita Press, Gorakhpur, 1971.

Bodhicaryāvatāra of *Śāntideva* with a commentary of Prajñākaramita: (Ed) P.L. Vaidya, Mithilā Insitute, Darbhanga, 1960.

Brahmasiddhi of Madana: (Ed) S. Kuppuswami Sastri, Madras Government Oriental Mss Series No. 4, Madras, 1937.

Brahmasūtrabhāṣya of Śaṅkarācharya: (Tr) Swami Gambhirananda, Advaita Ashrama, Calcutta, 1977.

Brahmasūtra with the commentary of Śaṅkara and *Bhāmatī:* (Ed) Durgācaraṇa Sāṃkhya Vednta Tīrtha, Calcutta, 1970.

Bṛhadāraṇyakopaniṣad with a commentary of Śaṅkarācharya: (Ed) Durgacharaṇa Sāṃkhya Vedānta Tīrtha, Calcutta; (Text with Tr) Swami Madhavananda, Advaita Ashrama, Calcutta, 1934; (with Śaṅkarabhāṣya), Gīta Press, Gorakhpur, 1972.

Bṛhaddevatā: (Ed) A. A. Macdonell, 2 Vols, Motilal Banarasidass, Delhi.

Bṛhajjātaka of Varāhamihira: (Ed) B. Suryanarayana Rao, Motilal Banarasidass, Delhi, 1957.

Bṛhatsaṃhitā of Varāhamihira: (Ed) M. R. Bhatt, 2 Vols., Motilal Banarasidass, Delhi, 1978.

Buddhacaritam: (Ed) E. H. Johnston, Panjab University Oriental Publications, Lahore, 1936.

Buddhadarśanamīmāṃsā: (Ed) B. Upadhyaya, Chowkhamba Vidya Bhavana, Benares, 1954.

Buddhavaṃśa: (Ed) B. C. Law, Sacred Books of the Buddhists, 1938.

Cārvākasaṣṭi (Indian Materialism): (Ed) Dakshina Ranjan Sastry, The Calcutta Book Co., Calcutta, 1963.

Carakasaṃhitā: (Tr) P. V. Sharma, 4 Vols. Jayakrishnadas Āyurveda Granthamālā, Chowkhamba Oreintalia, Varanasi, 1996; with the commentary of Cakrapāṇidatta: (Ed) Vaidya Jagdaviji Trikumji Acharya, Niranaya Sagar Press, Bombay, 1941.

Chāndogyopaniṣad: (Tr) Vidyāraṇya and Sirisa Chandra Basu, Sacred Books of the Hindus, 1910.

Chāndogyopaniṣadbhāṣya of Śaṅkarācārya: Gita Press, Gorakhpur, 1962.

Citsukhī of *Tattvapradīpikā*: (Ed) Swami Yogananda, Varanasi, 1974.

Dhammapada: (Tr) Irving Babhitt, Oxford University Press, London, 1936.

Dharmasūtras: (Tr) Manmathanatha Datta, Society for Resuscitation of Indian Literature, Calcutta, 1908.

Dharamottarapradīpa of Durveka Mishra: (Ed) Dalsukhbhai Malvania, Kashi Prasad Jayaswal Research Institute, Patna, 1971.

Dīghanikāya: (Tr) C.A.F Rhys Davids, Vols. II and III, Sacred Books of the Buddhists, 1921.

Gommaṭasāra Karmakāṇḍa: (Tr) Brahmachari Sital Prasad Ji and Pandit Ajit Prasadji, Sacred Books of the Jainas, Vol IX. Arrah and Lucknow, 1927.

Gṛhyasūtras: (Tr) H. Oldenberg and F. Max Muller, Sacred Books of the East. Vol. XXIX and XXX, Reprint. Motilal Banarasidass, Delhi, 1964.

Hetubindu of Dharmakīrti: (Ed) Sukhalalji Singhvi and Munisri Jinavijyayaji, Gaekwad Oriental Series, No. 113, Oriental Research Institute, Baroda, 1949.

Īśa, Kena, Kaṭha, Praśna, Muṇḍaka and Māṇḍūkya: (Tr) Vidyaranya, Sacred Books of the Hindus, 1924.

Iṣṭasiddhi: (Ed) M. Hiriyanna, Gaekwad Oriental Series, Baroda, 1933.

Jaiminīya Brāhmaṇa: (Ed) Raghuvīra and Lokesh Chandra, Sarasvati Vihara Series, No. 31, Nagpur, 1954.

Jaiminisūtra or Mīmāṃsādarśana: (Ed) Bhutanātha Saptatirtha, Basumati Sahitya Mandir, Calcutta, 1938.

Kaṇādarahasya of Śaṅkara Miśra: (Ed) Damodar Shastri Goswami, Chowkhamba Sanskrit, Benares, 1917.

Kārikāvalī of Viśvanātha: (Ed) Rama Shukla Nyāyācārya, Benares, 1951.

Kaṭha Upaniṣad: in *Īśādinavupaniṣads,* Gita Press, Gorakhpur, 1959.

Kauṣītakī Upaniṣad and *Maitri Upaniṣad:* (Tr) S. C. Vidyaranya and Mohanlal Sandal, Sacred Books of the Hindus, **31,** 1925-26.

Kenopaniṣad with the Commentary of Śaṅkarācārya: (Ed) M. Hiriyanna, Sri Vani Vilasa Press, Kumbhakoṇam, 1912.

Khaṇḍanakhaṇḍakhādya: (Tr) Ganganath Jha, *Indian Thought,* Vol I, VII, 1907-15.

Kiraṇāvalī of Udayana: (Ed) Vindhyeshwari Prasad Dvivedi, Chowkhamba Sanskrit Series, Benaras, 1918; (Ed) Jitendra S. Jetley, Oriental Institute, Vadodara, 1991.

Kiraṇāvalībhāskara of Padnanābha Miśra: Sarasvati Bhavan Text, Benares, 1920.

Kiraṇāvalīprakāśa of Vardhamāna: Benares, 1941.

Kundamālā of Diṅnāga: (Ed) J. L. Sastri, Motilal Banarsidass, Delhi.

Laghudīpikā (A commentary on Varadarāja's *Tārkikarakṣā*): (Ed) Pandit Vindhyeshwari Prasad Dvivedi,Varanasi, 1903.

Laghīyastraya of Akalaṅka: (Ed) K. B. Nitabe, Bombay, 1915.

Lakṣaṇāvalī with Bhaṭṭakeśava's *Prakāśa:* (Ed) Sasinath Jha, Darbhanga, 1963

Laṅkāvatārasūtra: (Tr) Daisetz Teitaro Suzuki, George Routledge & Sons Ltd., London, 1930.

Mādhyamikakārikā of Nāgārajuna (Ed) L. De la valle Poussin, St. Petersberg, 1907.

Mādhyamikaśāstra of Nāgārajuna: (Ed) P. L. Vaidya, Buddhists Sanskrit Text No. 10, Mithila Insitute, Darbhanga.

Mādhyamika Sūtram of Nāgārjuna: (Ed) Raghunatha Pandeya, Motilal Banarasidass, Delhi, 1946.

Majjhimanikāya: (The Middle Length Sayings): Isaline Blew Horner, Vol I, Oxford University Press, London, 1954.

Mahāvastu: (Tr) John James Jones, Vols. II and III, Sacred Books of the Buddhists, 1952.

Mahābhārata: (Tr) Von Beutanin, 3 vols, Chicago University, Chicago, 1973-78.

Mahāvagga (The Book of Discipline): (Tr) I. B. Hormer, Vol IV, Sacred Books of the Buddhists, 1951.

Mānameyodaya: (Tr) C. K. Raja and S. S. S. Sastri, The Adyar Library, Madras, 1933.

Māṇḍūkyopaniṣad with *Gauḍapādakārikā* and *Śaṅkarabhāṣya:* (Tr) Swami Nikhilananda, Ramakrishna Centenary Publication, Ramakrishna Ashrama, Calcutta, 1936.

Maṇḍūka Upaniṣad: (Ed) Sāṃkhya Vedāntatīrtha, Calcutta, 1938.

Manusmṛti with *Manubhāṣya* of Medhātithi: (Ed and Tr) Ganganatha Jhā, Motilal Banarsidass, Delhi, 1916.

Manusmṛti, Gita Press, Gorakhpur, 1953.

Mīmāṃsānyāyaprakāśa of Āpadeva: (Tr) Franklin Edgerton, Yale University Press, New Haven, 1939.

Mīmāṃsāsūtras of Jaimini: (Tr) Pandit Mohan Sandal, Sacred Books of the Hindus, **32**, 1923-25.

Nāradīya Dharmaśāstra: (Tr) Julius Jolly, Triibener & Co., London, 1876.

Naiṣkarmyasiddhi of Sureśvara: (Tr) A. J. Alston, London, 1959.

The *Nighaṇṭu and Nirukta:* (Ed and Tr) Lakshmana Swarup, Motilal Banarasidass, Delhi, 1967.

Niyamasāra by Sri Kundakundācārya: (Ed and Tr) Uggar Sain and Brahmachāri Sital Prasadji, Sacred Books of the Jainas year.

Nyāyabindu of Dharmakīrti: (Ed) Chandra Shekhara, Kashi Sanskrit Series, Varanasi, 1954.

Nyāyabhāṣya of Vātsyāyana, with extracts from Uddyotakara's *Vārttika* and Vācaspati Miśra's *Tātparyaṭīkā*: (Ed) G. S. Tailanga, Vizianagaram Sanskrit Sereis, No. 9, Benares, 1896.

Nyāyakandalī of *Śridhara*: (Ed) Pandit Durgadhara Jha, Sampurnanand Sanskrit Series, Varanasi, 1977.

Nyāya-Kandalī of *Śridhara*: (Ed) Vindhyeswari Prasad Dvivedi, Chowkhamba Sanskrit Book Depot, Benaras, 1895.

Nyāyabinduṭīkā of Dharmottara: (Ed and Tr) Shrinivas Sastri, Sahitya Bhandar, Subbash Bajara, Saranath, 1951.

Nyāyadarśanaṃ: Nyāyasūtras of Gautama, Uddyotakara's *Vārtika* and Vācaspatimiśra's *Tātparya tīkā*: (Ed) Amarendramohana Tarkatirtha, Munshiram Manoharlal, Delhi, 1985.

Nayanaprasādinī: Commentary on *Citsukhī:* Swami Yogindrananda, 2nd edn., Vārāṇasi, 1974.

Nyāya Kumudacandra of Prabhacandra, Vol I: (Ed) Mahendrakumar Nyayasastri, Bombay, 1938.

Nyāya Kusumāñjali with commentaries: (Ed) P. Upādhyāya and Dhundiraja Sastri, Chowkhamba Sanskrit series, Benares, 1967; (Ed) Uttamur T. Viraraghavachar, Kendriya Sanskrit Vidyapeetha, Tirupati, 1980.

Nyāyalīlāvatī of Vallabhācārya: (Ed) Dhundiraja Sastri, Chowkhamba Sanskrit Series, Benares, 1970.

Nyāyamañjarī of Jayanta Bhaṭṭa: (Ed) Pandit Sri Surya Narayana Shukla, Chowkhamba Sanskrit Series, Benares, 1936.

Nyāyamūla of Diṅnāga: Geusuppe Tucci, Heidelberg, 1930.

Nyāyapariśiṣṭa of Udayana with *Pañcikā*: (Ed) S. N. Srirama Desikan, Kendriya Sanskrit Vidyapeetha, Tirupati, 1976.

Nyāya Praveśa of Diṅnāga: Part I, Gaekwad Oriental Series No. 38, Oriental Institute, Baroda, 1968.

Nyāyaratnamālā of Pārthasārathi Miśra Gaekwad Oriental Series, No. 75, Baroda, 1937.

Nyāyaratnākara of Pārthasārathi Miśra, (a commentary on *Ślokavārtika*): Chowkhamba Sanskrit Series, Benares, 1898-99.

Nyāyasāra of Bhāsarvajña: (Ed) V. S. Abhyankar and C. R. Devadhar, Oriental Book Supplying Agency, Poona, 1922.

Nyāya-Siddhāntadīpa of *Śaśadhara*: (Ed) V. P. Dvivedi and D. Shastri, Chowkhamba, Benaras, 1924.

Nyāyasūtras of Gautama: (Ed) S. C. Vidyabhusana, Oriental Books Reprint Corporation, New Delhi, 1975.

Nyāyasūtras of Gautama with the *Bhāṣya* of Vātsyāyana and the *Vārttika* of Uddyotakara: (Tr) Ganganatha Jha, 4 vols. Motilal Banarasidass, Reprint, Delhi, 1984.

Nyāyasūtras of Gautama with Vātsyāyana Bhāṣya and Vishwanatha Pañcānana's: (Ed) N. D. Joshi, Anandashram, Poona, 1922.

Nyāyasūtravṛtti of Viśvanātha: (Ed) Jivananda, Calcutta, 1919.

Nyāyavāttikatātparyaṭīkā of Vācaspati Miśra: (Ed) Rajesvara Śāstri Dravid, Kashi Sanskrit Series, Kashi, 1925.

Nyāya Vārttika of Uddyotakara: (Ed) V. P. Dvivedi, Bibliotheca Indica, 1887, 1914; Chowkhamba Sanskrit Series, Varanasi, 1916.

Nyāyāvatāra of Siddhasena: (Ed and Tr) S. C. Vidya Bhushana, Calcutta, 1909.

Padārthatattvanirūpaṇam of Raghunatha Siromani: (Tr) K. H. Potter, Harvard Oriental series, Cambridge, 1957.

Padarthatattvanirūpaṇa of Raghunatha (with Bengali tr): (Ed) Madhusudan Nyayacarya, Sanskrit College, Calcutta, 1976.

Padārthadharmasaṅgraha of Praśastapāda with *Nyāya Kandalī*: (Ed) Ganganath Jhā, Lauzarus & Co., Benares, 1916.

Pancāstikāyasāra of Kundakundācārya: Chakravartinayanar, Sacred Books of the Jainas, 1936.

Pañcāstikāyasāra of Kundakundācārya: (Ed) A. Chakrabarti, The Central Jaina Publishing House, Arrah, 1920.

Pañcadaśī of Vidyāraṇya: Nirnaya Sagara Press, Bombay, 1949.

Pañcapādikā of Padmapāda: (Tr) D.R. Venkataram, Government Oriental Series, Baroda, 1948.

Paralokasiddhi of Dharmottara: *Indian Culture*, Vol 15, 1941.

Parīkṣāmukha of Māṇikyanandi: (Ed) Sarat Chandra Ghoshal, Sacred Books of the Jainas, Vol XI, 1936.

Prakaraṇapañcikā of Śālikānātha : (Ed) A. S. Sastri, Banares Hindu University, Benares, 1961.

Pramāṇavārttikakārikā of Dharmakīrti: (Ed) Rahul Sāṅkrityāyana, Bihar and Orissa Research Society, Patna, 1940; (Ed) Dwarakadas Sastri, Bauddhabhāratī Granthamālā Prakashan, Varanasi, 1958.

Pramāṇavārttikavṛtti of Manorathanandini: (Ed) Rahul Sankrityayana, Bihar and Orissa Research Society, Patna, 1940.

Pramāṇavārttikālaṅkāra of Prajñākara Gupta: (Ed) Rahul Sankrityayana, Kashiprasada Jayaswal Anuśilana Saṃsthā, Pataliputra, 1953.

Prameyakamalamārtāṇḍa of Prabhacandra: (Ed) M. K. Shastri, Bombay, 1912.

Praśastapādabhāṣyam with Commentary *Kiraṇāvalī* of Udayanācārya: (Ed) J. S. Jetley, Oriental Institute, Baroda, 1971.

Puggalapaññatti: Pali Text Society Translation Series, Nalanda, 1924.

Pūrvamīmāṃsāsūtras of Jaimini: Ganganath Jha, India Press, Allahabad, 1916.

Pūrṇaprajñadarśana: The *Vedānta Sūtras* with the commentary of Madhvācārya (Tr) S. Subba Rao, Madras, 1904.

Ṛgveda Brāhmaṇas: (Tr) A. B. Keith, Harvard University Press, Cambridge, 1920.

Ṛgveda with Sāyaṇa's Commentary: (Ed and Tr) Manmathanath Dutt, 4 Vols, Wealth of India, Second Series, Calcutta, 1906-12.

The Hymns of the *Ṛgveda:* (Tr) R. T. H. Griffith, E. J. Lauzarus & Co., Benares, 1896.

Hymns of the Ṛgveda: (Tr) A. A. Macdonell, Oxford University Press, London, 1918.

Ṛgvedasaṃhitā: (Ed) Ram Prakash Arya and K. L. Joshi, Motilal Banarsidass, Delhi; (Tr) H. H. Wilson; Published by H. R. Bhagavat, Poona, 1925 (1st edn.,) 6 Vols; (2nd Edn) C. Ramanuja Iyengar, Bangalore Printing and Publishing House, Bangalore, 1946.

Śabdaśaktiprakāśikā of Jagadīśa: Chowkhamba Sanskrit Series, Benares, 1999.

Ṣaḍdarśanasamuccaya Sūtram of Guṇaratna: (Ed) F. L. Pulle, Giornalledella Societa, Asiatica Italiana, Rome, 1894.

Ṣaḍdarśanasamuccya of Haribhadra Sūri: Chowkhamba Sanskrit Series, No. 95, Benares, 1935.

Saddharmapuṇḍarīka: (Tr) Hendrik Kern, Sacred Books of the East, XXI, 1884.

Sāmānya Vedanta Upaniṣads: (Tr) T. R. Srinivasa Iyengar, Adyar Library, Madras, 1941.

Samayasāra of Kundakundācārya: Sītal Prasad ji, Sacred Books of the Jainas, VIII, 1936.

Saṃyuttanikāya (The Book of Kindred Sayings): (Ed) C.A.F. Rhys Davids and F. L. Woodward, Pali Text Society Translation Series, London, 1917-30.

Saṃuttanikāya (grouped Sūtras): Pali Text Society Translation Series, Vol I; (Tr) Frank Woodward Lee, PJSTS, Vols. IV and V, London, 1926-30.

Sāṃkhyadarśanam with the *Sāṃkhyapravacana bhāṣya* of Vijñānabhikṣu, Kashi Sanskrit Series, No. 67, Kashi, 1928.

Sāṃkhya kārikabhāṣya of Gauḍapāda: Poona Oriental Series, Poona, 1933.

Sāṃkhyasūtra of Kapila with Vijñāna Bhikṣu's Commentary: (Ed) Kavivara Vedānta Vāgīśa, Calcutta, 1960.

Sāṃkhyasūtras with the commentaries of Aniruddha and Mahadeva: (Ed and Tr) Richard Garbe, Baptist Mission Press, Calcutta, 1892.

Sāṃkhyakārikā of Īśvara Kṛṣṇa: (Tr) T. H. Colebrooke, Oriental Translation Fund, Oxford, 1837; (Tr) S. S. Sūryanārayaṇa Sastrī, Madras University, Madras, 1935.

Śāntarakṣita-Tattvasaṅgraha: (Ed) with the commentary of Kamalaśīla by Dwarikadas Sastri, 2 Vols, Benares, 1968.

Saṅkṣepaśārīrakam of Sarvajñamuni: (Ed) S. N. Shukla, Sarasvati Bhavan Texts, Benares, 1936.

Sarvasiddhāntasaṅgraha attributed to Śaṅkarācārya: (Tr) M. Rangacharya, Madras Government Press, Madras, 1909.

Saptapadārthī of Śivāditya: D. Gurumurti, Theosophical Publishing House, Adyar, Madras, 1932.

Sāṃkhyapravacanabhāṣya: (Tr) R. Garbe, Vol. II, Harvard Oriental Series, Cambridge, 1895.

Sarvadarśanasaṅgraha: (Tr) E. B. Cowell, Trübner & Co., London, 1914.

Śāstradīpikā of Pārthasārathi Miśra: Gaekwad Oriental Series, Oriental Institute, Baroda, 1940; also Chowkhamba Sanskrit Series, Benares, 1913.

Śatapatha Brāhmaṇa (Mādhyandina School): Chowkhamba Sanskrit Sansthān, Benares; (Kāṇvīya recension) (Ed) Calvand and Raghuvīra, Motilal Banarsidass, Delhi, 1942.

Siddhāntabindu of Madhusūdana: (Ed and Tr) Prahlada Chandrashekara Diwanji, Gaekwad Oriental Series, Oriental Institute, Baroda, 1933.

Siddhāntamuktāvalī: (Tr) J. R. Ballantyne, Calcutta, 1851; Nirṇaya Sagar Press, Bombay, 1916.

Śikṣāsamuccaya by Śāntideva: (Tr) Cecil Bendall and William Henry Denham Rose, John Murray, London, 1928.

Siddhāntaleśasaṅgraha: (Tr) S. S. Sūryanārayana Śāstrī, Madras University, Madras, 1942; (Ed) V. S. Iyer, Advaitamayam Sanskrit Series, Kumbhakoṇam, 1894.

Siddhānta-Bindu of Madhusūdana: (Ed and Tr) P. C. Dalvayi, Gaekwad, Oriental Series, Oriental Institute, Baroda, 1933.

Siddhitraya of Yāmunācārya: (Ed and Tr) Ramanujachari and K. Srinivasacharya, Annamalai University, Annamalai, 1943.

Ślokavārttika of Kumārila: (Tr) Ganganath Jha, Asiatic Society, Calcutta, 1906.

Sphuṭārtha abhidharmakośa–vyākhyā of Yaśomitra: (Ed) N. N. Law, Calcutta, Oriental Series, Calcutta, 1949.

Śrībhāṣya of Rāmānuja (Commentary on *Brahmasūtras*); Sāṅkhya Vedānta Tīrtha, Calcutta, 1922.

Śrīmadbhāgavatapurāṇam: (Tr) J. M. Sanyal, 2 vols, Munshi Ram Manoharlal, Delhi, 1973.

Śukranīti: Benoy Kumar Sarkar, Sacred Books of the Hindus, XIII, 1914.

Suśruta saṃhitā: (Ed) Lala Shyamalal Agrawala, Bombay Bhushan Press, Mathura, 1912; (Ed) Jyotirmitra, Jayakrishnadas Āyurveda Granthamālā, Chowkhamba Orientalia, Benares.

Suttanipāta: (Tr) Dharmaratna Bhikṣu, Bhikṣu Sangharatna Mahābodhi Sabha, Saranath, 1951; (Ed & Tr) E. M. Hare, Sacred Books of the Buddhists, 1948.

Sūryasiddhānta: (Ed) Phanindra Lal Gangooly; (Tr) Ebenezer Burgess, Motilal Banarsidass, Delhi, 1952.

Svārthānumānapariccheda of Dharmakīrti: (Ed) Dalsukh Malvaniya, Benares Hindu University, Varanasi, 1959.

Syādvādamañjarī of Hemacandra: (Ed) D. Goswami, Chowkhamba Sanskrit Series, Benares, 1900;

Syādvādamañjarī of Malliṣeṇa: (Ed) Dhruva, Bombay Sanskrit and Prākṛt Series, Bombay, 1933.

Taittirīyaṣaṃhitā: (Ed) Roer and Cowell with the commentary of Sāyaṇācārya, (Tr) A. B. Keith, Calcutta, 1914; (Ed) A. Mahadeva Shastri and K. Rangacharya, Motilal Banarsidass, Delhi, 1956.

Taittirīya Upaniṣad: (Ed) Vāmana Shastri, with the commentary of Śaṅkarācarya and of Anandagiri, Anandashrama Sanskrit Series, Poona, 1889.

Tarkabhāṣā of Keśava Miśra: (Ed) D. R. Bhandarkar and Sahityabhuṣaṇa Kedarnatha, Bombay Sanskrit and Prakṛt Series, 84, Bhandarkar Prācya Vidyā Saṃśodhana Mandira, Poona, 1937; (Tr) Ganganath Jha, Poona Oriental Book Agency, Poona, 1924.

Tārkikarakṣā of Varadarāja: (Ed) Pandit Vindhyeshwari Prasada Dvivedi, Varanasi, 1903.

Tarkasaṅgraha of Annaṃbhaṭṭa: (Ed) Y. V. Athalye, 2nd Edn. Poona, 1963.

Tattvārthādhigama Sūtra of Umāsvāti: (Ed) Jagamandiralal Jaini, Central Jain Publishing House, Arrah, 1920.

Tattvārthasūtra of Umāsvāti: (Ed) A. S. Sastri, Oriental Library Publications, Mysore, 1944.

Tattvārthādhigamasūtrabhāṣya of Umāsvāti: (Ed) Kesavalal, Calcutta University, Calcutta, 1902.

Tatvārtha-sūtra of Umāsvāti with commentary of Akalanka: (Ed) Gajadharlal Jaina, Sanātana Jaina Granthamala, Benares, 1915.

Tattvacintāmaṇi of Gangeśa Upādhyāya: (Tr) S. C. Vidyabhushana, Motilal Banarsidass, Delhi, 1958.

Tattvakaumudī, a commentary of Vācaspati Miśra on *Sāṅkhyakārikā:* (Ed and Tr) Ganganatha Jha, Oriental Book Agency, Poona, 1957.

Tattvasaṃgraha of Śāntarakṣita and Kamalaśīla's commentary: (Tr) Ganganatha Jha, Motilal Banarsidass, Delhi, 1986.

Upaniṣadbhāṣya, Works of Śaṅkarācarya: (Ed) H. R. Bhagavat, Vol. II, Ashtekar & Co., Poona, 1927-28.

The Upaniṣads and Sri Śaṅkaras Commentary: (Tr) Sri Sitarama Sastry and Ganganatha Jha, Publisher V. E. Seshahari, Madras, 1898-01.

Uttarādhyayanasūtra (Manuscript Illustrations): (Ed) Norman Brown, American Oriental Series, Vol XXI, New Haven, 1941.

Vācaspatibhāmatī: (Tr) S. S. Sūryanārayaṇa Sastri and C. Kunhan Raja, The Adyar Library, Madras, 1933.

Vaiśeṣika Lexicon of Technical Terms of Nyāya Philosophy: Bhimacharya Jhalkikar, American Oriental Society library, Yale University, Yale.

The Vaiśeṣika Aphorisms of Kaṇāda with *Upaskāra* and *Vivṛti* commentaries, (Tr) A. E. Gough, Munshiram Manoharlal Publishers, Delhi, 1975.

Aphorisms of Vaiśeṣika and Illustrative extracts from Śaṅkara Miśra's Commentary: (Ed) J. R. Ballantyne, Mirzapore, 1861.

Vaiśeṣika Sūtras of Kaṇāda: (Ed and Tr) B. Faddegon; (Ed) Dhundirāja Śāstri with the commentaries of *Praśastapādabhāṣya* and *upaskāra* of Śaṅkara Hiśra, Kāśī Sanskrit series, No 3, Benaras, 1923.

Vaiśeṣika Sūtras of Kaṇāda with Chandra Kānta's bhāṣya: (Ed) Muni Sri Jambuvijayi, Gaekwad Oriental Series, Baroda, 1961.

Vaiṣṇava Upaniṣads: (Tr) T. R. Srinivasa Iyengar, The Adyar Library, Madras, 1941.

Vaṭeśvara Siddhānta: (Ed) K. S. Shukla, Indian National Science Academy, New Delhi, 1981.

Vaiśeṣika Aphorisms with the Commentary of Praśastapāda and gloss of Udayana: (Ed) Vindhyeshwari Prasad Dube, Benares Sanskrit Series, Benares, 1885.

Vedanayaprakaraṇam Sambandhaparīkṣā ca of Dharmakīrti: Swami Dwarakadas Shastri, Dharamkīrti Nibandhāvalī, Bauddha Bhāratī Series, Varanasi, 1972.

Vedāṅga Jyotiṣa: (Ed) R. Shamashastri, Oriental Research Institute, Mysore, 1936.

Vedānta Paribhāṣā and *Vedanta kaustubha*, Commentaries on Brahma *Sūtras*: (Tr) Roma Bose, Royal Asiatic Society of Bengal, 3 vols, Calcutta, 1940-41.

Vedāntaparibhāṣā of Dharmaraja Adhvarin: (Ed and Tr) S. S. Suryanarayana Sastri, Adyar Library, Madras, 1942.

Vedāntasāra of Sadananda: (Tr) Swami Nikhilananda, Advaita Ashrama, Mayavati, 1941.

Vedāntatattvasāra of Rāmānuja, (Tr) J. Johnson, Lauzarus & co., Benares, 1898.

Vedāvalī by Jayatīrtha: (Ed and Tr) P. Nagaraja Rao, Adyar Library, Madras, 1943.

Vijñapti-mātratāsiddhi of Vasubandhu: (Tr) K. N. Chatterjee, Kishore Vidhya Niketan, Varanasi, 1980; (Ed) T. C. Sastri and R. S. Tripathi, Varanasi, 1972; (Ed) N. A. Sastri, Namgyal Institute of Tibetology, Gangtok, Sikkim, 1964.

Vijñaptimātratā-siddhi (Vimśika): (Ed) N. A Sastri, Namgyal Institute of Tibetology, Gangtok, Sikkim, 1964.

Viṣṇu Purāṇam: Gita Press, Gorakhpur, 1955.

Viṣṇutattvanirṇaya of Madhvācārya: (Tr) S. S. Raghavachar, Ramakrishna Ashrama, Mangalore, 1959.

Viśuddhimagga, The Path of Purity: (Ed) Rhys F. W. Davids, (Tr) Pe Maung Tin, Oxford University Press, London, 1898.

Vivaraṇa prameyasaṅgraha: (Tr) S. S. Suryanarayana Sastri and Saileshwara Sen, Sri Vidya Press, Madras, 1936.

Vivaraṇam of Prakāśātman: (Ed) S. Srirama Sastri and S. R. Krishna Murthy Sastri, Government Oriental Series, Madras, 1958.

Vigrahavyāvartinī of Nagarjuna: (Ed) P. L. Vaidya, Buddhists Sanskrit Text No. 10, Mithila Insitute, Darbhanga, 1960.

Vyomavatī of Vyomaśivācārya: (Ed) Gopinath Kaviraj and Dhundiraja Sastri, Chowkhamba Sanskrit Series, Benares, 1930.

Yajñavalkyasmṛti with the commentary of Vijñāneśvara: (Tr) Sirish Chandra Basu, Sacred Books of the Hindus, 1909.

Yatīndramatadīpikā by Srinivasa: (Ed) A. Govindasvāmin, Madras, 1942.

Yogadarśana with Vyasa's Commentary: (Ed) Ganganath Jha, Bombay, 1907.

Yogasaṅgraha of Vijñānabhikṣu: (Tr) Ganganath Jha, Theosophical Publishing House, Adyar, Madras, 1933.

Yoga sūtras with *Vyāsa Bhāṣya* the *Tattvavaiśāradī* of Vācaspati Miśra and Vṛtti of Bhoja: (Tr) J. H. Woods, Motilal Banarasidass, Delhi, 1914; (reprint) 1972.

Yogasūtra of Patañjali with Vyasaś Commentary: (Ed) Hariharananda, Calcutta University, Calcutta, 1938.

Yoga-Vasiṣṭha of Vālmīki: Text published by Munshiram Manoharlal, 3rd edn. Delhi, 1981.

Yogimunivar, *Vaidyacintāmaṇi*, Part I. Palani Devasthanam Trust Series, Madras, 1973.

SECONDARY SOURCES

Aaron, R. I.: *The Theory of Universals,* Clarendon Press, Oxford, 1952.

Abhedananda, Swami: *Vedanta Philosophy* (4th edn.) Vedanta Society, New York, 1899.

Acharya, Ananda: *Brahmadarśanam, An Introduction to the Study of Indian Philosophy*, Mac Millan Co., New York, 1917.

Agarwala V. S.: *Nāsadiyasūkta: Vedic Lectures*, Prithvi Prakashan, Varanasi, 1981, pp. 135,153.

Agarwala V. S.: *Matsya Purāna, A Study,* Benares Hindu University, Varanasi, 1963.

Agarwala V. S.: *India as known to Pāṇini*, University of Lucknow, Lucknow, 1953.

Aiyangar, T. R. Srinivasa: (Tr.) *Śaiva Upaniṣads*, The Adyar Library, Madras, 1953; (Tr) *Yoga Upaniṣads*, The Adyar Library, Madras, 1952.

Aiyar, Paramanneri Sivaswamy: *Evolution of Hindu Moral Ideals*, Calcutta University Press, Calcutta, 1935.

Aiyar, Krishnaswami: *Sri Madhava and Madhvism*, G. A. Natesan & Co., Madras, 1956.

Akhilananda, Swami: *Mental Health and Hindu Psychology*, Harper & Bros, New York, 1951.

Alexander, S.: *Time and Deity*, Vols. I & II MacMillan & Co., London, 1920.

Armstrong, D. M.: *Nominalism and Realism,* Cambridge University Press, Cambridge, 1978.

Armstrong, D. M.: *Theory of Universals*, Cambridge University Press, Cambridge, 1978.

Anand, Mulk Raj: *The Hindu View of Arts,* George Allen and Unwin, London, 1946.

Aristotle: *'De anima'* (Tr.) J. A. Smith; *'Metaphysics'* (Tr.) W. D. Ross, in *The Basic Works of Aristotle*, Random House, New York, 1941.

Atreya B. L.: *The Philosophy of Yogavāsiṣṭha*, Theosophical Publishing House, Adyar, 1936.

Atreya B. L.: *The Elements of Logic* (Tr) of *Tarkasaṃgraha*, University of Calcutta, Calcutta, 1934.

Atreya, Jagat Prakash: 'A Comparative and Critical Review of Mind' in *Mind and Its Function in Indian Thought,* Classical Publishing Company, New Delhi, pp. 258-271, 1982.

Aurobindo, Sri: *On the Vedas,* Aurobindo Ashram, Pondicherry, 1964.

Ayyar, R. S. Vaidyanatha: *Manu's Land and Trade Laws,* Higginbothams, Madras, 1927.

Bagchi, Sitamshu Shekhar: *Inductive Reasoning,* Calcutta Oriental Press, Calcutta, 1953.

Balslev, Anindita Niyogi: *A Study of Time in Indian Philosophy,* Otto Harrasowitz Wiesbaden, 1983.

Bandyopadhyaya, Nandita: 'The Buddhist Theory of Relation Between Pramā and Pramāṇa', *Asiatic Society Journal of Indian Philosophy,* Vol. II, pp. 43-78, 1979.

Bapat, V.: *2500 Years of Buddhism,* Publication Division, Ministry of Information and Broadcasting, Delhi, 1956.

Barrow, J. D. and Tripler, F. J.: *The Anthropic Cosmological Principle,* Clarendon Press, Oxford, 1986.

Barnett, L. David: *The Heart of India, Sketches in the History of Hindu Religion and Morals,* Wisdom of the East Series, 1908, 1913 and 1924.

Baily, Cyril: *The Greek Atomists and Epicurus,* Clarendon Press, Oxford, 1936.

Ballantyne, J. R.: (Ed) *A Lecture on the Sankhya Philosophy embracing the text Tattvasamāsa of Kapila,* Orphan School Press, Mirzapore, 1850; (Ed and Tr) *The Sāṃkhya aphorisms of Kapila* (3rd Edn) Trübner & Co., London, 1885.

Banerjee, Anukula Chandra: *Sarvāstivāda Literature,* Oriental Press, Calcutta, 1957.

Banerjee, R. Viharee: *Concerning Human Understanding,* George Allen and Unwin, London, 1958.

Banerji, Satish Chandra: *Sāṃkhya Philosophy with Gauḍapāda's Scholia and Nārāyaṇa's Gloss,* Harex & Co., Calcutta, 1898

Bareau, Andre: 'The notion of time in early Buddhism', *East and West,* 7(4) 1956, pp. 353, 364.

Barth, A: *The Religions of India*: Kegan Paul, Trench, Trübner & Co, London, 1891.

Barodia, U.D.: *History and Literature of Jainism,* Jain Graduates Association, Bombay, 1909.

Barua, Benimadhava: *Early Buddhism,* Cultural Heritage of India, Belurmath, Calcutta, 1937; *A History of pre-Buddhist Indian Philosophy,* University of Calcutta, Calcutta, 1921; *Prolegomena to a History of Buddhist Philosophy,* University of Calcutta, Calcutta, 1918.

Basak, Radha Govinda: 'The Hindu Concept of Natural world', *The Religion of the Hindus,* Ed. Kenneth William Morgan, New York, 1953.

Basham, A.L.: *The Wonder that was India,* University Press, Calcutta, 1918; *History and Doctrines of the Ājīvikas, A Vanished Tradition,* Luzac & Co, London, 1951.

Bhattacharya, Harimohan: 'The Jaina Theory of Prathyabhijñā', 'The Philosophical Quarterly,* Vol. XIV, Calcutta, 1939.

Banik, Berhard: *The Anatomy of Modern Science,* George Bell & Sons, London, 1932.

Beal, Sammuel: (Ed & Tr) *Texts of Buddhist Canons Commonly Known as Dhammapada,* Trübner & Co., London, 1878; *A Catalogue of Buddhist Scriptures from the Chinese Sources,* Trübner & Co., London, 1921.

Beck, L.W.: *Philosophic Inquiry,* Prentice Hall, New York, 1952.

Bernard, Theos: *Hindu Philosophy,* Philosophical Library, New York, 1947; *Philosophic Foundations of India,* John F. Rider, New York, 1945.

Besant, Annie: *An Introduction to Yoga,* Theosophical Society Press, Madras, 1912.

Besant, Annie and Bhagavan Das: *The Bhagavad Gītā,* The Adyar Library, Madras, 1940.

Bhaduri, Sadananda: *Studies in Nyāya–Vaiśeṣika Metaphysics*, Bhandarkar Oriental Series, Poona, 1948.

Bhandarkar, R. G.: *Vaiṣṇavism, Śaivism and Minor Religious Systems*, K. P. Trübner, Straussberg, 1913.

Bhatia M.C.: *Causation in Indian Philosophy*, Vimal Prakashan, Ghaziabad, 1973.

Bhatt S.R.: 'On the Validity of Inferential Knowledge in Indian Philosophy', *Indian Philosophic Quarterly*, Vol. X, No. 3, 1983.

Bhattacharya Aushutosh Shastri: *Studies in Pre-Shankara Dialectics*, University of Calcutta, Calcutta, 1936.

Bhattacharya N. N.: 'Buddhist and Jaina Cosmologies', *History of Cosmological Ideas*, Munshiram Manoharlal, New Delhi, 1971, pp. 74-83.

Bhattacharya, Harisatya: *Divinity in Jainism*, Devendra & Co., Madras, 1925.

Bhattacharya, H. C.: *Kālasiddhāntadarśinī*, Calcutta, 1941.

Bhattacharya, Kapileshwar: *An Introduction to Advaita Philosophy*, University of Calcutta, Calcutta, 1909.

Bhattacharya, Kalidas: *Alternative Stand-points in Philosophy*, Vol. I, Dasgupta & Co., Calcutta, 1953.

Bhattacharya, Krishna Chandra: *Studies in Philosophy*, Progressive Publishers, Calcutta, 1956.

Bhattacharya, Sankara: 'The five provisional definitions of Vyāpti by Gangeśa', *Indian Philosophical Quarterly*, Vol. III, 1946.

Bhattacharya, Vidhushekhara: *The Basic conception of Buddhism*, University of Calcutta, Calcutta, 1935.

Bhattacharya S: 'The Nyāya-Vaiśeṣika Doctrine of Qualities', *Philosophy, East and West*, 11 **(3)**, 1961, pp. 143-152.

Bloomfield, Maurice: *The Religion of the Veda*, G. B. Putnam Sons, New York, 1908; *The Hymns of the Atharvaveda and Gopatha Brāhmaṇa*, Straussberg, 1888; *Vedic Concordance*, Oxford University Press, Oxford; (Reprint) Delhi, 1964.

Bodas, Mahadev Rajasan: 'An Historical Survey of Indian Logic', *Journal of Asiatic Society*, Bombay, 1924, pp. 306-347.

Botra, Puspa: 'The Jaina Theory of Pramāṇa', in *The Jaina Theory of Perception*, Motilal Banarasidass, Delhi, pp. 21-30.

Bouquet, A.C.: *Hinduism*, Hutchinsons University Library, London, 1948.

Brahma, Nalini Kant: *Philosophy of Hindu Sādhanā*, Kegan Paul, Trübner & Co., London, 1932.

Brahmasūtrabhāṣya of Śaṅkara: Ānandāśrama Sanskrit Series, Poona, 1900.

Brown, Norman: 'Theories of Creation in the Ṛgveda', *Journal of American Oriental Society*, **85**(1), 1915, pp 23-34.

Brunton, Paul: *Indian Philosophy and Modern Culture*, Doulton & Co., New York, 1939.

The Cambridge History of India, Cambridge University Press, Cambridge, 1922.

Bühler, Johann George: *On the Indian Sect of Jainas*, (Tr) Jas Burgess, Luzac & Co., London, 1903.

Burnet, John: *Early Greek Philosophy*, A & C Black, London, 1920.

Carpenter, J. E.: *Theism in Medieval India*, Withams and Norgate, London, 1921.

Carre, M.H: *Realists and Nominalists*, Oxford University Press, London, 1962.

Carus, Paul: *The Gospel of Buddha*, Religions of Science Library, London, 1921.

Chakravarti G. N.: 'Concept of the Structure of the Space–Time', *Indian Journal of History of Science*, 1970, pp. 227-327.

Chakravarti, Pulimabihari: 'Sankhya—What does it mean?' in *Origin and Development of the Sankhya System of Thought*, Oriental Books Reprint Corporation, New Delhi, pp. 1-41, 1989.

Chakravarti, Suresh Chandra: *The Philosophy of The Upaniṣads*, Calcutta University Press, Calcutta, 1935.

Chalmers, Lord: *Buddha's Teachings Being the Suttanipāta Discourse Collection*, Harvard Oriental Series, Vol. XXXVII, Harvard University Press, Cambridge, 1932; *Further Dialogues of the Buddha,* Sacred Books of the Buddhists, Vols. V. and VI, Oxford University Press, London, 1926.

Chaudhuri, Anil Kumar: *The Doctrine of Māyā*, Dasgupta & Co., Calcutta, 1950; *A Realistic Interpretation of Śaṅkara Vedānta*, University of Calcutta, Calcutta, 1952; *Self and Falsity in Advaita Vedanta*, Progressive Publications, Calcutta, 1955; *The Doctrine of Nyāya*, Dasgupta and Co., Calcutta, 1950.

Chari C. T K: 'Quantum Physics and East-West Rapproachment, *Philosophy East and West*, 5, 1955, pp. 63-67.

Chatrapati Singh: 'The Concept of time', *Journal of the Indian Council of Philosophical Research*, Vol. IX, 1, 1996, pp.13-31.

Chatterjee A.K: *Introduction to Yogācāra School,* Mahabodhi, Vol. 64, 1956.

Chatterji S. C.: 'The Nyāya doctrine of Pramāṇa', *Journal of Department of Letters,* Vol. XVI, 1927, pp 1-61; 'The Theory of Prakṣatā in Indian Logic', *The Philosophical Quarterly*, Vol. XIV, 1938; *Nyāya Theory of Knowledge*, University of Calcutta, Calcutta, 1935; *Fundamentals of Hinduism, A Philosophical Study*; Dasgupta and Co., Calcutta, 1950; *The Hindu Realism*, The Indian Press, Allahabad: 1912; 'Science of Motion in India, A Historical Retrospect' *Indo-Asian Cultures*, 1970, pp. 41-45; *The Nyāya Theory of Knowledge,* 2nd edn, University of Calcutta, 1950.

Chattinatham, John B.: *Consciousness and Reality, An Indian Approach to Metaphysics:* Orbis Books, New York, 1971.

Chattopadhyaya Deviprasad (Ed): *Studies in the History of Indian Philosophy*, Bagchi & Co., Calcutta, 1978; *Lokāyata, A Study in Ancient Indian Naturalism*, New Delhi, Peoples Publishing House, Delhi, 1972.

Chattopadhyaya, Deviprasad and Gangopadhyaya, Vimalakanti: *Nyaya Philosophy* (Parts I & IV), Indian Studies: Past and Present, Calcutta, 1967-76.

Chaturvedi, Gajaviharilal: 'The Scope of Verbal Testimony', *Indian Philosophical Quarterly*, **20**, no. 4, Delhi, pp. 1-6.

Colebrooke, H. T.: *Miscellaneous Essays*, 2nd edn., Trübner & Co, London, 1878.

Conze, E.: *Buddhism, Its Essence and Development,* Philosophical Library, New York, 1954.

Coomarswamy, Ananda Kentish: *Buddha and the Gospel of Buddhism*, Harper, London, 1938; *Time and Eternity*, Ascona, 1947.

Cowell E B: *'Cārvāka System'*, JASB, XXXI, 1862.

Dahlquist, Allan: *Megasthenes and Indian Religion, A Study in Motives and Types*, Almquist and Wiskell, Uppasala, 1962.

Dhalka, Paul: *Buddhism and Its Place in the Mental Life of Mankind*, MacMillan & Co., London, 1927.

Dampier, William C. D.: *A History of Science and its Relation with Philosophy and Religion,* Macmillan & Co., New York, 1931.

Das, Saroj Kumar: *Towards a Systematic Study of Vedānta*, Calcutta University, Calcutta, 1935.

Dasgupta, S. N.: *Philosophical Essays,* University of Calcutta, Calcutta; *Hindu Mysticism: (Six lectures)*, The Open Court Publishing House, Chicago, 1922; *Indian Philosophy,* Vols. I–V, Cambridge University Press, Cambridge, 1922-25; reprint, Motilal Banarasidass, Delhi, 1992; *Indian Idealism,* Cambridge University, Cambridge, 1933; *Yoga Philosophy;* Motilal Banarasidass, 1930; reprint Delhi, 1974.

Dasgupta, S N and S. K. De: *A History of Sanskrit Literature,* Calcutta University, Calcutta, 1947.

Date, Vinayaka Hari: *Vedanta Explained, Śaṅkara's Commentary on Sūtras:* Book Sellers Publishing House, Bombay, 1954.

Datta, Dhirendra Mohana: *Six Ways of Knowing,* George Allen and Unwin, London, 1932.

Datta, Nrpendra Kumar: *Vedanta, Its Place as a System of Metaphysics,* University of Calcutta, Calcutta, 1931.

Datta, Manmathanatha: *Aspects Of Mahāyāna Buddhism and Its Relation to Hīnayāna,* Luzac & Co., London, 1913.

Davids, CAF Rhys: *Buddhist Psychology,* George Bell & Sons, London, 1914; *Buddhism, A Study of Buddhist Norms,* Sheldon Press, London, 1932; *Outlines Of Buddhism, A Historical Sketch,* MacMillan, London, 1934; *Buddhist Sutras:* Sacred Books of the East, Vol. XI, part I–VII; *Buddhist India* G. P. Putnam's Sons, New York, 1903.

Davies, Paul: *About Time,* Touchstone, New York, 1995.

Day, B. B.: 'Physical Concepts—doctrine of motion, heat, light, acoustics and magnetism', in *Scientific thought in Ancient India', History of Philosophy Eastern and Western,* London 1952, pp. 460-463.

Deussen, Paul: (Tr) Charles Johnston, *The System of the Vedanta,* Chicago, 1912; (Tr) A. S. Geden: *The Philosophy of the Upaniṣads*, T & T Cark Edinburgh, 1919.

Deussen Paul, J. H. Woods and C. R. Renkel: *Outlines of Vedanta System of Philosophy According to Śaṅkara,* Massachussets, 1927; *The System of the Vedanta*: (Tr) Charles Johnston, Open Court Publishing Co., New York, 1912.

Dravid N. S: 'Anomalies of the Nyāya Vaiśeṣika Concept of the Self', *Indian Philosophical Quarterly,* Vol. XXII, No. 1, 1995, pp 1-11.

Dravid, P. R.: *The Problems of Universal in Indian Philosophy:* Motilal Banarasidass, Delhi, 1972.

Drue: *An Experiment with Time,* Faber & Faber, London, 1934.

Durant, Drake: *Mind And Its Place in Nature,* Macmillan, New York, 1925.

Drummit, Cornelia and Van Beutanin: *Classical Hindu Mythologies,* Temple University, Philadelphia, 1979.

Dutt, Ramesh Chandra: *History of Civilisation of Ancient India,* Trübner & Co, London, 1893.

Dwarakanath, C.: An appraisal of the Doctrine of Pañcabhūtas and tanmātras', *Nagarjuna,* (**78**), pp 13-18.

Eliade, M.: *Images and Symbols: Studies in Religious Symbolism,* (Tr) Philip Maret, Sheed and Ward, New York, 1961.

Eliot, Charles: *Hinduism and Buddhism,* 3 Vols. Edwin Arnold & Co., London, 1921.

Edgerton, F.: 'Dominant Ideas in the Formation of Indian Culture', *Journal of the American Oriental Society,* Vol. 62, 1942, pp. 153 ff.

Faddegon, B.: *The Vaiśeṣika System Described with the Help Of The Oldest Texts,* Johannes Muller, Amsterdam, 1918.

Falk, Marly: *Nāmarūpa and Dharmarūpa,* Calcutta, 1943.

Farrington, Benjamin: *Greek Science,* 2 Vols., Penguin Books, Hamondsworth, 1949.

Farquahar, J. N.: *An Outline of the Religious Literature of India,* Oxford University Press, London, 1920.

Frank, Philipp: *Modern Science and Its Philosophy,* Harvard University Series, Cambridge, 1949.

Frankfort, H. et. al.: *Before Philosophy: The Intellectual Adventure of Ancient Man, An Essay on Speculative Thought in the Ancient Near East,* Pelican, Middlesex, 1951.

Frazer R.W.: *Indian Thought, Past and Present,* Unwin, London, 1915.

Fuller, B. A. G.: *A History of Philosophy,* Henry Hort and Co., 3rd edn., New York, 1955.

Fung Yu Lan: *A History of Chinese Philosophy,* Princeton University Press, USA, 1952.

Garbe, R.: *The Philosophy of Ancient India,* Open Court, Chicago, 1899

Gajendragadgkar, Veena: 'Atomism, Kaṇāda's Doctrine of the Padārthas', Sri Satguru Publications, Delhi, pp. 280-359.

Garbe, Richard: (Tr) R. D. Vardikar, *The Sāṃkhya Philosophy,* Poona, 1895; *The Philosophy of Ancient India,* Open Court, Chicago, 1897.

Garratt, Geoffeey Theodar: *The Legacy of India:* Clarendon Press, Oxford, 1926.

Geunon, Rene: *Introduction to the Study of Hindu Doctrines,* Luzac & Co., London, 1945; *Orient and Occident,* (Tr) William Nassey, Luzac & Co., London, 1941.

Ghate, V. S.: *The Vedanta, A Study of the Brahmasūtras with commentaries*; Bhandarkar Oriental Research Institute, Poona, 1926.

Ghosh, Jnāneshwar: *Sāṃkhya and Modern Thought,* The Book and Co., Calcutta, 1930.

Ghosh, Raghunath: 'Can there be Ontological Argument in Nyāya-Vaiśeṣika?' *Indian Philosophical Quarterly,* Vol. XXI, no. 2, 1994, pp. 119-127.

Gokhale, Pradeep P.: 'The logical structure of Syādvāda', *Journal of Indian Council of Philosophical Research,* 1991, pp. 73-81.

Gopalan, S. 'Jaina epistemology—an overview', *Outlines of Jainism,* John Wiley & Sons, New York, pp. 47-59.

Gough, Archibald Edward: *The Philosophy of the Upaniṣad and Ancient Indian Metaphysics,* Trübner & Co., London, 1882.

Govinda, Lama: 'The Conception of Space in Ancient Buddhist Art and Thought', *Mahabodhi,* **64**, 1956, pp. 181-88.

Govinda Lama, A.: 'The Mystery of Time, *Mahabodhi,* **65**, 1957, pp. 204-210.

Grumbaum: *Vaiśeṣika Sūtras with Upaskāra,* Oriental Books Reprint Corporation, New Delhi, 1975.

Griswald, Harvey D. Writt: *The Religion of The Ṛgveda,* Oxford University Press, London, 1923; *Brahman—a Study in the History of Indian Philosophy,* Cornell University Studies in Philosophy, Vol. I, New York, 1900.

Grims, George: *The Doctrine of the Buddha,* Leipzig, 1926.

Gupta, 'The Buddhist Doctrine of Momentariness, and its presuppositions, *Journal of Indian Philosophy,* 1980.

Gupta, Uma: 'Vedic naturalism', *Materialism in the Vedas,* Classical Publishing Company, New Delhi, pp. 148-179.

Guthrie, W. K. C.: *A History of Greek Philosophy,* Cambridge University Press, 1962.

Hari Shankar Prasad (Ed): *Time in Indian Philosophy,* Sri Satguru Publications, Delhi, 1992.

Hastings (Ed): *Encyclopedia of Religion and Ethics*, T. & T. Clark, Edinburgh, 1908.

Hattori, M. H.: *Diṅnāga on Perception*, Harvard Oriental Series, Vol. 47, Harvard, 1968.

Hawking S.: *A Brief History of Time*, Bantom Books, New York, 1988.

Harrison, Max Hunter: *Indian Monism and Platonism*, Oxford University Press, London, 1932.

Hazra, R. L.: *Studies in the Purāṇic Records on Hindu Rites and Customs*, Motilal Banarasidass, Delhi, 1975.

Heiman, B.: *Indian and Western Philosophy: A Study of Contrasts*, George Allen and Unwin Ltd., London, 1937.

Hillebrandt, Alfred: *Vedic Mythology,* (Tr) Sreeramulu, R; Motilal Banarasidass, Delhi, 1982.

Herberger, H. G.: 'Double Negation in Buddhist Logic', *Journal of Indian Philosophy*, 1975

Hiriyanna, M.: *Outlines of Indian Philosophy*, George Allen and Unwin Ltd., London, 1932; *Essentials of Indian Philosophy*, MacMillan & Co., New York, 1949; *Indian Philosophic Studies*, Kāvyālaya Publications, Mysore, 1957; *Popular Essays in Indian Philosophies*; Kāvyālaya Publishers, Mysore, 1952; *Vedāntasāra, A Work on Vedānta Philosophy*, Oriental Book Agency, Poona, 1929; *The Quest After Perfection*, Kāvyālaya Publishers, Mysore, 1952.

Hopkins, E. W.: *Ethics of India,* Yale University, New Haven, 1924.

Hobhouse, L.T.: *Theory of Knowledge,* Mac Millan & Co., London, 1896.

Hospers, J: *Śaṅkara Vedanta*, Allahabad, Law Journal Press, Allahabad, 1939.

Hughes, E.R.: *Chinese Philosophy*, E.P. Dutton and Co., New York, 1942.

Hume David: *A Treatise on Human Nature*, Clarendon Press, Oxford, 1896; *Dialogues Concerning Natural Religion*, Longmans Green & Co., Vol. II, London, 1890.

Humphreys, Christmus: *Buddhism*, Penguin Books, Hamondsworth, 1949.

Ingalls, D.H.H.: 'Comparison of Indian and Western Philosophy', *Journal of Oriental Research Institute*, Madras, XXII, 1954.

Jain G. F.: 'Space, Time and the Universe', *Perspectives in Jaina Philosophy and Culture*, Alimas International, Delhi, pp. 7-17.

Jain, Hiralal and A. N. Upadhye: *Jainendra Siddhanta Kośa* of Jainendramuni, Bharatiya Jnanapitha Prakashan, Varanasi, 1970.

Jayatilake, K. N.: *Early Buddhist Theory of Knowledge*, George Allen and Unwin, London, 1963.

Javeri, I. M.: 'The Concept of Ākāśa in Indian Philosophy', *Annals of Bhandarkar Oriental Research Institute*, 37, 1956, pp. 300-307.

Jha, Ganganath: *Pūrvamīmāṃsā: Its Sources*, Benares Hindu University, Benares, 1942; *Prābhākara School Of Pūrvamīmāṃsā*, Benares Hindu University Benares, 1918; *The Study of Patañjali*, University of Calcutta, Calcutta, 1920; *Nyāya Philosophy of Gautama*, Allahabad University, Allahabad; (Tr) *Nyāyasūtras of Gautama*, Motilal Banarasidass, Delhi, 1979.

Jhaveri, R. L.: *The First Principles Of Jaina Philosophy*, London, 1910.

Joanna Macy: Mutual Consality in Buddhism and General Systems Theory, State University of New York Press, 1992.

Johnston, Charles: *The Great Upaniṣads*, Vol. I, New York, 1927.

Johnson, W. E: *Logic, Parts I- III,* Dover Publication, New York, 1921-24.

Jwala Prasad: *Indian Epistemology*, Motilal Banarasidass, 2nd edn. New Delhi, 1958.

Kalupahana, D.: *Buddhist Philosophy, A Historical Analysis*, University of Hawaii, Honolulu, 1966.

Kamat, M.A.: *Hindusim and Modern Science*, Sharada Press, Mangalore, 1947.

Kane, P. V.: *History of Dharmaśāstra*, Vols. I - IV., Bhandarakar Oriental Research Institute, Poona, 1930-53; *A Brief Sketch of Pūrvamīmāmsā*, Bhandarkar Oriental Research Institute, Poona, 1924.

Kapali Shastri, T.V.: *Lights on the Veda*, Sri Aurobindo Library, Pondicherry, 1947; *Lights on the Upaniṣads*, Sri Aurobindo Library, Pondicherry, 1945.

Karmadasa, Y.: 'The Buddhist Theory of Matter', *Mahābodhi*, 77, 1969, pp. 11-17, 36-43.

Kant, I: *Critique of Pure Reason* (Tr) N. K. Smith, (7th Edn), MacMillan & Co., London, 1961.

Katzu, N.: (Ed) *Buddhist and Western Philosophy*, Sterling Publishers, New Delhi, 1981.

Keith A. Berridale: *Buddhist Philosophy in India and Ceylon*, Clarendon Press, Oxford, 1923; *The Karmāmīmāmsā*, Oxford University Press, London, 1921; *A History of Sanskrit Literature*, Geoffery Cambridge, Oxford, 1948; *Indian Logic and Atomism*, Clarendon Press, Oxford, 1921; *Religion and Philosophy of the Vedas and Upaniṣads*, Harvard University Press, Cambridge, 1925; *The Sāṃkhya System*: The Heritage Of India Series, Calcutta, 1949; *The Veda of the Black Yajus,* Harvard Oriental Series, Cambridge, 1914.

Keshar, H. K.: *Some Basic Concepts in Science and Mysticism*, New Age International Limited, New Delhi, pp. 61-97.

Kirthikar, Vasadeva Jagannatha: *Studies in the Vedanta*, D. B. Taraporewala Sons and Co., Bombay, 1924.

Kosambi D.D. See original p. 536.

Krishna, Daya: *The Nature of Philosophy*, Praci Prakashan, Calcutta, 1955; (Ed) *Modern Logic, Its relevance to Philosophy,* Impex India, New Delhi, 1969.

Kunhan Raja, C: 'Where Ancient Thought and Modern Science meet', *Brahmavidyā*, **16**, 1952, pp. 59-86.

Kumarappa, Bharathan: *The Hindu Conception of Deity*, Luzac & Co., London, 1924.

Lacey A. R.: (Ed) *A Doctrinaire of Philosophy*, Routledge and Kegan Paul, London, 1976.

Lange, F. A.: *The History of Materialism*, (Tr) E. C. Thomas, Brame & Co., London, 1925.

Law, Bimala Charana: (Ed) *Buddhist Studies*, Thacker Spink & Co., Calcutta, 1931; *A History of Pali Literature*, Motilal Banarsidass, Delhi, 1938.

Liehenthal, W.: 'Reality in India in Our World interpretations', *The Visvabharati Quarterly*, **20**(i) pp 34-35.

Lin Yutang: *The Wisdom of China and India,* Random House, New York, 1942.

Landesman, C.: *The Problem of The Universals*, Basic Books, New York, 1971.

Luccas, J. R.: *Treatise on Time and Space,* Methuen, London, 1973.

Macdonell A A: *India's Past*, Clarendon Press, Oxford, 1927; *Vedic Mythology,* K. P. Trübner, Strassberg, 1897; *A History of Sanskrit Literature*, D. Appleton & Co., New York, 1900; *Indian Theism from Vedic to the Mohammadan Period*, Oxford University Press, Milford, 1915; *Lectures on Comparative Religion*, University of Calcutta, Calcutta, 1925.

McGovern William Montgomary: *A Manual of Buddhist Philosophy*, Vol. I, Tübner & Co., London, 1922; *An Introduction to Mahāyāna, Buddhism* Trübner & Co., London, 1923.

Mahadevan, T.M.P: *The Philosophy of Advaita,* Luzac & Co., London, 1938; *Sankhya Philosophy, Lecture delivered at the Graduate School*, Madras University, Madras, 1951; *Time and Timeless*, Upaniṣadic Vihar, Madras, 1953.

Maitra, Sushil Kumar: *The Ethics of the Hindus*, Calcutta University, Calcuta, 1925; *Studies in Philosophy and Religion*, Calcutta, 1956; *The Sprit of Indian Philosophy,* Benares, 1947;

Madhva Logic, Calcutta University, Calcutta, 1936.; *Gauḍapāda A Study in Early Advaita*, Madras University, Madras, 1952.

Majumdar, Abhayakumar and Jatindra Kumar Maya, *The Sāṃkhya Conception of Personality*, Calcutta, 1930.

Majumdar, R. C.: *Medieval India,* MacMillan & Co, London, 1949.

Majumdar, R. C., Roy Chaudhuri, H.C. and Datta, K.: *An Advanced History of India*, MacMillan & Co., London, 1949.

Malkani, G. R.: *Vedantic Epistemology,* Indian Institute of Philosophy, 1933.

Malkani, G. R., Ray U. Das and T.R.V. Murthy: *Ajñāna*, Luzac & Co., London, 1933.

Masson, O Paul, Hellena and Philip Stem: *Ancient India and Indian Civilization,* Trübner & Co., London, 1934.

Mandal, K. K.: *A Comparative Study of the Concepts of Space and Time in Indian Thought*, Chowkhamba Sanskrit Series, Varanasi, 1968.

Matilal, B. K.: 'Ontological aspects and Jainism', *Journal of Indian Philosophy*, Vol. V, **1**, 1977; 'Gangeśa on the concept of universal property', *Journal of Royal Asiatic Society*, 1968; *Epistemology, Logic and Grammar in Philosophical Analysis*, Mountan, The Hague and Paris, 1971.

Maynell, H: *The Intelligible Universe, A Cosmological Argument*, MacMillan & Co., London, 1972.

Mayer, Frederich: *A History of Ancient and Medieval Philosophy*, American Book Co., New York, 1950; *History Of Indian Culture*, Routledge and Kegan Paul, London, 1952.

Mehta, Mohanlal: *Jaina Psychology*, Sohanlal Jaindharma Pracharak Samiti, Amritsar, 1955; *Outlines of Jaina Philosophy,* Jaina Mission Society, Bangalore, 1954.

Mehta, Rohit: *The Indian Philosophy*, The Theosophical Publishing House, Adyar Library, Madras, 1950.

Mehta, D. D.: *Positive Sciences in the Vedas*, Arnold Heinemann Publishers (India), New Delhi, 1974.

Mellor, D.H.: *Real Time*, Cambridge University Press, Cambridge, 1967.

Menninger, Karl: *Zahlwort und Ziffer*, Vanden hoeck and Ruprecht, Göttingen, 1958.

Milburn, R. Gordon: *The Religious Mysticism of The Upanisads*, Theosophical Publishing House, London, 1924.

Mishra, Umesh: *Conception of Matter According to Nyaya-Vaisesika*, Allahabad Press, Allahabad, 1936.

Mishra, Sisir Kumar: *The Vision of India*, Jaico Book Co., Bombay, 1949.

Mohanty, J. N.: *The Concept of Rationality, Phenomenology and Indian Philosophy*, Indian Council of Philosophic research, New Delhi, pp. 8-19.

Mookherji, Radha Kumud: *Hindu Civilisation*, Longmans Green & Co., London, 1936.

Mookerji, Satkari: *The Jaina Philosophy of Non-Absolutism*, Bharati Mahavidyalaya, Calcutta, 1944; *The Buddhist Philosophy of Universal Flux* (2nd Edn), Motilal Banarasidass, Delhi, 1975.

Mukherji, J. N.: *Sankhya or Theory of Reality*, published by S. N. Mukherji, Calcutta, 1930.

Mukherji, Nalini Mohan Shastri: *A Study of Śaṅkara*, Calcutta University, Calcutta, 1942.

Mukhopadhyaya, Pramathanatha: *An Introduction to Vedānta Philosophy*, The Books Company Ltd., Calcutta, 1942.

Mittal, Kewal Krsihan: 'Role of Materialism in Indian thought', *Indian Materialism*, Munshiram Manoharlal Publishers, Delhi, pp. 47-102.

Moore, Charles A.: (Ed) *Essays in East-West Philosophy*, Honolulu, University of Hawaii Press, 1951.

Munitz: *Cosmic Understanding*, Princeton University, Princeton, 1986.

Murthy, K.S.: *Revelation and Reason in Advaita Vedānta*, Motilal Banarasidass, Delhi, reprint, 1986.

Murthy, T.R.V.: *The Central Philosophy of Buddhism, A Study of Mādhyamika System*, George Allen and Unwin, London, 1956.

Nagaraja Rao, P.: *Essays in Indian Philosophy and Religion*, Lalvani Publishing House, Bombay, 1971.

Needham, Joseph: *Science and Civilization in China*, Vol. II, Cambridge University Press, Cambridge, 1956.

Nikhilananda, Swami: *The Upaniṣads*, 2 Vols., Harper and Bros., New York, 1949-51.

Northrop F.S.C.: *The Meeting of East and West*, Mac Millan & Co., New York, 1946.

Nath S. C.: (Ed) *The Mahābhārata*, The Philosophical Library, New York, 1956.

Nakamura, Hajime: *Ways of Thinking of Eastern people*, East West Center Press, Honolulu, 1964; *A Comparative History of Ideas*, Motilal Banarasidass, Delhi, reprint, 1986.

Narasimha, Roddam: 'A metaphysics of living systems: the Yoga-Vāsiṣṭha view', *Journal of Biological Sciences*, **27**, 7, pp. 645-650.

Oldenburg, Hermann: *Buddha*, Sein Libre, Stutgart, 1914.

O'Leary, D. Lacy: *How Greek Sciences Passed to the Arabs*, Routledge and Kegan Paul, London, 1951.

Pande, Ramachandra: 'Theory of Inference', in *Indian Studies in Indian Philosophy*, Ontological basics of the Buddhists, Motilal Banarasidass, Delhi, pp. 50-59.

Pandeya, R. C.: *Buddhist Studies in India*, Motilal Banarasidass, Delhi, 1975.

Panikkar, K.M.: *A Survey of Indian History*, Median Books, London, 1947.

Pal, Radha Vinod: *The Hindu Philosophy of Law in the Vedic and post-Vedic Times Prior to the Institutes of Manu*, Bishwala Bundar Press, Calcutta, 1938.

Pargiter, Frederick Eden: *Ancient Indian Historical Tradition*, Oxford University Press, London, 1922.

Patil, Rajendra Kumar Rajaram: *Cultural History from the Vāyu Purāṇa*, Motilal Banarasidass, Delhi, 1973.

Perry, Ralpha Barton: *Philosophy of The Recent Past*, Charles Seribuns Sons, New York, 1926; *Present Philosophical Trends*, Longmans Green & Co., New York, 1921; Ponniah, V. *The Sarvāstivāda Theory of Knowledge*, Annamalai University, Annamalai, 1952.

Pingle, Pratibha: 'Mahābhūtas: The Buddhists Approach', *Prakṛti*, Vol. 2, Indira Gandhi National Center for the Arts, New Delhi, pp. 97-104; *The Pilgrimage of Buddhism and a Buddhist Pilgrimage*, The MacMillan Co., New York, 1928.

Pollinghouse, J.: *Reason and Reality, The Relation between Science and Theology*, SPCK, London, 1991.

Prasadji, Brahmacaran Sital: *A Comparative Study of Jainism and Buddhism*, Jain Mission Society, Madras, 1953.

Pratt, Brisset James: *India and Its Faiths*, Houghton Millan Co., New York, 1915.

Potter, Karl: *Encyclopedia of Indian Philosophy*, Vols. I & II, Motilal Banarasidass, Delhi, 1977.

Pratapchandra: *Metaphysics of Perpetual Change*, Somayya Publication, Bombay, 1978; *Eastern Religion and Western Thought*, Oxford University Press, Oxford, 1940; *An Idealist View of Life*, 2nd Edn, George Allen and Unwin, London, 1947.

Radhakrishnan, S.: *Indian Philosophy*, 2 Vols., George Allen and Unwin, London, 1948; *Eastern Religions and Western Thought*, Oxford University Press; *Indian Philosophy*, 2 Vols., George Allen and Unwin, New York, 1959.

Radhakrishnan, S., Wadia, A. R. *et al*: *History of Philosophy, East and West*: George Allen and Unwin, London, 1952.

Raja, K K: *Indian Theories of Meaning*, The Adyar library Research Center, Madras, 1963; *Outlines of History of Sanskrit literature*, Bhartiya Vidya Bhavan, Bombay, 1968.

Raju, P. T.: *Idealistic Thought of India*, Harvard University Press, Cambridge, 1933; *Comparative Philosophy, Ideal Approaches, East and West*, M. S. University, Baroda, 1956; *Structural Depths of Indian Thought*, South Asian Publishers, New Delhi, 1985.

Rant, A.: 'Buddhism and Science', *Mahabodhi*, **58**, 1950, pp. 128-134.

Rant, A and R. N. Dandekar: *Indian Philosophy, A Survey*, Bhandarkar Oriental Research Institute, Poona, 1942; *Thought and Reality*, George Allen and Unwin, London, 1947.

Raghavendrachar, H. N.: *Dvaita Philosophy and its Place in Vedanta*, University of Mysore, Mysore, 1943; *The Concept of Svatantra*, Mysore University, Mysore, 1943.

Randle, H. N.: *Fragments from Diṅnāga*, Prize Publications Fund, Vol. IX, The Royal Asiatic Society, London, 1926; *A Constructive Survey of Upaniṣadic Philosophy*, Oriental Book Agency, Poona, 1926; *Indian Logic in the Earlier Schools*, Oxford University Press, Oxford, 1930.

Rawlinson, H. G.: *India*, Frederick A Praeger, New York, 1952.

Rawson, J. A.: *A Constructive Survey of the Upaniṣads*, Theosophical Publication House, London, 1934.

Ray, Christopher: *Time, Space and Philosophy*, Routledge, London, 1975.

Reacher, N.: *Coherence Theory of Truth*, Oxford University Press, London, 1973.

Renou, L: *Bibliotheca Vedique*, Paris, 1931; *Religions of Ancient India*, Athlone Press, Paris, 1957.

Richard, Pischel : *Realms of Value: A Critique of Human Civilisation*, Harvard University Press, Cambridge, 1954.

Ross, Leon: *Plato's Theory of Ideas*, Clarendon Press, Oxford, 1951.

Ross, W. D: *The Works of Aristotle*, Vol. IX, Clarendon Press, Oxford, 1925.

Roy, M. N.: *Science and Superstition*, Indian Renaissance House, Dehradun, 1925.

Russell, Bertrand: *A History of Western Philosophy*, Sunan and Schuster, New York, 1945; *An Inquiry into meaning and Truth*, George Allen and Unwin, London, 1940.

Sachau, E.C.: (Tr and Ed) *Alberuni's India*, Kegan Paul, London, 1910.

Sandal, Pandit Mohan: *Philosophic Technique of the Upaniṣads*, Sacred Books of the Hindus, V, 1926.

Santayana, George: *Reason in Religion*, Chargles Screbeners Sons, New York, 1924.

Sarkar, A. K.: *Changing Phases of Buddhist Thought*, Bharathiya Bhavan, Patna, 1975.

Santinatha Sandhu: *Māyāvāda and non-dualistic Philosophy*, 1938.

Sarkar, Benoy Kumar: *The Positive Background of Hindu Sociology*, ISBH XXXVI, 1914, 1921.

Sarkar, Pronoy Kumar: *Hindu Achievements in Exact Sciences*, Longman Green and Co., London, 1918.

Sarma, R: 'The Buddhists Theory of perception', *The Philosophical Quarterly*, **3**, 1929.

Sarma, Dattakavi Subrahmayan: *Studies in the Renaissance of Hinduism in 14ᵗʰ and 15ᵗʰ Centuries*, Benares Hindu University, Benares, 1944.

Sarton, George: *A History of Science through the Golden Age of Greece*, Harvard University Press, Cambridge, 1959.

Sasaki G. H.: The time concept in *Abhidhamma*, Proceedings of 26ᵗʰ Congress of Orientalists, 1969, pp. 471-420.

Sastry, Kokileshwar: *An Introduction to Advaita*, University of Calcutta, Calcutta, 1936; *A Realistic Interpretation of Śaṅkara Vedanta,* University of Calcutta, Calcutta, 1939.

Sastri, Pashupatinath: *Introduction to the Pūrvamīmāṃsā,*. Published by A. N. Bhattacharya, Calcutta, 1923.

Sastry, A. Mahadeva: *The Vedānta Doctrine of Sri Śaṅkarācārya*, Minerva Press, Madras, 1899; *A Realistic Interpretation of Sankara Vedanta*, University of Calcutta, Calcutta, 1939.

Sastry, A. Nilakanta: *A Comprehensive History of India*, Vol. II, Oriental Longmans Private Limited, Calcutta, 1957; *A History of India,* 2 Vols., S. Vishwanathan, Madras, 1950.

Saxena, S. K.: *Nature of Consciousness in Hindu Philosophy*, Motilal Banarsidass, Delhi, 1971.

Sastry, Prabhudatta: *The Doctrine of Māyā in the Philosophy Of The Vedānta*, Luzac & Co., London, 1911.

Schlutz, M.: *Hindu philosophy*, Theosophist, Madras, 1910.

Seal, Brajendranath: *The Positive Sciences of the Ancient Hindus*, Longmans Green & Co., London, 1915.

Sellers, Raywood: *The Philosophy of Physical Realism*, MacMillan Co., New York, 1932.

Sharma, D.: 'The Buddhists Theory of Apoha', *Philosophy East and West*, Vol. XVII, 1, 1968.

Sen, S. N: 'An estimate of Indian Science in ancient and medieval times', *Scientia*, **70**, pp. 1-12; 'Prasastapāda's Impetus Theory of Motion', XI International Congress of History of Science, Warsaw, 1968, p. 241.

Sengupta B. K: *A Critique of the Vivarana School,* Calcutta, 1951.

Shaw, J L: 'Buddhist Theory of Meaning', *Journal of Indian Philosophy*, VI. No.1, 1978.

Shaw, J. L: 'The Nyāya on Cognition and Negation', *Journal of Indian Philosophy*, Vol. VIII, no. 3, 1980.

Sharma, Chandradhara: *A Critical Survey of Indian Philosophy*, Nand Kishore and Bros, Benaras, 1952.

Sharma D. S.: *Dialectic in Buddhism and Vedanta*, The MacMillan & Co., New York, 1928.

Shastri, D. N.: *The Philosophy Of Nyāya-Vaiśeṣika and Its Conflict with Diṅnāga School*, Bharatiya Vidya Prakashan, Delhi, 1976; *Studies in Vaiṣṇavism*, Bombay, 1927; *Critique of Indian Realism: A Study of Conflict between Nyāya-Vaiśeṣika and Buddhist Diṅnāga School*, Agra University, Agra, 1964.

Sastry D. Dutta: *The Essentials of Eastern Philosophy*, Mac Millan & Co., New York, 1928.

Shastri, Dakshina Murthy: *A Short History Indian Materialism, Sensationalism, Hedonism*, Calcutta Book Co., Calcutta, 1930.

Siddhanta, N. K.: *The Heroic Age of India,* Trübner & Co., London, 1929.

Sikdar, J. C.: 'Jaina Atomic Theory', *Indian Journal of History of Science*, **5**(2), 1970, pp. 199-213; 'Jain Conception of Substance (dravya)', *Studies in Bhagavatīsūtra*, Research Insitute of Prakrit and Jainology, Mirzapur, 1964, pp. 557-561.

Sinha, Jadunath: *Indian Realism*, French and Trübner and Co., London, 1938; *History of Indian Philosophy*, Vols. I & II, Central Book Agency, Calcutta, 1952.; *Introduction to Indian Philosophy*, Lakhsminarayana Agarwal Publishers, Agra, 1949.

Sircar K. L.: *The Mīmāṃsā Rules, The Interpretation as Applied to the Hindu Law,* University of Calcutta, Calcutta, 1923.

Sircar, Mahendranath: *The System of the Vedantic Thought*, Calcutta University, Calcutta.

Sivananda Swami: *The Ten Upaniṣads*, S. P. League, Calcutta, 1941.

Sivarama Shastry and Hanumantha Rao, G.: *Mysore Hiriyanna Commemoration Volume,* Kāvyālaya Publishers, Mysore, 1952.

Smith, Vincent A.: *The Early History of India,* Clarendon Press, Oxford, 1924.

Singh, B: *The Conceptual Framework of Indian Philosophy*, MacMillan Co. of India Ltd, Meerut, 1976.

Smart, N.: *Nyāya-Vaiśeṣika Atomism* under 'Indian Philosophy', *Encyclopedia of Philosophy*, **4**, 1967, pp. 157-158.

Sorabji, R.: *Time, Creation and the Continuum*, Duckworth, London, 1981.

Spence, Lewis: *An Introduction to Mythology*, George G. Harrap, London, 1921.

Stcherbatsky Th: *Buddhist Logic*, 2 Vols., Leningrad, 1925.

Story, Francis: 'The Buddhists Concept of Four great elements', *Mahabodhi*, **64**, pp. 292-93; *The Central Conception of Buddhism and the Meaning of the World Dharma*, Royal Asiatic Society, London, 1923; *The Conception of Buddhist Nirvana*, Academy of Sciences of the USSR, Leningrad, 1927.

Srinivasachar, P. N: *The Theory of Bhedābheda*, Varadachari & Co., Madras, 1934.

Stephen, Dorothea Jane: *Studies in Early Indian Thought*, Cambridge University Press, Cambridge, 1918.

Subbarayappa, B. V.: 'Physical World: Concepts and Views': A chapter in *A Concise History of Science in India*, Indian National Science Academy, New Delhi, 1971; reprint 1989. pp. 485-481; 'The Indian doctrine of Pañcabhūtas', *Indian Journal of History of Science,* **1**(1), pp. 60-67; 'On Indian Atomism', *Bulletin of National Institute of Science of India*, **21**, 1963, pp. 118-189; (Ed) *Medicine and Life Sciences*, Centre for Studies in Civilizations, New Delhi, 2002; (Ed) *Chemistry and Chemical Techniques*, Centre for Studies in Civilizations, New Delhi, 1999.

Subbarayappa, B.V. and Mukunda, N. (Eds): *Science in the West and India*, Himalaya Publishing House, Mumbai, 1993.

Subbarayappa, B.V. and Sarma, K. V.: *Indian Astronomy: A Source-Book,* Nehru Centre, Bombay, 1985.

Sukthankar V. S: *Guest Lectures on the Ṛgveda*, Oriental Book Agency, Poona, 1926.

Sukhalaji, Pandit: *Indian Philosophy*, Institute of Indology, Ahmedabad, 1977.

Suzuki, Beatrice Lane: *Mahayana Buddhism*, David Marlow, London, 1948; *Essence of Buddhism* (4th edn), Schocken Books, New York, 1970; *Philosophy of Yogācāra*, 1904; *Essays in Zen Buddhism,* Luzac and Co., London, 1927; *Studies in the Buddhism in Japan*, Vol. I. Philosophic Library, New York, 1955.

Takakusu, Jyan: 'Buddhism as Philosophic of Thyness', *Philosophy East and West*, (Ed) Charles Moore, Princeton; *The Essentials of Buddhist Philosophy*, University of Hawai Press, Hanolulu, 1947.

Tatia, Nathumal: *Studies in Jaina Philosophy*, Jaina Cultural Research Society, Benares, 1951.

Tatya, Rajaram Tukaram: *The Twelve Principle Upaniṣads*, Tattvaviveka, Bombay, 1906.

Tripathi, Chotelal: 'The Nature of Reality in Yogācāra Buddhism', *East and West*, **19**, 1969, pp. 474-494; 'Knowledge and Its Validity', *Journal of Oriental Institute*, Baroda, XXI-1971, pp. 71-89; *The Problem of Knowledge in Yogācāra Buddhism*, Bharati Original Publications and Book Sellers, Varanasi, 1972.

Thakur, A.: *Nyāyadarśana of Gautama*, Part I, Mithila Institute of Post-Graduate Studies and Research in Sanskrit Learning, Varanasi, 1967.

Thadani, N. V.: *The Mīmāṃsā: The Seat of Sacred Doctrines of The Hindus*, Bharat Research Institute, Delhi, 1962.

Thomas, Edward J.: *The History of Buddhist Thought*, Alfred A. Knoff, New York, 1933.

Thomas, George Derwant: *Studies in Ancient Greek Society*, Lawrence and Wishcart, London, 1954-55.

Toynbee, Arnold J.: *Greek Historical Thought*, New American Library, New York, 1952.

Tucci, Guessuppe: *Pre-Diṅnāga Buddhist Texts on Logic from Chinese Sources*, Oriental Research Institute, Baroda, 1929.

Tulpule, S. G.: 'Ākāśa: From Space to Spacelessness', *Prakṛti*, Vol. 2, Indira Gandhi National Center for the Arts, New Delhi, 1993. pp. 123-129.

Ui, H: *The Vaiśeṣika Philosophy According to Daśapadārtha Śāstra*, Chinese Texts with Introduction (Tr and notes), FW Thomas, London, 1971.

Urquahart, William Spencer: *The Vedanta and the Modern Thought*, Oxford University Press, London, 1928.

Vidyārnanya, Satish Chandra: *A Cataclysm of Hinduism, Sacred Books of the Hindus* III, 1919.

Vedalankar, Jagannath: *Jyotiṣām Jyotiḥ: An Esoteric Exposition of Select Vedic Hymns*, Motilal Banarasidass, Delhi, 1988.

Verma, Rajendra: *Vedic Cosmology*, New Age International, New Delhi, 1989.

Verma, Siddheswar: 'The Vedic Concepts of Time', *Indian Linguistics*, **27**(1), 1966, pp. 114-130.

Vidyāranya, S. C. and Mohanlal Sandal: *Aitareya Upaniṣad and Taittirīya Upaniṣad*, Sacred Books of the Hindus, 1925.

Vidyabhushana, S. C.: *Nyāyavāda, The Earliest Jaina Work on Pure Logic*, Indian Research Society, Calcutta, 1931.

Vasu, S. C.: *Studies in the Vedānta Sūtras*, part I, Sacred Books of the Hindus, 1933.

Warren, Clarke: *Buddhism in Translations*, Harvard Oriental series, Cambridge, 1896.

Warren, Herbert: *Jainism in Western Garb as a solution to Great Problems*, Central Jaina Publishing House, Atribal, 1916.

Ward, C.H.S.: *Buddhism*, Vol. I, GRES, London, 1952.

Watanabe, Baiyau: *Thoughts, Literature and Monasteries in Earlier Buddhism*, Minshukai Bandu, Tokyo, 1948.

Weber, Aufrecht: *The History of Indian Literature*, Kegan Paul, Trench, Trübener & Co., London, 1914.

Webener, Max: *The Religion of India, the Sociology of Hinduism and Buddhism*, Free Press, 1958.

Whitrow, J.G.: *The Natural Philosophy of Time*, Clarendon Press, Oxford, 1963.

Wilkins, W. J: *Hindu Mythology, Vedic and Purāṇic*, Calcutta, 1980.

Winternitz, M.: *Gestichiste des Indishen Litreaturs*, Leipzig, 1915-22; (Tr) S. Ketkar, *A History of Indian Literature*, Vols. I –III, University of Calcutta, Calcutta, 1927-1933; *A History of Indian Literature*, University of Calcutta, Calcutta, 1927.

Williams, Monier: *Brahmanism and Hinduism*, John Murray, London, 1891.

Wilson, H.H.: *Analysis of The Purāṇas* (Reprint), Nag Publications, Delhi, 1979.

Woods, James Hughton: *The Yoga System of Patañjali,* Harvard Oriental Series VIII, 1927.

Wood, Earnest: *Great System of Yoga,* Philosophical Library, New York, 1954.

Wood, Ledger: 'Transmigration', *The Dictionary of Philosophy*, Columbia University Press, New York, 1937.

Yamakai, Sogen: *Systems of Buddhist Thought*, University of Calcutta, Calcutta, 1912.

Zeller, Edward: *A History of Greek Philosophy from the earliest period to the time of Socrates,* (Tr) S. F. Alleyne, 2 Vols., Longmans Green and Co, London, 1881.

Zuner, Joseph Campbel: (Ed) *Philosophies of India*, Pantheon Books, New York, 1951.

Index

Note: *n* in italics refers to the note number in the particular reference.

---

* Already Published
➤ In the Process of Publication
• Under Plan